AN INTRODUCTION TO H

In memory of my father, Raymond Houlgate

An Introduction to Hegel

Freedom, Truth and History

Second Edition

Stephen Houlgate

Blackwell
Publishing

BLACKWELL PUBLISHING
350 Main Street, Malden, MA 02148-5020, USA
9600 Garsington Road, Oxford OX4 2DQ, UK
550 Swanston Street, Carlton, Victoria 3053, Australia

First edition published 1991 by Routledge
Second edition published 2005 by Blackwell Publishing Ltd

2   2006

Library of Congress Cataloging-in-Publication Data

Houlgate, Stephen.
    An introduction to Hegel: freedom, truth and history / Stephen Houlgate. – 2nd ed.
        p. cm.
    Rev. ed. of: Freedom, truth, and history. 1991.
    Includes bibliographical references and index.
    ISBN 0-631-23062-9 (alk. paper) – ISBN 0-631-23063-7 (pbk. : alk. paper)   1. Hegel, Georg Wilhelm Friedrich, 1770–1831.   I. Houlgate, Stephen. Freedom, truth and history.   II. Title.

    B2948.H658 2005
    193–dc22

                                                                        2004015916

ISBN-13: 978-0-631-23062-5 (alk. paper) – ISBN-13: 978-0-631-23063-2 (pbk. : alk. paper)

A catalogue record for this title is available from the British Library.

Set in 10 on 12 pt Minion
by SNP Best-set Typesetter Ltd, Hong Kong

For further information on
Blackwell Publishing, visit our website:
www.blackwellpublishing.com

Contents

Acknowledgements to the Second Edition

This book was first published in 1991 and comprised five chapters: on Hegel's philosophy of history, science of logic, political philosophy, aesthetics and philosophy of religion. For this second edition I have added five new chapters: two on Hegel's *Phenomenology*, two devoted wholly to the philosophy of nature, and one covering both the philosophy of nature and philosophy of subjective spirit. I have also made some revisions to the five original chapters. Most of these are minor and simply tidy up passages that were not quite as clear as I initially believed. In one or two cases the revisions are a little more extensive and have been made in order to accommodate the new chapters.

There is likely to be little surprise at the fact that I have added chapters on the *Phenomenology*. This is perhaps Hegel's most famous text and should have been treated more fully in the first edition. Eyebrows might be raised, however, at the inclusion of so much new material on the philosophy of nature. Hegel's philosophy of nature has often been dismissed with disdain. Scholars such as Michael Petry, John Burbidge and Dieter Wandschneider have shown beyond doubt, however, that Hegel's dialectical conception of nature is central to his philosophical project and very much rewards close attention and study. I hope that my account of Hegel's views on space, time, matter and life will help to open up the philosophy of nature to a much wider audience than hitherto.

I have benefited over the past thirteen years from conversations and correspondence with many friends and colleagues on both the *Phenomenology* and the philosophy of nature. I would like to thank the following especially for their enthusiasm, patience and invaluable insights: John Burbidge, Ardis Collins, Will Dudley, Cinzia Ferrini, William Maker, John McCumber, Michael Petry, Robert Stern, Kenneth Westphal and Robert Williams. I am also grateful to Steve Bosworth for making helpful suggestions for revisions to the first edition, to Thomas Posch for reading and correcting chapter 6 on the philosophy of nature with such care and to Kenneth Westphal (again) for reading through the whole manuscript with such scrupulous attention to detail. The five new chapters could not have been completed without two terms of research leave granted by the University of Warwick. The chapters on the *Phenomenology* also owe much to the graduate students and undergraduates at Warwick with whom I have studied Hegel's great work over the last few years. Thanks are due to all of them.

Most of all I would like to thank my loving family for all the big and little things they have done to help this new edition see the light of day. My wife, Mary, and my children,

Mark, Michael and Margaret, gave me wonderful support during the writing of the first edition, and they have been every bit as supportive and tolerant during the (mercifully much shorter) gestation of the second edition. Special thanks should go to our fourth child, Christopher, born in 1993, who so graciously agreed to play his football in the hall 'without commentary' when I was struggling to understand what Hegel was trying to say in some particularly knotty passages.

Stephen Houlgate
Kenilworth

Acknowledgements to the First Edition

This book was started in 1986 in Edinburgh and completed in 1990 in Evanston. In the intervening years many friends, colleagues and students have helped to bring clarity to my thoughts on Hegel and, especially, to my attempts to express those thoughts in intelligible English.

I am particularly grateful to Jonathan Rée, both for suggesting that I write the book in the first place and for reading through and editing each chapter with such understanding and patience. Paul Gurowich, Vincent Hope, Nicholas Sagovsky and Robert Stern also read individual chapters and made many valuable suggestions as to how to improve them. For any remaining obscurities or infelicities of style, I take full responsibility.

In addition, I have profited over the last few years from many conversations with friends about Hegel and related issues. Those whom I would particularly like to thank for their, perhaps unwitting, contributions to the genesis of this book are Ken Alpern, John Burbidge, Tom Burdett, Paul Davies, Tim Engström, David Kolb, John Llewelyn, George Matthews, Ron Nahser, John Protevi, Sally Sedgwick, John Walker and Nick Walker.

I could not have written this book without the generous financial support of a Research Fellowship from the Faculty of Arts and the Institute for Advanced Studies in the Humanities at the University of Edinburgh and two summer research grants from the College of Liberal Arts and Sciences at DePaul University in Chicago. For this support, and for the encouragement which both institutions have given me during the preparation of this book, I am especially grateful.

Finally, and most importantly, I owe my greatest debt of gratitude to my family: to my wife, Mary, for her good humour, her understanding and her love at all times, and to my children, Mark, Michael and Margaret, for their endless patience on all those days when we never did get to mend those toys and never did get to the park.

Stephen Houlgate
Evanston, Illinois
August 1990

Abbreviations

The following abbreviations have been used to refer to the works of Hegel:

Werke   *Werke in zwanzig Bänden*, eds E. Moldenhauer and K. M. Michel, 20 volumes and index (Frankfurt: Suhrkamp Verlag, 1969ff).

A   *Aesthetics. Lectures on Fine Art*, trans. T. M. Knox, 2 volumes (Oxford: Clarendon Press, 1975).

Enc **I**   *The Encyclopaedia Logic* (with the *Zusätze*), trans. T. F. Geraets, W. A. Suchting and H. S. Harris (Indianapolis: Hackett Publishing, 1991). This is a translation of the first volume of Hegel's *Encyclopaedia* (1830) and is known as the 'Lesser Logic'.

Enc **II**   *Hegel's Philosophy of Nature*, trans. A. V. Miller (Oxford: Clarendon Press, 1970). This is a translation of the second volume of Hegel's *Encyclopaedia* (1830).

Enc **III**   *Hegel's Philosophy of Mind*, trans. W. Wallace, together with the *Zusätze* in Boumann's text (1845), trans. A. V. Miller (Oxford: Clarendon Press, 1971). This is a translation of the third volume of Hegel's *Encyclopaedia* (1830).

HP   *Introduction to the Lectures on the History of Philosophy*, trans. T. M. Knox and A. V. Miller (Oxford: Clarendon Press, 1985).

LHP   *Lectures on the History of Philosophy*, trans. E. S. Haldane and F. H. Simson, 3 volumes (London: Routledge and Kegan Paul, 1892, 1955).

LPR   *Lectures on the Philosophy of Religion*, ed. P. C. Hodgson, trans. R. F. Brown, P. C. Hodgson and J. M. Stewart, with the assistance of J. P. Fitzer and H. S. Harris, 3 volumes (Berkeley: University of California Press, 1984–7).

NP   *Naturphilosophie. Band I: Die Vorlesung von 1819/20*, ed. M. Gies (Napoli: Bibliopolis, 1980).

PH   *The Philosophy of History*, trans. J. Sibree, with an introduction by C. J. Friedrich (New York: Dover Publications, 1956).

Phen   *Phenomenology of Spirit*, trans. A. V. Miller, with analysis of the text and foreword by J. N. Findlay (Oxford: Oxford University Press, 1977).

PR   *Hegel's Philosophy of Right*, trans. T. M. Knox (Oxford: Oxford University Press, 1952, 1967).

PRH   *Philosophie des Rechts. Die Vorlesung von 1819/20 in einer Nachschrift*, ed. D. Henrich (Frankfurt: Suhrkamp Verlag, 1983).

PWH   *Lectures on the Philosophy of World History. Introduction: Reason in History*, trans. H. B. Nisbet with an introduction by D. Forbes (Cambridge: Cambridge University Press, 1975).

SL   *Hegel's Science of Logic*, trans. A. V. Miller, foreword by J. N. Findlay (Atlantic Highlands, NJ: Humanities Press International, 1989). This text is known as the 'Greater Logic'.

VNP Bon *Natur-Philosophie*, 'Nachschrift A', in W. Bonsiepen, 'Hegels Raum-Zeit-Lehre', *Hegel-Studien*, 20 (1985), 9–78.

VNP 1821 *Vorlesung über Naturphilosophie. Berlin 1821/22*, eds G. Marmasse and T. Posch (Frankfurt am Main: Peter Lang, 2002).

VNP 1823 *Vorlesung über Naturphilosophie. Berlin 1823/24*, ed. G. Marmasse (Frankfurt am Main: Peter Lang, 2000).

VNS   *Vorlesungen über Naturrecht und Staatswissenschaft. Heidelberg 1817/18, mit Nachträgen aus der Vorlesung 1818/19. Nachgeschrieben von P. Wannenmann*, eds C. Becker and others, with Introduction by O. Pöggeler (Hamburg: Felix Meiner, 1983).

VPG   *Vorlesungen über die Philosophie des Geistes. Berlin 1827/1828*, eds F. Hespe and B. Tuschling (Hamburg: Felix Meiner, 1994).

VPN   *Vorlesungen über die Philosophie der Natur. Berlin 1819/20*, eds M. Bondeli and H. N. Seelmann (Hamburg: Felix Meiner Verlag, 2002).

VPR   *Vorlesungen über die Philosophie der Religion*, ed. W. Jaeschke, 3 volumes (Hamburg: Felix Meiner, 1983–5).

VRP   *Vorlesungen über Rechtsphilosophie, 1818–1831*, ed. K.-H. Ilting, 4 volumes (Stuttgart: Frommann-Holzboog, 1973ff).

Chronology

1770   20 March: Friedrich Hölderlin born in Lauffen am Neckar. 27 August: Georg Wilhelm Friedrich Hegel born in Stuttgart. Wordsworth and Beethoven are born in the same year.

1775   27 January: Friedrich Schelling born in Württemberg.

1776   American Declaration of Independence.

1777   Hegel attends the Stuttgart Gymnasium until 1788. His reading during this time includes Homer, Thucydides, Sophocles, Aristotle, Cicero, Tacitus, Horace, Shakespeare, Klopstock, Lessing and Schiller.

1781   Kant's *Critique of Pure Reason* published.

1783   20 September: Hegel's mother dies.

1785   Hegel begins writing a diary, partly in Latin. Kant's *Groundwork for the Metaphysics of Morals* published.

1788   October: Hegel and Hölderlin begin studies in theology and philosophy at the Tübinger Stift. During their time at the Stift the two students develop a close friendship with one another and with Schelling (after he enters the Stift in 1790).

1789   14 July: The storming of the Bastille in Paris marks the beginning of the French Revolution, which is greeted with enthusiasm by students at the Stift.

1790   Hegel receives MA degree. Kant publishes his *Critique of Judgement*.

1792   Fichte's *Attempt at a Critique of All Revelation* appears.

1793   Louis XVI guillotined. Hegel graduates from the Tübinger Stift. Autumn: He becomes house tutor with the family of Captain Karl Friedrich von Steiger in Bern. Kant publishes *Religion within the Limits of Reason Alone*.

1794   Fall of Robespierre. Fichte begins to publish his *Foundation of the Entire Science of Knowledge*.

1795   Schiller's letters on the *Aesthetic Education of Man* published. Hegel works on 'The Life of Jesus' and on 'The Positivity of the Christian Religion'.

1796   Hegel (or Schelling or Hölderlin) writes the *Earliest System-programme of German Idealism*. Napoleon's Italian campaign.

1797   January: Hegel moves to Frankfurt am Main to take up a tutorship which Hölderlin had arranged for him with the family Gogel. Summer/Autumn: Hegel drafts fragments on religion and love.

1798   Schelling becomes Professor of Philosophy at Jena on the recommendation of Goethe. Hegel works on Kant's *Metaphysics of Morals*. Napoleon's Egyptian campaign.

1799   14 January: Hegel's father dies. Hegel writes the 'Spirit of Christianity and its Fate' and works on Sir James Steuart's *Inquiry into the Principles of Political Economy*.

1800   Schelling publishes his *System of Transcendental Idealism*. September: Hegel completes his 'System-fragment'.

1801   January: Hegel joins Schelling at the University of Jena. Begins lecturing as Privatdozent on logic and metaphysics. His first publication, an essay entitled *The Difference between Fichte's and Schelling's System of Philosophy*, appears. He completes his dissertation *On the Orbits of the Planets*.

1802   Hegel lectures on natural law. He begins publication of the *Critical Journal of Philosophy* with Schelling. Publication continues until the summer of 1803 when Schelling leaves Jena. Articles by Hegel published in the journal include *Faith and Knowledge, The Relation of Scepticism to Philosophy* and the essay on *Natural Law*.

1803   September: Hegel prepares manuscript known as the 'System of Speculative Philosophy', which includes material on the philosophy of nature and the philosophy of spirit.

1804   12 February: Kant dies. 2 December: Napoleon crowns himself Emperor.

1805   February: Hegel appointed Extraordinary Professor at Jena through the help of Goethe. 9 May: Schiller dies.

1806   July: Hegel draws his first regular stipend at Jena. October: He completes manuscript of the *Phenomenology of Spirit* as Napoleon defeats the Prussian troops at the battle of Jena.

1807   *Phenomenology of Spirit* published. 5 February: Christiana Burckhardt (*née* Fischer), Hegel's landlady and housekeeper in Jena, gives birth to his illegitimate son, Ludwig Fischer. (Ludwig is raised in Jena by the sisters-in-law of Hegel's friend, the publisher Karl Friedrich Frommann, until he is taken into Hegel's own home in 1817.) March: Hegel moves to Bamberg to become editor of a newspaper. Autumn: Period of reform begins in Prussia, initially under Freiherr von Stein, then under Karl von Hardenberg. This lasts until 1813.

1808   November: Hegel moves to Nuremberg to become rector of the Aegidiengymnasium. One of his tasks at the Gymnasium is to teach speculative logic to his pupils.

1811   15 September: Hegel marries Marie von Tucher (born 1791).

1812   Napoleon's Russian campaign. Volume 1 of the *Science of Logic* (the Logic of Being) published. 27 June: Hegel's daughter, Susanna, born. She dies on 8 August.

1813   7 June: Hegel's son, Karl, born. Volume 2 of the *Science of Logic* (the Logic of Essence) published. Kierkegaard, Wagner, Verdi and Georg Büchner born.

1814   29 January: Fichte dies. 25 September: Hegel's son, Immanuel, born.

1815   Napoleon defeated at Waterloo.

1816   Volume 3 of the *Science of Logic* (the Logic of the Concept) published. Hegel becomes Professor of Philosophy at the University of Heidelberg. At Heidelberg he lectures on the history of philosophy, logic and metaphysics, anthropology and psychology, political philosophy, aesthetics and the *Encyclopaedia*.

1817   First edition of the *Encyclopaedia* published.

1818   May 5: Marx born in Trier. Hegel is recruited by the Prussian Minister for Religious, Educational and Medical Affairs, Karl von Altenstein, to become Professor of Philosophy at the University of Berlin, where he remains until his death. During these years in Berlin Hegel's philosophy gains in popularity among academics and amateur philosophers from the business world and the professions, and Hegelianism develops into a philosophical school.

1819   August/September: The Karlsbad Decrees are passed authorizing press censorship and closer surveillance of universities in Germany. In the period of crackdown shortly before the decrees are passed, one of Hegel's students, Leopold von Henning, is arrested.

1820   October: *Philosophy of Right* published.

1821   Hegel lectures for the first time on the philosophy of religion. 5 May: Napoleon dies.

1822   Hegel travels to the Rhineland and the Low Countries, where he sees paintings by Rembrandt and van Dyck. In Berlin he lectures for the first time on the philosophy of history.

1824   The Brockhaus *Konversationslexikon* includes an account of Hegel's life and philosophy. Hegel visits Vienna where he attends several operas by Rossini.

1826   Hegel founds the *Yearbooks for Scientific Criticism*.

1827   Second edition of the *Encyclopaedia* published. Hegel visits Paris, where he sees Molière's *Tartuffe* and an operatic version of *Oedipus at Colonus*. He also sees the central section of the van Eyck Altarpiece in Ghent and paintings by Memling in Bruges. October: He visits Goethe in Weimar on the way home to Berlin.

1830   Hegel is Rector of the University of Berlin. Third edition of the *Encyclopaedia* published. July: Revolution in France.

1831   January: Hegel decorated by Friedrich Wilhelm III of Prussia. 28 August: Ludwig Fischer dies in the East Indies. 14 November: Hegel dies in Berlin (probably of a chronic gastrointestinal disease) without learning of his son's fate. 24 December: A contract is signed by Hegel's wife, students and friends for the publication of his collected works.

1832   22 March: Goethe dies.

1835–6 D. F. Strauss's *Life of Jesus* is published, marking the beginning of a conscious split between Left, Right and Middle Hegelians.

1841   Schelling called to the University of Berlin by Friedrich Wilhelm IV to counter the influence of Hegelianism. L. Feuerbach's *The Essence of Christianity* published.

1843   7 June: Hölderlin dies in Tübingen.

1848   Marx and Engels publish the *Communist Manifesto*.

1854   20 August: Schelling dies in Switzerland.

Introduction

Opinions about Hegel are, to say the least, mixed. Some see in him 'a thinker of great argumentative strength and depth of vision' and are profoundly convinced of the 'originality and permanent interest of his ideas'.[1] One recent commentator has even claimed that Hegel's philosophy is so important that existential and political problems in today's world 'cannot be adequately approached by those not thoroughly experienced in Hegelian dialectical analysis'.[2] Others are somewhat less certain of the value of Hegel's philosophical enterprise. Bertrand Russell, for example, thought that almost all Hegel's doctrines were false; Karl Popper saw little more in him than 'bombastic and mystifying cant'; and Arthur Schopenhauer, who was his colleague at the University of Berlin in the early 1820s, complained bitterly about the countless minds that had been 'strained and ruined in the freshness of youth by the nonsense of Hegelism'. As far as Schopenhauer was concerned, most of his philosophical contemporaries were beneath contempt, but

the greatest effrontery in serving up sheer nonsense, in scrabbling together senseless and maddening webs of words, such as had previously been heard only in madhouses, finally appeared in Hegel. It became the instrument of the most ponderous and general mystification that has ever existed, with a result that will seem incredible to posterity, and be a lasting monument of German stupidity.[3]

Intemperate though such remarks may be, it has to be admitted that a casual glance at a work of Hegel's such as the *Science of Logic* is more likely to confirm Schopenhauer's judgement than persuade the unbiased reader of the incisiveness and logical precision of Hegel's thinking. Consider, for example, the following sentences, chosen at random from the *Logic*:

Negation as quality is negation simply as *affirmative*; being constitutes its ground and element. The determination of reflection, on the other hand, has for this ground reflectedness-into-self. Positedness fixes itself into a determination precisely because reflection is equality-with-self in its negatedness; its negatedness is consequently itself a reflection-into-self.[4]

Given that much of Hegel's writing is like this, it is not hard to see why his work has met with something less than universal acclaim during the one hundred and seventy years since his death. Indeed, it is pretty hard to understand how Hegel has found any philosophical friends at all.

Yet, as has often been pointed out, despite the apparent obscurity of his·thought, Hegel has in fact had an unparalleled impact on the modern world. Marx's conception of historical dialectic and his analysis of capitalism are heavily indebted to Hegel; Kierkegaard's existentialism was developed in response to Hegelian philosophy; and the work of many modern theologians (such as Karl Barth and Dietrich Bonhoeffer) and modern aesthetic theorists (such as Theodor Adorno) would be inconceivable without the background of Hegel's ideas. Dewey's pragmatism, Gadamer's hermeneutics, Habermas's social theory and Derrida's deconstruction, indeed the whole modern interest in historical understanding, have all been deeply influenced by Hegel. Even modern analytic philosophy, which was severely critical of Hegel for most of the twentieth century, is indirectly his progeny, since two of its founding fathers, Russell and G. E. Moore, were originally drawn to Hegelian ideas and spent much of their subsequent careers trying to refute what they perceived to be their early Hegelian errors. Given the extraordinary way in which Hegel's thinking pervades modern intellectual life, it seems to be undeniably true that 'no one today who seriously seeks to understand the shape of the modern world can avoid coming to terms with Hegel'.[5]

Yet a more important reason for engaging with Hegel's ideas, in my view, is that, despite their difficulty, they are actually of great value and relevance to current social, political, aesthetic, theological and philosophical discussions. I do not share the opinion of some commentators that 'the Hegelian synthesis, if ever a genuine possibility, has broken down beyond all possible recovery'.[6] To my mind, Hegel's is still a viable philosophical endeavour with important things to contribute to modern debates, particularly the debates about historical relativism, poverty and social alienation, the nature of freedom and political legitimacy, the future of art and the character of Christian faith. The purpose of this book is to try to explain what Hegel has to say to just such issues and to show that, contrary to what his detractors claim, his philosophy is still worthy of serious and thoughtful consideration.

In the past forty years there has been a revival of interest in Hegel that has led to the publication of some excellent studies of his work.[7] Many of these studies, however, are quite specialized and do not cover all aspects of Hegel's mature thought, preferring instead to concentrate on his phenomenology or political philosophy. There is, therefore, still a need, in my view, for a comprehensive introduction to Hegel's philosophy that can help to render the whole range of that daunting but immensely rewarding body of thought accessible to non-specialists. With this book I try to offer such an introduction.

The book covers almost all of the main areas of Hegel's mature philosophical system: the philosophy of history, the sciences of logic and phenomenology, the philosophy of nature, the philosophy of subjective spirit, political philosophy, the aesthetics and the philosophy of religion. I have not dealt directly with Hegel's lectures on the history of philosophy (though I have briefly considered his relation to one or two of his philosophical predecessors, such as Descartes and Kant); nor have I included any discussion of Hegel's early writings, i.e. those written before the publication of the *Phenomenology of Spirit* in 1807. I trust, however, that readers whose main philosophical concern is with these particular areas will nevertheless find the issues that the book does cover to be of interest.

The interpretation of Hegel that is presented in this book is, I believe, a distinctive one. First, in contrast to most other commentators, I have taken seriously Hegel's claim to have developed a *presuppositionless* philosophy.[8] Furthermore, I have tried to show that Hegel's claim to presuppositionlessness can be seen to be quite compatible with his emphasis on the historical context within which philosophy emerges, if we recognize that, according to him, a philosophy that takes nothing for granted but develops all its concepts itself is demanded by the modern historical claim to freedom. The concept of freedom will thus turn out in my account to be central to Hegel's thinking and to be the one that connects the concepts of history and truth.

Second, I have given a lot of attention to Hegel's largely neglected philosophy of nature. I try to show that Hegel's account of nature is not the product of ignorance and arrogance (as some have thought), but is a sober, intelligent and well informed exploration of the natural world. Furthermore, I argue that Hegel's philosophy of nature should not simply be dismissed as an aberration, but forms an essential part of his presuppositionless philosophy of freedom.

Third, I have concentrated more than is usual on Hegel's treatment of art and religion, the two spheres of absolute spirit that prepare the way, in his view, for true philosophy. Sadly, too few commentators on Hegel have paid close attention to his lectures on aesthetics, despite the fact that they contain some of the clearest and most accessible statements of his ideas. His philosophy of religion has been studied more frequently, but there is still much disagreement among philosophers and theologians about whether his claim to be a Christian philosopher can be taken seriously. In this book I will try to defend his claim, and show that he views religious experience – together with aesthetic experience – as essential to human wholeness, openness and freedom.

The account of Hegel's philosophy that I offer here is by no means exhaustive and may not be as critical of Hegel as some readers would like it to be. No doubt it also raises many more awkward questions about Hegel than it answers. However, the aim of the book is not to erect an impregnable defence around Hegel's ideas, nor to embalm them in detailed, historical scholarship. It is to kindle an interest in Hegel among those who have no prior knowledge of him or have previously regarded him with suspicion or trepidation, and to encourage them to engage with his ideas themselves. If this book succeeds in helping one or two readers to work their own way into the *Science of Logic* or the *Philosophy of Right*, it will have served its purpose well.

1   *History and Truth*

The Historicity of Thought and Civilization

Perhaps the best way for a modern reader to approach Hegel's philosophy is to see it as challenging the claim that our experience of the world can ever be direct and unmediated. The idea that we could have simple, immediate access to things has been called into question from within both the 'analytic' and 'continental' traditions of philosophy, so whether our philosophical home is in the writings of 'analytic' thinkers such as Wittgenstein, Quine and Rorty, or of 'continental' thinkers such as Heidegger, Gadamer and Derrida, we should find Hegel's critique of the concept of unmediated knowledge intelligible, familiar and possibly even congenial.

Throughout his writings, Hegel stresses that we cannot ever simply perceive what is, without preconditions or presuppositions, because all human consciousness is informed by categories of thought which mediate everything we experience. In his lectures on the philosophy of history, he suggests that the first duty of the philosophical historian could be said to be that of 'accurately apprehending' the facts of history. However, he points out that expressions such as 'accurate' and 'apprehend' are not as straightforward as they seem.

> Even the ordinary, run-of-the-mill historian who believes and professes that his attitude is entirely receptive, that he is dedicated to the facts, is by no means passive in his thinking; he brings his categories with him, and sees the data he has before him through them. . . . Whoever looks at the world rationally will find that it in turn assumes a rational aspect; the two exist in a reciprocal relationship.[1]

What is present at hand is thus never simply 'given' to us in a pure, unmediated form. Rather, the world we encounter is always experienced through a framework of categories which we cannot set aside. We must certainly be open to the facts, in Hegel's view, but we must realize that we can only be open to them from within a specific perspective.

In his philosophical *Encyclopaedia* (1830) Hegel calls this framework of categories the 'metaphysics' which informs all our experience. At other times Hegel uses the word 'metaphysics' to refer to the traditional philosophical enquiry into the essence of the soul or the nature of being, or to a particular mode of understanding, namely that which seeks to comprehend objects in the world as either one thing or the other – as either finite or infinite, for example – and which is unable to think of anything real as uniting opposite qualities within itself. Here, however, 'metaphysics is nothing else but the entire range of the universal determinations of thought, as it were, the diamond net into which everything is brought and thereby first made intelligible'. Every form of human consciousness thus has its metaphysics, its 'instinctive way of thinking, the absolute power within us of which we become master only when we make it in turn the object of our knowledge'.[2] And one might add that this is true even of modes of thought – such as pragmatism – which deny that they adhere to any particular set of definitive principles. However 'unprincipled' or 'undogmatic' consciousness might wish to be, it will always presuppose some sort of 'metaphysics', according to Hegel. Hegel is, of course, well aware that human beings perceive the world through the network of their emotional, physical and practical needs and interests as well as through the network of their categories and concepts. However, he believes that those emotional, physical and practical interests are themselves mediated by the categories of thought, and that consequently these categories are most important in determining our world-view.

In claiming that all human consciousness presupposes certain categories of thought Hegel is following in the footsteps of the greatest philosopher of the German Enlightenment, Immanuel Kant. In his *Critique of Pure Reason* (1781, second edition 1787) Kant put forward the view that the mind is not simply the passive recipient of sensations produced by the things around us, but is also active in understanding those sensations in terms of certain categories and principles which it itself brings to bear on its experience. When we make a judgement such as 'the sun caused the stone to become warm', we are not simply describing what we perceive, in Kant's understanding, because – and here he follows Hume – we do not actually *perceive* any causal connection. All we perceive is the appearance of the sun and then the stone becoming warm. We make sense of what we perceive, however, in terms of the concept of causality which we ourselves bring to experience. For Kant, therefore, we do not simply accept what is given to us by perception, but we are active, rational beings who understand what we perceive in terms of concepts and categories which our own thought supplies.[3]

Hegel follows Kant and stresses that we presuppose categories and concepts in all our dealings with the world. However, he differs from Kant in two important ways. First of all, since, for Kant, the categories that we bring to experience are the products of our own thought, all we are entitled to claim is that *we* make sense of the world in terms of these categories. We are not entitled to claim that the world is *itself* structured in accordance with them. Kant maintains that as rational beings we have to organize our experience in terms of categories such as cause and effect, and that experience is organized in the same way by all of us. The ordered world that we experience is thus objective and real as far as we are concerned; but what the world might be like in itself we cannot tell. Indeed, Kant is not simply an agnostic about the nature of the world in itself. He suggests very strongly that it is *not* organized in terms of our categories: the categories through which we comprehend the world allow us to see the world in a light that is peculiar to us, but they do not allow us to see things in the true light in which they themselves stand. From such a position, it is clearly not too great a step to the view, adopted later by Nietzsche, that the world which we experience is made up of layer upon layer of human interpretation or fiction.

From Hegel's perspective, however, Kant's position rests on an unjustified assumption: namely that what we ourselves produce through our own thought cannot be true of things in themselves, that what we bring to bear on the world cannot be true of the world itself. For Hegel, by contrast, our categories do not keep us at one remove from the structure of things; rather, they are the very preconditions which give us access to the structure of things.[4] Our categories do not confine us within the alleged limits of human experience; they equip us to see and understand what *is*. We may come to the world predisposed by our reason and understanding to see it in a certain way, but the structure of our concepts and categories is identical with, and thus discloses, the structure of the world itself, because we ourselves are born into and so share the character of the world we encounter. This is not to say that all the particular judgements we make regarding, for example, causal connections in the world are correct, or that we always have a complete conception of what causality entails. But it does mean that we can rest assured that causality is a constituent feature of the world we inhabit, and not just a concept that we 'impose' on things.

Hegel thus agrees with Kant that we bring categories to bear on the world we perceive, but, in contrast to Kant, he maintains that those categories make possible genuine knowledge of the world itself and do not simply bring order into our own 'limited' human experience. For Hegel, it is only because our minds are conceptually prepared for the truth of things that we can gain access to that truth. The truth does not simply spring out at us; we must come to meet it in the right frame of mind. We must ourselves actively bring the truth to light, if that truth is to be known at all.

The second difference between Hegel and Kant is equally fundamental and concerns the question of history. For Kant, the conceptual framework through which we see the world is peculiar to us as rational beings and does not give us access to things 'in themselves'. However, that framework is fixed and universal for all finite rational beings. It constitutes the unchanging, timeless grid that gives to human experience a uniform conceptual structure. Different scientists and philosophers may have propounded different theories about the world, but the fundamental categories of human understanding with which these scientists and philosophers operated – categories such as unity, plurality, possibility or necessity – have remained constant, in Kant's view, throughout history. They were conceived by Aristotle in basically the same way as by Kant himself.

In Hegel's eyes, things are not so simple. Certain categories – being, for example – may well be universal; but others, such as cause and effect, or force and expression, are to be found, according to him, only in more advanced cultures. Furthermore, all concepts – those that are universal and those that are not – are conceived and understood by different ages and civilizations in different ways. The categories of thought are not fixed, eternal forms that remain unchanged throughout history, but are concepts that alter their meaning in history. The categories that, for Kant, constituted the permanent transcendental framework of knowledge thus constitute, for Hegel, the changing *historical* preconditions of knowledge.

But if this is so, then Hegel faces a considerable problem. We have seen that he differs from Kant in considering the categories to be the conditions which make knowledge of the world in itself possible. Yet, in his view, categories change in history, whereas the world – at least the natural world – is presumably always governed by the same laws. How are these two Hegelian claims to be reconciled? The solution to this problem, according to Hegel, is that the categories of thought do put us in contact with the world itself, but they do so more or less adequately in different ages and cultures. Hegel's conviction is that the categories as they are conceived in his own 'dialectical' philosophy are the categories in which the structure of being is fully revealed. These dialectical categories – which we will consider in more detail in the next chapter – thus represent the conceptual presuppositions which Hegel deems appropriate for the modern, fully self-conscious age. However, Hegel believes that the ways in which the categories have been understood by other civilizations, by earlier periods of European civilization and indeed by some of his own – less sophisticated – contemporaries in modern Europe also give us visions of the truth. It is just that those visions are simpler, less refined, less developed than that offered by dialectical philosophy. In Hegel's view, what previous ages and civilizations have thought about the world has often been crude and primitive; indeed, it has often been inextricably fused with gross errors and distortions of the truth. But it has never been wholly misguided. However alien a civilization may seem to us, however 'irrational' its understanding of the world may be, something of the truth always shines through. So the fact that our conceptual presuppositions have changed in history does not of itself mean that none of them can put us in touch with the truth. Rather, it seems that historical changes in our categories are what have allowed the truth to become gradually more apparent and accessible.

Now if all consciousness rests on conceptual presuppositions, we can have no immediate access to a simple, independent standard such as 'fact' by reference to which we could compare and evaluate different sets of presuppositions. The criterion which enables us to decide between rival sets of presuppositions – if there is one – must thus be found within the conceptual presuppositions of consciousness itself. Precisely how Hegel judges between different conceptual frameworks or cultural viewpoints will be considered later in this chapter. What I wish to stress here is simply that he is conscious that different civilizations *do* have different conceptual presuppositions. Indeed, he maintains that all the major differences between civilizations are reducible to the differences in the categories they employ. A civilization whose conceptual presuppositions are not explicit, but are embedded in myth and poetry, will be different from one that has articulated its categories in a rational form in philosophy or science. Similarly, a civilization that sees the heavens and human society as peopled by free individuals will be different from one that conceives of the world as governed by an all-powerful natural or divine necessity. In Hegel's eyes, the way in which a civilization understands itself and its world gives that civilization a distinctive historical character. Significant changes within civilizations, and major developments within history as a whole, are not just the products of technological advances, therefore, or of population growth or chance discoveries; they are results of profound changes in the categories – in the 'metaphysics' – which govern human life. 'All revolutions, in the sciences no less than in world-history, originate solely from the fact that spirit, in order to understand and comprehend itself with a view to possessing itself, has changed its categories, comprehending itself more truly, more deeply, more intimately, and more in unity with itself.'[5]

Hegel's views bear a striking resemblance to the theory put forward by Thomas Kuhn in *The Structure of Scientific Revolutions* (1962). Like Hegel, Kuhn is critical of the idea that experience provides us with a neutral stock of data that is permanently present for all to see. Natural science – which is Kuhn's main concern – is thus not simply a matter of collecting facts and giving ever more sophisticated interpretations of them. For Kuhn, as for Hegel, we do not first have immediate experience of things and then interpret them; we only have experience of things within a certain framework of conceptual presuppositions in the first place. What we see, therefore, we always see through what Kuhn calls a 'paradigm'. We are always *looking at* the same world, since the world of nature does not change with the emergence of new scientific theories; but what we *see* changes according to the paradigm we presuppose.

Since remote antiquity most people have seen one or another heavy body swinging back and forth on a string or chain until it finally comes to rest. To the Aristotelians, who believed that a heavy body is moved by its own nature from a higher position to a state of natural rest at a lower one, the swinging body was simply falling with difficulty. Constrained by the chain, it could achieve rest at its low point only after a tortuous motion and a considerable time. Galileo, on the other hand, looking at the swinging body, saw a pendulum, a body that almost succeeded in repeating the same motion over and over again ad infinitum. And having seen that much, Galileo observed other properties of the pendulum as well and constructed many of the most significant and original parts of his new dynamics around them. From the properties of the pendulum, for example, Galileo derived his only full and sound arguments for the independence of weight and rate of fall, as well as for the relationship between vertical height and terminal velocity of motions down inclined planes. All these natural phenomena he saw differently from the way they had been seen before.[6]

For Kuhn, as for Hegel, intellectual revolutions are thus brought about not simply by the discovery of new facts, but by changes in the fundamental concepts which we employ to understand things, by the transformation of the network through which we deal with reality. Where Aristotle saw one world, Galileo, Newton and Einstein saw another one – one that did not simply spring out at them from what they observed, but that emerged from their new conceptual paradigm.

Hegel and Kuhn are clearly very different thinkers, however. Kuhn's concern is with the history of science, whereas Hegel develops a more all-embracing theory of historical change. Kuhn is concerned with specific changes in scientific outlook, often within relatively recent history; for example, since Galileo. Hegel, on the other hand, is concerned with the broader sweep of history and is as interested in the differences between the cultural perspectives of the ancient Chinese and the Romans as in those between scientists and philosophers working within the same civilization or period. Kuhn's account of the reasons behind the changes or 'shifts' in paradigm which interest him is also quite different from the account given by Hegel of the historical changes with which he is primarily concerned. New scientific paradigms for Kuhn are produced in response to inexplicable anomalies in nature encountered in older paradigms, and are accepted in part because they seem to explain more things than earlier paradigms did, or because they seem to explain familiar things better. However, changes in paradigm are also governed by what Kuhn calls 'aesthetic' features, such as the greater simplicity or economy of the new paradigm, by changes in scientific convention or custom and by historical accidents, such as fortuitous technical innovations. Moreover, although new paradigms are marked by a movement away from primitive beginnings towards greater articulation and specialization, there is, for Kuhn, no endpoint to the process of scientific development, no final arrival at the 'truth', because no theory, in his view, however sophisticated it may be, can ever anticipate or explain all the facts with which it might be confronted. Kuhn's model thus presents us with a potentially infinitely extendable development of new, more sophisticated paradigms.

By contrast, the profound changes that interest Hegel have been produced, in his view, not simply by our response to anomalies in nature, or by changes in convention, but by our becoming more conscious of our freedom and potential for self-determination, and more aware of the way in which that freedom is to be realized and fulfilled in the world. In contrast to the scientific exploration of nature, this process of growing *self*-awareness has an endpoint: namely when we become fully conscious of the fact that all human beings have the potential to be free, self-determining agents. From a Hegelian perspective Kuhn lacks sufficient consciousness of and interest in this pattern of increasing self-awareness that underlies the most important historical changes in our conceptual frameworks.

Yet, despite these differences, the positions of Hegel and Kuhn are similar. Hegel should be seen as a thinker who is just as sensitive to the historical character of human knowledge, and to the different historical preconceptions that underlie different civilizations and forms of life, as are many twentieth-century writers. He is acutely conscious that in order to understand other civilizations one must uncover the distinctive preconceptions that inform them. All civilizations are *human* civilizations and therefore will have some features in common. All will have to cater for natural human needs, for example, such as the need for food and sexual satisfaction. However, all civilizations have their own distinctive way of thinking about things, in Hegel's view, and do not therefore share one universal, neutral framework of belief or understanding.

In stressing the unique historical specificity of different cultures in this way, it is likely that Hegel was greatly influenced by Goethe's one-time friend and collaborator, Johann Gottfried Herder. In an essay on Shakespeare published in 1773, Herder criticizes French classical dramatists and dramatic theorists for treating Aristotle's general characterizations of Greek tragedy as timeless, universal rules for tragedy which could still be applied in seventeenth-century France, rather than as descriptions of a historically specific form of Greek art. In Herder's view, by considering the Aristotelian 'unities' of time and action to be required by universal rules of tragedy, French dramatists such as Racine abstracted these principles from their historical context – that is, from their relation to the Greeks' under-standing of their own history and mythology – and deprived them of their historical meaning. Shakespeare, on the other hand, was far more in tune with the spirit of the Greeks because he departed from Aristotle's alleged rules and gave expression to a specifically English view of the world, just as the Greeks had given expression to their own myths and values in their drama.[7]

For all his Enlightenment faith in reason, Hegel learned Herder's lesson well. For him, philosophical ideas, religious beliefs, aesthetic forms and political constitutions do not have a permanent, unchanging validity, but are the specific products of specific times and places and must be understood in the context of the time and place in which they emerged. In the lectures on the history of philosophy Hegel makes this point particularly clear.

The specific form of a philosophy is thus not merely contemporaneous with the specific shape of the people among whom it arises. It is not merely contemporaneous with this people's constitution, form of government, moral and social life and the skills, habits and conventions involved, its undertakings and endeavours in art and science, its religions, wars, and foreign affairs. . . . Philosophy is the supreme blossom – the *concept* [*Begriff*] – of this entire shape of history, the consciousness and the spiritual essence of the whole situation, the spirit of the age as the spirit present and aware of itself in thought.[8]

This is not of course to say that, because a philosophy or a work of art is produced in one age, its interest is confined to that age. Philosophical principles and aesthetic values from a past age can be appreciated by us and can be recognized as intimating truths to which we subscribe, even if we can no longer produce works of art or think about the world exactly as that past age did. Hegel's position does mean, however, that we cannot simply take over the philosophical, religious, aesthetic or moral ideas and practices of another age or civilization lock, stock and barrel, any more than another civilization could simply adopt our practices. As far as philosophy is concerned, we may be able to incorporate some Platonic or Aristotelian principles into our present point of view and even continue to employ Aristotelian logic in many areas of enquiry (as we also still use Euclidian geometry), but there can now no longer be any fully fledged Platonists, Aristotelians, Stoics or Epicure-ans, because we belong to a different and, in Hegel's opinion, freer and more sophisticated age. Similarly, although the artistic techniques and achievements of earlier ages may be passed down through history, be appropriated by each new age and, as in the case of Greek art, even be seen as unsurpassed, the aesthetic practices of today can no longer follow those of Aeschylus or Sophocles. And as far as the political constitution and the concrete organi-zation of social life are concerned, Hegel believes that we inherit almost no permanent legacy from previous civilizations, except for abstract and highly general principles such as that government should be just and that insight and virtue should guide the rulers.

Hegel's conviction that all the practices and institutions of a civilization are intimately related to one another marks his position as one of holism. Yet his view is not simply that the various aspects of a civilization have great influence on one another. He claims that the aspects of a civilization are united much more deeply than is implied by the concept of 'influence' because they all reflect and give expression to the same basic *character* of the culture. Hegel understands how complex and multifaceted individual civilizations can be and he does not underestimate that complexity. But he wants to highlight what differentiates each civilization – ancient Greek civilization, Roman civilization or modern English, French or German civilization. What gives a civilization its specific identity, he claims, is the principle which constitutes 'the common character [*Gepräge*] of its religion, its political constitution, its ethical life, its system of justice, its customs, and also of its science, art, and technical skill'.[9] This does not mean that everywhere we meet a general name such as the 'British' or the 'Irish', we necessarily encounter a distinct culture or civilization, but rather that it is only where we encounter a common *character* informing the beliefs and practices of a community, and where the community is thereby distinguished as a community, that we can talk of a unified society or culture.

Note that Hegel's view is different from what has sometimes been taken to be a similar position in the writings of Karl Marx. Marx – at least in the interpretation of his thought which I find most persuasive[10] – sees technological change, change in the material forces of production, as the primary determining factor in history. Ideology, belief and forms of social organization are products of such technological change for Marx. In Hegel's view, on the other hand, what is primary in a society is its general character or 'spirit', and the development of the technological power of a culture or society itself stems from the kind of character the society has. This is why different civilizations have made differing use of technological innovations, such as printing, which have been invented by different civilizations at different times. As Hegel points out in the lectures on the philosophy of history, the Chinese

knew of many things at a time when the Europeans had not discovered them, but they did not understand how to make use of what they knew of, such as, for example, the magnet and the art of printing. . . . Gunpowder, too, they claim to have invented before the Europeans, but the Jesuits had to make their first cannons for them.[11]

Hegel does not claim that every detail of a civilization's history is explicable in terms of its general character. The attempt to establish what causes specific things to happen in a society requires specific historical or sociological study: such things cannot be accounted for by general theories about the civilization's make-up. However, Hegel thinks that in all the manifold events and interactions in a civilization's history the basic character of that civilization can be discerned, and it is that character which interests him. The most important thing to identify in a civilization, for Hegel, is thus not this or that specific occurrence or achievement, but the fundamental spirit which makes the civilization what it is. And this spirit or character is equated by Hegel not simply with the contingencies of race or geographical location – although these factors do play a role – but with a civilization's mode of *understanding* the world and itself. 'The legislature, the whole situation of a people is based solely upon the conception which its spirit has of itself, on the categories which it has.'[12]

Here one must guard against misinterpreting Hegel, however. He is not simply asserting that we are modelled according to our own self-image. He insists that a people's (or
indeed an individual's) image of itself may not always be a just one. It is not the favoured
image we have of ourselves that makes us what we are. Rather, our character is constituted
by the fundamental self-understanding – the basic shared assumptions, some of which are
conscious and some unconscious – manifest in our practices, creative activity and labour,
as well as in our beliefs. To determine the character of a people, therefore, we must not
only attend to what a people says about itself and the world, we must also examine how it
lives and what it does. These fundamental values and assumptions are not a mere ideo-
logical superstructure built upon a material or physiological base, for Hegel, but constitute
the substance of society.

This substance is manifest throughout the practices of a culture, but Hegel believes that
it is seen most clearly in the culture's religion, for it is in the beliefs and practices of its
religion that a people gives expression to what it reveres and values most highly. It is in its
religion that a people reveals whether it respects the dignity of humanity or subordinates
humanity to the dictates of a harsh natural or divine power, and whether it conceives of
humanity as capable of compassion for others or as born to aggression or even cruelty.
'Religion', Hegel says in the philosophy of history, 'is the place where a people defines for
itself what it holds to be true.' In part this means what a people thinks about nature, but
more importantly it means what it holds to be true of humanity itself. In religion, therefore, we give expression to our own fundamental self-understanding, to the categories
through which we comprehend our own spiritual life. Indeed, Hegel says that it is the same
conception of spirituality or of individuality that 'in religion . . . is represented, revered and
enjoyed as God; in art . . . is depicted as an image and intuition [*Anschauung*]; and in philosophy . . . is recognised and comprehended by thought'. And because religion, art and
philosophy give expression to the same substantial self-understanding of a people – to the
same conception of truth – they must belong together within one culture and one state.
'This particular form of state can only exist in conjunction with this particular religion,
and only this particular philosophy and this particular art can exist within this state.'[13]

Hegel is very concerned that we should not be misled by superficial similarities between
the religions or philosophies of different cultures. We should not be seduced, as some
of his contemporaries were, into saying that Chinese philosophy, the philosophy of the
Eleatics (such as Parmenides) and Spinozism are all 'basically' the same, because all are
founded on the principle of the unity of being. In his view, such judgements overlook what
is specific about Chinese, Eleatic and Spinozistic conceptions of unity and disregard the
specific cultural contexts from which these philosophies emerged. Like Wittgenstein, therefore, Hegel wishes us to eschew abstract generalizations and to attend to forms of life in
their particularity.

When considering another civilization, we can interpret its myths and explain meanings
that were not explicit within the civilization itself. Or we may, as in the history of philosophy, attend only to the principles that have been explicitly articulated by past philosophers
themselves. But we must always be sensitive to, and seek to bring out, the specific problems and questions, beliefs and presuppositions that occupied the particular civilization in
question. We must thus not seek in the writings of an ancient philosopher more than he
can deliver, and so must not seek in the writings of the Greek philosopher Thales, for
example, the kind of principle which only a Jewish or Christian theologian could have
entertained. In Hegel's judgement, we must not expect that the questions which interest us
will necessarily find answers in philosophers who belong to a different cultural world,
because our questions stem from our civilization and our beliefs – from our 'paradigm', to

use Kuhn's word – and would not necessarily even be intelligible to someone from a different culture. There are no unambiguous common standards of judgement which could be agreed upon by all ages and civilizations, therefore – except such principles as that we all need to eat – because we are all children of our time and understand things in the terms which our civilization and time permit.

To this extent Hegel shares the views of twentieth-century writers like Kuhn or Richard Rorty who stress the absence of a 'permanent, neutral, ahistorical, commensurating vocabulary' in human history.[14] Yet Hegel differs from such writers in one very important respect. For Kuhn, paradigm changes are ultimately the result of non-rational factors, such as shifts in convention. The developments in history which Hegel examines are, likewise, clearly not the product of purely rational argument. Christianity did not conquer the world through the power of its syllogisms. The early Christians did not refer to a common set of principles that they shared with the Romans, Jews and Greeks and *demonstrate* that theirs was the religion which was most rational or which did most justice to some common human experience of the world. Rather, Christianity ushered in a profound shift in human self-understanding which was not self-evidently compelling to all, indeed which could only appear foolish to most Romans, Greeks and Jews. Yet, although Christians and their predecessors may have had different and incompatible fundamental assumptions, Hegel believes that there was in fact a compelling reason for the adoption of the new religion, namely that Christianity represents a higher and more profound form of human self-awareness or self-consciousness.[15]

This is where Hegel and more recent writers like Kuhn and Rorty diverge. Hegel argues that the most important changes in history have involved shifts in the categories through which human beings understand their world, but that these have not been mere shifts in historical convention. They have been shifts brought about by humanity's growing self-awareness.

It is important to stress straight away, however, that Hegel does not see all change in viewpoint or all historical change as the result of increasing human self-awareness. Much in history, for him, is the product of custom or of contingent developments, and much therefore indicates no particular advance in human self-understanding. Some occurrences in history in fact testify to nothing other than humanity's enduring capacity for barbarism and destruction. The actions of the Mongol hordes under Genghis Khan and Tamburlaine, for example, are understood by Hegel in this way. Hegel thus clearly does not believe that we are all marching gloriously to full self-awareness in all that we do. Yet he does believe that within the manifold vicissitudes of human history there is an identifiable strand of development from humanity's initial, primitive self-understanding to the much more enlightened perspective of the modern age.

Hegel justifies this belief by examining what he sees as the fundamental characters or principles informing different historical civilizations and by comparing them with one another. He does not claim to give an exhaustive account of the civilizations he studies, but he does believe that he can identify the fundamental beliefs of a civilization which enable us to situate it historically in relation to other civilizations. What he looks for in a civilization is the extent to which it is or is not conscious of human self-determination or *freedom*.

Comparing Civilizations

The main difference, for Hegel, between African and Asiatic civilizations on the one hand, and the civilizations of ancient Greece, ancient Rome and the modern world on the other, is that the latter were and are informed by a lively consciousness of the significance of individual freedom, whereas in the former (at least prior to the influence of the Europeans) such consciousness has been largely dormant or indeed wholly lacking. In Hegel's view, this is a difference in fundamental outlook, and it determines the whole structure of the respective civilizations. Thus, from a Hegelian perspective, because no clear consciousness of individual freedom was alive in ancient China or ancient India, those civilizations did not provide for the freedom of political representation which was claimed in the Greek city-states or in the Roman republic. A civilization in which people are not *conscious* of themselves as free, therefore – that is, a civilization in which the claim to freedom is not made – *is* not free, in Hegel's view, and will not develop the institutions which human freedom requires. 'The Orientals do not yet know that the spirit or man as such is free in himself', Hegel tells us. And 'because they do not know this, they are not themselves free'.[16]

The China of the first Emperor, Qin Shihuang, was a highly bureaucratized, hierarchical society which allowed no room for the freedom of self-determination which Western European civilizations have claimed, except, perhaps, in the case of the Emperor himself. Moreover, whatever changes have since occurred in China – and Hegel does not deny that changes have occurred – they do not constitute any evidence that the spirit of individual self-determination which we prize so highly has played any significant role in Chinese history. Even in ancient Greece, where individual freedom was claimed and given expression in art, religion and political life, the conception of freedom with which the Greeks operated was, Hegel thinks, a limited one. It was a freedom to be enjoyed by the few, not by all. Greek art thus celebrated the noble heroes who stood out above all others, and Greek democracy, even at its height, only gave representation to some and was able to coexist with slavery. The Greeks and the Romans valued human freedom – albeit in subtly different ways – but they both confined that freedom to certain privileged groups. Only with the coming of Christianity, Hegel maintains, did people come to recognize that all human beings are in principle free because all are equal in the eyes of God. Of course, the acceptance of the Christian religion in Europe did not bring about the abolition of slavery and the realization of political freedom overnight. Nevertheless, the history of Western civilization is understood by Hegel to be the gradual process of developing the Christian recognition of the universal freedom and dignity of humanity before God into the social, political and ethical reality of the modern rational, constitutional state. European history is thus the process of matching the Christian demand for universal human freedom with the secular claim to universal human rights – a claim which grew out of the religious demand for freedom and which is characteristic of the modern period.

In Hegel's view, therefore, certain shifts in cultural perspective have resulted not merely from a *change* in human self-understanding, but rather from a *deepening* of human self-understanding. Such shifts constitute, for him, a progressive development towards the truth. They represent humanity's increasing awareness of the essential nature of our own character, activity and thought – a growing self-awareness that brings with it a more adequate understanding of the world around us.

Once again, we should be careful not to misunderstand Hegel. He does not presuppose that there is a given, fixed human nature or immutable human 'soul' – analogous to external, physical nature – which we gradually represent more and more accurately in our theories. For Hegel, there is no given, immutable human self, no 'entity' called the self which would be available for scientific scrutiny. There is only the human *activity* of producing our world, of producing or determining different forms of social life from different forms of philosophical, religious, aesthetic or ethical self-understanding. But, for Hegel, that activity of historical self-production, self-construction and self-determination *is* thus what we are. It is the universal form of all human activity, of all human life. Different cultures differ only in the degree to which they are conscious of themselves as self-productive and self-determining; that is, only in the degree to which they are explicitly, self-consciously and thus *freely* self-determining.

This does not mean that there is after all an agreed and acknowledged standard by which civilizations can be compared. Not all civilizations understand themselves in the same way and not all recognize or accept that human beings create their own identity and world. Some civilizations understand themselves as caught up in a fixed natural order (Hegel often cites the Indian caste system as an example), whereas other civilizations are much more confident of their ability and power to create their own world (Hegel sees this confidence as a characteristic of modern civil society in particular). Nevertheless, all civilizations, in Hegel's understanding, do in fact produce their own world, whether they do so consciously or not, because in all civilizations the way in which people see themselves fundamentally determines the social practices which they develop.

Essentially, human beings are nothing but the activity of producing and determining themselves and their identity; they are self-producing, self-determining beings. Human beings are born into a particular geographical and historical environment with certain natural characteristics, so they do not create themselves, as it were, out of nothing. However, mankind's natural constitution and specific historical and geographical context, while providing the conditions from which we must start, do not fix for all time what human beings can become. Rather, mankind's character changes as its self-understanding changes. When human beings become more conscious of themselves as self-determining beings, or, indeed, when a once sophisticated level of human self-understanding is sub-merged by that of a more primitive people and forgotten – as happened, at least in part, to classical learning during the Dark Ages – then the nature of the social, political and cultural world which human beings create and inhabit is transformed. The fundamental advances in history – the emergence of the classical world and the dawn of Christianity, for example – are thus the result, for Hegel, of mankind's becoming more aware of itself as freely self-determining and thereby actually coming to be more freely self-determining in history.

All peoples and civilizations are in fact self-productive and produce a different social order through the particular way in which they understand themselves and their world; but not all civilizations are fully conscious of the extent to which they are self-productive. Thus, there is a criterion for assessing the relative merits of different civilizations, namely the degree to which they are conscious of themselves as they are, as active and self-determining. But this criterion cannot be a generally acknowledged and accepted standard of evaluation, since only those civilizations which do evince a high degree of self-awareness will recognize that mankind is essentially self-productive. The criterion of evaluation that Hegel establishes is thus not a neutral standard available to all which would allow a neutral comparative evaluation of different civilizations. It is a standard that is only available to those civilizations that are in fact conscious of human self-determination.

Clearly, there is an asymmetry between civilizations, for Hegel, that makes his model of historical change different from that of Kuhn or Rorty. For Hegel, the fact that there may be no agreed standard of judgement in all cultures or forms of life does not mean that rival cultural (or religious or philosophical) viewpoints are incommensurable, or that they are equal partners in a conversation. In Hegel's eyes, there is an absolute standard of judgement which is laid down precisely by the fact that human beings are self-productive, historical beings with no agreed universal values or standards. But this absolute standard of judgement can only be known to those civilizations which are *aware* that they are histori-cally self-productive.

But how can this make sense? How can different civilizations have fundamentally dif-ferent conceptions of themselves yet not be incommensurable? Hegel's answer to this ques-tion is that, despite the absence of common assumptions between civilizations, a more self-aware civilization can *prove* its greater understanding of human 'nature' and potential and its consequent greater strength. It does so by making space for degrees of self-consciousness and freedom that other civilizations cannot contain (at least not without huge and sometimes destructive upheaval). Hegel claims, for example, that democracy in ancient Greece was founded on a deep sense of the identity of the interests of the individ-ual and the community. In democratic Greek city-states – Hegel has fifth-century Athens in mind – individuals took a free and active part in debating public affairs; but they did so largely in a common spirit of upholding the customs and practices of the community. What was right and proper was thus not determined by individual reflection or personal con-science, but was embodied in the living customs and practices of the community in which individuals participated. The strength of Greek democracy, for Hegel, lay in this shared sense of the value of common practices and institutions, which meant that individuals drew their moral ideas from their ethical customs rather than from autonomous, individual conscience. Once the principle of critical, individual reflection entered Greek life, however – Hegel points to the Sophists and Socrates as the major philosophical sources of this prin-ciple – the immediate bond between the individual and the community was weakened. People were encouraged to follow their own convictions, to seek guidance in their own critical reflection and ideas, rather than in established common practices. Hegel argues that this principle of subjective reflection undermined the trust that the Greeks had placed in their institutions and in leaders such as Themistocles and Pericles, and therefore ultimately undermined the ethical basis for their particular forms of democratic cooperation. Thucy-dides revealed his awareness of this development, Hegel tells us, in his complaint that citizens were coming to believe that things were going wrong if *they* were not personally involved in them in some way.[17] In Hegel's view, therefore, the principle of critical freedom, which reached its height in the great philosophers of the fourth century, such as Plato and Aristotle, posed a serious threat to Greek religion and Greek democracy because it no longer allowed belief and action to be guided by custom, but subjected everything to critical scrutiny. The reason why Socrates was put to death by the Athenians, according to Hegel, was thus that the principle of critical inquiry which he espoused proved to be revolutionary and subversive in the Athenian state.

The flourishing of free, rational thought in philosophers such as Plato and Aristotle was magnificent, Hegel says, but it was not compatible with the equal magnificence of Greek democracy. For all its grandeur, therefore, Greek culture was not able to accommodate this new sense of subjective human freedom – the dawn of reflective, critical thought – and remain the splendid political and aesthetic culture that it had been in the fifth century. Rome, however, and, to a much greater extent, Christian civilization have been able to incorporate and indeed build their strength upon this subjective, critical freedom. In fact Hegel believes that it is precisely this subjective freedom – which proved to be the ruin of ancient Greece – 'which constitutes the principle, and the peculiar form, of freedom in our world, [and] which forms the absolute foundation of our state and our religious life'.[18] He believes that the emergence of humanity's sense of its own freedom of critical reflec-tion marks a real development or progress in human self-awareness, but that Greek culture as it was constituted in fifth-century Athens could not accommodate this progress and remain what it was. Modern Christian, constitutional states, on the other hand, can accommodate that freedom – indeed they derive their strength from that freedom and from their ability to integrate it into the 'substantive unity' of the community and the state[19] – and thus in this respect at least have proved their historical superiority over ancient Greece.

Even though all civilizations do not share the same world-view, therefore, they can be evaluated by comparing the extent to which they can incorporate new levels of human self-consciousness and freedom. The more self-conscious civilization, according to Hegel, can thus prove its greater self-awareness to another, less advanced civilization with which it coexists by showing that less advanced civilization aspects of human freedom and potential of which that civilization either is not conscious or has not taken full account. In the modern world, Hegel considered the English in particular to have taken on this educative role and to be the 'missionaries' of modern European civilization to the rest of the world – missionaries who are driven by interests of commerce and trade 'to form connections with barbarous peoples, to awaken needs within them and to stimulate their industry, and first and foremost to establish among them the conditions necessary for commerce, viz. the relinquishing of violence, a respect for property, and hospitality'.[20] Yet Hegel is well aware that the moment the more advanced civilization makes the less advanced civilization share in and adopt its higher or deeper level of human self-understanding, it transforms that civilization completely. The less advanced civilization can be shown what it had previously not recognized; to that extent a more advanced civilization can *prove* the advantage it has over its neighbours. But the less advanced civilization can only incorporate what it had previously not recognized by radically altering its way of life, as we ourselves see only too clearly today, as Third World countries often struggle painfully to adopt Western freedoms and at the same time seek to avoid the evident excesses of Western life and hold on to their own traditional values and beliefs. In Hegel's hard-headed, in some ways tragic but to my mind deeply realistic view, such Third World countries face an extremely difficult road ahead, because no civilization can become more self-aware and more free and also expect to retain all of its old values and practices. To that extent, for Hegel, civilizations are indeed incommensurable.

It should be evident from what has been said so far that Hegel's philosophy offers a solution to one of the most important questions occupying philosophers today: the question whether our modern consciousness of the changing historical character of human existence is reconcilable or compatible with the traditional philosophical belief in, and search for, the *true* nature of humanity. In the lectures on the history of philosophy Hegel poses the problem of the relation of history and truth in the following way:

The first thought that may strike us in connection with the history of philosophy is that this subject itself involves at once an inner contradiction, because philosophy aims at knowing what is imperishable, eternal and absolute [*an und für sich*]. Its aim is *truth*. But history relates the sort of thing which has existed at one time but at another has perished, superseded by its successor. If we start from the fact that truth is eternal, then it cannot fall into the sphere of the transient and it has no history. But if it has a history, and history is only a display of a series of past forms of knowledge, then truth is not to be found in it, since truth is not something past.[21]

This at least is how ordinary reasoning conceives of the matter: if truth is to be absolute, it can't have a history, and if it is to have a history, it can't be absolute. Nietzsche, for example, insisted that what has a history cannot be defined,[22] and many writers, from pragmatists like John Dewey to neo-Marxists like Theodor Adorno to Aristotelian neo-Hegelians like Alasdair MacIntyre, have welcomed Hegel's sense of history while rejecting his 'metaphysical' concern for absolute truth. It is invariably the case in fact that declared critics of metaphysical oppositions and dualities, like Nietzsche, find the opposition between history and absolute truth to be the main one they are unable to overcome or undermine. They are usually led to drop one side of the opposition – absolute truth – and to stick with history. But, from Hegel's perspective, the opposition between history and absolute truth is a false one, and the reasons for rejecting absolute truth (either in the guise of philosophy or religion) in the name of history are therefore spurious. For Hegel, the absolute truth of humanity is that human beings have no fixed, given identity, but rather determine and produce their identity and their world in history, and that they gradually come to the recognition of this fact in history. History is indeed essentially the process whereby mankind becomes aware of itself as free, self-determining and therefore historical. The absolute truth of humanity is that we are historical, and the history of humanity is the process of coming to recognize our absolute, historical character. History and truth are thus completely inseparable for Hegel, and it is not possible to drop or reject either term.

For Hegel, consciousness of human truth and consciousness of human historicity are not incompatible, because consciousness of human truth is essentially consciousness of human self-determination in history and of the historical process whereby humanity comes to recognize itself as essentially historical and self-determining. This connection between the truth of humanity and human historicity is not merely contingent. If human beings are indeed historically self-determining, they cannot simply *be* this, but must actively *determine* themselves in history to be self-determining. In other words, we must make ourselves into self-determining beings in history, because we are self-determining, self-*producing* beings. However, if we always already *are* self-determining beings, then the process of making ourselves into self-determining beings cannot simply bring into being something which is not already a reality. Rather, it must be the process of making us into what we already are. To put the point a little less paradoxically, this process involves humanity making itself *explicitly* what it already is *implicitly*. This means that we must come to be self-consciously what we already are 'unconsciously'. Hegel thinks that all the major developments in history as he understands it are to be explained in terms of this process.

What is implicit in man must become an object to him, come into his consciousness; then it becomes *for* him and he becomes aware of himself, explicit to himself. In this way he duplicates himself: first, he *is* reason and thinking, but only implicitly; then, secondly, he thinks, makes his implicit self into an object of his thought. . . . What was *potentia* comes into appearance *actu*. On further reflection we see that the man who was potentially rational and now makes this rationality the object of his thought has got no further than he was at the beginning. What a man brings before his mind he potentially *is*. His *potentia* is maintained and remains the same; the content [what he has become] is nothing new. This seems to be a useless duplication, yet the difference between *potentia* and *actus* is tremendous. All knowing, learning, insight, science, even all action has no other interest but to bring out, produce, make objective, what was potential and inner. . . . The whole difference in world-history arises from and depends on this difference. All men are rational, and the formal side of this rationality is that man is free; this is his nature, inherent in the essence of man. And yet there has been, and in some cases still is, slavery in many lands, and the population is content with this. Orientals, for example, are men and, as such, are implicitly free, and yet they are still not [explicitly free]; they have no consciousness of freedom because they have all submitted to a despotism, whether religious or political. The whole difference between Orientals and peoples amongst whom slavery does not prevail is that the latter know that they are free and are aware of it explicitly. The Orientals are free too – implicitly – but they are not free in fact. The tremendous difference in the world-historical situation is whether men are only implicitly free or whether they know that it is their fundamental truth, nature or vocation to live as free individuals.[23]

History is thus the process whereby human beings come to new levels of awareness of their freedom, of their productive, active nature, and thereby produce new forms of social and political life. The human activity of self-production is, therefore, at the same time the process of self-discovery and self-revelation – a fusion of making oneself and finding oneself, of acting and of coming to know, which is perhaps best expressed in English by the word 'self-realization'.

Self-consciousness and Historical Progress

What I have said so far should have made it clear that Hegel's philosophy is a profound and challenging body of thought that has important ideas to contribute to current debates. However, I have given only the barest outline of Hegel's understanding of history and the historical nature of truth, and that outline needs to be fleshed out rather more if the new student of Hegel is to avoid certain popular misinterpretations of his thought.

First of all, it is important to point out that, although Hegel believes that history is the process whereby humanity gradually awakens to itself, he is not the naive Enlightenment optimist caricatured by Nietzsche or Schopenhauer. He does not regard the process of awakening as a smooth, continuous development in which new levels of human self-understanding just grow out of one another. The civilization of the Romans, in Hegel's view, was able to contain the principle of subjective particularity which precipitated the decline of Greece, but Roman civilization did not simply 'develop' out of Greek civilization. Rome owed much to the achievements of the Greeks and was influenced by them in many ways, but it had its own distinctive roots. The only area of history in which Hegel does see a continuous development is in the emergence and growth of modern European states within Western Christendom. Hegel's claim, then, is not that there is one simple, continuous tradition which constitutes 'history', but rather that within history we see a series of civilizations – the main ones being the Persian Empire, Greece, Rome and Western Christian civilization – each with its own distinctive roots, but each able to appropriate the achievements of its predecessor and accommodate a level of self-consciousness and freedom which its predecessor could not accommodate.

Nor, indeed, is this progress in human self-consciousness quite the steady, unproblematic development which some have understood Hegel to have in mind. Roman civilization, for Hegel, had a much more developed sense of the claims of the private individual than Greek civilization (at least, than fifth-century Athens), and this is made manifest in the institutions of Roman law. Rome thus developed a concept of the formal rights of private citizens which surpassed anything the Greeks had achieved. But this advance was purchased at a heavy cost. In Hegel's understanding, the Roman concern for the formal rights of the particular subject or citizen degenerated all too easily into a willingness to indulge private interest and self-will, and Rome was consequently not able to develop the sense of ethical community which was the glory of Greek democracy at its height. Rome in fact came to manifest the worst excesses of selfishness, force and even bestiality. Rome's artistic achievement is also much inferior to that of the Greeks in Hegel's view (as, of course, in the view of many others). In the transition from the cultural supremacy of the Greeks to that of the Romans, therefore, the world gained and lost something at the same time. The history of Christian civilization, in Hegel's understanding, shows a similar combination of progress and regression – the degeneration of the Catholic Church which followed upon the extension of Church power in the Middle Ages and which led to the Reformation, and the Terror which followed the French Revolution being perhaps his most important examples. But Hegel never claimed that progress in human self-consciousness is a smooth or easy affair. After all, he called the history of the world 'the slaughter-bench on which the happiness of peoples, the wisdom of states and the virtue of individuals have been sacrificed'.[24] The point, for him, is not to present a bland, idealized view of history, but to consider where in all this historical confusion and bloodshed progress does actually show itself, and to what extent massive historical upheavals – such as the Thirty Years War between Protestant and Catholic states in seventeenth-century Germany or the French Revolution – were the tragic results of *advances* in human religious or political self-understanding. And, rightly or wrongly, Hegel believes that he can see progress in these upheavals, despite the horrors which they brought in their wake, since the Thirty Years War led to the consolidation of Protestantism in Germany (and Protestantism, for Hegel, is a more profound and liberating form of Christianity than Catholicism), and since the French Revolution, whatever else it showed about our capacity for exercising terror in the name of freedom, demonstrated the powerful modern desire to remould our political world in accordance with the principles of free, rational self-determination.

Another misconception of Hegel's philosophy of history, fostered to a certain extent by Marx, is that he sees the development of human self-consciousness as a purely intellectual matter, as simply the development of human ideas. Hegel does indeed say that the thought of the early Greek philosopher Anaxagoras was 'epoch-making', because it introduced into human consciousness the idea that there is reason in nature,[25] and he clearly thinks that the philosophy of Descartes had enormous historical influence too. But, in his view, the changes in categories, and the consequent reformation of the human spirit, that underlie all revolutionary historical transformation involve changes in our material interests and practical, socio-economic activity (as well as in religious belief) as much as changes in intellectual or philosophical perspective. Having said that, history, for Hegel, is not primarily (as it is for Marx) the development of material productive power, but is 'the spirit's effort to attain *knowledge* [*Wissen*] of what it is in itself'.[26] In history, human beings gradually come to recognize and will the truth about themselves (and the world), and it is this that brings about changes in both our beliefs and our practices.

Note that this is not a claim about everything that has happened in the past, but a claim about what is to be understood by the word 'history'. What Hegel is arguing is that only those sequences of events which have been brought about by the development of human self-consciousness and by the pursuit of consciously articulated goals can really count as *historical*. But why should Hegel define history in this way? The answer lies in the distinction he draws between natural and historical change.

Natural change, for Hegel, is determined by unstated natural laws (and by certain contingencies). The laws of the movements of the planets are not written up on the heavens, and natural objects such as planets do not obey such laws consciously or purposefully. Indeed, whatever purposes may be fulfilled in nature, they are never pursued as self-conscious goals.

History, on the other hand, is different. The word 'history', Hegel points out, means both what happens and the narrative record of what happens, and, he adds, this coincidence of meanings is not arbitrary. 'We must . . . suppose', he says, 'that the writing of history and the actual deeds and events of history make their appearance simultaneously, and that they emerge together from a common source'.[27] Historical change or activity, therefore, is self-recording, self-narrating, self-interpreting activity; that is, *self-conscious* activity. Change is historical when those involved in it understand it as fitting into a narrative scheme of things, when they are conscious of its having historical significance.

Historical activity is self-conscious activity, for Hegel, not only because it is self-narrating, but also because it is directed at the achievement of deliberately pursued, self-conscious ends. And in Hegel's understanding, people come to pursue genuinely self-conscious, as opposed to merely natural, ends when they have formed themselves into communities which are held together not merely by the natural bonds of family affection, or by custom, but by self-consciously determined laws. Such is the case in states. A state, for Hegel, is a body of people held together by consciously willed general laws, rather than mere force or natural association. States may be created by the forceful unification of people, but they must be sustained by some commonly acknowledged conscious purpose or identity if they are to count as true states. Now, it is precisely because states are not based on the merely natural bonds of kinship, but are held together above all by a *consciousness* of a common social or political identity and purpose, that historical narrative is required to objectify and preserve the achievements of the state and thus consolidate its sense of identity.

It is the state which first supplies a content which not only lends itself to the prose of history but actually helps produce it. Instead of the merely subjective dictates of authority – which may suffice for the needs of the moment – a commonwealth in the process of coalescing and raising itself up to the position of a state requires formal commandments and laws, i.e. general and universally valid directives. It thereby creates a record of, and interest in, intelligible, determinate, and – in their results – enduring deeds and events, on which Mnemosyne, for the benefit of the perennial aim which under-lies the present form and constitution of the state, is impelled to confer a lasting memory.[28]

The writing of history thus contributes to the preservation and consolidation of the self-conscious identity of the state by giving it a sense of where it has come from, what it is essentially concerned with and where it is going; that is, by enabling a state to develop a *historical* identity which nature alone does not provide.

Historical change is change that is produced by our self-conscious pursuit of the goals of the self-conscious communities – the states – in which we live. History, in other words, is the working out of the conflicts, clashes and interactions between and within different states. It is clear, therefore, that history, as Hegel conceives it – history as the progressive development of humanity towards greater self-understanding – is inseparable from the *political* history of human development towards greater self-consciousness and freedom in states. It is not the history of our intellectual – i.e. scientific, aesthetic or philosophical – achievements in abstraction from their social and political context. Shifts in human self-understanding, which entail shifts in our religious, aesthetic, philosophical and ethical viewpoints, thus also involve the transfer of political and historical power from one state – such as Greece – which reflects a particular level of human self-consciousness to another state – such as Rome – which reflects a more advanced level of self-consciousness. Or, alternatively, as happened in the development of modern Europe, shifts in human self-understanding, such as the transition from the Mediaeval world to the post-Renaissance and post-Reformation world, involve enormous social and political upheavals within one civilization and within individual states. Hegel's view of history is not therefore as 'ideal-istic' as it might first appear. Rather, it entails understanding major *political*, *social* and *economic* transformations in history in the light of major reformations or developments in human self-consciousness. Technological developments in history also play an important role for Hegel in the transformation of human life – witness the importance he sees in the invention of printing in Europe in the fifteenth century – but such technological innovations, in his view, themselves derive their power to change our lives from the social and political expectations of the people who are able to exploit them. The course of history is thus determined not by technological advances alone, but by our growing consciousness of our power and freedom of self-determination.

History, Truth and Relativism

Hegel is often referred to as the greatest philosopher of German Idealism, but it should be clear from what I have been saying that his view of history is not 'idealistic' if that term is meant to suggest either that he has a bland, optimistic theory of historical progress or that he reduces history to the history of ideas. Nor is Hegel an 'idealist' in the manner of Kant, since he clearly believes that human beings live in a world that is intrinsically spatio-temporal and that space and time are not mere forms of intuition that have no reality apart from human sensibility. Hegel is an 'idealist' (in his philosophy of history, at least) because he does not understand human character or identity to be some fixed, immutable 'reality', but rather conceives of human beings as actively producing their character and identity in history. Human beings have a true, essential nature according to him, but it is not 'an essence that is already finished and complete before its manifestation, keeping itself aloof behind its host of appearances, but an essence which is truly actual only through the specific forms of its necessary self-manifestation'.[29] As Hegel puts it in the lectures on the philosophy of history,

the spirit is essentially active; it makes itself into that which it is in itself, into its own deed, its own creation [*Werk*]. In this way, it becomes its own object, and has its own existence before it. And it is the same with the spirit of a nation; it is a specific spirit which makes itself into an actual world which now exists objectively in its religion, its ritual, its customs, constitution and political laws, and in the whole range of its institutions, events and deeds. That is its creation – that *is* this people.[30]

The goal of historical activity, for Hegel, is thus for human beings to become conscious of themselves as freely and historically self-productive and self-determining – not something fixed by nature – and for them to build their world in accordance with that recognition. In other words, 'the entire development of the spirit is nothing else but the raising of itself to its truth'.[31]

Here we see the great subtlety of Hegel's historical conception of truth. Becoming aware of the true character of human existence does not mean for him simply becoming conscious of a given, fixed reality or gaining a more accurate picture of what we were like at the beginning of history. Rather, it means learning that what we are is the process of producing and determining ourselves. Furthermore, it means learning that this process of self-production is itself the process of coming to *understand* more clearly that we are self-producing beings. Indeed, we learn that it is above all through changes in our self-understanding that we actually make ourselves into and so *become* something new: we produce ourselves precisely through developing a fuller understanding that we do so. At the culmination of history, human beings recognize more explicitly than in earlier ages that they are and have always been free, self-productive beings; but they also realize that this more explicit recognition has itself made new beings of us and has produced a new world. What we achieve at the culmination of history is thus a full consciousness of what we *are* and a full consciousness of what we have *become* through understanding what we are.

History and truth necessarily belong together in Hegel's philosophy, (a) because our true nature is to come to understand ourselves through a process of historical development and to produce a new world in the process, and (b) because genuinely historical, as opposed to natural, change is generated by our gradual awakening to our true nature. Consciousness of the truth is thus crucial to historical existence, for Hegel, since the deepening of such consciousness is what drives history forward. Equally, it is only when we have become fully aware of our true character that we are fully conscious of our historicity and of our real historical possibilities. This, of course, is where Hegel is out of line with a certain relativist trend in philosophy which has been fashionable at various times since his death. Nietzsche, for example, can only see the concept of absolute truth as restricting humanity within one limited perspective and so believes that doing away with the concept will liberate humanity to a more open future with new, infinitely varying possibilities. However, to Hegelian eyes, Nietzschean 'openness' seems dangerously vague and indeterminate. We are genuinely freed to our human possibilities, for Hegel, only when we know who or what we truly are, when we recognize that we are free, self-determining, historical beings and when we understand fully the form that our freedom must *necessarily* take if it is to be real freedom. A religious or philosophical consciousness of the truth that, for example, human beings must give up clinging to their narrow self-interest in order to find freedom with others does not confine us within one 'limited' human perspective or stand in the way of human self-realization, but rather makes real freedom possible by preventing us from destroying ourselves in the name of a false image of freedom.

Hegel recognizes, however, that the rejection of truth and the privileging of individual, partial or local 'opinions' has become a 'great sign of the times'.[32] What he had in mind in his own day was what he took to be the championing of subjective piety and intuition at the expense of reason by writers such as Jacobi, theologians such as Schleiermacher and Romantics such as Friedrich Schlegel. In the twentieth and twenty-first centuries Hegel would have seen the danger coming from open subjectivism – above all in the arts – and from the historical relativism associated, for example, with certain forms of pragmatism. By stressing the conventional element in belief above all else, such writers as Richard Rorty argue that no absolute justification for our beliefs can be given or is even desirable. In Rorty's view, we should be less concerned with making grandiose claims to truth and more concerned with fostering 'conversation' between different perspectives. In Hegel's view, however, although many of the variations in human outlook and belief are the result of different geographical conditions and of different national or local conventions – factors that cannot be given any ultimate justification – the prime factor determining the outlook and character of a people is the level of its self-consciousness and self-understanding. From a Hegelian perspective, an unwillingness to make definitive judgements about human practices betrays a wilful refusal to recognize that there are *necessary* constraints imposed upon us by our essential nature as self-determining beings.

What many critics of Hegel fail to grasp is that he is not a historical thinker despite his retention of the idea of truth, but *because* of his retention of the idea of truth. Hegel understands human beings to be *essentially* self-determining and therefore historical beings. Like Herder, he is a deeply historical thinker who believes that we should seek to understand particular cultures and particular thinkers in their own terms, and not by reference to some abstract, neutral standard. Indeed, where possible, he believes that we should try to employ the 'actual words' of the people we are considering.[33] We should therefore always enter into the strength of our opponents' terms and try to grasp the point that they want to make, rather than simply interpret our opponents' interests in the light of our own. On the other hand, Hegel does not believe that we should give up looking for truth in what past ages or other civilizations have said. Where it is clear that one civilization's self-understanding is more advanced – more free – than that of another, then we should not be afraid to say so. This involves no doctrine of 'cultural imperialism' or 'racial superiority'. (Hegel does not give particular priority to racial differences between people because, in his view, human self-consciousness is what determines a civilization's character, and this self-consciousness can be changed and developed through education.) Hegel's position does, however, commit him to the view that certain civilizations are more advanced than others and that the culture and civilization of the Western Christian tradition is the most profoundly self-aware and thus most advanced in history.

But is this not an intolerably smug, Eurocentric position? Is Hegel blind to the unmistakable deficiencies of the modern world? Not at all. Hegel was acutely concerned with the problem of modern subjectivism and, like the Scottish Enlightenment before him and Marx and Engels after him, he was acutely concerned with the problems of poverty and the division of labour which modern European industrial power has brought in its wake. However, he did not think that such problems expose fundamental deficiencies in modern society or in Western civilization, but rather that they result from our failure to grasp the true nature of the freedom to which we lay claim. For Hegel, post-Reformation Western civilization has recognized that the nature and purpose of humanity is to be fully free and self-determining. In the modern age, therefore, we lay claim to freedom of speech, freedom of representation, freedom of conscience, freedom of national self-determination and a host of other freedoms, in a way that no other civilization has ever done before. We also extend that claim to freedom over the whole globe and proclaim the right of all peoples to self-determination – sometimes with tremendous consequences. Out of this modern claim to freedom there have emerged in Western European civilization – and in this respect Hegel sees America as an extension of Europe – social, economic and political institutions such as open law-courts, relations of legally regulated economic exchange and representative assemblies which more or less successfully satisfy our demands. These institutions are not by any means perfect, in Hegel's view, but have grown up painfully and with many imperfections out of Europe's political, religious, economic and social struggles. Nevertheless, they are for him essentially the products of the emerging modern consciousness of freedom and of the corresponding demand for greater extension of human power and control over human affairs.

The basic character of the modern age is thus determined by the modern claim to freedom. However, Hegel also believes that the modern age has the tendency to seize on one aspect of human freedom at the expense of others. The evident deficiencies of modern Western society, of which Hegel was well aware, are thus not the result (as they are for Heidegger) of some fundamental blindness running throughout Western civilization, but rather of our understanding our freedom in a partial, one-sided way. The 'freedom' of opinion which rejects the constraints placed upon it by truth, the 'freedom' of economic competition which ignores its ethical responsibilities, the 'freedom' of aesthetic experimentation which undermines the wholeness and dignity of human beings and the 'freedom' of self-righteous political virtue which rides roughshod over the rights of others to make their views heard are all examples of modern freedom gone badly wrong. The modern evils of economic poverty (which Hegel discusses in the *Philosophy of Right*), of political tyranny in the name of political freedom (which he discusses in the context of the French Revolution in the *Phenomenology* and the philosophy of history) and of modern subjectivism (which he discusses throughout his philosophy) are all products of our understanding our freedom in a one-sided way and of our consequent neglect of the true nature of human fulfilment.

Hegel's defence of the Christian and modern secular conception of self-determination is not therefore smug or complacent, for he is acutely aware that modern consciousness does not always fully understand what true self-determination means. Consequently, our

᾽frequent failure to grasp the true nature of freedom or to make freedom a reality for many people today does not mean we are wrong to see the concern for freedom as the defining characteristic of the modern age. However, it does mean that we moderns have a duty to understand freedom properly, especially if we are going to export it to the rest of the globe. The task of Hegel's philosophy, as commentators such as Joachim Ritter have recognized,[34] will thus be to try to develop the true conception of the freedom and self-determination to which modern consciousness now lays claim, and so perhaps to enable modern consciousness to avoid its worst excesses.

History and the Absolute

Two questions regarding Hegel's historical conception of truth now need to be briefly addressed. The first is this: Hegel has insisted that all civilizations understand the world from the perspective of their own self-understanding, but does this apply to the modern age as well, and, if so, does it limit the value of the modern conception of truth and freedom? The answer to the first part of this question, for Hegel, is yes. We moderns do bring our own categories to bear on our experience and view nature and history through these categories just as any civilization does. The categories we employ – or at least should employ – are, as we have seen, categories such as freedom, development and self-determination. But these categories are not just conventional categories; they are not just the product of technological changes or of 'paradigm shifts' which are ultimately a matter of chance. They are the categories which derive from our becoming conscious of the essentially historical character of human activity, and they are the only categories in which that character can be fully revealed. The categories of modern consciousness are *historical* products, but they are not therefore intrinsically *limited* categories because they are the categories through which we have become fully aware of our historicity and freedom.

As we have seen, however, the problem which Hegel recognizes with modern consciousness is that we do not always properly understand the character of historical activity and of free self-determination. We often prefer to understand ourselves in terms of the restricted categories of natural science, or in terms of abstract, one-sided conceptions of freedom. Or, like Nietzsche or Richard Rorty, we are often misled by our preconceptions into believing that our recognition of our historicity puts our claim to truth out of order. The task of Hegel's philosophy will thus be to provide a proper understanding of the categories appropriate to the modern age that will free us from such one-sided misconceptions of ourselves (and of the world around us).

The second key question is this: what has happened to Hegel's Absolute in this discussion? In one sense, I hope that my account will have shown that the infamous Hegelian Absolute which is supposed to be the all-powerful puppet-master governing history and using human beings as the vehicles for its schemes is in fact an absolute fiction. Such an Absolute does not exist in Hegel's philosophy, but only in the minds of his critics. Hegel is quite clear that history is the sphere of *human* activity. In all events and occurrences in history, he says, 'our first concern is with the deeds and sufferings of men; we see elements of ourselves in everything, so that our sympathies constantly oscillate from one side to the other'. Historical activity, therefore, has its source 'in the needs, impulses, inclinations and passions of man'.[35] However, like David Hume and Adam Smith before him and Karl Marx after him, Hegel believes that human beings are not in complete control of their historical activity. Human beings make history but not always as they intend to make it. Human interest, which for Hegel is always at least interest in satisfying individual human needs, thus leads human beings, *despite* their initial intentions, to become interdependent, to form communities and to organize themselves into self-conscious groupings such as states. In this way they come to recognize that the satisfaction of their particular interests requires them to pursue common, social goals. Human beings' own needs, therefore, drive them to the recognition that they are essentially self-conscious, social animals who are able to find freedom only in self-conscious community with other human beings. This initially unintended course of action is, in Hegel's view, rational and necessary and is nothing other than the course of action to which human beings are driven by their own free activity. We are thus not at the mercy of some transcendent Absolute, but we are guided by the *logic* that is immanent in our own activity – a logic which we come more and more to understand as we progress in history, but which, tragically, we are also always able to *misunderstand* and, in so doing, turn into a force which threatens us rather than leads us to true freedom.

There is reason in being, nature and history for Hegel. Such reason, or, as Hegel calls it, the 'Idea', is a reality, not a fiction. It is not, however, a transcendent power that dominates from on high the world in which we live. In that sense, it is not the infamous 'Absolute' attacked so frequently by Hegel's critics. The Idea is, rather, the rationality that is *immanent* in the world itself: the world's own inherent logic. In nature the Idea is the logic that is immanent in and generated by space as such and that leads to the emergence of freely moving matter and eventually to life. In history the Idea is nothing other than the logic that is immanent within and generated by human action and that leads human beings to become more social and more self-conscious as they seek to satisfy their interests.

Reason, or the Idea, in history is thus not some abstract, domineering cosmic power. It is the dynamic, *immanent* logic through which human beings are led – despite themselves but by their own actions – to full self-understanding. This 'divine' logic of human development – which is also the logic of certain developments in nature – is understood by Hegel to be dialectical in character. In order to understand precisely what Hegel means by 'dialectical' reason, we must now turn our attention to Hegel's most difficult and unforgiving text: the *Science of Logic*.

2   *Thinking without Presuppositions*

Thought and Freedom

In the preface to the *Phenomenology*, published in 1807, Hegel proclaims the dawn of a new age. 'It is not difficult to see', he says, 'that ours is a time of birth and transition to a new era. Spirit has broken with the world it has hitherto inhabited and imagined, and stands prepared to submerge it in the past and in the labour of its own transformation.'[1] This same theme is taken up five years later in the preface to the first edition of the *Science of Logic*, when Hegel refers to the 'new spirit which has arisen in science no less than in actuality'.[2] What has brought about this transformation of consciousness, and what has thus ushered in the new age? As we saw in chapter 1, Hegel believes that the tremendous changes which have been taking place in Europe and America since the 1770s and 1780s are ultimately the result of one thing: human beings have at last become aware that their essence lies in freedom and self-determination. In art, artists have acquired an unprecedented freedom of style and subject-matter; in politics – notably in the American and French Revolutions – freedom has been made into the ground and principle of legitimate authority and activity; and in philosophy – particularly in the writings of Kant and Fichte – free self-determining and self-critical reason has been established as the highest authority in human life. Humanity has thus come to realize that its fundamental nature and destiny is to be free, and it has proceeded to create a new social, political, aesthetic, religious and philosophical world on the basis of its new consciousness of freedom.

This modern turn towards freedom is one that Hegel wholeheartedly endorses, although, as I pointed out in the previous chapter, he is well aware that unless freedom is understood properly, it can easily degenerate into a destructive selfishness and subjectivism. One particularly unfortunate consequence of the modern turn towards freedom, in Hegel's view, is that early nineteenth-century philosophers and writers have largely given up the traditional 'metaphysical' enquiry into the essence of the human soul and the nature of being, preferring instead to concern themselves with 'practical education'.[3] Owing to the influence of Kant's critical philosophy and to the pressing needs of an age of political revolution and social and intellectual upheaval, the traditional metaphysical enquiries into, for example, the immateriality of the soul or the nature of causality appear to Hegel to have been pushed aside or forgotten by most of his contemporaries.

Hegel considers this turn away from metaphysics[4] to be unfortunate because he believes that modern social and political freedom rests on our *consciousness* that we are free and self-determining, and because he construes metaphysics as the science which clarifies our consciousness and our understanding of ourselves and of our world. A modern world without metaphysics is thus a world without a clear conception of the freedom of which it has become aware. It is a world geared towards self-determination, practical activity and cultural, social and political change, but without a clear idea of what self-determination actually is. What is needed, therefore, is not an outright rejection of metaphysics in the name of 'practice', but the transformation of metaphysics from an enquiry into elusive (and, in Hegel's view, questionable) 'entities', such as an independent soul, into a modern discipline concerned to articulate the essential nature of free, self-determining spirit. Hegel's philosophy will attempt to present just such a new, reformed metaphysics of freedom in order to provide the modern age with the clear self-understanding which he believes it requires.

The main source and element of human freedom, for Hegel, is thought. Of course, the institutions of modern freedom owe their existence not only to the exercise of human thought and reason but also to social and economic factors, such as the growth of cities in the late Mediaeval period and the emergence of modern exchange relations. Nevertheless, in Hegel's view, human thought has proven to be the most powerful liberating force in history and has brought about significant changes in both our self-understanding and our material and religious practices. In the *Encyclopaedia* Hegel makes this point particularly clear.

In earlier times people saw no harm in thinking and happily used their own heads. . . . But, because they pushed on with thinking in this way, it turned out that the highest relationships in life were compromised by it. Thinking deprived what was positive of its power. Political constitutions fell victim to thought; religion was attacked by thought; firm religious notions that counted as totally genuine revelations were undermined, and in many minds the old faith was overthrown. . . . In this way thinking asserted its validity in the actual world and exerted the most tremendous influence.[5]

For Hegel, therefore, it is above all as *thinking* beings that we are free and self-determining.

This is of course a development of Kant's conception, presented in the *Critique of Pure Reason*, that theoretical understanding is the power of spontaneity and active, groundless synthesis, and of his idea, set out in the *Groundwork for the Metaphysics of Morals*, that practical reason is the power of autonomous self-legislation. It is also a development of Descartes's idea that philosophy may take nothing for granted in its search for truth and that thought is the principle of doubt or criticism that frees us from the authority of habitual but unwarranted belief. The connection between thought and freedom is perhaps more implicit than explicit in Descartes's writings, since his explicit aim is not so much to liberate human consciousness as to provide a solid foundation for the sciences. In Kant's philosophy, however, especially his moral philosophy, this connection between thought and freedom is made fully explicit. We are moral beings for Kant in so far as our will is capable of being determined not simply by particular interests and desires, but by self-legislating reason. And it is this capacity of our reason to determine the will independently of particular interests that constitutes our autonomy and freedom, and our ultimate human worth.[6]

What Hegel learns from Descartes and Kant is that human thought frees us from arbitrary authority by subjecting everything to the scrutiny of self-determining reason. The connection between thought – specifically philosophical thought – and freedom was of course made by both Plato and Aristotle, too; but it is in the post-Reformation period that free, *self-grounding* thought comes to be recognised as the highest principle for humanity. It is in the modern period, therefore, when human consciousness at last recognizes that it is the essential nature of all of humanity to be free, that the demand that thought should make itself as explicitly autonomous and self-grounding as it can becomes most urgent. The supreme demand of the modern age, in Hegel's view, is thus that thought should endeavour to derive all its knowledge and values freely and autonomously through reason. Imagination and empirical science have their roles to play as well, but it is the tribunal of reason that constitutes the highest authority for us.

This modern demand that rational thought should subject all human assumptions and presuppositions to critical scrutiny means, of course, that reason should not make any unwarranted assumptions about itself either. It is for this reason that Hegel maintains that the modern consciousness of freedom requires us to develop a new presuppositionless account of the nature of thought; that is, a new science of logic. If thought is to be truly free in the modern age, it must determine for itself what its true character is and not simply take that character for granted. It may not therefore – and this is perhaps Hegel's most controversial claim – take the categories and rules of formal or 'ordinary' logic for granted.

Much ink has been spilled over Hegel's alleged violation of the sacred rules of valid reasoning, specifically over his alleged rejection of the laws of identity and non-contradiction. Many have dismissed Hegel's philosophy out of hand because of its apparent irrationalism. Some, like Nietzsche, have seen Hegel's apparent willingness to embrace contradiction as a virtue of his thinking. Others have tried bravely to 'formalize' Hegel's logic in order to establish whether it is, after all, compatible with ordinary logical rules.[7] Whatever one's opinion of Hegel's thinking may be, however, it is important to realize that his reasons for wanting to develop a new logic have nothing to do with any desire simply to throw the traditional rules of thought overboard. He merely wants to provide an account of the character of thought which presupposes nothing about logical validity, but which allows thought to determine itself *freely*.

What is it about the rules of formal logic that needs revising, in Hegel's opinion? Surely all intelligible thought must assume that a thing is what it is (that A is A), and that a thing cannot be both what it is and what it is not (A and not-A) in the same respect. And all rational thought must surely respect the rules of rational inference in order to be rational. Hegel's point, however, is that that 'surely' is not good enough. It is not sufficient to assert or assume that rational thought must proceed according to the rules of formal logic; truly rational thought can take nothing for granted, not even its own rules. Until reason has been shown to determine and justify its rules *itself*, therefore, we must abstain from assuming anything about reason. Hegel is thus not deliberately violating any of the principles of formal logic; he is just turning thoroughgoing scepticism against those principles and suspending them until they have been validated by thought itself. Whether Hegel's presuppositionless account of thought will be successful or even intelligible remains to be seen. It is important at this stage simply to recognize why he believes the science of logic needs to be revised.

Hegel's call for a presuppositionless science of logic is a response to the modern historical situation. We are now fully aware that we are free, self-determining beings and that we are free above all as rational, thinking beings. This is clear from the demands we make in our social, political, aesthetic, religious and philosophical life. We need therefore to develop an understanding of what it means for thought to be truly free and self-determining. Furthermore, we need to fulfil the demand of post-Reformation philosophy that thought be fully self-critical. This we can do only if we take nothing for granted and accept as legitimate only what reason determines to be so. Hegel's demand for a presuppositionless science of logic is thus not, as some have claimed, an unfortunate throw-back to pre-Kantian dogmatism, but a demand for a thoroughly free and self-critical modern science.

But what are the 'presuppositions' of traditional formal logic, for Hegel? The first thing to mention is that formal logic operates under the assumption that the fundamental distinctions drawn by our ordinary understanding are valid. Formal logic is not necessarily restricted to the categories set out by Aristotle or Kant, but it does assume – as indeed ordinary consciousness assumes – that apparently opposed or distinct categories are indeed opposed to or distinct from one another. Formal logic presupposes, therefore, that 'infinity is different from finitude, that content is something other than form, that what is inner is other than what is outer, that mediation, similarly, is not immediacy'.[8] Hegel himself does not assume either that these categorial distinctions are valid or that they are not. He simply points out that formal logic and ordinary thinking take such distinctions for granted and do not even consider whether it really makes sense to think of form without its own content, of content without its own form, or of something inner that is not expressed in some way.

In Hegel's view, this assumption that apparently distinct categories are indeed distinct from one another reflects a deeper assumption that all thought is founded upon the laws of identity and non-contradiction. The formal logician assumes that 'what is inner is other than what is outer', therefore, because he assumes that whatever is, is what it is, or, in Aristotle's words, 'that a thing cannot at the same time be and not be'.[9] Once more, we must realize that Hegel is not dismissing this principle. He is simply pointing out that the principle constitutes an axiom of formal logic that cannot be proven or established by formal logic itself. Perhaps this principle will turn out to be indispensable after all; as yet we cannot know. What we can say, however, is that any thinking that claims to be fully self-critical and self-determining cannot simply take the laws of identity and non-contradiction for granted. The formal logician may assert that all intelligible thought requires that we acknowledge those laws, but Hegel wants him to prove it.

Formal logic not only presupposes axiomatic laws of thought, it also presupposes rules of deductive inference. Furthermore, specific inferences themselves require certain premises: they show only what will follow *if* something else is presupposed. Given that all men are mortal and given that Socrates is a man, formal logic tells us that Socrates must be mortal. The premises of this argument, and indeed the rule of inference employed here – namely that the particular must share the property of the universal under which it is subsumed – are not themselves proved by the argument, but are presupposed by it. Formal logic is thus concerned with the rules of *valid* inference from given premises in accordance with general logical principles. It is not concerned with determining *truth*. By the rules of formal logic, the following argument is valid, even though its conclusion and major premise are untrue: all men have wooden legs, Socrates is a man, therefore Socrates has a wooden leg. By itself formal logical reasoning cannot show that there is anything wrong with the conclusion we have just drawn. All it can tell us is that it is derived by valid logical deduction. We need information drawn from some other source – for example, experience – to show us that the major premise is incorrect and that the conclusion is thus untrue.

Formal logical reasoning cannot prove the truth of its premises and conclusions or the necessity of the rules and principles by which it determines validity. This is what Hegel means by saying that thought as construed by Aristotle is 'a formal activity, which indeed proceeds correctly, but whose content is given to it'.[10] Hegel does not dispute the fact that if one wants to make valid inferences from given premises, one must understand and respect the rules of formal logic. He does not accept, however, that a form of thinking which seeks to call into question, and to avoid relying on, *all* presuppositions should be bound in advance by a conception of logical validity that simply takes for granted its own rules. Fully self-critical thought, in Hegel's eyes, must endeavour to determine the true character of thought *freely*; that is, without assuming in advance that thinking and reasoning is valid only when it observes certain prescribed rules. Once thought has freely determined its own intrinsic nature, it may well become evident that, in certain circumstances, thinking must after all observe the rules of deductive inference. However, it may also become clear that truly free, self-determining thinking does not *itself* proceed according to the rules and principles of Aristotelian syllogistic logic, but observes a rigorous presuppositionless logic of its own. These matters cannot be decided before the new science of logic is developed. All we can say is that the science of logic that Hegel has to develop cannot be 'guided or legitimated by any propositional calculus, rules of syllogism, logic of discovery, semantic analysis or doctrine of intentionality', but must follow the path that it determines for itself.[11]

Hegel was, of course, familiar with the development of logic only up to the first quarter of the nineteenth century. He did not experience the profound transformation of formal logic brought about by Frege and Russell at (and just after) the end of the nineteenth century. From a Hegelian perspective, however, the developments initiated by Frege and Russell, such as the turn away from traditional 'subject–predicate' logic towards a more mathematical conception of formal logic, do not make any difference to the significance of his project. Modern symbolic logic is still a logic of formal validity, not a logic of truth, and it still presupposes axioms such as the laws of identity and non-contradiction. Were he faced with a textbook in symbolic logic, therefore, Hegel would still raise the question: should freely self-determining and self-critical thought think in this way? Should we, for example, take it for granted that a concept should be understood as a class? Indeed, should we assume that mathematics provides any kind of model at all for free, self-critical thinking? In raising such questions, the Hegelian is raising questions about the status and value of any formal logic, however it be conceived. And he is clearly suggesting that the new logic of self-determining thought must not be approached in the unself-critical conviction that the rules of formal or symbolic logic provide established standards of legitimate logical procedure by which to evaluate and pass judgement on whatever might call itself rational.

From Indeterminate to Determinate Thought

Hegel is not asking readers of his *Science of Logic* to abandon themselves to flights of wild Romantic fancy. He is asking us to follow Descartes and suspend judgement about what we have previously taken for granted until some way has been found to show whether or not our traditional ways of thinking are justified. He is insisting that 'science should be preceded by *universal doubt*, i.e. by total *presuppositionlessness*'.[12] He is asking us, therefore, to be more self-critical than we have hitherto been, not less, and to approach his logic in a spirit of openness.

But how are we to make sense of Hegel's new science of logic? What precisely will it be trying to do? It will first of all seek to determine – without presuppositions – which categories must logically (if not always and everywhere in fact) be employed in thinking and which are 'either illusory attempts or illegitimate combinations of genuine categories'.[13] Furthermore, it will seek to determine how the necessary categories of thought are to be conceived and whether the distinctions that are traditionally drawn between categories really hold. Hegel will thus attempt to discover the *true* determinations of thought and the *truth of* those determinations. The categories disclosed by freely self-determining thought will be those that are best suited to modern free, historical self-consciousness. In chapter 1 I argued that all experience of the world, for Hegel, presupposes certain categories. It is now clear, however, that the appropriate conceptual presuppositions of modern self-consciousness must be determined by a science of logic that is itself free and – systematically, though not historically – presupposition*less*.

By showing how specific categories are generated by freely self-determining thought, Hegel will provide a genuine derivation or 'deduction' of those categories and make good what he sees as the deficiencies of Kant's critical philosophy. In the *Critique of Pure Reason* Kant provided a 'metaphysical deduction' of the categories by showing that they can be derived from the fundamental forms of judgement. (He also provided a 'transcendental deduction' of the categories by arguing that they constitute the indispensable conditions of our knowledge and experience of objects.) In his 'metaphysical' deduction, however, Kant simply *assumed* that the basic activity of thought is judgement and that judgement thus provides the key to understanding the true character of the categories. He did not consider the possibility that judgement itself might be a derivative mode of thought that is based upon inadequately determined categories and so might not actually ground an adequate understanding of the categories at all.

Hegel praised Kant for locating the source of our categories in the spontaneity of thought, rather than in sensation or imagination. He criticized Kant, however, for not deriving his conception of the categories from a consideration of the free activity of thought *as such*, but simply reading them off from the structure of judgement (as he understood it). In Hegel's view – which is, of course, indebted to that of Fichte – Kant's failure in this regard meant that he was unable to demonstrate definitively which categories thought by its very nature should employ and how those categories are properly to be conceived.

In addition to determining the necessary categories of thought, Hegel's science of logic will also attempt to determine how far thought must respect the rules of formal logic and how far it must proceed in ways that formal logic cannot comprehend. If Hegel can derive his conclusions on this matter immanently from the free self-determination of thought, then he can claim to have provided a definitive understanding of the function and limits of all modes of reasoning – including mathematical, syllogistic and inductive reasoning – and to have avoided taking their unconditional or conditional validity for granted.

But how, exactly, is Hegel's logic to proceed if it is to take nothing for granted (except, of course, the modern historical demand that philosophy be free and self-critical and so take nothing for granted)? If thought is to determine its own necessary characteristics and presuppose no determinate categories or principles in so doing, it must begin by abstracting from and suspending all given, determinate thoughts and must think a thought in which nothing determinate is thought, a thought which is thus utterly *indeterminate*. For Hegel, that thought is the indeterminate, empty thought of *being* (*Sein*).

One should be careful, however, not to be misled at this point. Hegel is not inviting us to think of concrete 'reality' or 'nature' or any particular determinate being. Each of these thoughts represents the thought of some determinate content, the thought of *something*. But Hegel wants us to begin by merely thinking the indeterminate thought of being as such. Remember that the logic is an attempt by thought to determine anew its own intrinsic character, categories and rules. Now consider what is the least that can be said about thought – the least that we can *think* about thought – to begin with. It is not that thought is syllogistic or that it is concerned with objectivity or that it is opposed to feeling; that is already to think too much. The least that thought can think about itself is simply that it *is*. The outcome of Hegel's turning of Cartesian doubt against thought itself is thus not the conviction that I am, but merely the ineradicable thought that thought is. Thought can abstract from everything, but it cannot abstract from the thought that it is, from the thought of its own being. But, equally, since that thought is still wholly indeterminate, we cannot yet give any determinate meaning to the idea that we are thinking the simple being of *thought*. All we can do, therefore, is think the presence to thought of utterly indeterminate being that cannot as yet even clearly identify itself as thought.

Thought that presupposes nothing does not yet think of itself as thought. It thinks utter indeterminacy: '*being, pure being* – without any further determination'.[14] This is not the thought of some transcendent 'beyond', nor is it the traditional metaphysical thought of the totality of all beings. It is simply the very least that thought can think – the only 'thing' that thought can think if it is not to think of anything determinate.

But, the wary reader is likely to object, thought surely cannot think simply of utter indeterminacy; it must think *something* if it is to think at all. If it tries to abstract from all content, thought surely ends up thinking nothing whatsoever. Hegel agrees. The indeterminate thought of being does indeed amount to the thought of nothing whatsoever. Being, construed in such an indeterminate way, is merely an empty word. At the beginning of Hegel's logic thought thinks – or tries to think – the utter indeterminacy of *being*, but that thought is so utterly indeterminate that it evaporates in the very attempt to conceive it. The thought of pure, indeterminate being thus slides into the thought of *nothing* (*Nichts*) because of its sheer indeterminacy.

Yet that does not simply put an end to presuppositionless thinking. We have abstracted from all determinate thoughts and been left thinking nothing at all, but we do not thereby stop thinking altogether. Thinking of nothing is not the same as simply not thinking. Thought that suspends all its presuppositions and so ends up thinking of nothing determinate still remains thought, albeit utterly indeterminate and inchoate thought. Thus, even as we admit that we are actually thinking *nothing whatsoever* when we think of being, we must recognize that we are none the less still thinking. Moreover, we must recognize that nothing whatsoever *is* what we are thinking of. The moment we do this we acknowledge that sheer and utter nothing actually has an immediacy of its own for thought: sheer nothing is understood by thought precisely *to be* nothing rather than something. This means, however, that sheer and utter nothing in fact vanishes before our very eyes: for when we think of nothing, we necessarily think of sheer indeterminacy that *is* purely and simply what it *is*. That is to say, we think of empty, indeterminate *be-ing*. Just as the thought of sheer, indeterminate being slides into the thought of nothing, therefore, so the thought of nothing inevitably slides into the thought of being.

The attempt to begin to think without presuppositions has led us into an apparent impasse. We have begun with the most indeterminate thought that can be thought, the thought of sheer, indeterminate being. However, the sheer indeterminacy of that thought deprives us of any way of specifying the difference between indeterminate being and nothing whatsoever. If we attempt to think or determine a difference between pure, indeterminate being and nothing, that difference disappears the moment it is thought. Yet the thought of being is not reducible to the thought of nothing, is not simply and utterly nothing whatsoever. Being after all *is*. However, that in turn fails to establish any concrete difference between being and nothing, since the thought of nothing is the thought that 'nothing *is* . . . in our intuition or thought', and thus itself slides into the thought of being.[15] We are thus left thinking of a difference between two indeterminate thoughts which is ineliminable, yet which collapses and disappears the moment it is thought.

Is there any way in which this apparent impasse can point towards further determinations of thought, or are we condemned to listen, in Richard Winfield's words, to the 'perennial braying of the same vacant term'?[16] A way forward becomes clear if we attend to what happens to the thought of being as it is thought: it immediately collapses into the thought of pure nothingness. In thinking of pure being, therefore, thought does not simply think of pure *being*; it thinks the *disappearance* of pure being into its immediate opposite. Thought that thinks being thus thinks being not simply *as* being, but as something else, namely as the immediate transition into nothing whatsoever and back again into being. In this way thought becomes the thought of transition, of the immediate disappearance and reappearance of sheer, indeterminate being. In other words, the thought of pure being becomes the thought of pure *becoming* (*Werden*).[17]

Groundlessly, immediately, presuppositionless thought has begun to determine itself. We do not have much to think yet, but we have made a beginning. Simply by attending to the indeterminate thought of being we have learned that utterly indeterminate thought *is* not simply, but *becomes*. We cannot yet say that it becomes determinate thought, however. We merely recognize that it becomes the still indeterminate and unstable thought of *becoming* itself. But how does indeterminate, presuppositionless thought proceed from this meagre beginning to determinate thought, to the determinate thought of determinacy and of something? How, in other words, does presuppositionless thought actually proceed to *determine* itself properly and thus become explicitly *self-determining* thought? Once more, progress is achieved by simply attending to what is involved in thinking the thoughts that we have been thinking so far.

Wherein lies the thought of simple becoming at which we have now arrived? In the thought of pure being disappearing into pure nothing, and vice versa. It is because being is conceived in such a pure and indeterminate way that it leaves us nothing to think and thus immediately disappears into – and so becomes – the thought of nothing at all. The thought of becoming is thus generated by the sheer indeterminacy and emptiness of the thought of pure being with which we begin. However, the thought that pure being disappears into pure nothingness undermines the purity and simplicity of our initial thought of being and means that we can no longer still conceive of being as *pure* being. Yet it is the thought of being as pure and indeterminate – as sheer *being* – which leads to the disappearance of the thought of being into the thought of nothing in the first place. If we are no longer able to think of being as *pure* being, therefore, we are no longer forced by that thought to think its constant, restless disappearance into its immediate opposite. Rather, we are led by the very disappearance of pure being into pure nothing (and of nothing into being) to give up the idea that each is purely what it is and utterly different from the other, to give up the attendant idea that each simply *disappears into* its opposite, and to think both thoughts *together* as a single unity. The thought of pure being only disappears into the thought of pure nothing because it is the wholly indeterminate thought of pure and utter being. However, the very disappearance of pure being and pure nothing into one another undermines the pure and immediate difference between the two and causes them to collapse into one. In this way, we settle into the thought that being and nothing do not merely *pass over* into one another, but *are* in fact indistinguishable.[18]

We have tried to sustain the indeterminate thought of sheer and utter being and we have failed. The outcome of our failure is the recognition that pure being is not simply pure *being*, but is in fact indistinguishable from its immediate other, nothing (just as nothing itself is indistinguishable from being). This is the first settled, stable thought that we have had, the first thought that does not immediately disappear but that is – albeit to an utterly minimal degree – determinate. Note that, for Hegel, the difference between being and nothing is not altogether eliminated: he maintains that in their irreducible difference the *two* thoughts of being and nothing prove to be quite indistinguishable. This thought is clearly paradoxical, but it is one with which we can, at least for a moment, rest.

But what thought have we arrived at exactly? The thought that being is nothing and that nothing is being? But isn't that just empty verbiage? Doesn't it just leave us with one combined vacuous thought instead of two? And doesn't it just dissolve everything into conceptual chaos? By no means. Paradoxically, it is precisely what establishes the conceptual possibility of genuine determinate difference. Consider where we have arrived in our presuppositionless thinking. We have been forced to give up our initial attempt to think pure being by itself, and we have been forced to think being and nothing *together* as one. This means that we can now think the thought that nothing *is* without thinking that we thereby lose the thought of *nothing*. The thought of nothing does not have to be the thought of pure and utter nothing to be the thought of nothing. Nothing is no less nothing just because it *is* nothing. Conversely, we can now think the thought that being *is not* anything – is *nothing* – determinate without thinking that we thereby lose the thought of *being*. The thought of being does not have to be the thought of pure and utter being, without any 'contamination' by the thought of nothing, to be the thought of being. Indeed, not only *can* we think of nothing as *being* nothing, and of being as being *nothing* – as *not being* anything – determinate; we have no choice but to think of them in that way. Our initial attempt to think pure being distinct from pure nothing failed. Presuppositionless thinking which begins by thinking pure, indeterminate being must therefore come to think being and nothing in terms of one another.

Hegel's logic has not led us into conceptual chaos. Nor has it led us to the simple-minded positivist conclusion that the word 'being' means absolutely nothing at all and might as well be discarded. Nor, finally, has it led us into a kind of metaphysical nihilism which claims that, since being is nothing, only nothingness *is*. Hegel's presuppositionless logic has led us to the paradoxical thought that nothing is itself to be thought of as being, namely as being *non*-being or *not*-being, and that being can only be thought of as what it is in so far as it is thought of as *not* being what it is. Note that nothing mutates logically into 'not-being' (*Nichtsein*) and as such is indistinguishable from being (which is itself defined as *not being* what it is not). To say that being and nothing are indistinguishable is thus at the same time to say that being and *not-being* are indistinguishable. This baffling thought is, however, precisely what allows us to think the difference between being and not-being – a difference which is still ineliminably contained in the idea of the indistinguishability of the two terms – as a *determinate* difference.

At the beginning of the logic we thought of the difference between being and nothing as an immediate difference that did not require determination. We thought that all we needed to do was to think of being, to think that being *is*, in order to distinguish being from nothing. Now, however, we realize that we cannot sustain the thought of the *immediate* difference of being and nothing, and that we can only think the *determinate* difference between being and nothing or not-being if we think of each term *as* the other. The only way we can think even the most minimal determinate difference between being and not-being is by thinking that being *is not* not-being, and that not-being *is* not-being. Unless we can say of being that it is not what it is not, and of not-being that it is what it is, we cannot think any clear difference between the terms at all. The difference between being and not-being is, of course, still insufficiently determined by what we have said. However, that is not the point. We have not yet reached the stage of completely determinate thought; we have not therefore thought all that has to be thought in order to think determinate difference. We have merely thought the *absolute minimum* that needs to be thought to think determinate difference. Free, presuppositionless thinking has thus provided us with our first necessary and unavoidable principle: that, however strange the thought may be to ordinary understanding, the determinate difference between being and not-being can only be thought if being and not-being are recognized to be indistinguishable. In other words, it is only to the extent that we can say what something is *not*, that we can say what it actually *is*.

What I have sketched out in a simplified form in the past few pages is the process whereby, in Hegel's logic, thought leads itself from pure indeterminacy to the thought of bare determinacy. It is the process whereby – without taking anything for granted – thought freely determines the manner in which all determinacy, at least initially, is to be thought. However, Hegel's argument – if that is what it can be called – is likely to displease those trained in formal logic. Can we really say that because being *is not* not-being, being therefore *is* not-being? Is that not to confuse two distinct kinds of proposition and two distinct uses of the word 'not'? Is it not to overlook the distinction which Kant drew between a negative judgement in which the 'not' attaches to the copula (such as 'the soul *is not* mortal'), and an infinite judgement in which the 'not' attaches to the predicate (such as 'the soul *is* non-mortal')?[19] Further, is it not a flagrant violation of the laws of identity and non-contradiction to say that being is not-being, and should we not avoid such violations?

But such objections only carry weight if we presuppose that those distinctions and those laws should be respected. And we must remember that Hegel is trying to philosophize *without* presuppositions. If we are not going to prejudge the issue, therefore, we must not simply assume that there are settled distinctions between different types of judgement, nor must we assume that negation has a specific logical character or that the law of non-contradiction holds without qualification. Rather, we should study the categories and logical principles which self-determining thought itself shows to be necessary and discover whether or not there are such settled distinctions and laws, or whether we are not rather led ineluctably into thoughts which ordinary consciousness deems paradoxical.

What Hegel lays out in the opening chapter of his *Science of Logic* is the process whereby thought, which tries to think pure indeterminacy, is led by its own intrinsic necessity to the thought of becoming and to the thought of bare determinacy. The determinacy we arrive at is thought simply by means of the bare 'not', by saying that what is, is what it is by virtue of the fact that it is not what it is not, that is, by saying that being lies in not-being. If this appears to annul the very difference between what something is and what it is not which it is meant to determine, that is because the concept of determinacy which is thought here is still utterly primitive. Hegel is not trying to throw thought into chaos through his account of determinacy. He is pointing to an important ambiguity in the most primitive concept of determinacy that thought can think: which is, that to say that X is not Y and that Y is not X is the *least* we can say to determine the difference between X and Y, if we are not to lapse into the utter vacuity of simply saying that X and Y are whatever they are. But to say no more than this is still to fail to determine the difference between X and Y properly. In this primitive conception of determinacy each item is minimally distinguished from the other simply by being *not* whatever the other is. But, for that very reason, each is thought in precisely the same way as precisely the same thing: as being through not being. Hegel's point is that one cannot say less than this if one wants to think of something as determinate, but that if that is all one says then determinate difference is not thought concretely.

Understood in this way, what appears to some to be mystifying charlatanry turns out to be a powerful *a priori* analysis of the minimal meaning of determinacy. Hegel's account should not simply be dismissed because it – apparently – violates the law of identity, but should be evaluated on its own merits. Indeed, if one thinks carefully about what Hegel is saying, it is clear that he is not deliberately violating the laws of identity and non-contradiction at all, but is pointing to something paradoxical about determinate identity itself, something which ordinary thinking in fact takes for granted, but just does not reflect upon: namely that identity cannot be established simply by insisting that A is A, but that the determination of identity is inseparable, indeed indistinguishable from the determination of difference. If this thought seems or indeed *is* contradictory, that is not the consequence of Hegelian perversity or sloppy thinking. It is the unavoidable consequence of the categories which he is required by his science of logic to think through.

Hegel's point is that if one determines the categories of thought freely and self-critically, one will see that they *are* self-contradictory. However, one will also see that thought can and must develop ever more complex categories which resolve the contradictions that emerge. Thought, as Hegel conceives it, cannot simply avoid contradiction, therefore, or – like Russell – always regard it as a sign of error. Rather, thought must think through the contradictions in its categories and resolve them. The most advanced categories of Hegel's logic will thus be those in which contradictions are rendered most explicit and resolved at the same time.

Throughout the remainder of the text of the *Science of Logic* Hegel will attempt to derive further categories from the thought of bare determinacy that we have been considering. Those categories will present further determinations of what it means to be determinate and will show that determinacy resides in quality, quantity, specificity, form, content, possibility, actuality and necessity, to list but a few of the categories which Hegel develops. In the last part of the *Logic*, the 'subjective' logic or logic of the concept, it becomes clear that determinacy lies in having a conceptual or rational structure. It is in this part, therefore, that thought comes to recognize its categories not simply as determinations of determinate *being*, but as determinations of *thought* at the same time. At this point, one can say that presuppositionless thought has become explicitly what it has always been implicitly, namely the determination by thought of *itself*. The final concept of the *Logic* is, as one would expect, the concept of self-determining reason itself – what Hegel calls the 'absolute Idea' – and upon reaching that concept, one can say that presuppositionless thought has finally determined wherein its essential character lies.

The Method of Dialectical Thinking

What can we learn from this short account of Hegel's *Science of Logic* that can help prospective students of Hegel to come to terms with this difficult text themselves? Above all, we can learn something about the method of Hegelian logic. A science such as Hegel's, which seeks to determine the character of thought without presupposing any specific categories or rules of thought, cannot presuppose any given method of procedure, but must obviously determine its own method as it proceeds. The method of Hegel's logic is thus nothing other than the way in which the thought of indeterminacy determines itself to become the thought of other categories, and the way in which the thought of those other categories determines itself to be the thought of self-determination itself. There is, therefore, no Hegelian method that is separable from the process whereby specific categories transform themselves into other categories. Each category or set of thought-determinations develops in a manner which is peculiar to it. The categories of the logic of being, for example, 'pass over' into other categories with which they appear to be unrelated in the way that the category of being passes over into the category of nothing. The determinations of the logic of essence, on the other hand, 'posit' or entail one another in the way that the concept of form entails the concept of content and the concept of cause entails the concept of effect. The only concepts which actually *develop* into other concepts, in the strict sense of continuing to be the same concepts as they change into different ones, are those considered in the logic of the concept itself.[20] Since the method of progression is in each case subtly different, the initial moves of the logic that we have been considering cannot be taken as paradigmatic for the whole enterprise. Nevertheless, some general features of Hegel's way of thinking in his logic do become clear right at the beginning.

It is clear from the opening of Hegel's *Science of Logic* that presuppositionless, self-determining thought does not proceed according to the rules of conventional deductive or inductive logic. Obviously, Hegel's method of procedure is not inductive. He is not developing categories by generalizing from collected data, and the categories of his logic are clearly not empirical concepts. They are purely logical determinations which require to be understood in their own terms, not in terms of familiar empirical experiences – a fact which explains much of the difficulty of Hegel's text.

However, although Hegel's logic presents the *a priori* development of pure, 'unschematized' thoughts, the method it employs is obviously not that of syllogistic deduction either. In an Aristotelian syllogism a conclusion is drawn from two independently given premises. These two premises are not derived from one another, but are simply presupposed. Hegel's logic, however, does not begin with two independent premises. At most one could say that it begins with one 'premise', the 'premise' of pure being. But the ensuing procedure is still not syllogistic, since the category of being does not constitute a fixed point of reference for thought, as does a premise such as 'all men are mortal', but changes as we think it. Moreover, the category of becoming is not brought in as an independently established minor premise to be subsumed under the 'major premise' of being in order to reach a determinate conclusion. Hegel is thus not simply arguing that *since* thought thinks being and *since* thought thinks becoming, thought must *therefore* think determinate being. He derives or develops the categories of becoming and determinate being immanently from the thought of being itself. The syllogistic account of the opening of the logic is at best a crude approximation to what is going on and at worst a total distortion.

If Hegel's logic is not governed by the rules of deductive thinking, could it simply be an exercise in categorial analysis? Could it simply be the process of laying out what is 'contained' in an initial category? This gets us closer to what is going on, but is still not quite adequate.

Kant says that analytic judgements merely break up a concept 'into those constituent concepts that have all along been thought in it, although confusedly'. Nothing new emerges in this process. We do not proceed to a new and different determination, we simply gain greater clarity about what we began with. New information, according to Kant, is gained only through synthetic judgements in which connections are thought between concepts that are not analytically related. We can thus tell simply by analysing the concept of 'cause' that every cause has an effect, but the statement that every *event* has a cause, Kant maintains, is a synthetic one, since it makes a connection between the concept of an event and the concept of cause which is not 'contained' in the concept of an event itself.[21]

Hegel's logic is clearly not synthetic in this Kantian sense. It does not establish connections between two *given* and apparently unrelated categories. One could say, then, that the logic proceeds analytically. After all, the concepts of becoming and determinate being are derived by Hegel simply by considering what is involved in thinking pure being; that is, by 'analysing' that initial indeterminate concept. Indeed Hegel says as much in the *Encyclopaedia*: 'the deduction of their unity [the unity of being and nothing] is to this extent entirely *analytic*; just as, quite generally, the whole course of philosophising, being method-ical, i.e., *necessary*, is nothing else but the mere *positing* of what is already contained in a concept'.[22] However, can we really say that the concept of becoming was already thought or 'contained' in the concept of being in Kant's sense?

Here the difference between Hegelian and Kantian analysis becomes clear. In Kant's view, analysis uncovers relations of straightforward identity or equivalence between concepts: a bachelor is equivalent to an unmarried man and a cause is equivalent to that which pro-duces an effect. Hegel does not claim that the concept of being is *equivalent* to the concept of becoming, however, but that, when it is thought through, it *turns into* the concept of becoming. Hegelian logic is 'analytic' to the extent that it merely renders explicit what is implicit or unthought in an initial category. However, by explicating the indeterminate cat-egory of being, we do not merely restate in different words what is obviously 'contained' in it; we watch a *new* category emerge. It is this transformation of categories into new cat-egories which prevents the development of Hegel's logic being straightforwardly analytic.

In contrast to Kantian analysis, we are required by Hegel's method of 'analysis' to under-take constant and subtle revisions of the way we think. Initially, we think that to think being is simply to think *being*, but, in the course of the logic, we come to understand that to think being is to think becoming, quality, quantity, specificity, essence and existence, substance and causality, and, ultimately, self-determining reason itself. Each of these new determi-nations will be derived from the previous ones and will refine our initial thought of being. Each will reveal the *truth* of the previous determinations in two senses: it will render explicit what was implied by, but also concealed by the previous category, and it will reveal the lim-itation of the previous category itself. In this way, Hegel's science of logic determines the proper categories of thought and sets limits to those categories at the same time. It estab-lishes, for example, that we are right to enquire after the *ground* of something, and not merely accept the fact that it *is*; but it reveals that the *true* ground of something is not something other than it, but the *substance* of that thing itself or the rational *concept* that makes the thing what it is.

The absolute truth about the thought of being – the fact that, in thinking being, thought is thinking the self-determination of reason itself – only becomes completely clear at the end of the process. At this point the 'circle' of Hegelian pure conceptual analysis is com-pleted and what was unthought at the beginning is made fully explicit.

Hegel's method of immanent development and immanent criticism is, in my view, unique. No other philosopher has ever thought in quite this way, though Fichte, Schelling and Marx (and at times Plato) come close to it. It clearly has very little to do with the method of 'thesis – antithesis – synthesis' employed at times by Kant and Engels. Instead, it is the organic method whereby presuppositionless thought freely and necessarily deter-mines itself. Hegel's method of thinking may appear to many to be strange and irrational, but that is simply because he takes so seriously what he calls the *dialectical* moment in thought, the fact that, when thought properly, 'the initial universal determines itself out of itself to be the *other of itself*'.[23]

The dialectical principle, for Hegel, is the principle whereby apparently stable thoughts reveal their inherent instability by turning into their opposites and then into new, more complex thoughts, as the thought of being turns first into the thought of nothing and then into the thought of becoming. This principle, Hegel tells us, is 'the soul of all genuinely sci-entific cognition', and it is what gives his thinking its distinctive character by breathing life and freedom into the concepts that he thinks through, and by making his thought *move* in a way that ordinary thinking is simply not used to. Dialectic is not completely alien to ordinary understanding, in Hegel's view. It is recognized, for example, in many common proverbs, such as ' "summum jus summa injuria", which means that if abstract justice is driven to the extreme, it overturns into injustice'. Similarly, he says,

in politics, it is well known how prone the extremes of anarchy and despotism are to lead to one another. In the domain of individual ethics, we find the consciousness of dialectic in those univer-sally familiar proverbs: 'Pride goes before a fall', 'Too much wit outwits itself', etc. – Feeling, too, both bodily and spiritual, has its dialectic. It is well known how the extremes of pain and joy pass into one another; the heart filled with joy relieves itself in tears, and the deepest melancholy tends in certain circumstances to make itself known by a smile.[24]

However, despite such popular recognition of the principle of dialectic, ordinary under-standing still prefers to think of things (and concepts) as being either one thing or the other – as either right or wrong, as either being or not being – and for this reason it invariably finds the dialectical transformation of one thought into its opposite in Hegel's logic hard to come to terms with.

Dialectical thinking may strike ordinary understanding as strange or absurd, but – con-trary to what critics such as Schopenhauer and Popper have alleged – it is clearly not the product of any insidious desire on Hegel's part to undermine genuine rational thinking. It is the product of his readiness to take nothing for granted and to respond to the way thought itself develops. The best way to understand Hegel is to see him as exemplifying a Cartesian willingness to suspend his cherished beliefs and habits of thought, and to accept as true only what reason itself determines to be true. Hegel's *Science of Logic* should thus not be seen as the product of philosophical hubris. It is not the creation of some arrogant metaphysician who, heedless of Kant's call to philosophical self-restraint, claims to have penetrated through mystical intuition to the heart of the Absolute, only to make himself look foolish in the process. It is in fact – though it will seem remarkable to some to say so – the product of the profoundest philosophical *humility*, the product of a willingness to give up any claim to control the path of thinking, and to follow wherever thought may take him.

In the fifth Meditation, where he presents his version of the ontological proof of God, Descartes insists that it is not *his* thinking that makes God's existence necessary or that imposes any necessity on things, but, on the contrary, that 'it is the necessity of the thing itself, namely the existence of God, which determines my thinking in this respect'.[25] What appears to some to be the epitome of philosophical arrogance – the claim to know that God *must* exist – is thus seen by Descartes himself to be the unavoidable consequence of his submission of himself to the thought of God. Descartes does not think of himself as making claims of his own, therefore, but as thinking what thought itself requires of him.

This, I believe, is the attitude of mind that Hegel also asks of us. If we are to think prop-erly, he claims, we must give up our dogmatic insistence on certain rules of thought or our equally dogmatic insistence that thought is irredeemably limited, finite or perspectival, and we must submit ourselves to the movement of thought itself. If that leads us to thoughts which are strange and unsettling, so be it; that is a risk which we, as self-critical thinking beings, must accept. To refuse to think what must be thought is, in Hegel's view, to be guilty of unself-critical stubbornness or 'fear of truth'.

All too often, Hegel says, his new science of logic has been scorned and mocked by oppo-nents 'who fail to make the simple reflection that their views and objections contain cat-egories which are themselves assumptions and themselves need to be criticised before being employed'. The kind of reader he hopes for, however, is one 'such as Plato imagines [*dichtet*]', who is prepared to put aside his own views and reflections and simply follow the matter at hand.[26] Such readers will not attempt naively to escape from their historical perspective and get direct, unmediated access to 'things'. Rather, they will see the need to develop the proper categories in order to disclose the true nature of the world, and they will realize that, if they are going to come to an understanding of the true character of thought, they must come prepared – not least through religion, as we will see in chapter 10 – to be open to what thought determines itself to be.

In thinking through Hegel's logic, therefore, we need to be ready to let thought determine itself in our thinking, not to insist that we be the ones who do the thinking or who control the path that thought takes. This is why Hegel talks of categories determining themselves, rather than of our determining them. He wants to avoid the familiar Anglo-Saxon assumption that everything to do with thought boils down to what *people* think about a matter. He wants to insist that in fact, when they are truly thinking freely and self-critically, people are themselves moved by the thoughts that they think. Concepts, for Hegel, are not 'tools' which we employ to get things done. Nor, on the other hand, are they mysterious cosmic entities that 'reveal' themselves through us. They are the intrinsic, dynamic determinations of thought which it is the task of a fully self-critical science of logic to disclose and think through.[27]

One could respond to Hegel by pointing out that his general idea of what it means to be rational is shared by others who do not, however, see the necessity of thinking dialectically. Of course, anyone who is rational is going to let himself be guided by logic and is not going to insist on determining everything himself. However, Hegel thinks that our ordinary reasoning is rational only in a very imperfect way. We may submit ourselves to the rules of reasoning in our ordinary thinking, but *we* will be the ones who select or determine what to think about, and *we* will thus be the ones who determine the premises of our particular inferences. Much ordinary and philosophical thinking will select a topic, say poverty or the mind, and proceed to think about it because, for personal, social or historical reasons, it seems an important, perhaps even urgent thing to think about. Such thinking will involve sorting through various propositions which may or may not be true of the matter under discussion and finding good reasons or empirical evidence to support or reject them. Certainly, the thinker will endeavour to be as thorough as possible in the search for truth, but there will always be an element of arbitrariness about this procedure. Why think about this particular topic? Because it is interesting? Because it is socially important? And why consider this particular set of options and this particular set of reasons for supporting or rejecting them? Too much in this way of thinking is simply assumed to be relevant or is left to the experience, perspicacity or even the will of the person or people doing the thinking. Too much depends on what the individual *thinker* does. This way of thinking is perfectly valid for everyday purposes, Hegel believes, but it is not sufficient for free, self-critical philosophy which sets itself the task of determining the true categories of thought, because *too much is taken for granted.*

The difference between these two approaches to thinking explains many of the difficulties people have with Hegel's thought. Most people like to consider themselves to be the ones who are active when they are thinking and wish to reserve the right to judge for themselves what counts as a good or a bad reason. The procedure of Hegel's logic disturbs that 'freedom' to think for *oneself*. It disturbs our 'freedom' to stand above a topic and think about it as seems rational to us. It requires of us, instead, that we exercise 'restraint' (*Enthaltsamkeit*) and let ourselves be guided by the immanent self-development of the matter at hand.[28] This means that we cannot even determine *what* our thinking is to address itself to. Self-determining thought itself sets the agenda, and categories are dealt with as and when they arise. As Richard Winfield puts it, 'whereas foundational theories move from one topic to another according to the stipulation of their author, the philosophy starting with indeterminacy can only address contents when they emerge as stages in the self-determination that follows'.[29] In presuppositionless philosophy, therefore, it matters very much indeed in what order various topics are thought through. Understanding a particular topic involves understanding the systematic context in which it arises. But the style of thinking which settles on topics which *it* deems important deprives itself of that systematic context and so risks misunderstanding the issue it addresses simply because of the way it approaches that issue.

There is clearly a religious dimension to the method of thinking that Hegel is asking us to adopt. We are being asked to accept that 'whosoever shall seek to save his life shall lose it; and whosoever shall lose his life shall preserve it',[30] and we are being enjoined to recognize in that idea the key to true freedom and thus to true freedom of thought. We are being asked, therefore, to give up our self-certainty and self-assurance, to let go of everything we have held to in the past and to find true freedom of mind in the self-movement of self-determining thought. This self-critical – and, in Hegel's view, Christ-like – readiness to *let go* is the attitude we must adopt in approaching the science of logic, and it is one which we must be prepared to sustain throughout that science, too, because the logic will be the process of constantly positing and redefining categories. Throughout Hegel's logic, indeed throughout his whole philosophy, we will be brought to think certain categories that appear to be settled and determinate, and then to let go of them as it becomes clear that the proper determination of those concepts is more complex than we had thought. Logic is thus a continuous process of conceptual revision and redefinition that demands of us the greatest willingness to be transformed and challenged by thought.

This, to my mind, is what gives Hegel's logic its most distinctive characteristic. It does not build on firm, unshakeable foundations, premises or definitions, but presents concepts which change dialectically before our very eyes as their implicit determinations are thought through and rendered explicit. To follow Hegel's science of logic, that process of dialectical transformation must be thought through and understood. Philosophers who insist that concepts have fixed, static meanings or structures will find trying to understand Hegel like trying to grasp a bar of soap with wet hands. However, philosophers who focus their attention on the process of conceptual transformation itself, and who think *with* the rhythm of self-determining thought, much as they would go *with* the movement of a piece of music or a drama, will find Hegelian logic to be rigorous, intelligible and clear.

To think through and understand Hegel's logic (and indeed the rest of his philosophy) is to understand the *process* of dialectical thinking, not simply to look for conclusions (though conclusions are generated by that dialectical process). It is to understand the process whereby a category such as being is transformed into a category such as determinate being. To do this one must be prepared to let go of the initial determination of a category and to allow a more subtle determination of that category to emerge. But one must also be able to keep that initial category in view as the origin from which the more complex determination arose. One must always recognize, therefore, that the category of determinate being is a subtler and truer determination *of the category of pure being*, and indeed that all the subsequent categories are subtler and truer determinations of the initial, apparently simple thought of being. Only by keeping in mind the initial concept from which thought begins can one grasp the fact that concepts (such as being) develop and generate a logical 'history'. If one attends to the logical origins of a category, together with its own determinations and the process whereby it transforms itself into a new category, one can say that one is understanding a category in a Hegelian way. And if one always keeps in mind that, for Hegel, 'truth is its own self-movement', and that it is that *movement* above all that he wishes us to think, one need not feel apprehensive about engaging with Hegel's texts.[31]

But, the sceptic will inevitably ask, can we really call Hegel's logic *rational*? How can we judge its success? Can it be criticized? We have talked of submitting to the necessity of the matter at hand, but what if Hegel got some of the logical transitions wrong? He himself admits that he has not produced a logic that is perfect in every detail.[32] How, then, can we tell if his account of a particular transition needs improvement or even correction?

This is obviously a legitimate worry, but Hegel's position on this issue is, I think, clear. Self-determining thought determines itself; *it* therefore sets the standards of what is to count as true rationality, and so cannot be faulted for not conforming to the rules of 'valid' deductive inference. There are no external logical criteria which can be called upon to evaluate or criticize Hegel's new logic, because what he is proposing is itself nothing other than the scientific process of determining – *without* presuppositions – wherein genuinely rational thinking actually lies. Any rational principles which are brought to bear on presuppositionless thinking thus always beg the very question such thinking is trying to answer: how should we think? However, this does not mean that Hegel's logic is utterly uncriticizable. There are clear criteria for determining whether the development Hegel sets out in his logic is necessary, and these are set by the specific concepts under discussion at a particular point in Hegel's text. What needs to be established is whether Hegel succeeds in developing and rendering explicit *only* what is implied by the concept under review; that is, whether the derivation of the categories is strictly immanent, or whether Hegel introduces illegitimate external factors, such as metaphorical association or (as Schelling claimed) an anticipation of the result and goal of the science, to move the logic along.[33] That, it seems to me, can be assessed by anyone; it can be publicly determined. And it is clear that, if Hegel does not develop conceptual determinations immanently as he claims to, his presentation is open to criticism.

One should remember that Hegel is asking the philosopher to give himself over to the movement of self-determining thought, *not* to the authority of G. W. F. Hegel. We are certainly being asked to suspend our faith in the assumed rules of thought and to follow the process whereby thought determines itself, but we are not being asked to abandon *understanding*. Anyone who has ever worked on Hegel's logic knows that one can only follow the self-determination of thought if one pays rigorous and close attention to, and understands, the determinations implicit in the categories and renders those determinations explicit. I would claim, indeed, that we are required by Hegel's *Science of Logic* to exercise greater understanding and to pay greater and more precise attention to significant logical distinctions – and to take *less* on trust – than by any other text in the history of philosophy.

As John Burbidge has made admirably clear, *understanding* the precise determinations of concepts and their implications is in fact what provides the motor for Hegel's science of logic. It is thus the proper understanding of the categories that leads to the recognition of their dialectical character, not some mystical, neo-Platonic 'intuition'.[34] Dialectical transformation, in Hegel's view, is the work of the understanding itself; it is the process whereby understanding leads *itself* into contradictions. When the categories of finitude and infinity come up for discussion in the *Logic*, for example, the finite is initially understood to be that which is bounded and limited, and the infinite is initially understood to be that which is unbounded and unlimited. Each is thus – understandably – conceived to be distinct from the other. However, by construing the infinite in this way, understanding sets a limit to what the infinite can be: it says that the infinite cannot become finite while remaining infinite, or, as Kierkegaard puts it, that the Christian doctrine of the Incarnation of the infinite and divine in the realm of the finite and human is absurd.[35] Hegel's dialectical point is simply that such an infinite that finds its *limit* in what is finite is itself a bounded or *finite* infinite, and that the distinction between finitude and infinity, which the understanding wishes to cling to, thus undermines *itself*. Understanding may find dialectic disconcerting, therefore, but dialectic is something understanding itself must assume responsibility for and think through. If understanding is honest with itself, Hegel claims, it will acknowledge the wisdom of Christ's words, and recognize that if it clings on to its fixed and established conceptual distinctions, it will lose them, but that if it is prepared to give up its narrow self-understanding and accept its intrinsically dialectical character, it will discover a much deeper truth and freedom of movement within itself.[36]

Hegel's logic requires our ordinary understanding to transform itself into dialectical thinking, but it sets out that process of transformation in a way that ordinary understanding can clearly understand. Hegel's logic is thus not some esoteric exercise in mystical thinking that can only be grasped by specially gifted initiates. It is the presuppositionless study of thought which is assessable and understandable by anyone who is prepared to be fully self-critical. Ordinary consciousness can understand the need for a presuppositionless logic and, as long as it is prepared to see its categories redefined, and see itself transformed in the process, it can understand the development of such a logic as well. Difficult as Hegel's *Science of Logic* is, therefore, the reader can be assured that Hegel has endeavoured to make his text as intelligible to ordinary understanding as he possibly can and to present a logical science which is 'capable of being the property of all self-conscious reason'.[37]

Logic and Ontology

The *Logic*, as I have presented it in this chapter, is a presuppositionless science designed to meet the modern demand for free self-determination in the sphere of philosophical thinking. As such it is to be understood as the product of a specific set of historical circumstances and a specific form of historical consciousness. Yet, precisely because of its presuppositionless, self-determining character, it is to be understood as the science which determines the true, intrinsic determinations of thought. The claim of the *Logic* to *truth* is thus not undermined by its emergence from a specific historical situation, because the historical situation from which it arises is the one in which consciousness has at last become aware of what *true* freedom means. Hegel's philosophy can therefore be said to offer us a developmental account of thought in two senses. As I have tried to show in this chapter, it shows how the categories of thought are generated *logically* from one another and, ultimately, from the very nature of thought itself. At the same time, as I tried to show in chapter 1, it understands its own definitive study of the logical self-determination of thought to be the product of definite *historical* circumstances.

The Hegel who emerges from the pages of this book is a profoundly historical philosopher, but he should not be mistaken for the 'soft', hermeneutic, pragmatic Hegel who sometimes appears in modern commentaries.[38] The Hegel I have presented in this chapter is a rigorous, precise and logical thinker who is concerned with truth and necessity, not just suggestive associations between concepts. Yet those familiar with the interpretations of Hegel's philosophy offered by such commentators as Charles Taylor may still find my account of Hegel's logic strangely one-sided.[39] Yes, they will say, the *Science of Logic* sets out the necessary determinations of thought, but doesn't it also present what Hegel calls various 'definitions of the Absolute'?[40] Is not Hegel's logic a metaphysical or ontological logic which gives us an account of the essence of absolute spirit? Haven't I deprived Hegel's philosophy of its metaphysical heart and left merely a categorial skeleton of dialectical thought?

It is certainly true that Hegel conceives of his science of logic as a metaphysics and onto-logy, as well as a logic. In the preface to the first edition of the *Science of Logic*, for example, he talks of 'the logical science which constitutes metaphysics proper, or pure, speculative phi-losophy'; in the *Encyclopaedia* he claims that '*logic* coincides with *metaphysics*, with the science of *things* grasped in *thoughts*'; and in the general introduction to the *Science of Logic* he maintains that the objective logic – which contains the logics of being and essence – 'takes the place of the previous metaphysics which was a scientific edifice to be erected over the world by thought alone'. The metaphysical and ontological character of the *Logic* is also emphasized when Hegel asserts that the subject matter of his logic is the *logos*: 'it is least of all the logos which should be left outside the science of logic', he says. Speculative logic, for Hegel, is therefore 'objective thinking', '*thought in so far as it is just as much the matter [Sache] in itself*, or *the matter in itself* in so far as *it is equally pure thought*'. This metaphysical, onto-logical side to Hegel's logic – the fact that it determines the structure of *being*, as well as the structure of *thought* – cannot, in my view, be denied and is, indeed, part of what makes Hegelian logic a logic of *truth*, not just validity.[41]

However, it is also clear that Hegel's logic does not constitute a traditional metaphysics of the kind put forward by, say, Leibniz. Hegel is not providing an account of the world based on the 'either/or' logic of the understanding and, more significantly, he is not offer-ing us philosophical arguments and propositions *about* presupposed metaphysical entities. He is not, therefore, presupposing that there is an Absolute and enquiring into what it is. In this respect I agree with commentators such as David Kolb and Richard Winfield that Hegel's logic is not a metaphysical account of 'a wondrous new superentity, a cosmic self or a world soul or a supermind', and indeed that the *Logic* does not present an account of any determinate, given reality at all.[42]

In what sense is Hegel's logic metaphysical and ontological, therefore? The answer to this question can be found if we reflect once more on the fact that Hegel is seeking to provide a *presuppositionless* logic. Logic, for Hegel, seeks to understand the basic categories and rules of thought. In a presuppositionless logic such categories and rules cannot be taken for granted at the outset, but must be discovered by the science itself. Presuppositionless logic may begin, therefore, from nothing more determinate than the simple being of thought. That is to say, it must proceed from the thought of thought itself *as* sheer, inde-terminate being. It is from the sheer being of thought that the basic categories are then to be derived immanently.

Yet logic cannot just be an account of the nature of thought, but must also be an account of the nature of *being as such* – that which we otherwise call 'existence' or 'actuality'. The reason why is straightforward: in a fully self-critical, presuppositionless logic we cannot start out from anything more than the indeterminate being of thought, yet neither can we presuppose at the outset that being as such (or 'existence') is anything beyond the being of which thought is minimally aware. If we are to set *all* our presuppositions – including those about being – to one side, we cannot simply suppose that being constitutes a world of objects that are external to thought or that it exceeds the reach of thought in some way. Initially we may suppose nothing about being at all, except for the fact that it is minimally pure and simple being. This means, however, that we have no warrant to assume that being as such is anything other than or different from the indeterminate being of which *thought* is minimally aware. Conversely, we have no warrant to assume that the being of which thought is aware is anything less than *being as such*.

Hegel's claim is not that being is a mere postulate of thought. On the contrary, he argues that, for the fully self-critical philosopher who suspends all his determinate preconceptions about thought and being, our *thought* of being cannot be anything less than the thought of *being itself*. Thought cannot be assumed necessarily to fall short of what there is – to be confined, for example, to the realm of conceivable possibility – but must be understood to be the awareness and disclosure of being as such. This may seem to some to be presumptuous. How can thought be certain that it is able to bridge the gap between itself and being and disclose the true nature of what there is? From the point of view of the self-critical philosopher, however, this question is illegitimate, for we are not entitled to presuppose that there is such a gap in the first place. The fully self-critical philosopher may not assume that being is anything beyond what thought itself is aware of. Consequently, he or she may not assume that thought is aware of anything less than being itself.

For Hegel, then, no fundamental distinction can be drawn in a genuinely presuppositionless logic between the determinations of thought and the determinations of being. What we understand to be the determinations of things are always to be understood – after Kant – to be the determinations of *our* thinking; but conversely – and contrary to what Kant believed – what we know to be the true determinations of *our* thinking are always also to be understood to be the determinations of *things themselves*. The mode of consciousness which recognizes this is what Hegel calls 'absolute knowing' or philosophy.

Philosophy, as Hegel understands it at the start of the *Logic*, has given up the presupposition, which is never challenged by Kant, that the determinations of thought could be, or indeed are, utterly distinct from the determinations of things themselves. And to the extent that philosophy has freed itself from the fundamental 'opposition of consciousness'[43] and has realized that being cannot be thought to be utterly other than thought, philosophy must acknowledge its categories to be *ontological*. However, this does not allow us to say that Hegelian philosophy has returned to the traditional metaphysical conclusion that the categories of thought 'correspond' to the nature of a given reality. To say this would be to imply that one can distinguish clearly between our thought and reality and then recognize a correspondence between the two. But Hegel's point is that, at the start of the *Logic*, thought is not entitled to make such a clear distinction. Presuppositionless philosophy begins with *no* systematic assumptions. That means that it cannot begin from the assumption that the determinations or categories of thought and reality are conceivably distinct from one another, or that they might conceivably 'correspond' to one another. It cannot begin with any definite conceivable distinction between thought and being at all.

Since we can presuppose no conceivable distinction between thought and being at the beginning of the *Logic*, the categories set out in the *Logic* must be ontological. At the same time they cannot provide a description of any Absolute, reality or being that is presupposed as the *distinct*, *given object* of philosophical enquiry. The *Logic* thus does not seek to 'mirror' in pure thought a world that is assumed to stand over against us. To suppose that our categories 'correspond' or 'apply' to a distinct reality that is given to us is to take for granted, in David Kolb's words, 'what it means to be'.[44] It is to suppose from the start that reality or being is to be understood as some kind of *object* of enquiry which lies, as Heidegger puts it, 'present at hand' waiting to be known by us. We similarly beg the question if we assume that being is not an 'object' but spirit, or if we assume that being might elude or exceed thinking altogether. Presuppositionless thinking, however, cannot assume what it means to be any more than it can assume what it means to think. Hegel's logic may not presuppose from the outset that being is objective, substantial, absolute or in any way determinate, and then seek to provide a metaphysical account of such a determinate reality. Rather, it must start with pure *indeterminate* being as such and determine from scratch precisely *how* such being is to be conceived by letting being determine itself immanently in thought. Hegel's *Logic* does not, therefore, merely contain ideas and propositions *about* being. It presents in thought the self-determining and self-unfolding *of* being itself. In this way, it *discovers* 'what it means to be' and what it is to be, without taking anything determinate for granted at all. It is in this sense that Hegel's logic is ontological.

It should be clear from this why Hegel's logic does not presuppose any specific correspondence between *consciousness* and *nature*. This is because speculative logic considers the general ontological question of what it means to be, and this question must be considered *before* we can know what it means to be natural or to be conscious in particular. Indeed, Hegel insists that we must *derive* our understanding of what it means to be natural or to be conscious from our logical study of what it means to be as such, if we are not to take the character of natural things and of human consciousness for granted.

The transition from the logic to the philosophy of nature and consciousness in Hegel's system is thus not made by bringing in given material to which the categories of the logic are then 'applied', but is simply the result of further determining what it means and what it is to be. Hegel's logic shows that to be means to be qualitatively and quantitatively determinate, to be substantial and to be rational or the 'Idea'. The Idea itself then proves to be *self-external* or *spatio-temporal*. It turns out, therefore, that being-as-Idea is in truth *nature*. The further determination of what it is and means to be nature then reveals that nature requires there to be physical, chemical and organic structures and leads, ultimately, to the emergence of consciousness. The final part of Hegel's system shows that to be conscious is to be subjective, to be free, to be historical, to be aesthetic, religious and philosophical. The logic thus provides the categories and method by which the philosophy of reality proceeds, but these categories are not *applied* to a given reality; they are developed further to generate new and more complex determinations of what it means to be; that is, to generate the concepts of nature and consciousness freely and without presuppositions. As David Kolb puts it, 'what happens in the transition to concrete reality can only be a further thinking of the logical Idea in terms of itself'.[45]

Logic, Science and History

To end this chapter, I wish to add a few comments in order to guard against certain misinterpretations of Hegel's position that may have arisen during the course of the chapter. First of all, Hegel claims that thought can determine *a priori* what it means to think, what it means to be and thus what being must be, but that does not mean that he is endorsing the ontological presumptions of all thought. He is maintaining that thought can only aspire to determine what it means to be if it is prepared to give up its conventional presuppositions and become freely self-determining. This is not to claim that all of *Hegel's* thoughts are guaranteed to be true, but to claim that the only way to seek truth properly is to take nothing for granted. The reader should recognize, therefore, that Hegel's science of logic is profoundly critical of the ontological aspirations of thought that does not make the effort to be freely self-determining. Hegel is not simply opening the door to any form of *a priori* thought to set itself up as providing the way to truth.

Second, it is important to realize that Hegel does not see his philosophy as being in competition with natural science or empirical history. He does not claim to have privileged insight into the workings of some cosmic superentity which empirical science cannot see. He does claim that only freely self-determining thought can determine properly what it means to be; but one of the conclusions of presuppositionless philosophy is that to be means to be subject to natural laws and to be subject to empirical contingencies. These are ineradicable for Hegel. Thus, although he recognizes that nature leads through its intrinsic logic or 'Idea' to the emergence of consciousness, he also understands that consciousness can in fact emerge only *if* the natural conditions are right. In Hegel's view, therefore, philosophy and natural science must work together, not conflict with one another. Philosophy understands that nature is so constituted that it is necessarily predisposed to generate organic life and consciousness at some time and place through its own natural processes; it is up to natural science, however, to discover *which* specific physical and chemical processes are required for life and consciousness actually to arise, and *where* in the universe those processes are in fact at work. In this way science can show what natural processes lead to the emergence of consciousness, while philosophy can show that it makes sense, given the concept of nature, that consciousness should arise *somewhere*.

The same is true of the relation between philosophy and empirical history. Philosophy recognizes that to be conscious means to be, or to become, historical; however historians must study how historical consciousness has actually emerged and when and where specific historical events have occurred. Free, self-determining philosophy shows us that human consciousness is impelled by its own inherent logic or 'Idea' to develop an awareness of its own freedom over time, and so to generate the process of history. However, such philosophy also recognizes that, if certain things had been different – if disease or some other natural disaster had destroyed human civilization, or if people such as Caesar or Napoleon had never been born – then the emergence of freedom (and of history as we understand it) could have been delayed or even been deferred indefinitely. Philosophy thus recognizes the emergence of modern freedom to be both a necessary *and* a contingent product of history. It also understands itself to be a product of certain natural and historical conditions that could have been different. But, equally, philosophy understands itself to be a product of a history which, *given* those particular natural and historical conditions, had to lead to the emergence of the consciousness of freedom, because it was generated by the drive towards self-consciousness which is a necessary and intrinsic characteristic of human consciousness itself. Hegel's philosophy is thus able to understand itself as a product of actual history, and to explain why it is – and must be – a product of history, at one and the same time.

In chapter 5 I consider further the relation between necessity and contingency in Hegel's philosophy of nature. The next two chapters, however, are devoted to Hegel's most famous text: the *Phenomenology of Spirit*.

3   *Phenomenology and Natural Consciousness*

Logic and Phenomenology

In chapter 2 I argued that Hegel's *Logic* is both an ontology and a logic. It determines not only what it means to think, but also what it means to be. The 'element' of the *Logic*, as Hegel calls it, is, in other words, the unity or identity of thought and being.[1] This is not to say that Hegel is a subjective idealist for whom the character of things or even their very presence depends in some way on the human mind. For Hegel, being is what it is in its *own* right and will continue to be such long after human beings have disappeared from the face of the earth. His claim, however, is that the structures or fundamental determinations of thought and being are identical. The process of discovering the immanent structure of *thought* – by letting the indeterminate being of thought determine itself – is thus at the same time the process of discovering the immanent structure of *being* itself. In this process being shows itself – within thought – to be intrinsically rational and dialectical. As Hegel puts it, 'being is [thus] known to be the pure Concept [*Begriff*] in its own self, and the pure Concept to be true being'.[2] In the *Logic*, therefore, being is not regarded primarily as that which stands over against thought and to which thought must somehow gain access. It is understood to be that which is what it is in its own right, but whose structure can nevertheless be discerned *within* thought itself.

Yet how can Hegel justify what many would regard as the height of philosophical presumptuousness: the claim that thought can divine the nature of things *a priori* without, as it were, ever leaving the comfort of its armchair? The justification for such 'presumptuousness' lies in the fact that it is actually the consequence of being radically self-critical and setting all one's determinate assumptions about thought and being to one side.

As I noted in chapter 2, if thought is to be truly presuppositionless, it cannot take any determinate categories or rules of thought for granted but can begin from nothing but the sheer, indeterminate immediacy or being of thought. Furthermore, it may not at the outset make any determinate assumptions about the nature of being itself. We cannot start out from the idea that being is substance, nature or will to power, because in each case we would first need to prove that being necessarily takes this form. Initially, therefore, before any such proof has been provided, the most we may understand being to be is sheer being as such. But that means that at the start of philosophy we have no warrant to regard being as anything beyond the sheer immediacy of which thought is minimally aware. If, therefore, we are truly self-critical and suspend all determinate preconceptions about being, we have no alternative but to regard being as that which *thought* understands there to be and so to regard thought in turn as the awareness of *being as such*. This means that the true nature of being will be disclosed simply by determining what is entailed by the thought or category of being and that the structure of being and thought (properly understood) cannot but be identical. The apparently presumptuous claim that thought and being are identical in structure is thus, from Hegel's point of view, the very opposite of presumptuous. It is the claim that we are required to make by the demands of radical self-criticism.

By contrast, the seemingly more modest claim that being should be conceived from the outset as 'that-which-might-possibly-differ-in-structure-from-thought' is in fact far from modest, because it takes for granted being's possible difference from thought without first showing that the very idea of being as such entitles us to conceive of it in this way. It is easy to think that sceptical doubts about our ability to understand being properly are founded simply on the idea that our thought and understanding may be limited. But this is not the case: they are founded just as much on the idea that being itself might differ from the way we understand it. In Hegel's view, however, this conception of being is one that we are not automatically entitled to adopt. Indeed, we will only be entitled to adopt it if and when it can be shown to be entailed by the very idea of being itself. In the absence of such a demonstration, all that the self-critical philosopher may assume being to be is pure and simple *being* – the very being of which thought is minimally aware. Hegel meets the challenge of the sceptic, therefore, not by showing how we can, after all, gain access to the realm of being that the sceptic deems to be beyond our reach, but by rejecting as unwarranted – at least initially – the conception of 'being' (as possibly other than thought) on which such scepticism rests.

For Hegel, therefore, nothing is needed to begin presuppositionless onto-logic except a willingness freely to suspend one's favoured assumptions about being and thought and to start from the bare thought of being as such. This is made clear in both the *Science of Logic* and the *Encyclopaedia Logic*. In the former, Hegel writes that at the beginning of speculative logic all that is needed is simply 'the resolve [*Entschluss*], which can also be regarded as arbitrary, that we propose to consider thought as such'. Acting on this resolve and actually setting all presuppositions to one side leads directly, Hegel explains, to the thought of pure *being*:

> the beginning must be an *absolute*, or what is synonymous here, an *abstract* beginning; and so it *may not presuppose anything*, must not be mediated by anything nor have a ground; rather it is to be itself the ground of the entire science. Consequently, it must be purely and simply *an* immediacy, or rather merely *immediacy* itself. . . . The beginning therefore is *pure being*.[3]

This, then, is the direct route into Hegel's ontological logic: 'To enter into philosophy . . . calls for no other preparations, no further reflections or points of connection'.[4]

A similar case is made in the *Encyclopaedia Logic*. In §78 Hegel writes that 'all . . . presuppositions or assumptions must equally be given up when we enter into the Science, whether they are taken from representation or from thinking; for it is this Science, in which all determinations of this sort must first be investigated'. Philosophy, or 'Science', thus requires that it be 'preceded by *universal doubt*, i.e. by total *presuppositionlessness*'. Hegel goes on to note that 'this requirement is fulfilled by the freedom that abstracts from everything, and grasps its own pure abstraction, the simplicity of thinking – in the resolve [*Entschluss*] of *the will to think purely*'.[5] Here, too, therefore, Hegel points out that there is a direct route into speculative logic. All one needs to do is freely suspend and abstract from all determinate presuppositions about thought and being and render explicit whatever is entailed by the indeterminate thought (of sheer indeterminate being) that results from this act of abstraction. Since any rational person is capable of performing this act of abstraction, anyone is able to begin speculative logic.

Hegel recognizes, however, that not everybody will in fact be *willing* to perform such an act of abstraction and suspend his or her deepest assumptions about thought and being. He anticipates resistance in particular from what he calls 'natural consciousness'; that is, ordinary, non-philosophical consciousness. Such consciousness, Hegel believes, is invariably convinced that its everyday assumptions about the world are beyond dispute and is unlikely to be minded to throw them all overboard in the interests of what it can only regard as the absurd demand for total 'presuppositionlessness'. Furthermore, such consciousness cannot fail to consider perverse the idea that the true nature of things can be discovered *a priori* within thought simply by 'unfolding' what is contained in the bare thought of being.

Everyday consciousness draws a clear distinction between itself and the objects it knows: it considers itself to be 'here' and the things it is aware of to be 'over there'. As Hegel puts it, it 'knows objects in their antithesis to itself, and itself in antithesis to them'.[6] From the perspective of ordinary, natural consciousness, therefore, one cannot just close one's eyes and work out by pure reason what the world is like; one has to go over and look. For ordinary consciousness, indeed, Hegelian 'Science' is the complete 'antithesis of its own standpoint'. It overturns our common-sense conviction that things are irreducibly *other* than us and it presumes that we can know in some mysterious way purely from within thought what the world 'out there' is like. Hegel is well aware of the perplexity that is bound to overcome consciousness when it first encounters speculative philosophy:

> When natural consciousness entrusts itself straightway to Science, it makes an attempt, induced by it knows not what, to walk on its head too, just this once; the compulsion to assume this unwonted posture and to go about in it is a violence it is expected to do to itself, all unprepared and seemingly without necessity. Let Science be in its own self what it may, relatively to immediate self-consciousness it presents itself in an inverted posture [*als ein Verkehrtes*].[7]

Remarkably, Hegel does not just dismiss the bewilderment of ordinary consciousness as of no concern to the philosopher. He accepts that philosophy must show ordinary consciousness why it is rational, rather than perverse, to believe with the speculative philosopher that the true structure of being can be found within the structure of thought itself. In other words, Hegel acknowledges that, if philosophy or 'Science' is to demand of consciousness that it raise itself to the standpoint of ontological logic, 'the individual has the right to demand that Science should at least provide him with the ladder to this standpoint, should show him this standpoint within himself'.[8] Such a ladder will be provided by the *Phenomenology of Spirit* (1807).

The *Phenomenology*, as I understand it, can be bypassed by those who are prepared to carry out the free act of suspending all their presuppositions about thought and being, begin with the bare thought of 'pure being', and accept that, initially, being itself may not be understood to be anything beyond the bare, indeterminate immediacy of which thought is minimally aware. The *Phenomenology* is essential reading, however, for those who are deeply attached to the ordinary view of the world as something that stands over against us and who want to know why they should be persuaded to give up that common-sense view and adopt the standpoint of ontological logic. The role of the *Phenomenology*, on this interpretation, is thus to justify the standpoint of ontological logic (or 'absolute knowing') *to ordinary, natural consciousness.* It aims to provide such justification by demonstrating that, paradoxically, the seemingly 'perverse' standpoint of philosophy is actually made necessary by the very certainties of ordinary consciousness itself. For ordinary consciousness (and those philosophers who are wedded to the ordinary view of things) the *Phenomenology* is, therefore, the indispensable *presupposition* of presuppositionless logic. Without it, Hegel believes, such consciousness cannot but regard the standpoint of ontological logic or speculative philosophy as illegitimate. The role of the *Phenomenology* is clearly set out by Hegel in these lines from the *Logic*:

> In the *Phenomenology of Spirit* I have exhibited consciousness in its movement onwards from the first immediate opposition of itself and the object to absolute knowing. The path of this movement goes through every form of the *relation of consciousness to the object* and has the Concept [*Begriff*] of science for its result. This Concept therefore . . . needs no justification here [in the *Logic*] because it has received it in that work [the *Phenomenology*]; and it cannot be justified in any other way than by this emergence in consciousness, all the forms of which are resolved into this Concept as into their truth.[9]

At least, it cannot be justified in any other way to a consciousness that refuses to suspend its cherished preconceptions about the world of its own accord.

The Method of Phenomenology

Phenomenology is a discipline, developed by the speculative philosopher, to show that the standpoint of speculative, ontological logic – the identity of thought and being – is necessarily entailed by the perspective of ordinary, natural consciousness itself (though ordinary consciousness does not initially realize this). If, however, the philosopher-as-phenomenologist is to succeed in persuading consciousness that its ordinary certainties, taken on their own terms, do indeed lead to the standpoint of philosophy or absolute knowing, the philosopher may not simply assume from the start that the ordinary perspective will inevitably be overcome or undermined. The philosopher must, rather, put his own expectations to one side, examine consciousness with an open mind and seek to discover *whether or not* ordinary certainties lead to absolute knowing. Otherwise, ordinary consciousness may justifiably complain that its point of view is not being taken seriously, but is being subjected to an examination whose outcome is predetermined. If ordinary consciousness is to be given a 'ladder' to philosophy that is acceptable to consciousness, it cannot be given one whose rungs are already fixed in advance. In fact, strictly speaking, the philosopher may not himself provide consciousness with a 'ladder' or 'map' of any kind whatsoever, but must simply analyse the certainties of ordinary consciousness and note where, if anywhere, they lead. As Quentin Lauer puts it, Hegel must allow consciousness 'to follow out its own implications'.[10] During the course of the *Phenomenology* Hegel shows that such certainties do take us necessarily to the standpoint of philosophy; but he shows that they do so *immanently* – wholly by themselves – without any guidance from the philosopher. Hegel demonstrates, indeed, that ordinary consciousness actually builds its own ladder to absolute knowing, and that it does so not through any effort to reach some anticipated height, but precisely by endeavouring to stay where it is and adhere to its own certainties.

Yet in the minds of some commentators, there lingers the suspicion that, behind the back of consciousness, Hegel is actually pulling puppet-strings all along. This is because phenomenology is an examination of the development of consciousness that is undertaken by *philosophical thought.* The phenomenologist does not go out into the street, like a modern-day Socrates, engage people in dialogue and then watch them argue themselves into an acceptance of the philosophical point of view. The phenomenologist works out for himself – *in thought* – the paradoxical consequences of espousing the various perspectives of ordinary consciousness. According to some, however, the very fact that the examination of consciousness is carried out by philosophical thought means that the path that consciousness must take is, in Paul Redding's words, already 'rigged from the start'.[11] For such commentators, to *think through* the perspective of consciousness in a Hegelian manner is from the outset to think consciousness dialectically; that is, to think consciousness according to a prior conception of teleological development or, as Heidegger claims, 'in accordance with a predetermined idea of being'.[12]

According to Hegel himself, however, philosophical thought is not inevitably bound by predetermined concepts of 'development' or 'dialectic', but is capable of entering into the perspectives of consciousness and understanding them wholly in their *own* terms. Hegel does not deny that phenomenology is a discipline undertaken by philosophical thought or 'absolute knowing'. It is undertaken, however, by absolute knowing that *sets to one side* its ontological conviction that being can be understood from within thought (as well as concepts such as 'dialectic') and seeks to understand the immanent character of ordinary consciousness itself. For Hegel, indeed, every form of consciousness is 'a complete individual shape, and one is only viewed in absolute perspective [*absolut betrachtet*] when its determinateness is regarded as a concrete whole, or the whole is considered in the *specificity of this determination* [*Eigentümlichkeit dieser Bestimmung*]'.[13] These lines make it clear that, for Hegel, philosophical thought considers consciousness from an 'absolute' perspective only when it attends to and lingers over the unique specificity of each shape of consciousness and does *not* assume in advance that such shapes lead necessarily and dialectically to absolute knowing. Phenomenology must, therefore, be an open-minded and open-ended examination of consciousness, undertaken in the hope that it will lead to the standpoint of philosophy, but with no prior assumption that we will be taken beyond the shape of consciousness with which we start.

The Preface and Introduction to the *Phenomenology* do, of course, tell us in advance that consciousness will lead dialectically to the standpoint of philosophy; but they also tell us that consciousness will be shown to do so only when it is considered *immanently* on its own terms without assuming in advance that it will lead anywhere. Science, Hegel writes in the Preface, requires that one 'enter into the immanent content of the matter, . . . surrender oneself to the life of the object, or, what amounts to the same thing, confront and express its inner necessity'; and this applies as much to phenomenology as to philosophy proper.[14]

How does Hegel ensure that his examination of consciousness is rigorously immanent? By refraining from comparing the claims of ordinary consciousness with the world as philosophy comprehends it, and confining himself instead to studying the relation between consciousness and what consciousness itself takes its object to be. Hegel notes in the Introduction that consciousness is minimally aware of *something* and so draws a distinction between itself and the object it knows. Furthermore, he notes that consciousness regards its object in two ways: once as being whatever it is in itself and once as being known by – or being *for* – consciousness:

Consciousness simultaneously *distinguishes* itself from something, and at the same time *relates* itself to it, or, as it is said, this something exists *for* consciousness; and the determinate aspect of this *relating*, or of the *being* of something for a consciousness, is *knowing*. But we distinguish this being-for-another from *being-in-itself*; whatever is related to knowledge or knowing is also distinguished from it, and posited as existing outside of this relationship; this *being-in-itself* is called *truth*.[15]

This is not to say that there are two distinct objects of consciousness: the object in itself and the object known. There is only one such object, but consciousness distinguishes between what it takes the object itself to be and the way *it* actually knows or experiences that object. Moreover, consciousness itself is able to establish whether its knowledge or experience of the object concerned actually matches what it understands the object in itself to be:

for consciousness is, on the one hand, consciousness of the object, and on the other, consciousness of itself; consciousness of what for it is the True, and consciousness of its knowledge of the truth. Since both are *for* the same consciousness, this consciousness is itself their comparison; it is for this same consciousness to know whether its knowledge of the object corresponds to the object or not.[16]

It is important to note here that consciousness is not being asked to compare its knowledge of things with things as they might be outside the perspective of consciousness altogether. Such a comparison would clearly be impossible. It is also unnecessary, for, as Hegel points out, consciousness has a standard or 'criterion' (*Maßstab*) within itself by which to judge the merits of its own knowledge, namely the object as consciousness *itself* understands it to be in itself: 'in what consciousness affirms from within itself as *being-in-itself* or the *True* we have the standard which consciousness itself sets up by which to measure what it knows'.[17] Consciousness is thus in a position to establish from within itself whether its knowledge is adequate, because it can directly compare the way it knows and experiences things with what *it* takes them to be in themselves. For this reason the analysis of consciousness undertaken in the *Phenomenology* is wholly immanent: it makes reference to no standard of judgement other than one that is set up by consciousness itself. It seeks to determine not whether consciousness's knowledge of the world meets the standards established by philosophy, but whether such knowledge is satisfactory in consciousness's own terms.[18]

As I pointed out above, the examination of consciousness carried out in the *Phenomenology* is undertaken by philosophical thought. Yet it has now become clear that such thought brings no standards of its own to bear on consciousness. The task of thought is, instead, to describe and articulate the experience that consciousness itself makes of the objects it declares to be the 'truth'. To be more precise, thought describes not the contingent experiences made by ordinary consciousness in history, but the experience that, *logically*, consciousness must make, given the way it initially understands its object to be in itself. It should be noted that, although philosophical thought tells the story of consciousness's experience, such thought does not undertake any active comparison of its own between the object of consciousness and consciousness's knowledge of that object. Consciousness examines itself and its own object, so, in fact, 'all that is left for us to do is simply to look on [*zusehen*]' and describe what must occur.[19]

Hegel believes that the actual examination of consciousness shows that its knowledge or experience turns out *not* to accord with its initial conception of the object itself. The object as it is known in experience proves to be different from what it is first understood to be. Now in everyday circumstances, if we note such a discrepancy between our experience of an object and what we understand the object itself to be, we might suspect that our experience is deficient and in need of revision. If we understand the object to be a dog, but find that it looks like a large cat, we might assume that something is wrong with the way we are looking at it and try to see it properly. Similarly, one might think that consciousness in the *Phenomenology*, upon finding that its experience or knowledge does not correspond to what it holds the object in itself to be, would seek to revise its 'knowledge' to make it accurately reflect the object: 'if the comparison shows that these two moments do not correspond to one another, it would seem that consciousness must alter its knowledge to make it conform to the object'.[20]

The experience described in the *Phenomenology* cannot, however, be revised in this way because it does not misrepresent the object, but discloses what the object *itself* necessarily proves to be. In the course of its experience, Hegel argues, consciousness's knowledge of its object changes; that knowledge, however, is not something wholly detached from the object, but is knowledge *of the object itself*, of what that object itself turns out to be. As the knowledge changes, therefore, so the object itself changes for consciousness: the object proves to be not just what it is first understood to be after all, but what it is revealed to be *in the experience of it*. 'In the alteration of the knowledge, the object itself alters for it too, for the knowledge that was present was essentially a knowledge of the object: as the knowledge changes, so too does the object, for it essentially belonged to this knowledge.'[21] Since consciousness's experience is experience of the *object itself*, consciousness cannot simply reject that experience and revert to its initial conception of the object. Rather, it must recognize that through such experience the initial conception of the object has been undermined and the object shown to be other than it is first taken to be. That is to say, consciousness must acknowledge that what it initially took to be the object in itself was in fact merely what it *took* to be the object in itself, and that the object has now shown itself in the experience of it to be somewhat different. As Hegel puts it, 'it comes to pass for consciousness that what it previously took to be the *in-itself* is not an *in-itself*, or that it was only an in-itself *for consciousness*'.[22]

Needless to say, such a recognition will only 'come to pass' if Hegel can prove that the experience in which the object of consciousness is transformed is, indeed, genuine experience of what the object proves to be, and does not simply misrepresent that object. He can prove this only if he can demonstrate that such experience is made necessary by nothing other than the object as it is itself *initially* conceived to be. Hegel must show, therefore, that the object itself, as it is first understood by consciousness, generates the very experience in which it is transformed.

When consciousness accepts that its object must be understood in a new way and has in fact turned out to be a different kind of object, it becomes a new shape of consciousness. This new shape now declares its object to have its own distinctive character, and the phenomenologist has to describe the experience that the new shape of consciousness makes of this newly conceived object. If the object again proves in the experience of it to be other than what it is first declared to be, then consciousness must mutate logically into a further shape, and so on. In this way, Hegel maintains, consciousness can be shown to develop logically through a series of different shapes as more and more of the character of the object of consciousness is disclosed in the experience of consciousness itself. Hegel's claim that such a development must occur will, of course, only be justified, if he can prove that the experience in which the object of consciousness is transformed is *in each case* made necessary by the object as it is initially understood.

Logic in Phenomenology

Hegel's project in his most famous text is, as the title indicates, that of pure phenomenology. Hegel does not put forward his own philosophical conception of being in that work, nor does he examine whether consciousness knows the world as philosophy knows it. Rather, he examines whether consciousness knows the very objects *it* knows quite as *it* thinks it does. The *Phenomenology* argues that consciousness does not do so, because the object it knows constantly proves in the very experience of it to be other than it is first known to be. Hegel's project is rigorously phenomenological, therefore, because it starts from the object as it is initially taken to be by consciousness itself – the object as it first *appears* to consciousness – and considers the transformation that this object undergoes in the further experience of it.

It is important to remember, however, that Hegel provides a phenomeno-*logical* account of consciousness. He does not undertake an empirical survey of the ways in which people in everyday situations actually learn by experience that, say, this animal is in fact a cat rather than a dog or that this action is in fact bad rather than good. He examines abstract types or 'shapes' of consciousness – such as 'sense-certainty' or 'perception' – that do not exist in the world on their own but that constitute (or have constituted) recognizable aspects or 'moments' of concrete historical life; and he analyses the experience that, *logically*, each shape of consciousness must make, given the way it understands its object to be.[23] Furthermore, Hegel focuses specifically on the changes in the *logical form* of the object that must occur in such experience. He is not interested in explaining how we learn more about the empirical character of things. He seeks, rather, to explain how the object that sense-certainty initially takes to have the form of simple immediacy – of simply being *this, here, now* – necessarily proves in the very experience of it to have the form of something complex and manifold, and how, in turn, an object with this form – the object of perception – proves in the experience of it to have an inner, invisible unity.

The various forms that the object turns out to exhibit are described by Hegel using logical categories, such as 'being-in-itself', 'being-for-itself' and 'universality'.[24] These categories may seem to be alien to ordinary consciousness itself: after all, in everyday situations we are more likely to say 'there's the bus' than 'there's a complex universal'. Indeed, Hegel acknowledges that the individual shapes of consciousness analysed in the *Phenomenology* do not themselves explicitly employ such categories to describe their objects: sense-certainty, for example, says that it is aware of *this, here, now*, not of 'pure being'. Nevertheless, Hegel's use of such categories does not prevent his phenomenological account of consciousness from being genuinely immanent: for they capture, in abstract, logical terms, the form that the object actually has *for consciousness itself*.[25]

Hegel's phenomenological analysis is thus an examination of the experience that, logically, consciousness must make, given that its object has this or that logical form for it. This analysis discloses the ways in which, in such experience, the object necessarily changes its logical form for consciousness and so ceases to be *for consciousness* what consciousness itself initially took it to be. In so far as the experience of consciousness is determined by the *logical form* exhibited by its object, one might say, as Hegel himself puts it in the first preface to the *Science of Logic*, that the development of consciousness in the *Phenomenology* 'rests solely on the nature of the pure essentialities [*Wesenheiten*, i.e. the categories] which constitute the content of logic'.[26] This does not mean, however, that the *Phenomenology*, which is meant to serve as an introduction to the *Logic*, itself *presupposes* the *Logic*. It means simply that the categories that are discovered in the *Logic* to be immanent in pure thought (and being) are *discovered* in the *Phenomenology* to be immanent in consciousness, too – namely, as constituting the logical form of the object as it appears and transforms itself in the experience of consciousness itself.

Now if Hegel's analysis of consciousness is to be genuinely immanent, he clearly cannot assume in advance that consciousness will be led necessarily by the logic of its own experience to new and more complex conceptions of its object. For all we know at the start, we might begin with sense-certainty, find that its object proves in experience to be exactly what it initially appears to be, and so discover nothing in consciousness that would move us on to the standpoint of absolute knowing. Once Hegel has begun his analysis of consciousness, however, he learns that the object of consciousness does actually prove in experience *not* to be what it initially appears to be. We are thus, indeed, taken forward to a new and richer knowledge of the object. That is to say, the object proves in experience to have a more complex logical form than it is first deemed to have. In this way, Hegel argues, the *Phenomenology* traces the *progressive* transformation of consciousness from sense-certainty through numerous more complex forms of consciousness to absolute knowing. The latter is thereby shown to be made necessary logically by the very certainties and experience of consciousness itself, and so to be justified.

In the *Phenomenology*, therefore, progress is not achieved by simply abandoning one conception of the object in favour of another, as one might abandon a flawed scientific theory for one that is more successful. Nor is it achieved by externally introducing a wholly new object in order to resolve the problems or 'contradictions' that are generated by a previous object. Progress is achieved by watching the object from which consciousness begins transform itself – reveal itself to have a different logical form – in the very experience of consciousness itself. Progress is achieved, in other words, because consciousness is taken, by its own experience of the object, from what it first understands the object to be *in itself* to what it now *knows* the object to be or to what the object actually proves to be *for consciousness*. In this process consciousness acquires a new conception of its object and, with this, a new object as such; that is, an object of a different logical form. The new conception of the object consists in nothing but the knowledge we have gained of the object as it was first taken to be in itself. The new object is thus itself nothing but what the (initial) object in itself has been disclosed to be in such knowledge, or what it has come to be *for consciousness*. This is what Hegel means when he states that 'our knowledge of the first object, or the being-*for*-consciousness of the first in-itself, itself becomes the second object'.[27]

Consciousness gains a new understanding of the object, as the true character of the object comes to be known by – and so to be *for* – consciousness. At the same time, consciousness is deprived of its initial certainty that it knows the object in itself, because the object as it is first understood to be in itself is shown merely to be what consciousness *took* to be the object in itself; that is, to be what first constituted the object *for consciousness*. These two processes of gain and loss together make up the one process whereby the object of consciousness is transformed in the experience of it. They are both to be borne in mind, therefore, when considering Hegel's statement that consciousness in its experience becomes aware of 'the being-*for*-consciousness of the first in-itself': as the true character of the object in itself comes to be *for consciousness*, so the object as initially conceived shows itself merely to have been what the object in itself was *for consciousness*.

The Role of the 'We'

Hegel concludes the Introduction to the *Phenomenology* by modifying slightly the account just given. It remains the case that the new object emerges in and through the experience of consciousness. It now becomes apparent, however, that the particular shape of consciousness under consideration does not recognize *explicitly* that an altogether *new* form of object has arisen in its experience. A given shape of consciousness – say, sense-certainty – certainly becomes aware in its experience that its object has changed and is no longer what it is first taken to be: as Hegel writes, 'it comes to pass for consciousness that what it previously took to be the *in-itself* is not an *in-itself*, or that it was only an in-itself *for consciousness*'.[28] Yet this shape of consciousness understands such experience to entail the transformation and loss of *the object that it all along regards as its own*. A new form of object has, indeed, emerged *implicitly* in this experience, but, Hegel notes, it is only we – the readers and the phenomenologist – who recognize this fact. It is only for us, therefore, that the experience of any particular shape of consciousness issues in a completely new conception of the object.

For consciousness itself to see before it an altogether new form of object, it must undergo what Hegel calls a 'reversal' or 'turn-around' (*Umkehrung*) and become an altogether new and different shape of consciousness. Hegel argues, however, that no individual shape of consciousness in the *Phenomenology* actually undergoes and experiences such a reversal itself. It is, rather, *we* who turn consciousness around by making the transition to a new shape that explicitly takes up the new object and considers it to be what there is in truth:

the new object shows itself to have come about through a *reversal of consciousness itself*. This way of looking at the matter is something contributed by *us*, by means of which the succession of experiences through which consciousness passes is raised into a scientific progression – but it is not known to the consciousness that we are observing.

Hegel adds that the new shape of consciousness analysed by the phenomenologist is not itself aware that its object has *emerged* from the experience of a prior shape. We know this, but the new shape itself is simply conscious that its object has a certain logical form:

the *origination* [*Entstehung*] of the new object, that presents itself to consciousness without its understanding how this happens, . . . proceeds for us, as it were, behind the back of consciousness. . . . The *content*, however, of what presents itself to us does exist *for it*; we comprehend only the formal aspect of that content, or its pure origination. *For it*, what has thus arisen exists only as an object; *for us*, it appears at the same time as movement and a process of becoming.[29]

To my mind, nothing that is said in these lines contradicts the basic argument of the Introduction. The new object arises necessarily in the experience that consciousness makes of the object of which it is initially aware. This new object is, indeed, nothing but what the initial object is known in truth to be. It is simply the 'being-*for*-consciousness of the first in-itself'.[30] Consciousness can see its new object explicitly *as* a new and different form of object only in so far as it takes up and accepts that new object as the truth and thereby becomes a new shape of consciousness that is not wedded to the assumptions of its predecessor. According to Hegel, however, no particular shape of consciousness itself mutates into the succeeding shape; rather, consciousness becomes a new shape in the transition that *we* make to that new shape. It is we, therefore, who understand the shapes of consciousness to form a progression or development. The various shapes themselves are simply aware of the object they take to be before them and of the experience they make of this object, and they do not regard themselves as stages in any development. Yet this development is necessitated by nothing but each shape itself and its experience. Each shape of consciousness can thus be said to generate the succeeding shape immanently of its own accord, since all we do is render *explicit* the new shape that is *implicit* in the experience of the preceding one. Our role may be said to be passive in so far as we simply 'look on' as consciousness makes its own experience of its object. Yet we are active in so far as we think through and articulate that experience and in so far as we effect the transition, made necessary by a given shape, from that shape to another.

Sense-certainty

Hegel's account in the Introduction of the way in which phenomenology progresses from one shape of consciousness to another is borne out by his opening examination of sense-certainty. Sense-certainty, according to Hegel, is the simplest and most primitive form of consciousness in that it takes its object to be *immediately* present to it. Indeed, it declares itself to be aware of nothing but the sheer immediate presence of the object. Since it takes itself to be directly acquainted with the object, it does not see any need to bring the object into focus by describing it, by means of general empirical concepts, as a 'tree' or a 'house'. It certainly beholds a rich array of objects before it, including trees and houses, and it is interested in the unique singularity and specificity of such objects. All it says and thinks, however, is that its object is *this, here, now*, and it is certain that in being aware of *this* – without the mediating clutter of concepts – it knows the specificity of the object itself.

Consciousness learns, however, that thinking of its object purely as *this* does not actually bring the unique specificity of the object to mind in quite the way it thought it would: for such pure, immediate certainty is utterly indeterminate. To stare at something and think not 'I see a tree' but simply 'I see *this, here, now*' might seem to put me in direct contact with the thing itself, but in fact it brings nothing determinate to mind. Indeed, it leaves me conscious of nothing but the empty universal form of 'being this, here, now' that fails utterly to distinguish one thing from anything else.

Hegel thus argues that 'sense-certainty demonstrates in its own self that the truth of its object is the universal'. This is not merely something that *we* note about sense-certainty, but something it experiences for itself when it discovers that, wherever it directs its attention, it has the *same* indeterminate consciousness of a thing's simply being *this, here, now*:

Here is, e.g., the tree. If I turn round, this truth has vanished and is converted into its opposite: no tree is here, but a house instead. 'Here' itself does not vanish; on the contrary, it abides constant in the vanishing of the house, the tree, etc., and is indifferently house or tree. Again, therefore, the 'This' shows itself to be a *mediated simplicity*, or a *universality*.[31]

Hegel points out, however, that consciousness does not now give up on the idea that it is directly acquainted with the singular immediacy of the tree or house before it. Rather, it declares that it can bring such immediacy to mind by focusing not just on *this* but more specifically on what *I* mean by this. 'The force of its truth thus lies now in the "I", in the immediacy of my *seeing, hearing*, and so on; . . . "Now" is day because I see it; "Here" is a tree for the same reason'.[32] Yet consciousness again learns that it does not thereby bring anything particular or determinate to mind. In this case, this is because what I mean by 'I' is itself left indeterminate. I *mean* this 'I' in particular – the I that I am – but I do nothing to distinguish my 'I' from that of anyone else. I simply insist that I am conscious of what *I* mean by this, and I think that that is sufficient to give specificity to myself and the object of my consciousness. As Hegel points out, however, 'everyone is "I", this singular "I"'. By saying merely that I have in mind what *I* mean by this, therefore, I leave myself with nothing but the empty, universal certainty that is claimed by every 'I'. My bare insistence that *I* am conscious of what *I* mean by this thus fails to bring to mind precisely what I mean.

Again Hegel claims that sense-certainty itself experiences the indeterminacy and empty universality of its object. 'Sense-certainty thus comes to know by experience that its essence is neither in the object nor in the "I", and that its immediacy is neither an immediacy of the one nor of the other; for . . . the object and "I" are universals in which that "Now" and "Here" and "I" which I *mean* do not have a continuing being, or *are* not.'[33]

Yet consciousness still does not give up on the idea that it can be conscious of the sheer immediacy of the object. It seeks to secure such consciousness by deliberately *excluding* from its perspective any objects other than the one it means to have in view and the viewpoint of any 'I' other than its own.

I, *this* I, assert then the 'Here' as a tree, and do not turn round so that the Here would become for me *not* a tree; also, I take no notice of the fact that another 'I' sees the Here as *not* a tree, or that I myself at another time take the Here as not-tree, the Now as not-day. On the contrary, I am a pure [act of] intuiting; I, for my part, stick to the fact that the Now is day, or that the Here is a tree; also I do not compare Here and Now themselves with one another, but stick firmly to *one* immediate relation: the Now is day.[34]

In this way, I endeavour to banish all indeterminacy from my consciousness and guarantee that I am, indeed, conscious of the specific object that *I* mean, even though I think of it as nothing but *this*.

Hegel notes, however, that consciousness must now point out to us precisely what it is aware of, since it has retreated into a purely private view of things and so 'will no longer come forth to *us* when we direct its attention to a Now that is night, or to an "I" to whom it is night'.[35] Indeed, consciousness must also point out *to itself* what it is aware of. This is because the very act of excluding other objects from its point of view requires it to pick out from a range of such objects the specific one on which it is focusing. As we have seen, sensuous certainty remains indeterminate for itself unless the I specifies for itself that it is conscious of *this* (not that) and of what *it* (not another I) has in mind. This means that consciousness can lay claim to knowledge of a specific *this* only if it brings such a 'this' explicitly into view by pointing it out to itself. Hegel argues, however, that in the process of pointing out its object to itself and to us, consciousness learns that its object is not in fact the simple, immediate *this* that it took it to be, but rather something complex.

This is especially evident in the consciousness of what I take to be before me *now*, or of what Hegel calls 'the now' (*das Jetzt*). The problem, according to Hegel, is that, in the very act of pointing out the 'now' it is certain of, consciousness moves on from that now to another moment, another 'now'. Thus, precisely because it has been *pointed out* – and the act of pointing out takes time – any such now is necessarily brought to mind at a *later* now. This means that it can only be brought to mind as a now that no longer simply *is*, but that *has been*.

The Now is pointed to, *this* now. 'Now'; it has already ceased to be in the act of pointing to it. The Now that *is*, is another Now than the one pointed to, and we see that the Now is just this: to be no more just when it is. The now, as it is pointed out to us, is Now that *has been*, and this is its truth; it has not the truth of *being*.[36]

This does not mean that consciousness fails to point out the now it has in mind. In the process Hegel is analysing consciousness succeeds in its endeavour: the now is, indeed, pointed out and as a result *is now* present to consciousness. It is present, however, as a now that *has been* pointed out. In other words, it is present as a now that necessarily has a past. In the very act that is meant to secure for consciousness its certainty of the *now*, the now thus proves *not* to be the pure immediate presence – the pure and simple *now* – that consciousness has taken it to be. Rather, the now necessarily shows itself, in the very experience of it, to be the now-that-has-been or the continuity of present *and* past moments. As such, the object of sense-certainty proves to be 'an absolute plurality of Nows'.

Hegel's argument, by the way, does not presuppose that time is actually divided up into atomic units called 'nows'. Hegel is doing phenomenology, not philosophy of nature, and is not putting forward any conception of time of his own, and certainly not an atomistic theory of time. His claim is that sense-certainty conceives of its object as the simple imme- diacy of the *now*, but that it necessarily goes beyond such simple immediacy in the very act of pointing it out to itself. In the process, sense-certainty itself reveals its object not just to be the pure now, but to be the now-that-has-been: for the object can be known in its immediacy only in being pointed out, but as pointed out it necessarily has a past.

In the same vein, sense-certainty's act of picking out a specific *here* from other heres shows any such here to be inseparable from those other heres and so itself to be 'a simple complex of many Heres'. As Hegel explains, 'the *Here pointed out*, to which I hold fast, is similarly a *this* Here which, in fact, is *not* this Here, but a Before and Behind, and Above and Below, a Right and a Left. The Above is itself similarly this manifold otherness of above, below, etc.'[37]

Such a complex continuity of different moments is called by Hegel a 'universal'. It is, however, a concrete, internally differentiated universal, rather than the empty, abstract uni- versal that sense-certainty first experienced the this and the I to be. Hegel writes that 'the dialectic of sense-certainty is nothing else but the simple history of its movement or of its experience', and he notes that such experience is itself nothing but the discovery that the object is more complex than consciousness first thought. 'The pointing-out of the Now', he states, is 'itself the movement which expresses what the Now is in truth, viz. a result, or a plurality of Nows all taken together; and the pointing-out is the experience of learning that Now is a *universal*'.[38]

It is evident to us as readers and phenomenologists that the object has proven in the experience of sense-certainty itself to be a wholly new form of object. The object has turned out not just to be the simple immediacy that consciousness first took it to be, but rather to be a complex unity of different moments. Sense-certainty, however, does not itself explic- itly recognize that an altogether *new* form of object has thereby emerged in its experience. It merely learns that its *own* object proves in the experience of it *not* to be what it initially took it to be. This, Hegel maintains, is because sense-certainty does not actually 'take over the truth' that has been disclosed in its own experience.

As we have seen, sense-certainty's 'truth' is the 'universal'. None the less, Hegel notes, such certainty still 'wants to apprehend the This'.[39] Despite all it has learned about its object, therefore, sense-certainty does not let go of its own conception of the object altogether. It starts out wedded to the idea that its object is pure immediacy, and it experiences this very immediacy as complex and so as not what it initially takes it to be. It does not, however, relinquish its identity as *sense-certainty* and cease seeking immediate certainty of *this*, *here*, *now*, even though it experiences the impossibility of such simple sensuous certainty. Sense- certainty does not, therefore, grasp the full implication of its own experience and accept that the object of consciousness has actually been shown to have a new logical form.

The shape of consciousness that does accept this and 'take over the truth' revealed by sense-certainty is perception or *Wahrnehmung* (literally, 'taking truly'). 'Perception', Hegel tells us, thus 'takes what is present to it *as* a universal'.[40] In Hegel's account, sense-certainty does not turn itself around and become perception; it is *we* who make the transition to perception. Nevertheless, this transition is made necessary by the experience of sense-cer- tainty itself, since perception is simply the shape of consciousness that *accepts* the truth disclosed by sense-certainty and takes the object as it is actually known by sense-certainty – the 'being-*for*-consciousness of the first in-itself' – to be the *new* object of consciousness.

In the transition that *we* make, consciousness itself thus mutates immanently and logically – through its own experience – into a new shape.

From Certainty to Truth

This pattern is repeated throughout the *Phenomenology*. The object proves in the experience of it to have a new logical form. The shape of consciousness concerned does not, however, regard what has been disclosed in its experience *as* an altogether new form of object; it understands its experience to reveal the complexity of its *own* object. In this sense, the new form of object as such is merely implicit in consciousness, as indeed is the subsequent shape of consciousness that explicitly takes up this new form of object as its own. A given shape of consciousness does not, therefore, actually become the following shape. The slave does not itself become a stoic, and the sceptic does not itself become an unhappy consciousness. Rather, the later shape of consciousness takes up the *truth* that is disclosed by the previous shape and understands that truth – the newly conceived object – to be the object of its own specific experience.

The relation between the shapes of consciousness in the *Phenomenology* is thus not historical, but *logical*. The *Phenomenology* has been interpreted by some as essentially a dialectical retelling of the history of human development.[41] It is clear, however, that many shapes of consciousness – such as perception – cannot be assigned to any particular period of history, and that some of those that can are not arranged in the correct chronological order in Hegel's text (Greek religion and Christianity, for example, are discussed after the French Revolution). Furthermore, throughout the *Phenomenology*, even when – as in chapter 6 on 'spirit' – shapes do follow one another in roughly chronological order, the connection between the shapes is always one of logical necessity, rather than historical causality. That is to say not that later shapes constitute the 'transcendental' presuppositions of the earlier ones, but that the later shapes take full cognizance of the *truth* that is necessarily revealed in the experience of the preceding shape.

Each new shape has a new object, an object of a new logical form. Such an object is not, however, quite separate from the one that precedes it in the *Phenomenology*, but is what the previous object proves *in truth* to be. With each new object, therefore, more of the true character of the object of consciousness as such becomes apparent. The *Phenomenology* thus traces the continuous process whereby, through a series of logically connected shapes, consciousness gradually acquires a richer understanding of the truth of which it is initially only imperfectly aware. Consciousness learns that the object or 'content' of which it is aware is not just the sheer immediacy of this, here, now, but a unified thing with manifold properties. Then it learns that the object is not just this either, but is in fact a realm of things governed by invisible forces and laws. Then it learns that the object is not just this, but is that through which consciousness achieves self-consciousness. Then it learns that the object is not just this, but is the realm in which reason is actualized. Then it learns that the object is not just this, but is also the world that is produced by the activity of self-consciousness itself, the world of culture, enlightenment and morality. Lastly, it learns that object is not just this, but is 'absolute being' that reveals itself to be the process of becoming self-conscious in and as human self-consciousness. As Lauer puts it, 'in the consistently sustained *experience* of the object the object [thus] reveals itself more and more as what it truly is'.[42]

Each individual shape of consciousness sees a dimension of the truth that is not explicitly acknowledged by the previous shape, but is nevertheless brought to our attention by the experience of that previous shape itself; and, in so far as each shape does, indeed, see an essential dimension of the *truth*, its insights are carried over and incorporated into later shapes. The *Phenomenology* does not, therefore, merely move on from one form of object to another, but in each new shape of consciousness preserves what has been learned up to that point. Self-consciousness thus retains a relation to the sensuous, perceivable things disclosed by *consciousness*, reason remains conscious of *itself*, even as it recognizes how its own reason is actualized in nature, and later shapes retain the insight that the object, whether it be natural or human, embodies *reason* in some form.

Yet each individual shape of consciousness elevates the dimension of truth that it understands into the principal – one might even say, *absolute* – truth. In each shape, as Hegel puts it in the Preface, 'whatever the content may be, the individual is the absolute form, i.e. he is the *immediate certainty* of himself and, if this expression be preferred, he is therefore unconditioned *being*'.[43] Consciousness thus takes its object above all to be *other* than itself; self-consciousness, by contrast, is fixated on *itself* and its freedom (or lack of it) in relation to the things and other self-consciousnesses that confront it. Each subsequent shape of consciousness is similarly absorbed by the object as it conceives it to be.

To the extent that each shape is characterized by this overwhelming preoccupation with its *own* object, it is not preserved as the *Phenomenology* progresses from shape to shape, but is left behind. Perception certainly incorporates the idea that the things it perceives have an immediacy in their very complexity and occupy definite positions in space and time; but it no longer regards its object as *simply* this, here, now, and in that sense it leaves sense-certainty behind. Similarly, the world of culture or 'self-alienated spirit' preserves the idea that self-consciousness must mould itself into a community, but the immediate form that such a community takes in the world of Sophocles' *Antigone* is not itself preserved. The unhappy consciousness is left behind, as self-consciousness mutates into reason, and natural religion and the Greek 'religion of art' are also abandoned as consciousness enters the stage of 'manifest' religion or Christianity.

The dimension of *truth* disclosed by a given shape is taken up and incorporated into the next, more developed shape of consciousness. Yet the actual shape that arises when a particular aspect of the truth is assumed to be the *whole* truth is consigned to phenomenological 'history' (though in certain cases 'traces' of earlier shapes can, indeed, be detected in later shapes).[44] Hegel insists, however, that we must take each shape seriously and 'linger over' it (*bei jedem sich verweilen*).[45] Otherwise, we will never understand the immanent necessity that takes us from shape to shape and so causes consciousness itself to mutate into different shapes in the very transitions that we make.

Hegel describes the series of shapes which consciousness goes through in the *Phenomenology* as 'the *education* [*Bildung*] of consciousness itself to the standpoint of Science'.[46] Consciousness is 'educated' in so far as it is taken, via the transitions that we make from shape to shape, from its initial immediate *certainty* of its object as 'this' to the deeper understanding of the *truth* achieved in religion and absolute knowing. Consciousness in fact educates itself, since its own experience of the object undermines its favoured conception of that object and makes the transition to the next shape necessary. As Hegel puts it, in this process 'consciousness suffers . . . violence at its own hands: it spoils its own limited satisfaction'.[47]

Not only does the consciousness analysed in Hegel's text – referred to by Hegel as 'phenomenal consciousness' – receive an education, but the 'natural consciousness' of the *reader* is also educated by being shown that the certainties of consciousness lead logically and necessarily to other, more profound conceptions of the truth. This process of education has positive significance for the reader in that it constitutes 'the path of the natural consciousness which presses forward to true knowledge'. Yet this process is also experienced by the reader's natural consciousness as negative, because 'it loses its truth on this path' and thereby suffers 'the loss of its own self' in so far as it witnesses various shapes of consciousness undermine their own certainties. The *Phenomenology* can thus be said to be a work of 'scepticism', since it casts doubt on the certainties of consciousness, or rather shows how those certainties cast doubt upon themselves. As the reader follows the course of such 'thoroughgoing scepticism', and understands its intrinsic necessity, he is brought to do what the fully self-critical philosopher was prepared to do of his own free will: namely, *let go* of the natural certainties of life. This in turn renders the reader capable of undertaking the presuppositionless, philosophical study of the truth:

The scepticism that is directed against the whole range of phenomenal consciousness . . . renders the Spirit for the first time competent to examine what truth is. For it brings about a state of despair about all the so-called natural ideas, thoughts, and opinions, regardless of whether they are called one's own or someone else's, ideas with which the consciousness that sets about the examination [of truth] *straight away* is still filled and hampered, so that it is, in fact, incapable of carrying out what it wants to undertake.[48]

Just as the reader's natural consciousness is educated by the immanent development of sense-certainty to absolute knowing, so the philosopher-as-phenomenologist gains the assurance that consciousness itself – *not* the philosopher – constructs the ladder that takes the reader to the standpoint of philosophy. It is true that the phenomenologist makes the logical transitions from shape to shape and so in that sense puts each rung in place. Yet it is the experience of the consciousness thematized in Hegel's text that makes each rung necessary, and so it is such consciousness that effectively builds its own ladder (with the phenomenologist's help).

The reader is, in this respect, in a slightly different position from the phenomenologist. Like the phenomenologist, the reader also makes the transition in thought from one shape of consciousness to another. However, these shapes of consciousness represent numerous certainties to which the reader – in so far as he or she is, indeed, a 'natural consciousness' – is still to a greater or lesser degree wedded. No reader's consciousness will be exhausted by any particular shape (and none, clearly, can be a character from Sophocles' *Antigone*). Furthermore, every reader must have some interest in learning about speculative philosophy, as otherwise there is little point in ploughing through Hegel's vast book. Nevertheless, the reader may very well consider perception or 'observing reason' to be the best source of knowledge, or be profoundly sceptical about truth altogether, or regard conscience as unassailable, or consider religious experience to reveal the ultimate truth. In this sense, the shapes of consciousness examined in the *Phenomenology* govern the natural consciousness of the reader in a way that they no longer govern the philosopher (or philosopher-as-phenomenologist). For this reason, one can say that the reader's *own* natural consciousness builds the ladder that takes him to philosophy.

Absolute Knowing: The Standpoint of Philosophy

The *Phenomenology* does not set out Hegel's own philosophical account of the world, but is the 'science of the *experience* which consciousness goes through'.[49] Through such experience consciousness learns more and more about the logical form of its object (and of itself). The experience of consciousness culminates in the recognition that the object of consciousness is not merely the *object* (*Gegenstand*) of consciousness after all – not merely something distinct from consciousness to which consciousness stands in relation – but is in fact *identical in form* to consciousness itself and so is that wherein consciousness 'finds itself'. With this recognition consciousness becomes 'absolute knowing'. Absolute knowing is thus 'the *truth* of every mode of consciousness', because it takes over and explicitly acknowledges the truth that has emerged in the experience of consciousness itself.[50]

Absolute knowing – sometimes referred to as 'pure knowing' – is the final shape of consciousness in the *Phenomenology*. Yet it is actually no longer a shape of *consciousness* as such, because it no longer accepts as ultimate the distinction between the object of consciousness and consciousness itself – or between the *truth* that is known and the *certainty* of that truth – that characterizes consciousness. As Hegel writes in the *Logic*, 'in absolute knowing . . . the separation of the *object* from the *certainty of oneself* is completely eliminated: truth is now equated with certainty and this certainty with truth'.[51]

The various shapes analysed in the *Phenomenology* include not only the three forms of object-directed consciousness or consciousness in the narrow sense – sense-certainty, perception and understanding – but also self-consciousness, reason, spirit and religion. Yet, in so far as all of these shapes contain 'the two moments of knowing and the objectivity negative to knowing . . . they all appear as shapes of consciousness'.[52] Absolute knowing, by contrast, is the shape in which consciousness ceases being consciousness and becomes speculative, philosophical *thought* or 'science'. Hegel explains the principal difference between shapes of consciousness and philosophical science in these lines from the end of the *Phenomenology*:

Whereas in the phenomenology of Spirit each moment is the difference of knowledge and Truth, and is the movement in which that difference is cancelled, Science on the other hand does not contain this difference and the cancelling of it. On the contrary, since the moment has the form of the Concept [*Begriff*], it unites the objective form of Truth and of the knowing Self in an immediate unity.[53]

A similar point is made earlier in the Preface:

What Spirit prepares for itself in [the Phenomenology of Spirit], is the element of [true] knowing. In this element the moments of Spirit now spread themselves out in that *form of simplicity* which knows its object as its own self. They no longer fall apart into the antithesis of being and knowing, but remain in the simple oneness of knowing; they are the True in the form of the True, and their difference is only the difference of content. Their movement, which organises itself in this element into a whole, is *Logic* or *speculative philosophy*.[54]

What should be noted here is that absolute knowing still has an object or *Gegenstand*. It thus still knows a realm of being or 'substance' that it takes to have its own objectivity and not merely to be something constructed or posited by consciousness itself. Yet this object is understood not just to be an *object* and so to be fundamentally *distinct* from consciousness, but to be *identical* in form to consciousness – or thought – itself: 'it unites the objective form of Truth and of the knowing Self in an immediate unity'. This form, as Hegel points out, is the form of the *Concept*. Absolute knowing thus knows its object to be *being* that is *conceptual* or *rational* in form. It is for this reason that in absolute knowing spirit 'knows its object as its own self'. Absolute knowing, for Hegel, is thus clearly a form of self-consciousness. Yet it is not mere *self*-consciousness, because it knows the patterns of its own self-determining reason to be immanent in *being itself*. Absolute knowing, in other words, has for its object 'being [as] absolutely mediated'; that is, as 'a substantial content which is just as immediately . . . self-like [*selbstisch*] or the Concept'.[55]

This is why Hegel characterizes the 'ground and soil of Science' as '*pure* self-recognition in absolute otherness'.[56] Strictly speaking, being or the 'object' is not regarded by absolute knowing as fundamentally *other* or 'alien'; it is consciousness that regards the object in this way. Yet Hegel's well known expression reminds us that absolute knowing is not merely *self*-consciousness, but ontological knowledge – knowledge of *being* – too. In the *Logic* Hegel explains that in pure knowing or pure thought – the element of speculative logic – 'being' and 'Concept' are 'known to be *inseparable*, not as in consciousness where each *also* has a separate being of its own'. He adds, however, that they are 'known as *different* (yet not with an independent being)' and that for this reason 'their unity is not abstract, dead and inert, but concrete'.[57]

Absolute knowing thus acknowledges the identity of *thought* and *being*, which has emerged in the experience of consciousness, as the true logical form of its object. Since being has now proven to be identical in form to thought, thought must be able to understand the structure of being from *within* thought itself, and thought can be said to have 'internalized' its object.[58] Yet at the same time, what is known from within thought by absolute knowing must be understood not just to be its own concepts and categories but to be *being itself* – being that is 'in its being its own Concept'.[59]

In the experience of consciousness the very opposition between consciousness and its object is overcome, and consciousness thereby mutates of its own accord (in the transition that we make) into absolute knowing. In this way the *Phenomenology* proves to natural consciousness that the standpoint of philosophy is by no means as perverse as consciousness first believed, but is in fact made necessary, and so justified, by the certainties of consciousness itself. Yet why should we assume that the necessary identity between thought and being-as-it-is-*experienced* allows us to claim that the structure of thought and *being itself* is identical? For the simple reason that a fully self-critical philosophy may not assume at the outset that 'being' is anything beyond what is disclosed by thought or absolute knowing and the experience that generated such thought. Consciousness takes itself all along to be consciousness of *being*, and as phenomenologists endeavouring to provide an immanent analysis of consciousness we may not assume that being is anything more than consciousness takes it to be. At the end of the *Phenomenology* and the start of the *Logic*, we are still not permitted to assume that being is anything more than it has proven to be in the experience of consciousness and the thought to which it leads. Consequently, we have no warrant to assume that absolute knowing is confined 'within' experience and that being could definitively exceed such experience. 'Being' at the start of the *Logic* must be taken to be what *thought* or absolute knowing is minimally aware of – no more, no less.

Indeed, if we are to be genuinely self-critical philosophers, being may be understood to be no more than sheer *indeterminate* being. This means that, as we start the *Logic*, we must even set aside what we have learned in the *Phenomenology* about being through the experience of the various shapes of consciousness, except, of course, for the fact that it has proven to be identical in form to thought. The final chapter of the *Phenomenology* does not, therefore, lead directly to the opening of the *Logic*. It takes us to absolute or pure knowing, but 'to ensure that the beginning remains immanent in its scientific development', we must 'rid ourselves of all other reflections and opinions whatever' and simply 'take up *what is there before us*'; that is, pure being.[60]

At the start of the *Phenomenology* we may hope, but may not presuppose, that consciousness will mutate of its own accord into absolute knowing. By the end of Hegel's text, we have seen consciousness do precisely that. The readers are thereby shown the legitimacy of the standpoint of absolute knowing, and the philosopher-as-phenomenologist is once again permitted to assert that the structure of being can be discerned from within thought

– a claim that had to be suspended throughout the *Phenomenology* itself since it was at odds with the beliefs of consciousness. At the end of the *Phenomenology*, therefore, the perspectives of 'phenomenal' consciousness and of the reader coalesce with that of the philosopher who has been undertaking the task of phenomenology in order to justify his philosophical standpoint. All three now occupy the position of absolute knowing, and speculative philosophy may begin.[61]

4   *The Path to Absolute Knowing*

Hegel's *Phenomenology* shows how simple sensuous certainty mutates into a series of more advanced shapes of consciousness and, finally, into absolute knowing or speculative philosophy. It is we, the readers and the phenomenologist, who effect the transition from one shape to the next, but such transitions are made necessary by the experience undergone by each shape itself. Consciousness changes into absolute knowing because the object of consciousness eventually proves, in the very experience of it, to be nothing less than being that is identical in structure to thought.

Unlike Hegel's *Philosophy of History*, the *Phenomenology* does not trace the historical development of consciousness over time. Its task is to show how, *logically*, consciousness transforms itself into absolute knowing, as it learns more about both its object and itself and finally takes full account of what both turn out in its experience to be. Ordinary, natural consciousness may regard philosophy as a somewhat perverse enterprise. Hegelian phenomenology, by contrast, argues that it is only in philosophy that the truth disclosed in human experience is rendered fully explicit.

In this chapter I propose to give a brief account of some of the principal shapes of consciousness that emerge in the course of Hegel's analysis. My intention here is by no means to be exhaustive. Nor do I plan to discuss the numerous different interpretations of each shape of consciousness to be found in the secondary literature. My aim is simply to flesh out somewhat the account of the *Phenomenology* provided in chapter 3 and in so doing to introduce the reader to some of Hegel's most important analyses.

In the course of this chapter it will, I hope, become evident that, throughout the *Phenomenology*, Hegel adheres faithfully to the method of phenomenological analysis set out in the work's Introduction. It will also become abundantly clear that consciousness is caused to develop both by changes in the object in the strict sense *and* by changes in the 'object' that consciousness is *for itself*. The experience of consciousness traced in the *Phenomenology* will thus prove to be just as much its journey of self-discovery.

Self-consciousness and the Master–Slave Relation

The *Phenomenology* starts with the analysis of sensuous certainty, which – as we saw in chapter 3 – mutates logically into perception. Perception then transforms itself into understanding (*Verstand*). In each of these shapes of consciousness, there is an element of self-awareness, since each distinguishes *itself* from the object to which it relates. Yet the principal focus of each shape is on its *object*, rather than itself. Each one takes 'what is true for consciousness' to be 'something other than itself'.[1] Consequently, these three shapes are described by Hegel as shapes of *consciousness* in the narrow sense, as opposed to shapes of self-consciousness, reason or spirit. (In the broader sense, of course, all the shapes analysed in the *Phenomenology* – with the exception of absolute knowing – count as shapes of 'consciousness', since all fail to recognize fully the essential structural identity between being and thought.)[2]

Hegel then argues that consciousness in the narrow sense turns logically into self-consciousness. Such self-consciousness does not merely consist in the self-awareness that accompanies all consciousness of objects. It consists, rather, in being wholly preoccupied with and absorbed by itself, and it sees objects as little more than the means to reinforce and deepen its sense of itself. The transition to such all-embracing self-consciousness is made necessary by the third shape of consciousness, 'understanding'. Its object proves in its experience not just to be simple immediacy, nor just to be a perceivable thing with properties, but to be an object governed by inner forces and laws. In such laws, however, consciousness recognizes principles of its *own* understanding. This, according to Hegel, is why 'explaining' something in terms of laws affords such satisfaction: 'because in it consciousness is, so to speak, communing directly with itself, enjoying only itself; although it seems to be busy with something else, it is in fact occupied only with itself'.[3]

Explanatory consciousness, or understanding, is explicitly directed towards objects standing over against it; but it is implicitly concerned with itself above all. The next shape of consciousness analysed by Hegel is the one that *explicitly* affirms what is implicit in the experience of understanding and openly places itself at the centre of its own world. Such explicit self-consciousness, as its name suggests, is principally absorbed by *itself*. Yet it also remains conscious of what is *other* than itself, and its certainty of itself is mediated by the other things and selves to which it relates. Such mediation, Hegel argues, takes two forms. On the one hand, self-consciousness affirms its certainty of itself by negating the independence of objects and pressing them into the service of the self; that is, by turning them into means to the satisfaction of *desire*. On the other hand, self-consciousness sees its identity confirmed by another self-consciousness that 'negates itself' through setting its own interests to one side and according *recognition* to the first self-consciousness.[4]

Fully developed self-consciousness, according to Hegel, is to be found only where such recognition is mutual, indeed where two (or more) self-consciousnesses '*recognise themselves as mutually recognising* one another', as, for example, in the modern constitutional state.[5] Hegel turns first, however, to examine primitive or 'immediate' self-consciousness which is not yet committed to genuine reciprocity but seeks recognition for itself alone. Such primitive self-consciousness, we are told, wants to be recognized by another self-consciousness as pure 'being-for-self' (*Fürsichsein*) or *freedom*.[6] This freedom is understood in a wholly negative way as freedom *from* all limitation and determination by others or by one's own given nature and, accordingly, is taken to reside in what Hegel calls 'absolute negativity'. Such negativity is held, more specifically, to consist (a) in being governed in oneself by nothing determinate, such as one's sex, age or skin colour, and so being in essence *nothing in particular*, and (b) in the corresponding ability to *negate* anything and everything outside oneself, including not only objects but also any other self-consciousness to which one relates. Since primitive self-consciousness seeks to be recognized by another as nothing but such sheer negativity, and the other self-consciousness seeks similar recognition for itself in turn, there necessarily ensues a 'life and death struggle' in which each tries to prove to the other how free and 'negative' it is. Each does so by endeavouring to kill the other and by risking its own life in the process.

Hegel points out, however, that there is a contradiction in this struggle: for if either self-consciousness were actually to end up dead, the other would not gain the desired recognition. The survivor would prove his freedom to himself, but he could not be recognized by the other as the one who was prepared to risk his life in seeking the other's death. The logical 'experience' of self-consciousness thus reveals that both the combatants must emerge from the struggle alive, and indeed that one of them must give way to the other, if there is to be any conferral and enjoyment of the recognition that they both desire. The one that backs down will do so out of the fear of dying: he will cling on to life, abandon his effort to be recognized as free 'negativity' and subordinate himself to the other as his 'bondsman' or 'slave' (*Knecht*). The other self-consciousness, who is recognized by the slave as free negativity, becomes the 'lord' or 'master' (*Herr*).[7] Note that Hegel's claim is not that all such life and death struggles in history issue in relations of dominance and subservience. Hegel well knows that the combatants in such struggles often end up dead. His point is that the recognition sought by both self-consciousnesses in the struggle can be achieved only if the struggle gives way to the master–slave relation. The life and death struggle thus leads *logically* to mastery and slavery, even if actual historical struggles do not always obey this logic.

In his famous account of the master–slave relation, Hegel shows that each self-consciousness discovers through its own experience that it is actually the opposite of what it initially takes itself to be. The master takes himself to manifest the freedom and power of unfettered 'negativity' or desire, but learns that his freedom is in fact *dependent* on the labour and service of the slave. The slave, by contrast, takes himself to be wholly unfree, but learns that he does in fact enjoy genuine freedom in his very servitude.

> Just as lordship showed that its essential nature is the reverse of what it wants to be, so too servitude in its consummation will really turn into the opposite of what it immediately is; as a consciousness forced back into itself, it will withdraw into itself and be transformed into a truly independent [*selbständig*] consciousness.[8]

The slave is forced by the master to work on things and prepare them for his consumption; but in the very activity of labour the slave discovers that he, too, has a certain freedom and power to negate and transform things: 'the bondsman realises that it is precisely in his work wherein he seemed to have only an alienated existence that he acquires a mind of his own [*eigener Sinn*]'. Furthermore, the slave is able to do what the master cannot do, namely give positive, objective expression to his freedom by giving a new form to, rather than merely destroying, objects around him: 'in fashioning the thing, the bondsman's own negativity, his being-for-self, becomes an object for him only through his negating the existing *shape* confronting him'.[9]

In itself such labour is the *particular* expression of a particular skill – the particular ability to bake bread or to make chairs. Hegel points out, however, that the slave also harbours within himself an awareness of a profound freedom *from* all particularity and givenness – an awareness of himself as 'pure negativity and being-for-self'.[10] Yet how can the slave think of himself in this way? In the life and death struggle, each of the rival self-consciousnesses sought recognition for itself as sheer negativity, but the one that became the slave abandoned its search for such recognition. In so doing, it also forfeited its own sense of being purely 'negative' by clinging on to the concrete determinacies of life. Paradoxically, however, the slave gains a new sense of being purely negative through his fear of death. The slave experiences such fear because, in the struggle, he envisages himself being dead, and so being nothing, and quakes at the thought of his utter destruction. This is not to say that slave is simply fearful that he will die at some unspecified time in the future. What fills him with all-consuming terror is the fact that he stares death directly in the face and envisages himself *being* dead and *being* nothing *now*. In other words, he is terrified by the thought of himself, now, *as* nothing whatsoever.

This fearful thought, in Hegel's view, is double-edged. On the one hand, it is the thought that everything about oneself is under threat of being 'inwardly dissolved'.[11] On the other hand, it entails a new and highly abstract thought of *oneself* – the thought of oneself *as* nothing determinate, *as not-a-thing*. The slave's confrontation with his own death in fear is thus not purely and simply an experience of loss, because in such fear the slave actually gains a renewed consciousness of himself. As Kojève puts it, the slave in the fear of death catches 'a glimpse of himself as nothingness, . . . a Nothingness maintained in Being'.[12] Indeed, the slave sees himself as nothing but pure and empty *being* itself – pure being that is *for itself*. For this reason, Hegel argues, 'in fear, being-for-self is present in the bondsman himself [*an ihm selbst*]'.[13]

The master's consciousness of his own pure negativity expressed itself in the form of sheer unrestrained desire. The slave's consciousness of his own pure negativity takes a far less rapacious form. It is sheltered within a fear that by itself is 'inward and mute' and is no more than a silent quaking within the slave.[14] Such fearful consciousness of being in essence *nothing in particular* is not, however, impotent; on the contrary, it radically trans-forms the slave's understanding of his own labour. For if the slave labours out of an under-lying mortal fear, he can regard his labour as giving active expression to the pure negativity that, in his fear, he experiences himself to be.

Were the slave to labour without fear, Hegel argues, such labour would be for the slave himself nothing more than the exercise of a particular talent. In such a case, the slavish consciousness's 'formative activity cannot give it a consciousness of itself as essential being'; that is, as 'negativity *per se*'. Furthermore, the slave would regard the particular labour in which he engages as the sole locus of his freedom and so would cling to it stubbornly – with *Eigensinn*.[15] Since the slave would be bound to and dependent upon this particular labour for the freedom he enjoys, his freedom would in fact still be 'enmeshed in servitude'.[16]

If, however, the slave labours out of fear and the accompanying experience of himself as pure negativity, he can regard any particular activity as the particular, concrete expression of his *universal* freedom from, and freedom to negate and transform, everything given and determinate around him, or what Hegel calls his 'universal formative activity'.[17] Accord-ingly, he will understand himself to be capable of all kinds of labour and not to be depend-ent on, or slave to, any one of them. To paraphrase Marx, he will regard himself not just as a painter but as a person who engages in painting among other possible activities.[18] In this way, the slave who labours out of fear acquires a consciousness of freedom that incor-porates and fuses together the *concrete* ability to transform particular objects and the *abstract* consciousness of oneself as pure negativity that initially appeared to be reserved for the master alone. Such consciousness of freedom belies the slave's initial understand-ing of himself as no more than a slave.[19]

In the experience described by the phenomenologist, the slave discovers that, thanks to the fear of death, he possesses a freedom that is not just the partial, slavish freedom of labour and service alone. Yet despite this, the slave still knows himself to be in servitude to the master. He thus regards himself as non-slavishly free *in his very slavery*. At this point, however, we make the transition to a new shape of consciousness that takes over and renders fully explicit the new understanding of freedom attained by the slave, without the slave's lingering conception of oneself as bound in servitude. This new shape of consciousness is *thought* or 'Stoicism'.

Stoicism

Kojève regards the transition from the slave's consciousness to 'stoical' thought as a historical transition: the slave himself *becomes* a stoic who claims that he is free in his thinking in order to compensate for his lack of real freedom in the world and, indeed, 'to justify . . . his refusal to *fight* to *realise* his libertarian ideal'.[20] As is the case throughout the *Phenomenology*, however, this transition is logical, not historical. Stoical thought is a new shape of consciousness that renders explicit what is implicit in the slave's experience.

The slave sees his own freedom embodied in the object of his labour. He works on the object, gives it a new form and sees that form as manifesting, in the object itself, his own free activity. In this way, 'consciousness, *qua* worker, comes to see in the independent being [of the object] its *own* independence'.[21] The slave, however, continues to regard the object as *other* than consciousness and, of course, as an inanimate *object* lacking any consciousness, selfhood or freedom of its own. He sees the master as another 'being-for-self', but he does not regard the object of his labour in this way. Consequently, he does not see his own selfhood as such duplicated in another self-consciousness, but instead sees his freedom embodied 'in the *form of the thing* he has fashioned'.[22]

Yet *for us* what is implicit in the slave's relation to his object is the fact that he finds *himself – qua* self-consciousness and being-for-self – in the form he has given to the object. As Hegel puts it, 'the form and the being-for-self are *for us*, or *in themselves*, the same'.[23] We now make the transition, therefore, to a new shape of consciousness that takes over explicitly the truth revealed in the experience of the slave.

This new shape of consciousness does not cease to relate to objects – objects that lack any self-consciousness of their own. Yet, at the same time, it finds *itself* explicitly as such in these objects. But how can it see itself and its own consciousness in objects that are inanimate? By recognizing that 'thinghood which received its form in being fashioned is no other substance [*keine andere Substanz*] than consciousness' itself. And what is this 'substance' that is identical in both inanimate things and consciousness? It is *intelligible*, *conceptual* form. The new shape of consciousness that explicitly recognizes *itself* in things is thus *thought (Denken)* that sees in the object's intelligible structure its very *own* concepts and categories.

When consciousness perceives something, its attention is directed outside itself to the object perceived. It knows itself to be perceptual consciousness, but it considers the object and the properties perceived in the object to be quite other than itself. When thought understands something through concepts, however, it is immediately aware that such concepts are its own: 'the Concept is for me straightway *my* Concept'. At the same time those concepts are understood to articulate and bring to mind the true structure of things themselves – a structure that is itself understood to be conceptual. Conceptual thought thus discerns in its object an intelligible structure that it understands also to belong to concepts it immediately knows to be its own: 'since this content is at the same time a content grasped *in thought*, consciousness remains *immediately* aware of its unity with this determinate and distinct being'. There is, therefore, a subtle but important difference between thought and the self-consciousness of the slave: whereas the slave relates to *another object* in which it finds itself embodied, thought relates principally to *itself* and its *own* concepts in the objects it finds before it. Such thought thus actually attains a higher degree of *self*-consciousness and freedom than does the slave: 'in thinking, I *am free*, because I am not in an *other*, but remain simply and solely in communion with myself, and the object, which is for me the *essential* being, is in undivided unity with my being-for-myself; and my activity in conceptual thinking is a movement within myself'.[24]

Yet does this not mean that the *Phenomenology* has now reached its goal: a shape of consciousness in which the opposition between subject and object has been overcome and in which thought and being are known to be completely identical in form? Not quite, because the mode of thought under discussion at this point in the text – associated by Hegel with Stoicism – does not give equal weight to being and to its own thought, but remains above all a shape of *self-consciousness*. Some critics have suggested that Hegelian absolute knowing is itself nothing more than self-consciousness writ large and for this reason fails to make genuine space for what is other than consciousness and its own determinations.[25] Yet a brief comparison between absolute knowing and stoical thought shows this charge to be misplaced.

Stoical thought prefigures absolute knowing in so far as it understands thought and being to be identical in structure. It insists on such an identity, however, not because it discovers through its experience that its object is itself independently and immanently logical, but because it 'withdraws' (*sich . . . zurückzieht*) into its *own* thought and finds therein the categories that it then discerns in the object.[26] Its understanding of the identity of thought and being is, therefore, one-sided, since it comes to recognize that identity by looking first to *itself* and then through itself and its own concepts at things. Since stoical thought is primarily conscious of itself in relating to its objects, it remains a shape of *self-consciousness*. (This, by the way, distinguishes stoical thought from 'understanding', which, as a shape of consciousness rather than self-consciousness, remains explicitly focused on objects standing over against it rather than itself.)

In so far as stoical thought withdraws into itself in order to learn the truth about things, it continues – like the previous shapes of self-consciousness – to stand in a *negative* relation to objects. True, it no longer consumes things to satisfy desire or transforms them through labour. None the less it negates them by 'turn[ing] away' from them, abstracting from their concrete, given individuality, and 'return[ing] into itself' in order to discover their essence.[27] For by abstracting from things in this way, thought declares that their true character lies *not* in what they are immediately found to be in nature, but only in what they are understood to be within *thought and self-consciousness*.

Since stoical thought finds the true structure of things within thought *as opposed to* their 'natural existence', it fails to overcome the characteristic 'opposition of consciousness', even though it recognizes an identity of substance between itself and being. Furthermore, such thought renders itself quite abstract: it is, as Hegel puts it, the 'abstraction' that 'cuts itself off from the multiplicity of things' and seeks the truth by withdrawing into its own abstract self-identity. Due to its abstractness, Hegel argues, thought leaves itself with 'no content *in its own self*'. This is not to say that it operates with no determinate concepts at all. It means, however, that such concepts are not understood to be generated by thought itself – and so to be truly its own – but are simply *found* within abstract thought as given concepts: 'this determinateness of the Concept is [thus] the alien element that it has within it'.[28] Note that thought's intrinsic abstractness, and its resultant dependence on *given* determinacies, is the direct consequence of its looking away from the immediate individuality of things and withdrawing back into *itself*. Stoical thought is thus inherently abstract because it is still a shape of *self*-consciousness.

Like stoical thought, absolute knowing also knows the structure of thought to be identical to that of being. It knows this, however, both because it explicitly recognizes itself and its own concepts in being *and* because being proves in the preceding experience of consciousness to be 'spiritual' and rational *in itself*. It is this knowledge that being has proven to be logical and rational in itself – that 'substance' has proven to be 'subject' – that enables absolute knowing to go on, in speculative philosophy, to 'go down into the depths of its own being' and discover the structure of being within thought.[29]

There is, therefore, a subtle but significant difference between absolute knowing and stoical thought, even though both find the true nature of things within thought. Stoical thought is a shape of *self*-consciousness and so thinks of itself as withdrawing from nature and being into itself in order to find the truth about things. Absolute knowing, by contrast, understands itself to be thought that is both self-conscious and wholly open to what *being* discloses itself immanently to be. Absolute knowing thus understands itself to be 'neither merely the withdrawal of self-consciousness into its pure inwardness, nor the mere submergence of self-consciousness in substance', but rather '*this movement* of the Self which empties itself of itself and sinks itself into its substance, and also, as Subject, has gone out of that substance into itself'. Since such knowing does not 'turn away from the independence of things' to find their truth, but seeks that truth by 'sinking itself into' substance or being in thought, it stands in an affirmative rather than negative relation to being.[30]

Since absolute knowing understands itself not just to be conscious of its own concepts but also to be open to and conscious of being itself, it does not cling abstractly to *itself* but is prepared in the spirit of ontological openness to let being unfold itself and its intrinsic determinations in thought. In this way, absolute knowing or speculative logic discovers a self-determining content within itself that it understands to be the rational, categorial structure of both thought and being. Stoical thought, by contrast, holds on to *itself* and its abstract identity as thought, and insists that the truth is to be found within its *own abstract* thought and concepts. It does not, therefore, adopt the more open posture of *letting* being disclose itself through *letting* the thought of being develop. Consequently, stoical thought does not discover any self-determining content within itself, but remains dependent, in its very abstractness, on *given* conceptual determinations.

Both stoical thought and absolute knowing certainly determine the truth about being from within thought. Nevertheless, there is a clear difference between them. For, whereas stoical thought is thought that has '*withdrawn* from existence only into itself', absolute knowing is thought that 'giv[es] up the *fixity* of its self-positing, by giving up not only the fixity of the pure concrete, which the "I" itself is, in contrast with its differentiated content, but also the fixity of the differentiated moments which, posited in the element of pure thinking, share the unconditioned nature of the "I"'. In this way, the thoughts entertained by absolute knowing become true '*concepts*, . . . self-movements, circles, spiritual essences', whereas the 'concepts' entertained by stoical thought remain quite abstract and dead – truths 'lacking the fullness of life'. The subtle difference between the ways in which each shape of thought conceives of its relation to being thus brings in its wake a difference between the ways in which they conceive of the very nature and method of thought itself.[31]

This, to my mind, is one of the profound lessons of the *Phenomenology*: that the perspective of absolute knowing can be attained by ordinary consciousness, if it is prepared to *let go* of itself and its natural certainties and let being determine itself in thought. Indeed, the *Phenomenology* shows that these very certainties themselves require us to let go of them, since they lead logically (if not always in fact) to the adoption of new standpoints in which they lose their privileged status.

The Unhappy Consciousness and Reason

Not only are we readers moved to give up a succession of certainties as the *Phenomeno-logy* progresses from one shape of consciousness to another, but at certain important points in Hegel's text the shape of consciousness under discussion brings about the transition to a further shape by itself letting go of or 'renouncing' itself. The first example of such renun-ciation is to be found at the end of the section on self-consciousness, where the 'unhappy consciousness' mutates into 'reason'.

Stoicism, as we have seen, is thought that 'negates' things in so far as it abstracts from their concrete individuality and withdraws into the realm of its own thought and concepts. Scepticism then takes over and radicalizes the idea that thought is conscious of itself only in actively *negating* what is given to it. For the radical sceptic, indeed, thought is the thor-ough negation of things, in that it denies that they enjoy any reality outside of thought at all. Hegel calls stoical thought the 'incomplete negation of otherness', because it simply withdraws into itself out of a sphere of otherness which it continues to regard as inde-pendently real, in order to discover within thought the true, intelligible structure of such otherness. For scepticism, however, 'thought becomes the concrete thinking which annihi-lates the being of the world in all its manifold determinateness, and the negativity of free self-consciousness [thereby] comes to know itself in the many and varied forms of life as a real negativity'.[32] Hegel's analysis of scepticism thus continues the theme that runs throughout the section on self-consciousness, namely that 'it procures for its own self the certainty of its freedom' through 'self-conscious negation'.[33] Indeed, Hegel's great insight is that radical scepticism is the logical consequence of the insistent concern to secure and preserve one's *own* (negative) freedom of thought above all else.

The price paid by scepticism for its freedom is, however, internal contradiction. On the one hand, sceptical consciousness retains its certainty of itself and its own freedom in the very act of calling everything else into question. As Hegel puts it, 'sceptical self-consciousness . . . experiences in the flux of all that would stand secure before it its own freedom as given and preserved by itself. It is aware of this stoical indifference [*Ataraxie*] of a thinking which thinks itself, the unchanging and genuine certainty of itself.' On the other hand, such consciousness confesses that it remains a changeable, contingent, empir-ical consciousness 'which takes its guidance from what has no reality for it': 'it affirms the nullity of seeing, hearing, etc., yet it is itself seeing, hearing, etc.' Sceptical consciousness is contradictory in itself, therefore, both because 'its deeds and its words always belie one another' and because 'it has itself the doubly contradictory consciousness of unchange-ableness and sameness, and of utter contingency and non-identity with itself'.[34]

Yet Hegel points out that scepticism does not bring these two thoughts of itself together but flips back and forth between asserting its sceptical freedom to dissolve into nothing-ness everything given to it and its inevitable dependence on the very testimony of sight and hearing that it declares to be illusory. It is, in other words, 'the unconscious, thoughtless rambling which passes back and forth from the one extreme of self-identical self-consciousness to the other extreme of the contingent consciousness that is both bewildered and bewildering'.[35] Yet, of course, these two extremes fall within *one* sceptical self-consciousness. The shape of self-consciousness that takes over the truth revealed in the experience of scepticism, and that knows itself explicitly to be one single, internally contradictory self-consciousness, is the unhappy consciousness.

It may seem strange for self-consciousness, which throughout its course appears to achieve freedom and self-certainty and in that sense to be 'happy', to culminate in unhap-piness and alienation. Such unhappiness is, however, the logical consequence of the idea that freedom and self-consciousness lie above all in the active, insistent *negation* of otherness, givenness and contingency: for this idea leads eventually to the further idea that freedom lies in the negation of the very contingency and changeableness that belong irreducibly to self-consciousness *itself*. This in turn leads to the thought that true freedom and self-consciousness do not reside within actual, living, individual self-consciousness at all, but are to be found beyond the self in a being that Hegel (perhaps following St Augustine) calls the 'Unchangeable' (*das Unwandelbare*).[36] This Unchangeable embodies what self-consciousness in truth is meant to be and so constitutes for self-consciousness its own 'essence'. At the same time, however, it is experienced as an 'alien' (*fremd*) being from which self-consciousness is separated by its own changeable contingency and individuality. Self-consciousness thus knows the Unchangeable to contain its own essence, 'although in such a way that . . . it does not take *itself* to be this essence'.[37] This alienation from its own true freedom is what makes this self-consciousness 'unhappy'.

Yet the unhappy consciousness does not, as it were, rest content in its unhappiness. The fact that it regards the unchangeable being beyond itself as embodying true self-consciousness drives it to attempt to free itself from itself, cast off its merely contingent individuality and raise itself to indissoluble communion with the Unchangeable – for example, through acts of religious devotion (*Andacht*). The problem is that self-consciousness cannot turn a blind eye to the fact that the very activity through which it seeks to unite itself with the Unchangeable is its *own* activity. At the same time as it brings self-consciousness close to its goal such activity thus constantly reinforces self-consciousness's sense of *itself* as that which is infinitely divided from the Unchangeable (and its own essence). At the very moment, for example, at which it feels itself to have become one with the Unchangeable in prayer, it realizes that this is merely its *own* feeling and the feeling of unity itself is thereby dissipated: 'instead of laying hold of the essence, it only *feels* it and has fallen back into itself'.[38]

Hegel goes on to point out that the unhappy consciousness understands its own talents and powers and the world about it to be 'a gift from an alien source, which the Unchangeable makes over to consciousness to make use of'. The Unchangeable is thereby understood to 'surrender' (*preisgeben*) part of itself for our benefit. This affords the unhappy consciousness another opportunity to become one with the Unchangeable, for it can seek to emulate the latter's self-surrender by surrendering itself to the Unchangeable in turn in an act of thanksgiving:

> The fact that the unchangeable consciousness *renounces* and *surrenders* its embodied form, while, on the other hand, the particular individual consciousness *gives thanks* [for the gift], i.e. *denies* itself the satisfaction of being conscious of its *independence*, and assigns the essence of its action not to itself but to the beyond, through these two moments of *reciprocal self-surrender* of both parts, consciousness does, of course, gain a sense of its *unity* with the Unchangeable.[39]

Once again, however, self-consciousness spoils its own satisfaction by seeing that 'even its *giving of thanks* . . . is its *own* act which counterbalances the action of the other extreme, and meets the self-sacrificing beneficence with a *like* action'. Consequently, 'consciousness feels itself therein as this particular individual, and does not let itself be deceived by its own seeming renunciation, for the truth of the matter is that' – by virtue of the very fact that it has felt the need to give thanks in return for the gift of its own powers – 'it has *not* renounced itself'. (At this point Hegel's analysis of the unhappy consciousness merits comparison with Nietzsche's account of gratitude in *Human, All-too Human*.)[40]

The unhappy consciousness learns, therefore, that it cannot hope to free itself from itself *by itself*, and to unite with its alienated essence, as long as it regards everything about itself and its own contingent individuality as keeping it irrreducibly separate from that essence. The only hope self-consciousness has, therefore, is to abandon all its *own* efforts to seek salvation and genuinely to renounce and let go of everything about itself. This it does not just by acknowledging its debt to the Unchangeable, as in giving thanks, but by giving itself over wholly to the 'will' of the Unchangeable, in the form of its representative on earth, the mediator or priest.

In the mediator, then, this consciousness frees itself from action and enjoyment so far as they are regarded as its own. As a separate, independent extreme, it rejects the essence of its will and casts upon the mediator or minister [priest] its own freedom of decision, and herewith the responsibility for its own action. This mediator, having a direct relationship with the unchangeable Being, ministers by giving advice on what is right. The action, since it follows upon the decision of someone else, ceases, as regards the doing or the *willing* of it, to be its own.[41]

Of course, such an act of submission and renunciation is still an act performed by *self-consciousness*. It does not, however, simply reinforce the individual's sense of himself and his own distance from the Unchangeable, because it entails actually allowing one's own will to be determined by that of the Unchangeable itself – to the point, indeed, of thinking and speaking 'what is meaningless to it' (i.e. Latin).[42] This act of letting go of oneself is, therefore, one through which self-consciousness actually succeeds in freeing itself from itself, because it welcomes into itself a will that is *not just its own*. In so doing, however, the unhappy consciousness does not (as one might imagine) revert to the standpoint of the slave, who submits himself to the will of the master that is wholly alien to his own. For the unhappy consciousness unites itself with another will – that of the Unchangeable – that it understands to be not only the will of another, but also its own true and essential will, indeed the *universal* will of all truly free self-consciousness.

By letting go of itself at the lowest point of its unhappiness and admitting the Unchangeable into itself, self-consciousness thus succeeds in overcoming its alienation from its own essence and so recovers something of its happiness. As Hegel puts it, 'in the sacrifice actually carried out, consciousness, having nullified the *action* as its own doing, has also *in principle* obtained relief from its *misery*'. The unhappy consciousness, however, does not fully appreciate just how happy its new situation is. This is because it understands itself to be taking into itself its own true and essential will in the form of the will of *another*, and so preserves a lingering sense of its separation from its own unchangeable essence that now lives and moves within it: 'for consciousness, its will does indeed become universal and essential will, but consciousness itself does not take itself to be this essential will'.[43]

The consequence of this is that 'the universal, which thereby comes to be for it, is not regarded [by self-consciousness] as its *own doing*'. That is to say, the unhappy consciousness does not recognize that its *own individual will* has in fact now become one with the universal will of the Unchangeable, and that this occurred precisely because that individual will, by renouncing itself, *opened itself* to the universal will. The (only partly happy) unhappy consciousness does not recognize, therefore, that its own contingent, individual will is *itself* implicitly (*an sich*) a free will that wills the 'universal', in so far as it has the intrinsic capacity to let go of itself and its own contingencies and welcome the universal into itself. The shape of self-consciousness that does recognize that 'the *single* individual consciousness is *in itself* [*an sich*] Absolute Essence', and that is thus completely happy with itself, is *reason* (*Vernunft*).[44]

It should be noted that the act of self-renunciation carried out by the unhappy consciousness leads logically to a new shape of consciousness – reason – that is no longer absorbed by *itself* above all but is conscious of and interested in what is universal. Furthermore, this new shape no longer stands in a primarily *negative* relation to what is other than itself and to its own contingent individuality. The slave consciousness, because of the specific circumstances of its emergence, affirms the other in the very act of negating it. It accepts that things have an independence of their own and so does not seek to do away with them. The negation of the thing, wherein it becomes conscious of its own freedom, thus stops short of destruction and takes the form of labour. The other shapes of self-consciousness, however – the master, stoical thought and scepticism – endeavour to establish their freedom through the more thorough negation of things, either by consuming them or withdrawing from them into thought or dissolving them into illusion. In so doing, each shape of self-consciousness, in the attempt to achieve certainty of itself, places itself in opposition to the sphere of givenness and contingency.

With the entry of self-consciousness into the 'happiness' of reason, however, this opposition is overcome. Reason no longer insists on maintaining *itself* in opposition to what is other than the self, and it no longer conceives of true freedom as the *negation* of given, contingent individuality (including the contingent individuality of self-consciousness itself). Rather, it finds true freedom *in* the very sphere of contingency itself, specifically in contingent, individual self-consciousness that is prepared to let go of itself and welcome into itself the will of the universal. Reason thus has an explicitly *affirmative* attitude to contingency, individuality and otherness (more affirmative even than that of the slave).[45]

Self-consciousness must let go of its own contingent individuality, if its will is actually to become 'universal' and rational. Once attained, however, rational consciousness itself is quite reconciled to, and happy to live with, its own contingent individuality, since it knows *explicitly* that that individuality is itself *implicitly* rational. Indeed, reason extends this judgement to cover the whole world of given, individual objects – nature – that surrounds it: it is happy to let that world of individuality stand and be what it is, because it regards all of it as implicitly rational. Reason remains a form of self-consciousness, in so far as it is confident that it can find itself and the patterns of its own rationality in the world. In that sense, as Hegel puts it, 'reason is the certainty of being all *reality*', or 'of being all *truth*'.[46] Yet reason does not believe that it has to negate the objects around it, either in thought or in acts of consumption, in order to secure its certainty of itself. It finds itself in a world whose existence it affirms as *implicitly rational in its own right*. With the emergence of reason, therefore, 'the [continuing] *existence* [*Bestehen*] of the world becomes for self-consciousness its own *truth* and *presence*; it is certain of experiencing only itself therein'.[47] Hegel sums up the difference between reason and mere self-consciousness in these lines:

Now that self-consciousness is Reason, its hitherto negative relation to otherness turns round into a positive relation. Up till now it has been concerned only with its independence and freedom, concerned to save and maintain itself for itself at the expense of the *world*, or of its own actuality, both of which appeared to it as the negative of its essence. But as Reason, assured of itself, it is at peace with them, and can endure them; for it is certain that it is itself reality, or that everything actual is none other than itself.[48]

By mutating logically into reason, consciousness thus takes a further step towards becoming absolute knowing. Simple *consciousness* was directed primarily towards objects, which it regarded as immediately given (as *this*, *here*, *now*), and then as unified things with manifold properties, and then as objects governed by inner forces and laws. *Self-consciousness* then related to itself by means of the negation of such objects. *Reason* now relates to itself by finding itself to be *implicitly* present *in* the world itself – a world 'which in its permanence holds an interest for it that previously lay only in its transiency'.[49] Reason thus could be said to combine into one the subjective self-certainty of self-consciousness and the objective certainty characteristic of consciousness. It understands *itself* to be immanent in that which it allows to stand as something *other* than itself.

Here lies the principal difference between reason and Stoicism. Like Stoicism, reason recognizes an identity between itself and the world around it: it is conscious that 'self-consciousness and being are the same essence'.[50] Unlike Stoicism, however, reason does not simply withdraw into itself to discover the concepts that articulate the true nature of things; rather, it looks also to the world itself and finds reason to be implicit *in* the very objects and individuality it encounters. Consequently, whereas Stoicism – like all self-consciousness (with the exception of the slave) – is interested principally in *itself* and its own thoughts, 'reason now has . . . a universal interest *in the world*, because it is certain of its presence in the world, or that the world present to it is rational'.[51] When Hegel equates the standpoint of reason with that of 'idealism', one should thus remember that such idealism does not reduce the world to a mere 'posit' or reflection of the self, but affirms the independent existence and implicit rationality of the world itself. Genuine (as opposed to subjective) idealism, for Hegel, is the point of view that knows the *world* to have a rational, and therefore 'ideal', structure.[52]

Yet reason still falls short of absolute knowing. This is because it remains too narrowly interested in immediate *individuality* – the individuality both of natural objects and of self-consciousness itself – which it understands to be *implicitly* rational.[53] This, indeed, is why reason takes the seemingly irrational forms of 'phrenology', in which rational self-consciousness believes that it can find reason embodied in the manifold bumps and depressions of an individual's skull, and 'the law of the heart', in which reason is identified with the immediate feelings of the individual heart. Reason is, however, driven by its own experience to mutate into a further shape of consciousness that knows itself to be *explicitly universal* reason and that knows the otherness to which it relates also to be universal reason that is conscious of itself as such: 'To begin with, . . . active reason is aware of itself merely as an individual [*Individuum*]. . . . Then, however, its consciousness having raised itself into universality, it becomes *universal* Reason, and is conscious of itself as Reason, as a consciousness that is already recognised in and for itself'.[54] Such self-conscious universal reason, that also recognizes its other to be self-conscious universal reason, is *spirit* (*Geist*).

Spirit and Absolute Freedom

Spirit, for Hegel, is not some disembodied cosmic consciousness, manipulating human activity from on high, but is a distinctive shape of human consciousness. It is not mere consciousness of objects, however, nor is it mere self-consciousness. It is, rather, consciousness that knows itself to be the embodiment of reason – reason that it understands also to be immanent within the world and so to be genuinely objective. Furthermore, spirit is self-conscious reason that relates to an other, whom it recognizes also to be self-conscious reason and who recognizes the first in turn as such reason. Spirit, therefore, takes the form of a community of reciprocal recognition: 'self-consciousness that is recognised and acknowledged, and which has its own self-certainty in the other free self-consciousness, and possesses its truth precisely in that other'.[55]

In such a spiritual or 'ethical' (*sittlich*) community each self-consciousness sees both itself and the other as specific individuals, but it also understands both to embody explicitly *universal* reason or what Hegel calls 'universal self-consciousness'.[56] Such reason is regarded as 'universal', because it takes the form not of the dictates of an individual's heart, but of *publicly acknowledged* law (*Gesetz*) and custom (*Sitte*) which are held to govern the whole community (and, indeed, humanity as such).

Laws and customs are, of course, the products of a *particular* community and give expression to its particular understanding of what it is rational to do. Yet at the same time, law and custom are *universal* within the community in that they constitute the very 'substance' and life-blood of every member of that community. As Hegel writes, 'the single individual consciousness . . . is only this existent unit in so far as it is aware of the universal consciousness in its individuality as its *own* being, since what it does and is, is the universal custom'. Indeed, individuals not only find their common identity as citizens expressed in the laws and customs, they also see their own *individual* identities protected and promoted by them. Conversely, the individuals who abide by the laws of the community and observe its customs know themselves to be the concrete embodiment of the explicit 'universal' itself: 'the laws proclaim what each individual is and does; the individual knows them not only as his universal objective thinghood, but equally knows himself in them, or knows them as *particularised* in his own individuality, and in each of his fellow citizens'. Spiritual or ethical self-consciousness thus not only recognizes reason *in* itself and its other, it also recognizes itself and its other *as* self-conscious universal reason.[57]

Note that Hegel is not here describing his personal vision of the ideal state. He is analysing a shape of consciousness that is made necessary logically by the experience of *reason*. Reason that knows itself to be self-conscious universal reason, and finds itself as such in both itself and the other, takes the form of spirit. At this point, therefore, Hegel's phenomenology of consciousness catches up with the title of his book and changes into a phenomenology of spirit. Such spirit is no longer simply a shape of consciousness or self-consciousness in the abstract, but is self-conscious universal reason in the form of a whole *community* or *world*. The succeeding shapes that emerge in the *Phenomenology* are thus themselves all 'real Spirits, genuine actualities' that constitute 'shapes of a world' (*Gestalten einer Welt*), rather than mere shapes of consciousness (though, as I have already indicated, all the shapes discussed in the *Phenomenology*, except absolute knowing, are shapes of consciousness in the broad sense).[58] Many of the shapes of spirit – though not, for example, the world of Sophocles' *Antigone* – have enjoyed a specific, independent, historical existence. Hegel continues, however, to trace the *logical* development of one shape into another, and is not concerned particularly with their historical interconnections.

Hegel's account of the various shapes of spirit is extraordinarily rich and I do not pretend to do it justice here. Suffice it to say that spirit does not merely remain an ethical *world*, but also develops 'an abstract *knowledge* [*Wissen*] of its essence'.[59] That is to say, it becomes more explicitly *self-conscious*. The initial effect of such heightened consciousness of itself is to cause spirit to split into two and so become divided or 'alienated' from itself. Specifically, it falls apart into an objectively existing world, the realm of *culture* (*Bildung*), and 'the realm of *pure* consciousness which, lying beyond the first, is not a present actuality but exists only for Faith'.[60] Eventually, however, spirit heals this rift within itself. It begins to do so in a shape of consciousness that Hegel calls 'absolute freedom'.

This shape is a genuine shape of *spirit*, since it knows itself explicitly to be universal reason. It knows itself to be such reason, however, not first and foremost in the public, embodied form of law and custom, but in the more abstract form of pure thought, pure reason and pure rational will. This will counts as a genuinely *rational* will, because it understands its principles not just to be the products of its own self-consciousness, but to be objectively and independently valid and authoritative. Furthermore, instead of withdrawing from the world or immuring itself within its own unassailable freedom, like the stoic or the sceptic, this free, self-conscious spirit understands itself and its own self-certainty to constitute, or be the 'essence' of, spiritual *actuality* itself. That is to say, it understands the concrete spiritual community to which it relates to be generated and sustained by the pure reason it knows *itself* to be. As Hegel puts it, 'it is self-consciousness which grasps the fact that its certainty of itself is the essence of all the spiritual "masses", or spheres, of the real as well as of the supersensible world, or conversely, that essence and actuality are consciousness' knowledge of *itself*'.[61]

Free spirit begins to heal the rift in self-alienated spirit, therefore, because it knows the spiritual world around it to be solely the creation and expression of its *own* universal, rational will: 'the world is for it simply its own will, and this is a universal [*allgemein*] will'. Furthermore, spirit knows its own will to be genuinely universal, because it understands it both to be governed by pure reason and to be the will that animates everyone in the community, 'the will of all *individuals* as such'. Free spirit thus understands its own pure rational will to be, in Rousseau's terminology, a truly *general* will. 'Will is in itself . . . the *self*-conscious essence of each and every personality, so that each, undivided from the whole, always does everything, and what appears as done by the whole is the direct and conscious deed of each'.[62] Such free spirit is a *revolutionary* spirit because the community it creates is one in which traditional social divisions have been dismantled and social hierarchies overturned in the name of universal reason. Indeed, everyone is understood now to be equal in pursuing the interests of universal reason and freedom:

In this absolute freedom . . . all social groups or classes which are the spiritual spheres into which the whole is articulated are abolished; the individual consciousness that belonged to any such sphere, and willed and fulfilled itself in it, has put aside its limitation; its purpose is the general purpose, its language universal law, its work the universal work.[63]

In such a revolutionized society each individual is thus held to be the direct embodiment of the general will. Individuals recognize that they could come into conflict with the general will, if they were to put their own particular interests above those of the whole. At the same time, however, they all understand themselves in fact to be committed to the pursuit of the general interest. In the community created by free reason, therefore, 'this *individual* consciousness is no less directly conscious of itself as universal will'. It knows, therefore, that 'in passing over into action and in creating objectivity, it is doing nothing individual, but carrying out the laws and functions of the state'.[64] Once again, one should remember that Hegel is not here setting out his own personal vision of a just and rational society. He is simply describing the community of rational individuals that is made logically necessary by the experience of spirit so far (and which manifested itself in particular in the French Revolution).

The problem is that the will that creates and sustains such a community is, according to Hegel, an *abstractly* universal will. As such, Hegel argues, this will allows nothing but itself to hold sway. It allows no traditions to stand that have not been sanctioned by free reason, and it permits no deviation from the pursuit of the universal freedom and equality on the part of individuals. In short, it does not give space to any interest at all that is different from or opposed to its own. As Hegel puts it, 'it lets nothing break loose [*entläßt nichts*] to become a *free object* standing over against it'. Indeed, its principal concern is to assert itself against and to eliminate everything that is not free and rational. The free, rational will thus pursues universal freedom and equality by rooting out all irrational traditions and countering any recalcitrant 'individualism', and so manifests itself in 'the *fury* of destruction'.[65]

After it has dissolved the old social order, Hegel maintains, the only work left for it to do is to negate and destroy the last vestiges of self-interested individualism. 'The sole work and deed of universal freedom', Hegel writes (clearly with the French Revolutionary Terror in mind), 'is therefore *death*, a death too which has no inner significance or filling, for what is negated is the empty point of the absolutely free self'. Such death, inflicted in the righteous conviction that those who suffer it are enemies of the revolution and of the people and so dispensable, 'is thus the coldest and meanest of all deaths, with no more significance than cutting off a head of cabbage or swallowing a mouthful of water'.[66]

This death, however, is one that the principal and most committed champions of the universal also inevitably call down upon themselves. This is because they cannot enforce the rule of universal reason without forming themselves into a government that stands over, and over *against*, the rest of the people. Yet by constituting such a government, they turn themselves into a ruling *faction*, whose members will always be subject to the suspicion – even though they speak on behalf of the universal interest – that they are abusing their office to pursue their own particular and individual interests. Once they are suspected of betraying the cause of universal reason, they can, of course, expect no other fate than the death that is inflicted on all undesirable counter-revolutionaries.

In the experience of such terror, the free spirit comes to recognize that its pursuit of universal freedom and reason to the exclusion of all else logically entails the *negation* of sheer individuality and thus the death of many in the community. Accordingly, through its own experience, 'absolutely free self-consciousness finds this its reality quite different from what its own Concept of itself was'. For it set out from the conviction that its will aimed at the freedom *of all*, 'that the universal will is merely the *positive* essence of personality, and that this latter knows itself in it only positively, or as preserved therein'.[67] Once again, therefore, Hegel's phenomenological account shows the experience undergone by consciousness to undermine its own conception of itself and its object. Implicit in the now chastened revolutionary consciousness, however, is a new shape of spirit.

In its experience of terror and death, revolutionary spirit witnesses its own actuality – the community of individuals that it creates – 'vanish and pass away into empty nothingness' thanks to spirit's own power of negation.[68] Yet spirit does not prove thereby to be merely negative, for via such negation it establishes *itself* as properly universal reason. Even if the community and the world betray the cause of universal reason by falling back into individualism, free spirit itself ensures that its *own* inner will is genuinely universal and rational, precisely by negating and abstracting from any will that is immediately individual, whether it be the will of another or its own. In other words, free spirit guarantees that its own will is rational by turning it into a will that is definitely *not* just individual but *pure*. In this way, free spirit detaches the will of universal reason from the individualistic world and takes that will back into itself, thereby becoming in its own pure willing and knowing – in its own interiority – the *sole* embodiment of that universal, rational will. The truth disclosed in the experience of free spirit is thus that 'the *universal will* is its *pure knowing and willing* and [that] *it* is the universal will *qua* this pure knowing and willing'. The shape of consciousness that takes over this truth and explicitly equates true, universal reason and true spirit with its *own* self-consciousness alone is the *moral* spirit. Free, revolutionary spirit thus mutates logically (though not necessarily historically) into moral spirit because, as a result of its experience, 'absolute freedom leave[s] its self-destroying reality and pass[es] over into another land of self-conscious Spirit' – the land of pure thought – 'where, in this unreal world [*Unwirklichkeit*], freedom [itself] has the value of truth'.[69]

Moral Spirit

In becoming moral, spirit appears to have regressed to the level of pure self-consciousness (such as we found in Stoicism). Yet moral self-consciousness remains a form of spirit, since its object continues to be explicitly universal, objectively authoritative reason, rather than just the self and its concepts. Moral spirit is, therefore, *self-conscious spirit*, or 'spirit that is certain of itself', since it knows its *own* inner will and thought to be the sole realization of *universal* reason. Such reason enters moral consciousness in the form of universal *duty*. This is not say that moral spirit considers reason to be its purely private possession. It regards its own will as the sole expression of true reason, but it does not think that its own will belongs to itself alone. Its own will – the moral will that is subject to duty – is equally the will of every moral agent. In that sense, it is a truly *universal* will. The point on which the moral will insists, however, is that reason is to be found *within* the interiority of self-conscious thought as such, and not 'out there' in and as the world. Indeed, the moral spirit initially understands itself to stand in relation to a world of – non-human, but also human – nature that is quite indifferent to the demands of morality.[70]

In so far as the moral spirit understands its own self-conscious thought and will to be reason incarnate, it takes spirit's alienation from itself to be definitively at an end. It also appears to bring us to the end of the *Phenomenology* as a whole, for we seem now to have reached the point at which the distinctive 'opposition of consciousness' has finally been overcome. Consciousness in general is characterized by the *difference* or 'antithesis' between itself and its object. Such a difference has been evident in all of the shapes analysed by Hegel up to this point in the text (including even Stoicism and reason, which see an 'identity' between thought and its object). With the moral spirit, however, this difference appears to disappear altogether, since the object – universal reason – is identified totally with self-conscious spirit itself. For the moral spirit, moral interiority itself, or self-conscious universal duty, *is* the only form that true reason takes: 'Here, then, knowledge appears at last to have become completely identical with its truth; for its truth is its very knowledge'.[71]

So is the moral spirit absolute knowing? Not quite; for it turns out that, although it finds the principle of duty within itself, moral consciousness considers '*actual* morality' (*wirkliche Moralität*), or actual conformity to duty, to lie quite *beyond* itself.[72] At the same time, it understands that 'beyond' to be its *own* postulate and so to lack any true being of its own. One might say, therefore, that moral consciousness proves to be both too other-directed *and* too self-enclosed to constitute truly absolute knowing.

The moral consciousness that Hegel considers at this point is a quite specific one that resembles, but is not simply to be equated with, the moral consciousness described by Kant in his *Groundwork* and *Critique of Practical Reason*.[73] Such moral consciousness regards itself as bound by the idea of pure duty alone. Indeed, it is a highly abstract consciousness that is concerned always to respect and conform to the demands of pure, *universal* duty as such, and that does not believe that the idea of duty by itself justifies different *particular* duties in different circumstances.

This abstract moral consciousness understands duty to be imposed upon it by its own self-conscious reason; and it considers such duty to be not merely an object of contemplation but that which should guide our action in the world. Furthermore, duty is understood to be directed *against* a world that by its very nature is indifferent to, and falls short of, the requirements of duty. This world – that is not what it ought to be – is held to include not only the objects and people around us but also the natural drives and inclinations of moral agents themselves. Moral consciousness thus necessarily understands itself to turn against an aspect of its own selfhood in the name of duty and so to be what Hegel calls a 'negative essence, for whose pure duty sensuousness has only a *negative* significance, is only *not* in conformity with duty'.[74]

Moral consciousness, however, endeavours to bring the world and its own drives into accord with the demands of universal duty and so to bring about the harmony of morality and 'actuality'. Yet, at the same time, such consciousness judges that the world and its own inclinations will always resist efforts to make them moral and that moral agents will thus never attain complete satisfaction or 'happiness' in their action: 'consummation . . . cannot be attained, but is to be thought of merely as an *absolute* task, i.e. one which simply remains a task'. The harmony of morality and the world, of duty and inclination – and of morality and happiness – is thus understood by moral consciousness to be forever beyond its reach and to be no more than a *postulate* or ideal that guides it in its efforts.[75] (In this respect moral spirit resembles somewhat the unhappy consciousness.)

Moral consciousness also postulates, or frames the image or representation (*Vorstellung*) of, another *consciousness* beyond itself. This other is postulated by moral consciousness in order to justify or 'sanctify' (*heiligen*) particular, determinate duties in the world. As was noted above, moral consciousness understands itself to stand under the obligation to act in accordance with the demands of pure, universal duty. Such consciousness also acknowledges, however, that the world confronts us with many different, particular circumstances. The problem is that, as far as moral consciousness is concerned, nothing in the very idea of duty as such can justify particular duties that we are required to perform in certain circumstances but not in others. Duty alone may require, for example, that we respect other rational beings, but it cannot establish that in these circumstances we should call on our neighbours unannounced to show our friendship, but in other circumstances we should leave them alone to protect their privacy. Furthermore, where a specific way of behaving is commonly regarded as the right thing to do in the circumstances, and so as a particular duty, moral consciousness can find no ground within its own understanding of universal duty to regard that particular duty as sacrosanct. Its own moral understanding requires it simply to ensure that such particular 'duties' do not conflict with the universal requirements of duty as such: 'as regards the *many* duties, moral consciousness as such heeds only the *pure duty* in them; the many duties *qua* manifold are *specific* and therefore as such have nothing sacred about them for the moral consciousness'.[76]

Yet moral consciousness also accepts that, as *moral*, it must be guided by an understanding of what duty requires – of what is right and proper – in everything it does; that is, *in every particular circumstance*. That is to say, it accepts that its actions must conform not only to the demands of universal duty but also to a range of *particular, determinate* duties. Since, however, moral consciousness can find no warrant for such particular duties within itself, it must postulate *another* consciousness beyond itself that sanctions the particular duties that it must observe:

for the consciousness of *pure duty*, the determinate or specific duty cannot straightway be sacred; but because a specific duty, on account of the actual 'doing' which is a *specific* action, is likewise *necessary*, its necessity falls outside of that consciousness into another consciousness, which thus mediates or brings together the specific and the pure duty and is the reason why the former also has validity.[77]

This other consciousness is understood by moral consciousness to be what Kant calls a 'holy will'. In Hegel's terminology, it is 'the master and ruler of the world', who 'brings about the harmony of morality and happiness' that lies beyond the reach of moral consciousness itself, and who at the same time 'sanctifies duties in their multiplicity'.[78]

Note that, in Hegel's view, moral consciousness necessarily postulates a holy or 'divine' consciousness that is other than and beyond its own, even though it considers itself to be wholly *self*-determining. This is not to say that moral consciousness in history will always think of itself in relation to such a holy will: there are and have been many historical moral agents who consider themselves to be atheists. The *Phenomenology*, however, does not give an account of moral consciousness in history, but traces the experience that *logically* moral consciousness must make. What becomes apparent in Hegel's account is that, whether it wishes to or not, an abstractly moral consciousness devoted to doing its pure, universal duty as such must logically postulate a holy will beyond its own as the source of its different, *particular* duties in the world.

Yet this holy consciousness is not only conceived as the ground of particular duties; it is also understood as the voice of authority that commands us from the outside to do our pure duty as such. The reason for this is as follows: Moral consciousness knows within itself that it is bound by the requirements of pure, universal duty and that it must act to bring its own inclinations into accord with duty. It also believes, however, that its own inclinations – as *natural* – will always resist being rendered moral in this way. This means that moral consciousness cannot but regard the actual action it carries out – its *wirkliche Handlung* – as ultimately directed towards the pursuit of non-moral interests, rather than duty. Consequently, it is not able to understand duty to be that which actually informs its own action and guides it from within. Rather, it must regard duty as that which 'falls outside' and stands over against its action in the form of a *law* that it must, but does not in fact, obey. In so far as this law is thought to fall outside of actual, acting consciousness as such, it must be understood to be brought to bear on us by the *other*, 'holy' consciousness whose existence moral subjects necessarily postulate – a consciousness which is thus regarded as 'the sacred lawgiver of pure duty'. In contrast to this holy consciousness, moral consciousness necessarily understands itself to be *imperfectly* moral. It thinks of itself in this way, and so projects its duty outside of itself in the form of an externally imposed law, because it believes its own actions and purposes always to be 'affected with sensuousness'.[79]

Yet moral consciousness continues to understand that it possesses *within* itself a '*pure will and knowledge*' that acknowledges the supremacy of duty. Thus, even though such consciousness understands its *actions* to be irredeemably imperfect, it nevertheless knows that 'in *thought* [*im Denken*], it is perfect'.[80] Moreover, moral consciousness provides further proof that it has a genuinely moral will precisely by postulating a 'holy will' beyond its own, in which it not only encounters its own duty in the form of law but also sees embodied the 'perfect morality' and conformity to duty that it strives impossibly to achieve in its actions. In this latter sense, moral consciousness finds *itself* – its own truly moral will – reflected in an *object* that is other than itself, albeit an object that it knows itself to have postulated in thought and imagination.[81]

Moral consciousness, which is initially said to overcome spirit's alienation from itself, thus proves to be divided in itself. On the one hand, it believes that its own inclinations prevent it from acting in complete accordance with duty. On the other hand, it knows that its own pure will is none the less truly moral. Moral consciousness does not, however, simply revert to being self-alienated: for it understands its moral imperfection and perfection to be in indissoluble unity with one another and so to be two aspects of *one and the same consciousness*. That is to say, it understands its own imperfectly moral self to be genuinely moral, in so far as it recognizes the supremacy of duty *and* postulates and strives to attain a holiness beyond itself and its imperfections. To put it another way, the imperfectly moral consciousness understands itself to be truly moral, not in its actions, but in the *conception* it forms of itself and the *image* it frames of the holiness beyond itself to which it aspires. As Hegel himself puts it, 'the *actually non-moral* [consciousness], because it is equally pure thought, and is raised above its actual existence, is yet, *in imagination* [*in der Vorstellung*], moral, and is taken to be completely valid'.[82] Moral consciousness is thus by no means an unhappy consciousness, because it is quite happy with what it conceives and imagines itself to be (if not with its actual acts).

Moral consciousness began by declaring that its universal duty is to be found within its thought and pure will and also that it is that which should guide our actions. Such consciousness has now revealed that it actually understands its moral perfection to lie in the purity of its thought and will *as opposed to* its action. It has also shown that it understands true conformity to duty to lie *beyond* its own actions in another consciousness that it imagines or thinks to be holy. In both these respects, therefore, moral consciousness reveals that it locates genuine morality – willing duty and actual conformity to duty – *outside* or *over against* its own actions and actuality. This raises the suspicion, however, that moral consciousness is not as serious about morality as it first appeared to be: for its stated aim as a moral consciousness was precisely to bring its own *actions* into accord with the demands of duty.

Indeed, the next shape of consciousness that Hegel considers is one that charges itself explicitly with not being serious about morality in any respect, and that even goes so far as to accuse itself of dissimulation (*Verstellung*) and hypocrisy. Such consciousness admits, for example, that it is not serious about morality to the extent that it seeks to bring about a harmony between duty and actuality that it knows it can never achieve: 'that consciousness is not in earnest about the perfection of morality is indicated by the fact that consciousness itself shifts it away into *infinity*, i.e. asserts that the perfection is never perfected'.[83] On the other hand, to the extent that the moral agent accepts that such harmony is beyond its reach and rests content in its moral imperfection, it shows just as clearly that it is not really serious about morality, since moral agents are meant to *endeavour* seriously to overcome their imperfection and bring actuality into accord with the demands of duty.

Furthermore, the postulate of another, holy consciousness is not completely serious, since moral consciousness knows that it is itself responsible for conferring on that postulated consciousness the authority it enjoys to impose laws on to moral agents:

> moral self-consciousness is its own Absolute, and duty is absolutely only what *it knows* as duty. . . . what is not sacred for it is not sacred in itself, and what is not sacred in itself cannot be made sacred by the holy being. The moral consciousness, too, is not really in earnest about letting something be made sacred by *another consciousness* than itself; for that alone it holds to be sacred which it has itself made sacred, and is sacred *in it*. It is, therefore, just as little in earnest about the holiness of this other being, for in this something was supposed to obtain an essentiality which for the moral consciousness, i.e. in itself, it did not possess.[84]

Finally, moral consciousness shows its hypocrisy by proclaiming that it seeks to make its actions moral, while, at the same time, showing that it in fact believes its moral perfection is to be found in the purity of its thought and will *as opposed* to its actions.

Such hypocrisy, however, is not the product of any malicious intent on the part of moral consciousness. It is a necessary consequence of the relation in which such consciousness understands duty to stand to actuality and action. Moral consciousness cannot avoid falling into hypocrisy, because it declares its supreme moral task to be that of bringing its actions into accord with duty, yet it never *seriously* believes that this can be done, since it considers its actions – and the whole sphere of actuality – to be intrinsically and irreducibly at odds with duty.

By drawing attention to the hypocrisy that lies in its own moral standpoint, consciousness points to the fact that *true* morality will be achieved only when this fundamental opposition between duty and actuality is given up. The truly moral consciousness is not the one
that pits duty against actuality and pursues what it can only regard as the impossible task
of bringing its actions into accord with duty, but the one whose actions and inclinations
do actually accord with duty and *are* actually moral. The shape of consciousness that explicitly acknowledges this, and that locates its moral character in the actual harmony between
its actions and duty, is *conscience (Gewissen)*.

Conscience

Conscience does not lack a genuine sense of duty and of being bound by what is truly
authoritative. It understands itself to be moral, however, because it *acts morally*, rather than
just thinking that it ought to and hypocritically lamenting the fact that it does not. Conscience thus cannot but have a good conscience about itself, for it understands itself to be
'simple action in accordance with duty, which fulfills not this or that duty, but knows and
does what is concretely right'. It is what Hegel calls '*concrete* moral spirit' that actually per-
forms its duty and whose action, accordingly, 'is immediately something *concretely* moral',
or 'moral *action qua* action'.[85]
    Since conscience knows that it is moral in both its thought and its actions, it is what
moral consciousness pretends, but in fact fails, to be: the spirit that is conscious of *itself* as
the true and sole embodiment of universal reason, or 'spirit that is directly aware of itself
as absolute truth and being'.[86] It abandons the idea that consciousness is moral in so far as
it is pure thought *as opposed* to action; and, since it knows that its actions are themselves
moral, it does not think of itself as essentially imperfect and so project moral perfection
on to a holy consciousness *beyond* itself.[87] Conscience knows that universal reason or 'duty'
is adequately realized in its *own* action in the world.
    It is clear that Hegel believes that conscience manifests the spirit of genuine morality
more fully than abstract moral consciousness. None the less, conscience does not represent
the final stage in the logical development of spirit, but will be required by its own experience to mutate into a further shape of consciousness: religion. The problem with conscience is this: although it avoids the hypocrisy of moral consciousness and locates true
morality in concrete moral action, rather than well meaning, but ineffectual, 'good will', it
believes that *everything* it does is moral, as long as it is carried out with moral conviction.
It thus equates true moral action with whatever action it happens – conscientiously – to
be engaged in, and so effectively conflates the truly moral life with its own *immediate* and
contingent existence: 'It is itself in its contingency completely valid in its own sight,
and knows its immediate individuality to be pure knowing and doing, to be the true
reality and harmony'.[88] As a result, it proves to be an utterly inviolable consciousness
that believes that, provided its conscience is good, it can never do any wrong. Of course,
in a phenomenological study of consciousness, one may not simply *assume* that such
self-proclaimed moral inviolability is problematic or inappropriate for spirit, and Hegel
does no such thing. What he does show, however, is that it undermines its own claim to
absolute status by mutating immanently into the standpoint of religion. Yet this is to get
ahead of ourselves. Let us return to the start of Hegel's account of conscience.
    The point from which Hegel begins is this: conscience identifies moral action with its
own self-conscious activity, and so sees *itself* as adequately embodying the genuinely moral
life. Conscience, however, rejects the standpoint of moral consciousness, which judges its

actions against a distinct standard of duty. Consequently, it does not itself explicitly compare its actions with such a distinct standard and conclude *by means of* this explicit comparison that they are moral. On the contrary, it knows *immediately* that its actions conform to duty. Furthermore, it knows immediately within itself what its duty is in any given situation. Conscience is thus wholly *self-certifying* moral consciousness: it both knows immediately within itself what counts as acting morally *and* sees immediately by itself that its actions are moral in this sense.[89]

Conscience, then, is a form of immediate self-knowledge: it understands itself to be moral for no other reason than that it knows itself immediately to be such. By dispensing with any distinct, public standard of duty, however, conscience completely equates its being moral with its immediate knowledge or *certainty* of itself. Indeed, it reduces the former to the latter: in conscience's view, it *is* moral precisely and exclusively to the extent that it is *certain* that it is. As Hegel puts it, 'conscience [*Gewissen*] knows that it has its truth in the *immediate certainty* [*Gewissheit*] of itself'.[90] This identification of *being* moral with being *certain* that one is moral means that, as far as conscience is concerned, acting-in-the-certainty-of-being-moral is in fact the defining feature or form of all genuine moral agency.

Moral activity, according to conscience, requires different things in different circumstances. What is common in each case, however, is the fact that moral action is performed in the immediate certainty or *conviction* (*Überzeugung*) that it is the proper thing to do. Indeed, for conscience, there can be no other shared 'criterion' of moral action. Conscience refuses to invoke an independent, public standard of moral judgement which all moral actions must meet, but insists that it knows immediately in each individual case that its actions are what duty requires. In the absence of a common moral standard, however, the only characteristic that moral acts share is the fact that they are carried out in the conviction that they are moral. Moral action, for conscience, is thus action that is tailored to individual circumstances, and whose agents are *convinced* that they are doing the right thing. As Hegel himself words it, 'the *essence* of the action, duty, consists in conscience's *conviction* about it; . . . its duty lies in its pure *conviction* of duty'.[91]

Hyppolite points out, indeed, that this conviction suffices in the eyes of conscience to make *any* particular action moral.[92] There are, therefore, for conscience, no *intrinsically* moral acts. As far as it is concerned, whatever it does is moral, provided that it is seriously and honestly convinced that the act is moral. Conscience, it would appear, subscribes not to a shared, public ethic, but to an ethic of personal integrity and authenticity, for which acting morally simply means acting out of personal moral certainty and conviction. Yet such an ethic is not completely personal, because it requires of *all* conscientious moral agents – as their universal *duty* – that they act morally and so out of personal conviction. In Hegel's own words, it stipulates that conscience's '*own* knowing, as conviction, is duty'.[93]

Conscience is immediately certain within itself that its actions are in conformity with duty, and does not seek to justify its certainty to anyone else. In this sense it is an intensely private consciousness. However, in so far as it recognizes that it stands under a further duty to act only out of moral conviction – a duty that bears on everyone – conscience understands itself to be a genuinely *universal*, shared form of consciousness. We noted above that conscience understands universal reason or duty to be embodied in itself and itself alone. What has now become apparent is that conscience understands itself, or at least the *form* of its own conscientious certainty, to be duplicated in others. (In this regard, as in its respect for what it honestly takes to be its universal duty, conscience is clearly a form of self-conscious *spirit*, not merely of immediate *self*-consciousness.)[94]

Conscience also acknowledges that it needs to be *recognized* by those others *as* acting out of conviction. Moral consciousness never succeeds in its own eyes in acting morally. Conscience, by contrast, does take itself to succeed: it understands itself to step into the world and perform concrete moral acts. As we have seen, conscience deems these acts to be moral because they are carried out in the *conviction* that they are moral. For conscience, however, such conviction cannot be something merely inward and invisible. This is because conviction is held to make the action moral, not just within the mind of the agent, but *in actuality*; and, in so far as it is an irreducible feature of an actual moral action in the world, it must be evident *for others* to see. Conscience must, therefore, be satisfied that its own conviction is recognized by others, for only in this way can it understand that its action is *manifestly* moral.

This is not to say that conscience is in any doubt about its action and seeks confirmation from others that it is, indeed, *moral* at all. Conscience is quite certain of this within itself. The point is that conscience understands moral action in the world to be action that is *evidently* moral *to others*. This means not only that the act itself must be visible to others, but that its specifically moral character must be evident, too. For this reason, conscience holds that the conviction that grounds its action must be publicly recognized as genuine (or, at least, be capable of such recognition). For conscience, therefore, 'the action is . . . the translation of its *individual* content into the *objective* element, in which it is universal and recognised, and it is just the fact that it is recognised that makes the deed a reality [*Wirklichkeit*]'.[95]

Conscience, as we have seen, can perform any action in the conviction that it is moral. Other consciences, however, may not be similarly convinced that such actions conform to duty and so would be appropriate for them. None the less, they can recognize that the first conscience is at least acting out of his *own* conviction of the rightness of the act and in that sense is a perfectly moral agent: 'the doer . . . knows what he does to be a duty, and since he knows this, and the conviction of duty is the very essence of moral obligation, he is thus recognised and acknowledged by others'. As Lauer points out, therefore, in the world of conscience 'we may admire someone for always following his conscience', though 'we need not always admire what he does'.[96]

Conscience acknowledges, however, not only that others need to recognize its moral conviction, but also that it must show to those others in turn that its actions are, indeed, grounded in conviction. It realizes that other consciences cannot peer directly into its soul, and that, consequently, it needs to bear witness to its conviction in *language*. Language in general, Hegel writes, is the medium in which we make public our inner thoughts and intentions: it is 'self-consciousness existing *for others*'. Conscience uses words to make public its specific conviction that its actions are moral:

The content of the language of conscience is the *self that knows itself as essential being*. This alone is what it declares, and this declaration is the true actuality of the act, and the validating of the action. Consciousness declares its *conviction*; it is in this conviction alone that the action is a duty; . . . what is valid for that self-consciousness is not the *action* as an *existence*, but the *conviction* that it is a duty; and this is made actual in language.[97]

The conviction itself is immediate and falls within conscience. In language, however, conscience translates that inner conviction 'into the form of an *assurance* [*Versicherung*] that consciousness is convinced of its duty and, as conscience, knows *in its own mind* what duty is'. This public assurance, Hegel writes, 'thus affirms that consciousness is convinced that its conviction is the essence of the matter'; and since the assurance is given by a conscience that is, indeed, *convinced* of the morality of its actions, it is automatically true.[98]

By recognizing the need to express its conviction to others, conscience acknowledges their right to know that its conviction is, in fact, genuine. In return, conscience receives recognition for itself as a sovereign consciousness that acts, and has the duty to act, on the basis of its *own* moral conscience alone. Each conscience involved thus understands itself to be inviolable: no one can impugn its moral character, provided that it is convinced within itself that it is doing the right thing. Each one is thus, in Hegel's words, a 'moral genius which knows the inner voice of what it immediately knows, to be a *divine* voice'.[99] Such moral geniuses do not, however, stand alone, because they need to receive and enjoy *public* recognition of the fact that their *own* conviction suffices to make their actions moral. They thus form themselves into a society of good consciences, each of which assures the others that it is, indeed, convinced of its moral goodness and that it *is* good precisely because it is so convinced. 'The spirit and substance of their association are thus the mutual assurance of their conscientiousness, good intentions, the rejoicing over this mutual purity, and the refreshing of themselves in the glory of knowing and uttering, of cherishing and fostering, such excellence.'[100] Each conscience in this society sees itself as 'divine', because it understands itself to be in perfect conformity with duty in so far as it acts out of conscientious conviction. For each conscience, indeed, its action is nothing but 'the contemplation of its own divinity'.[101] It might appear that such self-congratulatory conscience represents the ultimate in moral self-apotheosis. It soon becomes clear, however, that this is not the case.

Such conscience certainly sees itself as embodying divinity, but it does not for that reason set itself apart from others. It acknowledges that divinity or moral perfection is to be found only in conscientious action and speech that are recognized as such *by others*. It also accepts that 'divinity' is something universal, in so far as it is to be found in the conscientious action of *all* moral agents. Conscience, then, is still an overtly – if only formally – *rational* consciousness, because it understands itself to embody an objectively authoritative and universal idea of personal integrity and conscientiousness. As Hegel puts it, conscience, in its public expression of personal conviction, affirms that its is 'a universal self', and 'on account of this utterance . . . the validity of the act is acknowledged by others'.[102]

Yet, of course, such public acknowledgement serves precisely to confirm each conscience in its sense of being *personally* inviolable. Conscience may well endeavour to show that it acts out of conviction like everyone else, but it does so in order to prove to everyone that it harbours divinity within *itself*. The next shape of consciousness that Hegel examines is the one that focuses explicitly on its *own* inviolable divinity, rather than that of anyone else. Such utterly self-absorbed conscience locates its perfection and 'divinity' in a self that it sets *apart* from other selves and regards as *absolutely its own*. It has thus acquired what Hegel calls 'absolute *self-consciousness*' and believes that it is perfect and divine in so far as it is *this* singular, unique self.[103] (This fact that it finds *divinity* within itself is, by the way, what prevents such conscience falling back to the level of immediate *self*-consciousness, such as we saw in Stoicism and scepticism.)

The Beautiful Soul, Evil and Forgiveness

In this transition there actually emerge two representatives of the new shape of consciousness. Each one sets itself apart from others in some way, but each stands in a different relation to public morality. Public morality in turn is represented in this sphere by a further conscience that is sincerely and openly committed to upholding universal duty, but that proves in fact to be much closer in spirit to the other two consciences than it initially appears.

The first representative of the new shape turns its back on public morality and retreats into itself. For this conscience, Hegel writes, 'all life, all spiritual essentiality, has withdrawn into this self and lost its difference from the *I* itself'. Such conscience thus finds perfection away from public view in the inner 'purity of its heart'. It is divine in its own eyes not because it acts out of publicly declared conviction, but simply because it harbours deep *within* itself the noblest thoughts and intentions. Indeed, such conscience shies away from action altogether, because it fears that by engaging in such action it will inevitably become embroiled in selfish, worldly concerns and so sully the purity of its moral heart. The only way it can give expression to its inner purity and nobility, therefore, is through speech. Yet such speech is not understood – or perhaps even intended – to meet with any voice of recognition from others, but is, rather, the narcissistic disclosure of itself to itself: it is speech that is 'immediately heard' by conscience itself and 'only the echo of which returns to it'.[104]

This conscience is what Hegel – following Rousseau, Schiller and Goethe – calls the 'beautiful soul'.[105] Such a soul pronounces itself beautiful and holy, because it holds its intentions to be pure and free from narrow self-interest. In fact, however, its self-proclaimed moral purity itself testifies to its supreme self-absorption, for conscience secures such moral purity only by refusing to *let go of itself* and enter into real social inter-action and communion with others. In Hegel's own words, 'in order to preserve the purity of its heart, it flees from contact with the actual world, and persists in its self-willed [*eigensinnig*] impotence to renounce its self . . . or to transform its thought into being'. Such refusal to let go of oneself comes at a price, however, because, as Christ declared, 'whoever seeks to gain his life will lose it'. Accordingly, the 'transparent purity' of its heart fills the beautiful soul not just with a feeling of its own beauty but also with 'a sense of emptiness'. This purely inward soul is so inward and abstract that it vanishes before its very eyes 'like a shapeless vapour that dissolves into thin air', and so 'finds itself only as a lost soul'.[106]

Together with this beautiful soul there arises a second consciousness – one that does not simply remain submerged in itself but goes out into the world and acts. Like the beautiful soul, this consciousness understands that action is always ultimately self-serving. Unlike the beautiful soul, however, it openly embraces, rather than shies away from, such self-serving action. Yet such consciousness is not nakedly self-interested like the protagonists in the life and death struggle: it still wants to be recognized by others as a *moral* conscience.

Public morality, at this stage in the *Phenomenology*, does not prescribe specific courses of action, but requires that whatever one does be undertaken – and be *seen* to be under-taken – in the sincere conviction that it is right and dutiful. Indeed, such morality demands that all persons aim explicitly to exhibit the same universal, and universally recognized, personal integrity in their actions. Their task is thus not to set themselves apart from, or above, others, but to see themselves as equal members of a community of good consciences. The new, self-interested conscience realizes, therefore, that, in order to count as moral in society, it must *declare* publicly that it is acting out of personal conviction in accordance with the universally recognized idea of conscientious, dutiful action. It must state that it is seeking to be good and dutiful *like everyone else*. Within itself, however, such conscience does not regard itself as bound by a shared, public ideal of morality. It believes itself to be free, under the cover of its public declaration, to put its own interests *above* those of others and, indeed, to pursue them *against* those of others. Such conscience recognizes, therefore, that in its public declaration it does no more than pay lip-service to the public conception of duty. As Hegel puts it, self-interested conscience is 'the *specific* individuality that exempts itself from the universal, [and] for which pure duty is only a universality that appears on the *surface*'; that is, for which 'duty is only a matter of words'.[107]

Such conscience pretends to be dutiful in the publicly recognized sense, but is all the while 'conscious of the antithesis between what it is for itself and what it is for others, of the antithesis of universality or duty and its reflection out of universality into itself'. It is thus well aware that it is a *hypocritical* consciousness that pursues its own self-interest while feigning to display an integrity and authenticity that seeks public recognition as something universal and equally shared by all. Indeed, it acknowledges to itself that it is 'evil' (*böse*) in so far as it aims to outdo others in direct contravention of recognized public morality.[108]

Yet such conscience does not by any means regard itself as simply and straightforwardly evil or hypocritical: for when it is charged by others with such hypocrisy, it immediately insists that it is justified in what it does by its own *particular* conception of duty and entitlement. Such conscience takes itself, therefore, to be a *rightfully* and *righteously* self-serving consciousness. Hegel sums up the complex self-understanding of such conscience as follows: 'It admits, in fact, to being evil by asserting that it acts, in opposition to the acknowledged universal, according to its *own* inner law and conscience.'[109] The fact that this conscience acts out of the conviction that its self-serving actions conform to its own particular sense of duty, and so justify its hypocrisy and evil, confirms that it is, indeed, the twin of the beautiful soul, born in the same logical transition that gave rise to the latter: for both see their self-ascribed moral qualities as setting them quite *apart* from others. (Since both do, however, regard themselves as *moral* – albeit in a highly idiosyncratic way – their sense of separateness does not turn them back into shapes of mere self-consciousness.)

The self-interested acting conscience is explicitly judged to be hypocritical by a third consciousness that speaks on behalf of universally recognized public morality and sees through the agent's initial attempt to pass itself off as genuinely conscientious in the publicly recognized sense. This judging conscience appears initially to be quite different from the two representatives of the new shape of conscience. Hegel points out, however, that this judging conscience is closer to its hypocritical counterpart than it thinks (and also closer to the beautiful soul than we might imagine).

First of all, the very fact that the acting conscience does not respect public morality shows that that morality is not in fact truly universal. The judge is thus actually placed in the same position as the agent: namely, that of appealing to a law that has *particular* authority for him.[110] Second, the judging conscience is guilty of a certain hypocrisy of its own. The judge belongs to the same world as the acting conscience and the beautiful soul and shares their view that *action* carried out by individuals in the name of duty is invariably selfish (a view that led the beautiful soul to shy away from action). The judge sees through the hypocrisy of the acting conscience, therefore, because he is already on the look out for such hypocrisy. He looks at the agent's particular action and 'explains it as resulting . . . from selfish *motives*'; but this is in part, at least, because he looks at *every* action in this way:

just as every action is capable of being looked at from the point of view of conformity to duty, so too can it be considered from the point of view of the particularity [of the doer]. . . . This judging of the action thus takes it out of its outer existence and reflects it into its inner aspect, or into the form of its own particularity. If the action is accompanied by fame, then it knows this inner aspect to be a *desire* for fame.[111]

This means that – like the 'Kantian' moral consciousness we considered earlier – the judge is not completely serious and honest in his advocacy of public morality: for, although he *says* that his judgements on others promote genuinely conscientious action, his critical eye does not really allow for the possibility of such action. All action stands under the suspicion of being self-serving. As Hegel points out (expanding on the well known French saying), 'no man is a hero to his valet: not, however, because the man is not a hero, but because the valet – is a valet, whose dealings are with the man, not as a hero, but as one who eats, drinks, and wears clothes, in general, with his individual wants and fancies'. Equally, Hegel continues, 'for the judging consciousness, there is no action in which it could not oppose to the universal aspect of the action, the personal aspect of the individuality, and play the part of the *moral* valet towards the agent'.[112]

Third, the judge is also a hypocrite in so far as he advocates conscientious action, but contents himself with passing *judgement* on others, and, indeed, proclaims such judgement itself to be truly conscientious action. The judge suspects that action in the world will always be self-serving, and so keeps himself pure by avoiding such action altogether. In this respect, he is himself a kind of 'beautiful soul'. Yet, unlike the first beautiful soul, he does not simply withdraw from the world into his own divine interiority. He passes judgement on the world, exposes the hypocrisy of others, and claims that he is 'acting' conscientiously in the process. Like the hypocritical conscience, therefore, the judge hypo-critically *declares* that he is acting conscientiously without actually doing so. As Hegel writes, the judging conscience 'does well to preserve itself in its purity, for it *does not act*; it is the hypocrisy [*Heuchelei*] which wants its judging to be taken for an *actual* deed, and instead of proving its rectitude by actions, does so by uttering fine sentiments'. Consequently, the judge's 'nature . . . is altogether the same as that which is reproached with making duty a matter of mere words. In both alike, the side of reality is distinct from the words uttered.'[113] The difference between the two consciences is that the agent acts out of conscious self-interest while proclaiming his conformity to duty, whereas the judge does not act at all.

A further important difference is that the agent knows that he is being hypocritical, whereas the judge does not. Due to the fact that the acting conscience enjoys this clear understanding of itself, it is able, as Hegel puts it, to 'see its own self in this other consciousness': for it can recognize in the judge the very hypocrisy it acknowledges within itself.[114] Such a recognition in turn ushers in a significant change in the consciousness of the agent.

Up to this point the agent has held himself *apart* from others by putting the satisfaction of his own individual interests above those of others, while hypocritically declaring himself to be acting according to a shared conception of moral integrity. He now sees, however, that there is in fact a profound continuity and equality between himself and his accuser, for both are equally hypocritical. Note that the agent is necessarily led to recognize this equality by his experience of his own hypocrisy and of the hypocritical judgement passed on it. Such equality is thus something that, logically, he cannot disavow. On the contrary, he has to accept it as the new truth of his situation: he may always have thought of himself as someone special, whose interests should be privileged, but he now has to acknowledge that in truth he is *just like those who judge him*. The agent gives expression to this newly recognized equality in words and, in so doing, he automatically bares his soul to the judge: he *confesses* his own hypocrisy. This confession completes the transformation of the agent: for in the very act of confession the agent explicitly ceases holding himself apart and openly affirms the continuity between himself and his accuser. He says 'Yes, I admit it: I am a hypocrite, *just like you*'.

Confession of guilt need not, of course, always indicate that the agent has turned away from 'evil' self-interest: the confession may be made out of a desire to continue to be *visibly* evil. In the current case, however, things are different: for the confession is made not just to allow the agent to pursue his selfish interests without hypocrisy and thereby to set him more firmly against others, but specifically to acknowledge the *equality* between the agent and his judge. The agent does not say 'Yes, I'm evil and there's nothing you can do about it', but 'We're alike, you and I – both hypocrites together.' In his confession, therefore, the agent renounces his desire to stand apart from everyone else and put himself first, and seeks common ground with those who judge him. The acting conscience, Hegel writes, becomes one that has 'renounced its *separate being-for-self*, and thereby expressly super-seded its particularity, and in so doing posited itself in continuity with the other as a universal'.[115]

Accordingly, the confession is an invitation to the judge to reciprocate and confess his own hypocrisy as well, and so to establish a bond of mutual acceptance between the two. The judge, however, is not aware that he is a hypocrite and refuses the invitation contained in the agent's confession. He holds fast to his view of himself as the one who passes right-eous judgement on the iniquities of the agent, and he denies that the two share anything in common at all or are in any way 'equal'. The judging conscience thus 'repels this com-munity of nature, and is the hard heart [*das harte Herz*] that is *for itself*, and which rejects any continuity with the other'.[116] In this way, Hegel claims, the judge again shows himself to be a 'beautiful soul', who remains immured within his own moral perfection, unwilling to let go of himself and to acknowledge any common identity with those who are not sim-ilarly pure of heart.

In refusing to acknowledge such an identity, the judge denies both that he is in any way hypocritical himself *and* that the agent can ever be anything but hypocritical and evil. In so doing, Hegel maintains, the judge denies that the human spirit has the freedom to change and reform itself: 'It thereby reveals itself as a consciousness which is forsaken by and which itself denies Spirit; for it does not know that Spirit, in the absolute certainty of itself, is lord and master over every deed and actuality, and can cast them off, and make them as if they had never happened [*ungeschehen machen*].'[117] In other words, the hard-hearted judge refuses to *forgive* those who confess their hypocrisy, and to accord them the freedom, in spite of their past evil, to act morally in the future. As a result, the *judge* – rather than the agent himself – becomes the one who perpetuates the idea that the agent cannot be anything but selfish and evil.

The figure of the judge represents, for Hegel, the pinnacle of moral self-righteousness: the one who most explicitly locates his moral perfection in a self that stands *apart* from those it deems 'sinful'. Such a judge is rigorously unforgiving, even when sinners confess their hypocrisy to him. Indeed, he sees it as his moral duty to refuse to utter words of forgiving reconciliation to such sinners.

Hegel argues, however, that – logically, if by no means always in fact – the hard heart of the judge must 'break' and concede that it does, after all, share a common identity with the agent. This is because the judge cannot continue to remain blind to the fact that the agent, through his very confession, has become a genuinely *moral* conscience that seeks to be part of a community of equals; and as soon as the judge recognizes this, he cannot but see *himself* – and his own stated moral commitment to universally recognized duty – in the agent. At this point, Hegel writes, the judge necessarily

renounces the divisive thought, and the hard-heartedness of the being-for-self which clings to it, because it has in fact seen itself in the first [i.e. the agent]. The first consciousness . . . makes itself into a superseded [*aufgehoben*] *particular* consciousness, thereby displaying itself as in fact a universal . . . and therein the universal consciousness [i.e. the judge] thus recognises itself.[118]

Like the acting conscience, therefore, the judge comes to recognize an equality between the two of them, where beforehand he had seen only an absolute difference.

With this change of heart the judge *forgives* the 'evil' agent: for he no longer holds the agent's hypocrisy and deeds against him as an indelible stain on his character – as something 'imperishable'[119] – but acknowledges his freedom to cast off his hypocrisy and become moral. The readiness to forgive another, for Hegel, is thus rooted in the recognition of the other's fundamental *equality* with oneself as a free being. Such forgiveness, it should be noted, does not here mean simply letting someone off the hook willy-nilly and forgetting whatever he has done. It means granting to those who confess their 'sins' – and thereby turn to seek moral communion with their fellow human beings – the freedom to be moral, and not condemning them eternally for what they have done. It thus means letting moral judgement eventually give way to reconciliation. The judgement that hypocrisy is evil is not itself suspended; but the agent is not simply identified with, and reduced to, such hypocrisy or evil. He is recognized as being capable – *whatever* he may have done in the past – of letting go of evil and doing good from now on. As Lauer comments, the judgement of the judge thus forms part of a larger process in which 'there is (*a*) recognition that an evil deed has been done, (*b*) confession of guilt on the part of the one doing it, (*c*) forgiveness on the part of the one passing judgement, and (*d*) reconciliation in the emergence of spirit'.[120]

In his act of reconciliatory forgiveness, the judge gives up being no more than the one who passes critical *judgement* on the agent, and in this way 'renounces himself' (*auf sich Verzicht leistet*).[121] (In the process he also casts off his own hypocrisy.) This act of renunciation on the part of the judge mirrors that of the agent in his confession in which he, too, *lets go of* his 'evil' and 'hypocrisy'. In each case, the act of self-renunciation is also an act of *reconciliation*: it is the act in which each lets go of the identity that sets him apart from the other, and thereby establishes a new identity for himself in *communion* with the other. Such a communion is one in which each one recognizes himself in the other, and also sees himself recognized and accepted by the other. It is thus a moral community of mutual recognition, established not just by law or tradition (or the coming together of self-congratulatory consciences), but by renunciatory acts of confession and forgiveness. Such a community, Hegel writes, constitutes 'absolute spirit': 'The word of reconciliation is the *objectively* existent spirit . . . a reciprocal recognition which is *absolute* Spirit.'[122]

This community is what the moral spirit turns out in truth to be. Moral spirit initially understands itself to be subject to a duty that is impossible to fulfil in worldly action. Conscience, by contrast, believes that it can act in conformity to duty and that every conscience does so when it acts out of authentic conviction and 'good conscience'. The beautiful soul, the righteous hypocrite and the moral judge then locate their moral perfection in a self that sets them *apart* from others. Now, finally, we reach *truly* moral spirit. Such a spirit does not just endeavour fruitlessly to act in accordance with an unrealizable 'ought', but knows that its behaviour is *actually* moral. Yet it does not identify moral behaviour with whatever it undertakes in 'good conscience'. It understands moral behaviour to be that which specifically generates and supports a moral community of mutual recognition.

Truly moral individuals are not blind to the possibility of their own faults, and are prepared to confess their hypocrisy if they should fall into it. Furthermore, they do not mercilessly and self-righteously condemn faults in others, but are ready to forgive those who truly repent and to give them a further chance to do good. Such consciences know themselves to be moral, therefore, in their words and actions of *reconciliation*. These individuals do not cease acting and judging altogether, but their actions are informed by, and their judgements tempered by, the spirit of reconciliatory forgiveness. As such, they cease being the actions and words of evil or self-righteous hypocrites; and the shared hypocrisy that the agent recognizes within both himself and the judge, and which formed the basis of his initial confession, gives way to a shared concern for reconciliation. This may not be the community in which most people in the world actually live; but it is the community that is *truly moral*.

With the emergence of this moral community of mutual recognition, consciousness takes a further step towards absolute knowing. As we noted earlier, the initial moral consciousness appears already to have become absolute knowing because it closes the gap between itself and the truth by considering itself and its own consciousness of duty to be the true manifestation of reason. Yet it also imagines or postulates a holiness beyond itself which it aspires to emulate. Conscience does away with this postulate and identifies reason *absolutely* with itself and its own self-certainty – to the point of considering itself and its inner voice of conviction to be divine. Finally, the acting conscience and, even more so, the judge see their own *separateness* as absolutely justified and 'righteous'. Conscience thus undermines the distinction between its own certainty and the truth because it regards its own self *as* the ultimate truth and as *absolute in itself*. As Hegel puts it, referring to the agent and the judge, 'each of these two self-certain Spirits has no other purpose than its own pure self, and no other reality and existence than just this pure self'.[123] Note, however, that they are not for that reason mere shapes of *self-consciousness* (such as the master and the stoic). They are shapes of *spirit* that have as their object not just themselves but universal *reason*; but they completely identify such reason or 'the Absolute' with *themselves* alone.

With the change of heart that occurs in the agent and the judge, however, moral consciousness or spirit comes to a new understanding of its relation to reason or truth. Such consciousness still understands itself to be moral or divine; but it regards itself as divine in so far as it is *no longer just itself*. That is to say, it locates its moral 'perfection' or 'divinity' in its act of *letting go* of its separate – evil or hard-hearted – self and finding a new identity in communion with others. Such a communion is grounded in words and acts of forgiveness and reconciliation. For the truly moral conscience, therefore, forgiveness and reconciliation constitute, in Lauer's words, 'the divine dimension of the human'. Or, as Hegel himself puts it: 'The reconciling *Yea*, in which the two "I"s let go [*ablassen von*] their antithetical *existence*, is the *existence* of the "I" which has expanded into a duality, and therein remains identical with itself . . . : it is God manifested in the midst of those who know themselves in the form of pure knowledge.'[124] The abstractly moral conscience understands its 'divinity' to reside in its immediate certainty of *itself* and its *own* righteousness. By contrast, the truly moral conscience locates its divinity in its fellowship and relation of mutual recognition with *others*. That is to say, it knows itself to be 'divine' in so far as it is 'the universal knowledge *of itself* in its *absolute opposite*'.[125]

The shape of consciousness that takes over this new idea of 'divinity' or absolute reason is *religion*. True religious consciousness, for Hegel, is thus not self-righteous consciousness. It is not consciousness that considers its moral 'purity' to set it apart from 'sinners' and to give it the right to condemn them utterly for their sins. True religious consciousness retains a sober awareness of the ever-present possibility of hypocrisy and evil, but it is essentially a forgiving, loving consciousness that seeks reconciliation with others. It is, as Hegel insists, a consciousness 'which forgives evil' (when the evil soul confesses and repents) 'and in so doing relinquishes its own simple unitary nature and rigid unchangeableness'.[126] Genuine religious consciousness, in other words, locates divinity not just in the *self* alone (and its own sense of integrity or infallible judgement), but in the self that lets go of itself and finds its true self in its fellowship with others. Indeed, religious consciousness has emerged in the *Phenomenology* only because *two* shapes of consciousness have let go of themselves.

The unhappy consciousness first mutated into reason by letting go of its *alienated* self-consciousness and welcoming into itself the will of the 'Unchangeable' or the *universal*. Moral conscience then let go of its immediate *identity* with universal reason and so mutated into religion. True religious consciousness, therefore, is neither an unhappy consciousness that considers itself to be cut off from the truth, nor a self-righteous consciousness that thinks that it alone embodies the truth. It is a consciousness that finds the truth – absolute reason or 'God' – incarnated in its communion with other human beings.

Religion

Such forgiveness and fellowship may be regarded as the *moral* content of religion. What specifically distinguishes religion *as such* from morality, however, is the fact that it lets go of itself in another sense, namely by recognizing that 'divine' reason is not embodied solely in *human* self-consciousness, but constitutes being itself or 'absolute Being' (*das absolute Wesen*).[127] Religion thereby displays a humility that is altogether beyond the imagination of self-righteous conscience: for it understands universal reason to be the 'God' that is truly *absolute* and so encompasses more than mere human existence.

True religion does not, however, conceive of absolute being as something utterly separate from human existence. There are, indeed, shapes of proto-religious consciousness that conceive of absolute being in this way. The 'unhappy consciousness', for example, regards the 'Unchangeable' as a transcendent reality that embodies the true nature of human freedom but remains forever beyond consciousness' reach. For religion proper, by contrast, absolute being is not simply an *object* – or *Gegenstand* – that stands over against consciousness, because such religion understands being to become conscious of itself *in* religious consciousness itself. That is to say, true religious consciousness holds itself to be absolute being's own self-consciousness and in this way finds itself in absolute being. Religious consciousness thus sees itself in its opposite in two senses: for it sees itself both in the bonds of loving forgiveness it forms with others *and* in the very fabric of being as such.

Religion, as it has arisen in the *Phenomenology*, does not consider itself to be merely the product of human imagination or to be merely human self-consciousness. None the less, in religion, as Hegel conceives it, human beings do give expression to what they understand to be the ultimate truth about themselves. Accordingly, for Hegel, 'the self-knowing spirit is, in religion, immediately its own pure *self-consciousness*'.[128] Specifically, religious consciousness knows itself to be the consciousness that absolute being or the 'logos' has acquired of *itself*. Religious consciousness knows, therefore, that it is not just a human phenomenon, but rather absolute-being-that-has-become-conscious-of-itself-in-and-as-religion, or absolute being that has become (in religion) self-knowing *spirit*. As Hegel writes, 'in this religion the divine Being is known as Spirit, or this religion is the divine Being's consciousness of being Spirit'.[129]

This, at least, is how *true* religion understands itself. Hegel acknowledges, however, that not every religion attains this level of understanding and self-understanding. Every religion takes itself to be conscious of an Absolute or 'divinity' that encompasses more than human existence, and every religion sees in that Absolute some reflection of itself. Yet not every religion understands the Absolute explicitly to be self-knowing spirit or being-that-becomes-conscious-of-itself-in-human-religious-consciousness. The specific 'shape' (*Gestalt*) that the Absolute is conceived to have differs with each religion. Indeed, 'it is in accordance with the specific character of this "shape" in which Spirit knows itself that one religion is distinguished from another'.[130]

Natural religion, for example, believes that divinity takes the shape of light or of certain animals, and consequently it understands itself to be immersed in the immediacies of nature, too, and so to be a sensuous, natural consciousness. By contrast, in what Hegel calls the religion of art – ancient Greek religion – divinity is understood to take on the form of free, self-conscious individuality and so to constitute the realm of the heroic Olympian gods. Since these gods are deemed to manifest themselves above all in works of human poetic and artistic imagination, religious consciousness at this level understands itself equally to be aesthetic consciousness. Only in what Hegel names 'revealed' or 'manifest' religion (*offenbare Religion*) – Christianity – is absolute being conceived as the process of becoming Holy Spirit in and as the community of religious believers themselves.

Hegel's phenomenology of religion does not, however, start with manifest religion. It begins with natural religion and traces the process whereby each shape of religion is led by its own experience of the divine to mutate logically into a further shape and eventually into manifest religion. Only in this latter does consciousness understand absolute being to be the process of becoming self-conscious spirit and see *itself* as the very self-consciousness that divine being comes to acquire. Only in this latter, therefore, does religion recognize an *identity* between itself and the divinity that it knows to be greater than it – that is, an identity between its own 'certainty of itself' and the object or 'truth' of which it is conscious.[131] For Hegel, therefore,

the totality of Spirit, the Spirit of religion is . . . the movement away from its immediacy towards the attainment of the *knowledge* of what it is *in itself* or immediately, the movement in which, finally, the *shape* in which it appears for its consciousness will be perfectly identical with its essence, and it will behold itself as it is.[132]

Manifest religion first understands divine being to become self-conscious in a particular historical individual, Jesus Christ. Christ is not just a symbol of divinity for such religion, but is divine being itself in human form. Furthermore, the belief that God has become incarnate in Christ is not merely one aspect of manifest religion, but lies at its very heart: 'This incarnation [*Menschwerdung*] of the divine Being, or the fact that it essentially and directly has the shape of self-consciousness, is the simple content of the absolute religion'.[133]

Yet in so far as religious consciousness knows God to be incarnate in Christ, it still sees God as *other* than itself, namely as an individual removed from it in space and time. It does not yet know *itself* to be the divine being's self-consciousness. With the death of Christ, however, religious consciousness sees the gap between itself and divine being close, for it understands the departed God Incarnate to be 'resurrected' within religious consciousness itself: 'just as formerly He rose up for consciousness as a *sensuous existence*, now He has arisen [*ist aufgestanden*] in the Spirit'. In the experience of manifest religion, as Hegel describes it, Christ enjoys not a physical but a 'spiritual resurrection'. The Resurrection and Pentecost are thus understood to constitute one event: the process whereby Christ or God Incarnate becomes the Holy Spirit – of love and forgiveness – *within* religious believers themselves.[134]

At this point, religious consciousness understands itself and the community (*Gemeine*) it forms to be the self-consciousness of divine being itself. As a consequence, Hegel points out, the death and spiritual resurrection of Christ are regarded by religious consciousness as also the 'death of the *abstraction of the divine Being* which is not posited as Self'.[135] For, with Christ's death and resurrection, God is understood to cease being something other than and apart from human consciousness and to become *one with* such consciousness. In the experience of manifest religion God relinquishes his transcendence and comes to be divine-being-that-is-conscious-of-itself-*in-and-as*-human-self-consciousness.

Yet religion does not bring the *Phenomenology* to a close, because it points beyond itself to a further shape of consciousness: absolute knowing proper or philosophy. The source of the lingering problem with religion is the fact that the '*form of picture-thinking* [*Vorstellen*] constitutes the specific mode in which Spirit, in this community, becomes aware of itself'.[136]

The word 'spirit' in this quotation refers to religious consciousness that knows itself to be 'the mind of God'. Spirit is *human* consciousness that knows itself to be the consciousness that *divine* being acquires of itself, or absolute-being-that-has-become-spirit. Such spirit understands itself to be *actual* human self-consciousness. It does not see itself, as it were, as a figment of its own imagination. Yet its consciousness of *absolute being* is couched in images and metaphors that are the product of religious imagination. This is not to say that the idea of 'God', for Hegel, is simply a fiction dreamt up by religious consciousness (as, for example, Nietzsche will later argue): religion has arisen logically out of the experience of consciousness and understands the *truth* that it stands in relation to absolute being. It does not, however, conceive of such being explicitly as *being* that has become self-conscious in humanity. Rather it pictures such being as 'God the Father' who 'creates' the world and sends his 'Son' into that world to die and be 'resurrected' as 'Holy Spirit' within us.[137]

The content of religious consciousness, Hegel insists, is the truth;[138] but the form in which religion articulates this truth remains overly subjective, because it is shot through with images drawn from our own experience of nature and the world (such as those of 'father' and 'son'). Religion, therefore, remains enclosed within the perspective of *human* experience and self-consciousness and fails to understand being on its own terms as 'free actuality' and 'free *otherness*'. 'So far as Spirit in religion *pictures* [*vorstellt*] itself to itself, it is indeed consciousness. . . . But, in this picture-thinking, reality does not receive its perfect due, viz. to be not merely a guise [*Kleid*] but independent free existence [*selbständiges freies Dasein*].'[139] Religion, in other words, is not literal enough in its understanding of being and does not bring to mind the actuality of being *as such*.

Hegel also points out, however, that religion does not recognize a sufficiently intimate *identity* between absolute being and human self-consciousness, either. Religious consciousness certainly takes itself to be infused with God's Holy Spirit and in that sense understands God and humanity to become identical with one another in religious faith. None the less, religion pictures God as a being who is essentially *other* than us and who then *comes to be* one with humanity. Furthermore, religion pictures the process whereby God and humanity become one in faith as the activity of *God* – and so as the 'deed of an *alien* [*fremd*] satisfaction' – not as in some sense also our *own* activity.[140] Indeed, the whole divine story of God's becoming Holy Spirit is regarded as revealed to us by a God who is fundamentally *other*.

According to Hegel, absolute being appears to be essentially other than us – even in uniting with humanity in religious faith – precisely because of the distortions of picture-thinking:

Since this consciousness, even in its thinking, remains at the level of picture-thinking, absolute Being is indeed revealed to it, but the moments of this Being . . . partly themselves fall asunder so that they are not related to one another through their own Concept [*Begriff*], and partly this consciousness retreats from this its pure object, relating itself to it only in an external manner. The object is revealed to it by something alien, and it does not recognise itself in this thought of Spirit.[141]

There is, therefore, a clear difference between the way religion understands itself and the way it understands its 'content' or object, God. On the one hand, religious consciousness knows itself to be *actual*, concrete self-consciousness: 'Spirit is *self-knowing* Spirit; it knows *itself*; . . . it is also *actual Spirit* [*wirklicher Geist*].'[142] On the other hand, such consciousness *pictures* God as a being who is essentially distinct from us, lives and dies as Jesus Christ and is resurrected within us as Holy Spirit. Note that the distinction at the heart of religion is not simply one between humanity and God. It is one between humanity's own *actuality* and the God that is *pictured* or *represented* as other than humanity.

As a consequence of this difference, religious consciousness does not see an *absolute* identity between itself and its object. To recognize such an identity, consciousness would have to understand itself and its object to be *one and the same actuality*. Consciousness would have to understand its object *explicitly* as actuality – or *absolute being* – that has become self-conscious, and it would have to understand itself as the very self-consciousness that such actuality has come to be. Religious consciousness does not, however, recognize such an absolute identity between itself and its object, because religion's principal object is absolute being *pictured* as *other* than our own self-conscious actuality; that is, as 'God'. Consequently, as Hegel puts it, spirit's own 'actual self-consciousness is not the *object* of its consciousness' in revealed religion.[143]

This is not to deny the point made above, namely that in manifest religion consciousness finds *itself* incorporated into divine being. What has now become clear, however, is that religious consciousness – which knows itself to be actual – merely *pictures* itself as belonging to God by picturing God as the Holy Spirit at work within religious consciousness. Religious consciousness cannot, therefore, have as its object or 'content' its own *actual* self-consciousness, because 'in general, its content exists for it in the form of *picture-thinking*.'[144]

For religion, there is an essential difference between *actual* religious self-consciousness and the God who is *pictured* as becoming Holy Spirit within and as such self-consciousness. Yet, Hegel suggests, religion implicitly undermines the very difference between human consciousness and God that is central to religious belief. It does so, of course, precisely by picturing God becoming Holy Spirit *within* us and thereby becoming *one* with religious consciousness and faith itself. Moreover, in undermining the difference between humanity and God, religion implicitly calls into question the primacy of picture-thinking itself: for it is picture-thinking that holds God to be essentially other than humanity. In this way, Hegel suggests, religion implicitly points beyond itself to a new shape of consciousness that is no longer immersed in the images of picture-thinking. The new shape of consciousness that renders explicit the absolute identity between consciousness and absolute being is absolute knowing or *philosophy*.

Absolute Knowing

It is important to recognize that the transition from religion to philosophy is made necessary by religion itself. Religion undermines the idea that God is essentially *other* than humanity by understanding God to become Holy Spirit *within* us. In so doing, religion challenges the primacy of picture-thinking itself. Philosophy is simply the shape of consciousness that takes over and renders explicit the truth that is implicit in the very experience of religious consciousness: namely, that absolute being and human self-consciousness in fact form *one* single actuality. The content or object known by philosophy is thus, for Hegel, essentially the same as that known by manifest religion: 'God' or absolute being. It is just that philosophy or 'speculative knowing' understands the true form of that content.

God is attainable in pure speculative knowledge alone and *is* only in that knowledge, and is only that knowledge itself, for He is Spirit; and this speculative knowledge is the knowledge of the *revealed* religion. Speculative knowledge knows God as Thought or pure Essence, and knows this Thought as simple Being and as Existence, and Existence as the negativity of itself, hence as Self, as the Self that is at the same time *this* individual, and also the *universal*, Self. It is precisely this that the revealed religion knows.[145]

Note that in the transition to philosophy the logical form of the object of consciousness changes. On the one hand, it is no longer comprehended through images and metaphors drawn from human experience as 'God the Father' or pictured as 'Holy Spirit', but is understood to be *existence*, *actuality* or *being* as such. On the other hand, it is no longer held to be essentially other than human self-consciousness, but is known to be absolutely *one* with such self-consciousness. Accordingly, the object of philosophy is actuality or being that has itself become self-conscious in human beings (within a community of reciprocal recognition), or what Hegel calls 'absolute spirit'.

With the move from religion to philosophy, consciousness is thus taken in two different directions at the same time. In contrast to religion, philosophy understands its object to be both fully objective *and* fully united with consciousness. In becoming philosophical, therefore, consciousness finally turns into '*pure* self-recognition in absolute otherness'[146] or 'absolute knowing'. Other shapes of consciousness, including religion, come close to absolute knowing, but only philosophy, which understands its object to be 'absolute spirit', attains this goal because 'only Spirit that is object to itself as absolute Spirit both is conscious of itself as a free actuality and remains conscious of itself therein'.[147]

Yet philosophy recognizes an even deeper identity between being and consciousness than I have suggested so far. Philosophy understands that being becomes self-conscious in human beings, but also that it is *absolute* being and so encompasses more than mere human life and consciousness. It recognizes, however, that such being – even as nature, prior to becoming self-conscious – is identical *in structure* to human self-consciousness. 'In this self-like *form*', Hegel writes, 'existence is immediately thought, [and] the content is the *Concept* [*Begriff*]'.[148] According to Hegel, therefore, philosophical consciousness knows being to be actual and irreducible, but also understands being to be identical in form to thought in so far as it is absolute *reason* or 'Concept'.

Philosophical consciousness thus understands the course of the world not just to be 'the deed of an *alien* satisfaction', but to be the work of the very rationality that it knows to be at work within itself. In this sense, philosophy sees in the world 'its *own* action as such'.[149] This is not to say that the philosopher believes the world to be generated or 'posited' by human consciousness. That would be the position of 'subjective idealism' and is firmly rejected by Hegel. Philosophy, as Hegel understands it, understands the world to be immanently structured by reason – or the 'Idea' – that is absolute and ontological, but that comes to be self-conscious reason in us and in that sense constitutes our *own* rationality.[150]

With the emergence of philosophy, the object – being – is not reduced to a mere postulate of consciousness but is known to be irreducibly *actual* in its own right, to be 'free actuality'.[151] At the same time, it is understood to become self-conscious in human beings and to be identical in form to human reason and thought (in so far as the latter is conceived properly). At this point, therefore, the opposition between consciousness and its object, which characterized sensuous certainty at the start of the *Phenomenology*, is finally overcome and consciousness mutates into speculative *thought* in which 'being is known to be the pure Concept in its own self, and the pure Concept to be true being'.[152]

Yet, if philosophy is to be genuinely presuppositionless, it must at the start of the *Logic* set to one side the concrete conception of being as 'absolute spirit' – as being-that-becomes-self-conscious-in-human-being – that has emerged in the *Phenomenology*. Such a conception has been shown to be necessary, but it nevertheless is too determinate a conception from which to start presuppositionless philosophizing. Philosophy must, therefore, begin from the simple identity of thought and being as such – an identity, in which initially being is thought as nothing more than sheer, *indeterminate* being. Accordingly, the opening category of the *Logic* is simply '*being, pure being*, without any further determination'.[153]

Phenomenology and Philosophy

The account of the *Phenomenology* provided in this chapter has necessarily been truncated. I hope, however, that it has given readers an idea of the way in which Hegel's phenomenological study of consciousness develops. The *Phenomenology* does not describe the historical transformation of one shape of consciousness into another. It traces the experience that each shape *logically* must undergo. In the course of such experience, Hegel argues, the logical form of the object of consciousness and of consciousness itself is seen to change. The phenomenologist then moves on to consider a further shape of consciousness that takes over explicitly the new conception of the object and of consciousness that emerges within the experience of the shape he has just considered.

Note that subsequent shapes of consciousness are not introduced externally by the phenomenologist in order to resolve contradictions in earlier shapes. If that were the case, the course taken by the *Phenomenology* would depend partly on the judgement of the phenomenologist. Is this particular shape of consciousness the only one that removes the contradiction in the preceding shape, or might another shape do the job more efficiently? This would be up to the phenomenologist (and the readers) to decide. According to Hegel, however, the phenomenologist is not called upon to make such judgements, because later shapes are made necessary by the experience of the previous shapes themselves. It is true that *we* make the transition to a subsequent shape; but in so doing we simply move on to the shape that takes up the truth implicitly disclosed in the experience just examined.

The development of consciousness in the *Phenomenology* is thus understood by Hegel to be *necessary*, not just 'possible' or 'probable'. It is generated not merely by imaginative associations between different shapes drawn by the phenomenologist, but by the continuous *logical* transformation of consciousness and its object in the experience of consciousness itself.

This logical necessity determines what does and does not come up for discussion in Hegel's text. Hegel does not discuss every possible state of mind or form of human life in the *Phenomenology*. Indeed, many phenomena examined in Hegel's own *philosophy* – that is, in his *Logic*, *Philosophy of Nature* and *Philosophy of Spirit* – find no place in his *Phenomenology* (for example, the corporations and the free, constitutional state analysed in the *Philosophy of Right*). The *Phenomenology* considers only those shapes of consciousness that are made necessary by the experience of ordinary consciousness itself. These do, however, include what Hegel understands to be all the fundamental ways in which consciousness regards its object (as other than consciousness, as there *for* consciousness, as identical to consciousness, and so on).[154]

If one casts one's mind back over the shapes touched upon in this chapter and chapter 3, one will see that there is a clear structure to the development Hegel traces. Hegel first considers consciousness as such, whose focus is on the *object* or what is *other* than the self. Consciousness then mutates into self-consciousness, which focuses on *itself* and understands itself to be the negation of what is other than it. Self-consciousness then transforms itself into reason, which sees an implicit *unity* between the self and its other, in so far as it sees the other itself as implicitly rational. Reason then becomes spirit, whose object is explicitly, not just implicitly, rational, and for which such rationality or reason is explicitly *universal*. Such spirit understands both itself and its other to be self-conscious reason, and so relates to what it regards as a *world* of universal reason (for example, the ethical world of laws and customs).

As spirit becomes more conscious of *itself* as rational, however, it becomes alienated from the world of self-conscious universal reason. Spirit then heals this rift by understanding itself to be responsible for creating the world of self-conscious reason (through acts of revolutionary freedom). The fateful experience of such 'revolutionary' spirit leads it, however, to regard *its own pure self* as the *only true* realization of universal reason. At this point, spirit – in the form of moral spirit and conscience – completely identifies *universal* reason with its *own* self-consciousness and subjectivity (and so conflates its object and itself).

The penultimate transformation of spirit occurs when it learns to *let go* of itself and recognizes in confession, forgiveness and reconciliation its own absolute rationality and 'divinity'. At this point, the moral spirit mutates into religion. What distinguishes religion from moral conscience is ultimately a matter of emphasis, but it is none the less a highly significant one. Whereas conscience understands *itself* to be self-conscious universal reason, religion understands itself to be *universal reason* that has become conscious of itself. Religion, in other words, appreciates – in a way that conscience does not – that universal reason is not simply co-extensive with human self-consciousness, but is genuinely *absolute* being that comes to be self-conscious in humanity. Religion pictures this absolute being or reason as 'God' and in so doing places great stress on the difference between such absolute being and humanity. At the same time, however, in the doctrines of the Incarnation and the Holy Spirit, religion discloses that 'God' is actually the process of becoming *one with* humanity.

Philosophy, or absolute knowing, is the shape of spirit that takes over the truth implicit in religion. It understands absolute reason not to be an infinite *other* that joins together with humanity, but rather to be being itself – the one and only actuality there is – that becomes self-conscious *as* humanity. For philosophy, there is still a difference between being, or absolute reason, and human self-consciousness, since the former is not reducible to the latter but also takes the form of nature. Yet philosophy also recognizes an *identity* between the two and sees them as constituting *one and the same* actuality. This is to be understood in two ways. On the one hand, as we just noted, philosophy understands humanity to be nothing but *being* that has become self-conscious. On the other hand, philosophy understands being to have the very same logical form as self-conscious thought, namely that of the 'Concept' (a form articulated in the *Logic*). In philosophical thought, therefore, justice is finally done to both sides of consciousness: for thought relates to absolute being that is not reducible to thought – and in that sense is *other* than thought – but that is none the less identical in form to thought and so allows thought to recognize *itself* in it. Philosophical thought or absolute knowing, in other words, is '*pure* self-recognition in absolute otherness'.[155]

In the course of the *Phenomenology* consciousness transforms itself logically – through its own experience and the transitions that we make – into absolute knowing or philosophy. Many people may well remain opposed to speculative philosophy and reject it as perverse. Hegel's *Phenomenology* demonstrates, however, that speculative philosophy is the shape of consciousness (or thought) that is made logically necessary by the implications of consciousness's own experience.

If readers of the *Phenomenology* examine the experience of consciousness carefully, they will, Hegel believes, see that the numerous ways in which consciousness understands its object and itself are in each case more complex than they initially appear to be. Furthermore, if such readers are prepared to embrace the complexity disclosed by each shape, they will be taken necessarily on to further shapes and in this way progress towards greater understanding and self-understanding. Eventually, such readers will learn that the religious experience of being or 'God' requires them to go on to acknowledge the structural identity of being and thought. At that point, they will understand why philosophy is a logically necessary endeavour and not as perverse as they may at first have thought. Hegel's *Phenomenology* will in this way have provided these readers with a ladder to speculative philosophy, a ladder whose rungs are the shapes of consciousness itself.

Hegel argues that each rung in this ladder is made necessary by the previous one. This does not mean, however, that each of us must individually live out each shape of consciousness – and so actually *become* domineering, slavish, unhappy, revolutionary and morally self-righteous – before we are properly equipped to do philosophy. Many of the shapes Hegel discusses have, indeed, been lived out in history, often to very bloody effect. Our task as readers of the *Phenomenology*, however, is simply to understand the *logic* that leads from one shape to another and, eventually, to philosophy.[156] If we follow that logic, Hegel believes, we will see that philosophy does most justice to the deliverances of human experience and is thus a rationally justified endeavour.

At the same time, we will be brought to understand the *inadequacies* of each pre-philosophical shape of consciousness. For this reason, the *Phenomenology* can be regarded as a primarily critical, deconstructive text. It certainly shows how each shape of consciousness is made logically necessary by the experience of its predecessor, but it does so by explaining how each shape is *undermined* by its very own experience and so points beyond itself to a new shape. Hegel's text, in other words, reveals how shapes of consciousness themselves negate and subvert their own point of view. In this way, the *Phenomenology* serves the same purpose as radical self-criticism: for it frees us from the hold of non-philosophical consciousness and its manifold assumptions, and thereby prepares us for presuppositionless philosophy.

It is crucial to remember that the task of the *Phenomenology* is not to set out Hegel's speculative philosophy in its properly philosophical form. It does, indeed, contain a wide array of extraordinarily penetrating analyses of the nature and contradictions of human experience, many of which – for example, his analyses of the master–slave dialectic, the ethical world of Sophocles' *Antigone* and conscience – find echoes in Hegel's philosophy proper. Its principal role, however, is to clear the way for such philosophy by subjecting ordinary consciousness and its fundamental presuppositions to a radical, immanent critique.

Speculative philosophy is, of course, itself also critical. It demonstrates that being cannot merely be understood to be 'being' or 'essence' but must be conceived as 'Idea', that nature cannot merely be understood to be space, time and matter but must also be understood to include organic life, and that human spirit cannot merely be reduced to individual subjectivity and passion but must take the form of economic, political and religious intersubjectivity. Yet philosophy's principal task is to disclose the *enduring* necessity and rationality of the categories and forms of nature and spirit that it examines. Some phenomena, such as madness, slavery, injustice and evil, are shown to be necessary, only *if* the human spirit gets stuck within a specific perspective, and so are revealed in fact to be avoidable. In other cases, however, philosophy demonstrates that the phenomenon in question – be it habit, language, the state, art or religion – is and will always continue to be essential to human freedom. Philosophy is thus a more affirmative discipline, whose aim is to uncover the immanent rationality in being, nature and human freedom, whereas phenomenology may be said to be more 'sceptical' and deconstructive.

This difference between philosophy and phenomenology is, I think, reflected in the treatment of religion in the two disciplines. In his philosophy, as I argue in chapter 10, Hegel demonstrates that religion is absolutely necessary to the full human experience of the truth. Religious spirit is shown to be limited by the fact that it merely pictures and feels the truth. None the less, religion is also shown to be indispensable to a fully human life: for, although philosophical concepts give us the clearest and most adequate understanding of the truth, we cannot live by concepts alone but also need to satisfy the demands of feeling and imagination (just as we satisfy the demands of intuition in art). Philosophy thus affirms the central importance of religion for human individuals and societies by showing that it is the felt, pictorial consciousness of the *truth*.

In the *Phenomenology*, by contrast, Hegel is not concerned to explain why religion must be preserved. His aim, instead, is to show how religious experience undermines the very perspective of *Vorstellung* that defines it and thereby points logically *beyond itself* to philosophy. The account of religion provided in the *Phenomenology* is thus much more critical of religion than that given by philosophy (although both disciplines share a common understanding of the fundamental character of religion and of the central importance of, for example, forgiveness and picture-thinking to religious experience).

It is true, therefore, that Hegel's treatment of religion undergoes a subtle change between the *Phenomenology* and the Berlin *Lectures on the Philosophy of Religion*. In the former, philosophy or absolute knowing does, indeed, leave religion behind, whereas in the latter philosophy affirms and justifies the religious point of view.[157] This difference is, however, definitely *not* due to any growing conservatism on Hegel's part. It reflects the fundamental difference between the respective methods and purposes of phenomenology and philosophy. The whole point of phenomenology is to show that each shape of consciousness undermines itself and makes further shapes necessary. The *phenomenological* treatment of religion thus concentrates explicitly on the way in which religious experience paves the way for philosophy. Philosophy itself, by contrast, explains how phenomena are made necessary by and are essential to being as such, nature and human freedom. The *philosophical* treatment of religion thus emphasizes that religion is the wholly appropriate way in which to feel and picture the truth and so confirms the enduring significance of religion for our lives. If we have to choose between the two, it is clearly the philosophical account that must be given precedence, for philosophy discloses what Hegel understands to be the ultimate truth about things, including the truth about the religious experience of truth. Phenomenology, on the other hand, does not pretend to disclose the ultimate truth about religion, but contents itself with showing how and why religion makes the philosophical understanding of truth necessary.[158]

The *Phenomenology* is a magnificent work and both deserves and rewards careful, detailed study. To my mind, Hegel's analyses of the master–slave relation, the unhappy consciousness and self-congratulatory conscience in particular are unparalleled in their critical power and have quite justifiably been the focus of much scholarly attention since 1807.

Nevertheless, one should not forget that, for all its undeniable brilliance, the *Phenomenology* is intended only to prepare us for, not to replace, speculative philosophy. If we are to discover what Hegel understood being, nature and human freedom themselves to be, rather than the problems he saw in our pre-philosophical *experience* of them, we must look to the *Logic*, *Philosophy of Nature* and *Philosophy of Spirit*. We will now turn to consider Hegel's notorious and unjustly abused philosophy of nature.

5   *Reason in Nature*

From Logic to Nature

For a long time Hegel's philosophy of nature was regarded as the least convincing part of his philosophical system. Indeed, Karl Popper could see little in it but 'bombastic and mystifying cant'.[1] In recent years, however, scholars have begun to take Hegel's philosophy of nature more seriously. They have pointed out that, *pace* Popper, Hegel was well acquainted with the scientific literature of his day – in areas as diverse as mathematics, physics, chemistry, biology and geology – and they have begun to see merit in many of his own philosophical ideas about space, time, motion, light and organic life.

Why does Hegel deem it necessary to provide a philosophy of nature? Is it simply that nature is a *given* and as such commands the attention of philosophers? Or is a philosophy of nature made necessary by the internal structure of Hegel's own philosophical system? In my view, the latter is the case.

Hegel's philosophy proper begins with the *Logic* which seeks to provide an immanent, presuppositionless derivation of the basic categories of thought and being. This derivation of the categories is 'presuppositionless' because it takes for granted no specific rules of thought and, indeed, is preceded by the act of setting aside all our familiar determinate assumptions about thought and being (an act undertaken either in the interests of radical self-criticism or in response to the deconstructive arguments of the *Phenomenology*). Since it may not begin with any determinate conception of being (as, for example, 'substance' or 'nature'), presuppositionless logic must start, according to Hegel, with the wholly indeterminate category of pure being, and it must proceed by simply 'unfolding' or rendering explicit the various categories that are implicit in pure being itself. Such categories emerge in the *Logic* because, contrary to expectation, pure being turns out logically *not* just to be pure being after all, but to entail being 'something', being 'finite', being 'quantitative', exercising 'causality', and so on. The *Logic* culminates in the insight that being proves ultimately to be self-determining *reason* or what Hegel calls the 'Idea'. Hegel proves to be an idealist, therefore, not because he thinks that objects exist only in the mind, but because he understands being itself to be *rational*.[2]

At the very end of the *Logic* Hegel then argues that the Idea not only is self-determining reason, but also constitutes once again the simple 'immediacy of *being*'. The Idea constitutes this immediacy because it alone is what there truly is. As such, it has nothing outside itself but is pure and simple 'self-relation' (*einfache Beziehung auf sich*). In so far as it is purely self-relating, it is always and only itself, always and only what it is. Accordingly, the Idea is not just being that determines itself and develops in a certain manner, but also being that is *immediately* itself, being that simply *is* what it *is*. In this way, Hegel argues, the Idea necessarily 'contract[s] itself' (*sich zusammennimmt*) – through its own immanent logic – 'into the immediacy of *being*'.[3]

The immediate being we encounter at the end of the *Logic* is not, however, the same as the pure being with which the *Logic* began. Being, as it is initially conceived, is utterly abstract and indeterminate, whereas being as it emerges at the end of the *Logic* is '*fulfilled* being, . . . being as the *concrete* and also absolutely *intensive* totality'. This is because the being with which the *Logic* ends is constituted by self-determining, internally differentiated reason: it is 'the simple being to which the Idea determines itself'.[4]

To recapitulate: pure indeterminate being proves logically to be reason, but reason itself proves in turn to be immediate being and existence. Hegel goes on to claim that the immediate being constituted by reason is *nature*. It is not initially clear, however, why Hegel should identify the immediate being of reason with nature in particular, rather than, say, with God. We will thus have to return to this question later. At this stage, it is important simply to note that Hegel does, indeed, make this identification: 'The Idea, . . . contracting itself into the immediacy of *being*, is the *totality* in this form – *nature*'.[5] Hegel is thus required to develop a philosophy of nature because, in his view, being – the 'object' with which philosophy is always concerned – itself turns out to be nothing but nature. Nature, as it emerges in Hegel's philosophy, is in turn understood to be not just brute contingency or sheer givenness, but actually existing *reason* – 'the Idea as *being*', the 'Idea that *is*' (*diese seiende Idee*), or, as Hegel puts it in his 1819/20 lectures on the philosophy of nature, 'the embodied immediate Idea'.[6]

Hegel's account of the transition to the philosophy of nature is to be found at the end of both the *Science of Logic* and the *Encyclopaedia Logic*, and the formidable complexity and brevity of his arguments have led to widely differing interpretations of this crucial logical move.[7] In my view, however, the core of Hegel's argument is clear. Reason does not transform itself into nature gradually over time, nor does it precede nature in time and bring nature into being through a creative act. Rather, absolute reason discloses itself actually *to be* nature itself by proving logically to be immediately self-relating being. Note that absolute reason can be said to be the creative 'ground' of nature, in so far as it makes nature necessary. (This is the core of truth in the religious *Vorstellung* of 'divine creation').[8] Yet reason 'grounds' nature in a highly unusual manner: not by preceding it in time, but by proving itself logically *to be nothing less than nature itself*.

For Hegel, therefore, there is no 'being' prior to nature: nature is all there actually is (though later, of course, we shall see human consciousness or 'spirit' emerge out of nature). We reach this conclusion, however, by starting not directly with nature as such, but with pure indeterminate being and discovering that, logically, such being cannot be anything but nature.[9] This may seem to be a somewhat roundabout way to proceed. Why not begin straight away with nature? Because in a presuppositionless philosophy we cannot simply *assume* from the start that being is nature, any more than we can assume that it is substance or will to power. We must begin with sheer indeterminate being, about which no assumptions are made, and wait to see what such being proves logically to be. Furthermore, such philosophical patience brings its own reward: for it leads to a distinctive conception of nature that we might never have gained without undertaking the presuppositionless study of being.

It becomes clear, for example, that nature is an absolute logical necessity and not just a happy accident. It also becomes clear, however, that nature has no *transcendent* ground or cause that exists 'apart' from or 'prior' to it. The Idea 'grounds' nature by proving to be nothing apart from or less than nature itself. The Idea cannot, therefore, have an independent existence prior to nature. On the contrary, it must *inhabit* the very nature it makes necessary and so, to borrow the words of Spinoza, be the 'immanent, not the transitive, cause of all things'.[10]

At the end of the *Logic*, therefore, it becomes clear that to bring to mind only pure *being* or the *Idea* – as happens within the *Logic* itself – is not to think of something *other* than nature, but is to think of nature itself (including the conscious spirit that emerges from nature), in so far as it has been stripped of all or some of its defining characteristics. In other words, it is to underdetermine nature, in the same way that I underdetermine this book in front of me when I think of it merely as 'something', rather than as '*Hegel's Philosophy of Nature*'. The difference is that in ordinary life we are not led by the bare fact that something is 'something' to any deeper understanding of the object in question, whereas in philosophy we *are* led by the bare fact that being is pure and simple being to the deeper insight that being is in fact nature. Philosophy, in other words, understands how pure, abstract being *determines itself* logically to be nothing but nature.

The other thing that becomes apparent from Hegel's circuitous logical derivation of nature is that nature is essentially rational. This is necessarily the case because nature is simply the immediate existence of the self-determining *reason* or 'Idea' that being proves to be. The claim that nature is rational is thus not one that is asserted arbitrarily by Hegel, but one that he can claim to have proven at the close of the *Logic*.

Hegel emphasizes, however, that nature is by no means purely rational. This is because nature is reason in so far as the latter is *not* explicitly self-determining reason as such but immediate being and existence. This is no doubt a somewhat paradoxical idea, but it is an important one to grasp if we are to understand why Hegel conceives of nature in the way he does. To learn more about why nature is not fully rational – and, indeed, what it means for nature not to be fully rational – we must look more closely at the *Logic*.

Nature: The Idea as the 'Negative of Itself'

In the *Logic*, as we know, Hegel argues that pure being proves logically to be self-determining reason or the Idea. He also insists, however, that the process of being's logical development is not merely a means to an end which is then forgotten when the end is achieved. On the contrary, this process is itself an integral aspect of what being finally proves to be. For Hegel, therefore, the process whereby being *becomes* self-determining reason itself forms part of what it is for being to *be* self-determining reason. This is why in the *Encyclopaedia Logic* Hegel identifies the 'content' of the Idea or being-as-self-determining-reason with 'the entire system, the development of which we have been considering so far'.[11] Being is the Idea, for Hegel, not just in so far as it is self-determining reason *as opposed* to mere quality, quantity or substance, but in so far as it is the whole logical process that culminates in self-determining reason or the Idea itself. Being is the Idea, in other words, in so far as it is the progressive unfolding and systematic *interconnectedness* of all the logical determinations that are immanent in being.

Consider now what occurs when being-as-reason or the Idea proves to be nature. Being-as-reason determines itself to be nature, Hegel writes, because it 'contract[s] itself into the immediacy of *being*', and it 'contracts' itself in this way because it proves to be the totality of being, to relate only to itself and so to constitute a realm of immediate self-relation. In this logical move, however, being-as-reason *loses* the very character that defines it as self-determining reason, for it ceases being the dynamic process of determining and developing itself and gives itself the form of simple, static being that *is* purely what it *is*. In determining itself to be nature, therefore, being-as-reason determines itself to be being that is *not* in fact fully and explicitly rational. As Hegel puts it, in proving to be nature reason necessarily proves to be 'the negative of itself' (*das Negative ihrer selbst*).[12]

This is clearly not an easy thought to get one's mind around: being proves logically to be self-determining reason, but such reason in turn proves logically to be being that is *not* itself fully and explicitly rational. There must be nature, therefore, because, paradoxically, the Idea or being-as-self-determining-reason can in fact never be anything less than the sheer *negation* of itself.

This, I believe, is why Hegel describes nature as 'the Idea in the form of *otherness*'.[13] Hegel's claim is not that nature is something quite separate from reason – and that reason, correspondingly, is something separate from and independent of nature – but that nature is simply *absolute reason itself* existing in a form that is other than that of explicitly self-determining rationality. Hegel claims further that it is only as this imperfect embodiment of itself – as *nature* – that absolute reason actually exists (until, that is, nature itself gives rise to explicitly rational human consciousness).

If we continue to pursue this theme, we can answer the question that I raised earlier but have so far failed to address: granted that being proves to be reason and that reason 'contracts itself' into the immediacy of being, why must we think of such immediate being as *nature*? Couldn't it be that absolute reason determines itself to have an immediate existence as God, and might not this prove that there must exist a deity or *logos* that is quite separate from nature?

Hegel does, indeed, equate the Idea and God in so far as he maintains that religion pictures as 'God' what philosophy knows to be the Idea.[14] He insists, however – in a way that brings him close to Spinoza – that 'God' is not something separate from nature and the world, but actually exists as *nature itself*. But why does Hegel claim this? His argument is as follows: in 'contracting' itself into the immediacy of being, reason necessarily proves to be 'the *negative* of itself'; reason *qua* reason consists in the immanent interconnectedness of the logical determinations of being; the direct negation of reason that reason itself proves to be must, therefore, consist in being whose determinations are *not* immanently interconnected, but utterly external and indifferent to one another. The immediate being into which reason logically 'contracts' itself must thus be a realm of sheer, static *externality* and so, as Hegel puts it, be 'the Idea . . . in the form of externality'.[15] Such sheer externality is known to us through our experience as *space* – the minimal form of *nature*. Being-as-reason must, therefore, take the form of nature because it cannot be anything other than the negation of its own dynamic, dialectical fluidity and so cannot be anything other than the sheer externality we know to be space.

In this chapter I have argued that the emergence of nature is logically necessary. In the *Encyclopaedia Logic*, however, Hegel states (apparently to the contrary) that nature is the product of the Idea's *freedom*: 'the absolute *freedom* of the Idea . . . is that . . . it *resolves to release out of itself* into freedom the moment of its particularity . . . or itself as *nature*'. Similar wording is also to be found in the *Science of Logic*: 'the Idea *freely releases* itself', and 'by reason of this freedom, the form of its determinateness is also utterly free – the *externality of space and time* existing absolutely on its own account [*absolut für sich selbst . . . seiend*] without the moment of subjectivity'.[16] How exactly are these lines to be reconciled with the interpretation that I have been putting forward?

Taken at face value, the claim that the Idea 'resolves' (or 'decides' [*sich entschließt*]) to release itself as nature cannot be reconciled with my interpretation, since I argue that the Idea is not self-conscious spirit endowed with free will, but merely self-determining being as such, and so is not capable of making any 'resolutions' or 'decisions' in the ordinary sense of these words at all. In my view, therefore, Hegel's talk of free 'resolve' in this context should be regarded as metaphorical: the move to nature is in fact the impersonal, logical process whereby the Idea determines itself to be nature. (Resolution and decision in the ordinary senses of the words will be the prerogative of conscious human beings alone, whose reason does not 'ground' nature but emerges out of nature itself.)

This move to nature can, however, be regarded as an expression of the Idea's *freedom* in a different, more Spinozan, sense: for what makes nature necessary is precisely the logical process whereby the Idea *autonomously* determines itself to be nature. The Idea cannot but so determine itself – in this sense nature is necessary – and yet the Idea determines *itself* to be nature through its own, autonomous, immanent logic – and so in this sense nature is the result of the Idea's freedom. Reason is nothing but self-determination and, accordingly, it *determines itself* – without any external constraint – to be the 'simple being' that is nature. Reason's 'grounding' of nature is thus both necessary and free (in the sense of 'autonomous') at one and the same time.

Yet Hegel not only claims that the Idea's 'release' of itself as nature is free; he also maintains that the very externality of space and nature itself is 'utterly free'. It has to be admitted that the precise connection here between 'freedom' and 'externality' is by no means as clear as it should be. It becomes clearer, however, if we understand Hegel along the lines I have been suggesting (but do not in this case understand 'freedom' to mean 'autonomy'). On my reading, the Idea mutates logically into the externality of space because it 'releases itself' in a form that is *free from* – by virtue of being the *negation* of – that of the Idea itself. There must be space and nature, therefore, because the Idea or freely self-determining reason can never be anything less than the sheer *negation* of itself.

Hegel's account of the transition from the *Logic* to the philosophy of nature is abstract, condensed and highly paradoxical, and I do not pretend to have answered all the relevant questions about it. I hope, however, that my remarks may give readers at least an idea of why Hegel thinks nature is logically necessary. I hope also that they will enable readers to understand why Hegel considers nature to be so profoundly contradictory.

Reason and Nature's 'System of Stages'

Nature is the imperfect embodiment of reason, but it is none the less *reason* incarnate. The task of the philosophy of nature, in Hegel's view, is to reveal precisely how reason manifests itself in nature. In order to carry out this task philosophy must seek to discern the rationality that is immanent in nature in particular – the distinctive *logic of nature* – rather than that immanent in history or some other area of human life (such as art). This immanent rationality can only be discerned by focusing on what follows logically from nature at its most minimal, namely from the very *externality* of space itself. The philosophy of nature will not, therefore, simply try to fit the phenomena of nature into patterns of pure reason taken over directly from the *Logic* (as some commentators have suggested), but will endeavour to unfold what is made necessary by the externality of space in particular.

On the surface this would not appear to be a very promising way to proceed. Space, as understood by Hegel, is being whose parts are completely external and indifferent to one another and which is thus utterly lifeless.[17] Can such static externality harbour any immanent rationality of its own and make anything logically necessary? Hegel's answer is yes:

the lifeless externality of space will itself prove to be rationally self-determining and will give rise logically to a host of different aspects of nature. In Hegel's view, therefore, nature is profoundly contradictory because it is structured by the rationality that is immanent in the very 'unreason of externality' (*Unvernunft der Äußerlichkeit*) itself.[18]

As we learn in the course of the philosophy of nature, what is made necessary by the sheer externality of space includes time, motion, matter, gravitation, light, physical bodies (with cohesion and degrees of warmth), magnetism, electricity, chemical processes, geological formations, vegetable and animal life and, finally, human consciousness. From the philosophical perspective, therefore, these phenomena cannot be regarded as merely contingent, because they are made necessary by nature itself; that is, by the reason or 'Idea' inherent in the very fabric of space.

The necessity described by Hegel is a strictly logical necessity. Furthermore, it is timeless in the sense that it does not operate at one time rather than another, but is at work at all times, making the various aspects of nature discussed in the philosophy of nature necessary. As Hegel puts it, 'the Idea develops itself eternally, timelessly'.[19] It is always logically necessary, therefore, that there be time, motion, matter and light in nature.

But why is this the case? What is the precise character of this 'necessity'? It lies in the fact that each aspect or 'stage' (*Stufe*) of nature, beginning with space, has implicit within its logical structure a further, more complex logical structure. Each aspect thus points logically *beyond itself* to a further aspect of nature in which what is implicit in the first becomes explicit. Each further aspect of nature is made necessary by the preceding one, therefore, because it embodies the 'truth' contained in its predecessor. The logical 'necessity' that Hegel articulates in the philosophy of nature is thus nothing particularly mysterious. It is simply the process whereby one aspect of nature, in order to be fully what it is and to manifest all that is implicit within it, leads logically to the emergence of a new and more complex aspect of nature. The 'necessity of the Idea', in other words, consists in nothing more than the 'completion' (*Ergänzung*) of one stage by passing into another.[20]

In this process, Hegel maintains, nature comes to be more *explicitly* what it is implicitly: 'the movement of nature is then to posit itself as that which it is in itself [*an sich*]'.[21] What the sheer externality of nature is implicitly, of course, is self-determining reason or 'Idea'. The process whereby nature logically generates new levels of itself is thus at the same time the process whereby nature becomes more explicitly rational, self-determining and free. That is to say, the logical development of nature described by Hegel is the process in which the sheer externality of space progressively negates itself and transforms itself into the more integrated, unified and self-determining shape of *life*.[22] The ultimate goal of nature is, indeed, to progress beyond life itself and to give rise to the *conscious* self-determination and freedom found in human life in particular. Nature is thus not just a realm of lifeless externality, but space, time and matter whose intrinsic rationality or 'Idea' make the emergence of both life and human freedom necessary.

One must take care, however, to understand precisely what Hegel is and is not claiming. His claim is that each stage of nature makes the next one *logically* necessary and that stages are differentiated from one another by their relative logical complexity. He is not arguing that each stage necessarily generates – and so precedes – its successor *in time*:

Nature is to be regarded as a *system of stages*, one arising necessarily from the other and being the proximate truth [*nächste Wahrheit*] of the stage from which it results: but it is not generated *naturally* out of the other but only in the inner Idea which constitutes the ground of nature.[23]

Hegel's claim is thus not that space necessarily (and absurdly) comes before time *in time*, and that similarly time comes before motion, motion before matter, matter before light and so on. He argues, instead, that space is logically the least that nature can be and thus, in its sheer externality, is more abstract than the phenomena to which, logically, it gives rise.

As we shall see, some of the stages Hegel discusses can be separated in time, even though Hegel is interested only in their logical, not their temporal, relation to one another. Many of the stages, however, cannot be separated in time at all. For example, there cannot actually *be* any space that is not space-time, and there cannot *be* any matter that is not physical, chemical or organic. The first section of the *Philosophy of Nature* – Mechanics – considers matter in so far as it is characterized by different forms of motion that can be described mathematically; but Hegel acknowledges that there is in fact no matter that is purely mechanical: 'even the mechanical body must be a physical body'.[24] Mechanics, therefore, does not consider anything that can exist apart from or prior to physical matter, but considers physical matter itself in abstraction from its specifically physical characteristics.

The fact that the stages analysed by Hegel form a logical rather than temporal sequence does not, however, mean that the logical necessity he describes is not real. On the contrary, Hegel believes that that logical necessity – the Idea or 'God' – is at work in nature at all times, pressing, as it were, for the emergence of various natural phenomena. Evidence for the reality of this necessity is to be found in the fact that the phenomena necessitated and 'predicted' by the logic of nature do actually occur.

Some of the stages of nature are, of course, distinguished by their position in time as well as by their logical relation to one another. There was a time when there was no earth (with its metereological processes) and there was also a time when there was no life on earth. In such cases, however, Hegel's philosophy of nature does not seek to give an account of the *natural* processes that produced the earth or that gave rise to life. The philosophy of nature shows only why life and planets such as the earth are logically necessary, and it leaves it to science to explain the chemical processes that generated life and the cosmological processes that created the planets. Indeed, the philosophy of nature does not seek at all to compete with science by providing alternative natural explanations for natural phenomena. Rather, it supplements the work of science by demonstrating that each of these phenomena not only has its specific natural causes but also its own intrinsic *rationality*.

Note that the 'logic of nature' does not suffice by itself to account fully for the actual occurrence of natural phenomena. It works *through* the natural processes described by science, just as reason in history works through the passions and actions of historical individuals and states. Natural science, in Hegel's view, is incapable of discerning this logic, since it does not focus specifically on the *logical* structure of space and the subsequent stages of nature that are made necessary by it. It falls to philosophy, therefore, to demonstrate – in a manner that is alien to science itself – that there is, indeed, a logic of nature or 'divine' Idea working through natural processes and pushing nature towards the production of various natural phenomena in which it achieves the ends of reason. Philosophy and science are thus not in competition with one another but have quite different aims: philosophy restricts itself to showing the rational necessity of phenomena – the fact that they accord with the demands of reason – while science explores the details of how and why such phenomena actually arise in nature.

Contingency and the Limits of Philosophy

Hegel's philosophy of nature is much more limited in what it can tell us about the world than is sometimes believed. It can demonstrate that a particular phenomenon is made necessary *logically* by another, but it cannot by itself reconstruct the empirical natural history of any such phenomenon. Philosophy must, therefore, leave it to science to study the natural processes that actually give rise to phenomena such as planetary systems and life.

Hegel points out that philosophy is also limited in another respect, because the phenomena whose logical necessity it demonstrates are in every case beset by irreducible *contingencies* that the logic of nature alone cannot account for. The existence of such contingencies is itself made necessary by the fact that nature is not simply the embodiment of reason, but is reason as 'the *negative* of itself'; that is, reason in the form of 'the *unreason* of externality'.

We noted earlier that nature is contradictory, for Hegel, because the utterly lifeless and barren externality of space itself proves to be rationally self-determining and to contain the logical seeds of time, motion and matter. What now needs to be recognized is that nature is in fact contradictory in a further sense: for it is the embodiment of reason that is at the same time *not* purely or fully rational but shot through with illogical contingencies. The essential contradiction in nature is thus 'that on the one hand there is the *necessity* of its forms which is generated by the Concept [*Begriff*], and their rational determination in the organic totality; while on the other hand, there is their indifferent *contingency* and indeterminable irregularity'.[25] It is important to remember that such contingency is not just an accidental feature of nature but is itself made necessary by the fact that in nature reason manifests itself as the *negation* of itself, as reason that is not just reason alone. In nature, therefore, 'contingency and determination from without has its right' and must be acknowledged by philosophy.[26]

Contingencies in nature will not necessarily lack all explanation and may prove on further reflection to have definite, identifiable causes and so, from a scientific point of view, to be law-governed and necessary. They are deemed to be contingent by philosophy, however, because they are not made necessary by the inherent *logic of nature*.[27] From the perspective of philosophy, therefore, contingencies in nature constitute certain *givens* that ultimately have no rational foundation. The logic of nature may well make it logically necessary that there be organic life, that such life take the form of animals as well as plants, and – perhaps – that such life take to the air. It cannot, however, explain why in Hegel's day there were apparently over sixty species of parrot.[28] This and a whole host of other contingencies can only be explained – if they can be explained at all – by empirical science. They bear witness, therefore, to what Hegel calls the '*impotence* of nature' (*die Ohnmacht der Natur*): nature's inability to shape itself purely in accordance with the determinations of its own inherent logic and its consequent need to 'leave their detailed specification to external determination'.[29]

This does not mean that philosophy itself turns out to be utterly impotent in the face of nature's boundless and bewildering diversity. It does mean, however, that philosophy must restrict itself to determining what is made logically necessary by the sheer externality of space and must not aspire to explain every detail in nature. Hegel insists that 'this impotence of nature sets limits to philosophy' and that 'it is quite improper to expect the Concept to comprehend – or as it is said, construe or deduce – these contingent products of nature'.[30] As Gerd Buchdahl points out, 'Hegel's philosophy of nature is [thus] an enterprise that displays much more intellectual sanity than has often been attributed to it'.[31] It does not endeavour – in an act of monumental philosophical hubris – to deduce every aspect of nature from the 'Idea', but seeks to deduce only what the logic of nature demonstrably makes necessary. Hegel well understands that a great deal of what there is in nature remains beyond the understanding of philosophy, but he wishes to show that, amidst the vast array of contingencies it contains, nature is none the less *to a degree* rational:

Philosophy has to start from the Concept, and even if it does not assert much, we must be content with this. The Philosophy of Nature is in error when it wants to account for every phenomenon. . . . But what is known through the Concept is clear by itself and stands firm; and philosophy need not feel any disquiet [*Unruhe*] about this, even if all phenomena are not yet explained. . . . There is plenty that cannot be comprehended yet; this is something we must grant in the Philosophy of Nature.[32]

Hegel's aim, therefore, is a modest one. Yet it may still not be modest enough for some of his critics: for, although he clearly has no ambitions to explain the 'totality' of the universe philosophically, he does aim to provide a definitive, absolute, *a priori* account of what follows from 'the Idea in the form of externality'. Indeed, Hegel's modesty would make no sense without this ambition: for it is only by determining what follows necessarily from the logic of nature that one can know what counts (from a philosophical perspective) as contingent. As Hegel remarks in his 1823 lectures, 'the Concept is the judge that decides what is the True'.[33]

To conclude this section, I will briefly consider one of the most famous charges to be levelled at Hegel: namely that he attempted to prove by pure reason alone – in an act of egregious immodesty – that there can be at most seven planets and that no planet can be situated between Mars and Jupiter. This charge was made by Popper in *The Open Society and Its Enemies* and was repeated in Jacob Bronowski's *The Ascent of Man*, a book based on a television series that was seen by millions in the 1970s. Since many people may have been misled by Popper and Bronowski into thinking that Hegel was considerably more arrogant and foolish than I have been prepared to admit, it is important to set the record straight.[34]

In his 1801 dissertation, *On the Orbits of the Planets*, Hegel did try to explain why there were (as he thought) only seven planets, but as Olivier Depré has convincingly argued, he is in that work not by any means as guilty of mindless 'apriorism' as has often been claimed. Towards the end of the eighteenth century a group of scientists, guided by an arithmetical series of numbers known as the 'Titius–Bode Law', committed themselves to looking for a planet between the orbits of Mars and Jupiter. Hegel regarded this law as non-rational and inexact, and suggested that an alternative *exponential* series, inspired by Plato's *Timaeus*, would be much more rational and would account for the gap between Mars and Jupiter. Although Hegel would probably have heard reports that a minor planet had, indeed, been discovered precisely where he thought there was and should be a gap, he would not have had any reason at the time he was writing to regard the existence of this minor planet as anything more than conjecture. His motivation for preferring the exponential series was thus not only that it was more rational, but also that it corresponded more closely to what he took to be the currently known empirical facts. Indeed, from Hegel's point of view, it was actually the scientists looking for a planet between Mars and Jupiter on the basis of an arithmetical series alone who were guilty of uncritical apriorism. Moreover, as Depré points out, although Hegel was wrong not to take the reports of the discovery of the asteroid Ceres more seriously, he was actually right not to place uncritical trust in the Titius–Bode law, as the discovery in 1846 of Neptune, whose distance from the sun does not correspond precisely to that law, would later demonstrate.[35]

In his later lectures on the philosophy of nature, by which time he has accepted the existence of asteroids between the orbits or Mars and Jupiter, Hegel no longer maintains that he can account fully for the distances of the planets from the sun. In his 1821 lectures he does consider a law that might govern those distances, but he concludes that 'it fits only approximately'.[36] In 1823 he is even more cautious. He admits that 'it is a necessary demand that we also know this law [governing the distances of the planets]' but he states – perhaps echoing Newton's famous declaration, 'I do not feign hypotheses' – that he will not 'venture here to set up any hypotheses about [such a law]'.[37]

It is apparent from these passages, therefore, that Hegel is very far from being 'hypnotized by his own inspiring jargon' and does not set out 'to deceive and bewitch others' with his 'mystery method' of dialectical logic, as Popper alleges.[38] On the contrary, Hegel shows himself in his philosophy of nature to be capable of treating scientific issues with considerable circumspection and sanity. It is unfortunate that Popper and Bronowski were not similarly circumspect in the judgements they passed on Hegel.

Philosophy and Natural Science

The principal purpose of Hegel's philosophy of nature is not to reflect on the method and validity of the natural sciences, but to deepen our understanding of nature itself – to reveal what space, time and matter logically must be. None the less, Hegel does include in his philosophy of nature some brief remarks about the differences and relation between natural science and the philosophy of nature.

The most obvious difference between the two, he notes, is that natural science (or 'physics', as he sometimes calls it) proceeds from and is ultimately justified by empirical experience, whereas this is not the case with the philosophy of nature. A scientific theory is deemed to be true only if it is confirmed by observation or experiment. By contrast, a proposition in the speculative philosophy of nature is held to be true if it is derived logically – by pure *a priori* reason – from the very nature of nature itself (and, ultimately, from pure indeterminate being).[39]

Hegel points out that science does not consist solely in gathering empirical information but also employs thought and understanding to classify objects, identify the causes of events and formulate universal laws of nature. In particular, he notes, science interprets the world around us in terms of certain (non-empirical) concepts – such as 'force' and 'cause' – and certain logical and mathematical principles which together constitute what he calls the 'metaphysics' at the heart of science: 'the diamond net into which everything is brought and thereby first made intelligible'.[40] Nevertheless, science draws on such concepts and principles in order to make sense of *observed phenomena*. The scientist's aim is thus to *discover* the laws that best fit and explain the phenomena as they are currently known. In this sense, even though science is not a purely empirical and observational activity, it considers empirical observation to provide the ultimate warrant for its claims.

The relation between the philosophy of nature and empirical experience is somewhat more complicated. On the one hand, Hegel contends that the philosophy of nature 'does not need experience' because it derives the fundamental structures of nature *a priori* from the sheer externality of space. On the other hand, however, Hegel insists that philosophy's account of nature must 'be in agreement with our empirical experience of nature' and, indeed, that 'the *origin* and *formation* of the Philosophy of Nature presupposes and is conditioned by empirical physics'.[41] These two claims would appear to be incompatible. Let us consider how they might be reconciled.

Hegel recognizes that the philosophy of nature as such is an older discipline than natural science in the modern, post-Reformation sense, since it reaches as far back as Aristotle. Yet he maintains that modern science is the historical precondition of his own speculative philosophy of nature. As we saw in chapters 1 and 2, Hegel's philosophy as a whole is the distinctive product of the modern world, especially of the modern claim to freedom that finds expression in Kant's moral philosophy, the French Revolution and the modern constitutional state. One of the other developments that made the modern world possible is the emergence in the sixteenth and seventeenth centuries of modern experimental science: as Hegel puts it, human beings became 'free through knowledge of nature'.[42] Such science thus represents an essential historical presupposition of the development of Hegel's freely self-determining speculative philosophy, including the philosophy of nature.

Hegel acknowledges, therefore, that his philosophy of nature is *historically* indebted to the great scientists of the past, such as Galileo, Kepler and Newton: for it is their empirical discovery of the rationality in nature that paved the way for that philosophy to arise. At the same time, however, Hegel insists that the philosophy of nature itself is a speculative discipline that derives the basic structure of nature wholly *a priori* – and independently of science – from the simple externality of space. Indeed, he maintains, philosophy is able to derive *a priori* some of the very laws of nature that science discovered empirically before the speculative philosophy of nature was conceived, including, for example, Galileo's law of free fall and Kepler's three laws of planetary motion.[43] In this way, philosophy demonstrates its agreement with modern scientific experience. Philosophy secures this agreement, however, not by *basing* its insights on scientific experience but by proving *a priori* that laws formulated by empirical science are truly objective; that is, by establishing the logical *necessity* of laws that science discovers *empirically*: 'the Philosophy of Nature . . . has as its object the same *universal* [as science], but . . . it considers this universal in its *own immanent necessity* in accordance with the self-determination of the Concept'.[44]

Philosophy's historical indebtedness to empirical science does not mean, therefore, that science and empirical experience constitute the structural foundation of philosophy. On the contrary, science makes it possible for a philosophy of nature to emerge that demonstrates its agreement with such science through pure reason alone. In this way, the apparent contradiction noted earlier is resolved: the philosophy of nature is *historically* dependent on, but *structurally* and *logically* independent of, empirical science at one and the same time:

the *origin* and *formation* of the Philosophy of Nature presupposes and is conditioned by empirical physics. However, the course of a science's [i.e. philosophy's] origin and the preliminaries of its construction are one thing, while the science itself is another. In the latter, the former can no longer appear as the foundation of the science; here the foundation must be the necessity of the Concept.[45]

There is also a further sense in which the philosophy of nature is (or may be) historically dependent upon the development of science. The fact that one aspect of nature is made logically necessary by another does not mean that this will be immediately apparent to the philosopher. It may take a long time for the philosopher to see the logical connection between the two, and it may even be the case, in certain circumstances, that the philosopher would not be able to see the logical connection at all were it not for developments in empirical science. In this latter case, the logical connection between the aspects of nature in question would not itself depend upon the scientific discovery but would be wholly *a priori*. The ability of the *philosopher* to recognize that *a priori* connection would, however, depend on the disclosures of science. Hegel's ability to derive time, motion, matter, mass, free fall and solar systems logically from space does not, I think, depend on any specific scientific discoveries. In my judgement, however, he would not have been able to provide an *a priori* proof of Galileo's law of free fall and of Kepler's laws of planetary motion if those laws had not already been discovered by empirical science. In this respect, I agree with Buchdahl that Hegel did not claim that he could have *discovered* these laws by himself (in the way that he was able to deduce that time and motion are intrinsic to space).[46]

Hegel demonstrates *a priori* that such laws follow logically from the character of space, time, motion and matter, but he is able to do so only because they were first discovered 'empirically by induction'.[47]

Once again, therefore, we see that there is no contradiction in the idea that an *a priori* philosophy of nature is *historically* dependent on the deliverances of science. Indeed, it is not beyond the bounds of possibility that such dependence may extend into the future. Further developments in empirical science could, perhaps, alert the philosopher to hitherto unseen problems in his articulation of the logic of nature and require him to revise his account of that *a priori* logic (unless, of course, it is proven definitively that that logic is properly articulated already). Even if this were to occur, however, it would not mean that the *logical* structure of the philosophy of nature is itself founded on and determined by the current state of empirical evidence. That logical structure would still be determined by the immanent logic of nature, now correctly articulated. Science would simply have helped the philosopher to see more clearly precisely how that immanent *a priori* logic should unfold.

What has been said so far, however, is not quite the whole story, for there is a sense in which the philosophy of nature is dependent not only historically, but also structurally, on empirical science. Hegel makes it clear that, strictly speaking, the philosophy of nature does not derive *a priori* the *empirical* phenomena of nature themselves. What philosophy unfolds is a series of *logical* determinations or *Begriffsbestimmungen*. Such determinations incorporate, but are not reducible to, the categories and concepts articulated in the *Logic* because they are the specific logical structures immanent in the externality of nature, rather than the sheer immediacy of being as such. To complete its account of nature, philosophy must then match these determinations – which have been generated by the distinctive logic of nature – with phenomena known through 'representation' (*Vorstellung*), 'intuition' or scientific experience. Once this matching has taken place, philosophy can be said to have proven the logical necessity – albeit indirectly – of the empirical phenomena concerned. Hegel summarizes his philosophical procedure as follows:

> in the progress of philosophical knowledge, we must not only give an account of the object *according to its conceptual determination* [*nach seiner Begriffsbestimmung*], but we must also name the *empirical* appearance corresponding to it, and we must show that the appearance does, in fact, correspond to its Concept.[48]

Hegel claims, further, that if we were to make an error in identifying the empirical phenomenon that corresponds to a specific logical determination, this would not undermine the truth or validity of the logical determination itself. That determination would have been shown to belong necessarily to nature itself, and it would fall to us to look for the phenomenon that does actually correspond to it:

> Our procedure consists in first fixing the thought demanded by the necessity of the Concept and then in asking how this thought appears in our ordinary ideas [*Vorstellung*]. The further requirement is that, in intuition, space [for example] shall correspond to the thought of pure self-externality. Even if we were mistaken in this, it would not affect the truth of our thought.[49]

This suggests that new scientific discoveries cannot invalidate a natural-logical determination that has clearly been properly derived. If, therefore, an empirical phenomenon is initially judged to correspond with a specific logical determination, but science later reveals that it does not actually do so, the thing to do, in Hegel's view, is not automatically to

conceive the logical determination in a new way, but rather to associate the empirical phenomenon with a different determination (or consign it to contingency).[50] This appears to
be what happened to galvanism in Hegel's philosophy of nature between 1817 and 1819:
Hegel's conception of the logical structure of electrical and chemical relations does not
alter significantly, but galvanism itself comes to be regarded as a chemical, rather than electrical phenomenon.[51] Further advances in science could, of course, require other, similar
changes to be made to the philosophy of nature. In this respect, Hegel's *a priori* philosophy of nature proves to be open to new discoveries that science might make.

It has now become apparent that philosophy's derivation of actual phenomena in nature,
such as time, light and electricity – as opposed to its derivation of the natural-logical determinations to which those phenomena correspond – is not *purely a priori*, but requires the
support of empirical science and experience. To the extent that a given phenomenon as
described by science is correctly matched with a logical determination, then that phenomenon can, indeed, be said to have been shown *a priori* to be logically necessary. The
logical derivation of such a phenomenon is, however, indirect and requires the assistance
of science.

For Hegel, the philosophy of nature and empirical science are two distinct enterprises
with different aims and they should not be confused with one another. Philosophy's aim
is to set out what is made logically necessary by the externality of nature itself. Its task is
not to explain everything in nature, but to shed light on that *limited* range of natural phenomena that have their ground in nature's own inherent logic rather than contingency.
Science, by contrast, seeks to discover as much as it can about all aspects of nature and its
fundamental laws through a combination of mathematical reasoning and empirical investigation. Philosophy and science do, however, complement one another in the following
ways:

1 Philosophy complements science by demonstrating that certain phenomena described
   by science (and laws discovered by science) are not mere contingent givens but are made
   necessary logically by the very nature of nature itself (provided, of course, that the
   correct phenomena have been associated with each logical determination).
2 Science complements philosophy by (a) refining our empirical knowledge of the natural
   phenomena that philosophy associates with its logical determinations, (b) investigating
   the natural processes that produce such phenomena (processes that philosophy itself is
   not able fully to explain), (c) increasing our understanding of those phenomena that
   philosophy regards as 'contingencies' falling outside the scope of its comprehension, and
   (d) preparing the way *historically* for the philosophy of nature in two significant ways:
   (i) through contributing to the modern consciousness of freedom, out of which self-
   determining, speculative philosophy grows, and (ii) through discovering certain laws of
   nature – such as Galileo's law of free fall – whose logical necessity the philosopher then
   seeks to demonstrate. (As I noted above, the future progress of science could also alert
   philosophy to problems in its articulation of the logic of nature – though only if the
   philosopher has not been completely rigorous in the articulation of that logic in the first
   place.)

Philosophy and science are thus not regarded by Hegel as competing or mutually hostile
disciplines. He does not consider modern empirical science to be incompatible with *a priori*
philosophy of nature and so does not accept that the former has rendered the latter out-
dated. Nor does he harbour any insidious (or foolish) intention of his own to replace

empirical science altogether with a purely rational philosophy of nature. On the contrary, he recognizes that the philosophy of nature needs to *cooperate* with the empirical sciences, and he firmly rejects 'that humbug in natural philosophy which consists in philosophizing without wide knowledge'.[52] Evidence of Hegel's own commitment to such cooperation can be found in the long list of scientists on whose work he himself draws in the philosophy of nature, a list that includes among others Galileo, Kepler, Newton, Lagrange, Laplace, Herschel, Berthollet and Cuvier.

Hegel's openness to changes and developments in science does not, however, mean that he regards science as being altogether beyond criticism. As we have seen, the philosophy of nature demonstrates (albeit indirectly) the logical necessity of certain phenomena and it also determines the true logical structure of those phenomena. If scientists put forward a conception of those phenomena that is utterly incompatible with the insights of the speculative philosophy of nature, then philosophy is entitled to ask those scientists to look again at their observations and at the interpretations they put upon them (assuming, of course, that philosophy itself has not made an error in its logical derivation). In Hegel's view, therefore, the philosophy of nature does not have to accept without criticism *whatever* science claims about nature, but it is able to discriminate between different scientific conceptions of the world and, if necessary, can even act – as Manfred Gies puts it – as a 'corrective for natural sciences'.[53] Philosophy assumes this role because, for it, 'the *Concept* is the judge that decides what is the True'.[54] As we have seen, however, there are clear limits to what the Concept shows to be logically necessary. There are thus also clear limits to the extent to which philosophy is entitled to 'correct' science.

The idea that science might, under certain circumstances, be subject to such critical scrutiny or correction by the philosophy of nature is bound to make scientists uncomfortable. Yet this right of philosophy follows from the fact that philosophy and science both describe the same world. If the philosophy of nature has to agree with what empirical science shows us about the world, it can expect such science in turn to acknowledge and accept what philosophy demonstrates to be true. One of the tasks facing students of Hegel in the twenty-first century will thus be to determine whether post-Hegelian science – in particular, relativity theory and quantum mechanics – is able to meet this expectation or whether it requires 'correction' in some way by the philosophy of nature. Conversely, of course, scientists interested in Hegel will want to know to what extent his philosophy of nature can itself accommodate the insights provided by these two powerful theories. Such an investigation, however, lies beyond the scope of this study (though there are brief remarks on the relation between Hegel and Einstein in the next chapter).

In my view, the most significant criticism levelled at science by the philosophy of nature is that science sometimes employs categories that are appropriate for one set of phenomena to understand other phenomena that call for more complex categories. Consider, for example, the relation between chemistry and life. Although science may show that chemical processes produce life, philosophy makes it clear that life has a formal structure that is not reducible to that of mere chemical relations (and that similarly the structure of chemical relations cannot be articulated in purely physical or mechanical terms). Philosophy, indeed, teaches us that each stage of nature 'has its own proper category' (*ihre eigentümliche Kategorie*), which is 'not also a category of a higher [stage] and is not to be carried over into the category of another stage'.[55] In so doing, philosophy serves to remind science that it should not be *reductive* and conclude that, because life emerges out of chemical activity, it thereby consists in nothing more than such chemical activity. From the philosophical point of view, therefore, one of the tasks of natural science must be to explain how natural processes can produce a *new* phenomenon with a distinctive character of its own that is not itself intelligible purely in terms of the processes that gave rise to it.

Hegel notes, however, that science has a tendency precisely to try to reduce one phenomenon to another in the search for a single *universal* explanation for things. He remarks that

> physics looks on these universals as its triumph: one can say even that, unfortunately, it goes too far in its generalizations. Present-day philosophy is called the philosophy of identity: this name can be much more appropriately given to that physics which simply ignores specific differences [*Bestimmtheiten*], as occurs, for example, in the current theory of electro-chemistry in which magnetism, electricity and chemistry are regarded as one and the same. It is the weakness of physics that it is too much dominated by the category of identity; for identity is the fundamental category of the Understanding [*des Verstandes*].[56]

One should not, by the way, conclude from this passage that Hegel altogether denies the intimate connection between electricity and magnetism revealed during his lifetime or that he would necessarily have rejected the later insights of Faraday and Maxwell into the phenomenon of electromagnetism. Hegel knew of Oersted's discovery in 1820 that there is a magnetic effect associated with an electric current, and he appreciated its groundbreaking importance.[57] He believed, however, that it is vital to keep in mind the distinctive *differences* between such phenomena – differences that science, in its search for the universal principle underlying nature, sometimes risks obscuring – and he considered it to be the role of philosophy to remind us of precisely these differences.

Hegel sets out his views on electromagnetism in the Remark to §313 of the *Philosophy of Nature* and in the process clarifies what he sees as the different but complementary interests of science and philosophy:

> Here we must say a word regarding the *identity* of magnetism, electricity, and chemistry, an identity nowadays widely recognised and in physics even regarded as fundamental. . . . It is . . . to be looked on as an important advance in empirical science that the identity of these phenomena has been recognised in common thought, and goes by the name of 'electro-chemistry' or possibly of 'magneto-electro-chemistry' or something similar. It is just as important, however, to *distinguish from each other* the *particular* forms in which the universal exists and their *particular manifestations*. . . . Formerly, magnetism, electricity, and chemism were treated as wholly separate and uncorrelated, each being regarded as an independent force. Philosophy has grasped the idea of their *identity, but* with the express *proviso* that they also are *different*. Recent ideas in physics seem to have jumped to the other extreme and to emphasise only the *identity* of these phenomena, so that the need now is to assert the fact and manner of their distinctiveness.

Note that in neither of the cases I have touched on here does Hegel dismiss out of hand science's attempt to unify phenomena. He accepts both that life is a complex form of chemical activity and that electricity and magnetism are manifestations of the same natural process. His point is simply to remind us not to overemphasize the identity of such phenomena at the expense of their *differences*. For philosophy, life is chemical activity that has actually transformed itself into something more complex than mere chemical activity, and electricity and magnetism are two very different manifestations of electromagnetic activity.

As in the *Phenomenology* and elsewhere in his system, therefore, Hegel is concerned above all in the philosophy of nature not to reduce phenomena to mere expressions of a single, universal principle, but to understand the unique specificity of each phenomenon

in turn, as well as the distinctive logic immanent in that specificity that makes further speci-
ficities necessary.[58] In other words (and *pace* critics, such as Deleuze), Hegel endeavours
throughout his mature work on nature and on the human spirit to develop a fully articulated philosophy of *difference*. In the next chapter we look more closely at Hegel's account
of the different natural phenomena that make up the realm of mechanics in particular.

6 *Space, Gravity and the Freeing of Matter*

Space and Its Dimensions

This chapter considers Hegel's actual derivation of the necessary aspects of nature. It concentrates on the first section of the philosophy of nature – mechanics – for three reasons. First, this section is where most readers of Hegel's text will begin. Second, it shows that Hegel is not a Romantic fantasist but a thinker who engages intelligently with major scientific figures, such as Galileo, Kepler and Newton. Third, it reveals how supposedly 'dead' space and matter begin to determine themselves freely and so take the first steps in the direction of life. Life itself is considered in chapter 7.

Where, then, should we begin? Like the rest of Hegel's philosophy, the philosophy of nature is meant to be a fully self-critical study of its subject matter. We cannot, therefore, start by presupposing any determinate conception of nature inherited from natural science, pre-Hegelian philosophy or common experience. On the contrary, we must simply begin where the presuppositionless science of *logic* ended: with the recognition that being, or the Idea, necessarily takes the form of sheer externality to which corresponds the empirical phenomenon of *space*. The task of philosophy is thus to 'forget everything that was said about [nature] up till now' and to focus on what – if anything – is logically entailed by such externality.[1]

The important thing to note about externality, as Hegel understands it, is that it is a kind of *difference*. Specifically, it is difference in which the differentiated moments are not opposed to one another, like the poles of a magnet, but are utterly *other* than and *indifferent* to one another. When two things are opposed, they are not only different but also bound internally to one another. This is because the very identity of each is constituted by excluding the other from itself: 'hot' is in itself 'not-cold' and the 'positive' is intrinsically 'not-negative'.[2] When two things are external to one another, however, they lack this internal connection; they simply coexist as two separate things.

To think of space as sheer externality is thus to think of it as differentiated into moments that are quite indifferent to one another. The different moments of space are, of course, the infinitely many 'heres' that are contained within it. Space, therefore, is a 'multiplicity' (*Vielheit*) – or, as Kant calls it, a 'manifold' – of different 'heres', which 'all have a place next to one another and do nothing to one another'.[3]

Yet there is more to space than simple externality. Each 'here' is an instance of the same, universal space, so the difference between one 'here' and another 'here' is simply the difference between space and *more space*. In so far as it is differentiated into many 'heres', therefore, space actually differs from itself and falls outside itself. This in turn means that it extends *beyond itself*. The logical structure of space is thus not just that of externality, but that of 'self-externality' (*Außersichsein*) or 'being-external-to-itself' (*Sich-äußerlich-Sein*).[4]

This fact that the differences in space are differences of space from itself means that there is in fact no clear and *determinate* difference between one 'here' and another. One 'here' falls outside another 'here', but they are none the less all the same or 'equal' (*gleich*). The difference between them, therefore, is actually 'indistinguishable, wholly abstract and empty'.[5] Furthermore, not only are all 'heres' equal, and so only indeterminately different, but there is no definite boundary demarcating one from another: each 'here' extends beyond itself into the others that are external to it. Taken together the equality of the parts of space and the uninterrupted quality of space as a whole make space *continuous*. This means that there are no 'gaps' in space, no absence of space between spaces: 'between points of space there is no non-spatiality [*Unräumlichkeit*]'. Space is, rather, uniform and unbroken: the seamless continuity of 'heres' that are not clearly differentiated from one another and have no boundaries between them.[6]

As Hegel acknowledges, space understood as *external to itself* is in fact profoundly contradictory, for it is both differentiated from itself and continuous with itself at one and the same time: it is divided into 'heres' that are not determinately different and so is continuous in its very discreteness. We saw in chapter 5 that nature is made necessary by the fact that being-as-Idea proves to be the 'negative of itself'; that is, externality rather than the intrinsic interconnectedness of its moments. We have now seen that such externality or self-externality – space – is itself 'abstractly the negative of itself', since its own logical structure is contradictory.[7] Hegel goes on to claim that space proves to be even more 'self-negating' than we have suggested so far.

Space, we recall, is self-determining *reason* existing in the form of externality. Space is thus not sheer externality (or self-externality) alone, but 'the field of externality is itself Concept, totality, Idea'.[8] As a consequence, Hegel points out, spatial externality must 'contain within itself the *differences* of the Concept' or the Idea. The precise form that such differences will take in space cannot be predicted in advance but must emerge immanently from the minimal character of spatial difference as such. All we know at the start is that, as the embodiment of reason, space must minimally exhibit '*determinate*, qualitative difference'.[9]

Yet space, as we have seen, is essentially continuous and undifferentiated in its multiplicity. The *determinate* difference that space must contain will therefore be at odds with the seamless uniformity of space itself. In Hegel's own words, such spatial difference will be 'the *negation* of space', because space 'is immediate *differenceless* self-externality'.[10] At first this negation will itself be immediate and absolute. The determinate moments into which space is differentiated will thus be neither extended nor continuous, and so will be not just 'heres' but unextended *points*. Hegel goes on, however, to argue that the point in space never actually exists as *pure* point but immediately negates itself. In the process, he maintains, the point makes necessary the three-dimensionality of space.

Hegel first demonstrates that the point gives rise logically to the line, or what he also calls 'simple spatial direction', and he proves thereby that space must have at least one dimension.[11] His argument goes like this. A point is the negation of space. It is thus an *unextended* unity that is completely closed in on itself or 'for itself'.[12] Yet a point cannot be purely the negation of space, precisely because it is itself located *in* space and so is a point *of* space. Every point is thus itself something *spatial*. This means, however, that it must actually be *extended* and so cannot be a pure, unextended point after all. The point, therefore, is logically self-negating or 'self-sublating': simply by virtue of being a point in space, it ceases being a mere point and necessarily *extends itself* into a *line*:

> In the determination [of the point] lies spatiality; it is only the negation of space in so far as it is posited in space; it *is*, however, posited in space, it is spatial and is itself space. . . . In so far as it is this, it ceases being a point and becomes something extended: the line. Thus there arises spatial limitation that is no longer the point.[13]

This is not to say that there is no such thing as a point at all: there must be points in space because space must be definitively differentiated in itself. There is, however, no point that does not initiate a line in space. A *pure* point is thus simply 'a limit that ought to be' but that does not actually exist as such.[14]

The line, it should be noted, is not something separate from or other than the point, but is simply the spatially extended point. The point, however, is the place at which the continuity of space is interrupted and so, as we have seen, is the negation of space. The line must, therefore, itself be the *spatially extended* negation of space: '*räumliche Negation*'. The line interrupts space not just by constituting a pure point of rupture but by actually stretching out and dividing space in two. It is thus, as Hegel puts it, the first 'real limit [or boundary] of space'.[15]

According to Hegel, then, the line is both positive and negative. It is positive in that it is irreducibly extended space. Indeed, it is the minimal determinate form that spatial extension can take. Space cannot be purely punctiform and unextended, but nor can it merely be indeterminately continuous. It must minimally extend out along a line and so be continuous *in a definite direction*. Accordingly, space must have at least one dimension. At the same time, the line is negative in that it forms a boundary that breaks the continuity of space. Reason requires that space be differentiated into points that initiate lines. Through its intrinsic linearity, however, space both gives direction to *and* interrupts its own seamless continuity.

The line and the point are logically identical, since both constitute the simple negation of space. Yet the line and the point are different, since the line is positively extended, whereas the point (which, we recall, does not actually exist in its pure form) is not. By virtue of this difference, Hegel argues, the line is implicitly the *negation* of the simple negation of space that is represented by the point. In the terms used in the *Logic*, whereas the point is the '*first* negation' of space, the line is implicitly 'the second negation, the negation of the negation'.[16] In Hegel's view, however, this means that, logically, the line actually points beyond itself to that which is no longer merely a line. Why should this be?

Logically, the 'negation of negation' is negation that, as it were, doubles back on itself and 'relates itself to itself'.[17] In so far as the line is a mere *line*, however, it does not exhibit this structure of double negation and self-relation *explicitly*. Despite being positively extended, the line remains the *simple* negation of space because it does no more than introduce a limit or break into the continuity of space. If the line is to be the *explicit* 'negation of negation', therefore, it must become more than a mere one-dimensional line. Logically, it must be a line that negates its own linearity, becomes something *other* than a mere line, and in so doing 'relates itself to', or connects with, itself. The line that does this, Hegel maintains, forms an enclosed, bounded space or a *plane* (*Fläche*). If the continuity of space is to exhibit explicitly all that is implicit in it, it must thus be differentiated into points that initiate lines that in turn enclose planes. Space cannot, therefore, simply be extended in one direction but must have at least two dimensions: 'The plane has two dimensions (the line is one direction), because it contains two determinations within itself. The line is the first negative, and the negative of this negative is the plane.'[18] Hegel's claim, it should be noted, is not that space starts out *in time* as one-dimensional and then changes over time into two-dimensional space. His point is a logical one: space must be planar because only in this way is it *explicitly* the self-relating negation that linear space is implicitly.

The line, considered by itself, is positive, extended space. At the same time it is primarily negative, since it constitutes no more than a boundary in space. A plane also limits and so negates the continuity of space in so far as it is a *bounded* space. Yet it does not just interrupt or negate space, since it is the explicit *negation* of the mere negation of space. Accordingly, in contrast to the one-dimensional line, the two-dimensional plane constitutes an *affirmative* space enclosed within determinate limits.[19] Hegel notes, however, that the plane is not completely affirmative, because its principal characteristic is that it is *different* from, and so the *negation* of, the line. The plane, he says, is a 'determinateness *opposed* to line and point'.[20]

It has to be said that Hegel does not explain himself here as fully as he should. As I understand it, however, his point is this: the line extends in a single direction and is space in the form of a mere boundary; the plane, by contrast, encloses space *within* a boundary; the plane, therefore, is not just a further extension of the line – a figure generated by simply adding more lines to the line – but is a *different kind of space* altogether: an affirmative, self-relating, enclosed space, rather than merely negative, interruptive space. Logically, therefore, the plane is contradictory: for it is *affirmative* space that consists in being the explicit *negation* of the line; that is, the explicit *negation* of the negation of space. In this sense, the plane is not completely affirmative after all.

Yet this is not all there is to say about the plane: for precisely by being the negation of the negation of space, the plane is implicitly space that is not primarily negative at all but genuinely and completely *affirmative*. In so far as the plane is a mere plane, however, it does not explicitly exhibit this wholly affirmative character, as we have just seen. If space is to render explicit what is implicit in the plane, therefore, the plane itself must *cease being a mere plane*. In the process, it will cease being space that is merely *non*-linear and become truly affirmative space.

Note that the logical transformation of the plane into truly affirmative space requires a *third* negation: the plane must mutate logically into space that is not just the negation of space, but is not just the *negation* of the negation of space, either. By virtue of being constituted by this third negation, Hegel concludes, truly affirmative space must be *three*-dimensional. As such, space must give itself the form not just of the point, line or plane, but of what Hegel calls the 'geometrical body': the '*enclosing surface [Oberfläche]* which separates off a *single* whole space'. This body is 'a unit, but not the abstract unit of the point, but one that at the same time contains the three dimensions within itself'.[21] A complete statement of the nature of space is thus as follows: space is continuous self-externality that must be differentiated into points that initiate lines that connect up to form planes that in turn constitute three dimensional bodies.

Like the plane, the geometrical body constitutes bounded space and so in that sense negates the continuity of space; indeed, it is the 'total bounding of space'.[22] Yet it is the negation of space through which, from a logical point of view, space is restored to being fully *affirmative*. Logically, space starts out as essentially affirmative, self-external being, but, as the embodiment of reason, it must be determinately differentiated within itself. This means, as we have seen, that space must take the form of the point, line and plane. In each case, however, space takes a form that is primarily negative. In so far as it is merely punctiform, linear or planar, therefore, space falls short of what it intrinsically is, namely, truly affirmative space. Space is, however, restored to its true affirmativity when it gives itself a form that is no longer primarily that of negation. Logically, this must be a form that is not just that of the *non*-linear, two-dimensional plane. Such a form can thus only be that of an enclosed space that is raised out of its two-dimensional flatness into a further, third dimension: the geometrical body.

This body is 'the restoration of the spatial totality' and of truly affirmative space, since it is no longer the mere negation of linear space.[23] The affirmative being that is now restored to space is not, however, reducible to the simple continuity of indifferent 'heres' that defined space at the start. It is a new and richer – three-dimensional – affirmative being that has emerged logically from the fact that space must be determinately *differentiated*, and so explicitly *negative*, in itself.[24]

Yet why should we stop at the idea that space has just three dimensions? Is not the geometrical body logically in just as much need of further negation as the plane? Is it not itself the *negation* of the negation of the negation of space and does it not, therefore, require a fourth negation to turn it into affirmative space? Indeed, will not this fourth negation itself require a further, fifth negation, and so on *ad infinitum*? Does not Hegel's dialectical logic make it necessary that space be differentiated into an endless infinity of dimensions? No, it does not, because the third negation that logically generates the three-dimensional geometrical body is not simply a repetition of the second negation that defines the plane, and so it does not automatically call forth a further negation.

The plane, as I have suggested, is qualitatively different from the line, since it is not merely a boundary in space but a bounded affirmative space. Due to this qualitative difference between the two, the plane cannot be conceived simply as the product of more than one line, but must be understood as the definite *negation* of the line as such. The logical move from the plane to the three-dimensional geometrical body is different from this. It does not introduce an altogether new kind of space that is qualitatively distinct from that of the plane, but simply gives the self-enclosed, affirmative space found in the plane a form that is no longer restricted to that of the plane as such; that is, a form no longer characterized principally by being the *negation* of the line. The third negation of space does not, therefore, result in a space that is itself the explicit *negation* of the plane; rather, it produces self-relating space that has lost its primarily negative character and so, logically, is genuinely affirmative.

As Hegel puts it, the three-dimensional geometrical body is the 'sublated negation' (*aufgehobene Negation*) of space.[25] This means that, logically, it is negation that is no longer overtly negative at all and so – necessarily – is affirmative. Three-dimensional space is certainly space that is *not* just the negation of the negation of space. This third negation, however, is not just a repetition of the second, and so produces a space that is truly affirmative rather than one that is explicitly negative *once again*. For this reason, the third negation does not require further similar negations and so does not make necessary an infinity of spatial dimensions.

Three-dimensional space is thus, logically, all there is to space. It is space as 'totality'.[26] Logically, space must be: (1) the simple negation of itself, i.e. the non-dimensional point and one-dimensional line that do no more than interrupt the continuity of space, (2) the explicit negation of that simple negation, i.e. the two-dimensional plane that does not just interrupt space but constitutes bounded, affirmative space, and (3) the 'sublation' of negation altogether, i.e. the three-dimensional geometrical body that is no longer primarily negative but truly affirmative. Beyond these three 'negations' and their corresponding dimensions there is nothing, logically, that space is required to be.

Hegel asserts that geometry – by which he means Euclidian geometry – cannot prove that space must have three dimensions, but simply has to assume this to be the case. He believes, however, that philosophy can provide such a proof by demonstrating *a priori* that space must differentiate itself – through negation and self-negation – into points, lines, planes and geometrical bodies. Several things need to be noted about Hegel's philosophical account of space.

First, Hegel is not trying to prove the independent physical existence of geometrical figures. He is not arguing that, if we were to travel through empty space, we would actually see lines drawn across the vacuum or bump into geometrical bodies with tangible boundaries. He is arguing that the fabric of space itself is necessarily geometrical in structure and, for this reason, must be three-dimensional.

Second, Hegel argues that space must differentiate itself into lines, planes and 'total' bodies, all of which introduce ideal boundaries into the continuity of space, but he does not deny that space continues beyond any ideal boundaries that it may contain. In this sense, space is *unbounded*. He insists, however, that beyond any such boundaries space remains geometrically structured and so contains further ideal boundaries beyond which, of course, it continues uninterrupted. This is the fundamental contradiction or 'antinomy' at the heart of space: limits can be set anywhere in space but 'beyond its limit . . . space is still in community with itself, and this unity in asunderness is continuity'.[27]

Third, the geometrical figures into which space differentiates itself are generated in a logical sequence, one from the other. This does not mean, however, that lines 'consist' of points or that planes 'consist' of lines. Hegel's argument, rather, is that lines are what points prove in truth to be and that planes are lines that are explicitly self-relating. Indeed, once space has shown itself to be three-dimensional, it becomes apparent that geometrical points, lines and planes are in fact simply abstractions from the totality of space, rather than space's fundamental 'constituents'. All physical points, lines and planes (drawn, for example, on paper) will, of course, be three-dimensional.

Fourth, Hegel's philosophical demonstration that space must have three dimensions obviously accords well with our ordinary experience. It does not, however, accord with all sides of modern scientific thinking about space. The proponents of 'string theory', for example, argue that 'for string theory to make sense, the universe should have nine space dimensions and one time dimension, for a total of ten dimensions'.[28]

Does this mean that Hegel's philosophy of nature is incompatible with string theory? Not necessarily: for, whatever Hegel himself may have thought, he does not prove definitively that space *tout court* can have only three dimensions. All he proves is that space must be three-dimensional *to the extent that it is determined by its own inherent logic and so is rational*. This certainly rules out the possibility of purely two-dimensional space; but it leaves open the possibility that, as a matter of *contingent* fact, space might have more than the three dimensions its inherent logic requires it to have. It is beyond my competence to assess the plausibility of string theory. It seems to me, however, that, if space were indeed to be shown to have nine dimensions (or more), this would not automatically leave Hegel's philosophy of nature dead in the water. In that case, the Hegelian could argue that only three dimensions can be derived *logically* from the very nature of space, and that no philosophical explanation can be given for any dimensions space is found to have beyond the three with which we are familiar.

Time

The three dimensions of space are generated by the fact that space is necessarily the *negation* of its own uninterrupted continuity – and thus divided into points and lines – but also the negation of that very negation – and thus planar and 'total' or three-dimensional. Space differentiates itself into three dimensions, therefore, by logically *negating itself*. In Hegel's own words, 'negativity constitutes the dimensions of space'.[29]

Yet in giving itself three dimensions space negates itself in a relatively mild way, for in so doing it *preserves* its character as space: its dimensions exist outside one another and so do not alter the fact that space is self-external being. Hegel points out, however, that this renders space deeply contradictory. Since each spatial dimension is a negation of space (or negation of that negation), the *negations* that space introduces into itself actually take a *positive* form and subsist as real directions in space. As Hegel puts it, in space 'all negativity appears . . . as something that *is* [*als ein Seiendes*]'.[30] For this reason, he maintains, 'the negative in space does not . . . yet receive its due [*Recht*]', but is 'paralysed' or 'lamed' and so 'falls apart into indifferent subsistence'.[31]

This, however, cannot be the whole story: for space is *self-negating* and so, logically, must negate its very spatiality as such. That is, space must negate itself in a manner that does not just leave it *subsisting* as self-external being, but that causes it actually to *disappear* into nothingness. In this way, space will prove to be genuinely negative. Since space *qua space* does not negate itself in this way, however, it must mutate logically into a new form of being that is no longer simply spatial but is thoroughly self-negating. Such being, Hegel maintains, is *time*.

Time is thus not something independent of space, but simply what space itself logically proves to be: space that has become explicitly what it was implicitly. Space necessarily temporalizes itself through its own immanent logic: since it is self-negating, it cannot remain primarily affirmative being or 'indifferent subsistence', but must negate itself into being that is truly self-negating. According to Hegel, 'space is thus the pure negativity of itself or the transition into time'.[32] Ordinary consciousness, Hegel claims, tends to separate space and time from one another: 'we have space and *also* time'. Philosophy, by contrast, 'fights against this "also"' and understands time to be nothing but the passing away of space itself.[33]

Space, for Hegel, is the very least that nature can be, and time is the process of self-negation or vanishing that space itself proves to be. Time is thus nothing but 'the negative in nature' or nature *as* sheer negativity.[34] Indeed, it is negative and self-negating to such a degree that it is not even just the *vanishing* of being, but is equally the *emergence* or coming-to-be of the very being that vanishes. Since it is just as much the emerging as the vanishing of being, time is necessarily *continuous* and unending.[35]

Time thus has an even more contradictory structure than space, for it is neither purely affirmative being, nor nothing at all, but being that passes over into nothing just as it arises out of nothing. In Hegel's own words, time is 'being which, inasmuch as it *is*, is *not*, and inasmuch as it is *not*, *is*'. As such, time has the same logical structure as the pure becoming discussed in the *Logic* (see p. 33 above). Yet it is not sheer becoming by itself, but the becoming that *space* – the self-externality of nature – proves to be. It is, as Hegel puts it, '*intuited* becoming' (*das* angeschaute *Werden*), becoming that can, as it were, actually be seen to exist.[36]

As the continuous vanishing of being, time differentiates itself into three dimensions: past, present and future. Each dimension is made necessary by the contradictory logical structure of time itself. 'If we begin from positive being', Hegel states, 'this changes into non-being, and this changed being is the past.' On the other hand, 'the nothing that is destined [*bestimmt*] to change into being is the future'.[37] The present or the 'now' is being that both turns the future into a reality and immediately vanishes into the past. The whole process of time consists, therefore, in the present's becoming the past and the future's becoming the new present (that immediately becomes the past).

Note that the dimensions or 'divisions' of time do not exist next to or outside one another like the dimensions of space. The past and future cannot coexist with the present because they do not *exist* at all, but are, respectively, the *non-being* into which being vanishes and the *non-being* which has yet to come into being at all. Past and future can, perhaps, be said to exist 'in *remembrance* and *fear* or *hope*', but they have no independent existence in nature. In nature, Hegel insists, 'there is only the now' or the present.[38] Unlike space, therefore, time does not give each of its dimensions a positive reality of its own and thereby expand into rounded, three-dimensional being. On the contrary, it restricts itself to an exclusively one-dimensional existence. All time is, is the *present* that continuously vanishes and comes into being: 'neither the past is, nor the future, but only the present'.[39]

Thus, even though time is what space proves to be, time is utterly unlike space in its logical structure. It is the restless self-negating of being, as opposed to the expansive, 'indifferent unfolding of itself' that is space.[40] Hegel goes on to argue, however, that, just as space mutates logically into time, so time itself mutates logically back into space.

This logical transition is made necessary by the fact that the present is actually to be understood in two different ways. On the one hand, the present is the individual 'now' that vanishes as soon as it arises. Since each such 'now' immediately gives way to a new one, time is the unending, continuous *succession* of vanishing moments, each of which 'is the result of the past and is pregnant with the future' (and so is not merely a separate, 'atomic' now).[41] On the other hand, the present is also the *universal* 'now' that continues uninterrupted throughout this succession of vanishing moments. This 'now' does not itself vanish, but *endures*. Indeed, it endures eternally and in so doing constitutes all that Hegel understands by 'eternity'. Eternity, for Hegel, does not precede time or come after the end of time, but is simply irreducible, ongoing presence itself: 'eternity will not come to be, nor was it, but it *is*'.[42]

Note that this irreducible presence is constituted by, and inseparable from, the ceaseless vanishing of the individual 'now'. As one moment vanishes and yields to its successor, there is no 'gap' in time between the two; on the contrary, there is perfect continuity, since the vanishing of one moment *is* the arising of the next. Even though each moment immediately disappears, therefore, presence as such never vanishes (nor, indeed, does it come to be). Presence itself is thus not 'being which, inasmuch as it *is*, is *not*, and inasmuch as it is *not*, *is*'. It is being that just *is* what it *is* and thereby constitutes simple, affirmative 'subsistence' (*Bestehen*).[43]

The passage of time thus proves to be inseparable from being that is itself indifferent to time and in that sense 'timeless'. This is what Hegel means by saying that, logically, 'time is the immediate *collapse* into indifference'.[44] In nature, however, sheer 'indifferent subsistence', or simple, affirmative being that is not temporally differentiated, is nothing other than *space*.[45] By giving rise to irreducible, *timeless* being, therefore, time in fact makes space necessary. Space had to mutate logically into time in order to be fully and explicitly self-negating. We have now seen time mutate logically back into the explicitly affirmative being of space.

To repeat: time makes space necessary because (1) the very process of vanishing in which time consists itself gives rise logically to being that does *not* vanish but simply *is* affirmatively what it is, and (2) such immediately affirmative being, which does not itself explicitly differentiate itself into past, (fleeting) present and future, *is* nothing other than space. Note that, unlike Kant, Hegel is not claiming merely that *we* require intuitions in both space and time in order to have determinate knowledge of the world. He is arguing that time *itself* – as a fundamental feature of nature – requires that there be space: 'time collapses into itself, and the being-collapsed is space'.[46]

Place and Motion

Space and time each turn out to make the other necessary. Hegel concludes from this that they cannot ultimately be held apart from one another but must form a single, indissoluble *unity*. This is not to say that there is no difference between them: the qualitative difference between their respective logical structures remains ineliminable. Neither, however, can stand alone, but each, in order to be what it is, requires the other. 'As thus completed [*vervollständigt*] by one another', Hegel states, 'they are one.'[47]

Such a unity may (following Einstein) be called 'space-time' – though to my knowledge Hegel never uses this expression – since it consists in space that passes away in time but thereby continues to subsist as three-dimensional self-external being.[48] This space-time is divided into three-dimensional, *extended* points or 'heres', each of which is also irreducibly temporal and is called a *place* (*Ort*). For Hegel, therefore, a place is not just spatial but is a part of space existing in and enduring through time. It constantly vanishes into the past and yet, in so doing, persists as one and the same place: 'The here is at the same time a now, for it is the point of duration [*Dauer*]. This unity of here and now is place.'[49]

Yet the unity of space and time cannot only mean that space acquires the further 'fourth' dimension of time and that every 'here' thereby gains temporal duration. The unity must go deeper than this. If space and time are truly to constitute one reality in which neither is purely itself, then not only must each be inextricably bound to the other, but each must actually *take on the logical characteristics of the other* (while still retaining its own logical structure). In other words, with the help of space the dimensions of time must themselves come to *subsist* outside one another, and with the help of time space must itself become explicitly *self-negating* space. In this very intimate way, Hegel maintains, 'space is [thus] posited here as temporal, and time is posited here as spatial'.[50]

As we know, the past and the future do not exist as such, since only the present *is*. Each dimension of time gains a separate existence in space, however, when the present is *here*, the past is over *there* and the future is over *there* – that is, when 'there are three different places: the present place, the place about to be occupied, and the place which has just been vacated'. Equally, space comes to be explicitly self-negating space when place no longer simply remains the same place through time but also *ceases* being that place and comes to be a different one. In this way, place is, as it were, animated by time so that it *changes itself* into another place: 'place is spatial . . . and it is this only as a *spatial now*, as time, so that place is immediately . . . the negation of itself, and is *another place*'.[51]

This process whereby one place 'negates itself' into another place is logically quite complex. After all, place has been defined as a 'here' that *endures* through time. In ceasing to be *this* place and becoming another place, a place must thus also *remain* the place that it is. How is this possible? It is possible if an enduring place uncouples itself from the place it occupies – from the place that it initially *is* – and transfers itself to a new place. In this way, one and the same enduring place ceases being *here* and finds itself *there* instead. This process in which an enduring place changes its location from here to there through time is, of course, the process of *motion* (*Bewegung*): 'Something occupies its place, then changes it; another place arises, but, both before and after, something occupies its place and does not leave it. . . . That motion is what we have expounded is self-evident; this Concept of it conforms to our intuition of it.'[52]

According to Hegel, therefore, the intimate unity of space and time, in which each takes on the logical characteristics of the other and in this sense *becomes* the other, makes motion necessary. Indeed, Hegel argues, space and time have no existence apart from motion: 'it is in motion that space and time first acquire actuality'.[53] Philosophy begins by considering space alone; it has demonstrated, however, that nature is in fact nothing less than motion. This is not to deny that there can be such a thing as *rest* through time. Rest, however, is simply motion viewed from a different perspective. The difference between motion and rest is thus not absolute but relative, since all 'rest' is itself in reality motion.[54]

Hegel's account of motion may strike some readers as perverse, since he argues that motion can be understood without any reference to particular *things* that move. His position is especially likely to upset followers of Aristotle who insisted that 'there is no such thing as motion over and above the things'.[55] As we shall see, however, Hegel will go on to draw the same conclusion as Aristotle: there can, indeed, be no motion without bodies that move. In Hegel's view, this is because motion will prove logically not just to be purely itself but to be the motion of differentiated *matter*, just as space and time proved not just to be themselves in the abstract. Motion will therefore 'negate itself' logically into matter-in-motion. Hegel cannot, however, start out from the Aristotelian position, since he must restrict himself to unfolding what is made necessary by the very nature of space; and what space initially determines to be necessary is not the motion of material bodies but motion *as such*.[56]

This method of procedure allows Hegel to pinpoint, without making arbitrary assumptions, what it is that makes motion necessary and, indeed, what motion as such *is*. Through Hegel's account it becomes clear that motion is made necessary not by matter or by things in the world (or by a 'prime mover'), but simply by the union of space and time. Why must there be motion? Why can't the world just stand still? Because, logically, space and time must constitute *place that negates itself spatially as well as temporally* – place that, while retaining its identity, ceases to be *this* place and becomes *another* place. (*Pace* Spinoza, therefore, motion is not made immediately necessary by extension or space alone, but is generated by space-*time*.)[57]

Understood in this way, motion proves to be nothing but the *changing of place* (*Ortsveränderung*) *in time* – a logically derived conception that surely overlaps closely with our ordinary intuitions about motion.[58] In Hegel's view, therefore, although motion may not actually exist without matter, matter does not need to be invoked in order to comprehend what motion is. All one needs to understand is the nature of space, time and place. Accordingly, velocity (*Geschwindigkeit*) is simply 'space in relation to a specific time elapsed' – for example, metres per second (m/s).[59]

This conception of motion explains how it is, as we noted earlier, that the dimensions of time can come to subsist in space. 'In motion', as Richard Winfield puts it, 'the passage of time presents itself spatially as the move from one place to another.' The past and the future thus become 'paralysed' as the place that has been left behind and the place that lies ahead. In a sense, therefore, one can *see* the past and future by looking around oneself in space.[60]

Matter and Its Gravity

Space and time, Hegel maintains, are sometimes thought of as empty 'containers' (*Behälter*) that exist prior to matter and are subsequently 'filled' by the introduction of matter, as it were, from the 'outside'.[61] For Hegel, by contrast, matter is not something distinct from space and time in this way, but is made necessary *by* space and time. This is because matter is precisely what space and time themselves, in their indissoluble unity, logically prove to be. Space and time, as we have seen, have shown themselves to be abstractions that have no existence by themselves but exist only in the form of motion. Hegel now demonstrates that motion is also an abstraction that turns out to be logically inseparable from matter.

For Hegel, therefore, there is never anything less than *matter*, and in this sense the great German 'idealist' can actually be considered a 'materialist'. Note, however, that, unlike many other, self-proclaimed materialists, Hegel does not simply presuppose the existence of matter. He reaches the conclusion that matter is irreducible by demonstrating that pure, 'immaterial' space, time and motion undermine their own abstractness and 'make themselves into this reality which is matter'.[62] In this way, Hegel proves that the presence of matter is not simply something contingently given, but is a logical necessity.

Matter is made necessary by the distinctive logical structure of motion. The latter, as we know, is the process whereby a place ceases being the particular place that it is and becomes another place, and then another and another, and so on. Motion is thus the process in which a place changes from being *here* to being *there* and then *there*. In this process of change, the place itself is not destroyed but endures: it simply relocates itself in space over time. As Winfield puts it, therefore, in motion 'a determinate, reidentifiable space travels along the trajectory of motion'.[63] This determinate space that retains its identity as it moves is what Hegel understands by *matter*: 'since there is motion, something moves; but this something which persists is matter'. For Hegel, therefore, 'there is no motion without matter'. Equally, 'there is no matter without motion', since matter is simply enduring, self-identical space that moves.[64]

Later in the philosophy of nature matter will turn out to have distinctive physical and chemical qualities: it will have density, cohesion, produce sounds, give off heat and be metallic, acidic or alkaline, and so on. The first thing that matter proves to be, however – and thus the very least that matter can be – is reidentifiable space in motion. In Hegel's view, the science of mechanics is distinguished from that of physics proper by the fact that it seeks to understand only the various kinds of *motion* (and the specific relations between space and time they involve) that are characteristic of matter in general, regardless of its physical or chemical composition. As we shall see, mechanics, in Hegel's view, also seeks to account for such motion without invoking the concept of 'force' and so coincides with *kinematics*.[65] From a mechanical or kinematical point of view, therefore, matter and motion are actually the same thing, understood once as a settled unity and once as process. This explains why an object can produce the same effect in another object through an increase in its mass (or weight) *or* in its velocity.[66]

By virtue of the fact that it endures through the course of its motion, matter retains a distinct *identity* of its own. It remains one and the same 'self-relating' space as it relocates itself from one place to another. By preserving its identity in this way, Hegel argues, matter necessarily *excludes* from the space it occupies any other self-identical moving space that it encounters. At its simplest, therefore, 'matter is place that is exclusive'. To put this another way, matter necessarily *repels* any other matter that endeavours to move into its space. This is true of every material body and of every part of every material body. Each one resists the encroachment on its own space by other bodies or parts of matter. Consequently, 'matter is impenetrable [*undurchdringlich*] ...; where one matter is, there can be no other'.[67] Impenetrability is thus not a contingent quality of matter, but is made necessary by the fact that matter *preserves* its identity as it moves.

As impenetrable, matter constitutes what Hegel calls 'the first real limit in space'.[68] Geometrical lines and planes also bound space, but they constitute ideal rather than real barriers. Matter, by contrast, definitively bars the progress of other matter through the space it occupies. By virtue of doing so, it *fills* space in a way that geometrical figures alone do not. Since space has proven to be nothing less than matter, it would thus appear at this point that there is nothing in nature but filled space; and Hegel does, indeed, maintain that 'there is no empty space'. It becomes clear later, however, that, even if space necessarily proves to be filled space or matter, matter itself differentiates itself into independent celestial bodies – planets, moons and their sun – that are separated by empty space. Matter itself will thus make some empty space necessary.[69]

Hegel goes on to argue that matter consists not only in the mutual repulsion, but also in the mutual *attraction*, of its parts. Through its activity of repulsion, matter distinguishes itself into many distinct parts or units. All remain, however, units of *one and the same* matter. Despite its differentiation into manifold material bodies (and parts of bodies), therefore, matter actually forms a single, continuous unity and identity. All units of matter give expression to their essential unity through their mutual *attraction* for one another: 'there is One which posits itself as many, and those that are distinguished . . . are one and the same; this is the determination of attraction which thus lies immediately in repulsion'. Matter, for Hegel, is thus both the repelling of one unit of itself from another *and* the 'positing of the many as one' in attraction.[70]

Indeed, matter cannot be one without the other: for repulsion, as the holding apart of what is essentially one and the same, must entail the mutual attraction of what is held apart, and attraction, as the unifying of what holds itself apart, must entail the mutual repulsion of the units that draw together. Matter, in other words, is both *one* and *many* at the same time, and so is the concrete embodiment of unity-in-difference.

Note that, in contrast to Kant, Hegel does not regard repulsion and attraction as *forces* within matter causing it to move in certain ways.[71] He considers them to be the processes or *movements* in which matter consists. No forces are needed to explain such motion, because matter itself proves logically to *be* the very movement of repelling and drawing together with other matter. According to Hegel, this unity of attraction and repulsion that matter proves to be is *gravity* (*Schwere*).

In his *Principia* Newton understands gravity to be a centripetal force by which bodies are drawn or 'impelled' toward some point as their 'centre'. For bodies on the earth this centre is located in the centre of the earth itself and for the planets it is in the centre of the sun.[72] Since centripetal forces draw or pull bodies *down* or *in* toward such a centre, they are considered by Newton to be 'attractions'.[73] Gravity, unlike magnetism, is the force of attraction that is found to be operative in all bodies and so is universal. Despite this, however, gravity, for Newton, is not 'essential to bodies': it is not a property without which matter could not be conceived to be what it is.[74] Gravity must, therefore, have a cause that is distinct from the simple nature of matter itself. Yet Newton maintains that the cause of gravity remains unknown and that he will not frame 'hypotheses' about its possible character.[75]

Hegel's conception of gravity differs in significant respects from that of Newton. First, gravity (which is simply the unity of attraction and repulsion) is not a *force* within matter, in Hegel's view. It is nothing but the *motion* towards other matter (or the propensity so to move) that is characteristic of all matter. As Hegel puts it, matter 'is heavy [*schwer*], and the appearance of gravity is motion'.[76]

Second, gravity is not a contingent property of matter without which matter would remain what it is. Gravity is, rather, the very essence or 'substance' of matter itself.[77] It is the movement of uniting-with-other-matter that is intrinsic to matter as such (as opposed to magnetism which is the property of only certain kinds of matter). The statement that 'matter is heavy' is thus for Hegel – though not for Newton or, famously, for Kant – an analytic or 'identical' proposition.[78] Accordingly, gravity is not merely an unexplained force in nature. It is a phenomenon whose occurrence is explained by the logical development of space and time that makes matter itself necessary.

Third, since gravity is matter's *own* movement towards other matter, it cannot be a force that acts upon bodies from the outside and *pulls* them towards their centre.[79] One needs to exercise caution, therefore, when considering Hegel's claim that gravity is the unity of repulsion and *attraction*, because (unlike Newton) he does not understand gravity to be a force *by which* matter is passively *attracted*. True, he allows us to *say* (with Newton) that 'matter is attracted by the centre'; but he makes it abundantly clear at several points that gravity is actually matter's own, active 'seeking' or 'striving' to unite with other matter.[80] Interestingly, Newton also talks at times (like Hegel) of 'bodies seeking a center'.[81] He makes it clear at numerous points, however, that gravity is in fact an external force *by* which bodies are drawn or 'impelled' towards a centre.

Fourth, even if we understand 'attraction' as the active seeking of other matter, Hegel still insists that 'it is essential to distinguish *gravity* from mere *attraction*', because gravity is in fact the union of attraction *and* repulsion.[82] It is the movement in which matter seeks to unite with other matter that it simultaneously repels and excludes from the space it occupies. This moment of repulsion is an ineliminable feature of gravitating matter and, indeed, constitutes its distinctive impenetrability. Accordingly, it prevents matter from ever achieving its goal of *complete* unity with other matter. Newton, of course, also recognizes that matter is both attracted to other matter and impenetrable. For Hegel, however, the repulsion of matter is a constitutive moment of gravitational attraction itself.

Perfect unity would only be attained, in Hegel's view, if different parts of matter were able to overcome their own impenetrability and their separation from one another and occupy the same space. This, he maintains, would involve them collapsing into *one point*: 'if matter attained what it seeks in gravity, it would melt into a single point'. It is impossible for matter to collapse into such a pure singularity, however, because 'repulsion, no less than attraction, is an essential moment of matter' and this necessarily keeps all parts of matter apart from one another, even if in some cases only to a minimal degree. Accordingly, matter forever seeks an intimate unity with other matter that it can never achieve: 'the unity of gravity is [thus] only an Ought [*Sollen*], a longing, the most unhappy striving to which matter is eternally condemned'.[83]

The point in space at which matter seeks its impossibly intimate unity with other matter is called by Hegel (following Newton) a 'centre' (*Mittelpunkt*). Since this centre lies absolutely beyond the reach of the matter that seeks it, it must not only be located outside such matter but also be a point that in principle cannot be occupied by matter at all. It must, therefore, be a wholly immaterial, unextended, '*ideal* singularity': a purely geometrical point.[84] This ideal centre will itself, however, be located within another *material* body. When a terrestrial body falls, therefore, it seeks its 'centre' or point of unity not in the empty space on the other side of the earth but within the earth itself.[85] Since gravity is thus matter's movement – or propensity to move – towards an *immaterial*, geometrical 'centre' within another *material* body, it is, in Hegel's view, the 'confession' by matter of its essentially contradictory nature.[86]

Mass, Inertia and Weight

Matter, for Hegel, is enduring, self-identical space that excludes other such space. Consequently, he argues, matter cannot be a simple unity, but must *differentiate* itself into various 'bodies', each of which repels all others from the space that it occupies. These bodies will not be qualitatively distinct from one another, since they are all bits of the same matter. Any difference there may be between them – beyond the fact that they must occupy different places – will thus be purely *quantitative*. This means that each body will occupy a certain quantity of space and so have a volume that may or may not differ from that of other bodies. It also means, however, that each body will itself be made up of a certain *quantity of matter* that may or may not differ from that of other bodies. The quantity of matter that each body comprises is its *mass*.[87]

The mass of a body is the number of 'homogeneous parts' (*gleichartige Teile*) that it contains, however densely or thinly they are distributed through the space occupied by the body.[88] To determine the difference in mass between two bodies, one does not, however, need to cut them open, identify parts that are of the same kind in both, and then count them. As Newton argues, mass 'can always be known from a body's weight'. Yet the mass of a body is not the same as its weight. The weight of a body can vary from place to place; the body's mass, by contrast, is the unvarying quantity of matter in the body that is, as Newton puts it, 'proportional to the weight'.[89]

Philosophy, for Hegel, proves that material bodies must have mass, but it cannot determine by itself what the mass of any given body will be. From the perspective of philosophy, the mass of a body is thus contingent. Each body just happens to have the mass that it has, and so each body 'is a wholly *contingent* One'.[90] Hegel goes on to argue that finite, material bodies – as opposed to the celestial bodies we will consider later – are marked by contingency in another respect, too: for, although all matter is necessarily in some kind of motion, it is contingent *how* any finite mass moves in relation to other specified masses and, indeed, whether it is in motion or at rest in relation to them.

Some finite bodies, such as animals, have the capacity to move themselves freely. In so far as finite bodies are considered to be mere masses of matter, however, they are, in Hegel's view, 'indifferent' to motion and rest. That is because there is nothing in the simple fact that a finite body is *this* particular mass that requires it to move at any particular speed or in any particular direction. Each finite mass is capable of moving in a variety of different ways, but it does not itself determine – simply through being the particular mass that it is – how it will move in relation to other masses. Its state of motion or rest must, therefore, be determined by something *outside* itself; that is, by another mass that happens – contingently – to strike it or apply pressure to it. This quality of being open but 'indifferent' to motion and rest is the inertness or 'inertia' (*Trägheit*) of mass.[91]

Being inert, for Hegel, does *not* mean being at rest as opposed to being in motion. It means that 'mass is indifferent to them both and is equally capable of motion or rest'. Mass is inert, therefore, in so far as it is itself 'neither at rest nor in motion, but only passes from one state [*Zustand*] to the other through an external impulse'. Since its state of motion or rest (relative to other masses) is necessarily determined by one or more other masses, no inert mass can change its own state of motion or rest – and so accelerate or decelerate – by itself: 'when at rest it remains in that state and does not spontaneously set itself in motion; and conversely, when in motion it remains in motion and does not spontaneously pass over into a state of rest'.[92] It thus necessarily *preserves* its state of motion until that state is changed again by further, contingent contact with another mass.

The principle of inertia is the fundamental principle of modern mechanics (that is, mechanics from the seventeenth century onwards). According to the older, Aristotelian physics, I. B. Cohen explains, 'if the motive force applied to a body were to cease acting, the body would then seek its natural place and there come to rest'. All motion thus needs to be sustained by the continuous operation of a mover. According to modern physics, by contrast, if an external force were to cease to act on a body, 'inertness would tend to maintain a body in whatever "state" it happened to be [in], whether a state of resting or of moving "uniformly straight forward"'.[93] Inertial motion thus does not need to be sustained by any motive force, but continues in its current state until that state is altered by an external force. This principle finds its most famous expression – and is thereby established as the foundation of modern physics – in Newton's First Law of Motion in the *Principia*:

'Every body perseveres in its state of being at rest or of moving uniformly straight forward, except in so far as it is compelled to change its state by forces impressed.'[94]

This principle is one that Hegel allegedly failed to comprehend or deliberately rejected in favour of a 'pre-inertial', Aristotelian conception of motion. William R. Shea, for example, insists that 'Hegel never grasped this fundamental principle of mechanics and maintained the traditional Aristotelian view that motion requires a mover, namely that a moving body comes to rest as soon as the force that moves it ceases to be applied.'[95] It is evident from what was said above, however, that this charge is false. Hegel argues that matter must take the form of inert mass, and he conceives of inertia in the same way as Newton: he recognizes that when in motion a finite mass 'does not spontaneously pass over into a state of rest' and that its state can be changed only 'through an external impulse'. In this respect, he clearly aligns himself with modern, rather than pre-modern, physics.

For Hegel, the external *mechanical* (as opposed to, say, magnetic) cause of a change in a body's state of motion is always the impact of, or pressure applied by, another body. For Newton, that external cause can be 'percussion, pressure, *or centripetal force*'. The latter may in turn be magnetic force or the force of gravity.[96] Gravity is thus, in Newton's view, an external cause of changes in a body's state of motion. As we saw above, Newton does not regard gravity as 'essential to bodies'. He contends, none the less, that the force of gravity is directed *universally* by all bodies towards all other bodies.[97] All bodies, therefore, are attracted by, and have weight in relation to, one another.

The motion of any finite body is thus compounded of both inertial motion *and* motion caused by gravitational attraction (as well as the effects of any intervening bodies). 'Projectiles', for example, 'persevere in their motions, except insofar as they are retarded by the resistance of the air and are impelled downward by the force of gravity'.[98] Newton proves that the force of gravity – and thus the weight of a body in relation to another – is not constant but directly proportional to the product of the masses of the bodies concerned and *inversely* proportional to the square of the distance between them (this is the 'inverse square law' taken over by Newton from Huygens and Hooke).[99] The mass of a heavy body, however, is invariant, and so its capacity for inertial motion, or 'persevering' in its state of motion, remains in all circumstances undiminished.

Hegel's position is similar to Newton's, except for one thing. For Hegel, gravity is not a force that acts on a body from the outside, pulling it, for example, down towards the earth. Gravity is, rather, a body's own *inherent* tendency to unite with other matter in an immaterial centre. Bodies are thus not attracted *by* one another, but actively gravitate *towards* one another. Hegel accepts the inverse square law and so recognizes that weight decreases as the distance between the bodies concerned is squared.[100] He argues, however, that all matter is intrinsically, rather than contingently, *weighted* or heavy: 'gravity is the predicate of matter and constitutes the substance of this subject'.[101] Inert mass, for Hegel, is thus never purely inert, because all inert mass is itself inherently *gravitating* mass.[102]

In Hegel's view, therefore, finite bodies are not deflected by an *external* force of gravity from the path of uniform rectilinear motion along which their inertia would otherwise take them. They deflect themselves from that path through their *own* gravity or weight. Such bodies are thus fundamentally at odds with themselves. On the one hand, they are inert and so preserve the state of motion that results from external determination; on the other hand, however, their very own gravity *outweighs* their inertia and causes them to seek unity with the largest mass in their vicinity; that is, the planet or moon to which they belong.

In pre-inertial physics, bodies come to rest on the earth because a moving force has *ceased* to be applied to them. In Newton's physics, bodies moving under their own inertia can only be brought to rest *by* an external force. In Hegel's view, by contrast, finite bodies moving under their own inertia eventually come to rest on the earth's surface due to their *own gravity*: 'all motion that has been communicated to us passes over . . . into rest through gravity'.[103] Since bodies resting on the earth continue to seek their 'centre' within the earth, they necessarily exert pressure on its surface and on any other bodies lying underneath them. Their state of rest is thus not one of pure rest, but is in fact 'attempted motion which makes itself felt in another mass'.[104]

Hegel not only argues that a body's gravity always works to overcome its inertia. He goes further and contends that 'gravitation directly *contradicts* the law of inertia'.[105] His reason for claiming this is easy to see. In so far as a body is inert, it 'perseveres' in its state of motion and so may be said to preserve its *identity* – an identity that has been conferred on it by an external cause but has now become its own. This is why Hegel maintains that the principle of inertia rests on the 'principle of identity': inertia is the 'endeavour [*Bestreben*] to make this rest and this motion identical with itself'. Through its inherent gravity, by contrast, 'matter strives to get away *out of itself* to an Other'.[106] Gravity is thus matter's intrinsic endeavour to *lose* its identity in a union with other matter.

Popper derides Hegel's alleged proof that 'Newton's theories of inertia and of gravity *contradict* one another', pointing out that Hegel 'could not foresee that Einstein would show the *identity* of inert and gravitating mass'.[107] But Popper misunderstands Hegel's position. As we have seen, Hegel does acknowledge the identity of inert and gravitating mass (though whether Hegel's conception of this identity exactly coincides with that of Einstein is for others to decide). All inert matter, for Hegel, has an inherent tendency to gravitate towards other matter. Precisely for this reason, however, inert matter is not purely inert. Inertness is merely one aspect – an 'abstract moment' – of gravitating matter.[108] Furthermore, the inertness of matter is constantly negated by the very gravity from which it is inseparable. Indeed, as I have pointed out, a body's gravity eventually outweighs its inertia and brings it to rest on the earth. A body's inertness is thus identical with and at odds with its gravity at one and the same time.

Note that gravity and inertness are not equal partners in the constitution of matter. The inertness of matter stems from the particular fact that matter takes the form of a finite mass whose state of motion is determined by other material bodies. Gravity, by contrast, is inherent in *matter as such*. It is the very substance of matter itself. This allows us to clarify further the difference between Hegel and Newton.

For Newton, inertia is the only 'inherent force' in matter.[109] That is to say, matter is most properly itself when it is moving under its own inertia. Its essence consists, therefore, in preserving the *identity* – the state of motion – that has been given to it by an external force. Accordingly, gravity is to be understood as causing matter to deviate from its proper path of uniform, rectilinear, inertial motion. For Hegel, by contrast, matter is most properly itself precisely when it is *gravitating* towards other matter. Its essence consists, therefore, not in trying to preserve its own identity, but in seeking to reach a point of absolute union with something *else*. Newton, of course, also understands matter to act on, and be acted on by, other matter. For Hegel, however, such interaction is not just an unexplained given fact about matter: matter is inherently relational and 'other-directed' *within itself*.

Despite this difference, Hegel and Newton clearly offer similar accounts of the interactions between finite terrestrial bodies (and between similar bodies on other planets and moons). Both understand the motion of such bodies to be explicable through the combination of their own inertia and the effect of gravity. As the two thinkers continue, however, the differences between them become more marked. Newton claims that the motion of planets and satellites is also due to the combination of inertia and gravity. Hegel, by contrast, argues that the motion of celestial bodies, such as planets, is produced by matter's inherent gravity *alone*. The same is true, he contends, of the *free fall* of finite bodies.

Falling Bodies and Galileo's Law

In so far as matter is inert (*träge*), it is simply the 'bearer' (*Träger*) of states of motion that have been caused by external impact.[110] In so far as matter inherently gravitates towards other matter, however, it is the source of its own motion. The first form of *purely* gravitational motion, Hegel maintains, is *free fall*.

A body in free fall has not been given its speed and direction by the impact of another body, but simply falls of its own accord to the ground. It determines itself to fall through its inherent propensity to gravitate towards other matter. Its fall is *free*, therefore, because it is 'the manifestation of the body's own gravity'. Strictly speaking, as Hegel points out, free fall is only '*relatively free*' or '*conditioned*' motion, because it is contingent upon a body's first being raised to a certain height and then dropped. The fall of a body is thus not wholly determined by gravity alone. Nevertheless, after the body has been lifted up from the ground it does not need to be pushed into motion but, when released, sets itself in motion. Its *fall* as such is therefore quite free.[111]

Since a body falls through its own gravity, however, its free fall is also necessary. It cannot but fall because of its inherent gravity. Hegel argues that two further aspects of free fall are also determined, and so made necessary, by gravity: (1) the fact that free fall is not simply inertial motion but uniformly *accelerating* motion and (2) the fact that it obeys Galileo's law of fall, which states that 'the distance traveled is proportional to the square of the time elapsed'.[112]

According to Galileo's law, Hegel explains, if 'the body falls a little more than 15 [Parisian] feet in the first second', then 'in two seconds, the body falls, not twice but four times the distance, i.e. 60 feet; in three seconds it falls 9×15 feet, and so on'. This law, we are told, counts among the 'immortal discoveries' of natural science that 'redound to the greatest honour of the analysis of the understanding'.[113] Hegel contends, however, that the logical necessity of this law has never been properly demonstrated.

This is not to say that no *a priori* proof of Galileo's law has ever been developed: Hegel recognizes that such a proof has been provided by mathematics. He considers such a proof, however, to fall short of what is demanded by philosophy. This is because the mathematical proof of Galileo's law 'rests on the presupposition that the velocity of a falling body is *uniformly* accelerated', but does not explain why this should be the case. Hegel also claims that mathematics derives Galileo's law from the phenomenon of uniformly accelerated motion via the 'detour' (*Umweg*) of equating the latter with 'purely uniform velocity'.[114] In this way it effaces the distinctive *qualitative* difference between free fall and uniform inertial motion that philosophy wishes to preserve.

It is hard to tell from Hegel's own account precisely what it is about the mathematical proof of Galileo's law that prompts him to make this second claim. This is because he does not examine that proof in detail. A brief statement of the proof will, however, reveal what Hegel has in mind. Note that the proof establishes Galileo's law by considering the distance covered in a given time by an object *accelerating* uniformly from rest to a final velocity to be the same as the distance covered in that time by an object moving uniformly *without* acceleration at half that final velocity. The proof proceeds as follows:

1 The distance (s) travelled in uniform motion is equal to the velocity (v) multiplied by the time (t). A body thus covers 10 metres by going 5 m/s for 2 seconds:

$$s = v \times t$$

2 The final velocity (v_{final}) of a body *accelerating* uniformly from rest (such as a falling body) is equal to the rate of acceleration (a) multiplied by the time elapsed (t). A body accelerating at 5 m/s per second for 4 seconds thus reaches a final velocity of 20 m/s:

$$v_{final} = a \times t$$

3 The average velocity ($v_{average}$) of a body *accelerating* uniformly from rest is half of its final velocity. A body accelerating uniformly from 0 m/s to 20 m/s will thus travel with an average velocity of 10 m/s (where this average velocity is, of course, uniform):

$$v_{average} = \frac{1}{2}v_{final}$$

4 The distance (s) covered by travelling at this uniform average velocity is found by multiplying the velocity by the time elapsed (see 1, above). So travelling at an average velocity of 10 m/s for 4 seconds carries a body 40 metres:

$$s = v_{average} \times t$$

5 Since the average velocity of a body *accelerating* uniformly from rest is equal to half of its final velocity, we can replace $v_{average}$ in the previous equation with $^1/_2 v_{final}$ to determine the distance covered by such a uniformly accelerating body:

$$s = \frac{1}{2}v_{final} \times t$$

6 Since the final velocity of a body *accelerating* uniformly from rest is equal to the rate of acceleration (a) multiplied by the time elapsed (t), we can replace v_{final} in the previous equation with $a \times t$. The distance covered by a body accelerating uniformly from rest is thus found by multiplying the rate of acceleration by the time elapsed, then multiplying by the time elapsed again, and then dividing by half. So a body accelerating at 5 m/s per second for 4 seconds will cover a distance of 40 metres:

$$s = \frac{1}{2}a \times t \times t$$

or:

$$s = \frac{1}{2}at^2$$

7 Since the rate of acceleration of a *uniformly* accelerating body (such as a falling body) is by definition constant, the distance travelled by such a body is necessarily proportional to the square of the time elapsed, as Galileo's law states. A stone that falls with a rate of acceleration of 9.8 m/s per second increases its velocity from 0 m/s to 9.8 m/s in the first second. It thus travels at an average velocity in that first second of 4.9 m/s and so covers 4.9 metres. However, 'in two seconds, *twice* the time, it moves *four* times the distance, or 19.6 meters; and in *three* seconds it moves *nine* times as far, or 44 meters'.[115]

There are two things to note about this proof. First, it simply *assumes* that free fall is uniformly accelerated motion. Second, the distance travelled by a uniformly accelerating body is computed by finding the average velocity of that body and so equating it with a body that does not accelerate but *moves uniformly*. This involves precisely the 'detour' of 'treating velocity as purely uniform velocity' to which Hegel refers.

A cursory glance at the text of Hegel's *Philosophy of Nature* can leave the impression that he wants to replace this 'indirect' proof of Galileo's law of fall with a new mathematical proof of his own. Yet this impression is misleading: Hegel does not presume here to reform mathematics. It is true that he considers the mathematical manner of proving Galileo's law to be 'tortuous'. He never states, however, that it is formally invalid. On the contrary, he acknowledges that the detours of mathematics are 'perhaps necessary' and arise from the need to make what mathematics analyses 'more amenable to mathematical treatment, e.g. to reduce it to addition or subtraction or multiplication'.[116]

At one point Hegel does present, in a quasi-mathematical form, a 'simple, genuine proof' of Galileo's law that dispenses with the above mentioned 'detour'. This proof, however, is not designed to be an alternative *mathematical* proof of Galileo's law. It is meant to establish the *conceptual* point that Galileo's law is built into the very 'definition' of uniformly accelerated motion itself.[117] It aims to show that, *if* one starts from the assumption that free fall is uniformly accelerated motion, there is a much more direct route to Galileo's law than that provided by mathematics.

Hegel's principal concern, however, is not with this 'simple, genuine proof'. It is to present a different, properly *philosophical* proof of Galileo's law of fall. Such a proof must derive Galileo's law directly from the phenomenon of free fall itself. In the process it must demonstrate what both mathematics and Hegel's own 'simple, genuine proof' take for granted, namely that free fall is, indeed, uniformly *accelerated* motion. In addition, of course, it must avoid equating such motion with uniform inertial motion in the manner of mathematics. Hegel's philosophical proof will not supplant that provided by mathematics, but will – if successful – complement it. To understand this philosophical proof of Galileo's law, we need to bear the following things in mind.

The reason why matter must move at all is that, logically, it is exclusive space that endures throughout the *changing of place*. What makes it necessary for place to change is the fact that it is the unity of space and time: if space and time are to be truly united, the process whereby place 'negates itself' *temporally* must be identical with the process of its *spatial* self-negation. This means that as place passes through time, it must also change into *another place* – and another and another – and so *move* through space. Space and time in turn must form such a unity because the nature of each renders it inseparable from the other. Ultimately, therefore, the ground of matter's motion is to be found in the nature of space and time themselves.

Ordinary inertial motion has a further, more immediate cause: the initial impact of another body. Such motion is thus not generated by space and time alone. Free fall, however, is different. It is motion caused solely by gravity; that is, by matter's inherent propensity to move towards a centre. Since matter and its gravity are themselves made necessary by the very nature of space and time, the same must be true of free fall. What makes bodies fall is ultimately the nature of space and time themselves.

Now all motion involves a *quantitative* relation between space and time: a certain quantity of space is covered in a certain quantity of time. In ordinary, inertial motion that relation is contingent: the body may move 5 metres in 1 second, 2 seconds or 3, depending (in part) on the velocity of the last object that *happened* to strike it. In free fall, in Hegel's view, that relation is not just contingent but necessary. Free fall is not caused by the impact of other bodies but is generated solely by gravity and, ultimately, by the very nature of space and time. According to Hegel, therefore, the quantitative relation between space and time in free fall must also be determined by the nature of space and time. As Hegel himself puts it, 'their *quantitative determinations* [must] conform to their conceptual determinations'. This is not quite as obscure an idea as it may appear at first sight. Hegel's point is really quite simple: if we examine the logical structure or *quality* of space and time', we will find the key to the *quantitative* relation in which they must stand in free fall, because the latter is itself grounded in the former.[118]

One further point needs emphasis. Motion, matter, gravity and free fall are made necessary by the unity of space and time, but that unity is itself made necessary by the *different* logical structures of space and time themselves. It is the difference between space and time, as much as their unity, therefore, that is ultimately responsible for the fact that bodies fall: this, I think, is what Hegel has in mind when he says that in the generation of free fall 'time and space ... become *free* in regard to each other'.[119] Those *different* logical structures must thus also determine the quantitative relation between space and time in free fall. This means, in Hegel's view, that space and time in free fall cannot just be represented by a different quantum or number. Each one must be represented by a different *kind* of quantity that expresses its particular quality. We will now consider precisely what this means.[120]

Time, we recall, is the pure negativity or 'passing away' of space, and as such it differentiates itself into the three 'dimensions' of past, present and future. Only *one* of those dimensions, however, actually exists: the endlessly vanishing (yet enduring) present. Time, therefore, is the negativity that constitutes the singularity and unity of the now. This logical *quality* of time determines the kind of *quantity* that will be associated with time in free fall. As Hegel writes: 'seeing that *time* is the moment of *negation*, of being-for-self, the principle of the One [*Eins*], its magnitude (any empirical number) in relation to space is to be taken as the unit [*Einheit*] or denominator'. Free fall will thus be motion in which a certain distance is traversed in a given *unit* of time, where this unit is an immediately given number (1 second, 1 minute, and so on). From this point of view, therefore, free fall looks no different from inertial motion, and Hegel does not appear to be saying anything especially remarkable. Things get more interesting, however, when he turns to space.

Space, Hegel reminds us, is sheer 'externality' (*Außereinandersein*). Indeed, it is *self*-externality: being that expands beyond itself, but in so doing merely extends *itself* beyond itself. As is the case with time, this quality of space determines the kind of quantity that will be associated with space in free fall: that quantity must also be one that 'comes outside itself' (is '*außer sich kommend*'). Hegel understands this to mean that such a quantity must increase itself *by itself*; that is, through its own agency and by an amount that is equal to itself. Such a quantity, he explains, cannot be a simple unit or number, but must be a *square* (*Quadrat*). Note that Hegel does not consider the square of a number to be merely a different *quantum* from the number itself. He regards the square – and, indeed, every 'power' – to be an altogether different *kind* or *quality* of quantity from a simple number. It is the particular kind of quantity that *determines itself by itself*. As such, it perfectly reflects the distinctive logical character of space: 'the form of the externality of space ... is the *square*: magnitude as *coming out of itself*, raising itself into a second dimension and thus expanding itself, but *solely in accordance with its own* determinateness'.

In free fall, therefore, a certain quantity of space, or distance, will be travelled in a given time. In contrast to what occurs in the case of inertial motion, however, that distance will necessarily be represented by the square of a given number. But what number is to be squared? This, Hegel claims, is determined not by the quality or logical structure of time or space taken separately, but by the fact that free fall is the *unity* of space and time.

In uniform inertial motion, as was noted above, space (or distance) and time are contingently related: neither the magnitude of the distance covered nor the magnitude of the time involved is determined by the other. In free fall, by contrast, space and time stand in a logically determined, *necessary* relation to one another. *Given* the quantity of one, therefore, the other *must* have a corresponding quantity. Indeed, Hegel claims, the *given* quantity of the one itself dictates the corresponding quantity of the other, so that both together 'form a *single* determination'. As we have seen, it is time whose quantity necessarily takes the form of a given unit in free fall. It is the magnitude of the time, therefore, which must dictate the magnitude of the distance that is travelled. Consequently, the distance or space travelled in a given time must be determined by squaring the *time* that has elapsed: $s = t^2$. If a body falls y metres in 1 second, the distance it travels in 2 seconds is not $y \times 2$ but $y \times 2^2$ or $4y$ metres and the distance covered in 3 seconds is $y \times 3^2$ or $9y$ metres. 'This', Hegel writes, 'is the proof of the law of descent of a falling body as derived from the concept of the matter'.[121]

Since the distance travelled in free fall necessarily increases in a regular manner from one unit of time to another, free fall must be uniformly *accelerated* motion. Hegel thus proves what mathematics took for granted. Indeed, by deriving the law governing free fall from the very quality of space and time themselves, he demonstrates that uniformly accelerated motion is 'the living motion of nature conforming to law' – the form of motion that is inherent in freely gravitating matter itself.[122] In this way Hegel also shows that there is a clear *qualitative* difference between uniformly accelerated motion and uniform inertial motion (even though in the mathematical proof considered above they are treated as equivalent): for in the former, but not in the latter, the magnitudes of space and time stand in a *necessary* relation to one another.

Note, however, that Hegel's argument does not establish the specific *rate* of acceleration of any falling body. That varies from one planet or satellite to another and, from the perspective of philosophy, is a wholly *contingent*, empirical relation between given quantities of distance and time: on earth, for example, bodies fall with a rate of acceleration of 9.8 m/s per second, whereas on the moon they fall with a rate of 1.6 m/s per second.[123] What Hegel's proof establishes is the general point that, regardless of the planet one inhabits, free fall *must* be uniformly accelerated motion in which the distance covered is proportional to the square of the time.

Free fall is the form of motion that is generated by the gravity or propensity to move inherent in matter itself. The fact that an object falls when released is thus due simply to its being a unit of gravitating matter – a weighted material object as such – not to its having an especially large mass or weight. Since all material objects are *equally* material, all gravitate or fall towards the earth in the same way. This means that they all fall to earth at the same rate of acceleration, *regardless of their mass*. Furthermore their fall is in every case governed by the same law, since that law is determined by the distinctive qualities of space and time that are constituents of every material object. Hegel thus endorses Galileo's famous theory of falling bodies:

where the motion is posited by the Concept of matter, the quantitative difference between bodies has no significance; bodies fall simply as matter, not as masses. In other words, bodies fall simply on account of their gravity, and in this respect a large body and a smaller one, i.e. one smaller in weight, are equally heavy [*schwer*].

Or, rather, all bodies fall to earth at the same rate in those cases where air resistance can be discounted, since some objects, such as feathers, are slowed down by the air as they fall: 'we are well aware that a feather does not fall like a lead bullet; but this is on account of the medium which has to give way. . . . In a vacuum, however, bodies fall in the same manner [*auf gleiche Weise*].'[124]

The velocity of a terrestrial body whose state of motion has been altered by the impact of another body depends in part on the strength of that impact and in part on the mass (or weight) of the body whose motion is altered. By contrast, the velocity of a body falling freely through its own gravity towards the earth depends on the height from which it has been dropped and (discounting air resistance) is independent of the mass of the body. Free fall thus represents, as it were, the liberation of a material body from the contingencies of its own mass.

Free fall, however, is not independent of mass altogether, for the mass of the planet or moon to which the falling bodies belong determines the *direction* of their fall. Hegel accepts the idea that all bodies gravitate towards all others and that bodies gravitate most strongly towards the largest mass in their vicinity, that is, the planet or moon that serves as their 'central body': 'the universal gravitation, which [dependent bodies] as matter have towards one another, is subordinate to that which they have towards their common central body'.[125] Such a central body does not 'attract' other bodies towards itself, but those bodies gravitate towards that central body of their own accord. Terrestrial bodies thus fall down towards the earth, rather than up towards a passing asteroid, because they have an intrinsic 'tendency to move in the direction of the greatest mass'.[126] Nevertheless, the direction in which bodies fall is not determined solely by the bodies themselves, but is dictated precisely by the large mass of their central body. This represents another sense, therefore, in which free fall is 'conditioned' and so only relatively free.

Hegel does not draw attention to the fact that, strictly speaking, the inverse square law that underlies Newton's theory of universal gravitation is at odds with Galileo's law of fall. The tension between the two stems from the fact that 'Galileo has the object fall with constant acceleration (that is, with a uniformly accelerated motion), whereas Newton has the body fall under the action of a variable force and a consequent variable acceleration'.[127] Hegel would reject the idea that objects fall under the action of a 'force', since he takes them to fall freely. None the less, he accepts the inverse square law and might be expected to notice the tension between it and Galileo's law. Newton's law, however, only conflicts with Galileo's law at some distance from the surface of a central body. Near the surface of such a central body, where the rate of acceleration is effectively constant, Galileo's law holds for all falling bodies, as Newton himself acknowledged.[128] This may well be why Hegel neglects to mention the tension between the two laws: for him, the law of fall applies *only* to what he calls 'finite bodies' on or near the surface of a central body. It applies to bodies that actually *belong* to the central body itself, but are lifted from its surface and then released. Celestial bodies, such as planets and moons, do not, in his view, *fall* towards one another – at least, not in the sense of dropping *freely* towards another body from a position of rest relative to it.[129]

Hegel states that his aim is to show how Galileo's law of fall is 'connected to [*zusammenhängt mit*] the determinations of the Concept'. This suggests to commentators such as Kalenberg and Buchdahl that Hegel's proof of that law presupposes that the law itself has already been discovered and provides a philosophical 'reconstruction' of it.[130] I am in broad agreement with these commentators: without Galileo's discovery Hegel would not, I think, have been able to deduce the law of fall purely by himself. None the less, Hegel describes his proof as a 'deduction of this law' and clearly regards it as *a priori*.[131] To my mind, therefore, Hegel's proof of Galileo's particular law – unlike his proofs that space is temporal, that matter entails gravity and that finite bodies fall freely towards a central body – must be regarded as an example of a strict, logical derivation whose presentation was actually made possible by an *empirical* discovery by science.

Not all readers will be equally impressed by Hegel's proof. Some may find it elegant and persuasive, others will no doubt think it contrived. This proof, however, is a crucial part of Hegel's philosophical mechanics (or kinematics). Hegel's overall purpose in this mechanics is to show that matter is necessarily in *motion* without being governed by alleged 'forces', such as the 'force of gravity'. The importance of the philosophical proof of Galileo's law of fall, for Hegel, is that it demonstrates that gravitational matter itself – and its constituents, space and time – makes one particular form of motion necessary, namely uniformly accelerated motion. Such motion, therefore, is not a mere accident of nature, but is rather nature's '*essential* motion'.[132]

Hegel's proof also demonstrates that, in determining itself to move in this way, nature – or matter – gives itself its own *law*. Nature as space is sheer lifeless externality; but in giving rise to the law of fall – 'a *free* law of nature' – nature proves to be self-determining and *autonomous*.[133] The necessary logical transition from inertial motion to free fall thus represents the emergence of *freedom* in nature in two senses: objects come to be understood as moving freely through their own gravity, but matter itself also becomes freely self-determining by determining through its own logical structure how it is to move. (Such free self-determination is, of course, at the same time necessary self-determination.)

This is why I have devoted more space than one might have expected to Hegel's account of falling bodies. Hegel is well known as the philosopher of 'ethical life' or 'the cunning of reason', but not many realize that he also sees tremendous importance in the phenomenon of free fall (and is a strong admirer of Galileo). This is because in the simple fall of a book from a ledge, we can see nature make its first humble move towards becoming free, self-determining *spirit*.[134]

The Solar System

We have seen that matter differentiates itself into finite bodies. These bodies gravitate towards, and so weigh down on, their central body – a planet or moon – in proportion to their mass. Such bodies also fall freely towards their central body at a uniform rate of acceleration that is independent of their mass or weight. They do this, however, only after they have been raised to a certain height and then released. In such a case, the body's fall is due to gravity alone, but the condition of that fall, 'namely, [the body's] distance from the centre . . . is not posited by gravity'.[135] Hegel now goes on to argue that matter must also set itself at a certain distance from itself *through its very own gravity*. In this way, he claims, matter will become absolutely free, because its motion towards others and its separation from others will both be determined wholly by matter's inherent nature.

Yet why should gravity itself – which is the motion of matter towards other matter – put *distance* between matter and matter? Because, as we saw earlier, gravity is not mere attraction but the unity of attraction *and* repulsion. In Hegel's view, this means two different things. First, bodies gravitate towards and simultaneously repel other bodies that are *already* distinct from them, such as we see in the phenomena of weight and free fall. Second, however, matter's gravitational attraction towards other matter is *itself* what separates matter into different, mutually repelling bodies. But how is this latter possible?

It is possible if, in the very process of moving towards its centre, matter simultaneously sets itself apart from – and in that sense, *repels* – other matter moving towards another centre. This in turn, however, requires that centre-oriented matter split itself into the manifold processes of gravitating towards *different* centres. Each such centre will be surrounded by the matter that seeks it and so will constitute the core of a massive 'central body'. Matter can only be the explicit unity of attraction and repulsion, therefore, if it differentiates itself into many different central bodies, each of which is separated from the others by empty space: 'this is real repulsion where the centre repels itself, multiplies itself'. These *primary* central bodies, which are made necessary by the nature of gravity itself, are the *stars*.[136]

Hegel maintains, however, that stars do not manifest the unity of attraction and repulsion in its most explicit form. This is because stars do not exhibit, by virtue of their very nature, a fully explicit *attraction for one another*. Although each star contains within itself a centre towards which matter gravitates and to which that matter is thus 'attracted', 'the host of stars is a formal world' in which 'the one-sided determination of repulsion holds sway'. The stars are thus dispersed throughout the heavens as an 'abstract multiplicity' of separate, independent centres.[137]

This is not to say that stars do not exhibit any attraction for one another at all. Hegel accepts Newton's principle of universal gravitation and, following Sir William Herschel, points out that stars cluster into 'groupings' (*Figurationen*) which 'may express essential relations'. He notes in particular that the stars in the Milky Way are thought to 'form the shape of a lens'.[138] In his view, however, such groupings do not provide evidence of an inherent, fully *explicit* attraction between stars. A body is attracted to another when it seeks to unite with, and so to find its centre in, that other body; and such attraction is fully explicit when the first body actually changes its position and *moves* in relation to the second. Hegel, however, does not believe that stars seek to unite with other stars in this explicit way, but he understands them to remain at rest in relation to one another.

Ihmig calls Hegel's assumption that all stars are at rest relative to one another a 'weak point' of his argumentation.[139] Especially problematic for Hegel's account is the phenomenon of binary stars which move in separate orbits around a common centre of mass.[140] Such stars are not discussed by Hegel himself, but they were known during his lifetime and would appear to exhibit an explicit attraction for one another of precisely the kind Hegel denies to stars. In my view, however, Hegel would have considered such stars to be *contingencies* from the philosophical point of view. For Hegel, stars are made necessary by the fact that matter must *repel* itself from itself and coalesce around different gravitational centres. Logically, therefore, stars 'belong to the sphere of dead repulsion'.[141] This means that, for philosophy at least, it is inherent in the nature of stars that they stand *apart* from one another as separate worlds, but not that they join together in an orbital dance of mutual attraction around a common centre of mass. The fact that many stars are binaries engaged in just such a dance may well be the necessary result of circumstances in the natural history of galaxies and stars. It is not grounded, however, in the inherent, logical nature of stars themselves and in this respect is contingent.

This has one very important consequence. Since gravitational matter is the unity of repulsion and attraction, it must differentiate itself into central bodies whose inherent nature is both to repel *and* to be explicitly attracted to other such bodies. Stars fail to satisfy this logical requirement fully by themselves. Logically, therefore, there must exist, in addition to stars, other central bodies whose nature is precisely to seek to unite with a central body beyond themselves. These inherently 'attractive' central bodies are *planets*. Planets are thus not an accident of nature, for Hegel, but a logical necessity. They are central bodies that keep their distance from one another but that also openly seek their centre in *another* central body.

If matter is to be a true *unity* of repulsion and attraction, however, stars and planets cannot exist in splendid isolation from one another but must themselves form a unity. The character of this unity follows from the respective characters of stars and planets. Stars are the primary central bodies or 'absolutely *universal* centrality'; planets, by contrast, are inherently secondary or 'relative' central bodies.[142] Their unity must thus consist in planets relating to, and seeking their centre in, a star. Planets, in other words, must belong to a star and, together with that star or *sun*, form a system of central bodies or a *solar system*.

For Hegel, therefore, stars and planets are logically inseparable: 'the centre has no meaning without the periphery nor the periphery without the centre'.[143] This is not to deny that, as a matter of contingency, stars could exist without planets. The nature of gravitational matter, however, demands that there be stars with their own planetary systems, since only in this way can matter be the true unity of repulsion and attraction. Solar systems – and Hegel recognizes that ours is not necessarily the only one – are thus more rational than isolated stars (or binary stars). Indeed, for Hegel, every solar system is simply 'the system of reason as a reality in the heavens'.[144]

Yet a fully rational solar system is not composed solely of a star (or sun) and its planets. Stars and planets both enclose centres of gravitational attraction and so are central bodies. A star is an absolutely central body: it 'has its centre absolutely within itself' and so does not explicitly seek its centre in another body.[145] It serves, instead, as a centre of gravitational attraction *for* other bodies, namely the planets. This reflects the fact that the star embodies the logical moment of repulsion above all. Planets, by contrast, are *relative* central bodies, since they do explicitly seek their centre in another body, namely in their star. This reflects the fact that they embody more overtly than do the stars the logical moment of attraction. Yet planets are also relative *central bodies* and so have a 'centre' in themselves as well as in their star. As such they embody the logical moment of repulsion just as much as that of attraction, and so can also serve as centres of gravitational attraction for other celestial bodies. But what other celestial bodies are made necessary by the logical structure of gravity, except stars and planets? Hegel's answer is: bodies in which the logical moment of attraction *outweighs* that of repulsion (just as repulsion outweighs attraction in the stars).

In such bodies, the logical moment of repulsion is suppressed but not eliminated altogether, so they remain 'independent' (*selbständig*) bodies, separated by empty space from both the planets and their sun.[146] As such, they serve as central bodies for the 'finite' objects that belong to them: objects that weigh down upon them or fall towards them. They do not, however, serve as central bodies for other independent celestial bodies and so do not have a centre within themselves in the same sense as planets and stars. This is because they are defined primarily by their attraction for and relation to *other* bodies. Despite their 'apparently free existence', such bodies are thus thoroughly *dependent* celestial bodies; and their dependence is evident in the fact that they seek their centre in the two kinds of central body that inhabit the solar system: the planets and the sun.[147] The dependent bodies that are gravitationally oriented towards the planets are satellites or *moons*, and those that are oriented towards the sun are *comets*. Hegel contends, therefore, that both moons and comets – as well as planets and a sun – are logically necessary if a solar system is to embody fully the unity of repulsion and attraction inherent in gravitating matter. 'First of all, we have the absolute, central body, then dependent bodies without a centre in themselves, and lastly, relative central bodies. It is only with these three kinds of bodies that the system of gravity is completed into a totality.' Or, as Hegel puts it a little later, in recognition of the fact that moons and comets constitute two different types of 'dependent' celestial body, 'this quadruplicity [*Vierheit*] of the celestial bodies forms the complete system of rational corporeality'.[148]

Hegel began his philosophy of nature with the concept of sheer externality or space. He then demonstrated that space gives rise to time and that both together make motion and matter necessary. The substance of matter was then shown to be gravitational motion: the motion of seeking to unite with other matter that it simultaneously repels. This gravitational motion (or propensity to move) initially took the form of weight and free fall. Now we have seen that matter's inherent gravity requires that there be solar systems. This is because in the system of interrelated, independent celestial bodies matter fully manifests both its gravitational attraction towards and repulsion of other matter.

It is important to recognize, however, that Hegel is not telling a story here about the natural history of solar systems: he is not arguing that first stars are created *in time*, then planets and then moons and comets. The connections established by Hegel between these celestial bodies are logical, not temporal. It is up to natural scientists to explore the role that gravity (and perhaps collisions between celestial bodies) may play in the actual genesis of our solar system. Hegel's philosophy shows only that, whatever natural causes produce solar systems, these systems also meet the demands of reason. In this sense, philosophy demonstrates that reason is, indeed, at work in nature, operating through the natural causes discerned by science.

Kepler's Laws of Planetary Motion

For Hegel, gravitating matter is matter in motion. The solar system, which is produced by gravity, is thus a system of *moving* bodies. From the perspective of philosophical mechanics, indeed, nothing else about celestial bodies needs to be taken into account: what makes the sun and the planets different kinds of gravitating body is not the physical fact that the sun is a source of light whereas the planets are not, but the simple mechanical fact that they *move* in different ways. In Hegel's view, the character of celestial motion and the laws governing it are determined by the inherent gravity of matter itself in much the same way as free fall and Galileo's law.

Stars have their centres within themselves and do not (as a matter of logical necessity) explicitly seek their centres in another body. Accordingly, their essential nature is not to move, but to remain at rest, in relation to one another and to the planets. As material, gravitational bodies, of course, they cannot be absolutely immobile. Their motion, for Hegel, is, however, restricted to rotation around their *own* axis. Planets, by contrast, are not so unambiguously self-contained. This finds expression in the fact that 'they seek their centre' outside themselves and so always 'leave their place and occupy another one'. Planets, therefore, are necessarily in motion in relation to their sun.[149]

Planets, however, not only actively seek their centre within the sun, but also remain irreducibly independent of the sun. This finds expression in the fact that in their motion they preserve their distance from the sun and do not fall towards it. Accordingly, Hegel argues, planets move in an endless orbit *around* the sun, for only in this way can they show that they are both bound to the sun and free: 'in altering their position at various distances from one another they describe a curve and return into themselves. For it is only in this way that they express their independence in regard to the central body; just as their unity with the central body finds expression in their motion round it in this same curve.'[150] Similarly, comets must orbit the sun and moons must orbit their respective planets, because they, too, are independent bodies that explicitly seek to unite with a central body outside themselves.[151]

The orbital motion of the planets is thus made necessary by the fact that they are *attracted* to yet also set themselves apart from, and so *repel*, their sun. Planets combine explicit attraction and repulsion in this way because they are the most perfect and concrete embodiment of *gravitational* motion. What causes planets to orbit their sun, therefore, is nothing but gravity itself. In Hegel's view, the characteristic motion of the planets does not arise due to the impact of other bodies or the 'pull' of an external centripetal force; rather, matter *determines itself* – through its inherent gravity – to move in a closed orbit around a central body. Planetary motion is thus not only necessary but also '*absolutely free motion*'. It is the closed, curvilinear motion that is intrinsic to the planets themselves.[152]

Hegel maintains that the laws governing planetary motion are also determined by the inherent gravity of matter. These laws were discovered by Johannes Kepler in the seventeenth century and, in Hegel's words, concern 'the shape of the orbit and the velocity of the motion'. They are usually stated as follows:

1st Law: each planet moves in its own elliptical orbit around the sun, with the sun at one of the two foci.
2nd Law: an imaginary line joining the sun to a planet moving in its orbit around the sun sweeps out equal areas in equal times.
3rd Law: the squares of the orbital periods of any two planets are proportional to the cubes of their distances from the sun.[153]

Hegel notes that 'Kepler discovered his laws empirically by induction, based on the investigations of Tycho Brahe', but he believes that they can also be derived *a priori* from the nature of gravitational matter. He admits, however, that 'the difficulty of the task is such that this has not yet been fully accomplished'.[154] Hegel's proofs of Kepler's laws – like his proof of Galileo's law of fall – are, in my view, *a priori* proofs whose presentation is made possible by a prior *empirical* discovery. In this case, however, Hegel openly admits that he did not work out those proofs as fully as he would have liked to.

Kepler's laws are to be derived from the very nature of gravitational matter. From the mechanical point of view, however, matter is essentially motion. Motion in turn is generated by the unity of space and time; that is, by place negating itself into another place and then another in time. To derive the laws of motion from the nature of gravitational matter is, therefore, to derive them from the nature of space and time that ultimately give rise to matter. More specifically, philosophy must show how the distinctive *qualities* of space and time determine the *quantitative* relations between space and time in planetary motion.[155] The derivation of Kepler's first law proceeds as follows.

Planets move in a closed orbit around their sun, so their motion is either circular or elliptical. When a body moves in a circular orbit, Hegel claims, it covers equal arcs of the orbit in equal times. The magnitude of the space – that is, the arc – travelled in a given time thus always remains the same and, in this sense, the body orbits with a uniform velocity. Hegel recognizes that a circular orbit could conceivably be produced by a body accelerating and decelerating over the course of its orbit, but he regards such a possibility as a 'superficial' product of 'abstract imagination'.[156] In Hegel's view, there is nothing about circular orbital motion as such that requires it to involve acceleration, and it is more rational to conceive it as motion generated by covering equal arcs in equal times.

Whether one considers circular motion to be the product of uniform or accelerated motion, one thing is clear: regardless of their length, the arcs covered in equal times all have the same curvature and in that sense are all of the same kind. This is because they are all spanned between *radii vectores* of equal length. The *radius vector* is the straight line connecting the orbiting body to its central body, and a circular orbit is defined by the fact that the *radius vector* remains constant throughout the orbit.[157]

Now planetary motion, for Hegel, is *free* motion; that is, motion determined by gravity and, ultimately, by the nature of space and time alone. As we saw in the discussion of falling bodies, however, space and time play *different* roles in the generation of free, gravitational motion: in this sense they remain *free* and *independent* of one another in their very unity. In Hegel's view, this qualitative difference between space and time must determine, and find expression in, their quantitative relation in planetary motion: 'in the motion which is *free*, space and time come to assert themselves as what they are – that is, as *different* – in determining the magnitude of the motion'.[158] But what precisely does this mean? It means that the quantitative relation between space and time in planetary motion must itself be one in which the difference and independence of space from time is clearly evident. Space proves its independence from time by constantly *changing* the relation in which it stands to time in the course of the motion. A planet in orbit around the sun must, therefore, cover *unequal* distances or arcs in *equal* times. Hegel claims that this inequality must be twofold.

First, an orbiting planet must cover arcs of *different lengths* in equal times. This dictates that its velocity cannot be simply uniform, but must be '*uniformly accelerated* (and, as returning into itself, in turn uniformly *retarded*)'.[159] Hegel assumes here that free motion will be *uniformly* – rather than erratically – accelerated or decelerated, because it is self-determining and so (largely) unaffected by contingent factors. He also assumes that this suffices to prove that planetary orbits cannot be circular. Yet by his own admission it is *conceivable* – if only by 'abstract imagination' – that circular orbits can be generated by accelerating (and decelerating) bodies.

Hegel argues, however, that if arcs covered in equal times are to be genuinely unequal and different from one another, they cannot differ in length alone but must also differ 'in their function'. That is to say, they must play different roles in the constitution of the orbit. Arcs of the same orbit perform different functions when they have different *curvature*, and they have different curvature only when they span *radii vectores* of different lengths. It is this fact that proves definitively that the orbit followed by a planet covering unequal arcs in equal times cannot be circular: because the *radii vectores* in a circular orbit are all equal rather than different:

if different arcs are traversed in the same time, then they must differ not only empirically but in regard to their function. . . . The radius – the relation of the circumference to the centre – belongs essentially to the function of an arc. If the arcs differ, then so must the radii too, and thus the Concept of the circle is overcome [*aufgehoben*].[160]

Since planets move freely and continuously around the sun, with uniform acceleration and deceleration rather than in an erratic manner, their *radii vectores* must themselves increase and decrease in a regular way. The orbit followed by any such planet must, therefore, be *elliptical*.

The passage just quoted is taken from the addition to §270 of the *Philosophy of Nature*. In §270 itself Hegel presents his argument in a much more abstract form. As we have just seen, in free planetary motion the magnitudes of space and time are differentiated from one another not only because unequal spaces are covered in equal times but because those unequal spaces are themselves the product of *two* different determinations, namely the arc and the *radius vector*. In §270 Hegel condenses this idea into the following claim: time and space are distinct because time is simply a given magnitude whereas the space covered in that time is the product of a *difference within space itself*: 'in free motion, where the determinations of space and time come together in *diversity*, in a qualitative relation, this relation necessarily emerges in the *element of space* itself, as a *difference* of it, which accordingly demands *two* determinations'. It is this, Hegel maintains, that requires planets to move in elliptical orbits.

It has to be admitted that, taken by itself, Hegel's condensed argument in the lines just quoted is barely intelligible. If we read those lines in conjunction with those from the addition, however, his overall point is clear. The spaces covered in equal times are unequal due to differences in the respective *arcs* that are connected to differences in the respective *radii vectores*. The fact that these *two* determinations together differentiate the spaces from one another – as arcs with different curvature – is what makes planets move in elliptical orbits.

The elliptical orbit is thus the orbit that freely moving celestial bodies are required to follow by space and time themselves. Accordingly, it is inherent in the very nature of gravitating matter. This is not to say that planets can never follow circular orbits, but only that such orbits would be contingent from the philosophical point of view. Nor is it to say that planets will follow *perfectly* elliptical orbits: Hegel admits that 'observation shows that even the ellipse does not exactly correspond to the path of the planets, and so other perturbations must be assumed'. The task of philosophy, however, is simply to show that an elliptical orbit is the *rational* one for planets to follow – the one that is made logically necessary by gravitating matter itself. Accordingly, Hegel declares, 'it will be for future astronomy to decide whether the path has not functions more profound than the ellipse, whether it is not perhaps an oval, etc.'[161]

In contrast to his proof of Galileo's law of fall, Hegel's proof of Kepler's first law does not make direct reference to the specific qualities of space and time; that is, to 'self-externality' and 'negativity'. It rests on the general idea that there is a qualitative difference between space and time and on the claim that in free, planetary motion their respective magnitudes must also be genuinely differentiated. For this reason, in planetary motion *unequal* spaces (or arcs) must be traversed in equal times. Hegel's proof of Kepler's second law does, however, make reference to the particular quality of space, albeit indirectly.

This proof is founded on the idea that space in free motion must not only be differentiated from time but also *united* with time in a single determination. That is to say, space must be proportional to and determined by time. Hegel reminds us that this is also the case in free fall: in such motion, as we recall, the space travelled is proportional to and determined by the square of the time elapsed (so that a body falling *y* metres in 1 second will, in 2 seconds, fall 4*y* metres rather than 2*y* metres). Although the *time* has to be squared in free fall in order to calculate the distance travelled, it is actually the quality of *space* that requires there to be any squaring at all. Space is being that is external to itself and so constantly extends itself beyond itself; it thereby augments itself *by itself*. If this is to be reflected in the magnitude of the space travelled in free fall, that magnitude must also increase itself '*solely in accordance with its own* determinateness' and so be a *square*.[162]

In the free motion of the planets the space that is proportional to the time must also be a 'square', and Hegel's reference back to the law of fall suggests that now, as then, this is due to the quality or logical structure of space. In the case of planetary motion, however, the space concerned will not be proportional to the square of the *time* elapsed but will be a 'squared' *space* in its own right. That is to say, it will be a space that is itself a geometrical 'square'. But what exactly does this mean? It does not mean that the space proportional to and determined by time will have the particular shape of a square as opposed to a triangle or pentagon. It means simply that such a space will be an area or a *plane* – measured in, for example, square kilometres – rather than a mere line. What area will this be? It will be the area that corresponds to the line, or arc, that is covered by the freely orbiting planet.

We have already seen in the proof of Kepler's first law that the arcs traversed in free orbital motion span *radii vectores* of differing lengths. Indeed, the different curvature of each arc is determined by the different *radii vectores* that it connects: 'the arc is in this way essentially a function of the radius vector [*Radiusvektor*]'. Hegel points out that a given arc and its two principal *radii vectores* together 'constitute *a whole*', namely the space that they enclose. This space is 'a space-determination of two dimensions – the *sector*'. It is this sector, Hegel claims, that must be proportional to the time in free orbital motion. This is because such sectors constitute precisely the 'squared space' that must be proportional to time, if space and time are to be united in free motion as *qualitatively* distinct:

That the spatial determination should appear here, by means of time, as a two-dimensional determination – as a *plane* – is connected with what was said above (§267) about the exposition of the same determinateness in fall . . . as space in the *square* [*Quadrat*]. Here, however, the *quadraticity* or *squaredness* [*das Quadratische*] of space is, through the return of the line of motion into itself, confined to the sector.

Since the sectors – as 'squared' space – are directly proportional to the time elapsed, '*equal sectors are swept out in equal times*', as stated in Kepler's second law of motion.[163]

It might seem that there is no more than a superficial verbal connection between the idea of a 'squared' number and a 'squared' space and that Hegel's proof of Kepler's second law is thus spurious. In Hegel's view, however, there is a *logical* connection between the two ideas that goes beyond the fact that the same adjective is used in each case. What connects them is the fact that the specific quality of space requires the space that is proportional to time in free motion to have the following logical structure: it must become *other* than itself but, 'in becoming an Other, [be] related solely to itself'.[164]

Now in free fall the space traversed is one-dimensional: it is the straight line of descent. That space is thus not itself, and cannot ever be, explicitly *self-relating* space, since such space does not arise until the line connects up to itself and forms a two-dimensional plane (as we learn at the start of the philosophy of nature). Accordingly, the space in free fall cannot – *simply through being the space that it is* – satisfy the logical demand to become 'other' than itself and thereby explicitly 'relate to itself' in a given time. This logical demand can only be met if the space or distance covered increases by a *quantum* or *number* that 'becomes other than itself' and in so doing 'relates solely to itself'. Such a number that changes into *another* number purely by itself is, as we have seen, one that is *squared*. Thus, 'in the abstract motion of falling, the squares . . . are only numerical determinations; the square is not to be taken in a spatial sense, because in falling what is traversed is only a straight line. It is this that constitutes the formal element in falling.'[165] Precisely because space is not *itself* explicitly self-relating in free fall, however, it is not the numerical value of the *space* or distance travelled in a given time that is squared. Rather, it is the *time* that is squared, and the distance travelled is thus proportional to the square of the time.

In free orbital motion, by contrast, the space traversed is not merely a straight line but an arc that, together with its *radii vectores*, encloses a whole sector of space. Such a sector is an explicitly *self-relating* space or plane, since it is the product of a line that connects to itself. In free orbital motion, therefore, the logical demand that is made of space is immediately satisfied by space itself: for the space that is proportional to time necessarily 'relates to itself' in 'becoming other than itself' simply by virtue of being a sector rather than a line. For this reason, the space traversed in a given time does not need to increase itself by a squared number: that space is itself already 'squared' through being spatially or geometrically self-relating. And since this squared space does not increase from moment to moment, the sectors swept out in equal times are themselves equal.

This argument is highly abstract and is unlikely to win over all readers. There is no denying, however, that it is logical in Hegel's distinctive sense and, indeed, that it is intelligible even to those who may not be persuaded by it.

As Kalenberg notes, Hegel considers Kepler's third law to be the 'high-point and consummation of mechanics'.[166] Kepler's first law merely determines the shape of the orbit, and the second law merely determines the relation between time and individual sectors swept out by the *radius vector* connecting the planets to the sun. The third law, by contrast, concerns the relation between time and the *orbit as a whole*. More specifically, it concerns the relation between time and the orbit in so far as it is determined by the *distance* of the planet from the sun (which is to say, by the orbit's 'semi-major axis'). The actual circumference of a planet's orbit is dependent both on its semi-major axis and on the degree of its 'eccentricity' – the degree to which the orbit is squashed and elongated.[167] An orbit's eccentricity, however, is, from a philosophical point of view, a matter of contingency: reason determines that such an orbit should be elliptical but not *how* elliptical it should be. A purely rational law will thus relate the time of the orbit not to its actual circumference but to the orbit as determined by the planet's distance from the sun (or the semi-major axis) alone. As Hegel puts it, therefore, Kepler's third law establishes the relation 'of time, . . . as period of revolution, to the magnitude of the path, *or what is the same thing*, to that of the distance from the centre'.[168] In its usual formulation this law states that the squares of the periods of any two planets are proportional to the cubes of their distances from the Sun.

The principal thing to remember here is that the motion of planets around their sun is determined wholly by the gravity inherent in matter. Gravitating matter is itself generated by the nature of space and time. Solar systems arise, therefore, ultimately because space and time freely determine themselves to take the form of such systems. As we have seen, the distinctive logical structures of space and time make it necessary both that planetary orbits are elliptical and that equal sectors are traversed in equal times. They also, however, determine the relation between time and space over the orbit *as a whole*. Indeed, it is in determining this relation that space and time complete the process of their own logical self-determination and so, at last, become *fully self-determining*. This is the key to Hegel's proof of Kepler's third law: for he argues that the *quantitative* relation between space and time in planetary motion must bear witness to the fact that such motion is the product of two fully self-determining phenomena.

Yet how is this possible? It is possible if the quantitative relation between space and time in orbital motion is itself a relation between two fully self-determining magnitudes, rather than between two given magnitudes or between one given magnitude and a 'square'. If this relation is to reflect the qualitative difference between space and time, however, the two magnitudes must determine themselves in different ways in accordance with the respective qualities of space and time.

Time, for Hegel, is sheer negativity: it is the constant vanishing of the present into the past. In the course of this vanishing, however, the *form* of presence is itself preserved: *this* 'now' vanishes, and *this* one, and *this*, but the very form of the 'now' *as such* endures. Time is thus the constant vanishing of space that also produces the *formal unity* of the present. In so doing, time determines *itself* to be a formal unity or continuity. Furthermore, as we have seen, time – as space-time – goes on to determine itself logically to be free orbital motion. If such orbital motion is to bear witness to the fact that it is the product of time's self-determination, then this must be manifest in the magnitude of time in such motion. The magnitude of time must, therefore, also have a 'formal identity with itself' or 'formal relation to itself'. This means that it cannot merely be a simple *given* magnitude, but must be a magnitude that relates to itself, determines itself and so 'produces itself'. As Hegel argues, 'time that relates to itself and is determined by itself can only be time squared'.[169]

As we have seen, the magnitude of space also had to be a square in the law of fall and in Kepler's second law: in the former it had to be a numerical square and in the latter a geometrical square. Hegel now points out, however, that space, in so far as it is *fully* self-determined, is in fact not just a geometrical square but rather a geometrical *cube*. This is because it extends itself beyond itself in *three* different directions. If the magnitude of space in free orbital motion is to bear witness to the fact that such motion is the product of space's self-determination (as space-time), then that magnitude must itself be a cube. It cannot itself, however, be a *geometrical* cube, since the planet in the course of its orbit remains in the same plane. That magnitude must, therefore, be a numerical cube: the cube of the planet's whole orbit or – 'what is the same thing' – of its distance from the sun.

The *unity* of space and time in orbital motion is expressed by the fact that these two self-determining magnitudes are in necessary relation or 'proportion' to one another. That is to say, the *squares* of the orbital periods of any two planets are proportional to the *cubes* of their distances from the sun.

In Hegel's view, Kepler's third law – his so-called 'harmonic law' – is the most important of the three. This is because the quantitative relation between space and time that it describes gives fullest expression to the qualities of space and time themselves. It is thus the most rational of the three laws – the one that shows most clearly that planetary motion is determined by the inherent nature of space and time (and thereby of matter and gravity). As Hegel puts it, 'the greatness of this law is that it so simply and directly demonstrates the *rationality of the matter*'.[170]

Hegel thought it very important to provide a persuasive philosophical proof of Kepler's laws. Yet it is hard to disagree with his judgement that, despite his own best efforts, the philosophical derivation of Kepler's laws 'has not yet been fully accomplished': his arguments are by no means unintelligible, but they remain underdeveloped. Nevertheless, those arguments do make Hegel's principal underlying claim clear: the laws of planetary motion are not just contingent but are grounded in the nature of space and time and so are made necessary by nature itself. These laws are differentiated from one another (and from the law of free fall) by the fact that space and time enter into different quantitative relations in such motion. None the less, the *quantitative* relation between space and time laid down in such laws is in each case determined by the distinctive *qualities* of space and time alone (or at least, as in the first law, by the simple fact *that* space and time are qualitatively different). These laws are thus independent of the *mass* of the objects involved: whether the planets are large or small it is rational for them to move in an ellipse around their sun and to obey Kepler's 'areal' and 'harmonic' laws. They must do so because these laws are inherent in the very motion of matter as such. Kepler's laws are, indeed, matter's – nature's – *own* laws of motion: the laws that nature freely and necessarily gives to itself. As such, Hegel concludes, 'these laws are among the most beautiful to be found in the natural sciences'.[171]

It should be clear from what has been said, therefore, that Hegel's reverence for Kepler has nothing to do with any nationalistic desire to 'vindicate . . . the German way of philosophizing' or to champion an astronomer who happened to study at the same university as Hegel himself.[172] It rests on the fact that Kepler first revealed the *rational* character of celestial motion. Furthermore, he described such motion purely in terms of the relation between space and time without (as Hegel believed) invoking the dubious, abstractly 'metaphysical' concept of 'force'. Newton, by contrast, took Kepler's 'sublime' laws of celestial motion and converted them into 'the *reflective* form' of a law concerning the '*force of gravity*', namely the so-called inverse square law.[173]

Hegel and Newton

As we have seen, Hegel rejects Newton's idea that gravity is an external force 'pulling' bodies towards a central body: for him, gravity is matter's *inherent* propensity to move towards a centre. Yet Hegel accepts Newton's idea that all matter gravitates towards all other matter. Indeed, he notes, 'it is this generalisation of the law of gravity which is Newton's merit [*Verdienst*]'.[174] In Hegel's view, however, Newton fails to distinguish properly between the different ways in which gravity operates in the heavens, on the one hand, and on earth (or the other planets and moons), on the other.

According to Hegel, when the state of motion of finite bodies on earth is altered by the impact of other bodies, the bodies continue to move with the new velocity or in the new direction through their own inertia. At the same time their inherent attraction for the earth – their weight – deflects them from the direction in which their inertia carries them and causes them to fall towards or press down on the earth. The motion of the planets, by contrast, does not arise from such a combination of inertial movement and 'downward' pressure. Their motion is completely free motion and is *inherently* curvilinear. Hegel thus retains the ancient distinction between celestial and terrestrial motion. He does so, however, because he thinks that this distinction is made necessary by the *modern* idea of universal gravitation: properly understood, matter's inherent gravity itself makes the wholly *free* orbital motion of the planets necessary, as well as weight (and free fall) on earth.

In contrast to Hegel, Newton understands celestial motion to be essentially the same as terrestrial motion. Planets are just like terrestrial bodies in so far as they move around the sun only because they are deflected from the path along which they would otherwise be taken by their rectilinear inertial motion. Furthermore, they are 'drawn back from rectilinear motions and kept in curvilinear orbits' not by their own gravitational attraction for the sun, but by the *external* force of gravity that is exerted upon them by the sun.[175]

Hegel has been accused of misunderstanding Newton by attributing to him the view that orbital motion results from the action of *two* external forces on a planet, namely centripetal force (or gravity) and centrifugal force.[176] It is clear, however, that in his explanation of Newton's position Hegel – like Newton himself on rare occasions – uses the term 'centrifugal force' to refer to the *inertial* 'tendency to fly off at a tangent'. He thus recognizes that for Newton gravity and inertia are all that is needed to explain orbital motion.[177] Indeed, this is precisely what Hegel objects to in Newton's account. Hegel's fundamental critique of Newton is not, as Hegel's own critics appear to think, that Newton employs two external forces to explain orbital motion. It is that Newton *generalizes the principle of inertia* to cover all matter equally.

For Hegel, only finite objects, whose state of motion has to be altered by external impact, have an inertial tendency, if left alone, to follow a rectilinear path (and even in their case this tendency is outweighed by matter's intrinsic propensity to gravitate towards a central body). The planets have no such inertial tendency and are thus not kept in orbit by being deflected from what would otherwise be their rectilinear tangential path. They are required by their intrinsic gravity to follow a path that is intrinsically *curvilinear*. For Newton, by contrast, *all* matter has the inertial tendency to move uniformly in a straight line – or to remain in a state of rest – unless its state is altered by an external cause. On this view, the curvilinear motion of the planets is not free and natural but rather a *departure* from their intrinsically rectilinear inertial motion – a departure that can be explained only by invoking the action of an external 'force' of gravity.[178] Newton thus fails to understand that the planets move *freely* in an orbit around the sun, because he assumes that celestial and terrestrial motion are both governed in the same way by the principle of inertia. That is to say, in Newton's account 'the determinations of *inertia* [*Trägheit*], thrust, pressure, falling, etc., which are proper to the sphere of ordinary mechanics, and so to *finite motion*, are improperly carried over into absolute mechanics in which, on the contrary, matter and motion exist in their free Concept'.[179]

Yet Hegel is not hostile to every aspect of Newton's treatment of celestial motion. He acknowledges in particular Newton's ground-breaking contribution to the mathematical analysis of such motion. He argues, however, that the lines drawn by Newton to mark, for example, the tangent to the orbit and the *radius vector* should serve the purpose of mathematical calculation only and should not be taken to represent actual 'physical realities'.[180] They should not mislead us into thinking that free orbital motion is *actually* the product of inertial motion and a separate centripetal gravitational force.

As Hegel recognizes, Newton himself protests that he considers the force of gravity 'not from a physical but only from a mathematical point of view'. Indeed, he explicitly warns readers of the *Principia* to 'beware of thinking that . . . I am attributing forces in a true and physical sense to centers (which are mathematical points) if I happen to say that centers attract or that centers have forces'.[181] In Hegel's view, however, Newton did not heed his own warning strictly enough: for Newton clearly assumes that bodies *do* exert gravitational force on one another (even if he refrains from explaining what *causes* them to do so). If Newton were seriously committed to a purely mathematical analysis of celestial motion, he would abandon talk of a 'force' of gravity altogether.

Another contribution of Newton's whose importance is acknowledged by Hegel is the English physicist's precise mathematical proof and formulation of the 'inverse square law', which, according to Hegel, states that 'motion is controlled by gravity, the force of which is inversely proportional to the squares of the distances [between bodies]'. Hegel argues – following Louis-Benjamin Francoeur – that this law can be derived directly from, and so is implicit in, Kepler's third, 'harmonic' law. He points out, however, that 'Newton's merit . . . is that his form of the law possesses great advantages for mathematical treatment'.[182] Yet Hegel, of course, must reject the idea that the inverse square law describes the working of an *external* force of gravity. That law should instead be understood to describe the way in which the inherent tendency of one body – such as a planet – to gravitate towards another body – such as the sun – diminishes in strength in proportion to the square of the distance between them.

Finally, Hegel acknowledges that 'the really material addition made by Newton to Kepler's laws is the principle of *perturbation*'. Each planet, in Hegel's view, gravitates towards all the others with a strength that depends on the *mass* of the particular planet towards which it moves (and, of course, on its distance from that planet). They all stand, therefore, in a 'gravitational relationship' or 'relation of mass' (*Massenverhältnis*) with one another, through which 'disturbance' (*Störung*) is produced in their orbital motion.[183] For this reason, they do not move in a perfect ellipse.

Hegel's understanding of such perturbations is directly indebted to Newton, who writes that 'all the planets are heavy toward one another. . . . And hence Jupiter and Saturn near conjunction, by attracting each other, sensibly perturb each other's motions, the sun perturbs the lunar motions, and the sun and moon perturb our sea'.[184] The principal difference between Hegel and Newton, of course, is that, for Hegel, planetary orbits are perturbed not because planets are attracted *by* another planet but because they draw towards one another of their own accord.[185]

A further difference between the two thinkers is that Hegel does not take up Newton's point that the sun is affected by perturbations, as well as the planets. Hegel recognizes, with Newton, that the planets 'jointly give themselves a *particular* centre' or centre of mass, but he does not appear to see that, for Newton, the sun also shares a common centre of mass with the planets and actually moves *around* that centre. Newton, however, maintains that the sun 'never recedes far from the common center of gravity of all the planets'. He also states that 'the actions of the planets upon one another . . . are so very small that they can be ignored'. For Newton, therefore, the perturbations produced by the mutual gravitational attraction between the bodies in the solar system do not seriously challenge Kepler's laws (though he does point out that 'the action of Jupiter upon Saturn is not to be ignored entirely').[186]

Similarly, Hegel concludes that any disturbance of planetary orbits due to gravitational attraction is 'partly resolved again in the universal system, and partly, at least when such relation is permanent (in the mutual perturbations of Jupiter and Saturn), remains in subjection to it'.[187] For Hegel, therefore, Newton's principle of perturbation may well be an important consequence of the theory of universal gravitation, but it does not alter the fact that the motions of the planets are *essentially* – if not exclusively – governed by Kepler's laws.

It should now be clear that Hegel is not as relentlessly anti-Newtonian as he is sometimes thought to be. Hegel prefers Kepler to Newton because he finds greater *philosophical* interest in the laws that Kepler discovered. He is not, however, recommending that *science* should in future be based more on Kepler's than on Newton's work. He recognizes that Newton laid 'the foundation of the *analytic* treatment' of celestial motion and that there is no going back to pre-Newtonian mechanics (even if subsequent mathematical analysis, in Hegel's view, has gone beyond Newton in certain ways).[188] Furthermore, by pointing to the significance of perturbations, he implicitly acknowledges that Kepler's laws alone will not suffice to predict the precise motions of the planets but that Newtonian calculations, based on the assumption of universal gravitation, must also be employed.[189]

Hegel himself, however, is not trying to develop a comprehensive scientific theory that would enable accurate predictions to be made. He is developing a philosophical account of nature that discloses the forms of motion that are made logically necessary by, and so are inherent in, gravitating matter itself, namely free fall and the elliptical orbits of the planets around the sun. For Hegel, the fact that planets' orbits are not purely elliptical, but are perturbed by their attraction for one another, does not compromise the essential *rationality* of elliptical orbits. Kepler's laws – together with Galileo's law of fall – are of special interest to philosophy because they govern precisely the motions that philosophy has shown to be rational and necessary. Furthermore, they can themselves be shown to be grounded in the very nature of space and time. Newton's method of mathematical analysis certainly leads to more accurate scientific predictions than Kepler's laws alone. In Hegel's view, however, Kepler's laws – discovered 'empirically by induction'[190] – confirm the philosophical thesis that matter determines itself *logically* to move in certain ways and that *reason* is thus at work in nature.

Hegel's philosophy is meant to complement the work of science, not to usurp its role, and his philosophical mechanics is, indeed, quite compatible with Newton's powerful mathematical analysis of celestial motion (if not with his conception of gravity). Hegel challenges neither the empirical observations nor the mathematical calculations upon which Newtonian natural science rests. He offers an alternative *metaphysics* in the light of which such science can do its work. This metaphysics is one in which there is no 'force' of gravity but gravity is simply the inherent propensity of matter to *move* towards other matter. Such a metaphysics, in other words, is one in which matter is not 'pulled' towards other matter externally but gravitates towards other matter of its own accord and so exhibits a certain *freedom* of its own. Hegel's mechanics thus shows both that apparently 'dead' matter is in fact self-determining and self-moving and also that Hegel himself has a much more intelligent conception of the relation between philosophy and science than many of his critics have thought.

Hegel and Relativity

Since Hegel's death there have been further – revolutionary – developments in science, and it is appropriate to ask whether Hegel's philosophy of nature is compatible with such developments. This is not a question that can be answered fully here, but to end this chapter I offer a few thoughts on the relation between Hegel's philosophy of nature and Einstein's theories of relativity.

Dieter Wandschneider argues – in my view, convincingly – that Hegel accepts Galileo's principle of relativity. According to this principle, one cannot tell purely from the behaviour of physical objects within a closed space whether that space is in a state of rest or uniform motion. Which state an object is in can only be determined by comparison with *other* objects that serve as a frame of reference. Uniform motion is, therefore, always *relative* to other objects.[191] Hegel also explicitly acknowledges that light has 'absolute velocity' (*absolute Geschwindigkeit*).[192] Since the principle of relativity (in a more generalized form) and the constancy of the speed of light are the two postulates on which Einstein's special theory of relativity is founded, Hegel's philosophy of nature would thus appear *prima facie* to be compatible with that ground-breaking theory (even though Hegel clearly had no inkling himself that such a theory could ever be developed).[193] One can also point out that Hegel endorses another idea central to the special (and general) theory of relativity, namely the idea that space and time form a single unity: space-time.

Yet what about the startling effects predicted by Einstein's theory: time dilation and length contraction? The special theory of relativity states that 'time elapses more slowly for an individual in motion than it does for a stationary individual' and that 'observers perceive a moving object as being shortened along the direction of its motion.'[194] Could Hegel really countenance such revolutionary propositions? Perhaps.

Hegel maintains that space and time are universal in the sense that all matter is extended in three directions and is constantly vanishing into the past. By itself, however, this does not commit him to the view that time always and everywhere passes at the same rate or that the length of an object will always be the same, regardless of the frame of reference within which it is measured. Furthermore, Hegel denies that space and time themselves provide an *independent*, *universal* frame of reference for the measurement of distance or the passage of time. He states explicitly that space and time are not pre-existing 'containers' (*Behälter*) within which matter is located, but prove logically to be the extendedness and vanishing *of* matter itself.[195] This means that, for Hegel, motion is never motion in relation to 'absolute' space and time, but always only motion in relation to *other matter*: 'motion as such has meaning and existence simply and solely in a system of *several* bodies that stand in relation to each other'.[196] This is *not* to say that Hegel in some way 'anticipates' special relativity eighty years before Einstein: such a claim would be wholly inappropriate. Hegel's rejection of the idea that there is an independent, universal spatio-temporal frame of reference does, however, leave room for the idea that the rate of aging and the length of an object may depend on the velocity at which that object moves in relation to other objects. In this sense, his philosophy of nature is compatible with special relativity.

Einstein's *general* theory of relativity is a theory about gravity. It states that a body, such as the sun, warps or 'curves' the space around it and that the greater the mass of the body concerned, the greater the curvature it produces.[197] Other bodies moving without external buffeting through the space around a massive body like the sun will follow the nearest thing to a straight path in such curved space. Such a path, which is the path of minimum distance between two points but is itself curved, is called a 'geodesic'.[198] Due to the warping of space, bodies (or light beams) travelling 'straight ahead' in the vicinity of the sun will thus actually follow a *curved* trajectory rather than move in a straight line. This explains the phenomenon of gravity: the 'gravitating' of a body towards the sun is simply the motion that is produced by the curvature of the space through which that first body travels. If the curvature of that space is strong enough, and the body's speed and direction of travel are right, the body will be guided into an orbit around the sun. According to the general theory of relativity, therefore, a 'planet orbits the Sun in an elliptical orbit not because of a gravitational force of attraction exerted on the planet by the Sun, as Newton affirmed, but because the mass of the Sun warps the space around it, altering its geometry' and the motion of the planet is determined by the shape of that warp. For Einstein, there is thus no such thing as a *force* of gravity: gravitational motion is motion due to the distorted geometry of space.[199]

Einstein also made the suggestion that space might be not only locally warped by matter but positively curved or 'closed' *as a whole* in such a way that light travelling in a constant direction away from its source would eventually return to its point of origin. Such space would be unbounded in that it would have no discoverable limit or 'edge'; but the fact that light would ultimately return to its point of departure, rather than continue to move away from its source indefinitely, means that this space would be finite. The general theory of relativity, however, does not itself fully determine the global shape of the universe – it predicts only that the fabric of space will be *locally* 'warped' by the presence of matter – and there is currently no definitive proof that space overall is positively curved.[200]

Is Hegel's philosophy of nature compatible with general relativity? Two things suggest that the answer might be yes. First, as we saw earlier, Hegel insists on the identity of inertial and gravitational mass, and P. M. Kluit argues that this brings him close to Einstein, for whom the equivalence of the two types of mass is the starting-point for the general theory of relativity.[201] Second, Hegel agrees with Einstein – against Newton – that gravity is not a *force* exerted by one body on another. For Hegel, gravitational motion is grounded in the inherent nature of matter and, ultimately, in the very nature of space and time themselves. In this sense, one could say of Hegel, as Brian Greene says of Einstein, that he 'wove gravity into the basic fabric of the universe'.[202]

There are two things, however, that suggest Hegel's philosophy of nature might not be compatible with general relativity after all. The first is this. According to general relativity, 'figures constructed out of light rays do not satisfy Euclidian geometry if the light rays propagate in the presence of gravitating matter' because, in taking the *shortest* path between two points, those rays follow a *curved* rather than a straight line. In Einstein's own words, therefore, 'the space-time continuum cannot be regarded as a Euclidian one'.[203] Hegel, by contrast, clearly assumes that space is Euclidian. The proposition that the *straight* line is the shortest between two points is said by him to be 'the most correct definition'. Moreover, he argues that Pythagoras' theorem, with which Book 1 of Euclid's *Elements* concludes, can be derived directly 'from the Concept' and so be proven *a priori* to be true.[204]

Yet does Hegel's commitment to Euclid inevitably pit his philosophy against general relativity? I think not. Brian Greene notes that 'in the absence of any matter or energy, Einstein envisioned that space would be *flat*': light would thus propagate in straight lines that behave in accordance with the axioms of Euclid.[205] Einstein could also be said, therefore, to hold that space *in itself* is Euclidian. He argues, however, that the presence of *matter* warps space and thereby renders it locally (and maybe even globally) non-Euclidian. The question to consider is thus whether Hegel could also accept that matter might distort space that is otherwise intrinsically Euclidian.

For Hegel, there is no space *prior* to matter, because space-time itself proves logically to be nothing but matter-in-motion. In particular, it takes the form of independent central bodies – stars and planets – that are separated by the vastness of empty space. Hegel clearly assumes that not only the space far removed from matter but also that in the vicinity of matter will be Euclidian. As far as I can tell, however, there is nothing in Hegel's conception of matter that *logically* precludes the possibility of matter's distorting the surrounding space. Any such distortion would have to be considered contingent from the philosophical point of view, since nothing makes it logically necessary; but it does not appear to be definitively ruled out. In this sense, Hegel's understanding of space as inherently Euclidian is not irreconcilably at odds with general relativity.

Nor does the idea that space might be positively curved *globally*, and so finite, conflict with Hegel's claim that space must be continuous and unbounded. According to Hegel, one can travel as far as one likes, but one will always be able to go further and will never reach a definitive limit or edge to space: 'however remotely I place a star, I can go beyond it, for the universe is nowhere nailed up with boards'.[206] This conception of space as continuous and unbounded is, however, compatible with either the *infinity* of globally 'flat' (but locally curved) space or the *finitude* of space that is overall positively curved. After all, even in a positively curved, finite universe, one could still travel forever in a uniform direction without reaching an edge to space; one would just return at some point in time to one's place of departure. The fact that space is necessarily continuous and unbounded does not, therefore, determine by itself whether space is infinite or finite. It is thus a matter of *contingency*, from the philosophical point of view, which is the case – or indeed whether space is negatively curved (like a saddle) – and it is up to natural science to determine the true state of affairs.[207]

There is, however, a second problem. In Hegel's view, the fall or orbital motion of a body is due not to the action of an external force upon it but to the inherent tendency of matter to seek unity with other matter. Matter thus gravitates freely – of its own accord – towards or around other matter. According to general relativity, by contrast, bodies such as planets do not gravitate *of their own accord* around their sun. Their motion is determined by the curvature of the space through which they pass. In this sense, from the Hegelian point of view, Einstein's account of gravity closely resembles Newton's: for in neither account do bodies *actively* move or gravitate towards or around another body. In both accounts, bodies fall towards or orbit around another body because they are caused to do so by something *outside* themselves – either by a force exerted upon them or by the warping of the surrounding space. There is thus a clear tension between Hegel's conception of gravitational motion and Einstein's. This tension is, of course, of no concern to the physicist, but it is a serious problem for the philosopher who claims that philosophy and science study the *same* realm of nature and that 'agreement with actuality and experience' is essential to philosophy.[208]

So is it possible to dissolve this tension between the philosophy of nature and general relativity? Well, we could conclude that Hegel's derivation of gravity from the nature of space and time is misconceived. We would, however, have to show precisely where that derivation goes astray and how it can be amended. On the other hand, we could choose to reject the general theory of relativity. This would, however, be unwise, since 'no deviations from the predictions of general relativity have been found in experiments performed with our present level of technology'.[209] The third option is to suggest that, perhaps, both the philosophy of nature and general relativity capture something of the truth. Perhaps planets move in orbits around their sun *both* because the space through which they travel is warped by the mass of the sun *and* because they have an inherent tendency to gravitate around that sun – a tendency rooted in the fact that they form part of a unified system of celestial bodies into which intrinsically gravitational matter has organized itself.[210] If this third option has merit, Hegel's philosophy of nature would, after all, be compatible with general relativity.

These remarks are certainly not meant to be the last word on the relation between Hegel and Einstein. They are meant to do no more than prompt those better qualified than I to examine that relation in detail. In my judgement, Hegel's philosophy of nature is intended not just to systematize the scientific knowledge of Hegel's own day but to determine what is made logically *necessary* by nature itself. If it is successful in this task, there will still remain a huge amount of work for science to undertake, but no future scientific discovery will be fundamentally incompatible with the insights of philosophy. If discoveries incompatible with philosophy are made, however, then the philosopher will clearly have to think again. For this reason, although physicists may well be able to ignore Hegel, students of Hegel's philosophy of nature cannot, in my view, afford to ignore modern physics.

This concludes my examination of Hegel's mechanics. I have discussed this section of the philosophy of nature in some detail in order to help readers to follow the twists and turns of Hegel's logical analysis and see for themselves the subtle way in which Hegel relates his analysis to the findings of science. I also wished to explain as clearly as I could how it is that Hegel finds the seeds of freedom and spirit in the most unlikely of places, namely in the barrenness of space itself. Not all readers will be convinced that Hegel's philosophy of nature rewards intensive study, but I hope that some might be tempted to press on and examine the further dialectical development of nature.

Following his account of celestial mechanics, Hegel goes on to argue that matter must take the form of light, physical objects (with density, cohesion and heat) and chemicals. In the process matter proves to be held together not just by gravity but also by magnetism, electricity and chemical bonds. Matter also proves to be more and more explicitly self-determining and self-moving. The philosophy of nature culminates in an account of the most explicitly self-determining matter that nature produces, namely life. In the next chapter we consider Hegel's analysis of life and then briefly trace the logical process whereby life mutates into freely self-determining, embodied *spirit*.

7   *Life and Embodied Spirit*

The 'Ideal' Structure of Life

In the Introduction to the *Philosophy of Nature* Hegel writes that 'nature exhibits no freedom in its existence, but only *necessity* and *contingency*'.[1] This statement, however, requires further qualification: for, although non-human nature certainly lacks the self-conscious freedom enjoyed by human beings, finite natural objects fall freely towards their respective planets and those planets themselves orbit freely around their sun. Hegel goes on to argue that the highest degree of freedom to be found in nature is exhibited by life.[2] Life is free not simply because it is unhindered in its movement, like a body in free fall, but because it generates by itself, quite spontaneously and independently, all the processes and changes it undergoes. Life, for Hegel, is autonomously self-producing and self-renewing, and it is only through such self-renewal that it preserves itself and keeps itself alive.

A living organism continuously produces and renews both itself as a whole and its constituent parts. Indeed, the two processes are one and the same: the organism renews and preserves its whole self precisely *through* renewing its parts. A crystal is an organized structure that both grows and retains its fundamental form. It is not alive, however, because its parts are static rather than dynamic.[3] They do not regenerate themselves and thereby renew the whole structure of the crystal itself. Life, by contrast, is essentially the process of producing and *re*-producing itself. As Hegel puts it, 'it is only as this self-reproductive being [*als dieses sich Reproduzierende*], not as a mere being, that the living creature *is* and *preserves itself*; it only is, in making itself what it is'. Indeed, in his discussion of higher animal life he points out that 'nothing in the organism endures, but everything is reproduced, not excepting the bones. . . . It is said that after five, ten or twenty years the organism no longer contains its former substance, everything material has been consumed, and only the substantial form persists.'[4]

The parts of the organism, for Hegel, are thus 'fluid' and 'transitory': they are processes rather than mere 'things'.[5] Furthermore, their basic character is determined by the fact that they serve specifically to preserve the whole of which they are part. They are not like pebbles or stones that have an independent character of their own but can be put together to form various aggregates. They are, rather, integral *moments* of the organism itself – moments whose very identity is determined by the function they perform within the organism. To put it another way, the parts of the organism have a specific *purpose* to fulfil, namely to contribute in their distinctive way to the preservation and renewal of the whole individual.

Note that, for Hegel, the organism as a whole is nothing beyond the parts that constitute it. It is simply the organized unity or community of parts whose shared purpose is to preserve that community and their particular function within it. That is to say, the organism is nothing but the organized functioning and purposive activity *of* its constituent organs. Since this is the case, the organism as a whole necessarily pursues the purpose of preserving itself. Hegel follows Kant, therefore, in understanding an organism to be its *own* purpose or a 'purpose for itself' (*Zweck für sich selbst*): it is a being that does not just subsist, like a rock, but aims at its own survival.[6] Unlike Kant, however, Hegel maintains not just that *we* must think of organisms in this way, but that they are themselves ontologically oriented towards their own self-preservation.[7]

The parts of the organism not only sustain and renew the organism as a whole. They are in turn sustained by the whole, since they can only function properly within it (or, as we now know in the age of organ transplants, within a similarly structured organism). Such parts or organs of the body are characterized by Hegel as 'ideal'.[8] This does not mean that they are immaterial, or mere constructs of the mind, or especially beautiful. It means that they are irreducibly material but belong completely to the organism: they are dependent *moments* of the organism and have a specific function within it. Hegel similarly describes the whole organism as an 'idea': with life, he writes, 'the *Idea* has entered into existence'.[9] Once again, this does not mean that organisms are anything less than fully material entities. It means that they are (1) organized unities of 'ideal' moments, and (2) self-generating, *self-determining* entities.

As we saw in chapters 2 and 5, Hegel argues in the *Logic* that being, when fully understood, turns out to be self-determining reason or the 'Idea'. He then contends in the *Philosophy of Nature* that such self-determining reason first exists in the form of sheer externality – as space. Paradoxically, therefore, self-determining reason or the 'Idea' is initially neither self-determining nor rational, but static and barren. Hegel proceeds to demonstrate, however, that spatio-temporal matter actually *determines itself* to move in certain ways. In the elliptical motion of the planets around the sun matter thus shows that it is after all self-determining, rational and 'ideal'. With the emergence of life, matter shows itself to be even more explicitly self-determining and 'ideal'. Life, for Hegel, is an irreducibly material process: it is not something ethereal or supernatural. It is, however, the material process that most clearly embodies free self-determination – the process in which the 'Idea' is rendered incarnate.

We are now in a position to understand two of Hegel's more eye-catching statements about life. He says of the animal organism that in it 'the whole of inorganic nature is . . . idealized [*idealisiert*]', and he also remarks that 'the perpetual action of life is . . . absolute idealism'.[10] It is not hard to imagine an unwary reader being misled by these statements into thinking that life, for Hegel, is, indeed, some kind of immaterial vapour animating certain objects. Hegel recognizes perfectly well, however, that living organisms are made up of physical and chemical constituents just like other objects in nature. What distinguishes living organisms from inorganic things, in Hegel's view, is not that organisms consist of something radically different from other things but that the matter in them has the *form* or *structure* of 'ideality'. A living organism is a material entity whose parts are not independent of one another but interdependent – and thus 'ideal' – moments. Furthermore, it constitutes a whole that is self-determining and thus 'ideal'. Hegel's language may seem to some to be misleadingly abstract, but his point is actually quite straightforward.

He agrees with the modern-day physicist Paul Davies that 'what makes life so remarkable, what distinguishes the living from the non-living, is not what organisms are made of but how they are put together and function as wholes'.[11]

Life not only 'idealizes' matter into the organs of the body; it also 'idealizes' objects and materials outside the body by *assimilating* them into itself. 'If life were a realist [*Realist*]', Hegel remarks, 'it would have respect for the outer world.' In fact, however, 'it always inhibits the reality of the other and transforms it into its own self'.[12] Life, for Hegel is thus not only the process of preserving itself through renewing itself; it is also the process of taking into itself and making use of whatever it needs from the environment around it. Life, in other words, involves nutrition and metabolism, as well as self-regeneration and self-renewal.

Hegel refers to organic self-renewal as 'reproduction'. He understands reproduction, therefore, to be the process whereby an organism continuously produces and preserves *itself* as the singular organism it is – the process of 'self-producing' (*Sichproduzieren*).[13] He recognizes, however, that organisms also reproduce themselves by making copies of themselves in the form of offspring. Such self-reproduction through the production of new individuals can be asexual or sexual: an organism may simply divide or fragment into different individuals (or send out spores), or it may unite with another organism to create offspring.[14] The important thing to note in each case, in Hegel's view, is that the production of new individuals, which are identical or similar to their parent(s), sustains the *genus* or *species* (*Gattung*) to which the individual belongs. Life, for Hegel, is thus not merely the process in which individuals seek their own survival; it is at the same time necessarily 'the production and the preservation of the species'.[15] When the preservation and promotion of the species becomes the conscious, rather than unintended, consequence of the actions of individual organisms, we enter the realm of human beings or *spirit*.

Chemistry and Life

For Hegel, life is not a mere accident of nature but is logically necessary. It is made necessary, specifically, by chemistry. Hegel notes that acids and alkalis combine to form neutral salts in a process that does not continue indefinitely but eventually comes to an end. Similarly, Hegel points out, the process of galvanism ends with oxidation. Chemical processes are thus *finite* processes that cease at some point in time.[16] The product of one process can certainly be made to enter into a new process: two neutral salts, for example, can be 'combined in a solution of water and exchange their radicals, producing two quite different salts'.[17] The conclusion of one process, however, does not immediately and automatically initiate the next process. Processes involving chemicals, such as acids and alkalis, are thus not *living* processes because they are not self-renewing and self-sustaining.

Yet Hegel remarks that the product of one process constitutes the condition for another process and that the conditions of any chemical process are themselves products of previous processes. Chemicals, therefore, are not just independent, given objects, but are both the results and the conditions of processes. Their nature is thus essentially *relational*: each one owes its existence to other chemicals and is itself a set of ways of relating to and reacting with other chemicals.[18] Taken together, therefore, the basic chemical processes – such as galvanism, the production of acids and alkalis, the combining of acids and alkalis, and 'elective affinity' – can be thought of as stages of *one* overall chemical process in which the conditions of one stage are the products of a previous stage. Such a process, in Hegel's view, is *implicitly*, though not explicitly, a circular, self-producing, self-sustaining process: 'the infinite process which spontaneously kindles and sustains itself'.[19]

In the living organism, such a self-producing and self-sustaining process becomes an *explicit* reality. Life is thus made logically necessary by chemistry (in Hegel's distinctive sense of 'logical necessity') because it, and it alone, renders explicit what is implicit in chemical processes taken as a systematic whole. Life, in other words, fulfils the promise of chemistry that purely chemical processes themselves do not fulfil. Hegel states that 'if the products of the chemical process spontaneously renewed their activity, they would be life'. Accordingly, life is simply 'a chemical process made perpetual'.[20]

Hegel insists that life is qualitatively different from mere chemistry and irreducible to it: '*animal* and *vegetable* substances . . . belong to a quite different order; their nature, far from being understood from the chemical process, is rather destroyed in it; what we grasp therefrom is only the way of their death'.[21] Equally, however, he acknowledges that life is nothing but *chemical* activity so organized as to constitute an organic, self-preserving, self-renewing and self-replicating whole. Digestion, for example, can be understood as the chemical process of 'neutralizing' acids and alkalis; but digestive processes are not purely chemical precisely because they are moments of, and serve to sustain, the whole system of an organism. Hegel states that one can, indeed, 'analyse the individual parts of the living being chemically [*chemisch zerlegen*]'. Yet processes within the living organism should not be regarded as simply chemical, 'for chemistry applies only to what is lifeless, and animal processes always sublate [*aufheben*] the nature of what is chemical'.[22] Hegel notes that 'only at death or in disease is the chemical process able to prevail'.[23] Indeed, death occurs precisely when the whole organism stops sustaining and renewing itself and breaks up into different, finite chemical processes.

Hegel's account of the relation between chemistry and life is in striking accord with more recent biological thinking. Paul Davies, for example, unwittingly echoes Hegel when he writes as follows: 'life works its magic not by bowing to the directionality of chemistry, but by *circumventing* what is chemically and thermodynamically "natural". . . . Life succeeds precisely because it *evades* chemical imperatives'.[24] Hegel, of course, knew nothing of DNA – which Davies describes as 'a recipe for making an organism' – or of the genetic code. I see no reason, however, why Hegel should not have welcomed their discovery. For what DNA, RNA and the genetic code provide is a *chemical* means 'to *free* life from the shackles of non-random chemical bonding'.[25] They thus explain *how* chemical activity organizes and orders itself into living, self-replicating organisms. How DNA and RNA themselves first emerged is still not fully understood. The ultimate origin of life thus remains enigmatic. What is clear, however, is that Hegel is right to see life as a product of nature, rather than miraculous, supernatural intervention, and right to understand life as inseparable from but irreducible to chemical processes.

Hegel is a speculative philosopher, not a biologist. He does not see it as his task, therefore, to shed light on the *natural* processes that first gave birth to life. His concern is solely to prove that life is made *logically* necessary by chemistry and to uncover the fundamental structure of life. His proof of the logical necessity of life demonstrates, however, that there is (in Kalenberg's words) a clear 'tendency towards life' in nature. In Hegel's view, therefore, we live in what Davies calls a 'bio-friendly universe'.[26] Such a universe is not necessarily teeming with life; but it is one in which life is the unconscious *telos* of nature and should be expected to emerge wherever the conditions are right. It is the task of natural scientists to determine exactly what those conditions are and how frequently they arise and have arisen in the past.[27]

Plants and Animals

Hegel's concept is life is *a priori*. It is arrived at by considering what is logically implicit in chemical processes, not by trying to find an empirical description that fits everything we happen to call 'life'. It thus provides a rational criterion by which to judge whether an object is, indeed, alive or not. It also allows Hegel to rank phenomena in nature according to the degree to which they exhibit or fall short of the concept of life.

Hegel identifies two basic forms of life: plants and animals. He also maintains, however, that certain primitive organisms do not fall neatly into either category: 'everywhere', he claims, 'the earth covers itself with green vegetation – indeterminate formations which can equally be classed with animal life'. Some of these organisms, we are told, are not even unequivocally organic but are '*inorganic-organic* forms'. Hegel believes that some lower animals only get as far as 'a momentarily existing slime [*Gallert*]', though he adds (perhaps in pointed contrast to Kant) that he values such slime more highly than the 'starry host' above, since the former is at least organic. Other micro-organisms, he thinks, emerge from the sea spontaneously and then die. These are organisms without parents and without off-spring: 'organisms which originate immediately and do not procreate further'.[28]

Hegel's judgements about primitive organisms are sometimes bizarre. They are, however, invariably based on the scientific literature of the day, rather than on his own idle musings.[29] Furthermore, they bear witness to one of Hegel's most important insights: although philosophy unfolds the *a priori* concept of life, 'nature in its manifestations does not hold fast to the concept' but produces all manner of organisms that are 'indefinite intermediate beings, . . . neither fish nor flesh'.[30] Primitive life thus provides more evidence of what Hegel calls 'the *impotence* of nature' – its failure to be fully rational.[31]

Nature, however, is not utterly impotent and produces a host of organisms that are unequivocally organic and clearly plants or animals. Plants are self-preserving organic unities that grow, take in nutrition and produce offspring. In Hegel's view, however, their unity is less than fully organic, since many of their constituent parts have the capacity to become separate, *independent* plants in their own right. Depending on the plant, shoots, leaves or roots can be cut from the parent and grow into new individuals. In some cases, shoots that bend over and touch the ground can also give rise to new plants.[32] This is not just an accidental feature of plants, for Hegel, but is a fundamental consequence of the way they are organized. There is in the plant no clear distinction between the growth of the individual and the generation of new individuals: plants grow and renew themselves pre-cisely by producing *buds* that are able to develop into separate plants. 'In the plant world', Hegel states, 'the plant produces itself by coming out of itself, what it produces is an other – the bud [*Knospe*]'.[33]

Plants can also reproduce sexually, but Hegel regards such reproduction in plants as 'a play, a luxury, something superfluous for propagation'.[34] The essential characteristic of plants is that they produce new individuals directly from themselves. To put it simply, plants are organisms from which it is possible to take cuttings. Hegel notes that certain animals can also reproduce asexually or 'vegetatively', but he considers such animals to be 'undeveloped' or 'incomplete' (*unvollständig*) and so not animals in the full sense.[35]

Since their parts are not wholly dependent, 'ideal' moments of the organism, plants lack true organic unity or what Hegel calls 'genuine [*wahrhaft*] subjectivity'. As a result, they do not relate to the world around them as wholly autonomous beings. They have no capacity for independent locomotion and they do not interrupt the process of their own nutrition.[36] Furthermore, they have no *sense* or *feeling* of their own unity and individuality: 'the individual does not as such return into itself . . . and therefore has no *self-feeling* [*Selbstgefühl*]'.[37] The plant's lack of autonomy is evident, in Hegel's view, in the fact that it always turns in the direction of the *light* from which it derives its energy. Light is thus the 'supreme power' over the plant. It is, as it were, the plant's true 'self': 'Schelling therefore says that, if the plant had consciousness, it would worship light as its god'.[38]

In contrast to plants, animals are defined by Hegel as fully organic unities whose parts cannot form separate organisms in their own right. True animals, therefore, are organisms from which one cannot take cuttings: as Hegel points out (echoing Aristotle), 'if a finger is cut off, it is no longer a finger, but a process of chemical decomposition sets in'.[39] On this view, reproduction among true animals must thus be sexual rather than vegetative. (Hegel, of course, could not foresee the advent of animal cloning, but he would, I think, have to regard it as violating the distinctive organic integrity and independence of animals). Since animals possess the 'genuine subjectivity' that plants lack, they are capable of both independent locomotion and interrupted or periodical nutrition. Higher animals are also capable of giving *voice* to their subjectivity: 'the inorganic does not show its specific quality until it is stimulated from outside, gets struck; but the animal sounds of its own accord'.[40]

Hegel ranks animals from the most primitive – some of which are mere 'slime', some of which are plant-like in their structure or manner of reproduction and some of which are 'merely an intestinal canal' – to the most complex, namely mammals which have 'breasts, four articulated extremities, and all their organs developed'.[41] He picks out 'the human organism' in particular as the 'perfect animal'.[42] It is important to note, however, that Hegel's account of the animal organism does not rest on an uncritical anthropocentrism: he does not just *assume* that the human body is superior to all others and so set it up as the model against which all others are to be judged. As we have seen, Hegel derives the concept of life immanently from chemistry. Mammals and human beings (rather than primitive organisms) are privileged in his discussion for the simple reason that they fully realize the concept of life that has emerged. They are, for Hegel, the most properly *organic* organisms there are.

It is also important to note that Hegel's focus in the *Philosophy of Nature* is not on what distinguishes human beings as such from the rest of nature. This will be explored in the *Philosophy of Spirit*, in which Hegel analyses consciousness, thought and freedom. Hegel is interested in the *Philosophy of Nature* in clarifying what distinguishes the animal organism from plants and intermediate life-forms. To carry out his study Hegel looks primarily, though not exclusively, at animals in their most developed form. Human organisms are considered, therefore, because they are advanced *animal* organisms. Hegel abstracts from the fact that they can think, speak and lay claim to rights and examines only what they have in common with other animals. Humans are thus regarded not as beings set apart from nature but, like all other life-forms, as integral parts of nature itself.

Sensation in Animals

The most important and distinctive characteristic of animals, for Hegel (as for Aristotle), is *sensation* (*Empfindung*).[43] Sensation is the lowest form of awareness or inner, mental activity and is understood by Hegel to be common to both human and non-human animals.[44] Hegel recognizes, however, that sensation is present to a greater or lesser degree, depending on the nature of the animal concerned. In the lowest animals – microorganisms that, in Hegel's view, are barely animals at all – sensation is so rudimentary that it is in fact indistinguishable from simple irritability or the propensity to react defensively to an external stimulus.[45] More complex animals, by contrast – insects, fish, amphibians, reptiles, birds and mammals – are capable of more developed sensation in some or all of its familiar forms: touch, hearing, smell, taste and vision.

According to Hegel, sensation has two principal moments to it. On the one hand, it entails the feeling of being a unified self. As organic unities, all living things have an integrity, unity or 'selfhood' that they seek to preserve. In animals, however, 'the self is *for the self*'. As Hegel puts it, animals 'find themselves' within themselves and so have a certain awareness or sense of themselves. Their selfhood is not merely an objective fact about them; it is a selfhood that doubles back on itself and relates to itself. The animal is thus 'the subject as self-self [*Selbst-Selbst*], as self-feeling'.[46]

On the other hand, sensation does not consist only in the general feeling of being a self. It entails the particular feeling of being affected in some way by another thing: 'the animal in sentience does not merely sense itself, but itself as determined in a particular way; it senses a particularized form of itself'.[47] Sensation is thus equally the awareness of *something else* in so far as it affects the self. Sensations, for Hegel, are always individual: they are the feeling of being affected by *this* other in *this* specific manner. They are, however, related by the animal to the unity of its self as a whole. An animal does not just feel its nose or eye or ear to be affected by the thing it encounters. It feels *itself* – its very identity – to be affected in this or that particular way: 'in sensation such content is a determination of my whole (albeit . . . dull) being-for-self'.[48] In tactile sensation, for example, the sensation is felt wherever the skin is touched, but at the same time the animal feels that its *whole* being has been touched *there*. Each sensation thus engages the whole organism directly. When an animal sees or hears or smells something, therefore, it does not just neutrally register the presence of the object; the object is felt to be a source of pleasure or pain, comfort or danger to the animal's very *self*.

Non-human animals, for Hegel, are immersed in and restricted to a world of sensations. Their whole lives are spent feeling affected by things in manifold different ways. Often they derive pleasure and satisfaction from the things they encounter; but equally, and especially in the wild, their feeling can be 'an *insecure, anxious,* and *unhappy* one'.[49] Human beings, by contrast, can distance themselves from their sensations and the things they see and hear around them, consider rationally what affects them, and modify their behaviour accordingly. This capacity stems, however, from being free, spiritual beings, not from being animal organisms as such. The animal as such is capable of nothing but sensations (and the associations they establish within the animal's 'mind').[50]

Hegel states that the animal 'is not aware of itself in *thought*, but only in feeling and intuition'.[51] It feels itself to be a self and feels itself to be affected by other things, but it does not have a clear *conception* of itself as a particular individual or as an 'I' distinct from other individuals and objects in the world. It senses that it has a self to preserve but does not think to itself: 'I am a dog' or 'I am Rover'. Nor does the animal have a clear conception of the objects to which it relates. It does not identify them as 'trees' or 'flowers' within an objective public space, but simply feels them to be pleasant, painful, nutritive or threatening to itself. Animals, in Hegel's view, thus draw only a 'dull' (*dumpf*) distinction between themselves and the things they encounter.[52] They have no clear '*objective* consciousness, no knowledge of the world as a world actually *projected out of myself*'.[53] The animal's sense of self suffices, however, to allow it to feel needs and also to feel that those needs are met. Unlike the plant, therefore, the animal can interrupt its intake of nutrition and simply enjoy feeling satisfied within itself.[54]

Hegel's account of the animal organism is extraordinarily rich and nuanced and draws widely on the work of contemporary scientists, such as Treviranus, Lamarck and Cuvier.

My aim here, however, is not to examine Hegel's account of animal life in detail. It is to emphasize one simple but very important point: that animals, in Hegel's view, are capable of self-feeling, and thus of sensory awareness, because of the way their *bodies* are organized.

Animals are units of matter, subject to gravity like other finite masses. At the same time, they are organic unities whose material parts are moments that sustain and renew, and are in turn sustained by, the whole organism. The distinctive self-renewing unity of the animal constitutes its particular identity or 'self' – the self it seeks to preserve. The animal's self is thus simply the organic unity of its *material* body. That very organic unity or self, however, also has an *immaterial* relation to itself: it is 'for itself' and so senses and feels itself. Such self-feeling constitutes the 'soul' (*Seele*) of the animal.[55] Note that this soul is not something separate from the body, nor is it inserted into the body from the outside. The soul is the immaterial self-relation – or felt awareness of oneself – that is generated and enjoyed by the *material* body that constitutes the organism. The soul is thus what Murray Greene calls 'the simple ideality of its body' or, in Hegel's own phrase, the 'immateriality of nature' itself.[56]

Plants do not have self-feeling because they are not fully organic unities but unities whose parts can become separate individuals in their own right. Animals, by contrast, do have self-feeling, and it is clear that, for Hegel, this is because they are fully organic unities. It is thus their material structure and mode of organization that renders their immaterial self-relation and inner life possible. Indeed, Hegel thinks that this material structure makes such an immaterial self-relation *necessary*: animal bodies – especially in higher animals – are so well integrated that they cannot *not* have a sense of their own unity and of the way other things affect them. No true animal, therefore, can lack sensation and be a purely material object. Equally, no sensory awareness can be disembodied, since the sensory, feeling soul is simply the immaterial self-relation *of* the material organic body itself.

Three different features of the animal body enable it to have sensations. The first (which we have already mentioned) is the organic unity of the body as a whole. The second is the presence of the brain and nerves. Even though sensation, as a form of awareness, is itself an immaterial process, Hegel recognizes that it is dependent upon the workings of the nervous system. He states explicitly that 'the nerve is the condition for sensation where the body is touched'; and he goes on to note that in self-conscious human beings 'it is also a condition of the will, and generally of any self-determining end'.[57] The third feature of the body that makes sensation possible is, of course, the presence of the organs of sense – the eyes, ears, nose, tongue and skin that are affected by things outside the body.[58]

Unfortunately, Hegel does not explain in detail precisely how the body generates sensory awareness. He admits in particular that 'we still know very little about the organization of the brain'.[59] What he does provide, however, is a distinctive *philosophical* conception of the relation between the sensory 'soul' and the body. As we have seen, the sensory soul, for Hegel, is not separate from the body. Animal self-feeling and sensation arise because the body itself has become immaterially self-relating: it has become a *self-feeling, sensitive body*. Such sensation is made possible and necessary by the organization of the *whole* body. No particular parts of the body, such as eyes, ears and brain, should, therefore, be regarded by themselves as the ultimate foundation or underlying cause of the animal's mental activity. These organs are certainly the necessary conditions of such mental activity, but they are mere moments of the body as a whole. They can thus carry out their particular function only within the context of the whole body. From a Hegelian perspective, therefore, animals do not have certain sensations solely because of electro-chemical activity in the brain and in the nerves leading to it from the eyes or ears. Rather, such electro-chemical activity is itself but an indispensable *moment* of the self-feeling, sensitive organism as a whole.

If Hegel is right, machines are incapable of feeling or sensation; sensation is the prerogative of the animal organism. Sensory awareness is itself immaterial, but it is generated by the material body of the living being. Moreover, it is generated by the organism as a whole, not just by specific parts of the body working in isolation. The task of natural science is to understand precisely *how* the various processes within the organism cooperate to generate sensation and feeling. Hegel is also interested in the ways in which sensation and feeling can themselves produce particular bodily effects: he reminds us, for example, that 'cheerfulness preserves health, anxiety undermines it'. Accordingly, in the *Philosophy of Spirit* he suggests that a special science of 'psychic physiology' should be developed to study why human beings laugh or cry in certain emotional states and why 'anger and courage are felt in the breast'.[60]

Sensation and self-feeling are distinctive features of animal life. They constitute what Hegel regards as the lowest level of awareness. At the same time, they represent the initial stirrings of mental activity which in human beings also takes the further developed forms of consciousness and thought. For Hegel, the self that feels itself in sensibility is the very one that in humans produces an abstract conception of itself: the 'sentient self' is *itself* 'that which in spirit is the I' (*was im Geiste das Ich ist*).[61] This means that, since sensation is necessarily embodied, human consciousness, thought and spirit – in their very freedom and autonomy – must also be embodied. The human capacity to abstract in thought from its body and its immediate sensations and let itself be guided by reason must itself be rooted *in* and made possible *by* our organic, animal body.

Schopenhauer and Nietzsche are the German philosophers who are usually credited with emphasizing the irreducibly embodied character of consciousness and thought. It is clear, however, that Hegel also lays great stress on such embodiment. The embodied character of consciousness explains, for example, why human beings have to sleep and why we are subject to certain natural drives and inclinations. Even 'thinking', Hegel insists, 'has a corporeal manifestation, is felt and especially in the head, in the brain, in general in the system of sensibility'. This is the reason, he maintains, why 'want of habit and too-long-continued thinking cause headache'.[62] Unlike Nietzsche, Hegel does not deny that thought is freely self-determining; but he acknowledges that our organic, sensitive *body* is the necessary, enabling condition of such free, self-determining thought.

At first sight Hegel's insistence on the embodied character of spirit might appear to be at odds with his equally strong commitment to Christianity. Does not Christianity preach resurrection and life after death, and do not these ideas imply (as Plato also held)[63] that the soul or spirit can be separated from the body and continue after death on its own? As we shall see in chapter 10, Hegel does not share this 'Platonic' (and Nietzschean) understanding of Christian belief. For Hegel, as for the theologian Eberhard Jüngel, Christian 'life after death' does not lie beyond the grave. It is to be found in *this* world of nature and history. The 'life after death' promised by Christianity is precisely our present, embodied life in so far as it has been renewed and suffused with love through the anticipatory acceptance of our own death.[64] Whether such an interpretation accords with orthodox Christianity is for others to decide (my own view is that it does). My principal concern here is simply to point out that Hegel's conception of embodied spirit is not at odds with Christian faith as he himself understood it.

Life, Death and Spirit

There is a further difficulty to be considered. The problem is that at the end of the *Philosophy of Nature* Hegel understands the emergence of free spirit to require the *death* of the individual animal: 'death is the sublating of the individual and therewith . . . the procession of spirit'.[65] This makes it look as if Hegel is, indeed, part of an ascetic tradition, stretching back to Plato, for which spirit, consciousness and thought are the *negation* of life and the body – abstract forms of mental activity that achieve greater and greater maturity and freedom the closer the body comes to death.[66] Yet if Hegel is an ascetic thinker who sees death as the gateway to full spiritual freedom, how can he argue, and embrace the idea, that spirit is essentially embodied and alive?

The difficulty can be resolved if we recall that the transition Hegel describes from nature to spirit at the end of the *Philosophy of Nature* is a purely logical or conceptual one. Hegel is not claiming that we achieve full spiritual freedom only when we actually perish; he insists that spirit is inseparable from *life*. Indeed, he explicitly declares to be 'completely empty' the opinion of those ascetics 'who fancy that, strictly speaking, man should not have an organic body because this . . . diverts him from his purely spiritual life and prevents him from enjoying true freedom'.[67] He contends, however, that spirit and consciousness are made *logically* necessary by the fact that they render explicit what is implicit in the death of the animal. Throughout the *Philosophy of Nature* Hegel displays little interest in the way phenomena actually emerge in time; he focuses solely on the way in which one phenomenon makes another logically necessary. This remains his focus at the close of the *Philosophy of Nature*: 'when it was said . . . that the death of the merely immediate, individual form of life is the procession of spirit [*Geist*], this procession is . . . not to be understood as a natural procession but as a development of the Concept [*Begriff*]'.[68] This logical emergence of spirit from death is, in my view, perfectly compatible with the idea that spirit itself is actually, and necessarily, embodied and alive.

To understand why the death of the animal leads logically to the emergence of spirit, we must first recall that animals are not just separate individuals but members of a genus or species (*Gattung*). The species to which an animal belongs constitutes the 'substance' of that individual: it defines the kind of creature the animal is.[69] The species, however, is not limited to one individual (unless, of course, the animal is on the brink of extinction). It extends across several individuals and so is something *universal*. Animal life, in Hegel's view, is the process in which a given species or genus shows itself to be *explicitly* universal.

Animals have no articulated, conceptual consciousness of the fact that they are members of the same species: they do not think of themselves as, or know themselves to be, cats or dogs. They bear witness to a *feeling* of belonging to one species, however, in mating. The animal's instinct, for Hegel, is always to reinforce its feeling of being *itself*, 'to produce itself as a self-feeling, as totality'. In joining with another in copulation, however, the animal 'continues itself in this *other* and in this *other* feels its own self'. Copulation thus affords animals something of what mutual recognition grants to conscious human beings, namely 'hav[ing] their self-feeling only in the other'.[70] (Sexual relations and mutual recognition are, of course, brought together for human beings in the institution of marriage.) This feeling of being oneself with another is not merely a luxury or optional extra in an animal's life. Animals are driven to copulate by a strong *need* for one another; and this very sense of need for and dependence on another harbours, in Hegel's view, a feeling of being the same kind of animal, and of belonging to the same species or 'universal', as the other.

Hegel believes that this 'feeling of universality' in the sexual relation between two individuals is 'the highest to which the animal can attain'.[71] He also notes that mammals 'attain to the feeling of the unity of the one individual with the other, to the feeling of the genus or species' in the suckling and rearing of their young.[72] In neither mating nor suckling do animals attain a consciousness of their species *as* something universal: they do not form a *concept* of the species of which they are members. None the less, in Hegel's view, they *feel* that they belong to a single species and this feeling manifests itself in the strong bond they sense between themselves and other individuals.

In such feelings the species of which the individual animals are members acquires a certain degree of explicitness. That species proves to be genuinely *universal*, however, only when it shows itself not to be tied to, and dependent on, any particular individuals (and their feelings of belonging to it) but to continue in other individuals, and others, and others. According to Hegel, this means that an animal species shows itself to be truly universal only when an individual *dies* but the species itself lives on: 'the genus or species preserves itself only through the destruction [*Untergang*] of the individuals'.[73]

Animals, for Hegel, are thus destined to die not only because they are finite organisms, but also because it is through their death alone that they preserve and promote their species as something truly *universal*. Some animals, Hegel notes, die immediately after mating. Higher animals, by contrast, 'survive the generative act since they possess a higher kind of independence; and their death is the culmination of the process in their structure'. In all cases, however, animals – including human animals – carry 'the inborn *germ of death*' within them (and, indeed, an inherent propensity to sickness and disease). The very nature of the animal is to live and then *die*.[74]

Plants, of course, also die. Their death, however, is not essential to the process whereby species prove to be universal. This is because an individual plant can differentiate *itself* into the new individuals in which the species continues. These new individuals are identical in every respect to their parent. They thus do not replace their parent with something different and original, but simply duplicate it. They are the same plant *once again*.[75] In animals, by contrast, reproduction is essentially sexual, requiring the union of two different parents. The offspring produced in this way resemble the parents to a considerable degree, but they are not mere clones of either one (because, as we now know, they take different individual characteristics from each parent).[76] They are quite distinct individuals that *take the place* of their parents rather than duplicate them. Through sexual reproduction animals thus set in train the process of their own *supersession*. This process culminates in their death, at which point their offspring finally come into their own as truly distinct individuals. Among animals, therefore, the production of new individuals is completed only with the death of the parents. Accordingly, it is only with that death that the species to which the animals belong proves to be explicitly universal.

From a purely biological point of view, plants and animals are equally at risk of death.[77] There is, however, a higher, *logical* necessity to the death of the animal that is lacking in the case of plants. To recapitulate: the species to which an organism belongs proves to be truly universal only when it continues in new individuals; through sexual reproduction animals produce new individuals that are *different* from their parents; these offspring prove to be definitively different from their parents only by *outliving* them; an animal species proves to be explicitly universal, therefore, only by continuing after the death of individuals that belong to it. In animals the species or genus is thus 'the negative power over the individual', since it 'is realized through the sacrifice of this individual which it replaces by another'.[78]

Hegel celebrates life as the culmination of nature, but he understands that the death of individual animals is what gives their species an identity and continuity of its own. He reminds us, however, that an animal species in nature is never able to detach itself from individuals altogether and 'exist in and for itself', because such a species only exists in a continuing *series* of individuals, each of which must succumb to death in turn.[79] In proving to be continuous and universal, therefore, the species in fact becomes only partly independent. Yet this is not the end of the story, for Hegel sees in the death of the animal the promise of something more. He thinks that the absolute *negation* of the individual that occurs in death points logically towards a universal that is *wholly* free and independent – a universal or species that is a '*unity for itself*'.[80] Such a universal is not immediately generated by the death of the animal, but it is logically *implicit* in that death.

The individual animal that is 'for itself' has a sense or felt awareness of its own individual unity. The universal or species that is 'for itself' is similarly aware of itself. It is explicitly aware of itself as something *universal*. Such a 'universal that is for itself', Hegel maintains, is *thought* or *spirit*, rather than mere feeling.[81] Since the death of the individual animal points logically to a universal that is wholly independent and 'for itself', it thus points logically to spirit. In this sense, such a death makes spirit logically, but not empirically, *necessary*. In different circumstances spirit, thought and consciousness may never have emerged on the earth, but the death of animals would always have implied that they should.

This, briefly, is the logical transition from nature to spirit. 'With this', Hegel states, 'organic nature ends, for with the death of the individual the genus or species comes to its own self and thus becomes its *own* object: this is the procession of spirit.'[82] Since this transition is logical, not empirical, spirit itself does not have to be something dead. Indeed, as I suggested above, Hegel understands spirit and thought to be essentially alive and embodied. We must, therefore, take great care when interpreting the end of the *Philosophy of Nature*. Hegel maintains in the addition to the final paragraph that thought and spirit are simply 'the universal that is for itself'. For Hegel, however, there can be no purely *disembodied* spirit. The universal – the species to which we belong, and ultimately reason or the 'Idea' itself – must thus come to be 'for themselves', and so become conscious of themselves, in *individual* living beings. As Hegel puts it, 'the Idea exists *in* the self-subsistent subject, for which, as organ of the Concept, everything is ideal and fluid'.[83] The non-human animal is restricted to sensation and feeling; the individual subject in which the universal comes to consciousness *as* something universal must, therefore, be the human being. The human being is thus the sole living incarnation of spirit on earth. Human beings, for Hegel, are no less alive and no less embodied than other animals. What distinguishes human from non-human animals is simply the fact that – *in life* – 'man . . . raises himself above the singleness of sensation to the universality of thought, to self-knowledge, to the grasp of his subjectivity, of his I'.[84]

Human self-consciousness – 'spirit' – is made logically necessary by the death of the animal; but life – both animal and plant – is itself made logically necessary by chemistry, and chemistry in turn is made necessary by the nature of matter and ultimately by space and time. What requires there to be spirit and consciousness, therefore, is in fact nature as a whole understood as a series of stages, each of which renders explicit what is logically implicit in its predecessor. The logical, dialectical rationality leading from one stage of nature to another is the 'Concept' or 'Idea' that is immanent in nature itself.[85] Hegel's *Philosophy of Nature* shows, therefore, that nature's *own* inherent rationality makes spirit necessary. Contingent circumstances play a role in determining where and when spirit actually comes into existence; but Hegel proves that it is rational – given the nature of nature – that it should arise somewhere and at some point in time. In this sense, spirit is the product of nature.

The rationality or 'Idea' at work in nature can, however, itself be regarded as potentially or implicitly spirit: it is reason that has the capacity to become, but has not yet actually become, self-conscious. From this perspective, spirit is thus actually made necessary by its own possibility, by its own *implicit* presence in nature itself. As Hegel puts it, 'spirit which exists in and for itself is not the mere result of nature, but is in truth its own result. . . . The transition from nature to spirit is not a transition to an out-and-out Other, but is only a coming-to-itself of spirit out of its self-externality in nature.'[86] This is not to say, however, that there are two processes going on in the logical move from nature to spirit. There is only one process: the process whereby spirit is made necessary by a nature that harbours reason – and thus the potential for self-conscious spirit – within its own apparently barren and lifeless externality.

Evolution

Hegel has a profound interest in the way in which human consciousness develops through history. In his philosophy of nature, however, his focus on the logical connection between stages in nature goes hand in hand with a lack of interest in attempts to explain how natural phenomena emerge in time. As I argued in chapter 5, he leaves it to natural science to shed light on the natural history of the solar system or on the origin of life. In one case, though, he is not just indifferent but actively hostile to the idea that there is a natural history to be uncovered. To the discomfort of many who are otherwise persuaded by his philosophy, Hegel rejects outright the doctrine of the *evolution of species*. I do not propose here to provide a detailed study of Hegel's views on evolution or of the compatibility between his philosophy of nature and Darwin's theory of evolution through natural selection. A few words on these two topics are, however, necessary.

Hegel, of course, knew nothing of Darwin's theory: he died twenty-eight years before *The Origin of Species* was published in 1859. He would have been familiar, however, with the evolutionary theory of Lamarck, who assumed that lower organisms were generated spontaneously and that higher organisms then gradually developed from them (through, for example, the transmission of acquired characteristics).[87] Hegel makes his hostility to evolutionary theory clear at the beginning and towards the end of the *Philosophy of Nature*. In the Introduction, for example, he states that 'it is a completely empty thought to represent species as developing successively, one after the other, in time. . . . The land animal did not develop *naturally* out of the aquatic animal, nor did it fly into the air on leaving the water.'[88] In his discussion of geology in the section on organics he admits that the earth has a history during which life itself emerged, but he repeats his rejection of the idea that living species evolve into one another:

even *if* the earth was once in a state where it had no living things but only the chemical process, and so on, yet the moment the lightning of life strikes into matter, at once there is present a determinate, complete creature, as Minerva fully armed springs forth from the head of Jupiter. . . . Man has not developed himself out of the animal, nor the animal out of the plant; each is at a single stroke what it is.[89]

Hegel's anti-evolutionary stance obviously has its source in his philosophical interest in the *logical* rather than *temporal* relations between phenomena in nature. What he seeks to understand is not the historical process whereby phenomena in nature have come to be the way they are, but the *logic* that requires nature to have the structure that it now has: 'the point of interest is not to determine how things were millions of years ago . . . the interest is confined to what is there before us' and to recognize in the present character of nature 'the characteristics of the Concept'.[90] Hegel's philosophical interest in the logical relations between natural phenomena leads him to place a special value on the science of comparative anatomy whose 'great founder' was Cuvier.[91] Unlike evolutionary theory, in Hegel's view, Cuvier's science works towards the same systematic comprehension of nature as speculative philosophy, because it provides the empirical information that enables thought to discern rational, structural distinctions between animal species that now exist.

Given Hegel's commitment to a synchronic rather than diachronic understanding of nature and life, it is clear that he would have had no greater interest in the Darwinian theory of evolution than in the Lamarckian theory. *Pace* Findlay, Hegel in the *Philosophy of Nature* is not 'a philosopher of evolution'.[92] There is a difference, however, between a lack of interest in something and outright hostility to it, and I see nothing in the very idea of speculative philosophy that justifies Hegel in *rejecting*, rather than simply being *indifferent* to, the idea of the evolution of species. It is quite possible to focus one's own philosophical attention on the logical, structural differences between species, but also to allow other scientists to study the process whereby such species emerged in time (just as it is possible to let scientists study the origins of the solar system and of life). In my view, therefore, Hegel's philosophy of nature is not in principle incompatible with either the general idea of the evolution of species or Darwin's particular theory of evolution by natural selection.

There is one aspect of Darwinian theory, however, that might appear to set it at odds with Hegel's speculative philosophy: the emphasis placed by Darwinians on chance and contingency. According to modern Darwinian theory, accidental or 'random' mutations occur in organisms (due to errors in DNA replication) that can enable them to adapt to a changing environment better than other organisms. The organisms with advantageous mutations then survive and reproduce more successively than others, leading to the emergence of new varieties and eventually new species.[93] For the modern Darwinian, the emergence of higher forms of life, including human beings, is thus to a considerable degree, if not completely, a matter of chance.[94] As Vittorio Hösle reminds us, however, Hegel himself accords 'contingency' a significant role in nature.[95] For Hegel, there is a rational tendency towards life and consciousness in nature, but where and when they will emerge depends on circumstances that, from a philosophical point of view, are contingent. Furthermore, Hegel accepts that contingency plays a role in determining the different animal species that exist on earth.

Reason requires that life take the form not just of plant life but also of animal life, since only animal life is truly organic. There are also rational, structural differences between different kinds of animal (such as insects, fish, birds and mammals). Hegel acknowledges, however, that the element in or over which the animal moves – water, air or land – as well as the local geography co-determine the character of different animal species: animals are always suited to a specific environment. He also notes that 'the species of animals are exposed to contingency': hence the myriad of transitional forms that one finds in the animal world, such as mammals that fly and birds that don't.[96] For Hegel, therefore, reason, geography *and* contingency work together to create the species that populate the earth.

Hegel believes – *contra* Darwin – that species emerge fully formed and fixed. In my view, however, Hegel's systematic philosophical interest in rational distinctions between animal species (and in comparative anatomy) does not justify this anti-evolutionary position, but is in fact quite compatible with the idea that species evolved from one another. Furthermore, Hegel's recognition of the fact that contingency has a necessary place in nature suggests that his philosophy of nature may, indeed, be able to coexist with the Darwinian theory of evolution through natural selection. It is possible, of course, that 'contingency' does not mean exactly the same thing to Hegel and to Darwinians. In that case, much more work would need to be done to establish whether their respective views are compatible. Further exploration of the relation between Hegel's speculative philosophy of nature and Darwinian evolutionary theory must, however, await another occasion.[97]

Embodied Spirit

The non-human animal feels itself to be a unified self and also senses individual things in the world around it. The human spirit, by contrast, is the clear *consciousness* and *thought* of what is universal *as* something universal. It is explicitly aware of itself as an 'I' (and as a 'person') and it conceives of the things around it in terms of universal concepts, such as 'thing', 'plant' and 'animal'. Spirit is, however, *embodied* awareness. This is not to deny that humans are capable of free and rational self-determination; but such self-determination, for Hegel, is made possible by the organic structure of the human body.

The fact that human spirit is necessarily embodied means that it is inseparable from other aspects of our mental life that are determined by the body and by the natural environment with which our bodies are intimately connected. Hegel examines what he calls our 'natural soul' in his Anthropology, the first sub-section of the *Philosophy of Spirit*. He notes, for example, that the human spirit is subject to 'dull moods' (*trübe Stimmungen*) that change with the climate, the seasons of the year and the time of day. Like other animals, we thus live in a certain 'sympathy' with the rhythms of nature. These moods are, however, subordinate moments of our mental and spiritual life and do not get in the way of free, rational thought. Furthermore, their effect on us gets weaker, in Hegel's view, as we become more educated.[98]

The geographical region we inhabit gives rise to further aspects of our natural soul, namely to racial and national differences between human beings. Hegel believes that racial and national character sets limits to what certain peoples may achieve in history through their own efforts. It thus explains why political and religious freedom develops further in Europe than in Asia or Africa. He insists, however, that such naturally determined character does not prevent individuals or whole peoples being *educated* into the ways of freedom. He maintains, for example – notoriously – that Africans 'do not show an inherent striving for culture'. Yet he emphasizes at the same time that 'they cannot be denied a capacity for education'; and to prove the point he notes that they have 'adopted Christianity with the greatest gratitude and spoken movingly of the freedom they have acquired through Christianity after a long spiritual servitude'.[99]

This is not the place to consider the merits or inadequacies of Hegel's remarks on racial and national character. Readers must judge for themselves whether those remarks are largely fair and persuasive or, as some argue, patronizing and crudely stereotypical.[100] I wish only to highlight two things. On the one hand, Hegel believes that racial and national characteristics are not mere social 'constructs' but real products of the geography we inhabit. On the other hand, he thinks that, like the climate-related moods to which we are subject, they are no more than subordinate moments of our overall spirit and do not ultimately impair our capacity for free, rational thought. They provide no warrant, therefore, for the denial of basic rights and freedoms to individuals or peoples. Hegel is aware that some of his contemporaries have sought 'to prove that human beings are by nature so differently endowed with mental or spiritual capacities that some can be dominated like animals'. He makes it clear, however, that he rejects as a matter of principle any who would seek to enslave or deny rights to other human beings on racial (or nationalist) grounds. 'Man is implicitly rational', he reminds us; 'herein lies the possibility of equal justice for *all men* [*aller Menschen*] and the nullity [*Nichtigkeit*] of a rigid distinction between races which have rights and those which have none'.[101]

Hegel goes on to note that one's personal temperament is also determined by nature and that one's age and one's gender affect how one feels and thinks about things, as well.[102] Once again, however, he contends that such factors do not prevent us from being free and rational. Nor, he states, do they put insuperable barriers in the way of our becoming virtuous. 'Virtue', he maintains, 'is something universal, to be required of all men; it is not innate but is to be produced in the individual by his own efforts.' Virtue certainly has social and political conditions: it is hard to be virtuous other than in a state with good laws. In Hegel's view, however, 'differences in natural dispositions are . . . of no importance whatever for ethics'.[103] This is because they are nothing more than *dispositions* to feel, think or act in a certain way – dispositions which do not govern our lives but can themselves be mastered and integrated into a life of free self-determination.

As I have just noted, one of the factors disposing us to think and feel in a certain way is age. Below a certain age, however, our bodies do not allow us to think properly at all. As Hegel puts it, 'understanding does not come before its time'.[104] Equally, when we are asleep or when we are ill or when the body dies, thought is suspended, impaired or destroyed altogether. Apart from these cases, however, spirit's necessary embodiment does not prevent it from being free and rational. Indeed, the healthy organic human body is precisely what makes free spirit possible. If 'I behave in accordance with the laws of my physical organism', Hegel remarks, 'my soul is free in its body'.[105]

*   *   *

The human spirit's necessary embodiment means that it must be aware of itself and the world around it through feeling and sensation – like non-human animals – and not just through thought. It must also give involuntary bodily expression to its feelings, for example in laughter and crying. Spirit proves its freedom, however, by also giving *voluntary* bodily expression to its feelings and thoughts through hand gestures and facial expressions.[106] Furthermore, spirit can train the body to adopt certain habits. Habit formation is thus, in John McCumber's words, an 'emancipatory phenomenon', for it shows the spirit gaining freedom and control over the very body that is its own enabling condition.[107]

Spirit further proves its freedom by distinguishing itself from its body and turning itself into a 'completely indeterminate ideality' and 'purely self-relating universal'; that is, into an *I* (*Ich*). In so doing spirit also draws a sharp distinction between itself and what it sees, hears and feels, and it understands the latter to form a separate realm of *objects*. In this way spirit changes from a natural, feeling soul into the clear *consciousness* of things. Spirit becomes conscious of a world over against it only because it has come to conceive *itself* as having an abstract, ideal identity of its own: 'only when I come to apprehend myself as "I", does the Other become objective to me, confront me'.[108] It should not be forgotten, however, that what comes to this distinct consciousness of itself is nothing but the soul or the 'immateriality' of the *body*.

Hegel's account of consciousness is set out in a section entitled 'Phenomenology of Spirit'. This phenomenology, however, is not the same as the pure phenomenology that precedes speculative philosophy and was examined in chapters 3 and 4. It is, rather, a *philosophical* phenomenology that itself presupposes the science of logic and the philosophy of nature.[109] The difference between the two phenomenologies is subtle but significant. Whereas pure phenomenology traces the *experience* that consciousness itself logically generates, its philosophical counterpart uncovers what is logically implicit for the speculative philosopher in the *ontological structure* of consciousness. This latter discipline is none the less called 'phenomenology' because it studies the *'appearance (Erscheinen)* of spirit' – consciousness – rather than spirit proper.[110] Philosophical phenomenology begins in the same way as pure phenomenology by considering first sense certainty and then perception, understanding, desire and recognition. It does not, however, go on to consider stoical, sceptical and unhappy consciousness but moves straight to reason (via a phenomenon that Hegel calls 'universal self-consciousness'). Hegel then makes the logical transition to spirit proper (*der Geist*). Since we are examining forms of *subjective* spirit, however, spirit is considered here not in so far as it constitutes an objective social world (such as the world of Sophocles' *Antigone*), but in so far as it takes the form of *individual* subjectivity. Phenomenology thus gives way to psychology: the study of the human mind or spirit in its free theoretical and practical activity.

Intelligence and Its Signs

Consciousness, Hegel states, understands its object to be something immediately given and distinct from itself. Consciousness thus 'does not yet know that the object is in itself *identical* with spirit'.[111] This identity consists in the fact that both consciousness and its object – nature – have the same *rational* structure. The final mode of consciousness, 'Reason' (*Vernunft*), begins to discern this identity between itself and its object and so to 'possess the confidence that it will find itself in the world'. Only spirit proper, or *thought (Denken)*, however, is fully aware that the structure of its own categories and concepts is the structure of things themselves. Thought 'knows that what is *thought, is*, and that what *is*, only *is* in so far as it is thought'. It thus recognizes in its own concepts the 'simple identity of the subjective and the objective'.[112]

Such thought is not merely something given. It is the result of the free, self-determining activity of theoretical spirit or 'intelligence' (*Intelligenz*). Such intelligence at its simplest is the immediate sensuous *intuition (Anschauung)* of a world that does not just stand over against us – as the external object of consciousness – but surrounds us as an objective 'totality'.[113] Intuitive intelligence freely transforms itself, however, into thought: it actively produces its own conceptual understanding of itself and its world.[114] Intelligence transforms itself into thought by freeing itself from determination by its body and external nature. At the same time it remains irreducibly and definitively *embodied*.[115] It cannot, therefore, simply cut itself loose from its body, but must use that body to give expression to its spiritual freedom.

Hegel's philosophical psychology is a veritable treasure chest of insights that deserve extended and detailed discussion. My account here, however, will give only the barest outline of Hegel's argument. Human intuition, for Hegel, is not purely passive cognition, since it involves active attention to what surrounds us. The content of intuition, however, is given by sensation and so is determined by the external things that affect the sense organs of the body.[116] If intelligence is to become freely self-determining, in Hegel's view, it must learn to assert its *own* power and control over such intuitions. Intuitions themselves will always remain externally determined, but intelligence can learn to use them for its own ends. Intelligence takes the first step towards such control by internalizing its intuitions and turning them into images (*Bilder*) within the mind. These images are at first fleeting and so sink into what Hegel calls the 'nocturnal pit' of the unconscious. They can, however, be revived by the chance encounter – through one's eyes, ears, tongue, nose or skin – with objects. Intelligence, for Hegel, is thus necessarily subject to the *involuntary* recollection of images buried deep in the obscure recesses of the mind. Repeated involuntary recollection fixes an image in the mind and renders intelligence capable of recalling it *voluntarily*.[117]

Intelligence demonstrates its power over images not only by recalling them at will but also by freely associating them with one another and abstracting out their common features to form *general* representations (*allgemeine Vorstellungen*). As this free activity of recollecting, associating and abstracting, intelligence is 'reproductive imagination' (*reproduktive Einbildungskraft*).[118] Note that by internalizing intuitions and producing general representations from the resultant images, intelligence gives differentiated content to its own inner world: the general representations it forms acquire significance for it and so constitute its own inner realm of *meaning* (*Bedeutung* or *Sinn*).[119] Intelligence then extends its power and freedom over the concrete images in its mind by employing them to picture or *symbolize* these meaningful, general representations. In this way, Hegel maintains, intelligence mutates into '*phantasy* [*Phantasie*], *symbolising*, *allegorising* or *poetic* imagination' or what Hegel also calls 'productive imagination'.[120]

As deVries notes, 'symbolic fantasy is an important turning point in mind's growth to free self-determination'. This is because such imagination does not just focus its attention on the images themselves but freely appropriates them for its *own* expressive purpose. It thereby deprives the images of their independence.[121] A much more radical freedom is exhibited by imagination, however, when it gives expression to its own representations in *signs* (*Zeichen*) rather than symbols. Symbols can be internal images in the mind that we connect with a certain meaning, whereas signs are *external* – visible or audible – expressions of meaning, such as colours or sounds.[122] More importantly, whereas a symbol is chosen because of some similarity between it and its meaning, the connection between a sign and its meaning is wholly arbitrary. The image of the eagle symbolizes the strength of Jupiter because of the animal's own strength and power. The sounds 'Ju-pi-ter', by contrast, have no intrinsic connection with the god they stand for and so are signs rather than symbols.

The use of signs is normally governed by social and historical conventions – as in language – and so is not completely up to the individual. None the less, the very production and use of the sign as such, whose connection with meaning is *arbitrary* and so has to be learnt, manifests a clear freedom of intelligence: 'as *signifying*', Hegel states, 'intelligence demonstrates a much freer caprice [*Willkür*] and mastery in the use of intuition than as symbolising'.[123] Kathleen Dow Magnus points out, however, 'that the intelligence's ability to create the sign . . . arises out of its intuition, recollection, and imagination, elements of its experience that are intrinsically linked to the sensuous'.[124] That is to say, intelligence uses signs only because it is *embodied* spirit. Hegel argues, indeed, that the most perfect sign is generated by the human body itself.

When an intuited object is made into a sign, the 'sign-making phantasy' or 'productive memory' (*produktives Gedächtnis*) disregards – and thus *negates* – the visible or audible materiality of the object and turns it into a transparent, empty 'housing' or 'shell' (*Gehäuse*) for meaning.[125] In Hegel's view, the material object that is most suited to being a sign is thus one that actually *negates itself* and vanishes as soon as it arises and thereby, as it were, sets itself aside in favour of its assigned meaning. The best example of such an 'object', Hegel tells us, is the fleeting *sound*. Sounds that are deliberately emitted through the mouth as arbitrary signs of inner meaning – rather than just involuntary cries of pain or joy – are *words*. For Hegel, therefore, 'spoken words, which die away as they are uttered and thus negate themselves straightaway, are the most appropriate form of the sign'.[126] A system of such deliberately produced spoken signs, with agreed conventions and grammatical rules, constitutes a language. Intelligence must, therefore, give *linguistic* expression to its representations. This is because it is freely self-determining, *embodied* spirit and so must produce material signs of its immaterial inner life.

In his anthropology Hegel notes that a bodily gesture, such as a movement of the hand, can also serve as a '*sign* of inner feeling' to others.[127] Such a gesture, however, is in fact more likely to be a symbol – or, indeed, the actual physical incarnation – of feeling than a true, wholly arbitrary sign thereof. Furthermore, such gestures lack the airy, quasi-immaterial quality that makes words the most perfect material carriers of 'ideal' meaning. A language made up of true signs will thus be a system of speech, for Hegel, rather than a gesture-based 'sign language'.

Hegel has much of interest to say not only about spoken language but also about the role played by writing in stabilizing patterns of speech – ideas that have drawn the close attention of, among others, Derrida.[128] Here, however, there is space to give only a very brief sketch of the logical path from words to thought. Words are fleeting, immediately disappearing signs that bring ideal meanings to mind. They are preserved and turned into enduring *names* for things and ideas by 'name-retaining memory' (*das Namen behaltende Gedächtnis*). 'Reproductive memory' then learns to understand these names without the explicit presence of any accompanying representation or image. Such memory thus affords us a profound freedom not just over, but also *from*, the givens of the sensuous intuition and the image, because it fills the mind with nothing but arbitrary signs or names that we understand *immediately*. As deVries puts it, 'through our use of words we have eliminated the need for intuitions and images of the things we represent. The things we represent exist for us in the names themselves'.[129]

The last form of memory discussed by Hegel is 'mechanical memory'. Such memory holds together signs that have *lost* their meaning altogether. Intelligence itself is not thereby lost, however: on the contrary, in memorizing strings of meaningless words, intelligence comes to conceive of itself as the wholly abstract power and activity of connecting as such; that is, as '*wholly abstract subjectivity*'.[130] When intelligence discerns the different determinations or 'categories' that are immanent in such pure, abstract subjectivity, it begins to *think*.

Thought is an activity of the same self that feels its own unity and is conscious of itself as an 'I' over against a world of objects. Thought, however, is aware of a profound *identity* between itself and objects because it understands the true nature of those objects to be disclosed *within* its own concepts and categories.[131] Thought also understands itself to be *fully* free and self-determining: it knows that its fundamental logical categories are generated spontaneously by itself (and not abstracted from sensuous experience), and it knows that the way to discover the truth about things in the world is not through observation alone but through its own autonomous rational activity. In its most sophisticated form, however, thought is also aware that, even when it is silent and inward, its consummate freedom is dependent upon names and thus, ultimately, on the ability to use *spoken* signs: it knows that 'we *think* in names'.[132] Such thought understands, therefore, that it is fully free, self-determining, *embodied* thought. Consequently, it realizes that its concepts serve to clarify and render comprehensible what is given in sensation and intuition, that its free rational activity thus requires the aid of imagination and memory, and, indeed, that such activity is made possible by the organic structure of the human body.

This concludes our account of Hegel's philosophy of life and subjective spirit. Let us briefly review his principal theses: Matter, for Hegel, organizes itself into living beings, some of which exhibit an immaterial self-relation or 'self-feeling'. Feeling and sensation are thus not attributes of a wholly independent soul that is somehow inserted into the body; rather, matter mutates into sensitive organic life by 'immaterializing' or 'idealizing' *itself*. In human beings the immaterial animal self becomes conscious of itself and, indeed, becomes freely self-determining intelligence. Such intelligence gives expression to its representations through signs. Having 'idealized' itself into sensitive organic life, therefore, matter is even more radically 'idealized' by free intelligence by being reduced to the transparent carrier or sign of ideal meanings. By means of such idealized material signs, intelligence comes to conceive of itself as pure, abstract, but also fully free and self-determining subjectivity. As such, it is *thought*.

Hegel ends his psychology by noting that thought does not merely seek to understand the world around it through its own free reason. It also recognizes that it has the freedom and power to *remake* that world in accordance with purposes of its own choosing. In so doing it becomes practical spirit or *will*. As Hegel points out, not all of the will's purposes are themselves explicitly rational: many are governed by contingent needs and interests. None the less, the will is grounded in thought (rather than mere feeling or imagination) because it conceives of itself as *fully* free and self-determining: thanks to this self-conception alone is the will able to 'give itself its own content' in the form of self-chosen purposes and, through the pursuit of those purposes, put its own stamp on the world. As Hegel states, therefore, 'thought determines itself into will and remains the substance of the latter; so that without thought there can be no will'.[133] In the next chapter we consider the *rights* that such free will claims for itself and the objective social and political institutions that are needed in order to secure those rights.

8   *Freedom, Rights and Civility*

From Hegel to Hitler?

Hegel's *Philosophy of Right* is one of the greatest works of social and political philosophy ever written, equal in philosophical and historical importance to Plato's *Republic*, Aristotle's *Politics*, Hobbes's *Leviathan* and Rousseau's *Social Contract*, indeed exceeding them in the extraordinary range of topics with which it deals. In the *Philosophy of Right* Hegel draws on Rousseau, Montesquieu, Adam Smith, Kant and Schiller, as well as on political, legal, economic and social conditions in France, Britain and Germany, in order to develop his conception of political and social life. He offers a powerful analysis of the sources of industrial alienation and poverty that anticipates the thought of Marx, and he provides subtle analyses, among other things, of Roman law, Kantian ethics, the family, fashion, civil society, the jury system and the political constitution.

What binds all these topics together and to my mind makes Hegel the most important political philosopher of the modern, post-French Revolutionary era, is the fact that he integrates his social and political analyses into an all-embracing theory of *freedom*. I have suggested in previous chapters that the concept of freedom lies at the heart of Hegel's philosophy. In chapter 1, we saw how he interprets history as the development of the consciousness of freedom, and in chapter 2, we saw what it means to develop a speculative logic that is fully self-determining and free. In chapters 6 and 7 we learned that Hegel even understands there to be degrees of freedom in nature. In this chapter, I propose to pursue Hegel's understanding of freedom further by considering his account of what it means to be free in the sphere of 'objective *Geist*', the sphere of abstract right, morality, civil society and the state.

Richard Winfield is one of a growing group of modern commentators who recognize that Hegel is concerned to develop a conception of social and political freedom 'which gives due respect to the individual structure of the will'.[1] However, there is a strong tradition of Hegel criticism, running from Hegel's contemporary, Schopenhauer, through Rudolf Haym and Nietzsche, to Bertrand Russell and Karl Popper, which sees in Hegel little more than an apologist for the conservative (Prussian) status quo and an advocate of the subordination of the individual to the state. For some critics, indeed, Hegel's political philosophy is a direct precursor of corporate fascism and National Socialism, and is as hostile to the cause of freedom and tolerance as it is possible to be. In the minds of many people, then, Hegel is associated more with the veneration of the Prussian state, with proto-Hitlerian German nationalism, and with recommending 'war [as] an acceptable policy for vigorous nations', than with liberalism or democracy.[2] (A contributor to the journal of the Hegel Society of America even reported the discovery of a book entitled *From Hegel to Gaddafi* at Tripoli Airport in Libya, a title which would surely confirm all the worst fears of free-thinking Western democrats if it were ever to become widely known.)[3]

How is it possible for Hegel's political philosophy to have been interpreted in such conflicting ways? Part of the answer is that the severest critics of Hegel have frequently reacted to what they have perceived to be the deleterious effects of *Hegelianism* and have not actually read much of Hegel himself. However, even some commentators who have read Hegel relatively closely have found his philosophy to be inimical to the cause of freedom and therefore unpalatable. This can only be due, I think, to a failure to comprehend Hegel's philosophical method, and to a consequent inability to read and understand his texts properly. As we shall see, Hegel is critical of the traditional 'liberal' insistence that individuals are free to the extent that their activity is not restricted by society or the state, and he considers political patriotism and respect for the state to be essential to a healthy political community. However, in my view, Hegel's commentators would not be led to the conclusion that he is simply subordinating the interests of the individual to those of the state, or indeed advocating the suppression of individual freedom by the state, if they fully understood how his philosophy proceeds.

In the *Philosophy of Right*, Hegel reminds us that speculative philosophy does not proceed by setting up definitions or propositions and defending them through argument or supporting evidence, but that it seeks to understand and articulate the immanent development of the concepts which it considers. The task of a speculative philosophy of political and social freedom is thus not to argue for or against certain given conceptions of freedom, or to criticize an individualistic conception of freedom from an external perspective (such as that of the state), but simply to develop the idea of freedom or, as Hegel puts it, 'to look on at the proper immanent development of the matter [*Sache*] itself'.[4] In the course of this development, speculative philosophy will recognize that when freedom is conceived in certain ways it turns out to be contradictory or inadequate on its own terms. At the same time, however, speculative philosophy will discern within those conceptions of freedom further, more complex, but as yet implicit, conceptions of freedom which, when rendered explicit, enable the previous contradictions or inadequacies to be overcome. What many of Hegel's critics fail to recognize is that his criticisms of individualistic conceptions of freedom are not due to any prejudice in favour of state authority on his part, but arise during the course of a prolonged meditation on and determination of the proper meaning of *freedom* itself. If we are indeed taken beyond a merely individualistic conception of freedom by Hegel's analysis, this is simply because the very meaning or concept of freedom itself requires us to recognize that freedom is not just to be found in unrestricted individual choice or in the unregulated pursuit of self-satisfaction, but in living in accordance with law within a just political constitution.

The Limits of Choice

The concept of human freedom emerges necessarily in Hegel's system. The *Science of Logic* considers what it means to be and reveals that to be means to be rationally self-determining or 'Idea'. Furthermore, it reveals that rationally self-determining existence is to be understood initially as nature. Hegel's philosophy of nature develops the concepts of space, time, matter, gravity, light and so on and shows that the rational outcome of nature is the emergence of human consciousness. The philosophy of *Geist* then develops the concept of consciousness to the point at which it has become fully free and self-determining in the form of thought and free will. It is at this point that the *Philosophy of Right* begins.

The particular conception of human freedom that Hegel considers first is what Peter Singer calls the 'classical liberal conception of freedom': I am free, on this account, when I can do as I please and others do not force me to do what I do not want to do.[5] Not all liberals, of course, are complete libertarians. Liberals may well acknowledge that limits and restrictions need to be placed on freedom of choice in order that society may function properly. They may also recognize that choices are made for communal not just personal reasons, and so need not be driven by wholly egoistic motives. Nevertheless, the core of the liberal position is that the society which maximizes freedom maximizes individual *choice*, and that any limits or restrictions which might be placed on our freedom to choose, however necessary they may be, are always experienced as *restrictions*.

This common, liberal conception of freedom has three 'moments' or 'sides' to it in Hegel's view. First of all, it involves what he calls the 'pure indeterminacy' of the self, the 'absolute *possibility* of abstracting from every determinate state of mind in which I may find myself or which I may have set up in myself, my flight from every content as from a restriction'.[6] This is what Hegel terms 'negative freedom' and it is, in his eyes, the most primitive conception of freedom – of free will – that we can have. It involves not being tied down to any particular state of mind or interest, but rather having the ability to cut oneself loose from any particular engagement and remain free from the constraints and limitations of particular activities.

But freedom as commonly conceived does not simply mean not being tied down or restricted; it also entails the positive ability to engage in particular activities if one wishes. The second moment of liberal freedom is thus the ability to enter into a specific state of mind or activity and to concern oneself with something particular.

However, in exercising my freedom to engage in specific pursuits, I must still preserve my freedom to withdraw from them, if I am to remain *free* in the initial, negative sense. The third moment of liberal freedom for Hegel must thus be the unity of the first two moments: the freedom to engage in – to choose – some specific pursuit, but in so doing to preserve the sense that one is not irrevocably committed to that pursuit, because one has chosen it oneself and so could withdraw from it and engage in some *other* pursuit if one so wished. Construed in this way, freedom entails the ability to make commitments, but at the same time to keep one's options open. This, Hegel tells us, is the conception most people have of freedom: freedom as the safeguarding of one's possibilities and capacities in the face of whatever commitments one may make, freedom as the ability to choose (and do) as one pleases.[7]

As many commentators have pointed out, Hegel is strongly critical of this conception of freedom. However, he does not pass judgement on it from some presupposed conception of the good or of what constitutes a just, ethical or responsible life. Rather, he thinks through what this conception of freedom entails and discerns a contradiction within it.

The mode of freedom which we have been considering lies, as Hegel puts it, in not being 'tied to this or that content', in not being *required* to choose or do anything.[8] Individuals may be confronted by seemingly unavoidable needs (such as the need to eat or work for a living), but they will think of themselves as free if they are not actually forced into any particular course of action, but could, for example, refuse to work or eat. From the perspective of this conception of freedom, therefore, the fact that I am free is not understood to bring with it any necessary commitments of its own. I must certainly choose something if my freedom is to be a real freedom to choose, but I do not consider that I am committed to any specific course of action simply by virtue of the fact that I am free – because I consider my freedom to be nothing other than the ability to disengage myself and withdraw from any particular commitment which I may have made.

I can thus only preserve my freedom of choice if I consider the options which I am able to choose (or reject) to be separate from me, external to me; that is, to be activities or interests which do not follow from my freedom itself. But this, in Hegel's understanding, is where the intrinsic contradiction in this conception of freedom becomes evident. For if I wish to preserve the sense that my freedom lies in facing a set of options to which, as a free individual, I am not *necessarily* committed, then the following question arises: what determines the options among which I have to choose, if it is not my freedom itself? The only possibility is that those options are determined by factors other than my free will, such as circumstance, chance or nature, and that they are *given* to me to choose between or reject. But if this is the case, then my freedom of choice is *dependent* upon what is available to be chosen. Moreover, by insisting that freedom resides in being able to choose whatever I want, I limit myself to, and make myself dependent on, whatever I happen to want or wish for at the moment; that is, whatever my particular desires happen to be or whatever my circumstances (or indeed the pressures of the market or of advertising) lead me to desire. It is clear, therefore, that, when I lay claim to unrestricted freedom of choice, I am not actually as free as I think I am, since my commitments are not derived from my free will itself, and so are not determined by my own free will. 'The ordinary man in the street believes himself to be free, when he is allowed to act as he wants to [*willkürlich*], but this very arbitrariness entails that he is not free', because the content of his will – what it is that he wills – is 'not intrinsic to self-determining activity itself'. Such 'freedom' is thus in fact 'dependence on a content and material given either from within or without'.[9]

This contradiction can only be resolved when the will is no longer dependent on something given to it, and the will only frees itself from such dependence, in Hegel's view, when *what* it wills is determined, not by external or internal contingencies, but by itself. But what 'content' is determined by the free will itself? What am I committed to simply by virtue of the fact that I am, and know myself to be, a *free* will? The answer becomes clear if we think about what the will is trying to preserve and actualize in exercising freedom of choice. When we choose a particular course of action we clearly will whatever it is that we choose; however, by insisting that we are not irrevocably committed to it, we demonstrate that we are interested not just in this particular option, but more importantly in preserving our *freedom* to choose. Whatever specific commitments we make, therefore, our primary concern, in so far as we seek to preserve the possibility of other, different choices, is to safeguard and exercise our freedom itself. The content or 'object' which any free will wills simply by virtue of being free is thus nothing other than its own freedom.

When the free will wills its own freedom as its *explicit* object, it is a *truly* free will, since it wills a content which is 'intrinsic to self-determining activity itself' and so is not dependent on a set of contents which are given to it to choose between. 'The absolute goal or, if you like, the absolute impulse, of free mind, is to make freedom its object', Hegel tells us. True freedom thus lies not merely in doing or choosing what one wishes, but in being a 'free will which wills the free will'.[10]

Like Rousseau and Kant, Hegel understands the truly free will to be the will that explicitly wills itself and its own freedom. He derives this conception of true freedom from what he understands to be implicit in the structure of freedom of choice, but it is clear that with this conception his analysis has moved us on from choice to a new conception of freedom.

The will that wishes to be able to choose whatever it wants *must* look to preserve its own freedom to choose, even though it conceives of its freedom as the absence of necessity or constraint. However, the will that is explicitly and self-consciously free *acknowledges* that freedom is something that it must will simply by virtue of the fact that it is free, and so no longer insists on the priority of its own freedom to choose. Such a will is no longer dependent for its object upon external factors, but wills an object or content – namely freedom – which is derived from itself and is thus wholly its own. Yet it only gains its freedom through its willingness to give up its unlimited ability to choose, and let itself be determined by the character of its own freedom.

The truly free will understands freedom to be something to which, as free, it is necessarily committed, something which thus necessarily commands the recognition of any free will. Understood in this way freedom is a matter of simple and immediate *right*.[11] Hegel's philosophy of freedom thus turns out to be a philosophy of right, an account of what the free will must uphold if it is to be a truly free will.

This new conception of freedom might not appear to mark much of an advance over the conception of freedom as choice, especially if one reflects on the fact that one can insist on one's right to choose as much as on any other right. However, for Hegel there is a decisive difference between the will which sees freedom solely in terms of choice and the will which sees freedom as a matter of right, namely that the latter explicitly recognizes that freedom itself entails necessary commitments, indeed obligations and responsibilities, which derive immanently from the structure of freedom itself, and from which, as a free will, it cannot choose to disengage itself without denying its own freedom. Hegel thus puts forward a conception of true freedom in which what is traditionally viewed as the opposition between freedom and necessity or constraint is dissolved. The truly free will understands the requirement that it recognize rights or laws not simply as a necessary or prudent *restriction* on its freedom, but as something that has been determined as necessary by freedom itself and thus as a positive element of what it means to be free. Like Rousseau and Kant, therefore, Hegel understands the free will to be one whose obligations derive from itself; that is, to be a self-legislating and self-determining will.

This is where many critics of Hegel have gone badly wrong. They recognize that Hegel is critical of the ordinary, liberal conception of freedom and that, for him, the truly free will is the will which willingly submits itself to laws. But they fail to recognize that the laws, obligations and responsibilities to which the free will submits itself issue from the free will itself, not from some alien authority. They fail to recognize, therefore, that the alternative to freedom construed as choice is not subordination to the state, but self-determination; that is, understanding the laws and institutions within which one lives to be determined by the character or structure of one's own freedom. It is the task of Hegel's *Philosophy of Right* to show precisely which institutions are determined to be necessary by the structure of freedom, by deriving them immanently from the concept of freedom as inviolable right.

Rights, Property and Slavery

Hegel holds that we are free not when we indulge in unconstrained, arbitrary choice, but when we acknowledge that freedom is something the free will must will; that is, that freedom is a *right*. Our right is thus our freedom construed as something which commands our recognition.

The rights to which Hegel turns his initial attention are those to which one is immediately entitled simply by virtue of the fact that one is free, those which immediately 'objectify' one's freedom. Such rights include the right to own property, to exchange goods, to enter into binding contracts and to 'own' one's body (i.e. not to be enslaved). We do not possess these rights because of any special natural characteristics or talents we may have, nor do we *merit* them because of our status in society or moral virtue. We have them simply because we are conscious that we are free and that freedom must be respected.

To bear certain immediate rights is the same as being a person, Hegel says, and because anyone who is conscious of his or her freedom can lay claim to personhood, regardless of differences in natural or moral character, it follows that all persons are equal before the law in respect of their immediate rights. Matters of immediate right are thus not to be decided on the basis of specific needs or circumstances or what is conducive to an individual's welfare, but simply on the basis of entitlement.

The specific rights which belong to someone as a free person follow, according to Hegel, directly from the concept of the free person itself, and the most basic of these is simply the right to have one's freedom as a person recognized and respected as a right; that is, the right to be considered a bearer of rights. 'The absolute right is [the right] to have rights.'[12] By itself, of course, this does not yet establish a right to anything in particular, but it does at least establish that I have the right to consider my personhood and my entitlement to rights in general to be inviolable. This generates what Hegel considers to be the first imperative of immediate or 'abstract' right: 'Be a person and respect others as persons.' Since this imperative is purely formal (because it allows anything to be done provided that a person's rights are respected), it actually amounts to no more than the negative imperative: 'Do not infringe personhood and what personhood entails.' 'The result', Hegel concludes, 'is that there are only prohibitions in the sphere of right, and the positive form of any command in this sphere is based in the last resort, if we examine its ultimate content, on prohibition.'[13]

However, the right of inviolable personhood does bring with it certain specific positive rights as well, the main one being the right to own property. Hegel would agree that we need to own things because we need to have at our disposal the means to satisfy our basic human needs, such as food, shelter and clothing. But he insists that the *right* to property stems from our freedom alone, not from our natural needs. The right to own property follows from the fact that a person is only bound by his freedom to respect persons and their rights and is not bound to respect whatever is unfree and 'without rights'. As Article Four of the *Declaration of the Rights of Man* (1789) puts it: 'Each man's exercise of his natural rights has no limits but those which guarantee the other members of society the enjoyment of these same rights.'[14] Things that are not aware of themselves as free – natural objects, for example – thus have no rights over against persons and do not have the right to set a limit to the freedom of persons. For this reason, Hegel says, 'a person has as his substantive end the right of putting his will into any and every thing and thereby making it his. . . . This is the absolute right of appropriation which man has over all things [*Sachen*].'[15] By appropriating external natural objects as his property, the person transforms them from potential limits on his freedom into expressions of it, and so affords himself a way of giving his freedom an external, objective form which others must recognize and respect. But it should be remembered that, since property must be respected as the objectification of a person's right, my freedom to appropriate, own and use natural objects can only apply to those objects which do not already belong to others.

Just as I can appropriate an external object as my property by laying claim to it as an expression of my free will, so I can also appropriate my body by laying claim to it as an expression of my free will. My body is thus not simply my own as a matter of natural fact; it becomes my own when I have freely and self-consciously appropriated it. To the extent that I have taken charge of my body, it becomes the literal embodiment of my freedom and right, and so commands respect as much as my will does. Violence done to my body, therefore, is violence done to my free will and personhood, and is a violation of my right.[16]

This conception of personal freedom as expressed in and through my body underlies Hegel's comments on slavery. Critics can point to certain passages in Hegel's writings which suggest that he does not view slavery as an utter evil or wrong. In the lectures on the philosophy of history, for example, one can find the following remarks:

> The only essential connection that has existed and continued between the negroes and the Europeans is that of slavery. In this the negroes see nothing unbecoming them, and the English, who have done most for abolishing the slave-trade and slavery, are treated by the negroes themselves as enemies. For it is a point of first importance with the kings to sell their captured enemies, or even their own subjects; and viewed in the light of such facts, we may conclude slavery to have been the occasion of the increase of human feeling among the negroes [because they no longer eat their enemies]. . . . We find slavery even in the Greek and Roman states, as we do serfdom down to the latest times. But thus existing in a state, slavery is itself a phase of advance from the merely isolated sensual existence – a phase of education – a mode of becoming participant in a higher morality and the culture connected with it. . . . The gradual abolition of slavery is . . . wiser and more equitable than its sudden removal.[17]

Doesn't this show Hegel trying a little too hard to find the positive in the obviously negative? Perhaps; but towards the end of this passage, in lines which I deliberately omitted, Hegel also states quite clearly that 'slavery is in and for itself an injustice, for the essence of humanity is freedom'. In Hegel's view, human beings are born to be free and in the light of that human destiny, slavery is always 'absolutely unjust'.[18] For this reason, he claims that even though slavery may be legal in particular states (as it was of course in America at the time he was writing), slaves have the inalienable right to break their chains and run away if they so wish. The state may be obliged to pay compensation to the slave owners for their loss, but the slaves themselves have no duty to stay. Even if a man was born a slave and all his ancestors were slaves, his right to reject his slavery is 'imprescriptible' (*unverjährbar*), and his slavery has by right to end as soon as he asserts his will to be free and his right to freedom.[19] A person can only appropriate something that has no consciousness of its freedom, as we saw above, so as soon as the slave becomes conscious that he is, and should be, free, the slave owner forfeits any right he might have to own him.

However, Hegel insists that since our rights objectify our self-conscious freedom, and since we only own our bodies when we *freely* appropriate them, we must actively lay claim to our rights over our bodies as self-conscious, free agents, in order to acquire the right to reject slavery. We are thus only truly free, and so bearers of rights, in so far as we claim our freedom, in so far as we will freedom as our object. It is for this reason that there are no merely natural rights, and that animals have no rights, in Hegel's view. If I am to enjoy rights as a free person, I must actually *be* a free person who is conscious of, and committed to, his or her freedom. Once I am self-consciously free, I need do nothing more than lay claim to my rights to acquire them. I do not need to do anything to merit rights. But, if someone is not self-consciously free, if he does not will his freedom, then it does not make any sense to protest that his free will is actually being violated if he is enslaved.

The demand that people ought not to be slaves is quite correct, Hegel says, because people are meant to be free. But this demand is a *moral* demand, which merely tells us what we *ought* to do. What we are concerned with in the sphere of immediate or abstract right, however, is not just what we ought to do, but what we must actually do. In this sphere, we are concerned with actual rights and freedoms which command actual, immediate respect from all persons, and which are thus not just a matter for moral conscience to decide upon, but which can be enforced by law. From the point of view of immediate right, rather than that of morality, if people are enslaved with no expectation that they should be free and without claiming their rights as free persons, then, strictly speaking, no *actual* violation of their rights occurs and no *actual* injustice is done to them, because no *actual* free will exists to be violated.[20]

Here we see the crux of Hegel's theory of slavery. Slavery is always wrong from a moral point of view, but it only becomes an actual injustice when the slave claims his right to be free. If slavery is accepted by a people or an individual, then the slaves are, from a moral point of view, as much to blame as the slave owners, because they have a moral duty not to let themselves be enslaved just as much as the slave owners have a moral duty not to take slaves. After all, Hegel says, 'a people need not let itself be downtrodden', but could fight against enslavement, even if they might die in the attempt.[21]

This does not mean, however, that Hegel is sanctioning the enslavement of people who are apparently unconcerned about their freedom. Slavery, after all, is always *morally wrong*. What he is pointing out is that if we are to establish a sphere of actual, recognized personal right, and not just a realm of good intentions, it is essential that people be educated into self-respect and into an understanding of their freedom. In other words, it is essential that people be taught to think of themselves as free persons and to claim their rights. Viewed in this light, Hegel's point is an important and profound one. A sphere of actual freedom and right requires more than just good will towards others to be secured. It needs to be rooted in people's consciousness that they are free and in their own claim to rights and property. A rational state, for Hegel, is thus one which fosters this sense of freedom in its citizens and which so ensures that the rights which it enshrines in law are also laid claim to by the people themselves. The only real guarantee against slavery, therefore, is the education of people into the consciousness of their freedom so that they will not let themselves be enslaved.

The Problem with Being Moral

We have seen that, for Hegel, the sphere of abstract, immediate right is quite independent of the sphere of morality. Rights, such as the right to personal inviolability or the right to property, are not accorded to us merely because others think that we ought to enjoy them, but because we ourselves lay claim to them as free beings. Furthermore, precisely because we acquire such rights simply by laying claim to them, we do not merit such rights through moral virtue or forfeit them through lack of moral virtue. However, it becomes clear at the end of Hegel's discussion of abstract right that morality is nevertheless crucial to the realization of freedom.

Moral concern for another's freedom is not enough to liberate the other, if the other does not claim freedom for himself. In this sense, moral consciousness is insufficient to establish the sphere of immediate right, and indeed need play no role in establishing it at all. But it appears that moral consciousness is required to ensure that the rights which I claim for myself I also respect in others. This is because there is nothing in the self-consciousness of a *person* to guarantee that he will actually respect the rights of others. Anyone can lay claim to the rights of personhood, whether or not he or she is a virtuous individual and whether or not he or she feels a responsibility to respect another's rights. The fact that one recognizes that freedom and rights *must* be respected does not mean that one *will* actually respect them in others. One might, of course, respect other people's rights without question; but one might respect them only as long as such respect serves one's own interests; or one might only make a show of respecting those rights and so commit fraud; or one might actually violate those rights even though one knows that one must respect them. Precisely because any person can legitimately lay claim to immediate rights, regardless of his or her willingness to respect the rights of others, it will always be a matter of contingency whether a particular person does actually respect the rights of others or not. And this is not merely a *contingent* contingency, but a *necessary* contingency, which stems from the very concept of what it means to be a person.[22]

Once more, then, Hegel's analysis shows that a particular conception of freedom is problematic in its own terms. Freedom of choice was shown to be contradictory because it was shown to be dependent on certain given options. Now the immediate freedom of the person has been shown to be inadequate, because of the perpetual possibility that the person who recognizes that rights must be respected may also fail to respect them and so violate the rights of others. What follows from this inadequacy, Hegel argues, is that abstract right must always be thought together with the possibility of its violation. This means that, even though right must command immediate respect, it is always possible that it will need to be enforced against violators and have its authority restored through the punishment of criminals.[23]

The free will which acknowledges freedom to be something it must will and respect, but which nevertheless recognizes that it has the capacity to violate the rights of others, and which thus understands that it needs to be constantly on its guard against its own possible violations of right, is what Hegel calls a *moral* will. Such a will does not just think of freedom as an immediate right which commands immediate respect; rather, it realizes that respect for freedom is something which it must be held to, and indeed – since it is a free will – something which it must *hold itself* to. The moral will thus recognizes that it must make itself respect freedom, that it must take *responsibility* for promoting freedom.

Furthermore, since the moral will does not just construe freedom as something which people enjoy immediately – that is, simply by laying claim to freedom – it can no longer think of *itself* as being free simply by virtue of its immediate claim to freedom, either. Such a will acknowledges the immediate rights of personhood, but is led by its recognition of the precarious character of those rights to locate its real freedom in its ability to hold itself to what it deems valuable, to assume responsibility for what it does, and so to be self-determining. It understands, therefore, that true freedom resides not just in asserting one's freedom – though that is an important part of freedom – but more properly in active *self-determination*. Consequently, it claims such self-determination as its right. The moral will thus recognizes both that it must determine itself if it is to be free and to respect freedom, and that it has the inviolable right so to determine itself, since its freedom lies in that very self-determination.

Hegel's analysis of the concept of freedom has shown that there is a further sphere of right beyond that of abstract, immediate right, namely the sphere of moral right. As a moral subject, I lay claim not just to the right to consider my personhood inviolable, or to the right to own property, but rather to the right to *determine myself*; that is, to the right of the will only to acknowledge something 'in so far as it is its own [*das Seinige*] and as the will is present to itself therein as something subjective'.[24]

Free self-determination, for Hegel, initially takes the form of action (*Handlung*). My initial right as a moral subject is thus my right to determine myself freely – and, in Hegel's view, this means consciously and deliberately – through my actions. In laying claim to such a right, Hegel explains, the moral subject claims the right to have actions, which he himself willed and initiated, regarded as his own. In other words, he claims the right to be credited with having carried out those actions and to be regarded as *responsible* for them.

At the same time, however, the moral subject claims the right, as a free being, to be considered responsible for his actions *only* to the extent that he himself has freely and knowingly willed and determined what he has done. As Hegel puts it,

the will's right . . . is to recognise as its action, and to accept responsibility for, only those presuppositions of the deed of which it was conscious in its aim and those aspects of the deed which were contained in its purpose. The deed can be imputed to me only if my will is responsible for it – this is the right to know.[25]

Oedipus may well have heroically accepted responsibility for having killed his father and married his mother, even though he did not do these things knowingly, but the genuinely moral will, in Hegel's view, always disclaims responsibility for deeds done in ignorance.[26]

Indeed, the moral will not only disclaims responsibility for deeds committed in ignorance, it only accepts responsibility for the particular acts it has in mind when acting; that is, for what it specifically *intends* to do. A moral individual who knowingly kills another individual may thus accept responsibility for the death, but, if he intends to carry out an act of euthanasia by that killing, he will not consider himself guilty of murder.

By insisting on my right, as a free individual, to determine what I specifically intend by a given action, I am claiming the right to acknowledge as my actions only those deeds that have issued directly from my particular intentions. The will that lays claim to the right to determine itself through its actions thus lays claim to the right to see its actions as expressing its own *particular* intentions and will. Such a will, Hegel says, insists on 'the right of subjective freedom', the right to find my own particularity realized and confirmed in what I do; that is, 'the right of the subject to find satisfaction [*Befriedigung*] in action'. In Hegel's view, therefore, the freedom of the moral subject does not require us to forgo personal satisfaction in the name of duty, to 'do with abhorrence what duty enjoins'. Rather, such freedom entails knowing that one's particular interests and intentions are being given free expression through one's actions, and that one is thereby gaining satisfaction through what one does.[27]

The right of free individuals to feel that they are catering for their own personal satisfaction or welfare through what they do is an essential right, according to Hegel, and follows directly from the free individual's right to self-determination. Furthermore, Hegel considers this to be a right that is perfectly compatible with disinterested or altruistic action. There is no reason why one should not find personal satisfaction in being genuinely concerned for others, just as there is no reason why one should not find personal fulfilment in universal truth, or indeed – as in Christian faith – in letting go of one's own particularity and opening oneself to the mind of Christ. It is only philosophers such as Nietzsche, who think that selflessness means having (or at least claiming to have) no regard at all for oneself, that see an interest in personal satisfaction as being incompatible with altruism.

It also follows that any state that fails to enable its citizens to find satisfaction in the spheres of economic, social, judicial and political activity violates their freedom. This is why Hegel insists on the 'demand that those who pass judgement have my trust, and that their insight and will appear to be my own',[28] and, as we shall see later, why he considers poverty and alienation to be unjust.

However, Hegel does not think that the right to personal satisfaction gives me the right to do absolutely anything I please. The right to personal satisfaction is something universal, something to which every free, self-determining individual can lay claim. As a moral individual, I may not, therefore, claim the right to promote my own welfare at the expense of the right of others to promote theirs. Nor indeed – except where my very livelihood is threatened – can I claim the right to further my own welfare at the expense of others' rights to security of their property.[29] As a moral individual, I can further my welfare only to the extent that I recognize it as the right of any and every free agent to do the same; that is, to the extent that I recognize the sanctity of *rights*.

The moral will is thus conscious of its freedom to act; it acknowledges its responsibility for its actions, and it claims that all free individuals have the right to personal satisfaction. But it may not yet seem to be fully *moral*, since we have not yet made any reference to the will's commitment to will what is *good*. However, once we think of the moral will as a will which pursues its welfare only to the extent that it recognizes its own (and others') *right* to do so, we think of the will as moral in the full sense, because the unity of right and welfare, for Hegel, is nothing other than the good. In willing the good, therefore, we will personal welfare (and freedom) as something which it is right and proper to will and thus as the right and proper end of all action.

For the truly moral will, neither right nor welfare is of absolute value by itself. 'Welfare without right is not a good. Similarly, right without welfare is not the good.' Only the unity of right and welfare can be considered the good and thus the supreme goal of all action. Consequently, the good 'has absolute right in contrast with the abstract right of property and the particular aims of welfare', and right and welfare only have validity in the eyes of the truly moral will in so far as they accord with the good and are subordinated to it.[30] Thus, though it may be the concern of the person or the just will to insist that property be distributed solely on the basis of legal entitlement, that cannot be the overriding concern of the moral will, because legal entitlement can easily be used as a way of depriving others of the means of securing their welfare and so cannot be considered unambiguously good in itself.

For the moral will, Hegel tells us, 'the good and the good alone is the essential'.[31] The good is thus something which the moral will, as a *moral* will, is bound or obliged to will, for no other reason than that it is the good, the supreme goal of all free action. Conceived in this way, the good is understood to be our unconditional, objective *duty*. We must remember, however, that the moral will is not constrained by any outside force to will what is good, but is a will that knows itself to be freely self-determining. The ultimate right which the moral will may claim for itself is thus the right to determine for itself what its duty is. This, Hegel says, is the 'right of insight into the good'.[32] Like Kant, therefore, Hegel understands the free, moral will to be one which is able to determine for itself, or, in Kant's terminology, to 'legislate' for itself, what its duty is.

The question which now arises is whether any specific good actions or duties follow from the moral will's commitment to will and do only what is good. What is my duty exactly? We as philosophers know that my duty is '(a) to uphold right, and (b) to strive after welfare, one's own welfare, and welfare in universal terms, the welfare of others', because we have seen these goals emerge from the concept of the self-determining will.[33] The moral will itself, however, has now come to realize that it can recognize, and is bound to will, only what duty itself requires. This means that, if the moral will is going to acknowledge that it is bound to promote rights and welfare, it must understand them to be required by duty itself.

The dutiful moral will cannot proceed from the assumption that right and welfare are to be valued and promoted. Rather, it must begin with the concept of duty alone, determine what duty specifically requires of it and so determine *whether* duty requires respect for rights and welfare. But the problem, as Hegel sees it, is that the moral will's insistence that it should will only what duty prescribes actually deprives it of any definite goals, and leaves it willing merely the empty form of duty for duty's sake, because, on closer inspection, the specific duty of upholding right and welfare turns out *not* to be contained in the definition of pure duty after all.

In Hegel's view, the essentially 'empty formalism' of willing duty for duty's sake is made clear by Kant's moral philosophy. In the *Groundwork for the Metaphysics of Morals* Kant claimed that an individual who acts only for the sake of duty must conceive of the principle or 'maxim' determining his actions as a duty or a universal law binding on all rational agents. The supreme or 'categorical' imperative which follows directly from willing our duty is, in other words, simply this: 'I should never act except in such a way that I can also will that my maxim should become a universal law'. For the moral will, therefore, 'mere conformity to law as such . . . serves . . . as principle'.[34]

In Kant's view, if we hold to this principle, we will have a clear criterion for determining which of our actions are moral ones and which actions we are duty-bound to avoid. It will become evident, for example, that an individual who wills what is good may not make promises with the intention of not keeping them or borrow money without intending to pay it back:

> for the universality of a law which says that anyone believing himself to be in difficulty could promise whatever he pleases with the intention of not keeping it would make promising itself and the end to be attained thereby quite impossible, in as much as no one would believe what was promised him but would merely laugh at all such utterances as being vain pretenses.[35]

It cannot be moral to set out to make promises without intending to keep them, therefore, since such a principle could never be made into a universal law or duty without destroying the faith and trust which make promises possible in the first place, and so being utterly self-defeating.

The problem with Kant's principle of universalizability, however, is that, while it may show that the act of making false promises is incapable of being made into a universal law without being self-defeating, and so is immoral, it does not show why the act of making false promises with the specific *intention* of destroying the possibility of promising should be immoral, since I can perfectly well will that all promising be universally self-defeating and self-destructive. The same applies to theft and murder. It may be contradictory to make it a universal law that we should kill others to preserve our life or steal from others to gain property, since universal murder or theft would destroy life and property themselves. However, as Hegel points out, it is only a contradiction to commit theft and murder, 'if it is already established on other grounds that property and human life are to exist and be respected'. If, on the other hand, I am prepared to countenance the wholesale destruction of property or the total destruction of the human race (including myself), there is nothing particularly self-defeating about recommending theft or murder to everybody. Since 'the absence of property contains in itself just as little contradiction as the non-existence of this or that nation, family, etc., or the death of the whole human race', there would thus seem to be no reason why, from a Kantian perspective, theft and murder should always be considered immoral.[36]

As Hegel understands it, therefore, it is not at all clear that an unambiguous duty to keep promises, or to refrain from theft and murder, can be derived from willing duty for duty's sake. It could be objected, of course, that Kant's principle of universalizability is not intended to generate duties by itself, but only to provide a test to determine whether *given* actions or principles of action are universalizable or not. In Hegel's view, however, this still does not let Kant off the hook. Hegel realizes that 'material may be brought in from outside and particular duties may be arrived at accordingly'.[37] His point is simply that many more actions than Kant realizes pass the test – including abstaining from theft and murder *and* indulging in theft and murder.

But one might make the further point in defence of Kant that his second main formulation of the categorical imperative – 'act in such a way that you treat humanity, whether in your own person or in the person of another, always at the same time as an end and never simply as a means' – does rule out murder and theft (even if the first formulation does not), since it commands unconditional respect for persons.[38] However, Hegel could reply that Kant cannot legitimately draw on the principle of respect for persons to determine that we have a duty not to commit theft or murder, since he has first to show that we have a *duty* to respect persons and their life and property, yet, as we have seen, the principle of universalizability, which (as Hegel understands it) is meant to provide a criterion for determining what our duties are, fails to do this. (Furthermore, Hegel could point out that, since respect is due to persons as a matter of immediate right, not moral duty, it is not by itself an absolutely unconditional good, but can only be considered a good when it is pursued in conjunction with welfare, so another's right to property or to be told the truth (and perhaps to life) *may* in fact be violated when one's own life or livelihood is threatened.)[39]

Hegel claims therefore – in contrast to Kant – that the will's commitment to will only what duty requires of it does not by itself rule out such acts as murder or theft as morally wrong. Though from the perspective of abstract right theft and murder are certainly crimes, from the perspective of the good will they *may or may not* be justifiable. By itself, the concept of duty seems to provide no objective criterion which would decide this issue, since the act of committing murder *and* the act of refraining from committing murder are both conceivably universalizable actions and so compatible with doing one's duty for duty's sake. The moral individual who looks to duty as a guide to action thus has no objective way of determining whether he should refrain from murder or commit murder in any given situation, since either act seems to be morally permissible, depending on how it is understood. Consequently, Hegel claims, there is nothing that can tell the self-determining, moral individual what to do in a given situation except his or her own *conscience*. Conscience, moreover, can only distinguish between a moral and an immoral act by determining whether or not the act is committed out of a concern to do one's duty, out of a good will; that is, whether or not the act is *intended* to be good. The only way for the moral agent ultimately to determine what he should do, therefore, is for him to examine his conscience and to establish what he understands and intends by his actions.

Hegel acknowledges that it is actually the moral individual's right to refer all moral decisions to his conscience, because a moral individual's fundamental freedom and right is to *hold himself* to what he understands to be right, proper and good. 'Conscience', for Hegel,

is [thus] the expression of the absolute title of subjective self-consciousness to know in itself and from within itself what is right and obligatory, to give recognition only to what it thus knows as good, and at the same time to maintain that whatever in this way it knows and wills is in truth right and obligatory.[40]

'Conscience as this unity of subjective knowing with what is absolute', Hegel continues, 'is a sanctuary which it would be a sacrilege to violate.' And he notes that, provided that one's intentions are good, one may well come to the conclusion that one can kill and steal with a good conscience. Though one may recognize that it is wrong to take the property of others, one might nevertheless, like St Crispin, feel morally obliged to steal leather to make shoes for the poor. Similarly, though one may recognize that one should not to take another's life, one might nevertheless feel morally obliged to kill someone in order to save his honour or his soul, relieve his suffering, or perhaps prevent worse suffering to another innocent party.[41] In such cases, therefore, conscience and moral duty may not seem to prohibit theft or murder at all, but actually to *require* them.

What ultimately makes me a moral individual, for Hegel, is the knowledge that I cannot go wrong as long as I will what my conscience tells me is good, together with the corresponding realization that my conscience, as the source of my understanding of what is good, is inviolable and sacred. After all, who could blame a person who is making an earnest effort to abide by the dictates of his conscience and do only what he understands to be good? In Hegel's view, however, there is a problem with such a conception of moral goodness, namely that the moral individual's claim to the inviolability of his conscience threatens to blur the essential distinction between good and evil on which the possibility of a truly good will rests.

A good will, for Hegel, is one which puts what it understands to be objectively good above its own subjective preferences and potentially wayward inclinations, and which wills only what it understands to be good. The will that elevates its own interests above those of duty, on the other hand, is considered, from this perspective, to be bad or evil. However, since the only principle available to the good will – namely the principle of universalizability – is unable to determine whether one should commit murder or refrain from committing murder in a given situation, the good conscience, in pursuing the good, can only appeal to *itself* and its own intentions for a decision. And, so, because it recognizes no right, duty or good except what it itself has determined, and because it has no principle for determining what the good is except itself, 'conscience, as formal subjectivity, is [actually] . . . on the point of slipping into evil'.[42]

In the sphere of abstract right, because rights are not accorded to people on the basis of their moral goodness or willingness to respect the rights of others, there is always the possibility that those who claim rights for themselves might knowingly violate the rights of others. In the sphere of morality, however, the problem is different. Here the problem is not just that the moral individual might do something morally wrong, but rather that the moral will, which recognizes that it might violate the rights of others and so holds itself to what it conceives to be good, itself *becomes* evil precisely by adhering exclusively to the dictates of its own conscience and only willing what it itself determines to be good. The evil Hegel finds at the heart of the good will is thus not simply the criminal violation of rights, but the evil which lies in believing oneself to be doing what is truly good, while allowing no one but oneself to determine what the good actually is. This is the evil which lies in being convinced that one is doing good because one's sacred, inviolable conscience tells one so; the evil which lies in self-righteousness, in remaining true to oneself and one's moral convictions at all costs; the evil, as Ludwig Siep puts it, that lies in the 'veneration for the decisions of conscience as being beyond criticism'.[43]

For Hegel, in contrast to Kant, the profoundest danger facing the moral individual is not so much that he might be led astray by his selfish inclinations, but that his very commitment to will the good itself turns into evil at the moment he insists upon the sanctity of his own conscience. This danger cannot be averted by resolving to commit oneself more thoroughly to the good. It can only be averted by giving up the conviction that one's own conscience is the sole or primary source of moral guidance, by letting go of one's exclusive right to determine what the good is; that is, by becoming an *ethical* (*sittlich*) will which recognizes that the good must be something genuinely objective and publicly understood.

Freedom at Home in the World

The difference between the ethical and the moral will is a simple one: whereas the moral will understands the good to be something which it can recognize or determine by itself, the ethical will acknowledges the good to be something actual which it encounters in the world about it. The ethical will thus recovers an understanding which was present at the level of abstract right, and which the moral will believed it shared but actually obscured, namely that freedom and right – the good – has a determinate character of its own which is objective and necessary and which clearly transcends all 'subjective opinion and caprice'.[44]

But, as we have seen, Hegel's analysis has demonstrated that freedom cannot simply be something immediate, objective and necessary – cannot simply be abstract *right* – but must also take on the form of freely self-determining subjectivity. If the ethical will is to encounter in the world about it genuinely objective freedom and genuinely objective good, therefore, it cannot find what it is looking for in immediate 'natural' rights or in 'the sun, moon, mountains, rivers, and the natural objects of all kinds by which we are sur-rounded', but must find it in the objective world generated by free self-determining sub-jectivity; that is, the world of human laws and institutions.[45] Ethical life (*Sittlichkeit*), for Hegel, is thus the sphere of human *subjectivity* conceived as the realm of *objective* freedom and right.

Unlike moral consciousness, ethical consciousness does not have to search its conscience to determine what its duties are, because it recognizes, as Charles Taylor explains, that 'the common life which is the basis of my *sittlich* obligation is already there in existence'. Thus, in an ethical community, it is very easy to say what an individual must do, what the duties are which he must fulfil in order to be virtuous: 'he has simply to follow the well-known and explicit rules of his own situation'. He has simply to do what is required of him by law or custom.[46]

Many commentators have interpreted this conception of ethical life as a simple recipe for unfreedom and inauthenticity, as a recipe for the slavish submission of oneself to the dictates of the state or society, to 'what one does'. However, even a relatively cursory reading of Hegel's *Philosophy of Right* reveals that this interpretation cannot be correct. *Sittlichkeit* involves no servitude or loss of freedom, because the laws and customs which set out the duties of ethical consciousness do not constitute an alien authority to which consciousness must submit itself. Rather, they are recognized by the ethical individual to be institutional structures and practices in which and through which his or her *own* interests as a free being are actually articulated and fulfilled. The ethical individual may not have determined those laws and customs by himself or have personally decided what they should be, but 'his spirit bears witness to them as to its own essence, the essence in which he has a feeling of his selfhood, and in which he lives as in his own element which is not distinguished from himself'.[47] In other words, the ethical individual finds freedom in the laws and customs of the society in which he lives because he recognizes that they accord with his innermost will and make it possible for him to be who he is.

Hegel is not naively recommending unquestioning obedience to each and every law one encounters, however unjust it may be. He is pointing out that there is a form of freedom which the just will (which insists on asserting its own rights, often against others) and the moral will (which concentrates solely on what ought to be the case) can never share: namely the freedom of being at home in the world and recognizing that what ought to be is already realized in the laws and customs of one's community and in one's *own* habits and prac-tices in so far as they accord with those laws and customs.

The moral will always confronts the world with what *it* knows to be right and good, with what *it* knows ought to be, but invariably is not, the case. It finds itself permanently dissatisfied with a world which it knows could be better. And in the terms which the moral will sets, it is probably right: the world could always be 'better'. However, for all its moral integrity and rectitude, the moral will always has to forgo the deeper freedom of being at home in the imperfect world of real human beings, and of knowing that good behaviour has become second nature to it, has become habitual, not through its own efforts, but simply because it has been educated into the practices and customs of society. Furthermore, the moral will which insists on doing what its conscience dictates and on preserving its moral integrity, will never understand the freedom to be found in *civility*; that is, in doing as one's neighbours do in trivial matters such as fashion, or, where matters are more serious, in participating in a public discussion with a willingness to let one's deepest convictions be debated and perhaps be shown to be wrong, and a willingness even to defer to established customs and norms if one's own powers of persuasion fail to sway others. The moral will will also find it hard to understand that one can be morally in the right about a particular issue yet, at the same time, ethically in the wrong because of one's refusal to heed any voice other than that of one's own conscience.

Yet doubts will surely linger in the minds of some that Hegel's ethical individual is 'ever in danger of being asked by his community to do the unconscionable'.[48] Might not Hegelian *Sittlichkeit* or civility all too easily sanction passive acquiescence in abhorrent political practices such as those of the Third Reich? After all, does not Hegel himself admit that it is possible to find oneself at home in a despotic society such as ancient China, in which people have no expectation that they should be accorded individual rights? What this suspicion overlooks, however, is that true *Sittlichkeit*, if it is to be the genuine objectification of *freedom*, must incorporate the other forms of freedom which have been developed so far, namely freedom of choice, abstract right and freedom of moral consciousness. For this reason, Hegel says, 'the right of individuals to their particularity [*das Recht der Individuen an ihrer Besonderheit*] is also contained in the ethical substantial order'.[49]

Ethical freedom is partly a matter of having a disposition towards civility: of being able to let go of one's insistence that one's conscience is the ultimate moral authority in one's life, of being open to the value of laws, customs and institutions and of knowing how to trust them and find freedom in them. However, if ethical civility is to constitute a form of genuine freedom and not just open the door to tyranny, the laws and institutions in which trust is placed must merit this trust by guaranteeing the rights of personal inviolability, property and moral responsibility. A truly ethical state cannot be tyrannical, in Hegel's view, because 'individuals have duties to the state *in proportion as they have rights against it*' (emphasis added). 'Slaves, therefore, have no duties because they have no rights.'[50]

Moreover, the ethical state must not only guarantee the rights of its citizens, it must ensure that their welfare is catered for, as well.

The state is actual only when its members have a feeling of their own selfhood and it is stable only when public and private ends are identical. It has often been said that the end of the state is the happiness of its citizens. That is perfectly true. If all is not well with them, if their subjective aims are not satisfied, if they do not find that the state as such is the means to their satisfaction, then the footing of the state itself is insecure.[51]

The ethical individual does not slavishly obey the laws, but insists both that the community guarantee his individual rights and that the community provide opportunities for him to satisfy his basic needs. All individuals in an ethical state also have the right to participate in public debates – in the press or, if elected, in the representative assemblies – about matters of public welfare and concern. Thus, provided that they do not put their own understanding beyond criticism, and that they are open to the good which is actually present in the society about them, all individuals retain the moral right to share in determining what the good is. (In purely private matters, of course, they have the right to follow their consciences as much as they wish.) However, the individual cannot claim the right as a truly free, ethical individual to determine through his conscience alone what is to count as good in the society as a whole or what his public duties are, but must allow this to be determined either by public debate, by the legally constituted or publicly recognized institutions within the society, or by custom. The moral individual becomes an ethical individual, therefore, when he recognizes that his own voice need not always utter the last word on a given matter, but rather that he should be understood as participating in and giving life to ongoing social and political practices which no private individual or particular group of private individuals has the exclusive right to determine.

Hegel never claims that every existing state is in fact a truly ethical community in the sense he has outlined here (although every state must be held together by *some* ethical bonds simply to constitute a single body politic).[52] In existing states, therefore, there may well be many grounds for criticism of existing laws and institutions and for action to protect people's rights. The lesson to be drawn from Hegel's analysis, however, is that true reform of a society entails above all the engendering of a deeper sense of civility, and that consequently, if people lay claim to their own rights or level moral criticisms at one another or at institutions in such a way as to destroy the bonds of civility, to destroy the possibility of *trust* between people and between individuals and the state, the essential core of human freedom will be lost.

Civil Society and Poverty

Ethical life constitutes the third main sphere of freedom which Hegel analyses in the *Philosophy of Right* after immediate, abstract right and morality. The first form of ethical life that he discusses is immediate ethical life, which is based on natural affection: the family. The basis of the family, Hegel explains, is marriage, the act whereby two individuals come together, give up their claim to independence and autonomy from one another and form a union of love in which each individual finds his or her freedom and his or her identity as an individual. Instead of locating their freedom simply in their personal right to own property, or in their moral right to autonomous self-determination, therefore, the partners in a marriage find a new sense of selfhood and freedom in their union itself, in their mutual recognition of, and love for, one another.

The union involved in a marriage is ethical because it creates a new sphere of freedom for the two individuals involved, which, once it has been constituted, is understood to be objective and thus no longer simply dependent upon the subjective wills of the two partners. Marriage is thus not a contractual agreement between two people who could simply opt out of the relationship. Nor does it rest ultimately upon the moral commitment of each partner to the other. Rather, marriage constitutes an independent, objective sphere of ethical right, which not only cannot be violated by others, but cannot simply be dissolved by the mutual consent of the two partners either. This does not mean that divorce is utterly impermissible, but that, as an ethical bond, marriage requires the recognition of society as a whole to be instituted or dissolved, and that it cannot simply be entered into or dissolved at will.

Since marriage is the first form of ethical freedom, it is the first form of the genuinely objective good. For this reason, Hegel explains, it is 'our objectively appointed end and so our ethical duty to enter the married state'.[53] One should note, however, that Hegel considers marriage to be a duty not because it is required by the categorical imperative, but because it has been derived immanently from the consideration of what it means to be free. The duty to uphold the institution of marriage and to enter into marriage ourselves is thus considered by Hegel to be a necessary duty for any free being, and to demonstrate that, unlike Kant's moral theory, a speculative analysis of freedom *can* generate an 'immanent and logical doctrine of duties'.[54]

Despite its importance in the development of the idea of freedom, marriage is not the culmination of freedom for Hegel. The unity of the partners in a marriage is represented by their children; but children grow up into adults who are conscious of their rights and moral responsibilities as free, self-determining agents. These adults will in turn find freedom in an objective union of love with another human being, and will thus give rise to further generations of families. However, as we have seen, if ethical life is to be a form of genuine *freedom*, it must make space for individuals to assert their right to property and to exercise their right to autonomy and self-determination, and not simply require them to forgo those rights by entering into a union of love with another. The second form of ethical life that Hegel discusses, therefore, is civil society, the sphere that is produced by the *exercise* of our immediate and our moral rights. Consequently the second ethical duty which philosophy shows to be immanent in the very idea of freedom is that we should be participating members of civil society.

Civil society is the sphere of activity generated by free individuals who both assert their rights to own and exchange property and insist on their right to cater for their own welfare by satisfying their own needs and interests through their own activity and labour. In other words, it is the sphere of *economic* activity, in which individuals produce goods to meet their needs and to exchange for other goods that they themselves cannot produce. It should be noted that Hegel is concerned with economic activity not in so far as it is based on need alone, but in so far as it is based on our freedom and right as individuals to satisfy our needs through the free production and exchange of goods. What will emerge in Hegel's analysis, therefore, will not be an account of exchange relations which are restricted to certain 'naturally' privileged individuals or groups, but, as Seyla Benhabib has pointed out, an account of exchange relations which presuppose 'the norms of personality, property and contract'.[55] What will emerge, in other words, will be an account of *modern* exchange relations based on what Hegel calls 'bourgeois freedom'.[56]

Bourgeois freedom combines freedom of choice, freedom of personhood and freedom of self-determination into one basic freedom: the freedom to pursue one's own particular interests and to satisfy one's own particular needs by means of whatever objects one chooses to own and consume and through a form of activity and labour which one determines for oneself. 'Individuals in their capacity as *bourgeois* [*Bürger*] . . . are private persons whose end is their own interest', Hegel says.[57] This freedom to pursue one's own interest – to be self-interested – is not to be frowned upon as 'immoral', but is absolutely fundamental and commands our respect as much as any other form of freedom discussed so far. Indeed it is the fact that modern Western societies do respect this freedom, and have consequently developed thriving forms of civil society, which leads Hegel to consider them to be much more advanced than more rigidly hierarchical cultures such as ancient China or the society envisaged by Plato in the *Republic*.

Hegel points out, however, that the very process whereby individuals in civil society free themselves from the limits imposed upon them by nature also leads to and intensifies their economic interdependence. An animal's needs and its means of satisfying them are both restricted in scope, being determined by the nature of the particular animal concerned and by what it finds in its environment to satisfy its needs. Human beings, on the other hand, since they are able to entertain wishes and desires which arise from their own thought and imagination rather than instinct, and also reflect on different ways of satisfying their wants and needs, are able to develop new, more specialized wants and needs of their own. Instead of simply having a natural need for food, therefore, they may want a particular kind of food prepared in a particular way, for example. In this way, Hegel explains, the needs and wants of human beings become more and more specialized and refined. As a consequence, the means required to meet those needs also become more specialized, and, with increasing specialization, the individual's capacity for producing all he needs himself diminishes and his dependence on others increases.

The bourgeois individual's need – and freedom – to engage in the production and exchange of goods required to meet his needs and wants entangles him in a system of economic interdependence 'wherein the livelihood, happiness, and legal status of one man is interwoven with the livelihood, happiness and rights of all', and which he is thus not able to control by himself.[58] Consequently, through his efforts to satisfy his *own* interests, the bourgeois individual is brought to recognize that the economic system itself is the condition of his own freedom and satisfaction, and that he must further the interests of the others who participate in that system if he wishes to find fulfilment himself. In this way, he is forced by the logic inherent in human action – by the 'cunning of reason' – to become ethical or *sittlich* and to find his own freedom in his association with others. The distinguishing feature of bourgeois ethical life, however, is that the association and cooperation of producers and consumers is as yet only conceived as a *means* to furthering the aims of the individual.

As Hegel points out, the economic and social interaction between people, which the process of developing specialized needs brings about, itself generates new wants and needs, because new needs can be suggested by producers eager to market their goods and because consumers can develop desires for what other people have.[59] Social needs also arise due to the increasing complexity of social interaction. A watch, for example, may be considered by some to be a luxury, but the more complex our daily life becomes, the less able we are to do without one. (Had he lived in the later twentieth or twenty-first centuries, Hegel would no doubt have made the same point about personal computers.) Since human beings are thoughtful, imaginative, social beings, who can always develop new needs and new ways of satisfying them, it is evident that there is no limit to what people might want or need in the future. Consequently, there is no limit to the productive power which individuals or civil society as a whole might try to develop, or to the *wealth* which we might wish to acquire – wealth being simply the 'capacity to satisfy needs'.[60] In so far as civil society is founded on the pursuit of individual freedom, therefore, the dominant interest in such a society is necessarily the interest in increasing or maximizing personal and social wealth; that is, in extending our freedom of choice and securing the means to satisfy more and more of our needs and make our lives ever more comfortable.[61]

As we have seen, individuals can only secure their concrete freedom by participating in the economic system of production, exchange and consumption. However, Hegel points out that mere participation in that system will not by itself guarantee that an individual's needs are actually met. The economic system only holds out to individuals in society the *possibility* of, or *opportunity* for, freedom and satisfaction. Whether individuals do in fact find satisfaction within the system depends upon a variety of factors, including whether they have useful skills and whether others allow them to satisfy their needs. Yet my freedom and welfare is something I insist upon as a *right*, so it cannot simply remain a possibility that may be denied me. On the other hand, since all members of civil society also insist on the right to satisfy their needs through their own labour, they cannot claim the privilege of simply being maintained at society's expense. What producers and consumers do have the right to demand from society, however, is that the opportunity to find satisfaction in the economic system through their own labour be kept open to them, that 'the possibility of sharing in the general wealth is open to individuals and is *assured* to them'.[62]

The freedom of economic enterprise which underlies civil society is thus not absolute, since the public has the right to demand that the economic system be maintained as a place where freedom, right and welfare remain available to all those who wish to work to achieve it. That means that individuals do not have the right to violate the rights or destroy the welfare of others in the pursuit of their own interests. Economic competition may of course itself ensure that unscrupulous traders do not prosper at the expense of others, but, Hegel argues, whether or not I have the opportunity to find satisfaction in the economy should not be left to mere chance by being made to depend on the interests or consciences of other individuals. Rather, it should be secured as an objective right by a legitimate public authority. This authority should have the right to intervene in the economy and regulate the freedom of trade and competition by ensuring that I have regard for the rights and welfare of others in whatever I do.

The responsibilities which fall to the public authority, in Hegel's view, include a wide variety of consumer protection measures, such as ensuring that basic necessities are always available and that goods do not pose a health hazard, as well as defending 'the public's right not to be defrauded' by making sure that goods are sold at fair prices and that weights and measures are properly marked. It must also make sure that roads are safe and properly lit and that the bridges and ports which are required for the transport of goods are open to all. Hegel recognizes that private interest frequently objects to such 'restrictive' measures and 'invokes freedom of trade and commerce against control from above', but he also recognizes that 'the more blindly it [private interest] sinks into self-seeking aims, the more it requires such control to bring it back to the universal'.

> The individual must have a right to work for his bread as he pleases, but the public also has a right to insist that essential tasks shall be properly done. Both points of view must be satisfied, and freedom of trade should not be such as to jeopardise the general good [*das allgemeine Beste*].[63]

It should be noted that the role of the public authority is not to inhibit enterprise or to bring about enforced equality of income, but to ensure equality of *opportunity*, to ensure that public wealth is open to all. The role of the public authority is thus not to trample on personal freedom, but to secure it as an objective right for everybody. The goal of public intervention is indeed to increase the wealth of individuals in society by promoting the free and fair, but otherwise unregulated, production, exchange and consumption of goods.

Hegel claims, however, that even a flourishing economy which is free and fair cannot guarantee that the needs of all who participate in it will be met. The reason for this, in his view, is that an economy which is geared to the maximization of production and wealth always has to face the problem of poverty. In a competitive economy some individuals are always going to lack the skill, intelligence or physical ability to compete with others and so are going to fall into destitution. As Raymond Plant notes, however, 'in Hegel's view . . . poverty in general is a structural phenomenon in society, the result of the operation of civil society when it is in a state of "unimpeded activity" and not the result of some *personal* failing on the part of the poor'.[64] Like Marx, therefore, Hegel contends that poverty is necessarily generated by a wholly free enterprise economy. There are various reasons why this should be.

Since civil society is founded on the freedom of the individual to satisfy his own particular interests through his own particular labour, and since 'a particular man's resources . . . are conditioned . . . partly by his own unearned principal (his capital), partly by his skill', there will inevitably be disparities between individuals in a flourishing economy.[65] Not only will some people start their own enterprises and others become employees, but some entrepreneurs will obviously be more successful than others because they have a good workforce or because they are able to keep their costs down and so charge less for their products. The resulting pressure of competition between entrepreneurs, the increasing specialization and refinement of needs and the ever-present demand for greater productive efficiency within an expanding economy all lead, in Hegel's view, to the need for an increasing division of labour. Not only will different entrepreneurs often be forced to concentrate on producing different goods, but within the workplace or factory, tasks will need to be divided up between different workers. The reason for this, Hegel explains (following Adam Smith), is that 'by this division, the work of the individual becomes less complex, and consequently his skill at his section of the job increases, like his output'.[66] As Hegel sees it, however, there is a dark side to the division of labour, namely that as people become more specialized in their skills, they become less able to switch from one job to another, more dependent on the demand of others for their products and consequently more vulnerable to the fluctuations in demand in a free market economy. If demand for one particular product should drop, therefore, a large number of people can lose their jobs and fall into hardship and poverty. Furthermore, since the division of labour and mechanization leads to 'mass-production to satisfy . . . needs in more universal demand', and thus enables factory owners to produce far more goods (and far more cheaply) than craftsmen who 'work to satisfy single needs in a comparatively concrete way and to supply single orders',[67] the inevitable tendency of unregulated competition will be that some producers will be able to monopolize a particular sector of the market and put their competitors out of business, so providing another cause of unemployment and poverty. Such a development, Hegel believes, can best be seen in nineteenth-century England, where

the large capitalists [*die großen Kapitalisten*] oppress [*unterdrücken*] the others. In this way, a branch of industry comes into the hands of the few. These have no authorised monopoly, but they have one through their large capital, and this is the worst of all monopolies. Thus it is, for example, with the breweries. . . . Thus monopolies arise precisely through the freedom of trade.[68]

In addition to this, the increasing simplification of labour required by the demand for greater productivity renders many jobs more and more mechanical 'until finally man is able to step aside and install machines in his place'.[69] While machines can in this way liberate human beings from mind-numbing repetitive labour and so allow them to take up new, possibly more rewarding jobs, the most immediate effect of such mechanization is, of course, simply that it puts many people out of work.

The last and perhaps most important reason why bourgeois freedom should lead to poverty, in Hegel's view, is that an economy which seeks greater and greater productive efficiency will eventually produce more in certain areas than it can consume. Such overproduction will require many workers to be laid off (since their specialized training will invariably prevent them from simply switching from one trade to another), and so will deprive them of the opportunity to earn their living through their own labour. 'If a trade is especially flourishing, many people turn to it. However, the need for [specific] goods has its limits, and if a trade is overfilled, many people will not be able to see this, will enter into it and be ruined.'[70]

What should be noted here is that, according to Hegel's analysis (as indeed according to that provided by Marx some thirty years later), it is not the malfunctioning of civil society which causes poverty, but the smooth functioning of the free market itself. Poverty is generated by the very processes and conditions which lead to the production of wealth and which enable the economy to flourish.[71] In other words, it is immanent in the *logic* of bourgeois freedom that it generate poverty, just as it is immanent in the *logic* of moral freedom to be constantly in danger of slipping into evil. Clearly, conditions in different societies will affect how much poverty is actually generated in any given case. In certain states, such as nineteenth-century England or twentieth-century America, poverty may be severe and permanent.[72] In others, it may be less severe and more transitory. What is clear, however, is that – if Hegel's analysis is right – some degree of structural unemployment, and the poverty and hardship which unemployment brings with it, are permanent dangers in an economy based on free, fair but otherwise unregulated production and competition, and on the resulting fluctuations in demand. Hegel recognizes, of course, that unemployment *could* just be considered to be the inevitable price we have to pay for allowing the market to readjust when great shifts in public taste have occurred. After all, he says, 'the plague also comes to an end again, . . . a few hundred thousands have died of it, . . . [but] in this way everything is restored to order again'. However, his characterization of this attitude as one of 'complacency' (*Bequemlichkeit*) indicates that such a judgement is not one he finds acceptable.[73]

Hegel is one of the first major philosophers to recognize that the problem of poverty is central to modern economic life. Furthermore, he discusses not just the material hardship which poverty involves but the social and spiritual deprivation or 'alienation' which accompanies it. 'The poor still have the needs common to civil society', Hegel explains,

and yet since society has withdrawn from them the natural means of acquisition . . . and broken the bond of the family . . . their poverty leaves them more or less deprived of all the advantages of society, of the opportunity of acquiring skill or education of any kind, as well as of the administration of justice, the public health services, and often even of the consolations of religion.[74]

When poverty is so severe or so long-lasting that it leads to a 'loss of a sense of right and wrong, of honesty and the self-respect which makes a man insist on maintaining himself by his own work and effort, the result is the creation of a rabble of paupers [*Pöbel*]'.[75] The poor who have sunk to this level of deprivation and degradation come to feel excluded from and rejected by civil society, and develop a feeling of envy, resentment and indignation against, and consequent lack of respect for, society as a whole and the rich in particular – a resentment which frequently leads to crime. The profound sense of injustice which the alienated poor harbour invariably leads them to think that society owes them the living which they cannot secure for themselves, and so produces in them a self-righteous insistence that they have a right to freedom and welfare without having to work for it. Indeed, the insistence on one's *rights* with little or no regard for one's responsibilities is, for Hegel, a distinguishing feature of an alienated 'rabble' mentality. (Hegel points out, by the way, that the rich can also manifest a 'rabble' mentality, in so far as they come to regard everything as 'able to be purchased' (*käuflich für sich*), and pursue profit and personal gain with a callous indifference to the dignity and welfare of others.)[76]

Hegel describes poverty as a 'cancer' at the heart of civil society. 'Nowhere', he says, 'can one see the depth of the abyss into which human nature can sink' more clearly than among the urban poor of England.[77] Furthermore, Hegel argues that poverty is a problem which civil society, and the public authority which oversees it and ensures that trading is free and fair, is unable to solve. The two main courses of action open to the public authority in its effort to alleviate poverty within the framework of a free market are, in Hegel's view, (a) direct provision of goods to meet the needs of the poor and to secure their welfare, and (b) provision of the opportunity to work. However, in an economy based on the right of individuals to maximize their wealth through their labour, both of these measures are bound to prove inadequate. If the poor are supported by a public welfare system or by charities, 'the needy would receive subsistence directly, not by means of their work, and this would violate the principle of civil society and the feeling of individual independence and self-respect in its individual members'. On the other hand, though the public authority has a duty to provide opportunities for the unemployed to work for their living, the direct provision of jobs by the public authority would increase production, which was precisely the source of unemployment in the first place: 'the evil consists precisely in an excess of production and in the lack of a proportionate number of consumers who are themselves also producers'. As a result, Hegel concludes, the main methods available to a public authority to enable it to restore to the poor what is due to them by right as members of civil society are more likely to intensify the problem of poverty and the 'rabble' mentality than alleviate it. 'It hence becomes apparent that despite an excess of wealth civil society is not rich enough, i.e. its own resources are insufficient, to check excessive poverty and the creation of a penurious rabble'.[78] Or, to put it another way, a flourishing civil society is *too* rich and *too* productive to deal with the problem of poverty, since its own wealth and productivity are themselves the prime cause of poverty.

The public authority does have the option of helping industry find markets for its products abroad and of founding colonies and promoting emigration. But these are not likely to be long-term solutions, since Hegel's analysis suggests that international trade tends either to stimulate foreign countries to develop their own economies and thus become competitors in the hunt for markets, or to undermine them by flooding them with cheap products, thus creating unemployment in those countries and spoiling them as markets.[79] It would seem, therefore, that modern economies have no way of dealing with poverty effectively and that the only real alternative is 'to leave the poor to their fate and instruct them to beg in the streets'.[80] Initially, the division of labour works to bring members of civil society together and so forces them to become interested in one another's welfare. However, the end result of the increasing division of labour is that civil society becomes divided against itself and the gap between the rich and the poor keeps on growing. It would seem, then, that poverty is just something wealthy countries have to live with.

This, at least, is the view taken of Hegel's account by Shlomo Avineri. Avineri commends Hegel for his trenchant analysis of the problem of poverty, but criticizes him for apparently failing to offer any real solution to it.[81] However, while Hegel admits that there will always be some impoverished people in modern societies, it is clear that he also believes the creation of a 'rabble' must be prevented;[82] and, though he never claims that there is any simple and easy way to deal with poverty, he does offer one important suggestion. The main cause of poverty, according to him, is the drive to *maximize* production and wealth, a drive which is rooted in the bourgeois freedom to satisfy one's ever-changing and so potentially limitless needs through one's labour. This suggests that the way to guard against poverty is to introduce measures to regulate the amount of production, and to ensure that production opportunities are distributed fairly throughout the population and not left to depend on the contingencies of demand or productive efficiency. What is needed, then, is to ensure that production does not exceed consumption by too much, and that producers are not allowed to lower their prices so drastically that they come to monopolize certain sections of the market and so take away production opportunities from others. What such measures would ensure is that everyone is granted the 'security of a smoothly continuing profit', rather than the mere *chance* of acquiring greater wealth.[83]

As we noted earlier, since civil society is a form of ethical freedom, it is meant to secure the good (i.e. freedom and welfare) as a *right*, as something objective and actual, and not leave it as a mere possibility which may be denied me. Civil society must, therefore, be granted the authority to take measures to prevent large numbers of people falling into destitution. Consequently, Hegel recognizes that a state may have to regulate prices either by direct decree, by increasing taxes on certain goods or by controlling the supply of money in the economy and so dampening or stimulating demand.[84] It is also clear that a state could, if necessary, 'determine everyone's labour'.[85] However, the more drastic and interventionist the measures taken by the state, the more the state would risk violating the legitimate freedom of individuals to determine which jobs they will engage in to satisfy their needs, instead of simply protecting producers and consumers by ensuring that free enterprise is also fair. Since there is no clear limit to the control which can be exercised by the public authority, the public authority can easily go too far and 'acquire a measure of odium' (*etwas Gehässiges*).[86] This would then prevent individuals in civil society from enjoying genuine ethical freedom, because their basic desire to increase their personal wealth would remain unaffected and they would simply feel forced by the state to limit their own productive activity for the benefit of others. They would thus not find their own will realized through the action of the public authority.

Intervention by the state in the economy in order not just to ensure free and fair competition, but to regulate and control the distribution and the amount of production, may be unavoidable if poverty is extreme. However, if all members of civil society are to enjoy real, objective freedom, not only must their productive activity be regulated so that all can enjoy the opportunity to work, they must also recognize such regulation as issuing from their *own* will rather than from an authority which is seen to be external to them. Their own will must thus be *transformed* from one which looks primarily to increase personal wealth, into one which actively, consciously and willingly seeks to promote the welfare of all. This transformation of the will into a genuinely *ethical* or *social* will is initially effected by the corporations.

Corporations are voluntary associations of manufacturers, craftsmen or traders who have come together with the explicit intention of furthering the rights and welfare of those who work in a particular sector of the economy, and of ensuring that the labour of one person in that sector does not destroy the labour of another. They are thus essentially the same as guilds and are not to be confused with the large modern companies that are often called 'corporations' today. After the family, the corporations represent the second form of genuinely ethical life in which individuals find freedom in a willing union with others. In corporations, therefore,

the so-called 'natural' right of exercising one's skill and thereby earning what there is to be earned is restricted . . . only in so far as it is therein made rational instead of natural. That is to say, it becomes freed from personal opinion and contingency, saved from endangering either the individual workman or others, recognised, guaranteed, and at the same time elevated to conscious effort for a common end.[87]

The third duty which Hegel understands to be immanent in the very concept of ethical freedom is thus membership of a corporation. Since the corporations are embodiments of genuine ethical freedom, they must both rest on and promote an attitude of concern for the welfare of others on the part of its members. Within a true corporation, therefore, members will be freed from the desire to maximize personal wealth at the expense of their competitors and will be encouraged and inclined to work together with one another. Hegel clearly sees this *esprit de corps* as important in preventing the development of a rabble mentality among the rich and the corresponding emergence of a rabble that is destitute and impoverished.

When complaints are made about the luxury of the business classes and their passion for extravagance – which have as their concomitant the creation of a rabble of paupers – we must not forget that besides its other causes (e.g. increasing mechanization of labour) this phenomenon has an ethical ground. . . . Unless he is a member of an authorised corporation . . . , an individual is without rank or dignity, his isolation reduces his business to mere self-seeking, and his livelihood and satisfaction become insecure. Consequently, he has to try to gain recognition for himself by giving external proofs of success in his business, and to these proofs no limit can be set. . . . Within the corporation [however] . . . the wealthy perform their duties to their fellow associates and thus riches cease to inspire either pride or envy, pride in their owners, envy in others. In these conditions rectitude obtains its proper recognition and respect.[88]

As an embodiment of genuine ethical freedom, however, corporations must not only engender an ethical habit of mind, they must also have the authority and right to exercise control over the trading practices and modes of production which fall within their purview.

A corporation [thus] has the right, under the surveillance of the public authority, (a) to look after its own interests within its own sphere, (b) to co-opt members, qualified objectively by the requisite skill and rectitude, to a number fixed by the general structure of society, (c) to protect its members against particular contingencies, (d) to provide the education requisite to fit others to become members.[89]

This means that a corporation can not only limit the number of people producing a certain type of product within society as a whole, but can also ensure that within the corporation production opportunities are equitably distributed and that manufacturers and traders do not try to undercut one another.[90] In this way, *the measures needed to prevent overproduction can be taken by the producers themselves*, rather than by the state. This ensures not only that decisions about production are taken by people who understand it, but also that controls on the productive activity of members of civil society are *self-imposed*.

Hegel was aware that the spirit of the late eighteenth and early nineteenth centuries was strongly against corporations and for unrestricted freedom of trade, '*laisser aller, laisser faire*'.[91] He recognized that the corporations and guilds had largely died out in Britain by this time. He also knew, of course, that they had been deliberately abolished during the French Revolution under the *Loi le Chapelier* of June 1791. (This law had declared 'the abolition of every kind of corporate organization for citizens of the same condition or profession' to be 'one of the fundamental bases of the French Constitution', and had even declared 'assemblies consisting of or instigated by artisans, workers, journeymen and daylabourers in restraint of the free exercise of the right to employ and to work on any terms mutually agreed' to be 'seditious'.)[92] It is clear, however, that Hegel considered the promotion of free trade and the corresponding decline of the corporations, particularly in advanced industrial countries like Britain, to be largely responsible for the growth of poverty: 'in England there is also the most monstrous poverty and rabble mentality [*Pöbelhaftigkeit*], and a good deal of this cancer is due to the dissolution of the corporations'.[93]

The corporations are not the only means of converting people to a genuine concern for the freedom and welfare of others. Membership of the state is meant to achieve this in part by engendering a 'political sentiment' or sense of common citizenship.[94] And, as we shall see in chapter 10, religion – especially Christianity – is meant to fill us with a *love* for our fellow human beings. But the ethical consciousness which arises in the corporations is of more direct relevance to the problem of poverty, because it makes us aware of our ethical responsibilities as manufacturers, tradesmen or craftsmen, not just as citizens or creatures of God. Membership of a corporation thus enables us to manifest our love for our neighbours in our everyday secular activity. And it also renders our common sense of citizenship more concrete by enabling us to find common cause with a specific group of people with whom we are engaged in a common activity or profession. It is certainly important that individuals understand themselves to live in the larger circle of the state or even of humanity. But it is equally important, in Hegel's view, that, through shared membership of the corporation, individuals also understand themselves to live in 'small circles within [those] large circles'.[95] (Just how important such 'small circles' are, for Hegel, can be seen from the fact that he understands the absence of corporations in nineteenth-century England to have led to poverty despite the fact that England at that time had what he considered to be one of the most developed senses of common political identity, and was of course a Christian country.)

Like Marx, Hegel is concerned that human beings find freedom and individual fulfilment in society; like Marx again, he believes that an economy based on the self-interested pursuit of profit will end up preventing large numbers of people from enjoying such freedom and welfare. Unlike Marx, however, Hegel does not think that an exchange economy based on private ownership of the means of production, wage-labour and money is bound to lead to exploitation and poverty, and he thus does not think that production and distribution need to be taken out of private hands altogether and into public ownership. Hegel's analysis shows that bourgeois private enterprise is a fundamental freedom, and that the growth in productivity which such freedom generates is not necessarily destructive. Indeed it will be beneficial to all, provided that certain controls are placed on production and trade and that the attitude which pervades business and industry is an *ethical* one, one which recognizes that the satisfaction of individual self-interest is the right of all and that self-interest must consequently be harmonized with concern for the common good. Unlike Marx, therefore, Hegel considers the most important safeguard against poverty to be the institutions within civil society (such as the corporations) which transform and reform people's understanding of their freedom and their habits of mind, *not* the forcible, revolutionary restructuring of relations of production.

The advantage of Marx's solution to the problem of poverty is, of course, that it suggests a definite course of action, whereas Hegel seems to be left bemoaning the fact that the main institutions which might have prevented poverty from developing have largely disappeared. If Hegel is right, however, not only is Marx's solution a dangerous and illusory one, but modern economies will remain burdened with poverty until people come to realize that, in addition to a degree of state intervention, *voluntary* associations and institutions are needed to transform selfish business activity into business activity which is ethical.

Freedom and the State

Membership of a corporation promotes the understanding that freedom is essentially ethical in character. This means not only that members of a corporation recognize that their own individual freedom and welfare are rendered more secure by being made the objects of common concern, but also that – like the partners in a marriage – they recognize that there is a distinct form of freedom to be found in sharing a common identity and purpose with someone else; that is, in living *with* rather than *against* others. In the corporation, however, the sense of common purpose is restricted to a particular trade or profession. Despite their great value, corporations can thus be a potentially divisive force within society as a whole, because they can 'ossify, build themselves in, and decline into a miserable system of castes' unless they are placed under a 'higher surveillance'.[96] Ethical freedom is not *fully* realized, therefore, until individuals find freedom in the sense of identity which they share with the whole cultural or geographical community in which they live. Such a community, in which the 'union [*Vereinigung*] pure and simple is the true content and aim of the individual', is the *state*.[97] The fourth ethical duty which is immanent in the very concept of the free will is thus the duty to be a willing member of a state.

The state, for Hegel, is the most developed form of ethical freedom. It is not a simple, immediate form of ethical life, like marriage. Nor is it just a form of interdependence which is forced on to property-owning individuals by the division of labour, like civil society. And, in contrast to the corporations, it is not just a form of ethical life restricted to a single trade or profession. The state is the union of fully autonomous, rights-bearing individuals who consciously and willingly identify with one another simply on the basis of common membership of that union; that is, simply on the basis of common citizenship.[98]

Like marriage and the corporations, the state does not have an existence of its own, independent of the human beings who constitute it and who are conscious of being part of it, and so is not to be compared to natural objects which exist whether or not we are aware of them. The state is thus only a state 'when it is present in consciousness, when it knows itself as a really existing object'.[99] However, again like marriage and the corporations, the state constitutes the objective reality of human freedom, and so cannot simply be assailed or undermined by any individual who chooses to do so, but, once established, must be respected by all free beings within it as a sphere of inviolable right. Indeed, as the most developed form of objective freedom, the state constitutes the highest sphere of right for free beings and thus has a legitimate claim to ultimate authority over the less developed forms of human freedom which have been analysed so far.

The common interest of the members of a state is rendered objective and authoritative when it takes the form of law. The state, as Hegel conceives it, thus has two sides to it: (a) law (together with the legislature and the government), and (b) 'political sentiment',[100] the willingness or disposition on the part of the citizens of the state to abide by the law (together with the institutions of the state and civil society which promote such a disposition). Both of these 'moments' of the state are crucial, since a community constitutes a *state* only when the freedom and welfare of its citizens is understood to be objective and binding on all of them *and* to be something which the citizens themselves are interested in promoting. Hegel recognizes that states are frequently established through the forcible unification of people within a given area, and that some states may continue to be held together largely by force. However, if the state is a true state – and thus the highest form of ethical *freedom* – then what holds it together cannot just be force and constraint, but must instead be the disposition towards lawful behaviour within the people themselves, the 'trust . . . or the consciousness that my interest, both substantive and particular, is contained and preserved in another's (i.e. the state's) interest and end', an interest which may include passing laws regarding such matters as property and public health, but which, as we have seen, may also include a degree of public regulation of economic production and trade. 'Commonplace thinking often has the impression that force holds the state together',

Hegel says, 'but in fact its only bond is the fundamental sense of order which everybody possesses.'[101]

Without this sense of public order and the trust that the laws of the state secure freedom, there is the danger that the citizens will view the state as an alien power which interferes unnecessarily with their lives, and will thus come to regard it with constant suspicion. But the invariable corollary of this, of course, is that the state will itself come to question the reliability of its citizens and so become suspicious of them. Far from being a guarantee of individual freedom, therefore (as some liberal theorists believe), a people which does not trust its government is more likely to encourage the state to engage in secrecy and excessive policing of the society and so to infringe individual freedom. Hegel does not deny that resistance to the state may be necessary at times – 'it can certainly have occurred . . . that a power was present which had to be resisted'[102] – but he is concerned to point out that an enduring mistrust or suspicion of the state on the part of its citizens will set those citizens against the very authority which guarantees their rights and freedoms, and so prevent any genuinely ethical freedom – any sense of being at home in the state – from emerging.[103]

As we indicated earlier in this chapter, however, though a disposition towards lawfulness on the part of the people is essential to ethical freedom, the state's laws must themselves be recognized as expressions of the rational will of the citizens and as guaranteeing the citizens' rights to property, to freedom of thought, to free economic activity and to form free associations. The essence of the free state, manifested above all in modern constitutional states in Hegel's view, is thus that

> the universal be bound up with the complete freedom of its particular members and with private well-being, that thus the interests of family and civil society must concentrate themselves on the state, although the universal end cannot be advanced without the personal knowledge and will of its particular members whose own rights must be maintained.[104]

Indeed, if the state is to be one in which citizens find their freedom, they must not only have the ability to pursue their own interests under the law (and promote the welfare of others), they must also have the right to participate in framing and executing the law. The sovereignty of the state and the supreme authority of the law are represented, Hegel claims, by the monarch who must sign all laws into effect. However, positions in the ministries of the state and in the civil service must be public offices that are open to all qualified citizens. Similarly, the members of the two houses of the legislature must be drawn from the two main estates in civil society, the agricultural estate and the estate of manufacturers, craftsmen and traders. Furthermore, since the purpose of the legislative assemblies is to frame laws which codify the general interest, the representatives of the lower house in particular are to be drawn from the institutions within civil society which already promote a limited concern for the general good, namely the corporations.

Hegel's account of the state contains a wealth of details which it is not possible to enter into here. It should be clear from what has been said, however, that, broadly speaking, the state that Hegel describes is a constitutional state, such as is to be found in many modern democracies. The one major difference between Hegel's conception of the constitutional state and most twentieth-century accounts concerns voting. Hegel does not deny that voting has its place within a free, constitutional state. He acknowledges, for example, that the leaders of the corporations, who may represent their institutions in the legislature, can be elected by the members of the corporations.[105] However, he is not convinced that general elections in which anyone may vote for any group which wishes to constitute itself as a party are the best guarantee of freedom. He points out first of all that the more people who vote, and the larger the parties and constituencies, the less relevant each single vote becomes and the greater the danger of apathy on the part of the voters. Second, he maintains that, if seats in the assembly are not accorded to the various legitimate corporations and associations which represent essential interests within society, but are awarded simply on the basis of the *number* of people who vote for a particular party, then there is no guarantee that the interests of all the main sectors of civil society will be represented.[106] (Hegel's worries about the effectiveness of popular elections in guaranteeing freedom are born out most strikingly, of course, by the elections in Germany in July and November 1932, both of which returned the National Socialists to the Reichstag as the largest single party.)

Hegel holds that the free will constitutes the principle underlying the true state, and he credits Rousseau with having established this principle. However, he does not agree that the authority or legitimacy of the state derives from the 'arbitrary will', 'opinion' or 'capriciously given express consent' – in short, the unconstrained wishes – of the people.[107] The authority of the state, for Hegel, is rooted in the fact that the state is immanent in the very idea of the free will. The state *must* be recognized and respected as having the highest claim to right, because it is only when the state is present that human freedom is rendered objective and universal by becoming law for all. As we saw at the beginning of this chapter, Hegel does not think that true human freedom lies in mere choice (because choice is ultimately arbitrary and dependent upon whatever happens to be available to it), but that it lies in willing what is *required* for freedom to be an objective reality. His whole analysis in the *Philosophy of Right* tries to show that this includes immediate right, moral responsibility, family life, the freedom of economic enterprise and association *and* life in the state. The legitimacy of the state *is* derived from the free will, therefore, but it is derived from what the will must actually will in order to be free (even though it may not always realize it), not from mere opinion or choice.

Hegel thinks that it is much more important that all the elements of freedom be *secured* within the state, than that governments be elected by popular vote – especially since popular elections do not by themselves ensure that a government will be voted in which actually respects all the elements of freedom. In addition to a disposition towards respect for rights, welfare and law, therefore, the best guarantee of freedom, in Hegel's view, is for the state to be organized in such a way that the legislature reflects all the substantial interests within civil society, not just the 'will of the majority' or the interests of those particular parties (some of whom, like the Nazis, may be hostile to freedom) who happen to find a measure of popular support, and that the rights and responsibilities of the legislative, executive and judicial powers are kept distinct, so diffusing power in the state.[108] What is crucial, for Hegel, is that the monarch who signs bills into law does not actually frame the law; that the legislature which frames the law does not execute it; and that the executive which governs through applying the law neither frames the law nor signs it into effect. It is this *organization* of the state, in Hegel's view, which renders all the aspects of freedom objective and secure, and so best guarantees freedom. Voting is not necessarily incompatible with this system of state organization. The point Hegel wishes to make is simply that *by itself* voting does not guarantee freedom, but (as Rousseau also recognized) can just as easily give the majority a popular mandate to impose its own arbitrary will on the minority and possibly even take away their rights and freedoms.

*   *   *

The human will becomes fully free, for Hegel, when it issues in a fully developed constitutional state. However, the existence of the state is itself vulnerable and precarious, because it stands in a relation to other sovereign states that no authority can oversee. Treaties can be concluded with other countries and economic pressure can be put on them in order to try to guarantee mutual security, but ultimately there is nothing to stop states resorting to war if they so decide. The constant possibility of war thus shows up the limits of freedom in the state in the way that the constant possibility of crime showed up the limits of abstract right, the danger of evil showed up the limits of moral conscience and the problem of poverty showed up the limits of unrestrained economic competition. There will thus always be limits to the freedom to be found in the sphere of property, action, labour and law – the sphere of freedom construed as something *objective* which commands our respect as a *right* – because objective human existence is forever exposed to the risk of death and destruction. If absolute freedom is to be attained, therefore, it will not be through economic or political activity, but through an understanding of the absolute character or *truth* of existence in art, religion and philosophy.

9   *Art and Human Wholeness*

Art, Religion and Philosophy

The word 'truth', for Hegel, refers not merely to a property of certain sentences, but to the activity of dialectical reason in the world, unifying and reconciling what is distinct, contrary or contradictory. Sentences which accurately describe facts or states of affairs are, of course, true in the ordinary sense of correct, but 'the highest truth, truth as such, is the resolution of the highest opposition and contradiction'.[1] This process of unifying and reconciling opposites is manifest, in Hegel's view, throughout the natural and the human world: in nature, as the process of generating organic life, and in history, as the process whereby human activity leads to freedom in civil society and the state.

Hegel believes that human beings articulate their understanding of truth as the process of unification in the three forms of what he calls 'absolute spirit': art, religion and philosophy. In Christianity, which he regards as the highest religion, the activity and power of reconciliation in the world is represented as the universal love of God, which finds its fullest expression in the love of Christ for humanity. In speculative philosophy, this divine love is understood in a conceptual form as the dialectical rationality or 'Idea' immanent within the world, overcoming and resolving oppositions. Art, on the other hand, presents truth in the sensuous or imaginative form of unified, harmonious objects produced by human creative activity.

The clearest, and thus truest, articulation of the truth is provided, according to Hegel, by philosophy. However, he recognizes that truth must not only be understood conceptually, but must also be felt, loved and trusted, as in religion, and intuited or perceived in a sensuous or imaginative form, as in art: 'for in inwardness as such, in pure thought, in the world of laws and their universality man cannot endure [*aushalten*]; he also needs sensuous existence, feeling, the heart, emotion, and so on'.[2] From a historical point of view, religion is actually the most important of the three forms of absolute self-consciousness, for Hegel, because its mode of articulating the truth is the one which touches the hearts of people most closely and most readily inspires them to change their world. In art, however, the claims of our senses and our creative imagination are satisfied. Through art, truth can be *enjoyed* without the severe discipline of philosophy or the personal urgency of religion, as the fruit of our own creative activity.

The appropriate content for art is thus unity, reconciliation and harmony, the 'resting with oneself' (*Beruhen auf sich*), which constitutes aesthetic freedom.[3] This content is presented not as an abstract concept, nor as a divine, historical reality, but rather as sensuous or imaginative individuality created by human artistry. The harmony and unity expressed in art is consequently the harmony of an individual created form, of *this* sculpture, *this* painting or *this* piece of music, and such individual expressions of harmony are as many and varied as the creative talent and genius of artists will permit.

The main medium of artistic expression, according to Hegel, is sensuous externality – the stone, colour or musical sound which we are able to touch, see or hear. In poetry and drama also, although the medium of expression is imagination, imaginative representations must be externalized for the ear in language. Aesthetic experience is thus always mediated by the senses in some way or another. Yet aesthetic pleasure, for Hegel, is not primarily sensuous or sensual. If we cannot raise our minds from the pursuit of mere sensuous pleasure to the apprehension – for its own sake – of harmonious form, then we will not be able to produce or enjoy genuine art. Art thus appeals through the senses to the mind and the spirit; it is 'essentially a question, an address to the responsive breast, a call to the heart and the spirit'.[4]

It would be equally wrong, however, to give the impression that Hegel saw no place at all in aesthetic experience for sensuous or sensual pleasure for its own sake. Hegel's is not an intellectualized or de-sensualized theory of art such as that of Schopenhauer. In his book *The Nude*, Kenneth Clark maintains that 'no nude, however abstract, should fail to arouse in the spectator some vestige of erotic feeling, even although it be only the faintest shadow'.[5] Hegel, I think, would agree with this judgement. In nude statues of Aphrodite, for example, he says that 'the sensuous charm of woman' (*der sinnliche weibliche Liebreiz*) is not just one aspect of what we enjoy, it is 'a chief feature'.[6] But while aesthetic experience undoubtedly entails an element of purely sensuous or sensual enjoyment, it involves above all else delight in and enjoyment of the sensuous expression of *formal* harmony and unity. Hegel thus follows Kant and Schiller in locating the great value of art in its harmonization of our sensuous experience with the rational capacity of the mind to apprehend form and structure. In art, he claims, the sensuous is 'spiritualized' (*vergeistigt*) and the spiritual or rational is rendered sensuous (*versinnlicht*).[7] Aesthetic experience thus engages the whole person; it appeals to our senses and our rational mind at one and the same time and so reconciles the two sides of human life which are often seen as being in constant opposition to one another.

For this reason, Hegel says, aesthetic experience has been championed by eighteenth- and early nineteenth-century writers like Schiller and the Romantics as the way in which to counter the abstractness of Enlightenment understanding and to recover concreteness, richness and unity in our thought and experience. (Aesthetic experience has been given a similar status, of course, by post-Hegelian writers such as Nietzsche.) Hegel has great sympathy with this 'aesthetic turn'. The influence of Schiller, for example, is clearly present in a fragment attributed to the young Hegel, *The Earliest System-programme of German Idealism*, which espouses the view 'that the highest act of reason . . . is an aesthetic act, and that *truth and goodness only become sisters in beauty*', and the later Hegel also valued Schiller's interest in the integration of the sensuous and the rational in aesthetic experience very highly indeed.[8] The mature Hegel's disagreement with his aestheticizing contemporaries concerns not art as such, but the question whether wholeness and concreteness in our thinking can only be achieved through an aesthetic mode of discourse, or whether purely conceptual or 'abstract' thought can be brought to concreteness, too. In Hegel's view, a writer does not need to try to give his prose concreteness through the abundant use of poetic imagery and metaphor, as, for example, Herder and Schiller do, though he does not by any means reject such a style out of hand.[9] One can better achieve a *concrete* prose and a *concrete* understanding of concepts through a dialectical mode of thinking, which brings out the life within reason itself by transforming the one-sided abstractions of ordinary understanding into complex, developing concepts. Aesthetic expression, for Hegel, is one mode of recovering concreteness and life from the abstractions of the understanding, but it is not the only mode or the best one. It does not surpass the expression of truth in speculative philosophy.

Like philosophy, art expresses the truth that lies in the dissolution of opposites and in the emergence of unity and reconciliation. But art does not express this truth in its clearest and most determinate form. Art is not the logical articulation of the idea of unity as an *idea*; it is, rather, the mere *appearance* of the truth.

The Function of Art

In a famous phrase from the Berlin lectures on aesthetics Hegel calls art 'the sensuous appearance [*Scheinen*] of the Idea'.[10] This term *Scheinen* must be understood in two ways. On the one hand, it means the appearing of the Idea or self-determining reason in a mode which is different from that of concepts, namely sensuous externality. Conceived like this, *Scheinen* means appearance as revelation, albeit imperfect revelation, and art is thus held to let truth appear or *shine forth* for our senses and our mind as beauty. On the other hand, as Stephen Bungay points out, Hegel also talks of art as *Schein* or appearance in the 'usual sense of what is not real'.[11] If we take appearance in this sense, art – at least so-called 'representational' art – is held to create the illusion of empirical reality, an image that seems to be real but in fact is not, and to employ this illusion to disclose truth.

When considering Hegel's aesthetic theory, it is important to be clear what he understands by terms such as 'appearance' and 'truth', and to recognize that he often gives these words a special meaning. Truth, as we have seen, means unification and reconciliation above all; it does not just mean what is empirically real or given, nor does it primarily mean what corresponds to what is given. The main aim of art as the appearance of *truth* is thus not simply to imitate or represent accurately the things we see about us in everyday experience. Hegel acknowledges that art can imitate life to a startling degree. He points out that there have been artists skilful enough to paint pictures of grapes at which doves have been seen to peck, and indeed that the eighteenth-century zoologist and painter, A. J. Rösel von Rosenhof, painted a picture of a beetle at which a monkey actually tried to gnaw. In Hegel's view, however, such paintings can only ever be poor substitutes for the fullness of nature and life: 'for art is restricted in its means of portrayal, and can only produce one-sided deceptions . . . and, in fact, if it abides by the formal aim of *mere imitation*, it provides not the reality of life but only a pretence of life'. Art can never compete with nature, so, if it is natural objects we wish to see, we will always be better off, according to Hegel, looking in our own garden than in an art gallery.[12]

The purpose of art is not to replicate what we see in the world about us, but to reveal the unity and wholeness which in our everyday experience we often overlook.[13] The most perfect manifestation of wholeness, for Hegel, is organic life and, especially, the richness of conscious human existence; and the most adequate *sensuous* expression of such wholeness is the sensuous form which organic life and human consciousness inhabit, namely the physical body. The most perfect sensuous expression of unity which art can call on, therefore, is the body of the free, harmonious individual. This means that, although the aim of art is not the imitation of nature, the expression of truth will frequently involve the representation of living things and, above all, of human beings. Such representation is not meant to imitate empirical reality for its own sake, but to give concrete, living expression to the often unseen harmony and unity within life. The way in which art indicates that its representational content is intended to have this expressive, rather than imitative function, is through *idealization*.

Genuine art, for Hegel, does not present us with things as they are in ordinary experience, it idealizes them by investing their natural form with grace, balance and proportion which are not encountered in such a pure form in nature itself. Such idealization, which we see above all in classical Greek sculpture, transfigures the appearance or *Schein* of natural form in order to let the truth of unity and harmony shine through.

It could be objected, of course, that there are works of art, notably the paintings of the seventeenth-century Dutch masters, whose aim is not to idealize in the manner of the Greeks, but to present prosaic reality as accurately as possible. Hegel would agree that the painting of the seventeenth, eighteenth and nineteenth centuries, and indeed much Dutch and German painting of earlier periods, too, is often less idealized than Greek art, and that such painting frequently aims at creating the illusion of actual physical presence. However, in the best examples of such art Hegel believes that the purpose of the illusion is not merely that of trying to match nature's achievement through *imitating* reality. The best 'realistic' artists are attempting not to reproduce the mundane, prosaic ordinariness of things, but to raise things out of their ordinariness, to present them – metaphorically and sometimes literally – in a new light and thus to imbue them with new life.

In creating an illusion of natural forms the artist is thus understood by Hegel to be 'mocking' nature by *overcoming* space and time, not to be reinforcing their seemingly intractable presence. The 'realistic' artist overcomes time by giving permanence and meaning to moments which in reality are fleeting and soon lost.

What in nature slips past, art ties down to permanence: a quickly vanishing smile, a sudden roguish expression in the mouth, a glance, a fleeting ray of light, as well as spiritual traits in human life, incidents and events that come and go, are there and then forgotten – anything and everything art wrests from momentary existence, and in this respect too conquers nature.[14]

In this way, what is transient is not denied, as it may appear, but is given a value which in nature it cannot possess, because the artist is able to hold the transient and present it as something worthy of dwelling with and savouring, rather than as something which we rush on from and immediately forget.

The artist overcomes space by imbuing the density and impenetrability of spatial objects with a resonant vitality that makes them shine as they rarely do in real life. What we enjoy in these 'realistic' paintings is thus still a certain form of idealization; it is the non-natural, heightened shining of things which only art can produce. Painters who prefer not to idealize what they present, but rather to confront us with the stark 'reality' of life, would thus appear to Hegel to miss the point of art.

Hegel believes that we can certainly appreciate the artist's skill in accurately reproducing what is given in nature, but he believes that we appreciate that skill better, the more we sense that the artistic reproduction is actually a free, creative transformation of nature and an expression of the artist's idealizing power. The essence of art, for him, does not therefore lie in prosaic naturalism. He has no high-minded view of art, however. He does not think that art should deal only with the elevated passions and concerns of kings and princes. The ordinary and everyday has its place in art, too, but not in its mundane and often laborious ordinariness. The great merit of Murillo's paintings of beggar boys, for example, is, in Hegel's judgement, that they invest the unglamorous, indeed impoverished existence of the beggar boys with a feeling of freedom and well-being. In one painting, an old woman picks lice out of a young boy's hair while the boy calmly chews his bread; in another, two young boys in tattered clothes and bare feet eat grapes and a melon. The subject matter is hardly elevated or the stuff of grand drama and pageantry; the pictures depict scenes from the lowest stratum of society. Yet, Hegel says,

> in this poverty and semi-nakedness what precisely shines forth within and without is nothing but complete absence of care and concern – a Dervish could not have less – in the full feeling of their well-being and delight in life. This freedom from care for external things and the inner freedom made visible outwardly is what the concept of the Ideal requires.[15]

Similarly, in the paintings of the seventeenth-century Dutch masters Hegel sees everyday life informed by 'joy and exuberance'. In a recent German painting he has seen, which depicts a woman entering an inn to scold her husband, Hegel says we encounter nothing but a scene of vicious, snarling people. The Dutch, on the other hand, are infinitely more generous and humane in their portrayal of life.

> With the Dutch in their taverns, at weddings and dances, at feasting and drinking, everything goes on merrily and jovially, even if matters come to quarrels and blows; wives and girls join in and a feeling of freedom and gaiety animates one and all. This spiritual cheerfulness in a justified pleasure, which enters even pictures of animals and which is revealed as satisfaction and delight – this freshly awakened spiritual freedom and vitality in conception and execution – constitutes the higher soul of pictures of this kind.[16]

It is not the purpose of art to confront us with the drudgery of everyday existence or with the extremities of physical and material distress. But this does not mean that Hegel sees it as the task of art to be blandly and superficially idyllic. It means that whether the matter depicted is everyday life or great tragedy, art must give expression to a sense of freedom and unity which enables us to feel reconciled with the world and made whole by the aesthetic experience. Artworks can and very often do bring us face to face with the unredeemed darkness or the prosaic drabness of life, but this cannot be the highest purpose of art. It represents, rather, an impoverishment of aesthetic experience.

If it is not art's main aim to be prosaically realistic, nor is it right to see artistic idealization as essentially an act of falsification, concealment and veiling, as, for example, Nietzsche does. The modern insistence that art is artificial or fictional, rather than true, derives its force from the misconception that truth in art would lie in the accurate representation of reality, if such truth were possible. Art, many modern artists insist, can never 'represent the real', so the only honest art is that which openly acknowledges its fictional, artificial character and which ceases all attempts to be realistic. Indeed, if there is one theme that dominates modern, especially twentieth-century, painting and literature, to the extent that it is now largely taken for granted, it is surely the view that it is not the business of art to create the credible illusion of the real.

Of course, Hegel does not dispute the fact that art is created by human beings and in that sense fictional. But the important thing about art for him is not that it 'falsifies' reality or experience, but that the aesthetic forms which human beings create are able to reveal to us in a particular way the immanent unity and coherence – the *truth* – of life. Art does not just make us aware that we are the creators of our own world – although it can legitimately do that; art makes us aware that through our creations we can reveal and come to comprehend genuine freedom and harmony which is not always evident to our prosaic eyes. It

Figure 1 Murillo, *Domestic Grooming*, *c.*1670–5. Reproduced by kind permission of the Bayerische Staatsgemäldesammlungen, Alte Pinakothek Munich, inv. nr. 489. See p. 215.

must be remembered that, for Hegel, the value of such traditional techniques of representational art as the use of perspective and modelling in painting is not that the artist can thereby accurately imitate nature – though that may be part of his purpose – but that he can create the sensuous image appropriate to the expression of the richness, wholeness and freedom of life, especially human life. Since Hegel's death, of course, the traditional techniques of creating sensuous images of human wholeness have increasingly been set aside, and painters have experimented with a wide variety of styles and techniques, including abstract, non-representational styles. As Ernst Gombrich points out, some painters, like Courbet, have abandoned graceful poses and flowing lines, while others, like Manet, have begun to reject the concern (which arose with Duccio and Giotto in the late thirteenth and early fourteenth centuries) to create fuller, more rounded forms, by flattening the subjects' features and abandoning the quest for solidity of form.[17] Such painters turned against traditional techniques out of a desire for greater realism; that is, out of a desire to paint things as we *see* them, not as we idealize them. Other modern painters, like Cézanne, Seurat or Aubrey Beardsley, turned against traditional representational techniques not necessarily because of any interest in realism, but because of their desire to create new pictorial forms

Figure 2 Murillo, *The Grape and Melon Eaters*, c.1645–6. Reproduced by kind permission of the Bayerische Staatsgemäldesammlungen, Alte Pinakothek Munich, inv. nr. 605. See p. 215.

and perhaps, as in the case of Cézanne, a new 'non-realistic' solidity and harmony of form. However, from a Hegelian point of view, whatever we may have gained through this 'emancipation' of art – especially painting – from traditional representational methods, whatever experimental 'freedom' we might have acquired, the effect has been to deprive us of the means to give sensuous, bodily expression to the richness and wholeness of human character.

Twentieth-century painters, like Francis Bacon, who take a less sanguine view of humanity and who appear to have no interest in depicting human wholeness aesthetically, would not, of course, consider the modern questioning of the artistic tradition to constitute a loss, but rather a decided gain. Here, however, Hegel would side firmly with the tradition, because it is the very purpose of art, in his view, to depict or express the harmony of human life – the 'tranquillity of the soul' and the 'satisfaction of the self with and in itself' – which an artist like Bacon seems to find so uncongenial.[18] This wholeness and harmony is what human life, according to Hegel, is most profoundly concerned with, and it is what we must bring to consciousness in religion and philosophy, as well as art, as the goal of our existence. The highest truth, for Hegel, is that one-sided or partial abstractions are self-negating and that only the unification of opposing moments constitutes genuine life and freedom. To know this truth in art, religion and philosophy, to abide with it, and, through it, to be made free and whole within oneself, is thus the supreme end of human existence. As such, it is an end in itself, not a means towards some further practical purpose.

This has very important consequences for Hegel's view of art which, I believe, put him at variance with writers and artists who are somewhat more politically minded. Hegel's conviction is that art is not primarily intended to serve as a means to the attainment of social, political or moral goals which lie outside the aesthetic domain, but that it affords us a distinctive form of experience which is not reducible to any other. He does not deny that art can and does legitimately serve a number of practical, non-aesthetic ends. It can be employed to cultivate our emotions and our taste and judgement, for example, either by heightening our emotional responsiveness to situations we encounter or, as Hume and Schiller believed, by moderating and refining our barbarian passions. In this way, art can serve as an important element in the practical education of humanity into the ways of civilized society. Equally, art can serve simply to decorate our surroundings or to divert and entertain us. In addition, it can be employed as a means of furthering social change by exhorting us to take moral or political action to remedy social ills. Satire, for example, is the vehicle whereby the artist gives expression to his anger and indignation at the misery and injustices of social life. In these three ways, art can and does serve the broader aim of making our social existence enjoyable or bearable. But the art that makes this its primary aim is, in Hegel's view, 'ancillary art' (*dienende Kunst*), not truly *free* art.[19] To say this is not to denigrate the social aims which such ancillary art serves, nor to suggest that art ought never to be employed towards furthering such aims. Hegel is arguing, however, that the highest function of art is to make possible, amidst the labour and toil of everyday social life, a distinctive aesthetic experience of freedom through the harmony of the senses, imagination and reason.

The principal purpose of art, for Hegel, is not to change the world, but to afford us a breathing space in which to feel at one with ourselves and with the world. Art is thus a mode of theoretical, contemplative activity, not of practical engagement with social and political problems. Aesthetic production is, of course, practical to the extent that the artist labours on and transforms objects in order to express through them what he wants to express. But the frame of mind which the genuine artist wishes to engender in the observer, listener or reader is one of openness to what is shown, not one of eagerness to reform, revolutionize or replace what is shown. A properly aesthetic attitude for Hegel is one which lets the aesthetic object and the aesthetically communicated truth be what it is. Such an attitude does not use art for the purpose of moral or political action, nor indeed does it seek simply to judge or categorize the artwork. A properly aesthetic attitude involves refraining from imposing one's will on things, letting them stand free, allowing them to be as the artist has presented them and thus being able to enjoy aesthetically rendered individuality for its own sake. Whoever has such an attitude does not lack interest in what he beholds – indeed he derives positive delight and enjoyment from what he beholds – but he is, in Kant's sense, 'disinterested'. Hegel is well aware that all aesthetic experience takes place in a specific historical context with its own historical presuppositions. He also thinks, as we shall see, that each age has the right to adapt certain works of art from the past (i.e. those which can be performed) for its present interests and so need not always respect the intentions of the artist. Nevertheless, the character of a truly aesthetic attitude for him is always one of disinterested openness to whatever is shown or performed within the particular historical context in which we live.

> Thus the contemplation of beauty is of a liberal kind; it lets objects be, as inherently free and infinite [*deshalb ist die Betrachtung des Schönen liberaler Art, ein Gewährenlassen der Gegenstände als in sich freier und unendlicher*]; there is no wish to possess them or employ them as useful for fulfilling finite needs and intentions. So the object, as beautiful, appears neither as forced or compelled by us, nor fought and overcome by external things.[20]

Much art, as Hegel recognized, does not fulfil this principal aesthetic aim, but does serve non-aesthetic ends – or, at least, is used by us to serve such ends – and I think that Hegel regards this as acceptable, provided that we do not lose sight of the fact that the highest value of art, and what makes great art great, is its ability to afford us an aesthetic experience of freedom and reconciliation. Certain forms of art – notably architecture, but also at times satire – actually combine functional or practical qualities and properly aesthetic qualities in one work. The basic structure of a Greek temple, for instance, is determined by the simple need to provide somewhere for people to gather and for sculptures to be displayed. Such a temple does not exist just for its own sake as an end in itself, but to provide a setting for something else and is thus an example of ancillary art. However, a Greek temple can also be seen as an example of free art, for if the columns are just the right height, thickness and distance apart to bear the load of the roof with ease and grace, then the building as a whole will embody an ideal of proportion and balance which we can enjoy for its own sake. In this way, the building can both serve the function of housing sculptures of the gods and be worthy of contemplation and appreciation as an end in itself because of the harmony and balance of its functional constituents. In the best Gothic architecture, indeed, Hegel believes that the buildings create such an impression of freedom, height and lightness that we are invited to forget the stupendous task that the pillars and walls perform in carrying the massive vault and just admire the whole structure rising freely into the heavens like a huge forest of trees.[21]

Art can, therefore, be both functional and free. However, the greatest art, for Hegel, is that which allows us to dwell with it primarily for the sake of the harmony and beauty that it expresses or embodies. Such art is *free* art because the harmony it expresses is of value in itself and the response it elicits from us is one of free contemplation and enjoyment of what is shown. Paradoxically, however, the aesthetic response which free art elicits – a response which lets things be and which enjoys them for their own sake without feeling impelled to proceed to practical action in the world – is itself of *practical* value for Hegel. This is because learning to suspend one's immediate practical preoccupations and to cultivate an appreciation of human wholeness, freedom and openness – which is what art teaches us to do – itself tempers and refines our activity in the world. In this sense, Hegel agrees with Schiller that it is art's very autonomy and freedom from subservience to other practical purposes that constitutes its own practical, historical value. Art, for Hegel, may not have been as effective in transforming people's lives as religion, but it has nevertheless played an educative role in history; indeed, Hegel calls it 'the first *teacher* of peoples'.[22] It serves to bring different civilizations to consciousness of their own fundamental values and beliefs, and it serves to bring humanity as a whole closer to consciousness of the human freedom, wholeness and openness which Hegel believes is fully articulated in Christianity and speculative philosophy. If we in the modern world are perhaps losing sight of the distinctive value of aesthetic freedom, and are exploiting art for material, moral or political ends, we should realize that it is not merely our aesthetic experience which is suffering; we are losing sight of an important dimension of our overall social and historical education as well.

Hegel's recognition of the educative value of art is significant because it points to a tension within his conception of art which is crucial to his whole aesthetic theory. On the one hand, art has its end and purpose in itself and is therefore a distinctive, autonomous mode of consciousness. On the other hand, art is a mode of consciousness of the same truth expressed in religion and philosophy, but one in which that truth is expressed in a less clear and less universal fashion. Aesthetic expression of the truth thus paves the way, in Hegel's view, for religious and philosophical expression; it initiates us into a truth which finds its fullest articulation elsewhere. On the one hand, therefore, aesthetic experience is clearly irreducible: the ideal beauty of a Raphael Madonna is not replaceable by the unity of a dialectical transition. But on the other hand, aesthetic experience is also a means of bringing us to the truths of religion and philosophy: that is to say, the spirituality which is expressed in a Raphael painting of the Madonna and Child or in Bach's religious music only comes fully to comprehend itself in the Sacrament of the Holy Communion and in speculative philosophy. This is the paradox at the heart of art, for Hegel, and, as we shall see, it governs his understanding of the history of art.

Art is most absolute, Hegel maintains, when it is the supreme form of consciousness of the truth, as was the case in classical Greek art. The Greeks of the sixth and fifth centuries BC did not see art as secondary to religion and philosophy, but as the primary expression of the truths of their religion. Art for the Greeks was thus an end in itself since it was the true locus of their experience of the gods. In the Christian period, however, religious consciousness withdrew out of the aesthetic and the sensuous into the sphere of inward spirituality. Consequently, art became a subordinate mode of consciousness of the truth, because it was not able to achieve the degree of inwardness which Christian spirituality sought. In the Christian period, art at first remained religious, though it directed attention *beyond* the aesthetic itself to a fuller expression of the truth in the teachings and life of the Mediaeval Church. Later, in the period from the sixteenth century to the present day, art became increasingly secularized and separate from religious experience. In this latter form, in which it largely lost its explicitly religious character, art became most properly an end in itself, because it developed an autonomy and independence from religion which it had not possessed before. But equally, such art ceased being an *absolute* end in itself as it was in Greece, because it was only a subordinate mode of consciousness of a truth fully articulated in the distinct spheres of religion and philosophy. In gaining its autonomy, therefore, art lost its absolute status. The paradox of art, for Hegel, is that the history of art's growing autonomy is at the same time the history of the growing relativization of art's value, because it is only in religion and philosophy that the truth which art intimates comes to be fully revealed.

Beauty and Ideal Character

It is clear that Hegel's views put him out of tune with many other conceptions of art. He does not believe that art's role is primarily to entertain, nor that art should serve mainly as a means to effect social change, nor that art is meant simply to mirror prosaic, empirical reality. Art's primary function, for Hegel, is to give expression to the unity and wholeness of life – especially human life – that the contingencies of everyday existence frequently conceal. Art does not present this unity in a conceptual form, or through the precise description of social and historical reality. It shows us harmony, unity and freedom in a form that is not historically realizable but recognized to be the product of our artistic imagination.

Aesthetic unity can be found in the proportions of architectural structures and in the formal relations of musical notes to one another; but the most perfect form of such unity, Hegel believes, is found in the fusion of human consciousness or spirit with the human body. Such a fusion, in which the human spirit is fully revealed in and as bodily form, represents, according to Hegel, the purest aesthetic ideal. It constitutes *pure beauty*.

The purest aesthetic ideal is thus characterized by a deep sense of contentment, rest and harmony within oneself. By this Hegel means a nobility and freedom of spirit, which is open to the world around it because it rests on a profound assurance of its own worth and value, not narrowly complacent or arrogant self-satisfaction. Such freedom is expressed in art through idealized bodily poses or facial expressions which offer an image of peace and composure to the eye. Most famously, of course, Hegel finds such ideal beauty in the sculptures of classical Greek artists, but he also recognizes it in the pictorial representations by Renaissance painters of the divine blessedness and tranquillity of the Virgin Mary and the Christ Child. Hegel insists that ideal beauty is never, and must never be, insipid. There is character and life in the Greek statues of their gods and there is profound inner warmth and love, not just superficial sweetness, in the Madonnas of Raphael. Gombrich points out that Greek idealization did not involve simply 'omitting any irregularities' or 'deleting small blemishes', so that 'little remains but a pale and insipid ghost of the model', but rather that it involved 'infusing more and more life into the ancient husks'.[23] This is a point with which Hegel fully agrees. 'While the Egyptians', he says, 'represented the gods in their sculptures with legs closed together, unmoved heads, and tightly closed arms, the Greeks release the arms and legs from the body and give to the body a walking position and, in general, one moved in many ways.'[24] Nevertheless, such subjects are not presented in action; they are presented as resting at one with themselves and their freedom.

Hegel goes into considerable detail to explain his conception of ideal physical form. He points out, for example, that in the ideal sculptural profile, which gives bodily expression to the harmony of the body and the spirit, the nose continues in an almost straight line down from the forehead, this line forming a right-angle to a line drawn from the base of the nose to the ear. If the forehead protrudes too much, causing the nose to jut out at a sharp angle, as in much Roman sculpture, Hegel believes that the effect is too intellectual. On the other hand, where the forehead slopes back and the nose and the mouth protrude, Hegel thinks the effect too animal-like. The perfect balance between the body and the spirit of the individual, in which neither outweighs the other and both are fused together as one, is thus achieved through a continuous line from the forehead to the nose. This indeed is the style employed, for example, in Praxiteles' Hermes.[25] Hegel provides many other examples of ideal physical beauty. However, the example I have just cited will suffice to give an impression of the kind of detail he gives in order to explain the nature of the aesthetic ideal.

Chapter 2 argues that Hegelian concepts are always developing ones, and Hegel's concept of art and the aesthetic ideal is no exception. The aesthetic ideal, for Hegel, always involves a sense of self-presence, but it is not always realized in the pure form of sculptural composure and repose. The most concrete form of the ideal, he maintains, involves the *development* of human beings towards the fulfilment (or frustration) of their aims or towards self-understanding, and this entails presenting human beings not simply in blessed repose, but proceeding to action in time. This is an example of the paradox or tension within art mentioned earlier: in order to establish the most *concrete* form of beauty, art has to sacrifice and lose the *purity* of its highest ideal.

The purest aesthetic ideal, in Hegel's view, is that presented by Greek sculpture where the spirit expressed and the sensuous expression are in unmediated harmony. For beauty to become concrete, however, it must be developed or reconstituted out of its negation. The structure of concrete ideal beauty, for Hegel, is thus the temporal pattern of development which proceeds through conflict, discord and dissonance – the negation of harmony and unity – to the resolution of conflict or the restoration of harmony. This pattern constitutes the essence of beauty in epic poetry and much lyrical self-expression, and even in the concentrated expression of inner subjectivity in music. But, above all, it informs what Hegel considers to be the richest and most profound art, drama. If sculpture represents the most aesthetic art, for Hegel, and music the most inward art, drama is art at its most concretely human. Indeed, Sophocles' *Antigone* is considered by Hegel to be perhaps the most excellent and most satisfying artwork of all.[26]

Ideal beauty in drama consists of characters in action who bring themselves into situations of conflict which lead ultimately to a satisfying resolution. The unity in drama is twofold for Hegel. First, as Aristotle said, the action as a whole must be integrated and unified. That is to say, the conflict must be seen to flow from the characters themselves and their situation, and the resolution of the dramatic conflict, whether bloody and catastrophic as in *Antigone* or *Hamlet*, or peaceful as in the *Oresteia*, must be seen to issue from the conflict itself and thus to make sense. Where the action does not flow directly from the ambitions or decisions of the characters concerned, but is simply the product of blind chance or of brute external forces, then we cannot regard it as unfolding the immanent dialectic of human action itself, as revealing a truth about ourselves, and so we cannot be reconciled to the events we see on stage. This is not to say that all dramas do in fact exhibit this ideal structure, only that if they fail to do so, they do not constitute works of true dramatic beauty. When characters are presented as the victims of the hostile, bewildering world into which they are cast, rather than the victims of their own actions, then the unity of the dramatic action is lost. Such a spectacle, Hegel claims, can never satisfy us, can never make us feel reconciled to, and at home with, what we see, but can only disturb or offend us; and disturbance or offence, in Hegel's view, is contrary to the true purpose of art.

The second way in which drama discloses unity is through the presentation of unified, rounded characters. If the purpose of art is not to replicate the prosaic ordinariness of life, then genuine drama should not focus on the doubts, weaknesses and vacillations of ordinary people, but should present idealized figures whose characters are rich, unified and whole. In sculpture – at least in sculpture which does not depict frozen events – ideal beauty takes on the form of calm, self-contained repose and self-presence. In drama, characters are not at rest, but they must still evince and embody self-presence if they are to be ideal. What this means is that they must have a profound and firm sense of who they are and what they are pursuing, that they must feel themselves to be clearly defined characters with clearly defined purposes, even if they do not have a complete understanding of themselves and their world.

In comedy, Hegel says, particularly in the comedies of Aristophanes, the characters enjoy a deep sense of well-being and confidence in themselves, even when their aims are frustrated and shown up to be laughable. This sense of well-being is rooted in their unaffected openness of heart, which allows them to bear the exposure of their ridiculous foibles, and even to join in the laughter. What we see in Aristophanes' comedies, therefore, is the 'blessed laughter [*die lachende Seligkeit*] of the Olympian gods, their unimpaired equanimity, which has found its home in man and which can deal with anything'; and Hegel adds that without having read Aristophanes one scarcely realizes how 'damn good' (*sauwohl*) a human being can feel.[27]

In tragedy, too, the greatest characters have a strong sense of themselves. In the Greek plays, they show a single-minded commitment to the ethical cause they value most highly. They stand up for their family (like Antigone) or the authority of the state (like Creon), and they pursue their 'pathos' with a determination that frequently leads to bloody disaster. If they are modern characters – say, in the plays of Shakespeare – their greatness lies not in the energy and vigour with which they defend an ethical 'pathos', but in what Hegel calls their 'formal independence'.[28] Such characters can be of widely different types. At one extreme, for instance, stand those who are unshaking in their resolve and pursue their ambitions or suspicions unrelentingly, such as Macbeth, Richard III or Othello. At another extreme stand those who are inward and lyrical, such as Juliet, or Miranda in *The Tempest*.

In Macbeth, Hegel says, we admire 'reckless firmness, the identity of the man with himself and with the purpose which derives only from himself'. Macbeth is at first unsure what to do, but once he has resolved to act, nothing makes him deviate from his intended path, neither his respect for the holiness of royal majesty, nor the madness of his wife, nor the disaffection of his vassals. 'Neither divine nor human law makes him falter or draw back; instead he persists in his course'. By any civilized standards, Macbeth is deeply unethical; however, his greatness, for Hegel, lies in the power and determination of his character and in the force of his imagination. Although we find satisfaction in his downfall, we also experience tragic pain at the sight of greatness destroying itself.[29]

In Juliet, of course, we admire something very different. Her character is not outgoing or ruthlessly ambitious, but 'a heart enclosed within itself'. Nevertheless, Juliet's inner strength reveals itself in the force and passion with which she throws herself into her love for Romeo.

Suddenly we see the development of the whole strength of this heart, of intrigue, circumspection, power to sacrifice everything and to submit to the harshest treatment; so that now the whole looks like the first blossoming of the whole rose at once in all its petals and folds, like an infinite outpouring of the innermost ground of the soul in which previously nothing was distinguished, formed or developed, but which now appears as an immediate product of a *single* interest that has awoken, unbeknown to itself, in its beautiful fullness and force, out of a hitherto self-enclosed spirit. It is a fire lit by a spark, a bud, only now just touched by love, which stands there unexpectedly in full bloom, yet, the quicker it unfolds, the quicker too does it droop, its petals gone.[30]

Such ideal characters are by no means ethically ideal: they do not represent models of how we would wish people to behave in civil society. But they are aesthetically ideal, in that they bring before our eyes, in an imaginative and poetic form, the spectacle of human beings who are fundamentally unified and worthy of our admiration. Such characters are not one-dimensional abstractions, personifying narrow passions, but are rich, diversified souls held together by a strong sense of themselves. Indeed, Hegel says – in a manner reminiscent of Nietzsche – that the strength and greatness of a character is measured precisely by how much conflict and division characters can contain within themselves and weld into a coherent unity.

Greatness and force are truly measured only by the greatness and force of the opposition out of which the spirit brings itself back to unity with itself again. The intensity and depth of subjectivity come all the more to light, the more endlessly and tremendously it is divided against itself, and the more lacerating are the contradictions in which it still has to remain firm within itself. In this development alone is preserved the power of the Idea and the Ideal, for power consists only in maintaining oneself within the negative of oneself.[31]

Hegel's conception of ideal character will gain in sharpness and relevance if we contrast it with an alternative conception of character in art. Hegel points out that, although there are traces of what we identify as drama in China and India, as far as we know action in Asian theatre is not conceived as the 'carrying through of a free, individual action'.[32] Drama as the development of the actions of free individuals is, in his view, the specific product of Graeco-Roman and Christian civilization, in which human beings are understood as essentially active and self-determining. However, not all Western European dramatists are able, or willing, to present ideal characters in Hegel's sense. For instance, in the works of the seventeenth-century tragedians, Corneille and Racine, characterization falls short of his aesthetic ideal of human wholeness because of its fundamental abstractness. But the main opponents of the aesthetic ideal, for Hegel, are some of his own German contemporaries, particularly the Romantics.

In the work of certain German dramatists and writers, Hegel believes, the aesthetic ideal of wholeness, self-presence and self-determination is undermined by the increasing importance that is accorded to discord and dissonance. The main target of his criticisms is Heinrich von Kleist, who committed suicide in 1811 while still young, but whose short-stories were to be highly regarded by twentieth-century writers, such as Kafka. Kleist's departure from the aesthetic ideal of character is most clearly evident in his play *Prinz Friedrich von Homburg*. Hegel criticized particularly the character of Prince Friedrich himself, in whom 'magnetism' and somnambulism are given a higher status than 'the wakeful condition of firm consistency'. Prince Friedrich, in Hegel's view, is the most wretched general. He is distracted when given his instructions for battle; on the eve of battle his mind is agitated by visions and dreams, by what Hegel calls the 'stuff of sickness' (*krankhaftes Zeug*); and on the day of battle itself he behaves in a wholly inappropriate way for a military commander, allowing himself to be guided by his 'heart' rather than his official orders. The Prince is caught between his present position and duties as a military officer and his dreams of union with Natalie, the niece of his superior, the Elector of Brandenburg. His attention is not fully directed to the actual situation in which he finds himself; nor, however, is he fully absorbed by the love he feels for Natalie. The Prince is suspended in the middle ground between the two and is in a state of what Hegel calls 'duality, disruption and inner dissonance of character' – not fully self-present and engaged, but at the mercy of unconscious powers within him which are beyond his control. It is this which provokes Hegel's criticism. For the fact that an individual, who should be a concrete 'living individual', is represented as subject to 'dark powers' within him, which take on the status of an alien, mysterious beyond, determining and governing his actions, conflicts with the view that art is the presentation of what is 'clear and transparent'. For Hegel, 'a truly ideal character has no trace of the beyond or the ghostly about him, but has only real [*wirklich*] interests, in which he is at one with himself, for his content and pathos'.[33]

Hegel's mention of Antigone, Macbeth and Juliet illustrates the wide range of diversity that he regards as possible in the portrayal of ideal human character in art. Different as they are, however, in contrast with Kleist's Prince Friedrich, these characters all exhibit the quality of self-presence which the latter lacks. They know who they are and what they are engaged with. They may not be in complete control of their fate – indeed, some may plunge themselves into unforeseen disaster through what they do – but they are not portrayed as being at the mercy of forces beyond themselves. Rather, they make themselves into what they are and forge their own destiny through their own passion and energy. Hegel claims that Kleist, rather than trying to be revolutionary as a dramatist, was actually endeavouring to develop a dramatic style close to that of Shakespeare – a point which could be made about the equally 'revolutionary' Georg Büchner. But, in Hegel's view, the distractedness in

Kleist's characters – their *lack* of character – makes them as far removed from Shakespeare's concrete human beings as it is possible to be.

The characterlessness which Hegel found in Kleist's dramas is developed by another movement with which he was not wholly sympathetic, namely Romantic irony. Romantic irony, for Hegel, is the product of a post-Fichtean philosophy which equates freedom with the ability to dissolve any specific condition in which human beings find themselves. Whatever we are, on this view, our imagination is able to treat our situation ironically and thus to distance us from it. In this way, Romantic irony becomes the power to unsettle any determinate state of personality, including the condition of feeling oneself to be unified and self-present. As a consequence, Hegel claims, the principle of irony leads writers (such as, for example, E. T. A. Hoffmann) to introduce into their fictional creations diversity, division and disorder that do not come together into a unity, 'so that every character destroys itself as character'.[34]

Here, I believe, Hegel has identified a trend which dominates much nineteenth- and twentieth-century art and literature, and indeed much recent philosophy, too, namely the tendency to unsettle, sometimes even to destroy, the coherence and integrity of human character and identity.[35] In modern art human identity has become problematic in a way that has perhaps not been seen to the same degree before in the Western tradition. In the plays of Büchner, the music dramas of Wagner or the short stories of Kafka, characters are no longer as certain of themselves as in, say, the paintings of the seventeenth-century Dutch masters or the comedies of Aristophanes. In the art of Francis Bacon or in the Cubist works of Picasso, the human form is actually savagely distorted; and in the texts of Nathalie Sarraute the words 'he' and 'she', which are meant to mark the presence of an identifiable human being, are frequently banished. This trend is not universal, of course: many modern artists and writers do still retain the concept of wholeness of character, and some, like Tolstoy in *Anna Karenina* or Thomas Mann in *Buddenbrooks*, blend a formal interest in rich, compelling characterization with a thematic interest in the precariousness and vulnerability of human identity. But the concern to present fully rounded human beings which motivated Shakespeare or Titian has – at least in what is considered to be the mainstream of modern art – largely disappeared. Similarly, many modern philosophers have called into question the unity of the subject which Hegel considers to be so important for ideal aesthetic character and civilized social existence: think only of Nietzsche's deconstruction of the traditional 'subject', or of Wittgenstein's dissipation of the single, unified transcendental self in the *Philosophical Investigations*, or of Derrida's subtle querying of the possibility of genuine self-presence.

In many ways Hegel shares the desire of many modern artists and philosophers to break with what they perceive to be the narrow, monological self bequeathed to us by the Cartesian philosophical tradition. However, he does not believe that an expanded, more complex and variegated conception of the self need lack genuine unity and identity; nor does he think that the conception of selfhood and character which we find in Western art, religion and philosophy is always as narrow and reductive as some modern writers imply. Hegel certainly finds the characters in seventeenth-century French tragedy somewhat abstract, but those in Sophoclean and Shakespearean drama represent for him the epitome of richness and concentrated, integrated multiplicity. By comparison with Antigone and Macbeth it is modern figures such as Prince Friedrich who are really reduced, because their inner dissonance is purchased at the price of sacrificing the coherence, effectiveness and presence – the *Wirklichkeit* – of character.

In this respect Hegel is very much out of sympathy with the distinctive Romantic and post-Romantic move in art and philosophy towards the 'emancipation' of diversity, dissemination or dissonance from the alleged illusion or constraint of human identity. He does not deny that social conditions such as poverty can threaten people's sense of themselves and of their value and identity, and that this may well find expression in art. But what he protests against in modern art, he considers to be more the product of 'false theory' and of the abstractions of modern understanding or *Verstand*, than of dire social conditions. The error of the modern movement, in Hegel's view, is to take one aspect of human personality – difference, diversity or dissonance – and to see it as excluding, or at least as compromising, the other – unity and wholeness. For Hegel, however, the strength of human character and consciousness is precisely that it suspends and overcomes this opposition: 'for man is this: not only to carry [*tragen*] the contradiction of multiplicity within himself, but to endure [*ertragen*] it and to remain equal and true to himself therein'.[36] The failure of so many modern artists is that they do not seem to grasp this fusion of opposites as well as the great artists of the past have done.

For Hegel, dissonance and self-division have always been essential moments of Western art. The very nature of drama requires that situations of conflict and collision be presented, and the resolution of dramatic conflict is frequently bloody and frightful. In the tragedies of Shakespeare even outright evil figures prominently. In painting, there is an important place for ugliness, and in music for discord. True beauty and harmony are not insipid or bland; they are created out of the fusion of many different elements, and they may be created out of the furthest extremes of division and contradiction. Poetry, for example, 'has the right to proceed, in describing the inner feelings, almost to the extreme torment of despair, and, in describing the external world, to downright ugliness'.[37] All aspects of disharmony and disunity – ugliness, conflict, dissonance, pain, self-division or just simple multiplicity – are thus able to form part of the beautiful, provided that they are thought *together* with the unity of plot, the wholeness of character or the harmony of visual form or musical resolution. The danger ever-present in Western art, and in post-classical art in particular, is that disharmony will get the upper hand. This danger does not only beset modern art. It was particularly strong, in Hegel's view, in the Middle Ages in the pictorial representation of extreme religious spirituality. In paintings of the devotion and self-sacrifice of Christian martyrs, he says, the 'agonies, the unheard-of abominations, the distortions and dislocations of limbs, the physical torments, etc.' can be so frightful that the effect is no longer that of harmony but of repulsiveness. (Here, perhaps, is a hint as to what Hegel's reaction to the 'distortions and dislocations of limbs' in the Cubist paintings of Picasso might have been.) The appropriate way to depict martyrs in art, Hegel claims, is to show them achieving inner peace and reconciliation through their martyrdom: as 'the preservers of the divine against the crudity of external force and the barbarity of unbelief . . . they endure grief and death, and this courage, strength, endurance and blessedness must therefore appear in them equally'. Thus depicted, even martyrs can become aesthetically satisfying as subjects of art, revealing to us the sobering grandeur of souls that are at one with themselves in pain and death.[38]

The power of the negative has its place in art, but it must not be presented as external, alien and therefore unredeemable. Rather, it must be shown to arise from the dynamic of the whole – be that a drama, an epic poem or a piece of music – and to be resolved into an essential *moment* of that whole. The greatness of Haydn and Mozart, and of the Italian painters of the Renaissance, for Hegel, is that the pain which they undoubtedly express is always 'assuaged' (*gelöst*) in this way. 'Even in the deepest grief and the most extreme rending of the soul, that reconciliation with self which preserves the traits of peace and joyful assurance in the midst of tears and sorrows is not allowed to be lacking.'[39]

It is this moment of 'reconciliation with self' which Hegel fears is being undermined by artists such as Hoffmann and Kleist. Ideal characters may experience the extremes of self-division or pain, but they remain fundamentally at one with themselves despite that dissonance. Even Hamlet, who seems to be the epitome of self-division and self-doubt, is understood by Hegel to refrain from rushing headlong into action because of the nobility of his soul, rather than any Kleistian weakness or distraction. Ideal characters are not cast, as many of Kleist's are, into a mysterious, puzzling world; they are the products of their own thoughts and actions. Or, at least, they are able to achieve a certain inner peace and understanding through the pain inflicted on them by others.

Art shows us in an idealized form that we find our true humanity in the unity of our spirit with itself and in free self-determination. As has already been pointed out, art does not give us direct practical guidance, because the heroes and heroines it presents are aesthetic, not ethical or social ideals. Nevertheless, art initiates us into an appreciation of the value of unity and harmony which religion and philosophy translate into concrete social and historical terms. If we lose our faith in the possibility of free, harmonious life, however, and if – as Kleist does – we present the picture of a world in which alien powers hold sway, then we not only impoverish our aesthetic experience, we also run the risk of losing an important element – namely the aesthetic moment – of our education into civilized values. Kleist casts his characters into an irrational, inhumane world. As his play *Penthesilea* and his short stories *The Earthquake in Chile* and *Michael Kohlhaas* demonstrate, his world is one in which arbitrariness and violence can erupt without warning and with terrible ferocity. If this is the image of life that we present in our art, however, is there not a danger that we might be persuaded by that image and – consciously or unconsciously – foster precisely that kind of world?

In contrast to many modern writers, Hegel retains a deep faith in the value of the aesthetic ideal of an integrated character which is at home with itself and its world, and he displays a profound antipathy to the alienated spirit which is unable or unwilling to be and feel reconciled and at home. Hegel's distance from such unredeemed alienation can be seen in a remarkable passage in which he discusses the wars between the old and the new gods in Greek literature. In his view, the triumph of the new, Olympian gods over the Titans in Greek mythology represents the 'progressive transformation of man's natural condition into a condition of law'. The new gods such as Athene and Apollo still retain an element of natural, individual arbitrariness, but fundamentally they embody the self-conscious and self-assured clarity of Homeric consciousness and, as such, stand for and guarantee the new, aesthetic civilization of the Greeks. The Titans, by contrast, are altogether darker figures. They express the untamed powers of nature, what Nietzsche will later call the 'Dionysian'. The character of these Titans is reflected, in Hegel's view, in the punishments to which they are subjected after their defeat by the Olympians: the endless unquenched thirst of Tantalus, and the endless, absurd task of Sisyphus. 'Like the Titanic powers of nature themselves', Hegel says, 'these punishments are the inherently measureless, the bad infinite, the longing of the "ought", the unsatiated craving of subjective natural desire, which in its continual recurrence never attains the final peace of satisfaction'.[40]

Hegel associates this same absence of satisfaction and lack of self-presence with a strand of modern consciousness, a connection echoed in the twentieth century by Albert Camus in *The Myth of Sisyphus*. Hegel's association of modern 'longing' (*Sehnsucht*) with the sufferings of the Titans, and his unfavourable comparison of both with the clarity and self-possession of the Olympians, indicates that he views the modern insistence on the disruption, dislocation or constant deferral of self-presence not as an advance beyond the allegedly restricted perspective of post-Cartesian thought, but as a relapse back into the eternally unsatisfied condition of natural desire, a condition which Western civilization deemed unworthy of humanity many centuries ago. Hegel would have to admit that the strategies that have been employed since the Romantic period to unsettle human identity and self-presence – in both art and philosophy – have often been extremely subtle and sophisticated. Nevertheless, if he is right that the conception of unified self-present subjectivity, rich in itself and open to the world around it, is central to Western *civilization*, then it would seem that the modern insistence that 'we are not very reliably at home in the interpreted world',[41] that we are homeless, restless, held out into 'nothingness' or cast into an 'abyss', does have a trace of the primitive, the inhumane and the uncivilized to it.

Hegel does not deny that the restlessness of desire constitutes the origin from which we sprang. Nor, clearly, does he deny that it is a state into which we can fall back, if we convince ourselves that it is the truth of human existence. What he denies is that such restlessness and endless deferral of self-presence *do* actually constitute the truth of human existence, and that Apolline clarity of vision and form is merely an illusion, a veil or a nostalgic dream. For Hegel, human beings are not ultimately at the mercy of restless desire because they have the power to transform their natural origin into genuine self-presence and genuine civility. This self-presence is something which we ourselves have to sustain, however. It will not persist unless we constantly bring it before our consciousness. One of the ways in which we do this is through the aesthetic experience of beauty.

The Historicity of Art

Hegel believes that the function of art and the general nature of ideal beauty can be determined *a priori* from the structure of truth or the Idea: beauty is the aesthetic expression of the freedom, harmony and unity within life, in particular in human life. The nature of beauty is thus not determined merely by subjective taste or historical convention, but by reason. However, as we saw in chapter 1, reason itself develops in history, as human beings become more and more conscious of their rational, self-determining character. The truth is realized as a series of different historical conceptions of the truth, leading from the most primitive and abstract to the most advanced and complex (though moments of historical relapse are also possible). Beauty – the aesthetic form in which truth appears – must thus also be historical, and art – the attempt to give concrete expression to beauty – must develop through the various forms in which different historical cultures have conceived of beauty. Although the nature of beauty is determined by reason, therefore, that process of determination forms part of the historical process whereby reason comes to consciousness of itself.

Hegel claims that unity within life is conceived in different ways by different civilizations: as grounded in a transcendent principle (in Judaism), as the unity of individuated form (in Greece), and as the reconciling love of God and the unity of free human subjective inwardness (in Christianity). However, in so far as many cultures recognize unity in some form as an explicit principle of life and human existence and give expression to it in their art, we can say that that principle is to a great degree 'universal'.

This variety of national differences . . . and this course of development through centuries is permeated by something common to them all, and for this reason other nations and the tempers of different periods have in common something intelligible and enjoyable, namely what is universally human [*das Allgemeinmenschliche*] and what is artistic [*das Künstlerische*].[42]

This is not to say that ideal art will necessarily appeal to every people on earth. But those civilizations which have developed an explicit consciousness of the value of unity and harmony in human life – in the family, in social relations and in the state – will be able to come to recognize in the art of other such civilizations expressions of a shared human truth. Even within such a tradition of common understanding, however, each civilization will give aesthetic expression to the 'universal' human interest in unity in its own very different and distinctive way. These differences between the artworks of different civilizations can be explained, as was suggested in chapter 1, by the different levels of self-consciousness which Hegel believes must necessarily emerge in history. They are also the product of a certain irreducible contingency in history. Artworks will thus bear the stamp of different ages and countries, of different particular regions or locales within a country, of different individual artists and schools, and even of different periods or moments within an artist's life. Such particularities and contingencies mean that the philosopher cannot hope to be able to say in exhaustive detail what an ideal work of art will look like: he can only determine the general character of ideal beauty and of its historical development in art.

Like Herder, Hegel is acutely aware that a work of art is embedded in the total social and historical context of a people and an age, and that it gives expression to the way in which they see themselves and the world: 'to whatever age a work of art belongs, it is always marked by particularities which separate it from what is proper to other peoples and other centuries'.[43] Indeed, certain forms of art, for Hegel, such as epic poetry, constitute a major way in which a specific people first comes to define itself and its character, and for this reason he believes that the great epic poems of the past parade the great civilizations of history before our eyes and so present an aesthetic record of the essential stages of human history.[44]

One consequence of the historical specificity of art is that, in spite of certain universal themes, the art of one age or civilization will not be *immediately* accessible to other ages or civilizations. However, Hegel does not think that we are confined within the narrow bounds of our own concerns. Education takes us outside ourselves, or rather broadens our perspective so that we can embrace the concerns of other civilizations. Like Collingwood after him, Hegel does not believe that we can ever really feel what another culture feels or share their values and beliefs; but he thinks we can be educated to *understand* what they feel and what they value in such a way that the concerns of the other culture no longer appear wholly alien to us.[45]

This does not mean that we need prolonged specialized study or a high level of 'scholarship' (*Gelehrsamkeit*) to enjoy the art of another civilization. 'Art does not exist for a small enclosed circle of a few eminent *savants* but for the nation at large and as a whole.'[46] Hegel's claim is simply that we must enjoy enough general historical and geographical education to be able to understand and appreciate the concerns and interests of civilizations other than our own. Such education must give us a clear sense of the similarities and differences between the concerns of our own civilization and those of other civilizations, and it must also give us the ability to appreciate, though not necessarily to define philosophically, the nature of ideal beauty in general. An educated public will always have its own particular tastes, but it must be able to appreciate beauty in a wide variety of cultural and historical forms. Hegel thinks we even need a certain level of historical understanding and knowledge if we are to appreciate the art from different periods of our own tradition. Properly to appreciate the art of the Dutch masters, for example, we need to know how they reclaimed their land from the sea and protected it through their own industry, and how they were consequently filled with joy, exuberance and a vigorous sense of their own nationhood.[47] Similarly, if we are to enjoy the art of ancient Greece, we must know something of Greek culture and history, Greek religion and, above all, the role of art in classical Greece. In addition to this knowledge of the context of artistic production, Hegel thinks we also need to have some idea of the development of art throughout history and of the place of given artworks within that development. For this reason, he thought that the practice of arranging paintings in historical order, which was adopted in the new Royal Gallery opened in Berlin in 1830, would be particularly helpful.[48] Given the right kind of horizon-expanding education, Hegel saw no reason why modern Europeans should not be able to enjoy the art and ancient mythology of cultures, such as India, Egypt and pagan Scandinavia, which were quite different from that of modern Europe.[49] Indeed, his own attempts to understand and appreciate the art of civilizations such as China, Persia and India might well be seen as his contribution to the broader education of his age.

There is a historical dimension not only to our understanding and reception of art, but also to its production, especially where the subject matter of art is derived from a period or culture other than that in which the artist lives. Some artists, Hegel believes, tend to sacrifice everything to the expression of the present interests of their own society and neglect the historical character of the material they are employing. The sixteenth-century Mastersinger, Hans Sachs, for example, turned all his characters, including God, Adam, Eve, Cain and Abel, into citizens of Nuremberg – although the naiveté, liveliness and burlesque boldness with which the poet cast his characters in the mould of his time compensate, according to Hegel, for his total lack of historical sense.[50] The case of the French classical dramatists is somewhat different. Hegel believes – rather harshly perhaps – that the seventeenth-century French tragedians were led to treat their own cultural conventions as the sole valid ones, and to reduce any subject matter drawn from another period to the expression of those conventions, not by an abundant sense of their own vitality, but by a certain narrow cultural arrogance. Echoing the views of Herder before him, Hegel claims that the French took the works of antiquity and simply 'nationalized' them out of disdain for everything foreign or different: 'what was to please had to be frenchified [*französiert*]; what had a different nationality and especially a mediaeval form was called tasteless and barbaric, and was rejected with complete contempt'. Achilles, for example, in Racine's *Iphigénie*, is, in Hegel's view, simply a conventional French prince and 'if his name were not there no one would discover an Achilles in him'. Similarly, he maintains,

in Louis XIV's time Racine's *Esther* was popular chiefly because, when Ahasuerus came on stage, he looked like Louis XIV himself entering the great reception chamber; true, Ahasuerus had oriental trappings, but he was powdered from head to foot and had an ermine royal robe, and behind him a great crowd of curled and powdered chamberlains, *en habit français*, with wigs, feathered bonnets on their arm, vests and hose of *drap d'or*, silk stockings and red heels on their shoes. What only the court and specially privileged persons could gain access to, was seen on stage by the other classes – the entry of the King, rendered in verse.[51]

The opposite tendency, according to Hegel, is evident in Herder, Friedrich Schlegel and their followers. The French may invariably be quick to judge from the assurance that their own perspective is right; the Germans, on the other hand, are always at pains to be historically faithful to the material they are dealing with. Though sympathizing with this historical approach, Hegel believes it can degenerate into an arid concern for historical accuracy for its own sake, and can thus fail to engage the living interest of the present-day audience.[52]

For Hegel, the proper relation between historical authenticity and the expression of present interests involves the fusion of the two. The artist may draw out from the social and personal concerns of the past something which is still of interest to the present; or, better still, he can create a work of art which expresses the concerns of the *present* in such a way that they are rendered compatible with the concerns of the past. Such an approach, avoiding a slavish concern for historical authenticity, would infuse past events with a relevance for a present-day audience; but, none the less, it would represent characters and events in such a way as to make them clearly recognizable as belonging to a past age. This, in Hegel's judgement, is one reason for the greatness of Shakespeare. In his Roman plays, Hegel maintains, Shakespeare imbued his characters with an unmistakable Englishness; but at the same time they appear as credible Romans, not just as Englishmen with Roman names. Similarly, in plays such as *Oedipus at Colonus* or *The Eumenides*, Sophocles and Aeschylus are held by Hegel to have created dramas in which the interests of fifth-century Athens were clearly to the fore, but in which ancient characters such as Oedipus and Orestes remained recognizably what they had always been taken to be. Goethe's achievement in the *West-östlicher Divan* is comparable, Hegel claims, in that he is able to strike a tone that preserves a certain oriental flavour and yet at the same time gives expression to modern German individuality.[53]

This fusion of past and present exemplifies the moment of historical anachronism which Hegel believes is necessary in the artistic representation of past ages. Since our primary concern is always with what we are *now* – however educated we may be – Hegel also believes it is legitimate for each age to edit or revise past works of art for present audiences.[54] Yet mere pragmatic concern for the needs of the moment is insufficient. We must be educated so as to appreciate the achievements and concerns of other cultures and recognize truths about humanity which other cultures may share. At its best, therefore, art can bridge the gap between the present and the past and create an aesthetic world in which the two become one. The greatness of Homer, Sophocles and Shakespeare, for Hegel, is that they do just that. Whether he would feel that twentieth-century artists like Sartre in *The Flies*, or Anouilh in *Antigone*, have managed to strike the right balance is, of course, a matter for conjecture.

Symbolic and Classical Art

Beauty is the harmony and unity of different or opposing moments expressed in a sensuous or imaginative form. It can appear in different modes in different kinds of art: in sculpture and painting as the repose of the human spirit with itself, in poetry as the process of self-articulation through lyrical self-expression or through action which leads to conflict and resolution. As we have just noted, beauty also has a historical dimension to it. We shall now look at the three main historical conceptions of the aesthetic ideal identified by Hegel: symbolic, classical and romantic art.[55] (These three forms of art represent not just historical distinctions, but also systematic differences in the way aesthetic form and content can be related, which can appear at various times in history. Egyptian and Persian art – indeed, all early oriental art – is considered by Hegel to be symbolic, but symbolic features, such as metaphor, can also appear in classical or romantic art. Similarly, ancient Greek art is the only truly classical form of art, but the art of Renaissance painters such as Raphael or Michelangelo also displays classical features.)

The basis of symbolic art is the attempt to give sensuous or imaginative expression to a content which cannot be fully expressed in this way. In symbolic art, a particular content thus *seeks* adequate expression in an aesthetic mode, but cannot achieve it. The paradox of such art, of course, is that it is able to express adequately the fact that its content cannot be fully and adequately expressed. There are, in Hegel's view, several different forms of symbolic art, but mention of just a few should make clear what he has in mind.[56]

In the 'fantastic' symbolism of Hindu art, for example, what is given expression is thought of as something purely spiritual, not something sensuous or natural. However, this pure spirit is conceived in an utterly indeterminate way and so cannot be defined or comprehended in its own terms. The only terms available for the comprehension and representation of this indeterminate, pure spirit, therefore, are the sensuous, natural forms that it is meant to transcend. The sensuous images of Hindu art reflect the freedom of indeterminate spirituality from sensuous nature, in Hegel's view, by means of what he considers to be the wild, 'free' distortion of natural forms. Human figures with multiple limbs or animal heads are thus the aesthetic forms in which a spirituality, which knows that it is not tied to nature, but which cannot articulate its indeterminate spiritual freedom in other than natural forms, intimates its presence.

In Egyptian art the ideal or spiritual content also fails to find any adequate expression, but that content is now conceived as the essentially mysterious, as the riddle, rather than as the indeterminate and abstract. Egyptian art, in Hegel's view, does not therefore express or intimate the inexpressible simply by distorting natural, sensuous forms – though it does do that as well – but rather by creating sensuous images which seem to point to a mysterious, concealed truth which needs to be deciphered.

In the sublime symbolism of Judaic poetry, the spiritual content is no longer as indeterminate or indecipherable as in Indian or Egyptian art, but is conceived as the clear and independent power of God. But the essence of Judaic – and indeed Islamic – consciousness, for Hegel, is that it understands God as non-finite, non-sensuous and non-pictorial. The sublimity of the Judaic God can thus only be given indirect aesthetic expression through the presentation of human beings as finite, powerless and unworthy before God's infinite majesty. The wonder of the Psalms, in Hegel's eyes, is that they are able to intimate a sense of the majesty of the Judaic God through the expression of the lamentations of mortal men.

The final form of symbolic art Hegel discusses is conscious symbolism where a determinate content is again given indirect aesthetic expression, this time by means of a comparison with something sensuous or imaginative with which it is similar, and where what is expressed and the means of expression are thus still held apart from one another. Such symbolism is found in fable and allegory, or in metaphor and simile where love, for example, may be expressed by being compared to a rose.

In symbolic art the content and the form of expression are not fused in perfect harmony, either because the content is intimated as something indeterminate or mysterious, or symbolized as a sublime 'beyond', or because the form and the content, as in simile, are kept separate. Symbolic art thus cannot achieve the unity of ideal beauty, the direct presence of the content *in* the aesthetic form. It is important to recognize, however, that Hegel does not criticize symbolic art for failing to be imitative or mimetic. He is fully aware that many symbolic artists are perfectly capable of 'realistic' representation, should they choose to engage in it.[57] Symbolic artists do not lack technical skill; they lack the concrete conception or vision of the harmony of the human spirit with itself and with its sensuous, bodily form. They cannot grasp that the unity within life or the human spirit is not elusive or mysterious, but fully present to those who have eyes to see it, and that art is one way in which such unity and harmony is presented imaginatively to humanity.

From this perspective, many features of recent Western art suggest that in some ways it has returned to a form of expression that Hegel would call symbolic. Hegel himself thinks that modern reflective understanding tends to treat art as intrinsically symbolic by looking for meaning *behind* the expression, rather than in the form of expression itself, and he cites, as an example of this, Friedrich Schlegel's contention that 'in every artistic representation an allegory is to be sought'.[58] Post-Hegelian examples of 'symbolic' art might include Cubism, in which natural forms are distorted much more excessively than in Indian art; or the plays of Samuel Beckett, in which the status of meaning and understanding becomes so uncertain that it is not clear in some scenes – for example, the hat-routine in Act Two of *Waiting for Godot* – whether they are intended to convey meaning or not. Symbolic art is characterized not simply by the use of metaphor or allegory, but by the absence of any harmony between a clearly articulated meaning and the form of expression. Modern art is thus symbolic in a Hegelian sense whenever it intimates that meaning is indeterminate or not wholly articulable.

Symbolic art ends, Hegel says, when, 'instead of indefinite, general, abstract ideas, it is free individuality which constitutes the content and form of the representation'.[59] Such free individuality is manifest in human consciousness which brings itself to full, unified self-presence, and which determines and expresses itself clearly and openly in action and words or simply through the proportion and balance of its form. This free individuality constitutes the content of what Hegel calls classical art and is found supremely in ancient Greece.

The essence of classical art, for Hegel, is that meaning is not seeking, or struggling to find, adequate expression in an aesthetic, sensuous mode, but is fully present and clear in – at home in – that aesthetic mode. The classical work of art does not point to a meaning beyond itself; it is not mysterious or disturbing, and it does not suggest a power, force or truth that exceeds or fractures the aesthetic expression. Rather, the classical work of art reveals its meaning fully in the harmony of individuated sensuous form itself. Such art is therefore open, self-revealing, not elusive, secretive or hermetic. The classical ideal of beauty is that of the clear self-expression of spiritual freedom in and through *bodily* form, 'the spirit neither escaping the body nor emerging from it, but both one solid whole out of which the inner being [*Insichsein*] of the spirit gazes silently in the wonderful certainty of itself'. This classical ideal, which is found in its purest form in Greek sculpture and in its most concretely human form in Greek drama, represents the most perfect aesthetic ideal that Hegel can conceive: 'the consummation of the realm of beauty. Nothing can be or become more beautiful.'[60]

Greek art exhibits perfect harmony between sensuous form and spiritual content because human and divine spirituality are already conceived by Greek religion as being in harmony with bodily individuality. Greek religion conceives of the truth not as a single unifying principle underlying or informing life, but as a multiplicity of different individual forms. These forms find clearest expression in Greek art – in the Homeric epics and the classical sculptures and tragedies. The importance of art for the Greeks is the corollary of the fact that the Greeks' relation to their gods was different from the Judaic or Christian relation to God. The Christian reveres God as the absolute truth, as the living spirit of reconciliation which informs all things and which is most perfectly revealed in the historical figure of Jesus Christ. The Greeks, on the other hand, had a much more ambivalent relation to their gods. They revered them as real powers in the world, but they viewed the aesthetic form, in which the poets and sculptors represented the gods and in which the gods came most vividly to life, as the product of *human* creative activity. Whereas the Christian God is an ontological and historical reality, therefore, the Homeric gods, in Hegel's view, 'hover in a magic light between poetry and actuality [*Wirklichkeit*]'.

They are not brought so close to us that they appear to us in all the detail of everyday life, and yet neither are they left so indeterminate that they could have no living reality in our eyes. What they do can equally well be explained from the inner life of the human agents, and what compels us to believe in them is the substantial content which is the basis of their character. This is the aspect which makes even the poet take them seriously, although he treats their form and external reality ironically. Accordingly, it seems, antiquity, too, believed in this external form of appearance only as a work of art which acquires its meaning and authenticity from the poet.[61]

Greek art was so harmonious because Greek spirituality and religion were perfectly suited to aesthetic expression, indeed because art was the most appropriate form in which to apprehend the gods. However, Hegel does not consider this aesthetic, individualized conception of truth to be the highest conception. True unity and freedom are found not just in the harmony of the spirit and the body, but in the inward unity of the spirit with itself. This is the conception of truth and unity found in Christianity, Hegel believes, and it is its conception which underlies the third artform, romantic art.

Christianity, Aesthetic Autonomy and the 'Death' of Art

In Christianity, Hegel maintains, the Idea or the 'Absolute' is thought of as the infinite power of love and reconciliation within life, as God. The core of Christian blessedness lies in our consciousness of our unity with God; that is, in the unseen sphere of spiritual life, not in the realm of sensuous, physical being. Christianity thus cannot find its complete expression in the sensuous, individuated form of art, but only in the non-sensuous form of religious and philosophical inwardness. In this sense, Christian consciousness transcends aesthetic expression and can no longer view art, as the Greeks did, as the highest mode of consciousness of the truth.

Yet, as Hegel points out, Christianity also conceives of divine love as that which became incarnate in the physical person of Jesus Christ. A central tenet of Christian faith is thus that spiritual love does not just remain inward and unseen, but takes on a visible form and makes a visible difference to the way human beings lead their lives. Since Christian spirituality is essentially outgoing in this way, it must reveal itself, according to Hegel, in both a historical and an aesthetic form.

Christianity must thus satisfy the whole human being – not just the inner life of the soul – by bringing the whole person into harmony with the spirit of love. For this reason, the aesthetic moment of the harmony of the body, the imagination and the spirit must be integrated into the unity of the spirit within itself. What the art of the Christian era – romantic art – expresses, therefore, is the inner self-certainty and self-presence which withdraws out of the sensuous, bodily sphere into itself, but which equally shines in and through the sensuous sphere and transforms it, as the human personality shines in and through the face. Unlike symbolic art, in which the spirit seeks but cannot find fully adequate, direct aesthetic expression, in romantic art the spirit *achieves* direct aesthetic expression, although it finds its truest expression beyond the aesthetic sphere.

The inward unity of the spirit with itself expresses itself in many ways in romantic art. It is revealed as explicitly Christian love in the figures of Christ, the Apostles and the Virgin Mary in the masterpieces of the Italian Renaissance painters. It is also expressed in the form of music, especially early Italian religious music. In these cases religious inwardness is given expression in an aesthetic form that is suffused with, and idealized by, religious inwardness itself.

However, the value of Christianity, for Hegel, is not only that it opens up a much more profound inner world of religious piety than classical Greek religion, but that its spirituality is much more concretely human. In Christianity 'the Absolute is manifest as a living, actual, and therefore human subject, just as the human and finite subject, in virtue of his being spiritual, makes the absolute substance and truth, the spirit of God, living and actual in himself'.[62] This is where Hegel takes issue with Schiller, and would have taken issue with Nietzsche, both of whom consider Christianity to be other-worldly and see Greek civilization as giving human beings pride of place.

In Schiller's view, expressed in the first version of his poem, *Die Götter Griechenlands* (*The Gods of Greece*),

Da die Götter menschlicher noch waren,
Waren Menschen göttlicher.

When the gods were still more human,
Men themselves were more divine.[63]

In Hegel's view, however, the Greek gods were not more human than the incarnate Christian God. For him, 'Christ is much more *human*; he lives, dies, suffers death on the cross, which is infinitely more human than the human being of Greek beauty'.[64] The Greek gods were the idealized products of the aesthetic imagination; the Christian God, on the other hand, reveals himself in the historical figure of Christ and in the human community which is held together and sustained by Christ's love. For this reason, Hegel believes that it is Christianity, not Greek religion, which in fact gives pride of place to humanity – because Christianity gives humanity the role of realizing divine love.

Christianity has pushed anthropomorphism much further; for, according to Christian doctrine, God is not merely an individual in human shape [*ein nur menschlich gestaltetes Individuum*], but an actual single individual [*ein wirkliches einzelnes Individuum*], wholly God and wholly an actual man, drawn into all the conditions of existence, and no merely humanly shaped ideal of beauty and art.[65]

Whereas Greek religion celebrates humanity in an idealized, imaginative form, Christianity seeks to transform our actual historical existence by transforming our inner spiritual life. This, Hegel believes, has important consequences for the development of romantic art. In Hegel's view, the history of Europe since the time of Christ has been the process whereby the Christian religion has worked to bring our secular, historical existence into conformity with Christ's love and has thereby helped to civilize us. This process has been one in which much blood has been shed and in which, especially in the later Mediaeval and Renaissance periods, the Church itself became infected with the very secular corruption it was trying to combat. Nevertheless, Hegel believes that the modern world's insistence on freedom, self-determination and the infinite value of human life is essentially the product of centuries of Christian proclamation of the infinite value and dignity of humanity and of the infinite importance of love. Christianity is thus an absolute humanism, whose task has been, and still is, to liberate human beings from themselves to the ways of God, which are the true ways of humanity but not those we are naturally inclined to choose.

In the history of Europe Christian freedom has gradually become a secular reality, in Hegel's view, even if that secular freedom is by no means perfect or universal. This process has involved two seemingly contradictory developments. Christianity not only sought to bring the secular domain under ecclesiastical control and thus to bring people to religious self-consciousness and faith; it also endeavoured, above all after the Reformation, to allow people to develop an autonomous, secular form of the freedom which the Christian religion proclaimed. Mediaeval Catholicism, Hegel claims, tried to subordinate the secular to the religious: in politics, the Catholic Church sought to achieve a dominant influence over the secular force of the state, and in art Catholicism sought to give itself aesthetic expression as explicitly religious spirituality. In the Mediaeval period (and the Renaissance), therefore, as in classical Greece, religion and art were unified, art reflecting largely religious concerns and religion spreading the Word of God through images and icons. With the Reformation, however, Hegel believes Christianity became much more inward than Catholicism had been. Emphasis was placed much more on the spoken and written word than the image, and religious consciousness withdrew much more decisively out of the aesthetic sphere into the sphere of pure – religious and philosophical – inwardness. In Protestantism, therefore, the transcendence of art by Christian spirituality became fully manifest, and the break with the classical conception of the centrality of art in religious experience, which was only partly accomplished by Catholicism, was completed.

Protestantism, for Hegel, represents the completion of the withdrawal of Christianity out of the sphere of the aesthetic into the sphere of inner experience, out of the sphere of the external authority of the icons of the Church into the sphere of the authority of the Holy Spirit within humanity. At the same time, Protestantism grants to art and history much greater freedom and independence from religion. Protestantism is thus conceived as more inward than Catholicism, and yet also as more at home in the world, because – unlike mediaeval Catholicism – it is able to let the secular sphere enjoy its own distinct form of freedom. Although the development of civic, political and economic freedom is recognized by Hegel to have begun to emerge in the late Mediaeval period, it was given tremendous impetus, in his view, by the Reformation, because 'it falls to Protestantism alone to immerse itself fully in the prose of life, to make it absolutely valid in itself independently of religious associations, and to let it develop in unrestricted freedom'.[66] Protestantism may have led to the decline of religious art, but it has given art, more generally conceived, increasing autonomy and has engendered an increasing interest in secular, prosaic life.

With Protestantism, art remains a central mode of expression of freedom and truth, but the freedom which is expressed is much more the freedom of secular human character than the inward freedom of religious piety and divine love. Art thus becomes much more consciously a product of *human* self-reflection, and much less the revelation of the divine. Hegel is not, of course, denying that Protestant Europe produced magnificent religious art – he has particular praise for Bach's religious music, for example – but he thinks that what especially characterizes post-Reformation art is the greater emphasis placed on human character and on the particularities and contingencies of nature and human life. In the performing arts, for example, mystery plays and morality plays give way to the great tragedies of human character, and in painting the great achievement is the extension of portraiture. Art opens its door to subject-matter from a wide range of human situations, including, as we saw earlier, ones drawn from everyday life. Indeed, the sense of 'being at home in the commonplace' is a highly important theme of post-Reformation art for Hegel.

The thing which is newly satisfied is the thirst for this present and this reality itself, the delight of the self in what is *there*, contentment with self, with the finitude of man and, generally, with the finite, the particular and the portrait-like. In his present world man wants to see the present itself as it is – even at the cost of sacrificing beauty and ideality of content and appearance – as a live presence recreated by art, as his own human and spiritual work.[67]

After the Reformation the centre of art ceased to be a religious conception and became human life itself in all its abundance and variety. Even landscape painting is interpreted by

Hegel as essentially a way of exploring human responses to nature and thus of expressing human feelings and emotions. Dissonance, contingency and ugliness all find greater room for expression in post-Reformation art, but the task of art remains that of creating a vision of the richness, freedom and wholeness of *human* life: any dissonance or ugliness within art must always be ultimately redeemed by that human richness.

The emancipation of the secular and the human in art marks the liberation of art itself from religion. But this autonomy is acquired at a price, Hegel believes, because in being separated off from religion art loses its equality with religion as the full revelation of the highest truth. In gaining its freedom from religion, therefore, art also discovers its own limitations. This, I think, is what Hegel means by the 'dissolution' of art.[68] Hegel never says that art *dies*; or, rather, he says it only about one art, the epic poem, and even in that case he suggests that a future American epic may be possible and that the modern novel continues the tradition of the great epics of the past.[69] His claim is that art cannot – and should not – have the same status in the modern world as it had in Greece or Mediaeval and Renaissance Europe. We can justifiably hope that art will still have a future and that it will 'always rise higher and perfect itself', but it has ceased to be the highest form of self-consciousness for humanity. Art does not die in the modern world, because the spectacle of ideal aesthetic individuality will always remain an object of human interest. We will always remain aesthetic beings. Nevertheless, however ideal, profound or deeply moving art may be, we as 'moderns' will ultimately always feel that art is, after all, *only* art. 'No matter how excellent we find the statues of the Greek gods, no matter how we see God the Father, Christ and Mary so estimably and perfectly portrayed: it is no help; we bow our knee no longer.'[70]

In the modern world art does not die, but finds its place below religion and philosophy as an important, but subordinate, mode of consciousness of the truth and wholeness of life. As I suggested in my comments on Hegel's view of Kleist and Romantic irony, however, Hegel does not consider the modern situation to be unproblematic: modern developments have in fact raised the spectre of the *real* end or 'death' of art. The significant development in very recent history in Hegel's view – since the 1770s – has been the emergence of a sense of complete freedom of self-expression in art. Post-Reformation art generally had considerably widened the range of things that could be dealt with in art, but at the end of the eighteenth century and the beginning of the nineteenth century artists began to sense a radically new and unlimited freedom. Whereas the Greek, Roman, Mediaeval or seventeenth-century artist was more or less bound to specific subjects and stylistic conventions suited to the society to which he belonged, the contemporary artist, Hegel claims, has the freedom to select virtually any subject and indeed any style.[71] We can develop neo-classical or neo-Gothic styles. We can also draw on the achievements of other civilizations; indeed Hegel sees a more open and responsive – one might even say 'postmodern' – attitude to non-European civilizations such as India as a characteristic of his age.[72] The content of contemporary art is no longer the classical ideal, or religious love, or heroic greatness, but human life as such in all its facets and aspects. Modern art is thus freed from all fixed limitation to a specific conception of human life and sets up as the new 'holy' object of art *'Humanus* . . . i.e. the depths and heights of the human heart as such, the universally human in its joys and sorrows, its strivings, deeds and destinies'. In this way, Hegel claims,

the artist acquires his subject-matter in himself and is the human spirit actually determining itself and considering, meditating on, and expressing the infinity of its feelings and situations: nothing that can be living in the human breast is alien to that spirit any more . . . , for art does not need any longer to represent only what is absolutely suited to one of its specific stages, but everything in which man as such is capable of being at home.[73]

Hegel welcomes the emergence of modern aesthetic freedom, but he makes it clear at various points that the modern artist should nevertheless be subject to certain constraints. To put it another way, modern aesthetic freedom should not be *abstract* but should be *concrete* freedom that embraces unity, harmony and reconciliation. In the passage just cited, for example, Hegel tells us that contemporary art may represent everything in which man is capable of *being at home*, not simply everything under the sun. Art should still express the wholeness and richness of life, and must therefore find subjects and styles in which we can feel at one with ourselves. Similarly, Hegel maintains that the artist may choose any subject or style provided that 'it does not contradict the formal law of simply being beautiful and capable of artistic treatment'. Literary texts should still present 'a rounded entirety of action', therefore, and tragedy should still preserve the moment of positive resolution, 'the reconciliation which art should never lack'.[74]

The radical freedom which contemporary artists enjoy should not be totally abstract and unrestricted, in Hegel's view, because the purpose of art is always to afford us a sense of reconciliation and wholeness. He is realistic enough, however, to recognize that not all artists share this understanding of art. What has become crucial for many artists of Hegel's generation – and since – is that artists should be true to their own experience and give uninhibited expression to their own vision of the world, whether that vision exhibits unity and wholeness or not. In this absolute freedom of expression Hegel sees the danger of the destruction of beauty and of the *real* death of art. This is not to say that works of the creative imagination might cease to be produced, but that such works might cease to exercise the true function of art and thereby threaten to undermine our opportunity for, and our capacity for, genuine aesthetic experience.

Hegel identifies a number of modern aesthetic trends which he believes have exceeded the bounds of beauty. One is the emancipation of the prosaic, the natural and the ordinary. We have already seen that Hegel believes these to be legitimate fields for artistic representation as long as they are in some way transfigured and idealized by art. Hegel claims, however, that some artists have taken the prosaic to the extreme of unidealized mundanity or harsh, painful 'realism'. He himself singles out the dramatists Kotzebue and Iffland for particular criticism as lacking the poetic vision to make the everyday bourgeois reality they depict shine with life.[75] But we might also point to a painter, such as Courbet, as someone who willingly forfeits the techniques of idealization for the sake of rendering more realistically 'what he sees'. In the harrowing naturalism of dramatists, such as Hauptmann, O'Neill or Albee, realism is not necessarily everyday, but is often the deeply sobering, and even haunting, exploration of the extremes of human frailty, self-deception and despair: here drama is used to dis-illusion us and help us come to terms with the darker side of life. But the very grimness of the world these dramatists explore – though their writing may be motivated by genuine passion and compassion – prevents their dramas from ever creating the spectacle of ideal characters whom we can admire and wonder at. In this respect, their naturalism, unlike that of the painter Murillo, lacks the radiance of idealized life and is as far away from ideal beauty as the art of Kleist.

Another potentially corrosive trend in contemporary art, in Hegel's opinion, is subjectivism, especially the subjectivism of Romantic irony. Romantic irony expresses modern 'freedom *from . . .*' through its delight in dissolving fixed determinacy, whether of character or value. Unlike comedy, however, which affirms the well-being and integrity of the subject who sees his or her foibles exposed, such irony slips all too easily into the celebration of subjective arbitrariness, destructiveness and vanity. Romantic irony, Hegel believes, licenses the imagination to connect or dissolve natural forms or rational concepts in a wholly subjective way. Jean Paul, for example, 'is remarkable, beyond everyone else, precisely in the baroque mustering of things objectively furthest removed from one another and in the most confused disorderly jumbling of topics related only in his subjective imagination'.[76] More recent examples of subjectivism may be found in the Dadaist and Surrealist movements, in which the celebration of the power of the unconscious and the irrational often becomes the supreme aim. As with Cubism, one is tempted to interpret the dislocation and displacement of natural forms in many Dadaist or Surrealist paintings as evidence that such art is attempting to *symbolize* – in Hegel's sense – the artist's freedom from traditional conceptions of humanity and from traditional techniques of representing human wholeness. Interpreted in this way, such paintings mark an assault on the aesthetic ideal in the name of an abstract freedom uninformed by reason, reconciliation and harmony.

A third trend in contemporary art to which Hegel draws attention is not unequivocally identified by him as a direct threat to ideal beauty, but remarks which he makes at various points allow us to formulate Hegelian criticisms of it nevertheless. This is the growing interest of artists in the medium of art and the process of artistic production itself, rather than in any specific content. Hegel always recognized that a certain formal interest in the free improvisation of sounds or in the free interplay of colours has its place in music and painting, respectively. In painting, for example, he says that the 'mastery in the production of the most striking effects through the magic of colour and the secrets of its spell now has an independent justification', and he calls this harmonious interplay of colours 'an objective music, a peal [*ein Tönen*] in colours'.[77] However, the fact that he cites the fifteenth-century painters Jan van Eyck and Hans Memling as masters of such 'objective music' indicates that he considers the self-reflective concern with the medium of art itself to be a moment of the exploration in paint of the human spirit, not to be something which can be *abstracted* from that exploration as an end in itself. What has happened in contemporary art, Hegel suggests, is that to a certain extent a process of abstraction has taken place. The exploration of the possibilities of the artistic medium is now not always integrated into the exploration of the subject matter, but develops into the exploration of the process of artistic production for its own sake and thus becomes a form of subjective self-expression: 'interest in the objects depicted is inverted, so that it is the stark subjectivity of the artist himself which intends to display itself and to which what matters is not the forming of a finished and self-subsistent work, but a production in which the productive artist lets us see himself alone'.[78] In the twentieth century, of course, many artists have completely abstracted the self-reflexive investigation of the medium of art from the exploration of human life and nature and have developed a wholly abstract, non-representational art. Some of these – Kandinsky and Pollock, perhaps – might be accused of indulging in subjective self-expression through their art; others – Mondrian, for example – seem to be more concerned with the objective relations between colours or shapes. However, all such artists have separated painting from what Hegel considers to be its prime function and have turned their back on, or simply ignored, the presentation of the aesthetic ideal of concrete human life. For this reason, their work would surely be criticized by Hegel as perhaps appropriate for symbolic consciousness, but not for modern subjectivity. Furthermore, even if it *were* possible to give a Hegelian justification for abstract art, the fact that so many abstract painters – and indeed many non-abstract painters – no longer blend colours into the kind of harmony which Hegel praises in Jan van Eyck, but rather – like Mondrian – separate colours out from one another, would, in my view, prevent Hegel from considering such art to have attained the beauty and harmony which he sees as the goal of art.[79]

The last trend in contemporary art identified by Hegel as a possible threat to the aesthetic ideal is the increasing primacy of philosophical reflection and of abstract ideas in some art. Schiller's poetry is singled out by Hegel for mild criticism in this respect. This development is harmful to art because it endangers the aesthetic fusion of the sensuous and imaginative and the rational and spiritual into one living, individual form, and leads instead to ideas being presented in art more directly in the form of laws or maxims. However, although Hegel may see this as a regrettable development, he recognizes that it is the understandable consequence of the priority that the modern world gives to abstract reflection in so many areas of life. We are now profoundly reflective beings, not the aesthetic beings of ancient Greece, so our art is bound to be more conceptual than in the past. For this reason, although Hegel believes that art has a future and that beauty can be preserved from the excesses of the prosaic and the subjective, he recognizes that the modern age as a whole is not as favourable to art as other ages were: in the modern world 'thought and reflection have surpassed [*überflügelt*] fine art'.[80]

However, this very primacy of reflection in the modern world can be turned to the advantage of art through the development of philosophical aesthetics. Aesthetic theory, particularly speculative, dialectical aesthetic theory, can teach us how to safeguard the distinctive value of art in the modern world by reminding us of the nature of beauty, and by making us aware of the threats to beauty facing us now which we must try to avoid or at least mitigate. In this way, the very process of consciousness moving beyond art to religion and philosophy can allow us to understand more clearly the unique place that art has in life, rather than cause us to destroy it. Art may no longer be the highest form of human self-consciousness, for Hegel, but it still has great value in the modern reflective age; indeed it 'acquires its real confirmation [*Bewährung*] only in philosophy'.[81]

Hegel thus identifies a number of developments in modern art that depart from what he sees as the proper function of art. Art, for him, is not primarily intended – indeed may not be intended at all – to confront us with the irrational and subjective or with the starkly prosaic, or to present colours and sounds simply for their own sake. Nor indeed is the purpose of art best served when art becomes overly theoretical or didactic. Yet Hegel believes that modern art can continue to exercise its proper function of giving sensuous, imaginative expression to the richness, wholeness and concrete freedom of human life, if we retain a healthy understanding of our nature and possibilities as human beings.

Lecturing in the 1820s, Hegel could still be optimistic about the future of art. He thought, for example, that prosaic realism need not degenerate into the dull presentation of mundane ordinariness, but could become – as it had with the Dutch – the brilliant exploration of the details of rural and bourgeois life through which the artist could demonstrate his ability to make things *shine*. He also thought that modern irony need not degenerate into mere subjective arbitrariness, but – as in the writings of Laurence Sterne – could be developed into true humour in which the author 'lets what is substantial emerge from chance and mere whims'.[82] Furthermore, he thought that beyond prosaic realism and subjectivism there lay the possibility of 'objective humour' – developed, he believed, by Goethe – in which the subject explores his own feelings and inner life through the concentrated exploration of the object before him, thus fusing subject and object in a striking new way; and the continuing possibility of a radical but concrete aesthetic freedom, in which the artist is able to draw on all appropriate styles and subjects to explore the whole rich realm of *Humanus*.[83]

Hegel thus thought that modern aesthetic freedom *could* be contained within the bounds of beauty. However, looking back over the development of art since Hegel's death, it seems that many of his fears have been confirmed and that much – though by no means all – modern art has indeed 'emancipated' itself from the aesthetic ideal. As a consequence, we have gained a much greater licence to experiment than even Hegel was aware of. But we have also precipitated ourselves into an artistic crisis, because the immense variety of aesthetic styles now recognized, and the artist's insistence on his right to create whatever he wishes, have rendered the criteria for evaluating art extremely problematic. People still employ criteria, of course, including the most traditional one: 'does the form express the content effectively?' But is there really any consensus as to whether, for example, Carl André's bricks are good or bad art?[84] And are we always able to judge what is a good or a bad Jackson Pollock? Many post-Hegelian artists have undoubtedly produced works of art that we love and admire greatly, but can we honestly say that we always know *why* we admire them?

Perhaps Hegel was wrong and modern art has simply displaced his aesthetics of beauty and truth – either by creating a need for a new philosophical aesthetics (such as that of Adorno) which can do justice to the emancipation of art from beauty, or by making any general philosophical aesthetics superfluous or impossible. Or perhaps Hegel's aesthetics should force us, instead, to ask whether, through the emancipation of art from beauty, we have not lost as much as we have gained. We may welcome the inventiveness of modern artists, but we might ask whether some have not used that inventiveness to undermine, rather than sustain, the wholeness and richness of human life. Many modern artists are, of course, still dedicated to the creation of beauty in some form, and some – perhaps Thomas Mann might stand as an example – have consciously tried to fuse modern, 'deconstructive' with traditional, humanist concerns. But others have projected the image of a world of alienation or uncertainty in which the harmony of life is never anything more than an illusion or a nostalgic dream. And that, surely, is a sad state of affairs to have reached. For, however genuine the alienation of a Kafka may be, and however justified the savage indignation of a George Grosz, their art can never heal the wounds they expose, but can only serve to reinforce and deepen them.

10 *Philosophy and Christian Faith*

Philosophy, Reason and *Geist*

This book began by focusing on the Kantian element in Hegel's philosophy: Hegel's contention that we never have direct access to the world, because we always view it through the categories of our thought and experience. As we saw in chapter 1, Hegel differs from Kant in that he recognizes that these categories develop historically as we become more and more conscious of our capacity for freedom. Nevertheless, Hegel remains a Kantian to the extent that he insists that our understanding of the world always presupposes certain categories and can never be simply immediate.

Unlike Kant, however, Hegel does not assume that our categories necessarily confine us within a limited human perspective on things or prevent us from coming to know the true nature of the world itself. In Hegel's view, we cannot cast off the categories of thought and see the world without presuppositions, but we can ask whether the categories we employ are the right ones, the ones in which the truth can be disclosed. It is clear, however, that the appropriateness of our categories cannot be gauged simply by comparing them with the world. Hegel's claim, after all, is that it is only through the appropriate categories that the world itself can become accessible to us, so we cannot determine which are the right categories in which to think by laying claim to any independent access to things. Hegel thus needs to develop some alternative way of determining which are the categories of truth, and the method he proposes, as we saw in chapter 2, is that of a *presuppositionless* logic.

A modern logic which attempts to determine the categories of truth must be presuppositionless, Hegel believes, if it is to satisfy the modern claim to freedom and self-determination and the modern desire to take nothing for granted. In this sense, paradoxically, such a logic has definite historical presuppositions. It will be presuppositon*less*, however, in that it will not be founded on any determinate principles, rules or axioms which lay down in advance how thought should proceed. Hegel's logic has no necessary *systematic* presuppositions, therefore, precisely because it presupposes that we suspend our familiar assumptions about thinking and begin with an utterly indeterminate and empty thought: the category of being. By not simply assuming that the categories are to be understood in a specific way, but by following the path along which thought is led when it tries to think the utterly indeterminate thought of being, Hegel believes that we can come to understand the proper way to conceive of the categories; that is, the character that free, self-determining thought itself shows its categories to have.

Hegel's speculative, presuppositionless logic thus claims to determine the true conceptual presuppositions of experience. However, speculative logic does not just offer an account of how *we* must think, it also claims to determine what it means to be, what being *itself* is in truth. The logic must tell us about being itself, Hegel argues, because any attempt to cut thought off from being, and to claim that being, existence or reality is utterly other than, and unreachable by, thought, itself rests on certain presupposed conceptions about being which have no warrant in a truly self-critical, presuppositionless logic (and which are also called into question by Hegel's *Phenomenology*). At the start of presuppositionless logic, being may not be taken to be anything beyond the indeterminate immediacy of which thought is minimally aware. There is no justification, therefore, for regarding the true philosophical account of the *concept* of being as anything less than the true account of *being* itself.

In the course of the *Logic* Hegel shows being to be rational; that is, to be the dialectical process of becoming – of determining itself to be – fully and explicitly self-determining. He also argues, however, that rational being, or the 'Idea', actually exists as *nature* – as space, time and matter. The Idea does not therefore precede nature in time, but itself takes the form of nature. Nature is thus the initial, immediate existence of reason. Since nature is rational, in Hegel's view, it is itself the process of becoming explicitly self-determining, a process which culminates in the emergence of life and consciousness. Consciousness is in turn the process of becoming more and more explicitly self-conscious and self-determining in history. Rational existence is thus the process whereby nature leads to consciousness and consciousness leads to ever more self-conscious forms of human life. This process is not governed by a pre-existing rational Idea because the process of natural and conscious development is *itself* the existence of dialectical reason. Reason is thus immanent in natural and human existence; it is the substance of existence itself. For Hegel, then, the process of natural and conscious development is the process whereby being-as-reason itself becomes self-conscious *spirit*. This, I believe, is what is meant by saying that being is ultimately to be understood as 'absolute spirit'.

Spirit is thus not just a human product, not just human self-consciousness. Spirit is reason – being itself – become self-conscious. However, it is clear that, for Hegel, being only becomes conscious in and as *human* consciousness. *We* are the consciousness and self-consciousness of being, of absolute reason itself. There is, therefore, only one spirit, for Hegel – absolute spirit, self-conscious rational existence – and we, as it were, are its head. Absolute spirit is not a mysterious cosmic entity to which we are subject; it is simply being itself become conscious of its own intrinsic rationality in and as *us*. 'True spirit', Hegel says in the philosophy of history, 'exists in man, it is *his* spirit.'[1] Without us, therefore, being is not absolute spirit. At the beginning of history, spirit is only a possibility, not yet a reality. In this sense, it is *we* who bring spirit into being.

Yet we must remember that our activity is not simply our own to command and control. Our activity *is* our own, for Hegel, in the sense that we are not simply the plaything of external forces. In us, reason – being itself – has become conscious and self-conscious, and because we are that self-consciousness of being, we are the power to determine, choose and initiate actions. We are not just puppets on a string. But, at the same time, our activity is nothing but the activity of self-conscious *reason* in the world. We did not create ourselves; nature – rational nature – brought us into being. Furthermore, our actions have rational consequences of their own which we do not control. Since we are conscious beings, we think we are in control of what we do; but just because we are *conscious* beings, we are capable of misunderstanding or rejecting the rational consequences of our activity. When we fail to comprehend the character of genuinely rational activity, or when we seek to assert our freedom by choosing not to act in accordance with reason, then our own profound impotence becomes apparent as our actions lead to consequences which we do not desire or do not foresee. However, if we seek to understand the character of rational activity and to act in explicit accord with reason, then, as our activity becomes more properly rational, we can claim that the activity of reason becomes more properly our *own* activity. With this acknowledgement, we are now at the point at which we can turn to Hegel's understanding of Christianity and its relation to speculative philosophy – because, in Hegel's view, it is in Christianity and speculative philosophy that we come to understand the true, dialectical character of reason most clearly.

Philosophy and Religious Representation

In speculative philosophy, Hegel maintains, the true character of dialectical reason is given its clearest, most precise articulation. However, philosophy is purely conceptual knowledge of the truth and Hegel recognizes that humanity cannot live by concepts alone. If we are genuinely to take hold of the truth and be transformed by it, that truth must not just be the concern of our intellect, but must enter our hearts, resonate through our innermost feelings and permeate the whole of our life. 'Whatever I hold as true, whatever ought to be valid for me, must also be in my feeling, must belong to my being and character.'[2] For Hegel, it is in religion, and specifically Christianity, that we take hold of the truth in this less exact, but more vivid and more urgent way.

Hegel claims that the Christian religion and speculative philosophy express the same basic truth – namely that reason informs the world – but that they do so in different ways. (Other religions also reveal aspects of the truth, in Hegel's view, but only Christianity reveals the truth adequately. Unless otherwise indicated, therefore, all references to 'religion' or 'faith' in this chapter should be understood to refer to Christianity.) From the strictly cognitive point of view, philosophy is a more precise account of the nature of reason and its activity in the world than is religion. But religion is in many ways of greater value than philosophy because it penetrates so deeply into our consciousness and is much more effective than philosophy at transforming our lives and bringing them into accord with reason. Furthermore, Hegel is also well aware that philosophy plays no direct role in most people's lives. Philosophy is vital to the health of a society as a whole, in his view, since a society needs to develop a clear and precise understanding of the nature of reason, freedom and the rights and duties involved in public life, and to make that understanding publicly available. However, philosophy is a strict discipline which demands special training, and so, though in principle anyone can be trained to understand it, its insights are in practice not equally accessible to everyone, for the simple reason that not all individuals can devote themselves to philosophy, any more than they can all become politicians or doctors. Many people will be able to enjoy the fruits of philosophy through reading, but many more will have no contact with it at all. Religion, on the other hand, is available to all because it speaks to us about matters of ultimate concern in a concrete way which has a direct and immediate bearing on the conduct of our lives. For most people, Hegel believes, religion is the supreme mode of consciousness and experience of the truth. It is, as he puts it, 'the place where a people defines for itself what it holds to be true.'[3]

As far as the daily lives of most individuals are concerned, philosophy may be of no importance whatsoever. However, Hegel does not think that the quality of religious experience is diminished by a lack of a properly philosophical grasp of the truth. Provided that religious faith is not utterly lacking in understanding and is indeed genuine consciousness of the truth,

> the religiosity and ethical character [*Sittlichkeit*] of a restricted sphere of life (for example, that of a shepherd or peasant), in their concentrated inwardness and limitation to a few simple situations of life, have infinite worth; they are just as valuable as those which accompany a high degree of knowledge and a life with a wide range of relationships and actions.[4]

However, although Hegel clearly thinks that the religious believer can remain ignorant of philosophy and still know the truth through genuine faith, he does not think that the philosopher can do without religion. Philosophy itself must be totally independent of religious faith. But if the philosopher as an individual is to have a complete and pervasive comprehension of the truth, he must feel the truth of what he grasps with his intellect, and have profound faith in the presence of reason in the world as well as an exact conceptual understanding of it. Otherwise, his head will be, as it were, cut off from his heart and his body, and his experience of the truth will be one-sided and impoverished. In Hegel's eyes, both 'a philosophy without heart and a faith without understanding are . . . abstractions from the true life and being of knowledge and faith'.[5]

Like speculative philosophy, religion comprehends the fact that we are not just accidents of nature but owe our existence to the rational character and activity of being itself. Religion expresses this fact by saying that we are created and sustained by God. The word 'God', in Hegel's view, is thus religion's word for what philosophy knows to be reason or the 'Idea'; that is, absolute reason active in the world. 'God is essentially rational, rationality [*Vernünftigkeit*]', Hegel tells us, and to know something as created by God is essentially to know that it is informed by reason and that reason is at work in it.[6] This is why Hegel claims to the great distress of many more recent philosophers – friends and foes of Hegel alike – that philosophy has God as its sole object of study and enquiry. 'The object of religion, like that of philosophy, is the eternal truth in its very objectivity, God and nothing but God and the explication of God.'[7]

In understanding the activity of God to be nothing other than the activity of *reason* in the world, Hegel is continuing a line of thought developed, in the eighteenth century, by Enlightenment thinkers such as Lessing and Kant, both of whom believed that religion communicates rational truths to us in a non-rational, non-conceptual way. For Hegel, therefore, religious faith is a form of consciousness of the rational character or truth of being. However, it is not a reflective consciousness which comprehends the truth through philosophical concepts, such as substance or cause. Nor indeed is faith the belief in certain 'facts' produced by reflecting on the 'evidence' or 'compelling reasons'. Faith is thus not to be equated with the simple belief *that* God exists, the kind of belief which may be supported by pointing to the appearance of design in the world or by referring to the reports of miracles in the Bible; nor is it to be equated with the conviction that certain events – miraculous or otherwise – have actually occurred in the past, such as that 'this or that person existed and said this or that; or that the Children of Israel passed with dry feet through the Red Sea – or that the trumpets before the walls of Jericho produced as powerful an effect as our cannons'.[8]

Hegel recognized, of course, that Enlightenment critics of Christianity, like Voltaire, understood faith to be precisely this kind of belief in 'facts' about God or his supernatural intervention in the world, and that they claimed victory over religious faith by questioning the evidence for such belief. He also recognized that religious orthodoxy itself often construes faith in this way and thus makes itself a target for sceptical attack. (Indeed, there are still plenty of theologians today who exhort us to 'consider the evidence' – such as the 'fact' of the empty tomb – as if religious faith could be established by scientific proof. And, of course, there are plenty of gleeful sceptics ready to assault such 'evidence' in the firm conviction that thereby the whole edifice of religion will come tumbling down.) For Hegel, however, faith does not stand or fall with the ability to produce convincing arguments or evidence for factual claims, because faith is never simply a matter of believing *that* certain events took place or *that* God exists. Faith is a matter of *understanding* the true, divine character of ultimate reality, of understanding what Paul Tillich calls 'the ground of being'.[9] 'Whether the guests at the marriage of Cana received more wine or not is a matter of total indifference', Hegel maintains. What constitutes the core of faith is the recognition that the ground of our being is infinite, divine reason or love – God – together with the certainty 'that God is in Christ, . . . that this course of the divine life is and has been beheld [*angeschaut*] in the course of this [human] life'.[10]

The understanding we have in faith is an intuitive one, however; it is a felt understanding of the nature of God. Such faith has a definite content: it believes that God is love and that his nature is revealed in Jesus Christ. Faith, however, can supply no reasons or external evidence to support this belief. What grounds Christian faith, for Hegel, is the inward witness of the spirit, the inner feeling that in this image of God as love and in the person of Christ the ultimate truth about ourselves and about being itself is made known to us. Faith is thus, as it were, 'instinctive', Hegel says; it rests on the fact that Christ speaks to us and strikes a chord in our lives. It stems from our recognition that the love he reveals meets our deepest needs and liberates us. Faith rests, Hegel claims, on an inner sympathy with what Christian teaching discloses, a sympathy which leads us to open our hearts and say simply: 'Yes, that is the truth.'[11] Faith cannot be imposed on anyone, therefore, nor can we argue anyone into it. Ultimately, what decides whether or not we share a faith in Christ and the Christian God of love is the witness of our spirit, whether or not we feel, and know ourselves to be, liberated by Christ's love.

To the Enlightenment sceptic this must make faith seem irrational and unscientific. However, for Hegel, though it lacks the trappings of formal argumentation, faith is in fact deeply rational, because our felt, intuitive recognition of the truth of Christian doctrine is nothing other than the 'dim recognition' (*dunkles Anerkennen*) by our *reason* of the nature of absolute reason itself.[12]

Faith is not merely the expression of arbitrary subjective convictions; it is the intuitive grasp by our consciousness of the character of universal, dialectical reason. However, faith embraces reason not in an explicitly rational or logical form, but in the form of concrete images and pictorial representations or *Vorstellungen*, such as the 'grace' and 'love' of God.

Speculative, conceptual thought as Hegel understands it, is able to grasp the identity-in-difference of concepts such as being and not-being (as we saw in chapter 2) or reason and nature (as we saw in chapter 5). Representation or *Vorstellung*, on the other hand, tends to separate the elements with which it deals from one another and merely connect them externally with such words as 'and' or 'also', or simply arrange them in a temporal sequence. 'The means for combining representations are [the words] "and" and "also". . . . What we say is, "something happens", "change occurs", or "if it is this, it is also that, and then it is in this way".'[13] This means that where philosophical thought understands reason to be immanent in nature as the principle of dialectical development informing nature and leading to the emergence of consciousness, religion (at least initially) represents reason as a separate being – God – who exists prior to nature and who then creates and sustains the natural world and human beings. Religious consciousness recognizes the fundamental truth that the existence of nature is not simply contingent, but follows from the absolute, 'divine' Idea of being itself, but religion expresses this truth through the image of 'creation', which, Hegel believes, is not to be taken literally.

Hegel follows Lessing in arguing that there are in fact many 'concepts' in religion which philosophy recognizes to be merely metaphors or images which present the truths of reason in a more popular and widely accessible form and which are not to be taken literally.

For example, if we say that God has begotten a son, we know quite well that this is only an image; representation provides us with 'son' and 'begetter' [*Erzeuger*] from a familiar relationship, which, as we well know, is not meant in its immediacy, but is supposed to signify a different relationship, which is something like this one.[14]

Similarly, when we talk of the 'wrath' of God, this is just a metaphor or image. Hegel is thus conscious of the fact that in religious experience we draw on many images of relationships which are familiar to us from everyday life, such as the relationship of father to son, in order to make sense of the ultimate nature of things and of the ultimate ground of our being in terms which we can readily understand.

This would seem to raise a serious problem, however. How can philosophy and faith coexist if the believer thinks that there exists a personal God who has created the world and now sustains it through his love, but philosophy tells us that the world is really ruled by reason? Is not Hegel's philosophy profoundly anti-religious in its implications?

Hegel clearly believes that this is not the case. He declared himself to be a Lutheran and saw no conflict within his own experience between the account of truth given by speculative philosophy and that given by Christianity. We must remember that Hegel did not consider faith and philosophy to be offering two rival accounts of the world. Rather, he thought that they both tell the same story and reveal the same truth, but that they take hold of that truth in different ways: faith through feeling, images and the concrete historical person of Jesus Christ, and philosophy through concepts. John Robinson writes that 'to assert that "*God* is love" is to believe that in love one comes into touch with the most fundamental reality in the universe, that Being itself ultimately has this character', and it might appear as if Hegel's speculative philosophy would pose a challenge to such a statement by claiming that the fundamental reality – God – is ultimately *reason*, not *love*.[15] However, in Hegel's view, by saying that God is ultimately reason, we are not contradicting the tenets of faith, but are providing a more exact understanding of what divine love actually *is*, and are showing that love is indeed the appropriate image for rational existence. Philosophy, for Hegel, thus clarifies and confirms the perspective of faith, and shows that through the familiar images, metaphors and analogies which faith employs, faith does grasp the heart of the matter.

When we give expression to our faith that we are 'loved' by God, therefore, we are implicitly recognizing the fundamental truth that we are sustained and guided in our existence by the reconciling power of reason in the world, not by blind fate or harsh necessity. But we are not giving expression to our intellectual understanding of that truth. We are giving expression to the profound *feeling* – and felt certainty – which we have of being sustained and preserved by what is absolute, the profound feeling which we can only think of as that of being loved. Speculative philosophy clearly considers this religious conception of love to be an image of reason; yet it sees it not as a distortion of the truth, but rather as precisely the right way to express our deep, abiding *feeling for* and *trust in* the benevolence of the power which sustains and guides our life.

Hegel also recognizes that some religious representations – for example, the stories we have of the life and work of Jesus – are not metaphorical, but historical. He understands, therefore, that Christianity does not just give us an *image* of reason as love, but that, in the person of Jesus Christ and in the community of believers filled with his spirit, Christianity reveals to us that a life lived in the spirit of God, in the spirit of reason and truth, actually *is* love. When faith claims that the truth – God – is love, its claim can thus be understood by speculative philosophy to be both metaphorically and literally true at one and the same time.

In Hegel's view, faith and philosophy complement each other. Philosophy shows us through its concepts that ultimate reality, which faith interprets as divine love, is to be understood more precisely as reason. Faith recognizes, through the person of Jesus Christ, that a life led in the heartfelt readiness to let go of ourselves and be guided by the truth – a spirit which philosophy recognizes to be the embodied spirit of reason – is literally a life of love.

Conflict between faith and philosophy will only arise from the side of philosophy if it ignores the fact that the truth must enter our heart and imagination, not just our intellect, and if it ignores the fact that a rational human existence is not just a life which seeks to give reasons for all that it does, but one led in *Sittlichkeit*, fellowship and love. Conflict will only arise from the side of faith if faith neglects the fact that philosophy is not trying to set aside its account of God, but rather to clarify the meaning of its belief in God; that is, to help us come to a deeper understanding of the truth which faith grasps through images, analogies and the historical person of Jesus.

Charles Taylor finds it difficult to understand how someone who thinks of the world as governed by reason can ever pray.[16] But it should be clear from what I have said that a Hegelian philosopher can worship and pray as a Christian. In worship and prayer he will not contemplate his identity with reason or with absolute spirit; that is the province of philosophy. Rather, he will focus his attention on Christ in the trusting faith that Christ is 'the way, and the truth, and the life'[17] and that by opening himself up to Christ he will be filled with the spirit of love and thereby gain freedom and new life. As Taylor points out, Hegel may not be able to offer prayers of petition to God, if by that we mean direct requests to God. But this does not necessarily make his position incompatible with Christianity, since Christian prayer, at least as former Archbishop of Canterbury, Michael Ramsey, understands it, does not involve 'the bombardment of God with requests so much as the bringing of our desires within the stream of God's own compassion' and 'being for a while consciously with the Father'.[18]

What is clear is that a Hegelian philosopher cannot share the supernatural – perhaps superstitious – beliefs commonly associated with Christianity, or see sacred stories as literal narratives of supernatural events in history. Miracles, for example, are understood by Hegel to be 'things which those who stand at a certain level of culture [*Bildung*] no longer can believe'. But this, of course, does not by itself mark Hegel's faith as non-Christian. It simply means that like St Augustine (though much more consistently than he) Hegel is primarily interested in 'the spiritual meaning of texts which, taken literally, appear to contain the most unlikely doctrines', and that his theology probably lends more support to Paul Tillich than to Billy Graham.[19] For Hegel, belief in God has nothing to do with belief in a supernatural being who can overrule the laws of nature. Christian faith in, and understanding of, God is simply the profoundest understanding that we can have – short of speculative philosophy itself – of the activity of reason or the 'Idea' in the world. The question we now have to consider, therefore, is how a religion that has been deemed by so many modern thinkers – Christian and non-Christian, from Kierkegaard to Bertrand Russell – to be profoundly *irrational* can be understood by Hegel to reveal the nature of reason to us so clearly.

God as Reason and Love

Christianity gives us a clear image of the character of reason, Hegel believes, in the doctrines of the Incarnation and the Trinity. As we have seen, Christian faith represents absolute reason as God, as the Creator of all things, as the Father Almighty. However, through the doctrine of the Incarnation, Christian faith recognizes that God does not simply hold himself apart from the world, but has revealed his presence *in* the world in the divine love of Christ. In the understanding of God as Holy Spirit, Christian faith goes further and recognizes that God is present in the world not just in one man, but as the spirit of love that fills all who share a faith in Christ. Through these religious conceptions of the God Incarnate and the Holy Spirit, Hegel believes that Christian faith expresses its profound understanding of the fact that absolute reason is immanent in the world and comes to full self-consciousness – comes to be absolute spirit or *Geist* – in human beings. Hegel fully accepts the fact that Christian faith talks of God and the Holy Spirit, not of reason or absolute spirit. But it is his conviction that in its Trinitarian conception of God, Christian discourse is in fact revealing the truth about absolute reason. The heart of the Christian understanding of God, for Hegel, is thus that God is known to be present in the world as love and ultimately as spirit, and in this central doctrine Christian faith – albeit implicitly and in a pictorial, representational form – comprehends the immanent character of absolute, dialectical reason.

This is why Hegel distinguishes so sharply between Christianity and Judaism. In Judaism, he maintains, God is conceived solely as the Father Almighty; that is, as essentially transcendent. Christianity recognizes, however, that God is only understood in truth when he is seen not just as the Father but as the process of becoming the Holy Spirit actively present in us.[20]

The Christian God, moreover, is not ultimately to be conceived as *a being* who sends his Son and the Holy Spirit into the world. Rather, he is to be understood as the actual *process* of coming to be *Geist* itself. The religious *Vorstellung* of God as a wholly separate being is thus understood by Hegel to be called into question, not just by philosophy, but by Christian faith itself. Christian faith begins with the image of God as a separate being who creates the world and sends his Son into the world to redeem it, but it ultimately reveals God to be the process of becoming spirit in and through the community of Christian believers. In this way, the Judaic conception of God as transcendent is profoundly transformed and redefined by Christian faith.

We say that God eternally begets his son, that God distinguishes himself from himself, and thus we begin to speak of God in this way: God does this, and is utterly present to himself [*bei sich selbst*] in the other whom he has posited (the form of love); but at the same time we must know very well that God is himself this entire activity [*daß Gott dies ganze Tun selbst ist*]. God is the beginning, he acts in this way; but he is likewise simply the end, the totality, and it is as totality that God is the spirit. Merely as the Father, God is not yet the truth (he is known in this way, without the Son, in the Jewish religion). Rather he is both beginning and end; . . . he is the eternal process.[21]

The distinctive insight of Christian faith for Hegel – the hinge around which world-history turns – is that God (absolute reason) comes to be fully present in the world as spirit. The

Christian God lives and is active in human faith. He is not the dry, cold abstraction who appears in the thought of Enlightenment philosophers like Wolff and Kant. The God of the Enlightenment is the God of the understanding, for Hegel, 'the unapproachable God [*der unnahbare Gott*], whom man holds at a distance from his body and the spirit as the beyond'. This God of the understanding, Hegel remarks scathingly, 'is, out of pure infinity [*aus purer Unendlichkeit*], too high and mighty [*vornehm*] to clothe himself in our flesh and blood'.[22] But such a remote, passionless God is clearly not the loving Incarnate God of Christian faith. The Kantian conception of God as 'the highest reality, as a being that is one, simple, all-sufficient, eternal, etc.', is in Hegel's eyes an abstraction which, if anything, is closer to Judaism or Islam than Christianity.[23] And Hegel would surely have considered Nietzsche's attacks on the Christian God to have been largely (though by no means exclusively) provoked by this dead Enlightenment abstraction, by what Nietzsche calls this 'nothingness deified', rather than the living, present God of Christian faith.[24]

What is missing from the Enlightenment conception of God is a recognition of the central importance of the Incarnation to the full revelation of, and being of, the Trinitarian God. Christian faith, in Hegel's view, recognizes that God is only truly a God of love and only comes to be spirit through becoming the life, suffering and death of humanity and thus through *giving up* the very purity of divine transcendence which Wolff and Kant insist on as essential to God's divinity. 'The Father', Hegel says, 'is precisely that which only is in so far as it surrenders itself [*sich preisgibt*]; but which first exists as real(ised) spirit in self-consciousness'.[25] In understanding the Christian God in this way as revealing his true divinity through sacrificing his transcendent majesty, Hegel is focusing our attention on the central fact that the Christian God is marked above all, not by aloofness, jealousy or thundering, raging judgement, but by self-sacrificing *love*. In this respect, Hegel's understanding of God is uncontroversial and would find acceptance with most Christian theologians. It is echoed perhaps most closely by the Tübingen theologian, Eberhard Jüngel, who has been strongly influenced by Hegel, but is by no means uncritical of his thought. Commenting on (and rejecting) the idea that Jesus' death is to be interpreted as a sacrifice made to appease an angry God, Jüngel writes:

if, in connection with the death of Jesus, we are to talk of a sacrifice, then [we must talk] of the sacrifice of divine other-worldliness [*Jenseitigkeit*], divine impassibility [*Unberührtheit*], divine absoluteness, in short: of the sacrifice of God's simply oppositional stance towards his sinful creature.[26]

Michael Ramsey makes essentially the same point.

The divine Creator has humbled himself to take on himself the entire experience of existence as man, in all the conditions of humanity. . . . To act divinely is [thus] not to grasp, but to *pour self* out; that is the secret of the incarnation, and it is no less the secret of fellowship. Such indeed is the Christian way.[27]

The Christian God is nothing other than the process of revealing himself in the figure of Jesus Christ to be divine, self-giving love, and thereby of becoming Holy Spirit within us. This Holy Spirit comes alive in us to the extent that we open ourselves up to, and seek to bring our lives into accord with, Christ's love, which is the love of God. *God* comes to be Holy Spirit within us, therefore, as *we* become filled with the love of Christ. Indeed, as Hegel puts it, 'the Holy Spirit is eternal love'.[28]

What has this got to do with the revelation of the nature of *reason*, however? If we cast our minds back to the analysis of Hegel's speculative logic which we gave in chapter 2, the connection between reason and divine love should become apparent. Reason, in Hegel's view, is ultimately dialectical; that is to say, it develops (within our thinking) through producing concepts, or (within the world) through producing modes of existence, which negate themselves and transform themselves into something new. Hegel believes that such dialectical reason is at work in nature; but he sees it at work above all in human history leading us through our actions and choices to develop more self-conscious and thus more explicitly rational, self-determining and free forms of human life. We must recall that reason for Hegel is no transcendent puppet-master, but is rather the immanent – though frequently uncomprehended – dialectical structure of the actions we ourselves initiate and carry through. It is the logic inherent in what we do which consigns so many of our individual and communal actions to tragic self-contradictoriness and self-destructiveness, but which also leads us to freedom and reconciliation.

If we wish to understand the true character of reason in its purest logical form, Hegel maintains, we must suspend our conventional assumptions and allow the dialectical character of reason to direct our thoughts. This entails allowing the inadequacy, self-contradictoriness or 'negativity' of our most cherished conceptions to be revealed to us and letting those conceptions be redefined before our very eyes. It thus means being willing to give up our insistence on controlling our thoughts ourselves. This willingness to relinquish our autonomy, to sacrifice our right to control our thinking, and to follow wherever the truth leads us, is for Hegel the key to genuinely rational thought, and it is precisely this spirit of willing self-surrender which Christ reveals – in the sphere of concrete experience and practical life – as the way of divine love. The Christian doctrine of the Incarnate God thus reveals the true nature of *reason* by showing that *God* surrenders his transcendence to become human, and lets go of his human form by suffering even to the point of death. The structure of self-conscious dialectical reason *is* the structure of Christian love, therefore, because they both involve the readiness to let go of one's hold on oneself, to 'die to oneself' or, in Michael Ramsey's words, to 'pour self out'. Hegel recognizes that to the understanding which sees reason as simple deductive or syllogistic inference, the equation of reason and love will be nonsensical. Similarly, he acknowledges that, to the understanding which conceives of God as pure infinity wholly distinct from human finitude, the idea of an infinite God incarnated in a finite, mortal human being, or the image of a God actually dying on a cross, will seem to be utterly absurd. However, if one understands reason to be ultimately dialectical, then one will appreciate why Hegel claims – apparently against all good sense – that 'the Idea [i.e. reason] can find nothing unsatisfactory in Christianity'.[29]

Like Lessing and Kant before him, Hegel interprets religion as the non-conceptual consciousness of rational truth. But, unlike them, he equates the structure of reason with that of divine love. Furthermore, he sees reason as becoming conscious of itself in human self-consciousness or *Geist*. For Hegel, this conception of reason as dialectical is given pictorial expression in the Christian conception of God as love and as spirit. The Christian God is thus not to be conceived of simply as a transcendent creator or judge; nor, as Nietzsche asserted, are we to see in him 'a declaration of hostility towards life . . ., the formula for every calumny of "this world", for every lie about "the next world"!'[30] For Hegel, as for the Evangelist, the Christian God is the God of love, the God who 'sent the Son into the world, not to condemn the world, but that the world might be saved through him'.[31]

It is because God is essentially a loving, self-giving God that he cannot be a jealous God who withholds himself from view, but is *necessarily* a God who opens and reveals himself to the world, who lets his Holy Spirit enter our hearts and guide us and who allows us thereby to share in his divine life and love. God's revelation of himself to us is not arbitrary for Hegel. The Christian God cannot *not* be loving self-revelation, because he is *essentially* self-revelation, *essentially* the process of coming to be present within consciousness as the spirit of love.[32]

But God does not just become spirit out of love *for* us, in Hegel's view. He becomes spirit because it is his own essence to come to know himself, and this he can only do in and through human beings. Christianity thus tells exactly the same story about God as speculative philosophy tells about absolute reason: namely that God (reason) necessarily comes to full self-consciousness in and as human self-consciousness. Although he recognizes that it may seem to some to be blasphemous to say so, Hegel understands this Christian doctrine of God as spirit to mean that human consciousness and human finitude are not fundamentally distinct from God's existence, but are essential to the full being of God as spirit; that is, as truly *God*. 'The relation to consciousness . . . belongs to God's being; only as an abstract God is he something beyond, something other for consciousness'.[33] The Christian God, for Hegel, thus only comes to be fully God as he comes to know himself in us, and he only does this as *we* come to know him within ourselves. 'God is only God in so far as he knows himself; his self-knowledge is, further, his self-consciousness in man and man's knowledge *of* God, which proceeds to man's self-knowledge *in* God'.[34]

Though Christian faith distinguishes God from man, therefore, it ultimately only accepts the existence of one spirit, 'the universal divine spirit' which comes into existence *as* spirit in and as the community of believers. 'Faith itself is the divine spirit that works in the subject. But the subject is not a passive receptacle; rather Holy Spirit is equally the subject's spirit to the extent that the subject has faith.'[35] In so far as the community of believers is genuinely filled, through faith, with the spirit of divine love, it does not just constitute a community of those who know God; it actually constitutes the existence of God himself as present, active *Geist*, that is to say, the existence of self-giving love itself as consciously and explicitly active in the world. And such a community of believers marks for Hegel the first appearance on earth of a community which lives in explicit accord with *reason*. As we have seen, therefore, love is not just a metaphor for absolute reason active in the world. In addition to its existence as reflective thinking and law, reason actually becomes self-conscious and explicitly effective in history *as* love, as the love of the religious and ethical community.

Hegel's interpretation of Christianity has exercised enormous influence on nineteenth- and twentieth-century Christian theology, but it has not been without its critics. The Protestant theologian Karl Barth, for example, sees in Hegel's understanding of God as essentially self-revealing, and as necessarily coming to self-awareness in the community of faith, a serious restriction of the freedom of God.

This God, the God of Hegel, is at least his own prisoner. . . . Revelation can now no longer be a matter of God's free act; rather, God *must* function as we see him function in revelation. It is necessary for him to reveal himself. . . . The *community* is necessary for God himself, so that he can be the *spirit* of the community and thus be spirit and God. Were he not the spirit of the *community*, he would not be God. Only insofar as he is the spirit of the community *is* he God. I am necessary for God. . . . By making the dialectical method of the *Logic* the essence of God, Hegel rendered any knowledge of the real dialectic of grace, which is founded in God's freedom, impossible.[36]

Charles Taylor echoes Barth's criticism of Hegel and indeed states even more boldly than Barth himself that Hegel's position is simply not one that a Christian can accept.

In Hegel's system, God cannot *give* to man – neither in creation, nor in revelation, nor in salvation through sending his Son. To see these as acts of God is to see them in the medium of *Vorstellung*, and what makes them acts is just what belongs to the inadequate narrative medium, which we transcend in philosophy. For to see them aright is to see them as emanations of a necessity which is no more God's than it is man's. . . . Lacking the idea of God as giver, Hegel cannot accommodate the relations of God and man as they must be for Christian faith. He has no place for grace in the properly Christian sense. . . . And he has no place for divine love in the Christian sense, for God's love for his creatures is inseparable from its expression in giving.[37]

In my view, however, neither Barth nor Taylor properly understands what Hegel is saying. It is true that Hegel sees God as the process of self-revelation and not as a subject who initiates individual acts. It is also true that Hegel claims that God *must* reveal himself. But this does not mean that God is to be thought of as subject to a necessity that is not his own or 'which is no more God's than it is man's'. Hegel never subordinates God – or reason – to any alien necessity. Divine activity, he says, is nothing but 'a *play* of love with itself', and when he talks of the way the presence of the divine spirit in us causes us to be 'reborn', he insists that this stems from 'divine free Grace, for everything divine is free, it is not fate, not destiny'.[38] However, just because God *is* freedom, grace and love, he is not 'free' to withhold himself, to be jealous or a wanton tyrant or to refuse to be freedom, grace and love. The necessity of God's revelation of himself, for Hegel, is thus not a restriction of his love and freedom; it flows from them. The Christian God *must* reveal himself, therefore, *must* pour himself out into the souls of those who have faith in him, because that is what it means to *be* a loving, self-giving God. When Hegel claims that God's revelation is necessary, he does not in any way limit God's capacity for love; he is simply pointing out what Charles Taylor himself asserts, namely that 'God's love . . . is *inseparable* from its expression in giving' (emphasis added). A truly loving God cannot *not* open himself up to us, and the only God who could withhold himself would be one who was not through and through a loving God. But such, Hegel believes, is not the God of Christian faith.

A further criticism levelled at Hegel, during his lifetime and since, is that, by claiming that God comes to self-consciousness in humanity, he comes close to simply equating human beings with God. As Hegel puts it, 'if God, by knowing man, is himself man, so also is man, by knowing God, God himself; that, it is said, is the unavoidable consequence of absolute knowledge which it may not conceal from itself'.[39] It is clear, however, that Hegel does not want to deny that human beings and God are different, though he does want to reject the idea that God is ultimately *other* than humanity. Humanity is the self-consciousness of God, for Hegel, and thus does not simply stand over against God as his other, but is itself an integral part of the life of God. Furthermore, through the presence of Holy Spirit within us our activity can take on the form of explicitly divine love. In both these senses we can say that our activity is indistinguishable from that of God. However, this does not mean that we are simply to be equated with God in every respect. We are, after all, only the self-consciousness of God, the product of God's (reason's) work in nature; we are not the sustaining ground of nature itself. Furthermore, we can only become fully one with God – that is to say, our own activity can only take on the form of truly divine love – to the extent that we acknowledge our own limitations and ultimate impotence as finite beings, let go of our own finite concerns and purposes and let ourselves be filled and transformed by the Holy Spirit. Hegel thus does not simply declare our immediate, natural human finitude to be divine. According to Christian belief, Hegel contends, humanity is contained in the concept of God, so Christians believe in the essential unity of the divine and human natures. However, 'this unity must not be conceived superficially, as if God were only man and man, equally, were God. Rather, man is only God in so far he negates [*aufhebt*] the natural existence and finitude of his spirit [*die Natürlichkeit und Endlichkeit seines Geistes*] and raises himself to God'.[40]

Hegel acknowledges that, at one level, Christian faith conceives of God as *other* than us, as sending his Holy Spirit to us, as it were, from on high. He also recognizes that Protestant theologians in particular have a tendency to see a great gulf between the human spirit and the grace of God.[41] Nevertheless, he believes that the central focus of Christian faith is on the revelation of the essential unity of the divine and human natures through the figure of Jesus Christ. For Hegel, Christ reveals that it is the very nature of God himself to *become* human, and at the same time he shows us how human activity itself can take on the form of truly divine love. Indeed, Christ reveals that the path of divine love is itself the path to true humanity. The heart of Christian faith, on this interpretation, is not that we are ultimately other than God, but that we are central to God's life and that, through consciousness and trusting acceptance of God, we ourselves can come to be truly human. Christian faith, in Hegel's understanding, is thus consciousness of the true nature of God *and* humanity, that is to say, consciousness of the true nature of *Geist*, of that one, absolute *Geist* which comes to self-consciousness *in* and *as* human beings. We initially picture God as the infinite standing over against us as finite beings, but genuinely *Christian* faith comes to recognize that 'the true spirit exists in man, is *his* spirit, and [that] the individual gives himself the certainty of this identity with the Absolute in worship'.[42]

Whether we find Hegel's understanding of Christian faith convincing depends of course on our own understanding and, perhaps, experience, of that faith. The philosopher Robert Solomon, for example, claims that 'traditional Christianity has placed its stress upon the Father and the Son, leaving the "Holy Ghost" as the mysterious white dove or the ray of light in a Masaccio Trinity', so not surprisingly he finds Hegel's emphasis on spirit in his interpretation of Christianity somewhat suspect. Solomon, in fact, denies that Hegel was a Christian at all and claims that the much discussed 'secret of Hegel' is that he was in fact an atheist who thought of God or spirit simply as 'humanity made absolute'.

He [Hegel] may have stuck to the letter of Christianity, but in 'spirit' he was anything but a Christian. He was not the great abstract thinker of Christianity at all, but rather the precursor of atheistic humanism in German Philosophy. . . . His 'Christianity' is nothing but nominal, an elaborate subterfuge to protect his professional ambitions in the most religiously conservative country in northern Europe.[43]

Ingenious and arresting though it may be, Solomon's thesis, by his own admission, can rely on none of Hegel's public declarations, but must argue against the explicitly religious doctrines in Hegel's philosophy 'on the basis of conjecture and indirect evidence'. However, this very admission should surely make us as suspicious of Solomon's interpretation of Hegel as he is of Hegel's interpretation of Christianity. After all, Hegel did claim, in letters and in his lectures, that he was a devout Lutheran, and it seems to me to be somewhat wilful simply to dismiss this as mere 'subterfuge'.[44] Extreme though it is, however, Solomon's reading of Hegel is nevertheless helpful in focusing our attention on what seems to be the main issue at stake here: whether or not Hegel is Christian 'in spirit' and whether or not he has grasped the 'spirit' of Christian faith. To answer this question, we need to take a closer look at what Hegel thinks Christian faith actually involves.

Faith and Worship

The centre of Christian faith, for Hegel, is the certainty of our essential unity with God – the certainty that God comes into the fullness of his divinity in and through humanity, and that humanity has the capacity, through the grace of God, for living a truly divine life. This unity of the divine and human natures is revealed to us in the person of Jesus Christ. Through Christ, therefore, we know ourselves to be taken up into God, to be, as Hegel puts it, a 'moment' of God himself. But, precisely because Christ reveals to us that God's love comes into the world as *human* self-surrender and compassion, he reveals that we are all called upon to be the children of God, called upon to be the space in which God's love is made manifest, and that, consequently, the appropriate life for human beings is one which actually manifests divine love. Christ, for Hegel, is thus the 'universal individual' who, in revealing the true nature of God, at one and the same time reveals what it means to live a truly *human* life.[45]

What Christ reveals about human life, in Hegel's view, is that human beings come to live a divine – and thus fully human – life not by insisting on the satisfaction of their natural, egoistical will, but by giving up that will and living a life of love. Indeed, as James Yerkes puts it, Hegel sees in Christ's death 'the *consummate* expression of this yielding up of man's "natural will"' and thus the consummation of true humanity.[46]

Since man as such is this process of negating immediacy and of coming to himself, to his unity, out of this negation, so he should renounce [*entsagen*] his natural will, knowledge and being. This giving up of his natural existence is beheld in the suffering and death of Christ and in his resurrection and elevation to the right hand of the Father.[47]

In his life, and supremely in his willingness to meet death, Christ shows that human life can free itself from self-will and become a life of divine love, a life lived in the 'spirit', not the 'flesh'. He thus reveals to us the truth about human spirituality, what Hegel calls 'the eternal history of the spirit [*die ewige Geschichte des Geistes*] – a history which everyone has to complete in himself in order to be spirit or become a child of God, a citizen of his kingdom'.[48]

Hegel recognizes, however, that we cannot shed our self-will and become children of God simply through our own effort of will, because all efforts on our part to imitate Christ will simply reinforce our sense that we are caught within the circle of our own activity and forever cut off from God. We can thus never free ourselves from the sense that all that we do serves ourselves; we can only be *released* from this sense. What releases us from self-will and the feeling of being caught in the narrow confines of self-serving activity, Hegel maintains, is the recognition – the faith – that our activity is not simply ours to begin with, but that we are in fact taken up into God and are sustained by *his* grace and love. We can only renounce self-will, bridge the gap between ourselves and God and share in divine love, therefore, if we know that ultimately there is no fundamental gap between ourselves and God to be bridged, but that essentially we are already united and reconciled with him.

Philosophy for Hegel, as we have seen, does not presuppose anything except the collapse of all the usual assumptions about consciousness (including the assumption that there is a fundamental divide between thought and being). Religious consciousness views the world in a more concrete, more pictorial way, however, and so requires a positive *Vorstellung* of the essential unity of man and God in order to be brought into the way of truth. In language reminiscent of Kant's Transcendental Deduction, Hegel says that religious consciousness needs to grasp the *possibility* of living in accordance with divine love for it actually to be able to let go of itself and begin to live a life of divine love. Religious consciousness thus needs to understand that despite our being finite, we are nevertheless created in the image of God with the potential to do God's will, and that despite our being constantly prey to selfishness and sin, our sins are forgiven us and do not prevent our being filled with the grace and love of God.[49] It is this, in Hegel's view, that is made clear to us in Christ, for in him we see God, not shunning human finitude, but revealing himself in and as human finitude. Through the figure of Christ, therefore, we realize that our finite nature does not separate us fundamentally from God but is precisely the place in which God's love becomes manifest in the world. This realization is the faith of St Paul that 'neither death, nor life, nor angels, nor principalities, nor powers, nor things present, nor things to come, nor height, nor depth, nor any other creature, shall be able to separate us from the love of God which is in Christ Jesus our Lord'.[50]

Christian renunciation of self-will is not brought about simply by an effort of will, there-fore; it is not something we ourselves achieve through *working* to suppress our wayward desires and keep them under our control. It is our faith which enables us to let go of our-selves, Hegel claims, our faith that we are already essentially united with God, that what we are we are through God's grace working within us, and that through that grace we can be brought to a life of divine love.

Man becomes actual [*wirklich*] as a spiritual being only when he overcomes his natural existence. This overcoming is made possible only by the presupposition that the human and divine nature are essentially [*an und für sich*] one and that man, in so far as he is spirit, has the essence and substance which belong to the concept of God. . . . The intuition of this unity is given to man in Christ.[51]

This faith helps us to let go of ourselves and open ourselves to God by showing us not just that we should be leading a life of divine love but that we are capable of it. But, more importantly, faith enables us to let go of ourselves for the simple reason that in placing our trust in God, not ourselves, we have *already* let go of ourselves. We relinquish our self-will not by an effort of active suppression, therefore, but simply by accepting that ultimately our activity and achievements are not just our own, but are the gift of God. In this respect it may be said that 'the subject does not attain reconciliation from out of itself [*aus sich*], i.e. as this subject and through its [own] activity or conduct; [that] reconciliation is not brought about, nor can it be brought about, by the subject in its way of conducting itself', but rather that the subject is released from self-will by faith – because in accepting that what he does is made possible through the grace of God within him, he is, and finds himself to be, already released from himself.[52]

Our initial faith that we are taken up into God is just a beginning for Hegel, however. It is the faith that we are called to be children of God and that we are capable of being chil-dren of God. But the individual does not become holy simply through his initial recogni-tion of the promise and the possibility of holiness. For the individual to become a true citizen of the Kingdom of God, and thus truly human, his faith must penetrate deeper and deeper into his innermost being, must take root in his heart and suffuse his whole exis-tence. His faith must become the profound inner feeling and conviction that we are not our own masters but that we belong to God. The deeper this faith becomes, Hegel believes, the more profound and all-pervasive will be our sense of reliance on the grace of God, and the more profound and all-pervasive will be our sense of being freed from self-will and of being filled with divine love.

Faith thus does not relieve us of the need to work to bring our will more and more into accord with the will of God; it gives us the confidence that this is something we should and can do. It is in faith, therefore, 'that the subject works off [*abarbeitet*] his naturalness, does battle with it'; though the way we 'work' to free ourselves from self-will is not by increased efforts to control and master our desires, but by appropriating the truth ever more firmly, that is, by deepening, extending and rendering ever more intimate our faith and acceptance that we are subjects of the grace of God.[53] At this point Hegel's position is thus essentially that of Martin Luther that it is

the sole work and exercise of all Christians [*aller Christen einziges Werk und Übung*], properly to imprint the Word and Christ in oneself and constantly to exercise and strengthen this faith; for no other work can make one a Christian, as Christ says to the Jews, John 6: 28ff, . . . 'This is the only work of God, that you believe in him whom God has sent' [*Das ist das einzige göttliche Werk, daß ihr an den glaubet, den Gott gesandt hat*].[54]

For Hegel, the task of deepening and extending faith falls to the organized community of believers in which one lives; that is, to the Church. Furthermore, it is in the acts of communal worship which constitute the centre of our life within the Church that Hegel believes we attain our profoundest consciousness of our unity with God – the feeling of mystical union with God in the Sacrament of Holy Communion. Faith in Christ, for Hegel, is the witness of the spirit to the truth which is revealed in Christ, the truth that, despite humanity's sinfulness and selfishness, human beings and God are ultimately united with one another. In the Sacrament of Holy Communion, however, our faith that man and God are essentially united turns into the consciousness of the *actual* presence of the spirit of God and the love of Christ within us. It is in worship, therefore, that the believer experiences his profoundest spiritual release and rebirth, for it is in worship

that as a human being one feels and knows God within oneself, within one's subjectivity, that as this subject one elevates oneself to God, gives oneself the certainty, the pleasure, and the joyfulness of having God within one's heart, of being united with God, of 'being received by God in grace' [*von Gott in Gnaden aufgenommen zu sein*], as it is phrased in theological language.

This, for Hegel, is the centre of the Christian life, because it is the fulfilment of the Christian promise – 'the conscious presence of God, the unity with God, the unio mystica'.[55]

The experience of being filled with the Holy Spirit does not bring the work of faith to an end, however. It does not signal that – at last! – our lives have reached perfection and that nothing more is to be done. Worship is itself an element in the continuing and deepening transformation and rebirth of the human heart. Indeed, it is the most important element in that process of transformation because it is the moment of most profound release and most profound fulfilment. It is these moments of deepest intimacy with God in worship which above all deepen and quicken faith and which thus contribute to the continuing transformation of the soul into one that is filled with the spirit of love.

As is well known, Hegel considered his conception of the Sacrament of the Lord's Supper to be Lutheran. This means that, unlike the Reformer Zwingli, Hegel does not see the Lord's Supper primarily as 'a commemoration of Christ's death',[56] but that, like the Catholic tradition, he accepts the 'real presence' of Christ in the Eucharist. However, it means that he rejects the Catholic interpretation of real presence. He does not share the Catholic view that 'sacraments are . . . effective *of themselves*, because of a divinely given power which inheres in them' and that 'they work *ex opere operato* – in virtue simply of their having been performed'.[57] Consequently, he denies that Christ is present, as it were in an objective form, in the consecrated Host, independently of the state of mind, or faith, of the believer. Christ *is* present in the Eucharist, for Hegel, but he is only present in the faith and spirit of the believer, not in the consecrated Host by itself.[58]

Like Luther, therefore, Hegel believes that 'faith takes hold of Christ and has him present, enclosing him as the ring encloses the gem'. Moreover – again like Luther – he understands the presence of Christ in faith to mean that the human heart itself takes on the form of divine love as it is filled with Christ's spirit, or, in Luther's own words, that Christ 'adorns and informs faith as colour does the wall' and is actually 'the form of faith'.[59]

What makes the difference between our initial faith that we are taken up into God and our enjoyment in Holy Communion of the actual presence within us of Christ's spirit is, in Hegel's view, the depth of our repentance and penitence. To receive the gift of the Holy Spirit we not only have to accept in faith that our life is not our own, we have to let go of our self-will in a much more radical way by feeling that our own selfish will and our own efforts and intentions are utterly ineffective, worthless and 'as nothing' (*nichtig*). To 'repent' and 'be penitent', for Hegel, is thus essentially to experience a deep and painful sense of one's own 'nothingness' (*Nichtigkeit*) and to put one's trust wholly and utterly in the love of God.[60] Only such a complete and total offer of one's heart and will to God, and only such an utter trust in the grace and love of God, can release us from self-will and purify our hearts. And this is so for a simple reason: because it is only when we feel ourselves to be nothing that we gain the sense that all that is in us is God.

Here, once again, Hegel is very close to Luther. Luther's deep conviction is that a human being is only in a position fully to comprehend that he is the object of God's *unconditional* grace and love, if he has been 'truly humbled and reduced to nothing in his own eyes' and has recognized that he can – but also need – do nothing by himself to *merit* forgiveness. And, in Luther's view, only this faith – that 'without our merit . . . [God] wants to give us forgiveness of sins, righteousness, and eternal life for the sake of Christ' – can give us 'peace of conscience' and lead to 'the most precious affection of the heart, enlarging and deepening the human soul; that is, love as given by the Holy Spirit through faith in Christ' – because only such faith frees us from the burden of having to work to live up to an exalted moral or heavenly standard. Luther believes, therefore, that 'faith justifies because it takes hold of and possesses this treasure, the present Christ', and that 'where the confidence of the heart is present . . . there Christ is present, in that very cloud and faith'; but he recognizes that genuine faith in Christ and in the love of God only follows when we have *lost* all faith in ourselves.[61]

Despite this affinity between Hegel and Luther, there are, of course, important differences between them. Hegel emphasizes that faith in God's unconditional grace is faith in the essential unity of God and humanity. It is the faith that God becomes self-conscious *Geist* in humanity and that, therefore, our consciousness of God is in fact at the same time our consciousness of our own true nature and essence. In religion, Hegel says, 'the individual self-consciousness has . . . consciousness of its essence'; but, as he points out, 'the essence is not external to whatever it is the essence of. The essence of my spirit is in my spirit itself, not outside it.' The content of religion is not the nature of a God 'over there', therefore; it is the 'freedom of self-consciousness'.[62] And this is not just Hegel's *philosophical* interpretation of the content of Christian faith, as if he were saying that faith believes itself to be relating to a God who is other than us, but we philosophers know that 'really' faith is simply human consciousness of the truth about itself. As we have seen, Hegel admits that faith initially conceives of God as other than us, but he believes that in worship faith itself comes to consciousness of our essential *unity* and *identity* with God. Christian faith believes, therefore, that in Christ the true nature of God – love, *Geist* – is revealed to be essentially one with the true nature of humanity.

But, as Eberhard Jüngel points out, this view appears to overlook the definitive *difference* between humanity and God that is central to Luther's – and perhaps any Christian – position.[63] And this perhaps suggests that Hegel's 'faith' is not so Christian after all, just as Solomon and Taylor have argued. However, while it is certainly true that Luther emphasizes much more strongly than Hegel that God is other than man, and that the grace of God comes to us as a gift from outside ourselves, Luther also stresses that the human being 'should be so united with Christ and his saints and have all things in common with them, that Christ's suffering and life, and the life and suffering of all the saints, should become his own', and that Christ is thus himself 'the form of faith'.[64] In this respect, therefore, Luther agrees with Hegel that in worship we become conscious of our oneness with Christ and, through Christ, with God.

Despite the obvious differences in aim and temperament between Luther and Hegel, there is thus clearly a great similarity between them. Both accept that in faith and worship we become united with Christ and both accept that the transformation and rebirth of the human spirit which faith brings can occur only if we let go of – 'die to' – our own self-will. For both Hegel and Luther, therefore, the heart of Christian faith seems to lie in these words of Christ: 'Whosoever will save his life shall lose it; but whosoever shall lose his life for my sake and the gospel's, the same shall save it'.[65] Robert Solomon believes that Hegel offers us a 'gutted Christianity', 'a faith without icons, images, stories, and myths, . . . without a resurrection, without a nativity, without Chartres and Fra Angelico, without wine and wafers, without heaven and hell'.[66] In view of his profound affinity with Luther, however (and, of course, with St John and St Paul), it seems to me that Hegel's account of the nature of Christianity actually displays great insight and understanding, and, contrary to what Solomon claims, gets right to the heart of Christian faith.

Death, Freedom and New Life

At the centre of Christianity, in Hegel's understanding as in Luther's, is our recognition and acceptance that we are 'as nothing' and that we are only sustained through the grace of God. We come face to face with our own 'nothingness' or *Nichtigkeit* most clearly, of course, in death. At its heart, therefore, faith involves a profound acknowledgement of the fact that we are going to die. But faith does not simply see death as the end of life. Rather, faith sees death – and more specifically the willingness to accept death – as the gateway to a new understanding of ourselves and thus to a new life.

For some, of course, the Christian interpretation of death is simply an expression of wishful thinking. For Hegel, however, Christianity discloses the profound significance of death for our lives. The fact that we are finite – that our lives will come to an end and we will die – means, in Hegel's understanding, that ultimately we do not control or have power over our own lives, and that we are thus not completely self-sufficient or self-sustaining. Genuinely to understand and accept our finitude, therefore, is to recognize that we are not simply 'for ourselves', but rather that we are merely a 'moment' of an ontological process which calls us into being and which requires that we pass away, a process which philosophy understands to be rational. Christianity acknowledges this by understanding death to be, in Eberhard Jüngel's phrase, 'the end of life which God wills for man'. The believer who accepts and understands that he is to die, Jüngel says, 'already looks back on his death, even though he is yet to die'. And, 'because he already looks back on his death, his present life cannot at all be his own life'.[67]

To have recognized and accepted this, as the true believer must do, is to be defined as someone who, in Hegel's words, 'has really renounced oneself [*realiter auf sich Verzicht geleistet hat*], and knows oneself as finite'. From this perspective, therefore, to insist simply that we are mortal and that that is the end of the matter, and to deny the implication that we are a 'moment' of the rational – or 'divine' – process of being itself, is not only to misconstrue the nature of being, but actually amounts to a failure to let oneself be sustained or carried, a failure to let go of oneself, and thus a failure to understand and accept one's own *Nichtigkeit*.[68]

The Christian acceptance of death leads to what Jüngel calls 'a last passivity' or what Luther calls 'passive righteousness' in which 'we only receive and permit someone else to work in us, namely God'.[69] This means that we see death as God's will for us, that we let death come when God wills it, and that we thus do not fight death, but accept it for what it is and let it be. It is in and through this passivity that new life comes, because the trust and acceptance that death is God's will frees us from our anxiety about, and consequent obsession with, death, and so removes the shadow that death otherwise casts over our lives. The logic behind this attitude towards death is a simple one. Once we accept death as God's will, and once we trust that by accepting death and letting go of life, as Christ did, we will find new life, then we are no longer trying to cling to life and so no longer fear losing it. And it is through this removal of our fear of death that we gain the new life we are hoping for, because we gain the freedom and peace of mind to *live* in a new, open and unconstrained way, unafraid of death and therefore unafraid of life.

On this interpretation, the Christian emphasis on death and the Cross as the gateway to new life does not mean that we should look forward to death as a release from this life, nor that our lives should be spent in solemn preparation for death and for a life beyond the grave. Rather, it means that our trusting acceptance of death gives us a renewed capacity to live in freedom *now*, because, when we are able to *die* in peace and without anxiety, we are able to *live* without fear and anxiety – and that is what we are ultimately hoping for.

Luther writes that 'none has made himself master of terrors save Christ, who has conquered death and all temporal evils. . . . Wherefore all who believe on him are no longer subject to fear, but laugh at all these evils with joyous assurance.'[70] Neither Luther nor Hegel, however, thinks that a life of Christian faith and love is one of unadulterated cheerfulness. 'Sin is always present', Luther declares, 'and the godly feel it'; and Hegel maintains that the pain and struggle of life are not withheld from the believer, but only 'alleviated' (*gemildert*).[71] It is not quite accurate, either, to say that the believer knows no anxiety in the face of death. As Eberhard Jüngel points out, anxiety is natural to man; and even Christ himself was 'sorrowful and troubled' in the garden at Gethsemane.[72] This fear of death runs deep within all of us and it is not to be thought that it is easily allayed. It is profoundly difficult to avoid anxiety in the face of death because it is hard genuinely to let go of oneself and one's life. It is so hard, indeed, that Hegel talks of the need for our heart and will to be 'broken' in worship, and for God's grace to 'break through' into our lives – words which indicate that he considers there to be much pain and fear involved in letting go of oneself, even though we let go of ourselves through our faith in the love and grace of God.[73]

Our faith in the grace of God and in the essential unity of God and man is the faith that we *can* let go of ourselves; indeed, it entails the recognition that we have begun to let go already. But it also demands of us that 'the heart should break', that we let go further, and in this respect it confronts us with a task of rebirth before which we feel great trepidation and anxiety. However, it is our very *faith* that through the grace of God we can and have let go, that at the same time 'alleviates' our pain and fear and fills us with a deep sense of calm and freedom.

As our faith in the way of Christ grows deeper, and as we take more and more to heart that through the acceptance of death we come to renewed life, our anxiety gives way to happiness and satisfaction and our lives become freer. For Hegel, as for Luther, faith is not without pain, but it does afford us a fundamental sense of release, peace and fulfilment. Christian consciousness is not alienated or unhappy for Hegel; it is not, as Marx thought, simply 'the sigh of the oppressed creature'.[74] Luther writes that the fruits of faith are 'peace, joy, love to God and all mankind; in addition, assurance, courage, confidence, and hopefulness in spite of sorrow and suffering'; and Hegel says that our faith that we are reconciled with God gives us a 'good conscience' about ourselves and the feeling that we are of the highest importance in the life of God.[75] Christian consciousness, for both Hegel and Luther, is thus above all consciousness that has been made whole and is *free* – freed from death and freed to a life in the spirit of Christ's love.

Now, it is true that Hegel, like Luther, talks of man's faith in the *grace* of God and that that notion – especially when coupled with Luther's concept of 'passive righteousness' – could easily create the impression that Hegel sees faith as a relation of dependence on God rather than freedom. But that impression would be mistaken. We are objects of God's unconditional grace, in Hegel's view, not because we are dependent on a God who is ultimately other than us, but because we belong to a God who is our sustaining power and who comes to self-consciousness in us. In faith, Hegel maintains, 'man is no longer in a relation of dependence, but of love, in the consciousness that he belongs to the divine essence'. If religious consciousness were a matter of feeling dependent, Hegel claims (with a side-swipe at his colleague at Berlin, Schleiermacher), the best Christian would be a dog.[76]

Hegel accepts that all Christian faith begins as a relation of dependence to the extent that we are born and brought up in an established community of faith and are taught the central tenets of faith by a Church whose authority we initially just accept. And he recognizes that some forms of Christianity – Mediaeval Catholicism most of all – have endeavoured to keep the faithful dependent on the authority of the priestly hierarchy throughout their lives, and indeed have sometimes reinforced that dependence through 'compulsion and the stake'.[77] However, in his view, such violence and continued dependence represents a perversion of Christian faith, not its proper realization.

Faith, for Hegel, is consciousness of the truth – of the true nature of God as *Geist* and of the true nature of the human spirit. What should predominate in genuine faith, therefore, is not dependence on another or submission to authority, but a consciousness of our own true nature and of being freed to be our true selves through Christ. This, Hegel maintains, is what true freedom is: the understanding that we have become what we are meant to be and that we are now truly human, truly ourselves.

Although Luther emphasizes our passivity before God, he too believes that by taking hold of Christ in faith and by letting go of ourselves, we become truly *free*. Faith, for Luther, involves the acceptance that 'all your life and works are nothing before God' and the willingness to let God deal with you as he wills. However, he believes that, through this faith and trust – through this passivity, through opening our souls to Christ and letting him into our hearts – the soul actually becomes 'equal to the divine Word', 'united with Christ' and thereby 'full of all grace, free and blessed'. Passivity before God does not mean dependence, therefore; it means the 'freedom of the Christian'.[78]

This is a central part of what Luther means by saying we are 'justified' by faith. Being – and feeling – justified through one's faith, in Luther's eyes, clearly involves being – and feeling – assured of redemption beyond the grave: fulfilment or completion, he says, comes 'first in the world beyond'.[79] But being justified also involves having the form of righteousness – being free and full of Christ's love – now. 'Therefore faith justifies because it takes hold of and possesses this treasure, the present Christ. . . . Where the confidence of the heart is present, therefore, there Christ is present, in that very cloud and faith. This is the formal righteousness on account of which a man is justified.'[80] For Luther, as for Hegel, therefore, the heart of faith is not dependence, but freedom; that is, knowing oneself to be 'put right with God' within oneself.

Furthermore, both Hegel and Luther agree that the life of Christian faith and freedom within oneself is a life of openness to and love for other people, not one in which 'each only seeks his own'. This point is all too often overlooked by critics of Christianity. Nietzsche, for example, suggests in *Daybreak* that what is central to the Christian state of mind is the 'strictly egoistic fundamental belief in the "one thing needful", in the absolute importance of eternal *personal* salvation', and that the 'belief in "love", in "love of one's neighbour"' is 'subsidiary'. And Feuerbach writes in a letter to Hegel, written in 1828, that 'Christianity is nothing other than the religion of the pure self, of the person taken as a *solitary* spirit'.[81] Now, it is true that Christianity – especially Protestant Christianity – often gives the impression of being merely the expression of the desire for personal salvation and immortality. It is equally true that Hegel's view of religion and philosophy as forms of self-consciousness can easily lead us to think of Hegelian thinking as simply the search for *self*-certainty and *self*-confirmation. However, although both Luther and Hegel stress that the individual does attain a sense of inner freedom and personal justification through his faith, both stress that the individual is justified and free *within* himself only through being taken *out of* himself; that is, through being freed from egoistic love for self to Christ-like love for others.

The Christian, Luther tells us, 'does not live in himself, but in Christ and in his neighbour: in Christ through faith, in his neighbour through love'. The Christian life, for Luther, in the words of one of his commentators, is thus 'indefeasibly social' because what the individual receives in Christ is fully realized only in and through community with others.[82] The focus of the believer's attention should not, therefore, be merely on himself or his personal salvation. It follows that being justified by faith does not mean being confirmed in oneself through the strength of one's faith or through one's personal commitment to Christ. Luther's doctrine of justification by faith has nothing to do with self-righteousness or with being certain of the value of one's own commitment, because we are justified only when we despair of ourselves and feel 'sad, humble, disturbed, confused, and uncertain', and when we have Christ – and Christ's self-giving love – present in our hearts.[83] We are justified and free in ourselves, therefore, only when we allow ourselves and our own concerns to be displaced and when we can say, with St Paul, 'it is no longer I who live, but Christ who lives in me'.[84]

Hegel, similarly, emphasizes that we come to freedom and true selfhood through our openness to the truth and our love and respect for other people. We do not become who we are meant to be simply by dwelling on our own particular interests and concerns, but by coming to know our oneness with God in worship and philosophy, and by recognizing that 'the truth of personality is found precisely in gaining it through immersion, through being immersed in the other [*durch das Versenken, Versenktsein in das Andere*]'.[85] A life of Christian faith – a truly human life – is thus not a life spent in single-minded pursuit of personal salvation and well-being, but a life of *Sittlichkeit*, a life in which our hearts are turned towards the universal, towards the good of others. And Hegel adds that Christian love is not some 'feeble love' (*lahme Liebe*) that addresses itself abstractly to all mankind, but the concrete love of one's neighbour, the love shown by the Good Samaritan.[86]

Hegel's stress on the fact that our ultimate aim in life is to come to know *ourselves* in no way conflicts with this view, because, as he makes clear in the *Phenomenology*, genuine self-consciousness is the '*I* that is *We* and *We* that is *I*', so there can be pure *self*-recognition only through opening oneself to, and finding oneself in, those who are other than us.[87]

For both Luther and Hegel, individual freedom is inseparable from love for others. The connection between the two derives from the fact that both personal freedom and love have their source in faith, specifically in the faith that through a willing, Christ-like acceptance of death, we can find true life.

When we are indifferent to death – through callousness, stoicism, self-assurance, complacency or simply because we have yet to grasp its reality – we may feel 'free' in ourselves to the extent that we are unconcerned about what awaits us. But our freedom will be selfish, because we will not be able to appreciate the significance of death for others, nor will we be able to share in their suffering, anxiety or grief in any meaningful way. The possibility for a real meeting of hearts and minds – and thus for love – will therefore be limited. Furthermore, such 'freedom' will always be fragile, because it will always run the risk that death – one's own or someone else's – may begin to make a difference at any time, and that our sense of secure self-certainty may be destroyed.

When death does make a difference to us, however, and when we feel that death threatens our ambitions, our companions and our very selves, our lives will be dominated by anxiety about impending loss, perhaps masquerading under the guise of business, attempting to achieve as much as possible in the time allotted to us. But such anxiety is a profound concern for oneself. And where there is such an anxious concern for oneself, there can be no freedom, no breathing easily, no deep sense of joy in life. Moreover, when our lives are dominated by such an anxious concern for *self*, there can be no real engagement with and love for others.

Only when death does make a difference to us – when we realize the real loss and pain that it involves – but when we accept death and loss in the faith that through doing so we will be granted new life, only then can we actually breathe freely and find joy in life, because only then are we freed from 'the egoistical worry about one's own end'.[88] But it is precisely this freedom from anxious concern for *ourselves* – our readiness to let go of ourselves and not feel threatened or hindered by others – that opens our eyes and makes us attentive to the concerns and sufferings of others. It is precisely the freedom we acquire through faith, therefore, that gives rise to love. This is not, of course, to say that an interest in the welfare of others could not have its source in self-interest or in natural sympathy or in some Nietzschean overflowing 'generosity' of heart. But it is to say that our ability to be *genuinely* open to and responsive to others – our ability truly to love others, to find time for and make space for them in our lives – depends on the degree to which we are freed from selfish indifference to the fortunes of others and from our anxious concern to preserve ourselves from others, from self-loss and from death.

Both Luther and Hegel agree that freedom and love are inseparably bound up with faith, because it is faith that transforms and opens our hearts by freeing us from an anxious (or brazen) concern with oneself. Both agree, therefore, that true faith must and does issue in acts of love, in good works, and does not just remain inward and mute.[89] It is obvious, then, that, although Christian freedom comes from the acceptance of death, this does not mean that faith pursues pain or death or in any way welcomes violence as the bringer of death. Faith does not seek death, but is willing to accept it when it comes. Since this acceptance of death in faith frees us to *love*, it frees us to a concern to alleviate the suffering and misery of others, and so, as Eberhard Jüngel notes, it moves us to try to afford people the possibility of enjoying life and of dying a *natural* – non-violent – death wherever possible.[90]

The fact that Hegel and Luther both see faith as issuing in good *works* also means that both agree that the spirit of self-giving love can and must inform – and thereby transform – our daily secular activity, and not just be evident in Church. Indeed, Hegel credits Luther specifically with having stressed that Christian faith and love are properly expressed in the *sittlich* spheres of family life and civil society, and not in monastic chastity and poverty.[91] It should be clear from this, too, that self-giving love is not incompatible with a proper concern to provide for oneself and one's family, and that the Christian aim is not to inculcate utter indifference to what happens to one, but rather to free us from narrow, selfish interest in or egoistic anxiety about one's welfare and one's future. (The second commandment on which 'depend all the law and the prophets' is, after all, 'you shall love your neighbour *as yourself*'.)[92]

Yet, though both Hegel and Luther see faith as issuing in good works, they do not – like Kant, who understands religion as 'the recognition of all duties as divine commands'[93] – see faith as simply making us aware of what we *ought* to do. They see faith, rather, as releasing us from the sense of moral duty and obligation by transforming our will into one that issues in acts of love willingly and without constraint; that is, into one that Kant would regard as a 'holy' will. For Hegel, both Kant and Fichte represent the standpoint of a moral consciousness that understands itself to be bound by laws (albeit determined by its own free, self-determining reason) that constrain its ever reluctant will. Such a moral consciousness is, however, an 'unhappy consciousness' in Hegel's view, one that is forever bound by laws it cannot fulfil, forever caught in the struggle between duty and inclination. Faith, by contrast, does not feel bound by laws and obligations or by the burden of duty because it is the consciousness of being reconciled with God, of being filled with the spirit of love, and thus of actually having been transformed and reconstructed in accordance with God's will, with what is right. Faith knows that it is love, therefore, that it is *sittlich*; it does not just understand that it *ought* to be. For 'if you are led by the spirit you are not under the law'.[94]

Luther's position in this respect is, of course, essentially the same as Hegel's; indeed, Hegel's is simply a reformulation of the Lutheran view. The law and the commandments, Luther tells us (following St Paul), teach us what to do, but give us no power to carry it out. In fact the law specifically makes us aware that we are unable to carry it out through our own efforts, and thus leads us to despair of ourselves and to turn to God for help.[95] As we have seen, however, Luther believes that it is precisely this total loss of faith in ourselves that permits us to accept in faith that God's love for us, as manifested in Christ, is unconditional and unmerited. And he holds that it is through this faith that we feel unconditionally justified in the eyes of God and thus free and open within ourselves. Faith begins, therefore, from a sense that we ought to fulfil the law but that we cannot do so through our own efforts. However, our faith that we are the recipients of the unconditional, unmerited love of God through Christ frees us from any sense of inadequacy or selfish anxiety about ourselves that may be born of our falling short of the demands of the law, and so opens our hearts to the Holy Spirit and to other human beings. In this way, through having let go of ourselves and having become open to the spirit of Christ's love, our will is turned around and we are made 'equal to the demands of the law'. Through the 'unconstrained love . . . put into our hearts by the Holy Spirit', we are thus able to meet the requirements of the law 'gladly and lovingly'; that is, to 'live virtuous and upright lives without the constraint of the law, and as if neither the law nor its penalties existed'. The freedom we gain through faith relieves us of the burden of duty, therefore, but 'it does not abolish the law; rather it supplies what the law lacks, namely, willingness and love'.[96]

At the heart of the theologies of Luther and Hegel lie the words of St Paul: 'a man is not justified by works of the law but through faith in Jesus Christ'.[97] Luther, for example, writes that through faith we are placed once more in paradise and created anew. However, though he acknowledges that faith gives us righteousness and new life now, in this life, he also insists that our present faith is but the beginning of our salvation and that we will only be fully redeemed 'in the world beyond'.[98] For Hegel, on the other hand, there is no world to come beyond the grave. We gain eternal life here, in this life, through our faith.

But this takes us back to the central problem we touched on earlier: is Hegel's position really a Christian one and does he really understand the spirit of Christianity? For many people – both believers and non-believers – Christian faith is inseparable from the belief that once we have died we will move on to a new life – eternal life – in the presence of God. On this interpretation, therefore, Christianity is profoundly committed to belief in immortality. Lessing, for example, calls Christ 'the first *reliable, practical* teacher of the immortality of the soul'. And the philosopher and theologian, Keith Ward, states unequivocally that 'a Christian is committed to belief in immortality for two main reasons: the existence of a God of love and the resurrection of Jesus. The whole life of faith is one of trusting that the love which we fitfully apprehend in this life will be clearly seen hereafter.'[99]

If Christian belief truly involves this commitment then Hegel can hardly be considered a genuine Christian because it is clear that he rejects the notion of personal immortality. Yet he rejects it not just because there is no place for it within speculative philosophy, but because he denies that the idea of personal immortality as popularly conceived is really central to Christian belief itself. Hegel recognizes that the Church sees itself as the 'preparation for future eternity', but he does not make it clear whether the Church understands this future to be within history or beyond the grave. What is more important, in his view, is that 'the Church also has the spirit of God present in it, that it forgives sinners and is the present Kingdom of Heaven'.[100] Even though he acknowledges that the doctrine of the immortality of the soul is 'a specific doctrine of the Christian religion', therefore, he understands the true Christian *meaning* of that doctrine not to be that we look forward to continued existence once we are dead, but that 'the subject possesses infinite value for itself, . . . is the absolute object of the infinite love of God', and that 'God is concerned about the subject' (*es sei Gott zu tun um das Subjekt*).[101] Accordingly, when he comments on the early Christian martyrs, Hegel does not think that they necessarily endured their sufferings because of what they hoped for beyond death, but that they endured suffering 'for the sake of the highest truth'.[102]

Hegel insists on several occasions that the Christian idea of eternity does not mean 'duration' (*Dauer*), that eternal life is not life that continues forever, but a *quality* of life which we enjoy now – in this life – through our faith in and knowledge of God. We become 'immortal' and enjoy 'eternal' life, in Hegel's view, through our knowledge of the absolute – infinite – nature of God and through bringing our hearts and minds into accord with divine love; that is, through living a divine life. This life is eternal or infinite because it is not conscious of itself as simply bounded by death, but knows itself to be – through its acceptance of death – the self-conscious life of God himself, a life of freedom, wholeness and divine love, a truly human life.

Hence the immortality of the soul must not be imagined as though it first emerges into actuality at some later time; rather it is a present quality [*gegenwärtige Qualität*]. . . . Spirit in its freedom does not lie within the sphere of limitation. As pure knowing or as thinking, it has the universal for its object – this is eternity. Eternity is not mere duration but knowing [*Wissen*] – the knowing of what is eternal. Hence the eternity of spirit is brought to consciousness at this point, in this cognition.[103]

But is this truly a Christian conception of eternal life? Hegel clearly thought so, but Lessing and Keith Ward would have to say that it is not. There are other theologians who take a position which is closer to Hegel's, however. Michael Ramsey, for example, believes that 'Christianity shares . . . with the philosophy of Plato the belief in survival after death', but he maintains – like Hegel – that 'what is significant in Christianity is not life of endless duration, but life in fellowship with God through union with Christ'. Ramsey also points to the connection which Hegel sees between eternal life and knowledge of God, by citing the words of St John: 'This life is eternal, to know thee the one true God, and Jesus Christ whom thou has sent.'[104]

The Tübingen theologian Eberhard Jüngel goes even further than Ramsey and agrees with Hegel that there is no place at all in Christianity for belief in the immortality of the soul in the way that, for example, Socrates (or Plato) conceives it in the *Phaedo*. The Christian idea of redemption, Jüngel says, is that we are brought to share in God's eternity in this life, that '*this lived* life is redeemed, not that we are released *from* this life'. The reconciling power of the death of Christ must thus be to the good of the '*life* between the beginning and the end of the time that is given [to us]', not to the good of some future 'beyond'. Jüngel implies indeed that belief in immortality is a utopian, egoistic belief that, despite our physical death, we will never finally have to let go of life, and so is not a truly Christian belief at all. It would seem, in fact, that Jüngel would endorse Clark Butler's assertion that 'fixation on such individual immortality may be a last stronghold of the very egoism from which true salvation delivers one'. Jüngel emphasizes that Christian salvation and eternal life come not through trying to cling on to life and evade death by hoping for some continued future existence, but through confronting and accepting death as unavoidable and definitive. Christian hope in the possibility of new life must thus not be confused with the desire to overcome 'the temporal limitation of human life'.[105]

From this perspective, Hegel's conception of eternal life can be seen, not as inadequate, but as providing us with a Christian understanding of genuine life after death (or rather, life *through* death), because it conceives of freedom and renewed life as that which can be granted us only if we let go of ourselves and accept that death is *death* – the definitive loss and end of life – not merely a stage within a continuing life. Eternal life does not begin or continue when we have physically passed away, for Hegel. It comes rather when one has accepted the *finality* of death in the faith that death is not ultimately a barrier or threat to our lives, but that the Christ-like acceptance of death will take away death's sting, set us free from the empty concern for ourselves and fill us with Christ's love. Eternal life is not an escape from the finality of death, therefore. It is a life of freedom made possible *by* the finality of death, because it is only when we accept – willingly and without any sense of grudging resignation or absurdity – that death is final, that we can be seen to have truly *let go* and to have said, with Christ, 'not as I will, but as thou wilt'.[106] And it is only when we do that that we can find freedom from our egoistic anxiety about death and live a life in the spirit of unconstrained divine freedom, wholeness and love. The true believer does not hope for salvation in 'the world to come', therefore; rather 'he who hears my word and believes him who sent me, *has* eternal life; he does not come into judgement, but *has passed* from death to life'.[107]

This recognition that Christian rebirth comes only through openness to the finality of death clearly has implications for our understanding of Christ's resurrection. Jüngel states that Jesus's resurrection is not to be seen as a kind of 'taking back of his death', and so does not mean that we can say simply that Jesus is no longer dead, *but* alive. The resurrection, for Jüngel, is instead the event in which the infinite significance of Jesus' irreversible death becomes clear.[108]

Hegel's view is essentially the same: the resurrection of Jesus is not to be understood as a 'sensuous phenomenon' that could be 'verified historically'. Jesus was crucified and died and, from the point of view of the historian, he remains dead. However, Jesus *is* resurrected in the hearts and minds of those who believe in him. 'It is thought', Hegel says, 'that in the sacrament Christ is eternally sacrificed and that he is resurrected in the heart [*im Herzen sei er auferstehend*]', and he adds simply, 'this is correct'. In Hegel's view, therefore, 'the Resurrection belongs . . . essentially to faith. After his resurrection Christ appeared only to his friends; this is not external history for those who do not believe, but this appearance is only for faith.'[109] This is not to say that Christ's resurrection is simply a myth or 'in our minds', however. Hegel's point is not just that Christ is alive *for* faith, but also that he is resurrected *as* faith, *as* the spirit of love which fills and guides the community of believers in their actions in the world. The resurrection *is* a historical fact, therefore, since Christ is alive and present in the world; but he is alive and present as the spirit which informs, transforms and renews the hearts and minds – and indeed bodies, for Christians believe in the 'resurrection of the body' as well – of those who put their faith and trust in him. That is to say, simply, that Christ is resurrected wherever 'two or three are gathered in my name'.[110]

As far as Hegel is concerned, whether one is a believer or a non-believer – a Christian or a Jew, a Muslim, a Hindu or an atheist – the historical facts of Jesus' life, ministry and death, in so far as they can be disentangled from the interpretation given them in the Gospels, will look the same. Jesus was

born like any other human being, has as a human being the needs of other human beings, only he does not share the corruption, the passions and evil inclinations of the others, nor does he share in the particular interests of the worldly. . . . Rather he lives only for the truth, only for its proclamation.

He taught that we should love our neighbour, he proclaimed the coming of the Kingdom of God, and he was arrested and crucified by the Romans at the request of the Jewish religious authorities, and so on. 'This then is the external history of Christ as it is for those who do not believe in him.'[111]

Where the perspectives of belief and unbelief diverge, in Hegel's opinion, is not in what they take to be the historical facts about Jesus, but in their understanding and interpretation of those facts, in their understanding of Jesus' life and teaching and, specifically, in their understanding of Jesus' death. Faith, Hegel says, is the proper 'exegesis' of Christ's utterances and of his death, for what faith understands is that this man who died on the Cross is in fact the Son of God. This enables those who believe in him to see his death in a wholly different light from those who do not believe in him. From the perspective of what Hegel calls 'unbelief', that is, from the perspective of the historian, the death of Jesus simply marks – as does the death of Socrates – the death of an important teacher and martyr for the truth. From the perspective of faith, however, the death of Jesus marks not just the death of a man but the death of God himself. Jesus' death

must not then be represented merely as the death of this individual, the death of this empirically existing individual. Heretics have interpreted it like that, but what it means is rather that God has died, that God himself is dead. God has died: this is negation, which is accordingly a moment of the divine nature, of God himself.[112]

For Nietzsche, the expression 'God is dead' is a metaphorical way of saying that belief in God is no longer respectable.[113] For Hegel, however, the expression 'God is dead' tells us not about belief, but about God: it tells us that it is in the nature of God himself to become human and to suffer even to the point of death. To see the death of Jesus as the death of God enables us to understand that finitude, death and the willingness to die are not alien to God's majesty but are the *incarnation* of God's majesty. In this way, we see that our own finitude itself belongs to God's nature and that even in death we are one with God. By recognizing that death is central to God, therefore, we recognize that God is only God through sharing in human suffering and giving himself up to death. This lets us see that the true nature of God is not to be a transcendent judge or an impassive supreme being, but to let go of himself and be incarnate, self-giving love. For faith, therefore, God's death in Christ signifies not just his demise – the end of his divinity – but his emergence into new life as *love* – the fulfilment of his divinity. For faith, 'death is love itself; in it absolute love is beheld [*angeschaut*]. The identity of the divine and the human means that God is at home with himself [*bei sich selbst*] in death, in the finite, and that this [moment of] finitude in death is itself a determination of God'.[114]

What Christ reveals, in Hegel's view, is that God – absolute reason – can only be explicit, fully manifest love in and as human beings who are born to die and who open themselves in faith to death and self-loss. The Christian God of love lives and is incarnated, therefore, *as* human self-sacrifice and openness to death. By revealing death and the acceptance of death in faith to be the place in which God and humanity become one as love, Christ's death is understood by Hegel to signify (in words frequently used by Luther) the 'death of death'. Christ's death is not death pure and simple: for through that death God has actually 'put death to death [*den Tod getötet*], since he proceeds from death itself'.[115] God 'proceeds from death' because it is precisely through dying in Christ that he comes to be fully manifest love. It is in *this* sense that Christ's death 'overcomes' death. Christ does not physically overcome death but he turns death into the manifestation of God's love. Christ is thus not physically resurrected: once he has died on the Cross, Christ does not walk again on the earth as the man he once was. He does walk again, however, in and as the faith of those who believe that he is the incarnation of divine love, who entrust themselves to his way, and who are thereby filled with his loving spirit, filled with his willingness to let go and to die.

Jesus tells his disciples: 'it is to your advantage that I go away, for if I do not go away, the Counsellor will not come to you; but if I go, I will send him to you'.[116] Hegel's interpretation of these words is clear: it is only when Christ dies that we can see the true nature of God as *love* incarnated in Christ's life and death, and it is only when we take hold of Christ in faith as the incarnate truth that he can be resurrected in our hearts as the *spirit* of openness and love. The resurrection is represented in the Bible as a separate event which occurs prior to Pentecost, but, on a Hegelian reading at least, that is simply because faith – which quite rightly understands Christ's overcoming of death to be real, not imaginary – needs to be able to picture that overcoming of death first in order to be able to take hold of Christ in faith as 'the way, and the truth and the life'.[117] In Hegel's interpretation, however, it is only when Christ's resurrection *for* faith has led to the outpouring of the Holy Spirit into his disciples that Christ is truly resurrected *as* faith, as what Luther calls 'the form of faith'.[118] Pentecost and the resurrection thus constitute, for Hegel, *one* spiritual event.

Faith, Interpretation and Philosophy

Christian faith, for Hegel, is not a matter of believing that, two thousand years ago, the laws of nature were mysteriously overturned and a man named Jesus, who had been crucified, miraculously came back to life again. Faith is instead the belief that in the person of Christ God manifests himself as self-giving love and thereby reveals to us the way to true humanity. This faith does not, therefore, make extraordinary historical claims in need of historical verification. It simply expresses our understanding that God is in truth the most profound love. Such understanding is prompted by the historical events of Jesus' life and death, but it is verified by the witness of our own spirit: for, as we are told in the first letter of John, 'he who believes in the Son of God has the testimony in himself'.[119]

Note that, from Hegel's *philosophical* perspective, Christ does not introduce into our hearts and minds an understanding of God that is utterly new and foreign to us, but simply sparks within us our *own* deeper understanding of the truth. Christ does so by allowing our spirit to see its own true, 'divine' character concretely realized in the world in Christ himself. Indeed, in conscious reference to Plato's doctrine of recollection, Hegel maintains that true religious understanding cannot ever be mechanically 'injected' into human beings, but can only be 'aroused' (*erregt*) in us. Such understanding, in Hegel's view, is already latent within us, so the historical life and death of Christ do no more than bring that understanding to explicit consciousness.[120]

The justification for this claim becomes clear if we recall that, for Hegel, the Christian God of love is properly understood when he is known as absolute, dialectical reason, and when it is known that we are the self-consciousness of absolute reason. Human beings are thus always to some extent aware of the character of reason, or God, simply because we are *self-conscious reason* – the self-consciousness of God – even though prior to the life of Christ human awareness of the nature of reason necessarily remained implicit and undeveloped. Indeed, Hegel notes, in so far as faith rests on the recognition by our *reason* of its own absolute character, we can say that faith is not just *our* understanding of God's nature, but is at the same time the work of God himself within us, 'a faith brought about by God'.[121] This fact that God (reason) is to one degree or another at work within us, whatever we do and whether or not we wish him (it) to be, is what enables Hegel to agree with Luther that God's grace and love for us are unconditional.

In contrast to philosophy, religious faith itself initially understands God to be *other* than us and to reveal himself to us from the 'outside' through Christ. Yet faith ultimately moves close to the philosophical point of view, for it understands God to become fully present *in* us, and it recognizes that through God's indwelling presence we come to have the 'source of infinity' – that is, the source of truth – within ourselves.[122] Faith holds that God is fully present in us when we recognize our own impotence and inadequacy and open ourselves to Christ. It believes, therefore, that we have the source of infinity and truth most clearly within ourselves when we embrace Christ's way of self-giving love, are filled with his spirit and allow it to guide us into the truth.[123] Faith, for Hegel, is thus not simply the belief that truth has been revealed once and for all in its totality. It is the belief that the spirit of Christ is alive within us and *continues to lead us into* all truth. In Hegel's view, this implies a recognition on the part of faith that, filled with Christ's spirit, faith itself must work to develop further its understanding of the truth.

Since this is the case, Hegel argues, the core of Christian doctrine should not be sought immediately in the teachings of Christ himself. It lies instead in the doctrines, such as that of the Trinity, which were developed later by the original community of the faithful, namely the early Church. As Hegel puts it, 'the teaching of Christ is not Christian dogmatics . . . Christ did not expound what the church later produced as its doctrine'. Christ's teachings – especially his assertion in the Sermon on the Mount that the pure in heart are blessed since they shall see God – belong to what Hegel considers to be 'the greatest that can be said'. But, at the same time, those teachings are often polemical or 'abstract' and do not present the fully developed content of Christian belief. Some of Christ's teachings, indeed, such as his injunction to 'sell what you possess and give to the poor' are actually contradictory if followed through, because if everyone gave everything to the poor, then soon there would be no more poor to give anything to, or no more persons who would still have something to give. Or rather, the poor would now be rich, and those who had been rich would now be poor, so that what was previously theirs would be returned to them.[124]

It is not what Jesus says that forms the core of Church doctrine, for Hegel, but what he signifies for our understanding of God. To be filled with the spirit of truth is to be transformed by the spirit of Christ, but once the spirit of Christ is guiding our hearts and minds into the truth, Christ's own teaching will 'partly receive another [different] determination, [and] partly be left on one side'.[125]

Since Christ is understood by faith to release the spirit of truth and love within us, he gives us the assurance that that spirit can guide and transform all aspects of our own life and activity. He thus gives us the assurance that our own *thinking* can be led by that spirit. Far from seeking to supplant human thought and philosophy, therefore, Hegel thinks that Christian faith gives us the confidence that philosophy can help us articulate and develop the truth. The role that philosophy, especially Platonic philosophy, plays in the development of early Church doctrine does not represent a distortion of an original Biblical message, therefore. Philosophy has a perfectly proper role to play in the development of doctrine, in Hegel's view, because for him, as for the second-century theologian Justin Martyr, Christian faith is the faith that 'the light that all men have is implanted by the divine Reason, the Logos of God who was incarnate in Jesus and who is universally active and present in the highest goodness and intelligence wherever they may be found' – including, of course, philosophy.[126] This is one respect in which Hegel thinks Catholicism is to be preferred to Protestantism: Catholicism, he believes, has always recognized the important role that philosophy must play in the articulation of theological doctrine, whereas Protestantism has all too often tended to see itself in conflict with philosophy.[127]

It is clear, then, that Hegel is no religious fundamentalist. He thinks that the Bible represents the *interpretation* by faith of the life and death of Jesus. He believes – like Luther – that the Bible itself needs to be interpreted by faith. And he believes – this time contrary to Luther – that philosophy is essential to the development and clarification of the faith of the Church. Hegel acknowledges that the believer should 'hold to the Bible': the Bible is not for Hegel, as it is for Lessing, a document that gradually becomes dispensable as its truths are appropriated by reason.[128] However, he points out that as soon as we begin to consider what the words of the Bible mean, 'we embark upon the process of reasoning, reflection, thinking; and the question then becomes how we should exercise this process of thinking, and whether our thinking is correct or not [*ob sein Denken richtig ist oder nicht*]'. The Bible cannot serve as a simple foundation for faith, therefore, since everything depends on how it is interpreted. And Hegel goes on to stress that each age interprets the Bible in a different way.[129]

The way to determine the true meaning(s) of the words of the Bible is by ensuring that interpretation is carried out by 'the true, correct spirit' (*der wahre, richtige Geist*). But what is the true spirit? It is the spirit which has the *form* of truth, which does not itself seek to determine the truth, but which lets the truth determine or reveal itself in us. It is thus the spirit which Luther recognizes to be that of faith – the spirit which acknowledges its own impotence, which lets go of itself and which 'permits someone else to work in us, namely God'. In this spirit alone, Hegel believes, can the true meaning of Christian freedom and love be understood.[130]

It is Hegel's intention, I believe, to develop the first *philosophy* that is fully informed by this Christian spirit of truth. The neo-Platonism of the Church Fathers and the neo-Aristotelianism of certain Scholastics played a crucial and quite proper role in the development of Church dogma and theological understanding, but, as modes of philosophy, these were Greek in origin and temper, not Christian through and through. The various strands of post-Reformation philosophy have not been thoroughly Christian, either. Cartesian rationalism, British empiricism and Kantian critical philosophy are all forms of post-Reformation philosophy, since they are all based on the Protestant principle that the truth must be verified by my own insight.[131] However, though – as I indicated in chapter 2 – an anticipation of Hegel's speculative philosophy is to be found in Descartes's fifth Meditation (as it is in Plato), post-Reformation philosophy has not had as its centre the idea that thought comes to know the truth within itself through 'dying to itself'; that is, through becoming genuinely *dialectical*.

Despite the fact that many philosophers have contributed to the development of Church doctrine or have devised proofs for God's existence, there has yet to emerge, in Hegel's view, a philosophical articulation of the truth that is thoroughly suffused by the Christian spirit of truth, by the willingness to let go. Indeed, much modern philosophy is seen by Hegel as explicitly anti-Christian (e.g. Voltaire) or to have more affinity with Judaism than with Christianity (e.g. Kant).

A Christian philosophy, for Hegel, would not just be one that told us about God; it would itself be the completion of Christian worship. In worship we come to consciousness of the presence of God's love within us, of our identity with God, of the fact that 'we have the mind of Christ'.[132] But worship begins from a sense of the *difference* between myself and God. In worship I am reconciled with God, but this occurs through my 'surrender' (*Hingeben*) of myself *to* him and through my 'receiving' the spirit *from* him. What philosophy does is complete the reconciliation of man and God by deepening our consciousness of our *identity* with God; that is, by recognizing God to be reason – absolute reason – which comes to self-consciousness in me, which constitutes my 'essence' and which is immanent within my subjective activity. Whereas worship is a 'thinking towards God' (*Daranhindenken*), therefore, a thinking which *comes to* consciousness of its identity with God, philosophy knows itself to be God's thinking of himself in and as our thinking or, to put it in less theological, more philosophical terms, to be reason determining itself.[133]

Philosophy clarifies what faith feels, pictures and intuits, but it is essential to recognize that philosophy and faith are forms of the same spirit. The intimate connection between Christian faith and speculative philosophy is made clear – albeit indirectly – in a remark Hegel makes about the connection between thinking and death. It is not the connection between analytic understanding and death that interests Hegel. He sees understanding as essential to give structure and determinacy to *life*, though he does on occasion speak of the 'dead understanding' as well and he does claim, in a manner similar to Nietzsche, that Enlightenment understanding has made a 'ghost' or 'phantom' (*Gespenst*) out of God. Nor is Hegel pursuing the now depressingly familiar alleged connection between reason, authority, violence and death. Hegel's point is deeper than either of these: it is that both thinking and death signify a 'renunciation of' (*Verzichtleisten auf*) or 'disengaging from' (*Loskommen von*) finitude and self-will.[134]

To think is to let go of one's finitude, of one's particular insights and assumptions, and to let one's thinking be guided by the self-determining character of thought. This is not to say that philosophy is an enterprise that demands no discipline or effort. On the contrary, it requires the ability to hold in one's mind thoughts of the greatest abstractness, the ability, that is, to exercise understanding, as we saw in chapter 2. But, more importantly, it demands the ability to follow the course that the dialectical character of such abstract concepts determines for thought. To do this – to find truth through letting go of oneself – is, Hegel is

272 Philosophy and Christian Faith

suggesting, to do precisely what faith does when it accepts death as God's will. In each case we let go of our finitude, of our concern to preserve ourselves and our own thoughts, possibilities and intentions, and we allow ourselves to be displaced – that is, to die, to be truly finite – and to be determined by God, by reason, rather than our own perceptions and assumptions. And in each case we gain thereby the highest freedom and truth.

It is in this sense that Hegel's philosophy – despite Robert Solomon's reservations – is profoundly Christian. Speculative philosophy and Christian faith are simply two modes of the same spirit, two ways of experiencing freedom and new life through letting go of oneself. This is why 'the true, correct spirit', in the light of which the Bible and indeed all experience is to be interpreted, can be said – without contradiction – to be at one and the same time genuine faith and, as we explained in chapter 2, the pure self-determining reason of speculative philosophy.

As I have explained, Hegel does not believe that each individual needs to engage in philosophical thinking in order to live in the truth. However, it is clear that he believes modern rational culture as a whole does need speculative philosophy, because speculative philosophy overcomes the harmful modern division between faith and reason.

On the one hand, speculative philosophy could do for Protestantism what Aquinas did for Catholicism; that is, provide the believer with a clear understanding of the content of Christian faith in both theological and philosophical terms. Indeed, speculative philosophy could itself be seen as the culminating stage in the long development of Church doctrine, the stage at which the meaning which is inherent in the pictures and images of faith – and which faith has always understood, though sometimes indirectly and sometimes in conjunction with other extraneous, even superstitious beliefs – at last becomes fully explicit. Hegel recognizes that some believers might find themselves thereby confronted with hard challenges to their deepest assumptions. Yet such believers, especially those who find Hegel's rejection of personal immortality disquieting, ought perhaps to ask themselves whether clinging on to all their cherished assumptions, and clinging on to themselves through them, is really the Christ-like thing to do.

On the other hand, philosophy can show the modern rationalist that there is a profound need to break with what Hegel calls the 'vanity of the understanding'[135] if we are to enjoy true freedom and *Sittlichkeit* in the modern world, and it can also show the importance of faith, of the felt experience of letting go, in so doing. This is bound to make many non-Christian philosophical friends of Hegel extremely uncomfortable. But I see no way of avoiding this. Hegel himself claimed that a philosophy without a heart of faith is an abstraction, and to fail or perhaps to refuse to see the intimate connection between faith and philosophy is, to my mind, either to misunderstand the nature of faith or to be unwilling to relinquish the vanity of one's understanding as deeply as one might suppose. Hegel well knew that Enlightenment philosophers of the understanding would resist his attempt to show that Christian faith has a rational content, and he also knew that his religious views did not please many contemporary Protestant theologians (especially Schleiermacher). However, he recognized that if freedom is to become a reality in the hearts and minds of people in the modern world, the attempt to reconcile faith and philosophy must be undertaken.

Philosophy and Faith in History

I have suggested that Hegel's philosophy is a thoroughly Christian one, perhaps indeed the first genuinely Christian philosophy. However, in chapter 2 I emphasized that speculative philosophy has no systematic presuppositions, but that it is pure self-determining reason. How can these two views be reconciled? How can speculative philosophy be both Christian and presuppositionless?

The apparent contradiction begins to disappear when we remind ourselves, first, that Christian faith for Hegel is a form of human freedom and, second, that it reveals to us the spirit in which we can find freedom and truth throughout the whole range of human experience, including philosophy. It is in Christianity, Hegel believes, that the idea that all human beings are born to be free first becomes widespread in history. As we pointed out in chapter 1, Hegel thinks that oriental and classical cultures had a restricted conception of human freedom – of who could be free – and for that reason tolerated slavery. 'The Germanic nations', he believes, 'through Christianity, were the first to realise that man is free as man and that freedom is his very nature.' This clearly did not mean that with the advent of Christianity slavery immediately died out, but it did mean that a form of human understanding entered the historical stage which was fundamentally opposed to slavery and which was able to initiate the long and difficult process of human emancipation.[136]

Hegel recognizes, of course, that this principle of Christian freedom can easily turn into the harshest form of tyranny when it pits itself against a world it deems to be evil or 'enslaved to sin'. And although he considers Mediaeval and Renaissance Catholicism to exemplify the worst excesses of Christian barbarism, corruption and repression, he does not hide the fact that Protestantism also, especially in the witch-hunts of the sixteenth and seventeenth centuries, all too often violated and destroyed the very freedom it was meant to promote.[137]

Yet, despite the undeniable fact of Christian tyranny in history, Hegel insists that Christian faith is essentially a form of human freedom, and he thinks that Christianity comes to its profoundest understanding of the nature of religious freedom in the Lutheran Reformation. Furthermore, it is with Luther that Christianity gains its deepest sense that Christian freedom is not merely confined to the realm of religious experience, but that the freedom gained in faith must inform and transform the sphere of secular activity – that is, family life, civil society and the state – as well. Through so doing the Reformation fostered the sense that secular activity and ordinary occupations were the appropriate spheres in which to live a spiritual life and to serve God acceptably, and so gave added impetus to the incipient economic, civic and political rights and freedoms which were emerging during the late Middle Ages.[138]

Luther's Reformation had a more direct effect on the furtherance of freedom, of course, by challenging the authority of the Catholic Church and by putting in its place the Bible and the witness of the individual spirit, albeit still very much within a Church community. Instead of subordinating the witness of the layman's spirit to that of that of the ecclesiastical authorities, Luther maintained that we are all priests and that everyone should be able to recognize the truth of Scripture in faith for himself.[139] This is not to say that the truth is simply whatever we make of it, but rather that we should be able to recognize within ourselves and our faith – to *experience* – that the teachings of the Church are indeed true. This view not only ascribes tremendous importance to increased literacy and to translating the Bible into the vernacular, of course, it also reinforces the role of subjective insight in determining the truth.[140] But here is the point at which Luther's Reformation actually reinforces a form of freedom which goes beyond what Luther himself would be prepared to countenance: for, in stressing the importance of subjective insight, the Reformation also strengthens the claim of *secular* consciousness to determine *for itself*, through reason or empirical experience and without the help of religion, what is to count as true. In Hegel's view, therefore, the Reformation leads, through its own principle of the freedom of subjective insight, but contrary to Luther's own intentions, to the development of a form of consciousness – found in thinkers as diverse as Descartes, Hume and Voltaire – which jealously guards its autonomy, especially its autonomy from Christian faith, and which at times even openly opposes faith. Wittingly or unwittingly, it is thus Christianity itself that has effectively promoted the autonomy of reason from faith – as Nietzsche recognized as well as Hegel.[141]

As the culmination of modern philosophy, speculative philosophy must meet the modern historical demand for autonomy and freedom of thought (which Christianity itself has fostered) and for that reason may not presuppose any Christian dogma (or indeed any metaphysical or empirical assumptions at all) as a *systematic* presupposition. It is this very autonomy and presuppositionlessness which requires that the speculative philosopher let go of his dearest assumptions and allow himself to be guided by the self-determining process of his own free reason. However, if Hegel is right, it is that very process of reason's self-determination which leads speculative philosophy to the recognition that being is rational and that being becomes fully and explicitly rational as it comes to be *Geist* in history, philosophy and religion. It is autonomous, presuppositionless philosophy itself, therefore, which recognizes that religion is central to the life of *Geist*, which sees that religion and philosophy articulate the very same spirit of freedom, which recognizes philosophy's own historical debt to religion, and which consequently recognizes the need to justify religion through philosophy in the modern age. Speculative philosophy thus understands through its own free, autonomous self-development that there is a need for Christian philosophy in the modern age and that it meets that need. There is, then, no contradiction in describing speculative philosophy as at once free and Christian, since these two terms, as speculative philosophy itself shows, are ultimately connected with one another.

Modern philosophers are frequently reluctant to accept the importance of religion, no doubt due to the fear of losing their autonomy or of being forced to sacrifice their critical judgement to blind faith. If Hegel is right, however, religion is not only an indispensable element in the life of the philosopher, but is the root of all freedom and *Sittlichkeit* in the state and society, too. Religion is the place in which a people grasps what is ultimately true for it.[142] This means, therefore, that the authority of the state and its laws must itself be rooted in the recognition by faith that the state's laws are just. Hegel argues that in secular matters the state is a higher authority than the Church, but he understands that the propriety of the state's higher authority must nevertheless be acknowledged by faith. If not, the state's laws will not take root in the hearts of people and will thus threaten to become a superstructure at odds with people's convictions. Furthermore, this leads Hegel to recognize that any far-reaching social, economic or political changes in society, such as were attempted in France in the 1790s, must entail a reformation of faith if they are to succeed. For without such a reformation there can be no deep-seated change in people's character and practice.[143]

If faith is to provide the foundation for genuine social and political freedom, therefore, the state must not violate the freedom of religious consciousness or interfere in matters of faith, but must guarantee the Church's freedom to fulfil its religious function. On the other hand, however, faith itself must not be negative or polemical against the state, but must be genuine faith in freedom and must acknowledge the rights of the secular sphere, indeed see it as the appropriate sphere for God's work.

Hegel believes that these conditions are not easily met; indeed he believed that, at the time he was writing, they were only met – and even there imperfectly – in certain Protestant countries such as Germany and England. What is at issue here, however, is not Hegel's understanding of the place of Germany and England in world history, but the place of *faith* in history. It is clear that for Hegel true faith – and thus the fully realized spirit of divine love – is a precious, but rare creature. It constitutes the cornerstone of human freedom, but it can be weakened and destroyed – not least through the 'vanity of understanding' and through the failure of theologians to teach the central doctrines of the faith to the people. And faith cannot be easily re-created once it has been destroyed. It is for this reason that Hegel sees it as so important that speculative philosophy defend faith against attacks by the understanding, by clarifying and justifying its central doctrines.

It is one of the great ironies of philosophical history that Hegel, who saw himself as someone who justified Christian faith, should have been seen by so many supporters and detractors as 'the precursor of atheistic humanism in German philosophy'.[144] In this chapter, however, I have tried to demonstrate that Hegel's interest in Christianity was a genuine one and that the claim that he is a Christian philosopher is defensible. Indeed, the whole of this book has been an attempt to show that a profound commitment to freedom, openness and truth – a commitment which is both distinctively modern *and* deeply Christian – guides Hegel's entire philosophical enterprise. Whether this attempt has been successful is for the reader to decide.

Notes

Quotations from translations have occasionally been modified.

Introduction

1 See T. Pinkard, *Hegel's Dialectic: The Explanation of Possibility* (Philadelphia: Temple University Press, 1988), pp. 3–4; and J. N. Findlay, *Hegel: A Re-examination* (1958) (Oxford: Oxford University Press, 1976), p. 18.

2 A. White, *Absolute Knowledge: Hegel and the Problem of Metaphysics* (Athens, OH: Ohio University Press, 1983), p. 158.

3 See B. Russell, *History of Western Philosophy* (London: Allen and Unwin, 1946, 2nd edn 1961), p. 701; K. Popper, *The Open Society and its Enemies* (1945), 2 volumes (London: Routledge, 5th edn 1966), II, 28; and A. Schopenhauer, *The World as Will and Representation* (1819, 1844), 2 volumes, trans. E. F. J. Payne (New York: Dover Publications, 1969), I, xxiv, 429.

4 *Hegel's Science of Logic*, trans. A. V. Miller, Foreword by J. N. Findlay (Atlantic Highlands, NJ: Humanities Press International, 1989) (hereafter *SL*), p. 407. This text is commonly known as the 'Greater Logic'.

5 S. Smith, *Hegel's Critique of Liberalism: Rights in Context* (Chicago: University of Chicago Press, 1989), p. 14.

6 E. Fackenheim, *The Religious Dimension in Hegel's Thought* (Chicago: University of Chicago Press, 1967), p. 12.

7 For an account of some of these studies, see the Bibliographical Essay at the end of this book.

8 One commentator who does take Hegel's claim to presuppositionlessness seriously, and from whom I have learned a great deal, is Richard Winfield. See his *Reason and Justice* (Albany: State University of New York Press, 1988).

1 History and Truth

1 G. W. F. Hegel, *Lectures on the Philosophy of World History: Introduction: Reason in History*, trans. H. B. Nisbet with an introduction by D. Forbes (Cambridge: Cambridge University Press, 1975) (hereafter *PWH*), p. 29. For the German text, see G. W. F. Hegel, *Werke in zwanzig Bänden*, eds E. Moldenhauer and K. M. Michel, 20 volumes and index (Frankfurt: Suhrkamp Verlag, 1969ff) (hereafter *Werke*), XII, 23.

2 *Hegel's Philosophy of Nature*, trans. A. V. Miller (Oxford: Clarendon Press, 1970) (hereafter *Enc* II), §246 addition. This is a translation of the second volume of Hegel's *Encyclopaedia* (1830). For the German text, see *Werke*, IX, 20. For a discussion of Hegel's critique of 'either/or' metaphysics, see my *Hegel, Nietzsche and the Criticism of Metaphysics* (Cambridge: Cambridge University Press, 1986).

3 See I. Kant, *Critique of Pure Reason* (1781 [= A], 1787 [= B]), trans. P. Guyer and A. W.

Wood (Cambridge: Cambridge University Press, 1997), B xiii–xiv.

4 G. W. F. Hegel, *The Encyclopaedia Logic* (with the *Zusätze*), trans. T. F. Geraets, W. A. Suchting and H. S. Harris (Indianapolis: Hackett Publishing, 1991) (hereafter *Enc* I), §42 addition 3. This is a translation of the first volume of Hegel's *Encyclopaedia* (1830) and is known as the 'Lesser Logic'. For the German text, see *Werke*, VIII, 118–19.

5 *Enc* II, §246 addition; *Werke*, IX, 20–1. See also G. W. F. Hegel, *Introduction to the Lectures on the History of Philosophy*, trans. T. M. Knox and A. V. Miller (Oxford: Clarendon Press, 1985) (hereafter *HP*), pp. 74–5; for the German text, see *Werke*, XVIII, 40. Knox and Miller's translation of the introduction is based on the edition of Hegel's lectures on the history of philosophy published by J. Hoffmeister in 1940, whereas the text presented in volumes 18–20 of the *Werke* is based on the original edition of the lectures published by K. L. Michelet in 1833–6. Reference has been made to the *Werke*, rather than to the Hoffmeister edition, because, unlike the latter, they contain Hegel's lectures on the whole history of philosophy and for this reason tend to be the more popular edition.

6 T. Kuhn, *The Structure of Scientific Revolutions* (Chicago: University of Chicago Press, 1962, 2nd edn 1970), pp. 118–19.

7 J. G. Herder, 'Shakespeare', in *German Aesthetic and Literary Criticism: Winckelmann, Lessing, Hamann, Herder, Schiller and Goethe*, ed. H. B. Nisbet (Cambridge: Cambridge University Press, 1985), pp. 161–76.

8 *HP*, p. 25; *Werke*, XX, 482–3.

9 *PWH*, p. 138; *Werke*, XII, 87.

10 See, for example, G. A. Cohen, *Karl Marx's Theory of History: A Defence* (Oxford: Clarendon Press, 1978).

11 G. W. F. Hegel, *The Philosophy of History*, trans. J. Sibree, with an Introduction by C. J. Friedrich (New York: Dover Publications, 1956) (hereafter *PH*), p. 137. For the German text, see *Werke*, XII, 172.

12 *HP*, p. 166; *Werke*, XVIII, 116.

13 *PWH*, pp. 103–5; *Werke*, XII, 70–3.

14 R. Rorty, *Philosophy and the Mirror of Nature* (Oxford: Basil Blackwell, 1980), p. 391.

15 G. W. F. Hegel, *Lectures on the Philosophy of Religion*, ed. P. C. Hodgson, trans. R. F. Brown, P. C. Hodgson and J. M. Stewart, with the assistance of J. P. Fitzer and H. S. Harris, 3 volumes (Berkeley: University of California Press, 1984–7) (hereafter *LPR*), III, 165. For the German text, see G. W. F. Hegel, *Vorlesungen über die Philosophie der Religion*, ed. W. Jaeschke, 3 volumes (Hamburg: Felix Meiner, 1983–5) (hereafter *VPR*), III, 100.

16 *PWH*, p. 54; *Werke*, XII, 31.

17 See *PH*, p. 253; *Werke*, XII, 310.

18 *PH*, p. 252; *Werke*, XII, 309.

19 *Hegel's Philosophy of Right*, trans. T. M. Knox (Oxford: Oxford University Press, 1952, 1967) (hereafter *PR*), §260; *Werke*, VII, 407.

20 *PH*, p. 455; *Werke*, XII, 538.

21 *HP*, p. 11; *Werke*, XVIII, 24.

22 F. Nietzsche, *On the Genealogy of Morals*, trans. W. Kaufmann and R. Hollingdale, and *Ecce Homo*, trans. W. Kaufmann (New York: Vintage Books, 1969), *Genealogy*, II, §13: 'only that which has no history is definable'.

23 *HP*, pp. 74–5; *Werke*, XVIII, 40. The German version of this passage included in *Werke*, XVIII is shorter than the English translation which I have quoted in the text. This is because the two versions are based on different editions. See note 5.

24 *PWH*, p. 69; *Werke*, XII, 35.

25 *PWH*, p. 34; *Werke*, XII, 24.

26 *PWH*, p. 54; *Werke*, XII, 31, emphasis added.

27 *PWH*, p. 135; *Werke*, XII, 83.

28 *PWH*, p. 136; *Werke*, XII, 83. Mnemosyne, sometimes known as Memory, was one of the Titans and the mother (by Zeus) of the nine Muses.

29 *Hegel's Philosophy of Mind*, trans. W. Wallace, together with the *Zusätze* in Boumann's text (1845), trans. A. V. Miller (Oxford: Clarendon Press, 1971) (hereafter *Enc* III), §378 addition. This is a translation of the third volume of Hegel's *Encyclopaedia* (1830). For the German text, see *Werke*, X, 12.

30 *PWH*, p. 58; *Werke*, XII, 99.

31 *Enc* III, §379 addition; *Werke*, X, 15.

32 *HP*, p. 59; *Werke*, XVIII, 31–2.

33 *HP*, p. 105; *Werke*, XVIII, 63.

34 See J. Ritter, *Hegel and the French Revolution*

(1965), trans. R. Winfield (Cambridge, MA: MIT Press, 1982).

35 *PWH*, pp. 32, 70; *Werke*, XII, 97, 36.

2 Thinking without Presuppositions

1 G. W. F. Hegel, *Phenomenology of Spirit*, trans. A. V. Miller, with Analysis of the Text and Foreword by J. N. Findlay (Oxford: Oxford University Press, 1977) (hereafter *Phen*), p. 6. For the German text, see *Werke*, III, 18.

2 *SL*, p. 26; *Werke*, V, 15.

3 *SL*, p. 25; *Werke*, V, 14.

4 Note that the word 'metaphysics' is being used here to refer not to the 'range of the universal determinations of thought … into which everything is brought and thereby first made intelligible' (*Enc* II, § 246 addition; *Werke*, IX, 20), but to a specific type of traditional philosophical enquiry. See chapter 1, pp. 4–5.

5 *Enc* I, §19 addition 3; *Werke*, VIII, 71.

6 I. Kant, *Groundwork for the Metaphysics of Morals*, trans. J. W. Ellington (Indianapolis: Hackett Publishing Company, 1981), p. 50. Ellington himself employs the word 'Grounding' in the title of his translation.

7 See M. Kosok, 'The Formalization of Hegel's Dialectical Logic', in *Hegel: A Collection of Critical Essays*, ed. A. MacIntyre (Garden City, NY: Doubleday, 1972), pp. 237–87.

8 *SL*, p. 41; *Werke*, V, 33.

9 *The Complete Works of Aristotle*, ed. J. Barnes, 2 volumes (Princeton, NJ: Princeton University Press, 1984), II, 1575 [*Metaphysics*, 996b 29–30]. Such a principle is 'metaphysical' in the sense that it is characteristic of a way of understanding that thinks of things as *either* one thing *or* the other; see chapter 1, p. 4.

10 G. W. F. Hegel, *Lectures on the History of Philosophy*, trans. E. S. Haldane and F. H. Simson, 3 volumes (London: Routledge and Kegan Paul, 1892, 1955) (hereafter *LHP*), II, 220–1; *Werke*, XIX, 238. Much of the text of the Haldane translation is arranged in a different order from that of the *Werke*. This is due to the fact that the text of the *Werke* is based on the first edition of the lectures (1833–6), whereas Haldane's translation is based on the second, amended edition (1840–4).

11 Winfield, *Reason and Justice*, p. 142.

12 *Enc* I, §78 remark; *Werke*, VIII, 168.

13 D. Kolb, *The Critique of Pure Modernity: Hegel, Heidegger and After* (Chicago: University of Chicago Press, 1986), p. 56.

14 *SL*, p. 82; *Werke*, V, 82.

15 *SL*, p. 82; *Werke*, V, 83.

16 Winfield, *Reason and Justice*, p. 133.

17 *SL*, p. 83; *Werke*, V, 83.

18 *SL*, p. 106; *Werke*, V, 113.

19 Kant, *Critique of Pure Reason*, B 97–8.

20 *Enc* I, §§161, 240; *Werke*, VIII, 308, 391.

21 Kant, *Critique of Pure Reason*, B 10–14.

22 *Enc* I, §88 remark 1; *Werke*, VIII, 188.

23 *SL*, p. 831; *Werke*, VI, 557.

24 *Enc* I, §81 addition 1; *Werke*, VIII, 175.

25 *The Philosophical Writings of Descartes*, trans. J. Cottingham, R. Stoothoff and D. Murdoch, 2 volumes (Cambridge: Cambridge University Press, 1985), II, 46.

26 *SL*, p. 40; *Werke*, V, 31.

27 See Kolb, *The Critique of Pure Modernity*, pp. 48–9.

28 *Phen*, pp. 35–6; *Werke*, III, 56.

29 Winfield, *Reason and Justice*, p. 142.

30 Luke 17: 33.

31 *Phen*, p. 28; *Werke*, III, 47.

32 *SL*, pp. 31, 54; *Werke*, V, 19, 50.

33 A good defence of Hegel against Schelling is provided by Alan White in his *Absolute Knowledge: Hegel and the Problem of Metaphysics*.

34 See J. Burbidge, 'Where is the Place of Understanding?', in *Essays on Hegel's Logic*, ed. G. di Giovanni (Albany: State University of New York Press, 1990), pp. 171–82. For the view that 'the self-development of Thought … is sheer Neo-Platonic fantasy', see M. Rosen, *Hegel's Dialectic and Its Criticism* (Cambridge: Cambridge University Press, 1982), p. 179. For an extended critique of Rosen, see my 'Some Notes on Rosen's *Hegel's Dialectic and Its Criticism*', *Hegel-Studien*, 20 (1985), 213–19.

35 S. Kierkegaard, *Concluding Unscientific Postscript* (1846), trans. D. Swenson and W. Lowrie (Princeton, NJ: Princeton University Press, 1941, 1968), pp. 188–9, 194–5.

36 On the connection between understanding and dialectic, see *Enc* I, §81 and additions; *Werke*, VIII, 172–6. For Hegel's analysis of finitude and infinity, see *SL*, pp. 136–50; *Werke*, V, 148–66.

37 *Phen*, p. 43; *Werke*, III, 65.

38 See Bibliographical Essay.
39 C. Taylor, *Hegel* (Cambridge: Cambridge University Press, 1975).
40 *Enc* I, §85; *Werke*, **VIII**, 181.
41 For the passages cited in this paragraph, see *SL*, pp. 27, 39, 49, 63; *Werke*, **V**, 16, 30, 43, 61, and *Enc* I, §24; *Werke*, **VIII**, 81.
42 See Kolb, *The Critique of Pure Modernity*, p. 43, and Winfield, *Reason and Justice*, p. 137.
43 *SL*, p. 49; *Werke*, **V**, 43.
44 Kolb, *The Critique of Pure Modernity*, p. 43.
45 Kolb, *The Critique of Pure Modernity*, p. 86.

3 Phenomenology and Natural Consciousness

1 *SL*, p. 60; *Werke*, **V**, 57.
2 *SL*, p. 60; *Werke*, **V**, 57, translation modified.
3 *SL*, p. 70; *Werke*, **V**, 68–9.
4 *SL*, p. 72; *Werke*, **V**, 72.
5 *Enc* I, §78 remark; *Werke*, **VIII**, 168. See also *Enc* I, §17; *Werke*, **VIII**, 63.
6 *Phen*, p. 15; *Werke*, **III**, 30.
7 *Phen*, p. 15; *Werke*, **III**, 30.
8 *Phen*, pp. 14–15; *Werke*, **III**, 29.
9 *SL*, p. 48; *Werke*, **V**, 42. See also *SL*, pp. 68–9; *Werke*, **V**, 67, and J. Hyppolite, *Genesis and Structure of Hegel's Phenomenology of Spirit*, trans. S. Cherniak and J. Heckman (Evanston, IL: Northwestern University Press, 1974), p. 591: 'The *Phenomenology* sets out to establish this identity of self and being from which the *Logic* starts and which is a paradox for the common consciousness.'
10 Q. Lauer, *A Reading of Hegel's Phenomenology of Spirit* (New York: Fordham University Press, 1976), p. 12.
11 P. Redding, *Hegel's Hermeneutics* (Ithaca, NY: Cornell University Press, 1996), p. 136.
12 M. Heidegger, *Hegel's Phenomenology of Spirit*, trans. P. Emad and K. Maly (Bloomington: Indiana University Press, 1988), p. 82.
13 *Phen*, p. 17; *Werke*, **III**, 33, translation modified, emphasis added.
14 *Phen*, p. 32; *Werke*, **III**, 52, translation modified.
15 *Phen*, p. 52; *Werke*, **III**, 76.
16 *Phen*, p. 54; *Werke*, **III**, 77–8.

17 *Phen*, p. 53; *Werke*, **III**, 77.
18 See R. Stern, *Hegel and the Phenomenology of Spirit* (London: Routledge, 2002), pp. 40–1, and K. Westphal, *Hegel's Epistemological Realism* (Dordrecht: Kluwer, 1989), pp. 100–39. Stern notes that Hegel's method of immanent critique in the *Phenomenology* is motivated by his desire to establish the legitimacy of his philosophical position 'in a non-dogmatic and non-question-begging way' (p. 41), and Westphal, too, stresses Hegel's 'paramount concern to avoid question-begging' (p. 137). I wholeheartedly agree with both commentators on this point; see S. Houlgate, 'G. W. F. Hegel, *Phenomenology of Spirit* (1807): Thinking Philosophically without Begging the Question', in *The Classics of Western Philosophy: A Reader's Guide*, ed. J. J. E. Gracia, G. M. Reichberg and B. N. Schumacher (Oxford: Blackwell, 2003), p. 370.
19 *Phen*, p. 54; *Werke*, **III**, 77.
20 *Phen*, p. 54; *Werke*, **III**, 78.
21 *Phen*, p. 54; *Werke*, **III**, 78.
22 *Phen*, p. 54; *Werke*, **III**, 78.
23 Lauer puts the point well when he writes that the task of phenomenology is to 'watch consciousness in operation, to see not only what it does but also what the logic of its doing demands that it do next'; *A Reading of Hegel's Phenomenology of Spirit*, p. 35.
24 *Phen*, p. 35; *Werke*, **III**, 56.
25 *Phen*, p. 78; *Werke*, **III**, 106.
26 *SL*, p. 28; *Werke*, **V**, 17.
27 *Phen*, p. 55; *Werke*, **III**, 79. See also K. Dove, 'Hegel's Phenomenological Method', in *The Phenomenology of Spirit Reader: Critical and Interpretive Essays*, ed. J. Stewart (Albany: State University of New York Press, 1998), p. 57: 'The "new object" therefore must not be introduced by the philosopher; it must arise out of the course of the experience described – and not merely *qua* described, but through itself'.
28 *Phen*, p. 54; *Werke*, **III**, 78.
29 *Phen*, pp. 55-6; *Werke*, **III**, 79–80.
30 *Phen*, p. 55; *Werke*, **III**, 79.
31 *Phen*, pp. 60–1; *Werke*, **III**, 85.
32 *Phen*, p. 61; *Werke*, **III**, 86.
33 *Phen*, p. 62; *Werke*, **III**, 87.
34 *Phen*, pp. 62–3; *Werke*, **III**, 88.
35 *Phen*, p. 63; *Werke*, **III**, 88.
36 *Phen*, p. 63; *Werke*, **III**, 88.

37 *Phen*, p. 64; *Werke*, **III**, 89.
38 *Phen*, p. 64; *Werke*, **III**, 89–90.
39 *Phen*, p. 67; *Werke*, **III**, 93.
40 *Phen*, p. 67; *Werke*, **III**, 93. Note that Hegel does not start immediately with an analysis of the experience of perception, but first takes time to define the object of perception 'more precisely'. The analysis of the *experience* of perception does not begin until *Phen*, p. 70; *Werke*, **III**, 97: 'Let us now see what consciousness experiences in its actual perceiving'.
41 See, for example, G. Lukács, *The Young Hegel*, trans. R. Livingstone (London: Merlin Press, 1975), pp. 470–2.
42 Lauer, *A Reading of Hegel's Phenomenology of Spirit*, p. 37.
43 *Phen*, p. 15; *Werke*, **III**, 30.
44 See *Phen*, p. 16; *Werke*, **III**, 32.
45 *Phen*, p. 17; *Werke*, **III**, 33.
46 *Phen*, p. 50; *Werke*, **III**, 73.
47 *Phen*, p. 51; *Werke*, **III**, 74.
48 *Phen*, pp. 49–50; *Werke*, **III**, 72–3. See also Stern, *Hegel and the Phenomenology of Spirit*, p. 24: 'Hegel therefore gives the *Phenomenology* a role here too, helping consciousness to gradually question those conceptual certainties and thus to move to a position where it can see what it might mean to give them up.' An especially clear and persuasive account of the way in which the *Phenomenology* undermines the perspective and assumptions of consciousness is provided by William Maker in *Philosophy without Foundations: Rethinking Hegel* (Albany: State University of New York Press, 1994).
49 *Phen*, p. 21; *Werke*, **III**, 38.
50 *SL*, p. 49; *Werke*, **V**, 43.
51 *SL*, p. 49; *Werke*, **V**, 43.
52 *Phen*, p. 21; *Werke*, **III**, 38. Michael Forster, by contrast, understands only consciousness, self-consciousness and reason to be shapes of consciousness in the strict sense. He argues – in my view unconvincingly – that the *Phenomenology* was originally intended to cover only these shapes of consciousness, but that Hegel later altered his conception of the work and added the chapters on spirit, religion and absolute knowing; see M. Forster, *Hegel's Idea of a Phenomenology of Spirit* (Chicago: University of Chicago Press, 1998), pp. 505–43.

53 *Phen*, p. 491; *Werke*, **III**, 589. See also Hyppolite, *Genesis and Structure of Hegel's Phenomenology of Spirit*, pp. 17, 578.
54 *Phen*, pp. 21–2; *Werke*, **III**, 39.
55 *Phen*, p. 21; *Werke*, **III**, 39.
56 *Phen*, p. 14; *Werke*, **III**, 29.
57 *SL*, p. 60; *Werke*, **V**, 57, translation modified.
58 *SL*, p. 69; *Werke*, **V**, 68.
59 *Phen*, p. 34; *Werke*, **III**, 54.
60 *SL*, p. 69; *Werke*, **V**, 68, translation modified.
61 For three other essays of mine that cover similar ground to this chapter, see S. Houlgate, 'G. W. F. Hegel, *Phenomenology of Spirit* (1807): Thinking Philosophically without Begging the Question', cited above (note 18), S. Houlgate, 'G. W. F. Hegel (1770–1831)', in *The Blackwell Guide to the Modern Philosophers from Descartes to Nietzsche*, ed. S. Emmanuel (Oxford: Blackwell, 2001), pp. 278–305, and S. Houlgate, 'Absolute Knowing Revisited', *The Owl of Minerva*, 30, 1 (1998), 51–67.

4 The Path to Absolute Knowing

1 *Phen*, p. 104; *Werke*, **III**, 137.
2 See *Phen*, p. 21; *Werke*, **III**, 38.
3 *Phen*, p. 101; *Werke*, **III**, 134.
4 See *Phen*, pp. 105–11; *Werke*, **III**, 138–45. For a more extensive discussion of Hegel's account of desire and recognition (and of the life and death struggle and the master–slave relation), see S. Houlgate, 'G. W. F. Hegel: The Phenomenology of Spirit', in *The Blackwell Guide to Continental Philosophy*, ed. R. Solomon (Oxford: Blackwell, 2003), pp. 8–29. On the central importance of recognition in particular in Hegel's thought, see R. Williams, *Recognition: Fichte and Hegel on the Other* (Albany: State University of New York Press, 1992).
5 *Phen*, p. 112; *Werke*, **III**, 147.
6 *Phen*, pp. 113–14; *Werke*, **III**, 148–9.
7 *Phen*, p. 115; *Werke*, **III**, 150.
8 *Phen*, p. 117; *Werke*, **III**, 152.
9 *Phen*, pp. 118–19; *Werke*, **III**, 154.
10 *Phen*, p. 117; *Werke*, **III**, 153.
11 *Phen*, p. 117; *Werke*, **III**, 153. Miller's translation has 'quite unmanned'. The German is '*innerlich aufgelöst*'.
12 A. Kojève, *Introduction to the Reading of Hegel: Lectures on the Phenomenology of*

Spirit, ed. A. Bloom, trans. J. H. Nichols (Ithaca, NY: Cornell University Press, 1980), pp. 47–8.

13 *Phen*, p. 118; *Werke*, **III**, 154.

14 *Phen*, p. 119; *Werke*, **III**, 154.

15 *Phen*, p. 119; *Werke*, **III**, 155: 'having a "mind of one's own" is self-will' (*der eigene Sinn ist Eigensinn*).

16 *Phen*, p. 119; *Werke*, **III**, 155.

17 *Phen*, p. 119; *Werke*, **III**, 155.

18 See Karl Marx, *Selected Writings*, ed. D. McLellan (Oxford: Oxford University Press, 1977, 2nd edn 2000), p. 206 [*The German Ideology*, 'Artistic Talent under Communism'].

19 Of the commentators I have read, almost none – not even Kojève – appears to share the interpretation put forward here of the way in which the fear of death transforms the slave's consciousness of his labour in Hegel's account. The one who comes closest is Taylor, who notes that in fear the slave is 'shaken loose from his particular sense of self' and that 'work alone, uninformed by the fear of death, would have produced just particular abilities . . . not a universal consciousness of self'; Taylor, *Hegel*, pp. 155, 157. Lauer recognizes that the fear of death 'dissolve[s] all fixity' for the slave, but he does not see this as affecting the slave's conception of his labour. Indeed, he asserts that the slave 'builds up skills but builds up in himself no universal competence in relation to the totality of reality over against him'; Lauer, *A Reading of Hegel's Phenomenology of Spirit*, pp. 111–12.

20 Kojève, *Introduction to the Reading of Hegel*, p. 53.

21 *Phen*, p. 118; *Werke*, **III**, 154.

22 *Phen*, p. 120; *Werke*, **III**, 155, emphasis added.

23 *Phen*, p. 120; *Werke*, **III**, 155.

24 *Phen*, p. 120; *Werke*, **III**, 156.

25 See, for example, W. Desmond, *Being and the Between* (Albany: State University of New York Press, 1995), pp. 168–9: 'The *telos* is the goal of absolutely self-mediating thought. This goal is reached in absolute knowing when the otherness of the immediate is completely mediated, in its being dialectically subsumed in a self-knowing that is absolutely self-mediating.'

26 *Phen*, p. 121; *Werke*, **III**, 157.

27 *Phen*, p. 122; *Werke*, **III**, 158. See also *Phen*, p. 130; *Werke*, **III**, 168: 'the abstract thinking of Stoicism which turns its back on [and looks away from] individuality altogether' (*das abstrakte von der Einzelheit überhaupt wegsehende Denken des Stoizismus*).

28 *Phen*, p. 122; *Werke*, **III**, 158.

29 *Phen*, p. 146; *Werke*, **III**, 187.

30 *Phen*, pp. 122, 490; *Werke*, **III**, 158, 587. See also Hyppolite, *Genesis and Structure of Hegel's Phenomenology of Spirit*, p. 181: 'The ideal proposed here – to rediscover oneself in being . . . – is indeed characteristic of Hegel's idealism. Yet the stage reached here is only a stage, for the unity realised in it is still an *immediate* unity. . . . The concept at this stage is not yet the penetration of thought into the variety and plenitude of being.'

31 *Phen*, pp. 20, 122; *Werke*, **III**, 37, 158–9.

32 *Phen*, pp. 122–3; *Werke*, **III**, 159.

33 *Phen*, p. 124; *Werke*, **III**, 160–1.

34 *Phen*, pp. 124–5; *Werke*, **III**, 161–2.

35 *Phen*, p. 125; *Werke*, **III**, 162.

36 *Phen*, p. 127; *Werke*, **III**, 164. See Saint Augustine, *Confessions*, trans. R. S. Pine-Coffin (Harmondsworth: Penguin Books, 1961), pp. 26, 143, 147, 280, and H. S. Harris, *Hegel's Ladder*, 2 volumes (Indianapolis: Hackett Publishing, 1997), I, 395. Kant, however, also refers to transcendental apperception as 'this pure, original, unchanging [*unwandelbar*] consciousness'; see Kant, *Critique of Pure Reason*, A 107.

37 *Phen*, p. 127; *Werke*, **III**, 164, translation modified.

38 *Phen*, p. 131; *Werke*, **III**, 169.

39 *Phen*, pp. 133–4; *Werke*, **III**, 171–2.

40 *Phen*, p. 134; *Werke*, **III**, 172–3. See F. Nietzsche, *Human, All Too Human: A Book for Free Spirits*, trans. R. J. Hollingdale (Cambridge: Cambridge University Press, 1986), pp. 36, 49 [I: §§44, 92].

41 *Phen*, pp. 136–7; *Werke*, **III**, 175.

42 *Phen*, p. 137; *Werke*, **III**, 175.

43 *Phen*, pp. 137–8; *Werke*, **III**, 176.

44 *Phen*, pp. 138–9; *Werke*, **III**, 176–8.

45 Due to the fact that it has a more affirmative attitude towards its object than the other shapes of self-consciousness Hegel examines, the slave's self-consciousness

could perhaps be judged – retrospectively – to be the most *rational* shape of self-consciousness (with stoical thought running second).

46 *Phen*, pp. 142, 139; *Werke*, III, 181, 178.
47 *Phen*, p. 140; *Werke*, III, 179.
48 *Phen*, p. 139; *Werke*, III, 178–9.
49 *Phen*, p. 140; *Werke*, III, 179.
50 *Phen*, p. 142; *Werke*, III, 181.
51 *Phen*, pp. 145–6; *Werke*, III, 186, emphasis added.
52 *Phen*, pp. 141–5; *Werke*, III, 180–5.
53 *Phen*, p. 146; *Werke*, III, 187: 'Reason, as it *immediately* comes before us as the certainty of consciousness that it is all reality, takes its reality in the sense of the *immediacy of being*.'
54 *Phen*, p. 211; *Werke*, III, 263.
55 *Phen*, p. 212; *Werke*, III, 264.
56 *Phen*, p. 212; *Werke*, III, 264.
57 *Phen*, pp. 212–13; *Werke*, III, 264–6.
58 *Phen*, pp. 265, 21; *Werke*, III, 326, 38.
59 *Phen*, p. 265; *Werke*, III, 326.
60 *Phen*, p. 296; *Werke*, III, 361.
61 *Phen*, p. 356; *Werke*, III, 432.
62 *Phen*, pp. 356–7; *Werke*, III, 432–3.
63 *Phen*, p. 357; *Werke*, III, 433. See also *Phen*, p. 265; *Werke*, III, 327, where Hegel talks of the world being 'revolutionized' (*revolutioniert*) by the Enlightenment.
64 *Phen*, p. 358; *Werke*, III, 434.
65 *Phen*, pp. 358–9; *Werke*, III, 434, 436.
66 *Phen*, p. 360; *Werke*, III, 436.
67 *Phen*, p. 361; *Werke*, III, 437.
68 *Phen*, p. 362; *Werke*, III, 439.
69 *Phen*, p. 363; *Werke*, III, 440–1.
70 *Phen*, p. 365; *Werke*, III, 442.
71 *Phen*, p. 364; *Werke*, III, 441.
72 *Phen*, p. 368; *Werke*, III, 446.
73 See Taylor, *Hegel*, p. 192: 'Hegel is not strictly interpreting Kant here . . . but rather what he sees as the inner logic of the moral world-outlook to which Kant and later Fichte gave expression.'
74 *Phen*, p. 368; *Werke*, III, 446–7.
75 *Phen*, p. 368; *Werke*, III, 446. For a more detailed discussion of Hegel's account of the postulates of morality, see Stern, *Hegel and the Phenomenology of Spirit*, pp. 169–78.
76 *Phen*, pp. 369–70; *Werke*, III, 448.
77 *Phen*, p. 370; *Werke*, III, 449.
78 *Phen*, p. 370; *Werke*, III, 449. See also Kant, *Groundwork*, p. 24.

79 *Phen*, p. 371; *Werke*, III, 449–50. Hegel sums up this whole argument in these lines from later in the text: 'Morality, then, in the moral consciousness is imperfect; this is now what is put forward. But it is the essence of morality to be only the *perfectly pure*; imperfect morality is therefore impure, or is immorality. Morality itself thus exists in another being than the actual consciousness. This other being is a *holy moral lawgiver*'; *Phen*, p. 380; *Werke*, III, 460.
80 *Phen*, p. 371; *Werke*, III, 450, emphasis added.
81 *Phen*, pp. 373–4; *Werke*, III, 452–3.
82 *Phen*, p. 373; *Werke*, III, 452.
83 *Phen*, p. 378; *Werke*, III, 458.
84 *Phen*, p. 380; *Werke*, III, 460.
85 *Phen*, pp. 385–6; *Werke*, III, 466–7.
86 *Phen*, p. 384; *Werke*, III, 465.
87 *Phen*, p. 386; *Werke*, III, 467–8.
88 *Phen*, p. 384; *Werke*, III, 465.
89 *Phen*, pp. 385–6, 393; *Werke*, III, 466–7, 475–6: 'it is precisely the essence of conscience to have no truck with this calculating and weighing of duties, and to make its *own* decision without reference to any such reasons'.
90 *Phen*, p. 387; *Werke*, III, 468, translation modified.
91 *Phen*, pp. 388, 390; *Werke*, III, 470, 472.
92 Hyppolite, *Genesis and Structure of Hegel's Phenomenology of Spirit*, p. 509.
93 *Phen*, p. 387; *Werke*, III, 469.
94 See Harris, *Hegel's Ladder*, II, 466, 473: ' "Conscience" is the same "self" in everyone; it is a fully spiritual world. . . . Consciences are all (materially) *different*; and they are all (formally) *equal*.'
95 *Phen*, p. 388; *Werke*, III, 470.
96 *Phen*, p. 392; *Werke*, III, 474, and Lauer, *A Reading of Hegel's Phenomenology of Spirit*, p. 224.
97 *Phen*, pp. 395–6; *Werke*, III, 478–9.
98 *Phen*, p. 396; *Werke*, III, 479–80.
99 *Phen*, p. 397; *Werke*, III, 481. See also Lauer, *A Reading of Hegel's Phenomenology of Spirit*, p. 225.
100 *Phen*, p. 398; *Werke*, III, 481, translation modified.
101 *Phen*, p. 397; *Werke*, III, 481.
102 *Phen*, p. 398; *Werke*, III, 481.
103 *Phen*, p. 399; *Werke*, III, 483.

104 *Phen*, pp. 399–400; *Werke*, **III**, 483.
105 See T. Pinkard, *Hegel's Phenomenology: The Sociality of Reason* (Cambridge: Cambridge University Press, 1994), pp. 400–1, and Harris, *Hegel's Ladder*, **II**, 479–89.
106 *Phen*, p. 400; *Werke*, **III**, 483–4, and Luke 17: 33.
107 *Phen*, p. 400; *Werke*, **III**, 484.
108 *Phen*, p. 401; *Werke*, **III**, 485. See also Hyppolite, *Genesis and Structure of Hegel's Phenomenology of Spirit*, p. 520.
109 *Phen*, p. 402; *Werke*, **III**, 486. For Hegel's philosophical (rather than phenomenological) account of 'evil' conscience, see *PR*, §140, remark and addition; *Werke*, **VII**, 265–86.
110 *Phen*, pp. 402–3; *Werke*, **III**, 487.
111 *Phen*, p. 404; *Werke*, **III**, 488.
112 *Phen*, p. 404; *Werke*, **III**, 489. See also Harris, *Hegel's Ladder*, **II**, 495, 516, and Allen Wood's note in G. W. F. Hegel, *Elements of the Philosophy of Right*, ed. A. W. Wood, trans. H. B. Nisbet (Cambridge: Cambridge University Press, 1991), p. 424.
113 *Phen*, p. 403; *Werke*, **III**, 487.
114 *Phen*, p. 403; *Werke*, **III**, 487.
115 *Phen*, p. 406; *Werke*, **III**, 490–1.
116 *Phen*, p. 405; *Werke*, **III**, 490.
117 *Phen*, p. 406; *Werke*, **III**, 491.
118 *Phen*, p. 407; *Werke*, **III**, 492.
119 *Phen*, p. 407; *Werke*, **III**, 492.
120 Lauer, *A Reading of Hegel's Phenomenology of Spirit*, p. 228. On the close parallels between Hegel and Hannah Arendt on the issue of forgiveness, see Williams, *Recognition: Fichte and Hegel on the Other*, pp. 208–10.
121 See *Phen*, p. 407; *Werke*, **III**, 492.
122 *Phen*, p. 408; *Werke*, **III**, 493. Williams points out that at this point 'the concept of absolute *Geist* is first introduced [in the *Phenomenology*] as a reciprocal recognition qualified as forgiveness'; *Recognition: Fichte and Hegel on the Other*, p. 221. See also Harris, *Hegel's Ladder*, **II**, 501–8.
123 *Phen*, p. 408; *Werke*, **III**, 493.
124 *Phen*, p. 409; *Werke*, **III**, 494, and Lauer, *A Reading of Hegel's Phenomenology of Spirit*, p. 229. See also D. P. Jamros, ' "The Appearing God" in Hegel's *Phenomenology of Spirit*', in *The Phenomenology of Spirit Reader*, p. 338: 'A more careful analysis would link the "appearing God" to the

meeting of two people rather than to a single person.'
125 *Phen*, p. 409; *Werke*, **III**, 494.
126 *Phen*, p. 477; *Werke*, **III**, 572.
127 *Phen*, p. 410; *Werke*, **III**, 495.
128 *Phen*, p. 411; *Werke*, **III**, 496.
129 *Phen*, p. 459; *Werke*, **III**, 552, translation modified. Pinkard, in my view, turns Hegel into too reductive a humanist, when he claims that, for Hegel, 'the divine just *is* the human spirit reflecting on itself and establishing *for itself*, through its religious practices, the "absolute principles" governing human life'; *Hegel's Phenomenology*, p. 253. Harris also appears to overlook the fact that Hegel understands 'God' to be *absolute-being*-that-comes-to-self-consciousness-in humanity when he writes that, for Hegel, 'the "Father" of whom the Johannine Jesus spoke, is identical with the human community from Altamira to Nagasaki (and however long it may last after that)'; *Hegel's Ladder*, **II**, 691. Taylor, by contrast, errs in the opposite direction by conferring on Hegel's *Geist* 'a larger-than-human consciousness' and so turning it into a 'cosmic infinite subject' (albeit one whose vehicles we are); *Hegel*, pp. 197–8. Stern, I believe, comes closer to the truth, when he argues that, for Hegel, 'God remains a substance, for in becoming human He remains unconditioned and absolute', but that 'God will be seen as achieving self-consciousness *through* humanity'; *Hegel and the Phenomenology of Spirit*, pp. 190–1.
130 *Phen*, p. 417; *Werke*, **III**, 503.
131 *Phen*, p. 415; *Werke*, **III**, 501–2.
132 *Phen*, p. 414; *Werke*, **III**, 499.
133 *Phen*, p. 459; *Werke*, **III**, 552.
134 *Phen*, pp. 462, 475; *Werke*, **III**, 555–6, 570. See also Harris, *Hegel's Ladder*, **II**, 692–4. Cyril O'Regan maintains that this 'elision' of the Resurrection and Pentecost – together with other, similar 'elisions' – clearly demonstrates that 'Hegel's views deviate from confessional norms'; C. O'Regan, 'The Impossibility of a Christian Reading of the *Phenomenology of Spirit*: H. S. Harris on Hegel's Liquidation of Christianity', *The Owl of Minerva*, 33, 1 (2001/2), 59–60, 65. For O'Regan's full account of what he sees as the 'heterodox' character of

Hegel's interpretation of Christianity, see his magnificent book, *The Heterodox Hegel* (Albany: State University of New York Press, 1994). As becomes clear in chapter 10 of this study, I do not share the view that Hegel deviates from the spirit of orthodox Christianity as much as O'Regan and others (including Harris) believe.

135 *Phen*, p. 476; *Werke*, III, 572.

136 *Phen*, p. 463; *Werke*, III, 556.

137 *Phen*, pp. 465–7; *Werke*, III, 560–1.

138 *Phen*, p. 463; *Werke*, III, 556.

139 *Phen*, pp. 411–12; *Werke*, III, 497–8.

140 *Phen*, p. 477; *Werke*, III, 573.

141 *Phen*, p. 466; *Werke*, III, 560.

142 *Phen*, p. 476; *Werke*, III, 572.

143 *Phen*, p. 479; *Werke*, III, 575, my italics. See also Jamros, '"The Appearing God" in Hegel's *Phenomenology of Spirit*', p. 341.

144 *Phen*, p. 477; *Werke*, III, 573.

145 *Phen*, p. 461; *Werke*, III, 554.

146 *Phen*, p. 14; *Werke*, III, 29.

147 *Phen*, p. 412; *Werke*, III, 498, translation modified.

148 *Phen*, p. 491; *Werke*, III, 588–9.

149 *Phen*, pp. 477–8; *Werke*, III, 573.

150 See Hyppolite, *Genesis and Structure of Hegel's Phenomenology of Spirit*, p. 599: 'Thus infinite reason knows itself in human self-consciousness and is infinite only in this finite knowledge of itself'.

151 *Phen*, p. 411; *Werke*, III, 497.

152 *SL*, p. 60; *Werke*, V, 57.

153 *SL*, p. 82; *Werke*, V, 82.

154 *SL*, p. 48; *Werke*, V, 42: 'The path of this movement goes through every form of the *relation of consciousness to the object*'.

155 *Phen*, p. 14; *Werke*, III, 29. Michael Forster argues that, when Hegel first wrote his Introduction to the *Phenomenology*, the term 'absolute knowing' referred not to 'philosophy', but to 'law-giving reason', the penultimate shape of reason. Forster concludes from this that Hegel's text was originally intended to analyse only the shapes of consciousness, self-consciousness and reason, and that the current chapter on 'absolute knowing', as well as the chapters on 'spirit' and 'religion', were 'only added later as an afterthought'. Forster bases his argument in part on a sheet from an early draft of the *Phenomenology*, written by Hegel in 1805, which begins with the fol-

lowing words: 'Thus Absolute Knowing first emerges as Lawgiving Reason' (*Das absolute Wissen tritt so zuerst als gesetzgebende Vernunft auf*). (See Forster, *Hegel's Idea of a Phenomenology of Spirit*, pp. 532, 611, and J. Hoffmeister, ed. *Dokumente zu Hegels Entwicklung* [Stuttgart: Frommann-Holzboog, 1936, 1974], p. 353.) What Forster overlooks, however, is the fact that Hegel's claim in this fragment is quite compatible with his final position in the text as we know it. Absolute knowing may well *first* emerge as lawgiving reason, but it emerges *fully* only as philosophy, after spirit and religion have been discussed. In other words, absolute knowing makes its appearance gradually in Hegel's *Phenomenology*. Absolute knowing is characterized by the collapse of the distinction between the 'certainty of oneself' and the object known, and the disclosure of their identity. This identity does not simply burst on to the scene at the end of Hegel's book, but becomes more and more apparent as the analysis proceeds. It begins to emerge in 'reason', then becomes more intimate in 'moral consciousness', and finally emerges fully in philosophy after being prefigured in religion. (Indeed, Hegel claims that we actually enter 'the native realm of truth' as early as the chapter on self-consciousness; *Phen*, p. 104; *Werke*, III, 138. One could also point out that absolute knowing is partly anticipated by stoical self-consciousness, although, as I argued above, there are important differences between the two.) On this interpretation, therefore, Hegel's 1805 fragment provides no grounds for departing from the idea that Hegel originally intended his *Phenomenology* to have the very structure with which it ended up and to include chapters on consciousness, self-consciousness, reason, spirit, religion *and* absolute knowing (or philosophy).

156 *Phen*, pp. 16–17; *Werke*, III, 32, 34: 'The single individual must also pass through the formative stages of universal Spirit so far as their content is concerned, but as shapes which Spirit has already left behind, as stages on a way that has been made level with toil . . . the content is already the actuality reduced to a possibility, its immediacy overcome, and the embodied shape reduced

to abbreviated, simple determinations of thought'.

157 A similar point could, perhaps, be made about Hegel's treatment of morality in the *Phenomenology* and the *Philosophy of Right*.

158 Even though the *Phenomenology* focuses more on the inadequacies of religious experience than do the later *Lectures on the Philosophy of Religion*, Hegel nevertheless acknowledges in the earlier work that religion is an important historical and personal precondition of philosophy. If philosophy presents in its true, conceptual form the truth that is disclosed in experience, that truth must obviously be experienced – and be pictured by religion – *before* it can be understood philosophically: 'it must be said that nothing is *known* that is not in *experience*, or, as it is also expressed, that is not *felt to be true*, not given as an *inwardly revealed* eternal verity, as something sacred that is *believed*, or whatever other expressions have been used'; *Phen*, p. 487; *Werke*, **III**, 585.

5 Reason in Nature

1 Popper, *The Open Society and Its Enemies*, **II**, 28.

2 In the *Logic* reason first takes the form of the Concept (*Begriff*) and the Concept then mutates logically into the fully developed form of the Idea (see *SL*, pp. 755–60; *Werke*, **VI**, 462–9). The terms 'Concept' and 'Idea' thus refer to one and the same self-determining reason at different levels of development.

3 *SL*, pp. 842–3; *Werke*, **VI**, 572–3.

4 *SL*, pp. 842–3; *Werke*, **VI**, 572–3.

5 *SL*, p. 843; *Werke*, **VI**, 573. See Thomas Kalenberg, *Die Befreiung der Natur: Natur und Selbstbewußtsein in der Philosophie Hegels* (Hamburg: Felix Meiner Verlag, 1997), p. 98.

6 *Enc* **I**, §244 addition; *Werke*, **VIII**, 392, and G. W. F. Hegel, *Naturphilosophie. Band I: Die Vorlesung von 1819/20*, ed. M. Gies (Napoli: Bibliopolis, 1980) (hereafter *NP*), p. 6.

7 See, for example, the articles in *The Owl of Minerva*, 34, 1 (2002/3).

8 See G. W. F. Hegel, *Vorlesung über Naturphilosophie: Berlin 1821/22*, eds. G. Mar-

masse and T. Posch (Frankfurt am Main: Peter Lang, 2002) (hereafter *VNP 1821*), p. 14.

9 See *Enc* **II**, §248 addition; *Werke*, **IX**, 30: 'Nature is the first in point of time, but the absolute *prius* is the Idea.'

10 *A Spinoza Reader: The Ethics and Other Works*, ed. and trans. E. Curley (Princeton, NJ: Princeton University Press, 1994), p. 100 [I P18].

11 *Enc* **I**, §237 addition; *Werke*, **VIII**, 389.

12 *Enc* **II**, §247; *Werke*, **IX**, 24.

13 *Enc* **II**, §247; *Werke*, **IX**, 24.

14 *VNP 1821*, p. 14.

15 *NP*, p. 7.

16 *Enc* **I**, §244; *Werke*, **VIII**, 392, and *SL*, p. 843; *Werke*, **VI**, 573.

17 *VNP 1821*, p. 23.

18 *Enc* **II**, §248 remark; *Werke*, **IX**, 28.

19 G. W. F. Hegel, *Vorlesung über Naturphilosophie: Berlin 1823/24*, ed. G. Marmasse (Frankfurt am Main: Peter Lang, 2000) (hereafter *VNP 1823*), p. 96.

20 *Enc* **II**, §249 addition; *Werke*, **IX**, 32.

21 *VNP 1821*, p. 22.

22 *Enc* **II**, §248 remark; *Werke*, **IX**, 28. See also *VNP 1821*, p. 23.

23 *Enc* **II**, §249; *Werke*, **IX**, 31.

24 *VNP 1821*, p. 25.

25 *Enc* **II**, §250; *Werke*, **IX**, 34.

26 *Enc* **II**, §250; *Werke*, **IX**, 34. See also S. Houlgate, 'Necessity and Contingency in Hegel's *Science of Logic*', *The Owl of Minerva*, 27, 1 (1995), 37–49.

27 *Enc* **II**, §248 addition; *Werke*, **IX**, 30: 'there is contingency in nature, i.e. external necessity, not the inner necessity of the Concept'.

28 *SL*, p. 682; *Werke*, **VI**, 375.

29 *Enc* **II**, §250; *Werke*, **IX**, 34.

30 *Enc* **II**, §250 remark; *Werke*, **IX**, 35.

31 G. Buchdahl, 'Hegel on the Interaction between Science and Philosophy', in *Hegel and Newtonianism*, ed. M. J. Petry (Dordrecht: Kluwer, 1993), p. 71.

32 *Enc* **II**, §§270 addition, 268 addition; *Werke*, **IX**, 106, 82. See also *VNP 1821*, pp. 56, 67 and *VNP 1823*, p. 132.

33 *VNP 1823*, p. 83.

34 Popper, *The Open Society and its Enemies*, **II**, 27, and J. Bronowski, *The Ascent of Man* (London: BBC Books, 1973), p. 360.

35 See O. Depré, 'The Ontological Foundations of Hegel's Dissertation of 1801', in *Hegel*

and the *Philosophy of Nature*, ed. S. Houlgate (Albany: State University of New York Press, 1998), pp. 257–81. On the 'Titius–Bode Law', see K. R. Lang, *The Cambridge Guide to the Solar System* (Cambridge: Cambridge University Press, 2003), pp. 17–18.

36 *VNP 1821*, p. 67, and *Enc* **II**, §270 addition; *Werke*, **IX**, 106.

37 *VNP 1823*, p. 131, and I. Newton, *The Principia: Mathematical Principles of Natural Philosophy*, trans. I. B. Cohen (Berkeley: University of California Press, 1999), p. 943. See also C. Ferrini, 'Framing Hypotheses: Numbers in Nature and the Logic of Measure in the Development of Hegel's System' in *Hegel and the Philosophy of Nature*, pp. 283–310.

38 Popper, *The Open Society and Its Enemies*, **II**, 28.

39 *VNP 1823*, p. 72.

40 *Enc* **II**, §246 addition; *Werke*, **IX**, 20. See also *VNP 1821*, p. 3, *VNP 1823*, p. 73, and chapter 1 above, pp. 4–5.

41 *VNP 1823*, p. 72, and *Enc* **II**, §246 remark; *Werke*, **IX**, 15. See also *Enc* **I**, §6; *Werke*, **VIII**, 47, and G. Buchdahl, 'Hegel's Philosophy of Nature and the Structure of Science' in *Hegel*, ed. M. Inwood (Oxford: Oxford University Press, 1985), p. 125.

42 *PH*, p. 440; *Werke*, **XII**, 522. See also G. W. F. Hegel, *Vorlesungen über die Philosophie der Weltgeschichte*, eds. G. Lasson and J. Hoffmeister, 4 volumes (Hamburg: Felix Meiner Verlag, 1919, 1923), **IV**, 911–13.

43 *Enc* **II**, §§267 remark, 270 remark; *Werke*, **IX**, 75–8, 91–3.

44 *Enc* **II**, §246; *Werke*, **IX**, 15.

45 *Enc* **II**, §246 remark; *Werke*, **IX**, 15.

46 Buchdahl, 'Hegel's Philosophy of Nature and the Structure of Science', p. 131.

47 *Enc* **II**, §270 addition; *Werke*, **IX**, 94.

48 *Enc* **II**, §246 remark; *Werke*, **IX**, 15. See also *VNP 1821*, p. 76, and *PR*, §2 remark; *Werke*, **VII**, 31–2.

49 *Enc* **II**, §254 addition; *Werke*, **IX**, 42. See also *VNP 1823*, p. 104.

50 *Enc* **II**, §276 remark; *Werke*, **IX**, 117: 'The immanent philosophical element is . . . the inherent necessity of the conceptual determination, which must then be pointed out as *some* [*irgendeine*] natural existence.'

51 See S. Houlgate, 'Logic and Nature in

Hegel's Philosophy: A Response to John Burbidge', *The Owl of Minerva*, 34, 1 (2002/3), 116–17.

52 *Hegel: The Letters*, trans. C. Butler and C. Seiler (Bloomington: Indiana University Press, 1984), p. 309.

53 M. Gies, 'Naturphilosophie und Naturwissenschaft bei Hegel', in *Hegel und die Naturwissenschaften*, ed. M. J. Petry (Stuttgart: Frommann-Holzboog, 1987), p. 77. See also K.-N. Ihmig, *Hegels Deutung der Gravitation: Eine Studie zu Hegel und Newton* (Frankfurt am Main: Athenäum, 1989), p. 83.

54 *VNP 1823*, p. 83.

55 *VNP 1823*, pp. 78, 93.

56 *Enc* **II**, §246 addition; *Werke*, **IX**, 20. See also *VNP 1823*, p. 71.

57 *Enc* **II**, §326 addition; *Werke*, **IX**, 290. See J. Gribbin, *Science: A History* (London: Penguin Books, 2002), p. 416.

58 *VNP 1821*, p. 25: 'each stage has its own proper [*eigentümlich*] shape, and it is this above all that we have to comprehend'.

6 Space, Gravity and the Freeing of Matter

1 *VNP 1821*, p. 29.

2 See *SL*, pp. 424–31; *Werke*, **VI**, 55–64.

3 *Enc* **II**, §254 addition; *Werke*, **IX**, 42, and *VNP 1821*, p. 30. See also Kant, *Critique of Pure Reason*, B 39.

4 *Enc* **II**, §254; *Werke*, **IX**, 41, and *VNP 1821*, p. 30.

5 *VNP 1823*, p. 105, and G. W. F. Hegel, *Natur-Philosophie*, 'Nachschrift A', in W. Bonsiepen, 'Hegels Raum-Zeit-Lehre', *Hegel-Studien*, 20 (1985) (hereafter *VNP Bon*), 41.

6 *Enc* **II**, §254; *Werke*, **IX**, 41, and *VNP 1821*, p. 30.

7 G. W. F. Hegel, *Vorlesungen über die Philosophie der Natur: Berlin 1819/20*, eds. M. Bondeli and H. N. Seelmann (Hamburg: Felix Meiner Verlag, 2002) (hereafter *VPN*), p. 20.

8 *VNP Bon*, p. 39.

9 *Enc* **II**, §§255–6; *Werke*, **IX**, 44, emphasis added.

10 *Enc* **II**, §256; *Werke*, **IX**, 44.

11 *VNP 1823*, p. 108.

12 *VNP 1821*, p. 32.

13 *VNP 1823*, p. 107, *VNP Bon*, p. 46, and *Enc* **II**, §256; *Werke*, **IX**, 44.

14 *VNP 1821*, p. 33.
15 *VNP 1823*, pp. 107–8. See also L. Stepelevich, 'Hegel's Geometric Theory', in *Hegel and the Philosophy of Nature*, pp. 86–7.
16 *SL*, p. 116; *Werke*, **V**, 124. See also *VNP 1823*, p. 108.
17 *VNP 1823*, p. 108.
18 *VNP Bon*, p. 46.
19 *VNP 1823*, p. 108.
20 *Enc* **II**, §256; *Werke*, **IX**, 45, emphasis added.
21 *VNP 1823*, p. 108, *Enc* **II**, §256; *Werke*, **IX**, 45, and *VNP 1821*, p. 33.
22 *VNP 1823*, p. 108.
23 *Enc* **II**, §256; *Werke*, **IX**, 45.
24 *NP*, p. 16.
25 *Enc* **II**, §256; *Werke*, **IX**, 45.
26 *Enc* **II**, §256; *Werke*, **IX**, 45.
27 *Enc* **II**, §254 addition; *Werke*, **IX**, 43.
28 B. Greene, *The Elegant Universe* (London: Vintage, 2000), p. 203.
29 *VNP Bon*, p. 49.
30 *VNP 1821*, p. 35.
31 *Enc* **II**, §257 addition; *Werke*, **IX**, 48, and *VNP Bon*, p. 58.
32 *VNP Bon*, p. 58.
33 *Enc* **II**, §257 addition; *Werke*, **IX**, 48.
34 *VNP 1821*, p. 36.
35 *Enc* **II**, §258 remark; *Werke*, **IX**, 49.
36 *Enc* **II**, §258; *Werke*, **IX**, 48.
37 *VNP Bon*, p. 52.
38 *Enc* **II**, §259 remark; *Werke*, **IX**, 52, and *VNP 1821*, p. 37.
39 *VNP 1821*, p. 37.
40 *VPN*, p. 23.
41 *Enc* **II**, §259 addition; *Werke*, **IX**, 55.
42 *Enc* **II**, §258 addition; *Werke*, **IX**, 50. This means that Hegel would not accept that there is a 'beginning' to time itself.
43 *VNP 1821*, p. 37.
44 *VPN*, p. 23, and *Enc* **II**, §260; *Werke*, **IX**, 55.
45 *Enc* **II**, §257 addition; *Werke*, **IX**, 48.
46 *VPN*, p. 23. See also *NP*, p. 21.
47 *VNP Bon*, p. 60.
48 See A. Einstein, *Relativity: The Special and the General Theory* (London: Methuen, 1920, 1954), pp. 55, 91.
49 *Enc* **II**, §260 and addition; *Werke*, **IX**, 55–6, and *VNP 1823*, p. 112. See also D. Wandschneider, *Raum, Zeit, Relativität* (Frankfurt am Main: Vittorio Klostermann, 1982), p. 114.
50 *VNP 1821*, p. 43.
51 *Enc* **II**, §261 and addition; *Werke*, **IX**, 56, 58.
52 *Enc* **II**, §261 addition; *Werke*, **IX**, 58.
53 *Enc* **II**, §261 addition; *Werke*, **IX**, 59.
54 See *NP*, p. 26, and Wandschneider, *Raum, Zeit, Relativität*, p. 119.
55 *The Complete Works of Aristotle*, **I**, 342 [*Physics* 200b33].
56 See R. D. Winfield, 'Space, Time and Matter: Conceiving Nature without Foundations', in *Hegel and the Philosophy of Nature*, pp. 62–3.
57 For Spinoza, motion and rest constitute the immediate 'infinite mode' of extension; see *A Spinoza Reader*, pp. 100, 271 [I P21, Letter 64].
58 See *VNP 1823*, p. 113, and Wandschneider, *Raum, Zeit, Relativität*, p. 114.
59 *Enc* **II**, §261 addition; *Werke*, **IX**, 59.
60 Winfield, 'Space, Time and Matter', p. 63. See also *VNP 1821*, p. 43.
61 *VNP 1823*, pp. 110, 114.
62 *VNP 1821*, p. 40.
63 Winfield, 'Space, Time and Matter', p. 63.
64 *Enc* **II**, §261 addition; *Werke*, **IX**, 60.
65 See Ihmig, *Hegels Deutung der Gravitation*, pp. 137, 143, 151.
66 *VNP 1821*, p. 42, and *Enc* **II**, §261 remark and addition; *Werke*, **IX**, 57, 60.
67 *VNP 1823*, pp. 113–14, and *Enc* **II**, §262; *Werke*, **IX**, 60.
68 *Enc* **II**, §261 addition; *Werke*, **IX**, 60.
69 *NP*, p. 22, and *VPN*, p. 36.
70 *VNP 1821*, p. 45, and *Enc* **II**, §262 addition; *Werke*, **IX**, 63.
71 I. Kant, *Theoretical Philosophy After 1781*, eds H. Allison and P. Heath (Cambridge: Cambridge University Press, 2002), p. 211 [*Metaphysical Foundations of Natural Science*, ch. 2, expl. 2].
72 Newton, *Principia*, pp. 405, 806, 817.
73 Newton, *Principia*, p. 561.
74 Newton, *Principia*, p. 796.
75 Newton, *Principia*, p. 943.
76 *VNP 1821*, p. 46.
77 *Enc* **II**, §262 addition; *Werke*, **IX**, 63.
78 *VPN*, p. 27.
79 *VNP 1821*, p. 50, and *VNP 1823*, p. 120.
80 *Enc* **II**, §262 remark and addition; *Werke*, **IX**, 62–3.
81 Newton, *Principia*, p. 407.
82 *Enc* **II**, §262 remark; *Werke*, **IX**, 61. See also Ihmig, *Hegels Deutung der Gravitation*, p. 94.
83 *Enc* **II**, §262 addition; *Werke*, **IX**, 63.

84 *Enc* **II**, §262; *Werke*, **IX**, 61.
85 *VNP 1821*, pp. 51, 57. The 'centre' which one body seeks in another should not, therefore, be confused with the 'centre of mass' (or 'centre of gravity') around which both of them move and which can be located in the empty space between them. On the latter, see Newton, *Principia*, pp. 816–17.
86 *Enc* **II**, §262 remark; *Werke*, **IX**, 62.
87 *Enc* **II**, §263; *Werke*, **IX**, 64.
88 *VNP 1823*, p. 117.
89 Newton, *Principia*, p. 404. See also H. Reichenbach, *From Copernicus to Einstein*, trans. R. B. Winn (New York: Dover, 1942, 1970), p. 90.
90 *Enc* **II**, §264; *Werke*, **IX**, 64.
91 *VNP 1821*, p. 47, and *Enc* **II**, §264; *Werke*, **IX**, 64.
92 *Enc* **II**, §264 addition; *Werke*, **IX**, 65.
93 I. B. Cohen, 'Newton's concepts of force and mass, with notes on the Laws of Motion', in *The Cambridge Companion to Newton*, eds. I. B. Cohen and G. E. Smith (Cambridge: Cambridge University Press, 2002), p. 61.
94 Newton, *Principia*, p. 416.
95 W. R. Shea, 'Hegel's Celestial Mechanics', in *Hegels Philosophie der Natur: Beziehungen zwischen empirischer und spekulativer Naturerkenntnis*, eds. R.-P. Horstmann and M. J. Petry (Stuttgart: Klett-Cotta, 1986), p. 33.
96 Newton, *Principia*, pp. 405, 806.
97 Newton, *Principia*, pp. 796, 806, 810.
98 Newton, *Principia*, p. 416.
99 See Newton, *Principia*, p. 811, Shea, 'Hegel's Celestial Mechanics', p. 32, and Gribbin, *Science: A History*, p. 173.
100 *Enc* **II**, §270 remark; *Werke*, **IX**, 86.
101 *Enc* **II**, §262 addition; *Werke*, **IX**, 63.
102 See Ihmig, *Hegels Deutung der Gravitation*, p. 63, and P. M. Kluit, 'Inertial and Gravitational Mass: Newton, Hegel and Modern Physics', in *Hegel and Newtonianism*, pp. 229–47.
103 *VNP 1821*, p. 49.
104 *Enc* **II**, §266 addition; *Werke*, **IX**, 73.
105 *Enc* **II**, §269 remark; *Werke*, **IX**, 83, emphasis added.
106 *VNP 1823*, p. 116, and *Enc* **II**, §269 remark; *Werke*, **IX**, 83.
107 Popper, *The Open Society and Its Enemies*, **II**, 27.
108 Kluit, 'Inertial and Gravitational Mass', p. 234.
109 Newton, *Principia*, p. 796. Cohen points out that Newton's 'force of inertia' 'is neither an accelerative force nor a static force and is not, properly speaking in the context of dynamics, a force at all'; Cohen, 'Newton's concepts of force and mass, with notes on the Laws of Motion', p. 57.
110 See D. Wandschneider, 'Die Kategorien "Materie" und "Licht" in der Naturphilosophie Hegels', in *Hegel und die Naturwissenschaften*, p. 295.
111 *Enc* **II**, §267; *Werke*, **IX**, 75.
112 C. I. Calle, *Superstrings and Other Things: A Guide to Physics* (Bristol: IOP Publishing, 2001), p. 40.
113 *Enc* **II**, §267 remark and addition; *Werke*, **IX**, 75, 79. A Parisian foot equals 0.3248 metres, so 15 feet = $c.4.9$ m; see Depré, 'The Ontological Foundations of Hegel's Dissertation of 1801', p. 262.
114 *Enc* **II**, §267 remark; *Werke*, **IX**, 76.
115 Calle, *Superstrings and Other Things*, pp. 39–40.
116 *Enc* **II**, §267 addition; *Werke*, **IX**, 79–80.
117 *Enc* **II**, §267 remark; *Werke*, **IX**, 76. See also Kalenberg, *Die Befreiung der Natur*, pp. 161–2.
118 *Enc* **II**, §267 remark; *Werke*, **IX**, 78, and *VNP 1821*, p. 52.
119 *Enc* **II**, §267 remark; *Werke*, **IX**, 78.
120 All quotations in the following account are taken from *Enc* **II**, §267 remark; *Werke*, **IX**, 78. My account is especially indebted to that provided by Kalenberg in *Die Befreiung der Natur*, pp. 167–79.
121 Hegel's 1819 lectures present a different argument in which the magnitude of time must be squared because of the quality of time itself, rather than that of space. Time is self-relating negation; therefore, only by relating to and determining itself *by itself – and so squaring itself –* does the magnitude of time determine that of space; see *NP*, p. 30.
122 *Enc* **II**, §267 addition; *Werke*, **IX**, 79.
123 *The New Solar System*, eds. J. K. Beatty, C. C. Petersen and A. Chaikin (Cambridge: Cambridge University Press, 1981, 4th edn 1999), p. 387.
124 *Enc* **II**, §267 addition; *Werke*, **IX**, 79. See Gribbin, *Science: A History*, pp. 76–7, 81.
125 G. W. F. Hegel, *Enzyklopädie der philo-*

sophischen Wissenschaften im Grundrisse
(1817), eds. W. Bonsiepen and K. Grotsch
(Hamburg: Felix Meiner Verlag, 2000), §216.
See also Newton, *Principia*, pp. 810–11, and
Ihmig, *Hegels Deutung der Gravitation*,
p. 62.

126 See *Enc* **II**, §262 remark; *Werke*, **IX**, 62, and
Ihmig, *Hegels Deutung der Gravitation*, p.
93.

127 I. B. Cohen, 'A Guide to Newton's *Principia*',
in Newton, *Principia*, p. 144. See also S.
Büttner, 'Hegel on Galileo's Law of Fall', in
Hegel and Newtonianism, pp. 336–7.

128 Newton, *Principia*, p. 424.

129 *Enc* **II**, §270 addition; *Werke*, **IX**, 97, and
VNP 1823, p. 129.

130 *Enc* **II**, §267 remark; *Werke*, **IX**, 78, and
Kalenberg, *Die Befreiung der Natur*, pp.
173–4.

131 *VNP 1821*, p. 54.

132 *Enc* **II**, §266; *Werke*, **IX**, 69.

133 *Enc* **II**, §267 remark; *Werke*, **IX**, 77.

134 Kalenberg, *Die Befreiung der Natur*, p. 175.

135 *Enc* **II**, §268 addition; *Werke*, **IX**, 80.

136 *Enc* **II**, §268 and addition; *Werke*, **IX**, 80–1.

137 *Enc* **II**, §268 addition; *Werke*, **IX**, 81, *VNP
1823*, p. 124, and *VNP 1821*, p. 55.

138 *Enc* **II**, §268 addition; *Werke*, **IX**, 81–2.

139 Ihmig, *Hegels Deutung der Gravitation*,
p. 154.

140 See S. Malin, *The Greenwich Guide to
Stars, Galaxies and Nebulae* (Cambridge:
Cambridge University Press, 1989),
pp. 31–2.

141 *Enc* **II**, §268 addition; *Werke*, **IX**, 81.

142 *Enc* **II**, §269 addition; *Werke*, **IX**, 84.

143 *Enc* **II**, §269 addition; *Werke*, **IX**, 84.

144 *Enc* **II**, §268 addition; *Werke*, **IX**, 81. Hegel
mentions the possibility of other solar
systems at *VPN*, p. 33.

145 *Enc* **II**, §270 addition; *Werke*, **IX**, 100.

146 *Enc* **II**, §270; *Werke*, **IX**, 85.

147 *Enc* **II**, §270 addition; *Werke*, **IX**, 101–3.

148 *Enc* **II**, §270 addition; *Werke*, **IX**, 100, 104.

149 *Enc* **II**, §§270 addition, 269 addition; *Werke*,
IX, 101, 84.

150 *Enc* **II**, §269 addition; *Werke*, **IX**, 84.

151 Hegel accepts that planets also rotate
around their own axis, but wrongly denies
that moons do the same; see *Enc* **II**, §270
addition; *Werke*, **IX**, 103.

152 *Enc* **II**, §§268, 270 remark; *Werke*, **IX**, 80,
85–6.

153 *Enc* **II**, §270 addition; *Werke*, **IX**, 94, and

Gribbin, pp. 62–5.

154 *Enc* **II**, §270 addition; *Werke*, **IX**, 94.

155 *Enc* **II**, §270 remark and addition; *Werke*,
IX, 89, 96.

156 *Enc* **II**, §270 remark; *Werke*, **IX**, 91.

157 M. Nasti de Vincentis, 'Hegel's Worm in
Newton's Apple', in *Hegel and the Philosophy
of Nature*, p. 227.

158 *Enc* **II**, §270 remark; *Werke*, **IX**, 90.

159 *Enc* **II**, §270 remark; *Werke*, **IX**, 90.

160 *Enc* **II**, §270 addition; *Werke*, **IX**, 94.

161 *Enc* **II**, §270 addition; *Werke*, **IX**, 94. The
planets in our solar system in fact have
nearly circular orbits, though almost half of
the known extrasolar planets do not; see
Beatty, Petersen and Chaikin (eds) *The New
Solar System*, pp. 380–1.

162 *Enc* **II**, §267 remark; *Werke*, **IX**, 78.

163 *Enc* **II**, §270 remark; *Werke*, **IX**, 92.

164 *Enc* **II**, §267 remark; *Werke*, **IX**, 78.

165 *Enc* **II**, §270 addition; *Werke*, **IX**, 95.

166 Kalenberg, *Die Befreiung der Natur*, p. 191.

167 See Lang, *The Cambridge Guide to the Solar
System*, p. 10.

168 *Enc* **II**, §270 remark; *Werke*, **IX**, 93.

169 *Enc* **II**, §270 remark; *Werke*, **IX**, 93, and *VNP
1821*, p. 62.

170 *Enc* **II**, §270 remark; *Werke*, **IX**, 93.

171 *Enc* **II**, §270 addition; *Werke*, **IX**, 96.

172 Shea, 'Hegel's Celestial Mechanics', pp. 30–1.

173 *Enc* **II**, §270 remark; *Werke*, **IX**, 87. See also
Ihmig, *Hegels Deutung der Gravitation*, p.
161. Shea argues that Hegel was wrong in
his belief that Kepler did not employ the
concept of 'force' in his study of planetary
motion; 'Hegel's Celestial Mechanics', p. 33.

174 *Enc* **II**, §270 remark and addition; *Werke*,
IX, 82, 97, and *VNP 1823*, p. 127.

175 Newton, *Principia*, p. 805.

176 Shea, 'Hegel's Celestial Mechanics', pp. 35–7.

177 *Enc* **II**, §269 addition; *Werke*, **IX**, 85. See also
VNP 1823, p. 128, Newton, *Principia*, pp.
453, 805, and Ihmig, *Hegels Deutung der
Gravitation*, p. 45.

178 Cohen, 'Newton's concepts of force and
mass, with notes on the Laws of Motion',
p. 63.

179 *Enc* **II**, §264 remark; *Werke*, **IX**, 65.

180 *Enc* **II**, §270 remark; *Werke*, **IX**, 89. See also
Enc **II**, §266 remark; *Werke*, **IX**, 70.

181 Newton, *Principia*, pp. 408, 588, and *VNP
1821*, p. 58.

182 *Enc* **II**, §270 remark and addition; *Werke*,
IX, 86–7, 96.

183 *Enc* **II**, §270 remark; *Werke*, **IX**, 88–9, and *NP*, p. 33.

184 Newton, *Principia*, p. 806.

185 See *VNP 1821*, p. 51, and *Enc* **II**, §270 addition; *Werke*, **IX**, 98–9: ' "attracted" is an inept expression'.

186 *Enc* **II**, §270 remark; *Werke*, **IX**, 89, and Newton, *Principia*, pp. 816–18. On the solar 'wobble' caused by planetary perturbations, see Beatty, Petersen and Chaikin (eds) *The New Solar System*, p. 378.

187 *Enc* **II**, §270 remark; *Werke*, **IX**, 89.

188 *Enc* **II**, §270 remark and addition; *Werke*, **IX**, 88, 99.

189 In fact Newton's calculations alone do not suffice either, for they do not explain the anomalous orbit of Mercury; see Lang, *The Cambridge Guide to the Solar System*, pp. 204–5.

190 *Enc* **II**, §270 addition; *Werke*, **IX**, 94.

191 *Enc* **II**, §270 addition; *Werke*, **IX**, 100, *NP*, p. 26, and Wandschneider, *Raum, Zeit, Relativität*, pp. 118–19. See also Calle, *Superstrings and Other Things*, pp. 441–5.

192 *Enc* **II**, §275 addition; *Werke*, **IX**, 112, and Wandschneider, *Raum, Zeit, Relativität*, p. 202.

193 See Greene, *The Elegant Universe*, pp. 28–41.

194 Greene, *The Elegant Universe*, pp. 41, 47.

195 *VNP 1823*, pp. 110, 114.

196 *Enc* **II**, §269 remark; *Werke*, **IX**, 83. See also Ihmig, *Hegels Deutung der Gravitation*, p. 157.

197 Greene, *The Elegant Universe*, p. 70.

198 S. Hawking, *A Brief History of Time: From the Big Bang to Black Holes* (New York: Bantam Books, 1988), p. 29.

199 Calle, *Superstrings and Other Things*, p. 479.

200 See Einstein, *Relativity*, p. 112, Reichenbach, *From Copernicus to Einstein*, pp. 119–20, and I. Novikov, *The River of Time*, trans. V. Kisin (Cambridge: Cambridge University Press, 1998), pp. 160–1.

201 Kluit, 'Inertial and Gravitational Mass', pp. 235, 246.

202 Greene, *The Elegant Universe*, p. 76.

203 J. Bernstein, *Einstein* (Glasgow: Collins, 1973), p. 113; Einstein, *Relativity*, p. 93.

204 *VNP 1821*, p. 35, and *NP*, p. 19.

205 Greene, *The Elegant Universe*, p. 68. See also Bernstein, *Einstein*, p. 113.

206 *Enc* **II**, §254 addition; *Werke*, **IX**, 43.

207 Hegel's philosophy of nature is, however, clearly incompatible with the idea that *time* has a beginning and so is finite. See *Enc* **II**, §258 addition; *Werke*, **IX**, 50: 'in its Concept, time itself is eternal'.

208 *Enc* **I**, §6; *Werke*, **VIII**, 47.

209 Greene, *The Elegant Universe*, p. 83.

210 On the earth as part of the *system* of the planets and their sun, see G. W. F. Hegel, *Vorlesungen über die Philosophie des Geistes: Berlin 1827/1828*, eds. F. Hespe and B. Tuschling (Hamburg: Felix Meiner Verlag, 1994) (hereafter *VPG*), p. 35.

7 Life and Embodied Spirit

1 *Enc* **II**, §248; *Werke* **IX**, 27.

2 *NP*, p. 108; see also Kalenberg, *Die Befreiung der Natur*, p. 362.

3 See *VNP 1821*, p. 133.

4 *Enc* **II**, §§352, 356 addition; *Werke*, **IX**, 435, 460–1.

5 *Enc* **II**, §337 addition; *Werke*, **IX**, 339, and *VNP 1821*, p. 164.

6 *Enc* **II**, §337 addition; *Werke*, **IX**, 339, and *VNP 1821*, p. 167. See also I. Kant, *Critique of the Power of Judgement*, trans. P. Guyer and E. Matthews (Cambridge: Cambridge University Press, 2000), pp. 242–9 [§§64–6].

7 On the differences between Hegel and Kant concerning the status of teleological judgement, see D. O. Dahlstrom, 'Hegel's Appropriation of Kant's Account of Teleology in Nature', in *Hegel and the Philosophy of Nature*, pp. 167–88.

8 *Enc* **II**, §336 addition; *Werke*, **IX**, 336.

9 *Enc* **II**, §337; *Werke*, **IX**, 337.

10 *Enc* **II**, §§352 addition, 337 addition; *Werke*, **IX**, 435, 338.

11 Paul Davies, *The Origin of Life* (London: Penguin Books, 2003), p. 17.

12 *Enc* **II**, §337 addition; *Werke*, **IX**, 338.

13 *Enc* **II**, §§353 addition, 366; *Werke*, **IX**, 438, 497.

14 Hegel acknowledges, by the way, that some organisms are hermaphrodites; see *Enc* **II**, §§348 addition, 369 addition; *Werke*, **IX**, 421, 518. In the Miller translation, which follows Michelet's 1842 edition of the *Philosophy of Nature*, §369 has been renumbered as §368.

15 *Enc* **II**, §346 addition 1; *Werke*, **IX**, 395. In the Miller translation (following Michelet)

§346 is split into §346 and §346a with the two additions assigned to the two different paragraphs. The German word *Gattung* can be translated as either 'genus' or 'species'. Miller prefers 'genus', but I have preferred 'species' as it reflects more usual English usage.

16 *Enc* **II**, §§332 and addition, 335; *Werke*, **IX**, 321–3, 333, *VNP 1821*, p. 162, and *VNP 1823*, p. 217.

17 J. W. Burbidge, *Real Process: How Logic and Chemistry Combine in Hegel's Philosophy of Nature* (Toronto: University of Toronto Press, 1996), p. 165.

18 *Enc* **II**, §336 and addition; *Werke*, **IX**, 334–5.

19 *Enc* **II**, §336; *Werke*, **IX**, 334.

20 *Enc* **II**, §335 addition; *Werke*, **IX**, 333.

21 *Enc* **II**, §334 remark; *Werke*, **IX**, 328.

22 *Enc* **II**, §363 addition; *Werke*, **IX**, 479–80.

23 *Enc* **II**, §337 addition; *Werke*, **IX**, 338.

24 Davies, *The Origin of Life*, pp. 237–8.

25 Davies, *The Origin of Life*, pp. 83, 237.

26 Kalenberg, *Die Befreiung der Natur*, p. 366, and Davies, *The Origin of Life*, pp. 228–9.

27 Hegel does tell us, however, that human life depends upon the distance of the earth from the sun: humanity 'could not live at either a greater or lesser distance from the Sun'; *Enc* **III**, §392 addition; *Werke*, **X**, 54.

28 *Enc* **II**, §341 addition; *Werke*, **IX**, 363–6. Kant famously maintained that 'two things fill the mind with ever new and increasing wonder and awe ... the starry heavens above me and the moral law within me'; I. Kant, *Critique of Practical Reason*, trans. L. White Beck (New York: Macmillan, 1956, 1993), p. 169. According to Heine, Hegel called the stars 'a gleaming leprosy in the sky'; see W. Kaufmann, *Hegel: Reinterpretation, Texts, and Commentary* (London: Weidenfeld and Nicolson, 1966), p. 358.

29 See *Hegel's Philosophy of Nature*, ed. M. J. Petry, 3 volumes (London: Allen and Unwin, 1970), **III**, 245–53.

30 *Enc* **II**, §341 addition; *Werke*, **IX**, 367.

31 *Enc* **II**, §§250, 368 addition; *Werke*, **IX**, 34, 510. In Miller's translation of the *Philosophy of Nature* §368 has been renumbered as §370 (following Michelet).

32 *Enc* **II**, §345 addition; *Werke*, **IX**, 383.

33 *Enc* **II**, §346 addition 2; *Werke*, **IX**, 395. See

also Findlay, *Hegel: A Re-examination*, p. 285.

34 *Enc* **II**, §348 addition; *Werke*, **IX**, 423.

35 *Enc* **II**, §§345 addition, 368 addition; *Werke*, **IX**, 385, 510.

36 *Enc* **II**, §344 and addition; *Werke*, **IX**, 373, 376–7.

37 *Enc* **II**, §344 addition; *Werke*, **IX**, 378–9.

38 *Enc* **II**, §344 addition; *Werke*, **IX**, 374. See also Petry (ed.) *Hegel's Philosophy of Nature*, **III**, 255, and F. W. J. Schelling, *Ideas for a Philosophy of Nature*, trans. E. E. Harris and P. Heath (Cambridge: Cambridge University Press, 1988), pp. 130–1 (where the view attributed to Schelling by Hegel is not explicitly stated but, according to Petry, is implied).

39 *Enc* **II**, §350 addition; *Werke*, **IX**, 431. See Aristotle, *The Politics*, trans. T. A. Sinclair, rev. T. J. Saunders (Harmondsworth: Penguin Books, 1951, 1957), p. 60: 'Separate hand or foot from the whole body, and they will no longer be hand or foot except in name'.

40 *Enc* **II**, §351 and addition; *Werke*, **IX**, 431–4. Hegel remarks, however, that the child in the womb absorbs nutrients continuously from the mother in a plant-like manner; see *Enc* **III**, §396 addition; *Werke*, **X**, 78.

41 *Enc* **II**, §§354 addition, 368 addition; *Werke*, **IX**, 454, 514.

42 *Enc* **II**, §§352 addition, 368 addition; *Werke*, **IX**, 436, 504. See also *VNP 1821*, p. 200.

43 *Enc* **II**, §351 addition; *Werke*, **IX**, 432, and *VNP 1823*, p. 239. See *The Complete Works of Aristotle*, **I**, 693 [*Sense and Sensibilia*, 436b10].

44 *Enc* **III**, §400 addition; *Werke*, **X**, 99.

45 *Enc* **II**, §353 addition; *Werke*, **IX**, 438.

46 *Enc* **II**, §351 addition; *Werke*, **IX**, 432.

47 *Enc* **II**, §357 addition 2; *Werke*, **IX**, 465. In the Miller translation §357 is split, following Michelet, into two paragraphs (§357 and §357a) and the two additions are attached to the two different paragraphs.

48 *Enc* **III**, §400 remark; *Werke*, **X**, 98.

49 *Enc* **II**, §368 remark; *Werke*, **IX**, 502; see also *Enc* **III**, §381 addition; *Werke*, **X**, 20, 25.

50 Animals are, however, also driven by *instinct*; see *Enc* **II**, §360 remark; *Werke*, **IX**, 473.

51 *Enc* **II**, §350 addition; *Werke*, **IX**, 431.

52 *Enc* **II**, §358 addition; *Werke*, **IX**, 466.

53 *Enc* **III**, §402 addition; *Werke*, **X**, 121.

54 *Enc* **II**, §351 addition; *Werke*, **IX**, 435.

55 *Enc* **II**, §350 addition; *Werke*, **IX**, 430–1.

56 M. Greene, *Hegel on the Soul: A Speculative Anthropology* (The Hague: Martinus Nijhoff, 1972), p. 86, and *Enc* **III**, §389; *Werke*, **X**, 43.

57 *Enc* **II**, §354 addition; *Werke*, **IX**, 443–4.

58 *Enc* **II**, §358 addition; *Werke*, **IX**, 468, and *Enc* **III**, §401 remark; *Werke*, **X**, 101.

59 *Enc* **II**, §354 addition; *Werke*, **IX**, 444.

60 *Enc* **III**, §401 and addition; *Werke*, **X**, 102, 111. See J. Rée, *I See a Voice: A Philosophical History* (London: HarperCollins, 1999), pp. 59–60.

61 *Enc* **II**, §353 addition; *Werke*, **IX**, 437.

62 *Enc* **III**, §§401 addition, 410 remark; *Werke*, **X**, 113, 186.

63 See Plato, *Phaedo*, trans. D. Gallop (Oxford: Oxford University Press, 1993), p. 9 [64c].

64 See E. Jüngel, *Tod* (Gütersloh: Gütersloher Verlagshaus Mohn, 1979), pp. 107, 116, 151–2, 160.

65 *Enc* **II**, §376 addition; *Werke*, **IX**, 538.

66 See D. F. Krell, *Contagion: Sexuality, Disease, and Death in German Idealism and Romanticism* (Bloomington: Indiana University Press, 1998), pp. 155, 160.

67 *Enc* **III**, §410 addition; *Werke*, **X**, 189.

68 *Enc* **III**, §381 addition; *Werke*, **X**, 25.

69 *Enc* **II**, §367; *Werke*, **IX**, 498.

70 *Enc* **II**, §369 and addition; *Werke*, **IX**, 516–17.

71 *Enc* **II**, §369 addition; *Werke*, **IX**, 517.

72 *Enc* **II**, §368 addition; *Werke*, **IX**, 514. Hegel notes that birds also enjoy an 'imperfect' feeling for their species in hatching and caring for their young; see *VNP 1821*, p. 201.

73 *Enc* **II**, §370; *Werke*, **IX**, 519. In the Miller translation §370 has been renumbered as §369 (following Michelet).

74 *Enc* **II**, §§370 addition, 375; *Werke*, **IX**, 520, 535. See also *VNP 1821*, p. 203, and *VNP 1823*, p. 269.

75 *VNP 1821*, p. 177.

76 Gribbin, *Science: A History*, p. 541.

77 The question has been raised, however, whether all bacteria need to die; some have been discovered to have survived for three million years in the Siberian permafrost, and claims for even greater longevity have been made. See Davies, *The Origin of Life*, p. 215.

78 *Enc* **II**, §348 addition; *Werke*, **IX**, 424.

79 *Enc* **II**, §370 addition; *Werke*, **IX**, 520.

80 *Enc* **II**, §367; *Werke*, **IX**, 498.

81 *Enc* **II**, §376 addition; *Werke*, **IX**, 538.

82 *Enc* **II**, §367 addition; *Werke*, **IX**, 499.

83 *Enc* **II**, §376 addition; *Werke*, **IX**, 538.

84 *Enc* **III**, §381 addition; *Werke*, **X**, 25.

85 *Enc* **II**, §376 addition; *Werke*, **IX**, 539.

86 *Enc* **III**, §381 addition; *Werke*, **X**, 24–5.

87 See W. Bonsiepen, 'Hegels kritische Auseinandersetzung mit der zeitgenössischen Evolutionstheorie', in *Hegels Philosophie der Natur*, pp. 160–1, 167.

88 *Enc* **II**, §249 addition; *Werke*, **IX**, 32.

89 *Enc* **II**, §339 addition; *Werke*, **IX**, 349.

90 *Enc* **II**, §339 addition; *Werke*, **IX**, 348.

91 *Enc* **II**, §368 remark; *Werke*, **IX**, 501. See also *VNP 1823*, p. 261, and Kalenberg, *Die Befreiung der Natur*, p. 332.

92 Findlay, *Hegel: A Re-examination*, p. 272.

93 See Davies, *The Origin of Life*, pp. 18–19, 34, and Gribbin, *Science: A History*, p. 349.

94 On exceptions to this consensus, see Davies, *The Origin of Life*, pp. 234–6.

95 V. Hösle, 'Pflanze und Tier', in *Hegel und die Naturwissenschaften*, pp. 386–7.

96 *Enc* **II**, §368 addition; *Werke*, **IX**, 503–4, 512.

97 Darwin himself held the claim that variations are 'due to chance' to be, strictly speaking, incorrect, and he maintained that it served merely 'to acknowledge plainly our ignorance of the cause of each particular variation'; C. Darwin, *The Origin of Species*, ed. J. W. Burrow (Harmondsworth: Penguin Books, 1968), p. 173. On this interpretation 'random' mutations are not in principle beyond all explanation. It is just that we do not know the precise cause of each one. Such a view of contingency would, I think, be quite close to Hegel's own. As I suggested in chapter 5, contingencies in nature, for Hegel, lack any *philosophical* explanation, but they are not necessarily beyond all explanation whatsoever; it is up to natural science to determine whether any explanation for them can in fact be found. See p. 113 above. For other discussions of Hegel and evolution, see E. E. Harris, 'How Final is Hegel's Rejection of

Evolution?', in *Hegel and the Philosophy of Nature*, pp. 189–208, and (especially) Kalenberg, *Die Befreiung der Natur*, pp. 321–43.

98 *Enc* III, §392 and addition; *Werke*, **X**, 52–3. Hegel dismisses astrology, however, as 'superstition'.

99 *Enc* III, §393 addition; *Werke*, **X**, 60.

100 For a forceful critique of Hegel's views on Africa, see R. Bernasconi, 'Hegel at the Court of the Ashanti', in *Hegel After Derrida*, ed. S. Barnett (London: Routledge, 1998), pp. 41–63.

101 *Enc* III, §393 addition; *Werke*, **X**, 57.

102 *Enc* III, §§395 and addition, 396–7; *Werke*, **X**, 70–1, 75, 86–7.

103 *Enc* III, §395 addition; *Werke*, **X**, 72. See *PR*, §153 remark; *Werke*, **VII**, 303, and L. L. Moland, 'Inheriting, Earning, and Owning: The Source of Practical Identity in Hegel's "Anthropology"', *The Owl of Minerva*, 34, 2 (2003), 141.

104 *Enc* III, §396 addition; *Werke*, **X**, 77.

105 *Enc* III, §410 addition; *Werke*, **X**, 190.

106 *Enc* III, §411 and addition; *Werke*, **X**, 192–5.

107 See *Enc* III, §410 addition; *Werke*, **X**, 189, and J. McCumber, 'Hegel on Habit', *The Owl of Minerva*, 21, 2 (1990), 157.

108 *Enc* III, §413 addition; *Werke*, **X**, 199–201.

109 See *The Hegel Reader*, ed. S. Houlgate (Oxford: Blackwell, 1998), p. 254.

110 *Enc* III, §414; *Werke*, **X**, 201.

111 *Enc* III, §414 addition; *Werke*, **X**, 201–2.

112 *Enc* III, §§438–9, 440 addition, 465; *Werke*, **X**, 228–30, 283.

113 *Enc* III, §§443, 449 addition; *Werke*, **X**, 236, 254. See also S. Houlgate, 'Vision, Reflection, and Openness: The "Hegemony of Vision" from a Hegelian point of View', in *Modernity and the Hegemony of Vision*, ed. D. M. Levin (Berkeley: University of California Press, 1993), pp. 112–14.

114 *Enc* III, §§442, 443 addition; *Werke*, **X**, 234, 237.

115 *VPG*, p. 210.

116 *Enc* III, §§401 addition, 448 addition; *Werke*, **X**, 102, 252.

117 *Enc* III, §§453 remark and addition, 454 and addition; *Werke*, **X**, 260–2. See also K. D. Magnus, *Hegel and the Symbolic Mediation of Spirit* (Albany: State University of New York Press, 2001), pp. 80–1.

118 *Enc* III, §§455, 456 and addition; *Werke*, **X**, 262, 265–6. See also J. Sallis, *Spacings of Reason and Imagination in Texts of Kant, Fichte, Hegel* (Chicago: University of Chicago Press, 1987), pp. 144–51.

119 See *VPG*, p. 206.

120 *Enc* III, §456 and addition; *Werke*, **X**, 266–7, and *VPG*, p. 206.

121 See W. A. deVries, *Hegel's Theory of Mental Activity: An Introduction to Theoretical Spirit* (Ithaca, NY: Cornell University Press, 1988), p. 142, and *VPG*, pp. 206–7.

122 *VPG*, p. 209, and Magnus, *Hegel and the Symbolic Mediation of Spirit*, p. 86.

123 *Enc* III, §458 remark; *Werke*, **X**, 270.

124 Magnus, *Hegel and the Symbolic Mediation of Spirit*, p. 71.

125 *Enc* III, §§457, 458 remark; *Werke*, **X**, 268, 271, and *VPG*, p. 207.

126 See J. McCumber, *The Company of Words: Hegel, Language, and Systematic Philosophy* (Evanston, IL: Northwestern University Press, 1993), p. 224, and *Enc* III, §459; *Werke*, **X**, 271.

127 *Enc* III, §401 addition; *Werke*, **X**, 111.

128 See J. Derrida, 'The Pit and the Pyramid: Introduction to Hegel's Semiology', in *Margins of Philosophy*, trans. A. Bass (Brighton: Harvester Press, 1982), pp. 69–108.

129 *Enc* III, §§461, 462; *Werke*, **X**, 278, and deVries, *Hegel's Theory of Mental Activity*, p. 156.

130 *Enc* III, §463; *Werke*, **X**, 281. See also S. Houlgate, 'Hegel, Derrida, and Restricted Economy: The Case of Mechanical Memory', *Journal of the History of Philosophy*, 34, 1 (1996), 90–1.

131 *Enc* III, §465; *Werke*, **X**, 283.

132 *Enc* III, §462 remark; *Werke*, **X**, 278.

133 *Enc* III, §§468 addition, 469; *Werke*, **X**, 288.

8 Freedom, Rights and Civility

1 R. Winfield, 'Freedom as Interaction: Hegel's Resolution to the Dilemma of Liberal Theory', in *Hegel's Philosophy of Action*, ed. L. S. Stepelevich and D. Lamb (Atlantic Highlands, NJ: Humanities Press, 1983), p. 175.

2 *The Owl of Minerva*, 18, 1 (1986), 102. See also H. C. Graef, 'From Hegel to Hitler', *Contemporary Review*, 158 (July–December 1940), 550–6.

3 *The Owl of Minerva*, 18, 1 (1986), 128.

4 *PR*, §2 and remark; *Werke*, **VII**, 30–1.

5 P. Singer, *Hegel* (Oxford: Oxford University Press, 1983), p. 25.

6 *PR*, §5 and remark; *Werke*, **VII**, 49–50.

7 See *PR*, §§6, 7, 12, 14; *Werke*, **VII**, 52, 54, 63, 65.

8 *PR*, §14; *Werke*, **VII**, 65.

9 *PR*, §15, remark and addition; *Werke*, **VII**, 66–7.

10 *PR*, §27; *Werke*, **VII**, 79.

11 *PR*, §29; *Werke*, **VII**, 80. See also Hegel's handwritten note to §29, which is included in the German edition (*Werke*, **VII**, 81–2), but not in the Knox translation.

12 G. W. F. Hegel, *Philosophie des Rechts: Die Vorlesung von 1819/20 in einer Nachschrift*, ed. D. Henrich (Frankfurt: Suhrkamp Verlag, 1983) (hereafter *PRH*), p. 127.

13 *PR*, §§36, 38; *Werke*, **VII**, 95, 97.

14 J. Hardman, *The French Revolution: The Fall of the Ancien Régime to the Thermidorean Reaction, 1785–1795* (London: Edward Arnold, 1981), p. 114.

15 *PR*, §44; *Werke*, **VII**, 106.

16 *PR*, §§47, 48 and remarks; *Werke*, **VII**, 110–12.

17 *PH*, pp. 95–6, 98–9; *Werke*, **XII**, 124–5, 128–9.

18 G. W. F. Hegel, *Vorlesungen über Naturrecht und Staatswissenschaft: Heidelberg 1817/18, mit Nachträgen aus der Vorlesung 1818/19. Nachgeschrieben von P. Wannenmann*, eds C. Becker and others, with Introduction by O. Pöggeler (Hamburg: Felix Meiner, 1983) (hereafter *VNS*), §8.

19 *PRH*, p. 78.

20 *PRH*, pp. 73–4.

21 G. W. F. Hegel, *Vorlesungen über Rechtsphilosophie, 1818–1831*, ed. K-H. Ilting, 4 volumes (Stuttgart: Frommann-Holzboog, 1973ff), (hereafter *VRP*), **III**, 226.

22 *PR*, §§84–92; *Werke*, **VII**, 174–9, and *PRH*, p. 84.

23 *PR*, §99; *Werke*, **VII**, 187.

24 *PR*, §107; *Werke*, **VII**, 205.

25 *PR*, §117; *Werke*, **VII**, 217.

26 Hegel acknowledges, however, that our ignorance does not always relieve us of responsibility for things we have done, because others can claim that, as rational beings, we *should* have known what we were doing even if we did not. When we should be held responsible for things done in ignorance, is something which Hegel believes cannot be determined by philosophy, but must be decided in the given context by the people involved. See *PR*, §120; *Werke*, **VII**, 225–6, and *PRH*, p. 95.

27 *PR*, §§121, 124 remark; *Werke*, **VII**, 229, 233, and *PRH*, p. 97.

28 *PRH*, p. 97.

29 *PR*, §§125–8; *Werke*, **VII**, 236–41.

30 *PR*, §130; *Werke*, **VII**, 243–4.

31 *PR*, §131; *Werke*, **VII**, 244.

32 *PR*, §132 remark; *Werke*, **VII**, 246.

33 *PR*, §134; *Werke*, **VII**, 251.

34 Kant, *Groundwork*, p. 14.

35 Kant, *Groundwork*, p. 31.

36 *PR*, §135 and remark; *Werke*, **VII**, 252–3.

37 *PR*, §135 remark; *Werke*, **VII**, 252.

38 Kant, *Groundwork*, p. 36.

39 *PR*, §127 and remark; *Werke*, **VII**, 239–40, and *PRH*, pp. 118–19.

40 *PR*, §137 remark; *Werke*, **VII**, 255.

41 *PR*, §§126 addition, 140 remark (d); *Werke*, **VII**, 239, 269–72.

42 *PR*, §§139 remark, 140 remark (d); *Werke*, **VII**, 261, 269–72.

43 L. Siep, 'The "Aufhebung" of Morality in Ethical Life', in *Hegel's Philosophy of Action*, p. 153. For a powerful literary representation of the evil that can be done by a will which is convinced that it is doing good, see J. Hogg, *The Private Memoirs and Confessions of a Justified Sinner* (1824), ed. J. Carey (Oxford: Oxford University Press, 1969).

44 *PR*, §144; *Werke*, **VII**, 293.

45 *PR*, §§144, 146 remark; *Werke*, **VII**, 294–5.

46 *PR*, §150 remark; *Werke*, **VII**, 298, and Taylor, *Hegel*, p. 376.

47 *PR*, §147; *Werke*, **VII**, 295.

48 Taylor, *Hegel*, p. 377.

49 *PR*, §154; *Werke*, **VII**, 304.

50 *PR*, §261 and remark; *Werke*, **VII**, 408–9.

51 *PR*, §265 addition; *Werke*, **VII**, 412.

52 *PR*, §§258 addition, 268 addition; *Werke*, **VII**, 403–4, 414.

53 *PR*, §162 remark; *Werke*, **VII**, 311.

54 *PR*, §148 remark; *Werke*, **VII**, 297.

55 S. Benhabib, 'Obligation, contract and exchange: on the significance of Hegel's abstract right', in *The State and Civil Society:*

Studies in Hegel's Political Philosophy, ed. Z. Pelczynski (Cambridge: Cambridge University Press, 1984), p. 162.

56 *PRH*, p. 150. It should be noted that Hegel uses both the German word *Bürger* and the French word *bourgeois* to refer to members of civil society. See also *VRP*, **IV**, 472.

57 *PR*, §187; *Werke*, **VII**, 343.

58 *PR*, §183; *Werke*, **VII**, 340.

59 *PR*, §§191 addition, 193; *Werke*, **VII**, 349–50.

60 *PRH*, p. 161.

61 *PR*, §191 addition; *Werke*, **VII**, 349, and *VRP*, **III**, 592–3.

62 *PR*, §237; *Werke*, **VII**, 385, my italics. See *VNS*, §118.

63 *PR*, §236, remark and addition; *Werke*, **VII**, 384–5.

64 R. Plant, *Hegel: An Introduction* (1972) (Oxford: Basil Blackwell, 2nd edn 1983), p. 228.

65 *PR*, §200; *Werke*, **VII**, 353.

66 *PR*, §198; *Werke*, **VII**, 352.

67 *PR*, §204; *Werke*, **VII**, 357.

68 *VRP*, **IV**, 627.

69 *PR*, §198; *Werke*, **VII**, 353.

70 *VRP*, **III**, 698.

71 See S. Avineri, *Hegel's Theory of the Modern State* (Cambridge: Cambridge University Press, 1972), p. 149. Also *PR*, §243; *Werke*, **VII**, 389.

72 An analysis of the causes of poverty in modern urban America and Britain would, of course, have to take account of one crucial factor which Hegel does not address: namely, the effects of racial prejudice on the distribution of economic resources and power.

73 *VRP*, **IV**, 625.

74 *PR*, §241; *Werke*, **VII**, 387–8.

75 *PR*, §244; *Werke*, **VII**, 389.

76 *PRH*, pp. 194–6, and *VRP*, **IV**, 495, 608.

77 *VRP*, **III**, 704, 711.

78 *PR*, §245; *Werke*, **VII**, 390, and *PRH*, p. 192.

79 *VRP*, **IV**, 508, 601.

80 *PR*, §245 remark; *Werke*, **VII**, 390–1.

81 Avineri, *Hegel's Theory of the Modern State*, pp. 153–4.

82 *VRP*, **IV**, 604.

83 *PRH*, p. 162, and *VRP*, **III**, 618–19, **IV**, 627.

84 *PRH*, p. 162.

85 *PR*, §236 remark; *Werke*, **VII**, 385.

86 *PR*, §234 addition; *Werke*, **VII**, 383.

87 *PR*, §254; *Werke*, **VII**, 396. See also *VRP*, **IV**, 618, and *PRH*, p. 204.

88 *PR*, §253 remark; *Werke*, **VII**, 395–6.

89 *PR*, §252; *Werke*, **VII**, 394.

90 *PRH*, pp. 203–7.

91 *VRP*, **IV**, 625.

92 Hardman, *The French Revolution*, pp. 112–13.

93 *VRP*, **III**, 711. See *PRH*, p. 206.

94 *PR*, §268; *Werke*, **VII**, 413.

95 *VRP*, **III**, 713.

96 *PR*, §255 addition; *Werke*, **VII**, 397.

97 *PR*, §258 remark; *Werke*, **VII**, 399.

98 On the connection between the state, culture and nationhood, see *PH*, pp. 38–53; *Werke*, **XII**, 55–74.

99 *PR*, §258 addition; *Werke*, **VII**, 403.

100 *PR*, §268; *Werke*, **VII**, 413.

101 *PR*, §268 and addition; *Werke*, **VII**, 413–14. See *Enc* III, §432 addition; *Werke*, **X**, 221.

102 *PRH*, p. 228.

103 See *PH*, pp. 450–2; *Werke*, **XII**, 532–5.

104 *PR*, §260 addition; *Werke*, **VII**, 407. See *VRP*, **IV**, 603.

105 *PRH*, p. 254.

106 *PR*, §311 remark; *Werke*, **VII**, 480–1.

107 *PR*, §258 remark; *Werke*, **VII**, 400.

108 *PRH*, pp. 230–1.

9 Art and Human Wholeness

1 G. W. F. Hegel, *Aesthetics: Lectures on Fine Art*, trans. T. M. Knox, 2 volumes (Oxford: Clarendon Press, 1975) (hereafter *A*), **I**, 99–100; *Werke*, **XIII**, 137.

2 *A*, **I**, 97–8; *Werke*, **XIII**, 135.

3 *A*, **I**, 177; *Werke*, **XIII**, 233.

4 *A*, **I**, 71; *Werke*, **XIII**, 102.

5 K. Clark, *The Nude* (Harmondsworth: Penguin Books, 1960), p. 6.

6 *A*, **II**, 745; *Werke*, **XIV**, 406.

7 *A*, **I**, 39; *Werke*, **XIII**, 61.

8 See H. S. Harris, *Hegel's Development: Toward the Sunlight (1770–1801)* (Oxford: Clarendon Press, 1972), p. 511, *Werke*, **I**, 235, and *A*, **I**, 61–3; *Werke*, **XIII**, 89–92.

9 *A*, **II**, 1010; *Werke*, **XV**, 288. Hegel's own style is indeed itself often rich in metaphors; see, for example, the passage cited on p. 223 (*A*, **I**, 582; *Werke*, **XIV**, 205–6).

10 *A*, **I**, 111; *Werke*, **XIII**, 151.

11 S. Bungay, *Beauty and Truth: A Study of Hegel's Aesthetics* (Oxford: Oxford Univer-

sity Press, 1984), p. 40. See also W. Desmond, *Art and the Absolute: A Study of Hegel's Aesthetics* (Albany: State University of New York Press, 1986), p. 140.

12 *A*, **I**, 42–3; *Werke*, **XIII**, 65–6.

13 See Desmond, *Art and the Absolute*, passim, especially p. 137: '*beauty is a sensuous image of being whole*'.

14 *A*, **I**, 163; *Werke*, **XIII**, 216.

15 *A*, **I**, 170; *Werke*, **XIII**, 224. See D. A. Iñiguez, *Murillo*, 3 volumes (Madrid: Espasa-Calpe, 1981), **III** (Láminas), figures 430, 438.

16 *A*, **I**, 169–70; *Werke*, **XIII**, 223.

17 E. Gombrich, *The Story of Art* (Oxford: Phaidon Press, 1972), pp. 403, 405–9.

18 *A*, **II**, 939–40; *Werke*, **XV**, 198.

19 *A*, **I**, 7; *Werke*, **XIII**, 20. See also *A*, **I**, 48–50, 515; *Werke*, **XIII**, 73–6, **XIV**, 124–5.

20 *A*, **I**, 114; *Werke*, **XIII**, 155–6.

21 *A*, **II**, 670–3, 688; *Werke*, **XIV**, 314–18; 335–6.

22 *A*, **I**, 50, **II**, 972; *Werke*, **XIII**, 76, **XV**, 239–40.

23 Gombrich, *The Story of Art*, p. 69.

24 *A*, **I**, 201; *Werke*, **XIII**, 263.

25 See *A*, **II**, 727–8; *Werke*, **XIV**, 383–4, and Gombrich, *The Story of Art*, p. 68, figure 61.

26 *A*, **II**, 1218; *Werke*, **XV**, 550.

27 *A*, **II**, 1220–2; *Werke*, **XV**, 552–4.

28 *A*, **I**, 573; *Werke*, **XIV**, 195.

29 *A*, **I**, 420, 578, **II**, 1227–8; *Werke*, **XIII**, 538, **XIV**, 200–2, **XV**, 561–2.

30 *A*, **I**, 581–2; *Werke*, **XIV**, 205–6.

31 *A*, **I**, 178; *Werke*, **XIII**, 234. Here is a concrete example, of course, of the unity of being and not-being which Hegel showed in his *Logic* to be essential to all true determinacy.

32 *A*, **II**, 1206; *Werke*, **XV**, 535.

33 *A*, **I**, 243, 578–9; *Werke*, **XIII**, 315, **XIV**, 201–2.

34 *A*, **I**, 243; *Werke*, **XIII**, 315.

35 For a more extensive discussion of the relation between Hegel's aesthetic ideal of wholeness and modern 'fragmentation', see Desmond, *Art and the Absolute*, chapters 5 and 6.

36 *A*, **I**, 240; *Werke*, **XIII**, 311.

37 *A*, **I**, 205; *Werke*, **XIII**, 268.

38 *A*, **I**, 545–6; *Werke*, **XIV**, 162–3.

39 *A*, **II**, 939; *Werke*, **XV**, 198.

40 *A*, **I**, 466; *Werke*, **XIV**, 62–3.

41 R. M. Rilke, *Duineser Elegien*, ed. E. L. Stahl (Oxford: Basil Blackwell, 1965), p. 1.

42 *A*, **II**, 978; *Werke*, **XV**, 246–7.

43 *A*, **I**, 264; *Werke*, **XIII**, 342.

44 *A*, **II**, 1045; *Werke*, **XV**, 331.

45 *A*, **I**, 265, 272, **II**, 1124; *Werke*, **XIII**, 343, 351–2, **XV**, 432. See also *PWH*, p. 177.

46 *A*, **I**, 273; *Werke*, **XIII**, 353.

47 *A*, **I**, 169; *Werke*, **XIII**, 222–3.

48 *A*, **II**, 870; *Werke*, **XV**, 108–9. See Bungay, *Beauty and Truth*, p. 124.

49 *A*, **I**, 272; *Werke*, **XIII**, 352.

50 *A*, **I**, 265–6; *Werke*, **XIII**, 344–5.

51 *A*, **I**, 266–8; *Werke*, **XIII**, 345–6.

52 *A*, **I**, 269–70; *Werke*, **XIII**, 348–9.

53 *A*, **I**, 274–5; *Werke*, **XIII**, 355–6.

54 *A*, **I**, 276–8; *Werke*, **XIII**, 357–60.

55 The word 'romantic' is used in this chapter to refer to the art of the whole post-Classical, Christian era in Europe, whereas the word 'Romantic' is used to refer to a distinctive form of late eighteenth- and early to mid-nineteenth-century European art.

56 For Hegel's account of the various forms of symbolic art, see *A*, **I**, 303–426; *Werke*, **XIII**, 393–546.

57 *A*, **I**, 74, **II**, 783–4; *Werke*, **XIII**, 105–6, **XIV**, 452.

58 *A*, **I**, 312; *Werke*, **XIII**, 404.

59 *A*, **I**, 313; *Werke*, **XIII**, 406.

60 *A*, **I**, 483–4, 517; *Werke*, **XIV**, 85, 127–8.

61 *A*, **II**, 1074; *Werke*, **XV**, 368.

62 *A*, **II**, 793; *Werke*, **XV**, 12.

63 *Schillers Werke*, ed. D. Schmidt, 4 volumes (Frankfurt: Insel Verlag, 1966), **III**, 192.

64 *PH*, p. 249; *Werke*, **XII**, 304.

65 *A*, **I**, 435; *Werke*, **XIV**, 23.

66 *A*, **I**, 598; *Werke*, **XIV**, 225–6.

67 *A*, **I**, 532, 573–4; *Werke*, **XIV**, 146, 196.

68 *A*, **II**, 1236; *Werke*, **XV**, 572–3. On the numerous different interpretations that have been put on Hegel's alleged thesis of the 'end' of art, see Bungay, *Beauty and Truth*, pp. 71–89.

69 *A*, **II**, 1062, 1110, 1143; *Werke*, **XV**, 353, 415, 457.

70 *A*, **I**, 103, 195; *Werke*, **XIII**, 142, 255.

71 *A*, **I**, 605; *Werke*, **XIV**, 234–5. See also Gombrich, *The Story of Art*, chapter 24.

72 *A*, **I**, 20; *Werke*, **XIII**, 37.

73 *A*, **I**, 607; *Werke*, **XIV**, 237–8.

74 *A*, **I**, 605, **II**, 1088, 1173; *Werke*, **XIV**, 235, **XV**, 386, 494.

75 *A*, **I**, 597; *Werke*, **XIV**, 224–5.

76 *A*, **I**, 601; *Werke*, **XIV**, 230.

77 *A*, **I**, 599–600; *Werke*, **XIV**, 228. On music, see *A*, **II**, 897, 956–7; *Werke*, **XV**, 143, 220.

78 *A*, **I**, 600; *Werke*, **XIV**, 229.

79 It should be noted that even music is concerned primarily with the exploration of human subjectivity, for Hegel. Thus, although it is non-representational, it is not 'abstractly' self-reflexive or concerned merely with the medium of art, in the manner discussed here.

80 *A*, **I**, 10; *Werke*, **XIII**, 24.

81 *A*, **I**, 13; *Werke*, **XIII**, 28.

82 *A*, **I**, 602; *Werke*, **XIV**, 231.

83 *A*, **I**, 607–11; *Werke*, **XIV**, 237–42.

84 For a picture of Carl André's *Equivalent VIII*, see R. Hughes, *The Shock of the New* (London: BBC Publications, 1980), p. 393, plate 248.

10 Philosophy and Christian Faith

1 *PH*, p. 381; *Werke*, **XII**, 458.

2 *LPR*, **I**, 403; *VPR*, **I**, 298.

3 *PWH*, p. 105; *Werke*, **XII**, 70.

4 *PWH*, p. 92; *Werke*, **XII**, 54.

5 *Werke*, **XI**, 385.

6 *LPR*, **I**, 139, **III**, 294; *VPR*, **I**, 53, **III**, 218.

7 *LPR*, **I**, 151, 116; *VPR*, **I**, 63, 33.

8 *PH*, p. 415; *Werke*, **XII**, 495.

9 P. Tillich, *Systematic Theology: Three Volumes in One* (Chicago: University of Chicago Press, 1967), **I**, 156.

10 *LPR*, **I**, 338, **III**, 369; *VPR*, **I**, 239, **III**, 285.

11 See *LPR*, **III**, 230, 257; *VPR*, **III**, 161, 184.

12 *LPR*, **I**, 400; *VPR*, **I**, 295.

13 *LPR*, **I**, 401; *VPR*, **I**, 296.

14 *LPR*, **I**, 398; *VPR*, **I**, 293.

15 J. Robinson, *Honest to God* (London: SCM Press, 1963), p. 53.

16 Taylor, *Hegel*, p. 494.

17 John 14: 6.

18 A. M. Ramsey, *Be Still and Know* (London: Collins, 1982), pp. 73–4.

19 Saint Augustine, *Confessions*, p. 116. See *LPR*, **I**, 338; *VPR*, **I**, 239.

20 *LPR*, **III**, 364, 279–80; *VPR*, **III**, 281–2, 204–5.

21 *LPR*, **III**, 284; *VPR*, **III**, 209.

22 *Werke*, **XI**, 362.

23 Kant, *Critique of Pure Reason*, A 580/B 608. See also T. M. Knox, *A Layman's Quest* (London: Allen and Unwin, 1969), p. 66.

24 F. Nietzsche, *Twilight of the Idols/ The Antichrist*, trans. R. J. Hollingdale

(Harmondsworth: Penguin Books, 1968), *Antichrist*, §18.

25 *LPR*, **III**, 236; *VPR*, **III**, 166.

26 Jüngel, *Tod*, p. 143.

27 A. M. Ramsey, *Introducing the Christian Faith* (London: SCM Press, 1970), p. 42, and *Holy Spirit* (London: SPCK, 1977), p. 76, emphasis added.

28 *LPR*, **III**, 276; *VPR*, **III**, 201.

29 *PH*, p. 342; *Werke*, **XII**, 414.

30 Nietzsche, *Antichrist*, §18.

31 John 3: 17.

32 *LPR*, **III**, 197; *VPR*, **III**, 130.

33 *LPR*, **I**, 335; *VPR*, **I**, 237.

34 *Enc*, **III**, §564 remark; *Werke*, **X**, 374.

35 *LPR*, **III**, 337; *VPR*, **III**, 260. See also *LHP*, **I**, 72–3; *Werke*, **XVIII**, 93.

36 K. Barth, *Die protestantische Theologie im 19. Jahrhundert* (Zürich: Evangelischer Verlag, 1946, 3rd edn 1960), p. 377.

37 Taylor, *Hegel*, pp. 493–4.

38 *LPR*, **III**, 292 (emphasis added), 235; *VPR*, **III**, 216, 165.

39 *Werke*, **XI**, 369.

40 *PH*, p. 324; *Werke*, **XII**, 392.

41 *LPR*, **I**, 140; *VPR*, **I**, 54, and *PH*, p. 438; *Werke*, **XII**, 520.

42 *PH*, p. 381; *Werke*, **XII**, 458.

43 R. Solomon, *From Hegel to Existentialism* (Oxford: Oxford University Press, 1987), pp. 57–8, 61, 66.

44 See, for example, *Hegel: The Letters*, pp. 520, 531, and *LHP*, **I**, 73; *Werke*, **XVIII**, 94.

45 *PH*, pp. 324, 377; *Werke*, **XII**, 392, 454.

46 J. Yerkes, *The Christology of Hegel* (Albany: State University of New York Press, 1983), p. 137.

47 *LHP*, **III**, 5; *Werke*, **XIX**, 526.

48 *PH*, p. 328; *Werke*, **XII**, 397.

49 *LPR*, **III**, 231–2, 296–7, 372; *VPR*, **III**, 162, 221, 288.

50 Romans 8: 38–9.

51 *PH*, p. 377; *Werke*, **XII**, 453.

52 *LPR*, **III**, 310–11; *VPR*, **III**, 234.

53 *LPR*, **III**, 372, 333; *VPR*, **III**, 288, 256.

54 M. Luther, *Von der Freiheit eines Christenmenschen*, ed. W. Metzger (Gütersloh: Gütersloher Verlagshaus Mohn, 1977), p. 165.

55 *LPR*, **I**, 180, **III**, 337; *VPR*, **I**, 88, **III**, 260. See also *LPR*, **III**, 240, 372; *VPR*, **III**, 169, 288.

56 *The Protestant Reformation*, ed. H. J. Hillerbrand (New York: Harper and Row, 1968), p. 115.

57 J. Whale, *The Protestant Tradition* (Cambridge: Cambridge University Press, 1955), p. 55.

58 *PH*, p. 416; *Werke*, **XII**, 495, and *LPR*, **III**, 338–9; *VPR*, **III**, 261.

59 Hillerbrand (ed.) *The Protestant Reformation*, pp. 102–4.

60 *LPR*, **I**, 446, **III**, 372; *VPR*, **I**, 334, **III**, 288.

61 Hillerbrand (ed.) *The Protestant Reformation*, pp. 9, 99, 102–3, and *Martin Luther: Selections from his Writings*, ed. J. Dillenberger (New York: Anchor Books, 1961), pp. 275, 291.

62 *LPR*, **III**, 164–5; *VPR*, **III**, 100, and *LHP*, **I**, 75; *Werke*, **XVIII**, 95.

63 E. Jüngel, *Gott als Geheimnis der Welt* (Tübingen: J. C. B. Mohr, 3rd edn 1978) p. 124.

64 Luther, *Von der Freiheit eines Christenmenschen*, pp. 140–1, and Hillerbrand (ed.) *The Protestant Reformation*, p. 103.

65 Mark 8: 35.

66 Solomon, *From Hegel to Existentialism*, p. 61.

67 Jüngel, *Tod*, pp. 116, 107.

68 *LPR*, **I**, 295–6, 306; *VPR*, **I**, 199–200, 210.

69 Jüngel, *Tod*, p. 116, and Hillerbrand (ed.) *The Protestant Reformation*, p. 88.

70 Whale, *The Protestant Tradition*, p. 101.

71 Hillerbrand (ed.) *The Protestant Reformation*, p. 105, and *LPR*, **III**, 372; *VPR*, **III**, 288.

72 Jüngel, *Tod*, p. 162, and Matthew 26: 37.

73 *LPR*, **I**, 362; *VPR*, **I**, 263, and *PH*, p. 424; *Werke*, **XII**, 504.

74 Marx, *Selected Writings*, p. 72.

75 *Martin Luther: Selections from his Writings*, p. 28, *PH*, pp. 407–8; *Werke*, **XII**, 488, and *LPR*, **III**, 208; *VPR*, **III**, 140.

76 *PH*, p. 334; *Werke*, **XII**, 404, and *Werke*, **XI**, 58.

77 *PH*, p. 378; *Werke*, **XII**, 455.

78 Luther, *Von der Freiheit eines Christenmenschen*, pp. 163–5, 167–9, 174.

79 Luther, *Von der Freiheit eines Christenmenschen*, p. 175.

80 Hillerbrand (ed.) *The Protestant Reformation*, pp. 102–3.

81 F. Nietzsche, *Daybreak*, trans. R. J. Hollingdale, with an introduction by M. Tanner (Cambridge: Cambridge University Press, 1982), §132, and *Hegel: The Letters*, p. 549.

82 Luther, *Von der Freiheit eines Christenmen-*

83 *Martin Luther: Selections from his Writings*, p. 291.

84 Galations 2: 20.

85 *LPR*, **III**, 286; *VPR*, **III**, 211.

86 *LPR*, **III**, 118, 218; *VPR*, **III**, 53, 149.

87 *Phen*, pp. 14, 110; *Werke*, **III**, 29, 145.

88 Jüngel, *Tod*, p. 168.

89 See *PH*, p. 335; *Werke*, **XII**, 405, Luther, *Von der Freiheit eines Christenmenschen*, p. 179, and Hillerbrand (ed.) *The Protestant Reformation*, p. 95.

90 Jüngel, *Tod*, pp. 161–2, 167.

91 *PH*, pp. 380, 422–3; *Werke*, **XII**, 457–8, 502–3.

92 Matthew 22: 39–40.

93 I. Kant, *Religion within the Limits of Reason alone*, trans. T. Greene and H. Hudson (New York: Harper and Row, 1960), p. 142.

94 Galatians 5: 18. See *LPR*, **I**, 349–50, **III**, 234, 337; *VPR*, **I**, 249–50, **III**, 164, 260.

95 Luther, *Von der Freiheit eines Christenmenschen*, p. 166, and Hillerbrand (ed.) *The Protestant Reformation*, pp. 103–4. See Romans 3: 20; 7: 7ff; 8: 3ff.

96 *Martin Luther: Selections from his Writings*, pp. 21, 30.

97 Galatians 2: 16.

98 Luther, *Von der Freiheit eines Christenmenschen*, pp. 175, 177.

99 *Lessings Werke*, ed. K. Wölfel, 3 volumes (Frankfurt: Insel Verlag, 1967), **III**, 556 [*Education of the Human Race*, §58], and K. Ward, *Holding Fast to God* (London: SPCK, 1982), p. 120.

100 *PH*, p. 342; *Werke*, **XII**, 414.

101 *LPR*, **I**, 351–2, **III**, 138; *VPR*, **I**, 251, **III**, 73–4.

102 *PH*, p. 329; *Werke*, **XII**, 398.

103 *LPR*, **III**, 208–9, 387; *VPR*, **III**, 140–1, 305.

104 See Ramsey, *Introducing the Christian Faith*, p. 62, and John 17: 3.

105 Jüngel, *Tod*, pp. 150–2, 160. See C. Butler, *G. W. F. Hegel* (Boston: G. K. Hall, 1977), p. 145.

106 Matthew 26: 39.

107 John 5: 24, my italics.

108 Jüngel, *Tod*, p. 123.

109 *LPR*, **III**, 227, 236, 323–4; *VPR*, **III**, 158, 166, 247.

110 Matthew 18: 20.

111 *LPR*, **III**, 316–17, 367–8; *VPR*, **III**, 240, 284–5.

112 *LPR*, **III**, 219; *VPR*, **III**, 150. See also *LPR*, **III**, 226–7, 316, 368–9; *VPR*, **III**, 156–7, 240, 285.

113 F. Nietzsche, *The Gay Science*, trans. W. Kaufmann (New York: Vintage Books, 1974), §§125, 343.

114 *LPR*, **III**, 219–20, 323; *VPR*, **III**, 150, 247.

115 *LPR*, **III**, 324; *VPR*, **III**, 247. See Jüngel, *Gott als Geheimnis der Welt*, p. 122.

116 John 16: 7.

117 John 14: 6. See *LPR*, **III**, 131; *VPR*, **III**, 67.

118 Hillerbrand (ed.) *The Protestant Reformation*, p. 103.

119 I John 5: 10.

120 *LPR*, **I**, 412; *VPR*, **I**, 307. See *LHP*, **I**, 70; *Werke*, **XVIII**, 91.

121 *LPR*, **III**, 150; *VPR*, **III**, 85.

122 *PH*, p. 333; *Werke*, **XII**, 403.

123 See I Corinthians 2: 16 and John 16: 13.

124 *LPR*, **III**, 152; *VPR*, **III**, 87. See also *LPR*, **III**, 216, 318–19, 367; *VPR*, **III**, 147, 241–2, 284. For the Biblical passages referred to, see Matthew 5: 8, 19: 21.

125 *LPR*, **III**, 317; *VPR*, **III**, 240.

126 H. Chadwick, *The Early Church* (Harmondsworth: Penguin Books, 1967), p. 76. See also *LPR*, **III**, 334; *VPR*, **III**, 256–7, *PH*, pp. 329–31; *Werke*, **XII**, 398–400, and *LHP*, **III**, 2; *Werke*, **XIX**, 524.

127 *LHP*, **III**, 152; *Werke*, **XX**, 54–5.

128 See *Lessings Werke*, **III**, 558 [*Education of the Human Race*, §72].

129 *LPR*, **III**, 258–9; *VPR*, **III**, 185.

130 See *LPR*, **I**, 168, **III**, 261; *VPR*, **I**, 78, **III**, 187,

and Hillerbrand (ed.) *The Protestant Reformation*, p. 88.

131 See *LHP*, **III**, 152; *Werke*, **XX**, 55. It should be pointed out, of course, that Luther himself thought truth was attested to by the witness of one's own spirit and by one's own faith, *not* (as the post-Reformation philosophers insisted) by one's own judgement, understanding or sense experience.

132 I Corinthians 2: 16.

133 *LPR*, **I**, 306, **III**, 240; *VPR*, **I**, 210, **III**, 169, and *LHP*, **I**, 63; *Werke*, **XVIII**, 83. Haldane translates *daranhindenken* rather weakly as 'the operation of reflection'.

134 *LPR*, **I**, 88, 290; *VPR*, **I**, 7, 194.

135 *LPR*, **III**, 246; *VPR*, **III**, 175.

136 *PWH*, p. 54; *Werke*, **XII**, 31. See also *PH*, p. 334; *Werke*, **XII**, 403–4, and *LPR*, **I**, 106, **III**, 340; *VPR*, **I**, 24, **III**, 262–3.

137 *PH*, pp. 377–8, 425–7; *Werke*, **XII**, 454–5, 506–7. See also *PR*, §270 addition; *Werke*, **VII**, 430–1.

138 *PH*, pp. 422–3; *Werke*, **XII**, 503, and *LHP*, **III**, 147; *Werke*, **XX**, 49. See also R. Bainton, *The Reformation of the Sixteenth Century* (Boston: Beacon Press, 1956), p. 246.

139 Luther, *Von der Freiheit eines Christenmenschen*, p. 173.

140 *PH*, pp. 417–18; *Werke*, **XII**, 497–8, and *LHP*, **III**, 147–52; *Werke*, **XX**, 49–55.

141 See Nietzsche, *The Gay Science*, §344.

142 *PWH*, p. 105; *Werke*, **XII**, 70.

143 *Enc* **III**, §552; *Werke*, **X**, 359–60, *PH*, pp. 449, 453; *Werke*, **XII**, 531, 535, and *PR*, §270 and remark; *Werke*, **VII**, 415–28.

144 Solomon, *From Hegel to Existentialism*, p. 57.

Bibliographical Essay

The best place to begin reading Hegel, in my view, is with the lectures on aesthetics or the philosophy of history. These present Hegel's main ideas in a relatively accessible form and include many perceptive and thought-provoking comments on individual works of art and civilizations. After these lectures, I would recommend reading the *Philosophy of Right* or the lectures on the philosophy of religion. Then, after a good night's rest and perhaps some encouragement from one's friends, one can begin to tackle the *Phenomenology* or the *Science of Logic*. (For bibliographical information on all the writings of Hegel that I have discussed in this book, see the list of abbreviations at the front of the book. A handy selection of Hegel's writings can be found in *The Hegel Reader*, ed. Stephen Houlgate, Oxford: Blackwell, 1998.)

Two of the best general surveys of Hegel's philosophy are the books which did so much to revive interest in him in the English-speaking world in the 1960s and 1970s: John Findlay's *Hegel: A Reexamination* (1958) (Oxford: Oxford University Press, 1976) and Walter Kaufmann's *Hegel: Reinterpretation, Texts and Commentary* (London: Weidenfeld and Nicolson, 1966). Both books certainly have their faults. Findlay's Hegel, in my judgement, is somewhat too 'soft': he is a philosopher whose thought has the coherence of a work of art rather than of rigorous logical necessity. Kaufmann, on the other hand, tends to see in Hegel too much of a turbulent Nietzschean. Nevertheless, both provide an admirably lucid and comprehensive account of Hegel's ideas, and Kaufmann's book in particular is invaluable for the way in which it situates him in the context of his contemporaries, such as Schiller and Goethe.

A 'harder', more rigorously logical and systematic Hegel is to be found in Stanley Rosen's *G. W. F. Hegel: An Introduction to the Science of Wisdom* (New Haven, CT: Yale University Press, 1974), as well as W. T. Stace's *The Philosophy of Hegel* (1924) (New York: Dover Publications, 1955). (Not the least of the charms of Stace's book is the pull-out 'Diagram of the Hegelian System' which provides an overview of over two hundred Hegelian categories.) Approximately half-way between the 'soft' and the 'hard' Hegel stands the Hegel presented by Charles Taylor in his impressive and popular study *Hegel* (Cambridge: Cambridge University Press, 1975).

For more advanced students, both Alexandre Kojève's *Introduction to the Reading of Hegel* (1947), ed. A. Bloom, trans. J. H. Nichols (Ithaca, NY: Cornell University Press, 1980) and Michael Inwood's *Hegel* (London: Routledge and Kegan Paul, 1983) are to be recommended. These two books demonstrate the extraordinary diversity to be found in commentaries on Hegel, with Kojève pioneering the 'existential' interpretation and Inwood providing a more 'analytical' examination of Hegel's arguments.

Of the smaller surveys of Hegel's thought in English, one of the best, in my view, is G. R. G. Mure's *The Philosophy of Hegel* (London: Oxford University Press, 1965). Also worthy of mention is Peter Singer's *Hegel* (Oxford: Oxford University Press, 1983), which gives a good account of Hegel's political philosophy, particularly his conception of freedom. Two other lucid and readable overviews of Hegel's thought are Tom Rockmore's *Before and After Hegel: A Historical Introduction to Hegel's Thought* (Berkeley: University of California Press, 1993) and Paul Redding's *Hegel's Hermeneutics* (Ithaca, NY: Cornell University Press, 1996).

Without any doubt the most comprehensive account of the 'young Hegel' in any language is contained in the two volumes of H. S. Harris's masterful *Hegel's Development* (Oxford: Clarendon Press, volume 1 1972, volume 2 1983). However, Laurence Dickey's *Hegel: Religion, Economics and the Politics of Spirit, 1770–1807* (Cambridge: Cambridge University Press, 1987) and George Luckács's *The Young Hegel* (1948), trans. R. Livingstone (London: Merlin Press, 1975) also contain much that is very useful. Good insight into the whole development of Hegel's thinking, from his early years to his death, can be gained from *Hegel: The Letters*, trans. C. Butler and C. Seiler (Bloomington: Indiana University Press, 1984). Also to be recommended is Terry Pinkard's *Hegel: A Biography* (Cambridge: Cambridge University Press, 2000), which not only sets Hegel's thought very intelligently in its social and historical context but is also a thoroughly good read.

The best book written in English on the *Phenomenology*, in my judgement, is Quentin Lauer's careful and detailed study, *A Reading of Hegel's Phenomenology of Spirit* (New York: Fordham University Press, 1976). In contrast to Lauer, who accepts Hegel's claim to be an orthodox Christian, Robert Solomon interprets Hegel in a decidedly left-Hegelian, humanist vein in his *In the Spirit of Hegel* (Oxford: Oxford University Press, 1983). Although Solomon's reading of the *Phenomenology* is undoubtedly lively and entertaining, he does not make sense of Hegel's theological claims, or explain the *logic* of the text, as well as Lauer. The classic French study, and still one of the most important books on Hegel, is Jean Hyppolite's monumental *Genesis and Structure of Hegel's Phenomenology of Spirit* (1946), trans. S. Cherniak and J. Heckman (Evanston, IL: Northwestern University Press, 1974). For the beginner, however, Richard Norman's *Hegel's Phenomenology: A Philosophical Introduction* (Brighton: Sussex University Press, 1976), Robert Stern's *Hegel and the Phenomenology of Spirit* (London: Routledge, 2002) and Kenneth Westphal's *Hegel's Epistemology: A Philosophical Introduction to the Phenomenology of Spirit* (Indianapolis: Hackett, 2003) are considerably more manageable. Other noteworthy studies include Merold Westphal's *History and Truth in Hegel's Phenomenology* (Atlantic Highlands, NJ: Humanities Press, 1979), Martin Heidegger's *Hegel's 'Phenomenology of Spirit'*, trans. P. Emad and K. Maly (Bloomington: Indiana University Press, 1988), Joseph Flay's *Hegel's Quest for Certainty* (Albany: State University of New York Press, 1984), Kenneth Westphal's *Hegel's Epistemological Realism* (Dordrecht: Kluwer, 1989), Terry Pinkard's *Hegel's Phenomenology: The Sociality of Reason* (Cambridge: Cambridge University Press, 1994), Michael Forster's *Hegel's Idea of a Phenomenology of Spirit* (Chicago: University of Chicago Press, 1998) and Kenley Dove's influential article, 'Hegel's Phenomenological Method', in *The Phenomenology of Spirit Reader: Critical and Interpretive Essays*, ed. J. Stewart (Albany: State University of New York Press, 1998), pp. 52–75. The most comprehensive and erudite study of Hegel's *Phenomenology* is undoubtedly H. S. Harris's *Hegel's Ladder*, two volumes (Indianapolis: Hackett, 1997). Newcomers to Hegel may, however, find Harris's magnificent work somewhat overwhelming. A more digestible – and highly insightful – examination of the relation between the *Phenomenology* and the *Logic* is provided by William Maker's *Philosophy without Foundations: Rethinking Hegel* (Albany: State University of New York Press, 1994).

John Burbidge's clear and perceptive *On Hegel's Logic: Fragments of a Commentary* (Atlantic Highlands, NJ: Humanities Press, 1981) is essential reading for those studying the *Science of Logic*. Also helpful are E. E. Harris's *An Interpretation of the Logic of Hegel* (Lanham, MD: University Press of America, 1983), J. M. E. McTaggart's *A Commentary on Hegel's Logic* (Cambridge: Cambridge University Press, 1910), Paul Johnson's *The Critique of Thought: A Re-examination of Hegel's Science of Logic* (Aldershot: Avebury, 1988) and Giacomo Rinaldi's *A History and Interpretation of the Logic of Hegel* (Lewiston, NY: The Edwin Mellen Press, 1992). Robert Pippin's *Hegel's Idealism: The Satisfactions of Self-consciousness* (Cambridge: Cambridge University Press, 1989) and Robert Stern's *Hegel, Kant and the Structure of the Object* (London: Routledge, 1990) both provide fine accounts of the relation between Hegel's logic and Kant's critical philosophy; and Richard Winfield, inspired by Kenley Dove, rightly stresses the rigorously presuppositionless character of Hegel's thinking in *Reason and Justice* (Albany: State University of New York Press, 1988) and *Overcoming Foundations: Studies in Systematic Philosophy* (New York: Columbia University Press, 1989). In contrast to Winfield, Klaus Hartmann interprets Hegel as a quasi-transcendental philosopher in his article 'Hegel: A Non-metaphysical View', in *Hegel: A Collection of Critical Essays*, ed. Alasdair MacIntyre (Garden City, NY: Doubleday, 1972). This article has spawned other noteworthy studies of Hegel, including Alan White's excellent defence of Hegel against Schelling, *Absolute Knowledge: Hegel and the Problem of Metaphysics* (Athens, OH: Ohio University Press, 1983) and Terry Pinkard's stimulating, but ultimately unconvincing, *Hegel's Dialectic: The Explanation of Possibility* (Philadelphia: Temple University Press, 1988). A controversial critique of Hegel's logic is to be found in Michael Rosen's *Hegel's Dialectic and Its Criticism* (Cambridge: Cambridge University Press, 1982).

Unfortunately, little has been written in English on Hegel's philosophy of nature or his philosophy of subjective spirit (which includes his anthropology and psychology). There is, however, much of value to be found on the philosophy of nature in *Hegel and the Sciences*, eds R. S. Cohen and M. Wartofsky (Dordrecht: Reidel, 1984), *Hegel and Newtonianism*, ed. M. Petry (Dordrecht: Kluwer, 1993), *Hegel and the Philosophy of Nature*, ed. Stephen Houlgate (Albany: State University of New York Press, 1998) and John Burbidge's exemplary *Real Process: How Logic and Chemistry Combine in Hegel's Philosophy of Nature* (Toronto: University of Toronto Press, 1996). Hegel's philosophy of subjective spirit is given detailed and helpful treatment in Murray Greene's *Hegel on the Soul: A Speculative Anthropology* (The Hague: Martinus Nijhoff, 1972), Willem deVries's *Hegel's Theory of Mental Activity* (Ithaca, NY: Cornell University Press, 1988), Daniel Berthold-Bond's *Hegel's Theory of Madness* (Albany: State University of New York Press, 1995) and Kathleen Dow Magnus's *Hegel and the Symbolic Mediation of Spirit* (Albany: State University of New York Press, 2001). Daniel Cook's *Language in the Philosophy of Hegel* (The Hague: Mouton, 1973) examines a much neglected topic and is one of the most accessible books in English on Hegel. A highly original study of the centrality of language to Hegel's systematic project as a whole is to be found in John McCumber's *The Company of Words: Hegel, Language, and Systematic Philosophy* (Evanston, IL: Northwestern University Press, 1993). Hegel's relation to Aristotle's philosophies of nature and spirit is greatly illuminated by Alfredo Ferrarin's *Hegel and Aristotle* (Cambridge: Cambridge University Press, 2001).

The profound influence of Scottish writers, such as Adam Ferguson and Adam Smith, on Hegel's social and political thought is demonstrated in Norbert Waszek's meticulous *The Scottish Enlightenment and Hegel's Account of 'Civil Society'* (Boston: Kluwer, 1988); and Shlomo Avineri's excellent *Hegel's Theory of the Modern State* (Cambridge: Cambridge University Press, 1972) shows clearly how much Hegel anticipated the analyses of Marx. Joachim Ritter argues for the central place of freedom in Hegel's philosophy in his *Hegel and the French Revolution* (1965), trans. R. Winfield (Cambridge, MA: MIT Press, 1982); and Raymond Plant traces the development of Hegel's social and political thinking in his *Hegel: An Introduction* (1972) (Oxford: Basil Blackwell, 1983). Also worth consulting are: *Hegel's Political Philosophy: Problems and Perspectives*, ed. Z. Pelczynski (Cambridge: Cambridge University Press, 1971), *The State and Civil Society: Studies in Hegel's Political Philosophy*, ed. Z. Pelczynski (Cambridge: Cambridge University Press, 1984), *Hegel's Philosophy of Action*, eds L. S. Stepelevich and D. Lamb (Atlantic Highlands, NJ: Humanities Press, 1983), Steven Smith's *Hegel's Critique of Liberalism: Rights in Context* (Chicago: University of Chicago Press, 1989), Allen Wood, *Hegel's Ethical Thought* (Cambridge: Cambridge University Press, 1990), Michael Hardimon, *Hegel's Social Philosophy: The Project of Reconciliation* (Cambridge: Cambridge University Press, 1994), Robert Williams, *Hegel's Ethics of Recognition* (Berkeley: University of California Press, 1997), Allen Patten, *Hegel's Idea of Freedom* (Oxford: Oxford University Press, 1999), Frederick Neuhouser, *Foundations of Hegel's Social Theory: Actualizing Freedom* (Cambridge, MA: Harvard University Press, 2000) and Dudley Knowles, *Hegel and the Philosophy of Right* (London: Routledge, 2002).

George O'Brien's elegant *Hegel on Reason and History* (Chicago: Chicago University Press, 1975), Duncan Forbes's excellent introduction to H. B. Nisbet's translation of Hegel's introduction to the lectures on world history and Joseph McCarney's marvellously clear *Hegel on History* (London: Routledge, 2000) all successfully put to rest many of the wilder distortions of Hegel's conception of history. Jack Kaminsky gives an admirably lucid account of Hegel's aesthetics in his *Hegel on Art* (Albany: State University of New York Press, 1962), and William Desmond offers a thought-provoking study of the relation between Hegel's aesthetics and 'the Nietzschean–Heideggerian heritage' in his *Art and the Absolute: A Study of Hegel's Aesthetics* (Albany: State University of New York Press, 1986); but Stephen Bungay's *Beauty and Truth: A Study of Hegel's Aesthetics* (Oxford: Oxford University Press, 1984) presents a somewhat idiosyncratic reconstruction of Hegel's theory of art, which is strongly influenced by Klaus Hartmann. Fine essays on Hegel's aesthetics are to be found in *Hegel and Aesthetics*, ed. William Maker (Albany: State University of New York Press, 2000). The best books in English on Hegel's philosophy of religion are E. Fackenheim's *The Religious Dimension in Hegel's Thought* (Chicago: University of Chicago Press, 1967), James Yerkes's *The Christology of Hegel* (Albany: State University of New York Press, 1983), Walter Jaeschke's *Reason in Religion: The Foundations of Hegel's Philosophy of Religion*, trans. J. M. Stewart and P. C. Hodgson (Berkeley: University of California Press, 1990) and Cyril O'Regan's *The Heterodox Hegel* (Albany: State University of New York Press, 1994). Clark Butler's *G. W. F. Hegel* (Boston: G. K. Hall, 1977) contains a useful account of Hegel's treatment of non-Christian religions, and Quentin Lauer's *Hegel's Concept of God* (Albany: State University of New York Press, 1982) is also very rewarding, though difficult. Glenn Alexander Magee provides an important reminder of Hegel's debt to hermetic thinkers, such as Jakob Böhme, in his scholarly and imaginative *Hegel and the Hermetic Tradition* (Ithaca, NY: Cornell University Press, 2001).

Several recent commentators have tried to relate Hegel's thinking to post-Hegelian developments in philosophy. Readers might like to look at David Kolb's *The Critique of Pure Modernity: Hegel, Heidegger and After* (Chicago: University of Chicago Press, 1986), Gillian Rose's *Hegel contra Sociology* (London: Athlone Press, 1981), David Lamb's *Hegel: From Foundation to System* (The Hague: Martinus Nijhoff, 1980), which considers Hegel in relation to Wittgenstein, Will Dudley's *Hegel, Nietzsche, and Philosophy: Thinking Freedom* (Cambridge: Cambridge University Press, 2002) and my own *Hegel, Nietzsche and the Criticism of Metaphysics* (Cambridge: Cambridge University Press, 1986). There are also some valuable thoughts on the relation between Hegel and Marx in Richard Winfield's *The Just Economy* (New York: Routledge, 1988) and in *Hegel and Modern Philosophy*, ed. D. Lamb (London: Croom Helm, 1987). A deconstructive reading of Hegel is offered by Jacques Derrida in *Glas* (1981), trans. J. P. Leavey and R. Rand (Lincoln and London: Nebraska University Press, 1986), though this should only be tackled after *two* nights' rest and a lot of encouragement from one's friends.

For readers who wish to find out about Hegel's predecessors and heirs, the following books are highly recommended: Frederick Beiser's *The Fate of Reason: German Philosophy from Kant to Fichte* (Cambridge, MA: Harvard University Press, 1987) and his *German Idealism: The Struggle Against Subjectivism, 1781–1801* (Cambridge, MA: Harvard University Press, 2002), Karl Löwith's *From Hegel to Nietzsche* (1941), trans. D. Green (New York: Doubleday, 1967), John Toews's *Hegelianism: The Path toward Dialectical Humanism, 1805–1841* (Cambridge: Cambridge University Press, 1980) and Terry Pinkard's *German Philosophy, 1760–1860: The Legacy of Idealism* (Cambridge: Cambridge University Press, 2002). Some of the writings of Hegel's heirs are collected in *The Young Hegelians: An Anthology*, ed. L. S. Stepelevich (Cambridge: Cambridge University Press, 1983). Marx's writings on Hegel can be found in Karl Marx, *Selected Writings*, ed. D. McLellan (Oxford: Oxford University Press, 1977, 2000); Kierkegaard set out his fundamental criticism of Hegel in his *Concluding Unscientific Postscript* (1846), trans. D. Swenson and W. Lowrie (Princeton, NJ: Princeton University Press, 1941, 1968); and Nietzsche's worries about the historical legacy of Hegelianism are given eloquent expression in his essay 'On the Uses and Disadvantages of History for Life', in *Untimely Meditations* (1873–6), trans. R. J. Hollingdale (Cambridge: Cambridge University Press, 1983).

Over and above the works I have mentioned, there are of course many others which merit attention, including several good collections of articles on Hegel in English, and numerous studies of his philosophy in German, French, Italian, Spanish, Dutch and even Welsh. In addition, many important articles and book reviews are published in journals, such as *Hegel-Studien*, *Hegel-Jahrbuch*, *Jahrbuch für Hegelforschung*, *The Owl of Minerva* (the journal of the Hegel Society of America), and the *Bulletin of the Hegel Society of Great Britain*. Finally, for the insatiably voracious, Kurt Steinhauer's *Hegel-Bibliographie* (Munich: K. G. Saur Verlag, 1980, 1998) lists more works on Hegel than one could read in a lifetime.

Index